PSYCHOPATHOLOGY TODAY
The Current Status of
Abnormal Psychology
THIRD EDITION

PSYCHOPATHOLOGY TODAY
The Current Status of Abnormal Psychology
Third Edition

Edited by

William S. Sahakian, Ph.D.
SUFFOLK UNIVERSITY

B. J. Sahakian, Ph.D. (Cantab)
INSTITUTE OF PSYCHIATRY
UNIVERSITY OF LONDON

Paula Leslie Sahakian Nunn, M.D.
VANDERBILT UNIVERSITY MEDICAL CENTER

F.E. PEACOCK PUBLISHERS, INC.
ITASCA, ILLINOIS 60143

Dedicated to the memory of

MABEL LEWIS SAHAKIAN

exceptional wife,
devoted mother,
valued colleague

Contents

Executives. Existential Neurosis. Taylor Manifest Anxiety Scale. Byrne Repression-Sensitization Scale. Neurotic Depression and Endogenous Depression.

INTRODUCTION: Definition of Schizophrenia. Does Schizophrenia Exist? Dimensions of Schizophrenia. Process and Reactive Schizophrenia. Process and Reactive Schizophrenia as Two Different Disorders. Process and Reactive Schizophrenia as a Continuum of the Same Disorder. The Somatic Cause of Process Schizophrenia and the Psychogenic Etiology of Reactive Schizophrenia. Schizophrenic Thought Disorder. Schizophrenic Thought as a Regression to a Childhood Stage of Development. The Von Domarus Principle. Overinclusive Thinking. Abstract-Concrete Deficit. Broken Associative Threads. Loss of Major Set. THEORIES OF SCHIZOPHRENIA: Genetic Hypothesis of Schizophrenia. Biochemical Theories of Schizophrenia. The Adrenocrome Metabolite Theory. Melatonin-harmine Hypothesis. The Taraxein Hypothesis. The Serotonin Hypothesis of Schizophrenia. The Dopamine Hypothesis. Other Biochemical Hypotheses. Vulnerability Hypothesis of Schizophrenia. Psychoanalytic Theory of Schizophrenia. Existential Hypothesis of Schizophrenia. Phenomenological Theory of Schizophrenia. Familial and Sociocultural Theories of Schizophrenia. The Double-Bind Hypothesis. The Quadruple-Bind Hypothesis. Marital Schism and Marital Skew Hypothesis. Mednick's Learning Theory of Schizophrenia. Interference or Segmental Set Theory in Schizophrenia. Progressive Teleological Regression Hypothesis of Schizophrenia. Multiple-Factor Psychosomatic Theory of Schizophrenia. Uncommon Psychiatric Syndromes.

Electroshock Therapy. Insulin Shock Therapy. Metrazol Convulsive Therapy and Carbon Dioxide Therapy. Psychosurgery: Prefrontal Leucotomy and Prefrontal Lobotomy. Sleep Therapy, Narcoanalysis, Hypnoanalysis, and Autogenic Training. Crisis Intervention.

INTRODUCTION: Social Class and Psychopathology. Downward Drift Hypothesis. Social Class and Post-Hospital Performance. Socially Shared Psychopathology. Sociocultural Criterion of Psychopathology. Preventive Psychiatry. Epidemiology of Psychopathology.
INTRODUCTION: Statistics on Mental Disorders.

Preface to the Third Edition

This third edition is more than an updating of the book. In keeping with the interests and trend of the times, new material has been added, especially in the area of anorexia nervosa, bulimia, and dementia, where there is growing interest among researchers. Psychotherapy has become an issue, and questions have been raised as to its effectiveness, and in areas where it is effective, Why is it? Accordingly, this debate is reflected in this new edition.

Psychology and psychiatry continue to be drawn closer together, with less contention and more cooperation in evidence. This results in part from the new independence gained by psychologists (from the medical profession) and the concomitant growing concern in professional issues, such as establishing a legal register of psychologists and developing psychological services. Psychologists with Ph.D.s are increasingly appointed to posts in medical schools throughout the United States.

Licensing of clinical psychologists by states in the United States is currently the vogue rather than the exception, thus legalizing the profession of psychology. Clinical psychologists are finding themselves increasingly included in an Individual Practice Association (IPA), Preferred Provider Organization (PPO), Exclusive Provider Organization (EPO), Health Maintenance Organization (HMO), and similar group plans and organizations delivering health services. Other accepted methods that are visible in the trend of the times include the registration of psychologists in practice in the *National Register of Health Service Providers in Psychology* by the Council for the National Register of Health Service Providers in Psychology. Their 1983 edition lists approximately 13,500 registrants.

Psychological services provided privately and by colleges and universities are very much in evidence. The Department of Psychological Services at colleges and universities is not ordinarily under the aegis of the Department of Psychology but independent from it.

Freudian psychoanalysis appears to be in greater degree yielding to behavioral and cognitive psychology, especially with respect to psychotherapy. Cognitive psychology is on the increase with a growing number of adherents.

To keep abreast of new and developing material and growing areas, introductory sections written by the authors have been expanded where necessary, while matter receding in current interest has been deleted. Thus the book continues to reflect abnormal psychology as it currently exists, and fairly depicts the status of psychopathology today.

WILLIAM S. SAHAKIAN, Ph.D.

Beacon Hill,
Boston, Massachusetts

B. J. SAHAKIAN, Ph.D.

Cambridge, England

PAULA SAHAKIAN NUNN, M.D.

Nashville, Tennessee
March 1985

Preface to the First Edition

No field of psychology since World War II has had the vertical progress and development of that found in psychopathology. Research, especially in the area of schizophrenia, has enlisted the efforts of many able professionals in advancing our knowledge to a markedly higher level of sophistication heretofore unknown, with some researchers believing that the problem of schizophrenia will be resolved in our own lifetime!

Such rapid progress has had the effect of relegating the giants of the past (such as Freud) to the background, where their value has been diminished to historical worth for the most part. These new and significant developments in psychopathology, ordinarily reported in numerous journals published throughout the world, are now made available in a single volume to the reader who does not have these articles or journals at his disposal or who is not prepared to review voluminous material requiring research.

In order to integrate the diverse selections of the many writers representing varying schools of thought, an introduction to each chapter has been provided as a point of orientation. In this respect, the present text is the first book of its kind in psychopathology to be offered to the reading public.

WILLIAM S. SAHAKIAN

Beacon Hill,
Boston, Massachusetts
January, 1970

CHAPTER I

Criteria of Mental Health

Psychiatry and Psychopathology

Perhaps the main distinction between psychology and psychiatry is that the former is a science whose principal subject matter is the study of human behavior, whereas the latter is an applied science, the application of science to those persons afflicted with behavior disorders. Accordingly, psychopathology would then be defined as the science dealing with behavior disorders, while psychiatry is the practice, art, or technique of treating mental, emotional, or behavioral disorders (Jaspers, 1963; Silverman, 1963). Although the two may not overlap in theory, yet in fact or practice they do.

Classification of Mental Disorders

The problem of the classification of mental disorders has posed a number of questions, such as: Which list of mental disorders should be adopted? Which diagnostic terms are preferable? Is it possible to classify mental disorders accurately, or is each case unique? Is the diagnosis and classification of mental disorder of a particular patient subjective on the part of the diagnostician?

One commonly accepted list of mental disorders is found in the *Diagnostic and Statistical Manual of Mental Disorders,* prepared by the Committee on Nomenclature and Statistics of the American Psychiatric Association (1980). A second one, adopted by the Nineteenth World Health Assembly, is published by the World Health Organization (1977) in their *Manual of the International Statistical Classification of Diseases, Injuries, and Causes of Death.*

Lists, however, must be continually revised because of the emergence of new facts, theories, and findings. For example, some psychologists see more intelligence in distinguishing schizophrenia by the *process or reactive* distinction

1

rather than by the simple, hebephrenic, catatonic, and paranoid types (Becker, 1959; Kantor, Wallner, & Winder, 1953; King, 1958). Mongolism is currently termed *Down's syndrome* (London & Rosenhan, 1968; Maher, 1966); and newer terms, concepts, and disorders are appearing, such as, noögenic neurosis (Frankl, 1958a, 1958b, 1959, 1962a, 1962b, 1966a, 1967a) and existential neurosis (Maddi, 1967).

Definition of Mental Disorder

Albee (1959, pp. 9-10) does not consider a definition of mental illness difficult, and dismisses it as an "unusually persistent pattern of behavior over which the individual has little or no voluntary control; it differentiates him from his fellows; it incapacitates him; it interferes with his normal participation in life." This sweeping definition of mental disorder is too encompassing, for it includes many physical disorders such as heart disease, or no disorder whatever such as old age.

Lately, a fairly acceptable definition of psychosis has been a loss or distortion of one's contact with reality. This definition, however, would not include neurosis, subnormality, and some other disorders. To avoid the problem of distinguishing among mental disorders, Wishner (1953, 1955) proposes *efficiency* as the criterion of mental disorder, a decreased efficiency being the concomitant of the severer or graver mental disorders. But, again, efficiency is too broad a concept, one which would fail to distinguish between physical and mental disorders.

Efficiency is an inadequate criterion, for a definitive criterion would discriminate among sensory-perceptual anomalies, motor anomalies, and thought disorders. Even though disorders would have to be subdivided into at least two categories: those relating to emotional problems and those disorders of logical thinking. Some work has been initiated in this area by Von Domarus (1944), who explored the logical thought processes of the schizophrenic, while emotional and logical components of schizophrenic thinking have been investigated by Arieti (1974). The significance of words in schizophrenic thinking has been studied by Chapman and Chapman (1965, 1973), while Payne (1961, 1962; Payne, Mattussek, & George, 1959; Payne, Caird, & Laverty, 1964) has been experimenting in the area of overinclusive thinking or thought disorder in schizophrenics. According to Bleuler, the thinking of some schizophrenics acquired a *negativism* (1912), while other schizophrenics developed an *autism* (1950). Sullivan (1953) has identified logical modes of experience, which he technically termed the prototaxic, parataxic, and syntaxic. In the prototaxic mode, the experience of an infant is lacking in serial connection and consists of an undifferentiated wholeness of experience between organism and environment; the parataxic mode is a slightly more mature stage of experience in which various experiences are differentiated. In the syntaxic, experience has reached its highest elevation of sophistication, one in which a person is capable of distinguishing logically and linguistically. Prototaxic and parataxic modes of experience are characteristic of psychotics.

Like Sullivan, Piaget (1928, 1929, 1930) studied the logical thought processes of children, and discovered many deficiencies in connection with abstract reasoning and class concepts, a mental state comparable to psychotic thinking. Gesell and Ilg (1949) report that the mind and behavior of the child grow in the direction of complex patterning processes. Mental life undergoes three levels of reality: "(1) *the vegetative functions* of respiration, alimentation, elimination; (2) *the world of things,* in time and space; (3) *the world of persons,* in home and community" (p. 20). The child, growing as a unit, develops as an integrated whole, and adjusts himself at all three levels of reality, but not on the "installment plan." Environmental factors do not beget progressions of development, but merely support them.

Recent reliable studies dealing with the thought processes of neurotics have been sparse. Freud (1963b, lecture 17) claims that the obsessional neurotic is "intellectually gifted above the average" as well as being highly ethical, over-conscientious, and "more than usually correct." Horney (1942) sees neurotic thinking stemming from 10 neurotic needs which serve as drives that the neurotic vainly strives to fulfill.

Criteria of Normality and Mental Health

Consensus regarding positive mental health (or even mental abnormality) is far from unanimous (Knutson, 1963). Some identify the mentally ill as anyone who seeks to see a psychiatrist (or has visited one); at the other end of the spectrum there are those who view the mentally ill as those who hallucinate, lose or distort contact with reality, or wish to do away with themselves. Hallucination is but an accessory rather than a fundamental symptom of schizophrenia according to Snyder (1974).

The criterion for mental health is accordingly the mere absence of mental illness (Redlich, 1957). Jahoda (1958, p. 13) points out that *"evaluation of actions as sick, or normal, or extraordinary in a positive sense often depends largely on accepted social conventions."* Mead (1967) elaborates on this point further.

Kubie, whose definition of normality is unsatisfactory because it merely distinguishes between neurosis and psychosis, states that

... we are justified in calling "normal" any act in the determination of which the alliance of conscious and preconscious forces places the dominant role, that is, forces that are accessible on need; whereas on the same grounds we are justified in calling abnormal or unhealthy or neurotic an act in the determination of which unconscious processes are dominant (1954, pp. 184-185).

Redlich, also noting this deficiency in Kubie's definition, comments: "In stating his hypothesis he limits mental illness to essential differences between normal and neurotic. He does not consider abnormal behavior determined by organic causes or the problem of mental deficiency" (1957, p. 150). Allport, however, favors Kubie and regards normal motivation as "flexible, largely conscious, and 'at age,'" while neurotic motivation is "blind, largely unconscious, automatic, and disconnected from the remainder of life" (1961, p. 152).

When normality is used as a criterion for mental health, then it is usually defined either as statistical frequency or normatively in terms of the way a person ought to behave. Cultural relativism results from the statistical frequency definition, accordingly resulting in the justification of the cruel behavior of the Nazis during Hitler's regime. However, to define mental health as normality is to beg the question, "What is normality?" hence to become involved in a circular definition. Coleman synthesizes the cultural with the individual by defining normal behavior as the "optimal development and functioning of the individual consistent with the long-term well-being and progress of the group" (1964, p. 18).

Jahoda (1958) cites six criteria for positive mental health: (1) the attitudes of a person toward himself; these would include the ability of self-objectification (Allport, 1937, pp. 213-214) and of bringing the self to consciousness, that is, being aware of one's motivations; the ability to see the self realistically and correctly as opposed to an ideal self (Cattell, 1957, p. 461; Horney, 1950, pp. 366-378); self-acceptance or the lack of ego-alien impulses; a sense of identity or Cattell's self-sentiment (1965, pp. 193-197; Cattell & Scheier, 1961). (2) A second criterion on positive mental health is growth, development, self-actualization, self-realization, or becoming (coming-to-be), that is, the successful realization of one's potentialities, a view shared by a number of psychologists, especially Goldstein (1939, 1940) and Maslow (1954, 1967, 1968). (3) Integration as a criterion of mental health (Freud) includes the balance or equilibrium of psychic forces, a unifying philosophy of life, and a reasonable resistance or tolerance to stress and anxiety, that is, a resiliency of character or ego, a frustration tolerance, or the ability to delay gratification (Allinsmith & Goethals, 1956). Shoben's model of integrative adjustment is "characterized by self-control, personal responsibility, social responsibility, democratic social interest, and ideals" (1957, p. 188). (4) Autonomy or a person's self-determination and relative independence from external influences (including internally regulating one's behavior and the independence of behavior) is also regarded as a criterion of mental health. (5) Still another criterion is the undistorted perception of reality, one free from need-distortion and from loss of contact with reality (Barron, 1955). (6) A sixth criterion for mental health is environmental mastery, one encompassing competency in problem-solving, adaptation or adjustment, adequate interpersonal relationships, a capacity for love, and efficiency in confronting situational requirements.

Approaching the question of mental illness from an operational point of view, Scott (1958) offers six definitions of mental illness: (1) exposure to psychiatric treatment; (2) maladjustment; (3) labeled mentally ill by psychiatric diagnosis; (4) the individual himself sensing that he is mentally ill or seeking assistance; (5) identified mentally ill by the outcome of psychological tests; and (6) the absence of mental health or positive striving for mental health.

Viewing the matter from a clinical psychologist's orientation, Dana (1966) lists five criteria for normality: (1) cultural-social; (2) legal, entailing the

McNaghten and Durham rules; (3) statistical; (4) ideal (which includes adjustment to society and personality adjustment); and (5) clinical criterion (judgment of a clinician).

Scott's (1968) list contains the following criteria of normality: (1) general adaptive capacity; (2) capacity for self-gratification; (3) competence in interpersonal roles; (4) intellectual capacity; (5) emotional and motivational control; (6) wholesome attitudes toward people; (7) productivity; (8) autonomy; (9) mature integration; and (10) favorable attitudes toward self. Accompanying these main heads are a number of subheads.

Martin (1977) envisions health as the ability to cope with stress and to be free from "psychological handicaps." This definition begs the question: How much stress is the normal person expected to bear before he yields? People who can cope with stress "enjoy mental health," this author claims. Yet many people enjoy stress. What a dull life it would be without any. Stress is not a good correlation of mental health. There is a lot more to it than stress per se.

Is Mental Health an Illusion?

Not only is mental health or normality virtually impossible to define, but some authorities even question its desirability. "It is not clear that normality is such a desirable state," challenges Kisker (1977, p. 3). He adds a comment from a distinguished mental health expert that "to be normal seems shockingly repellent to me. I see neither hope nor comfort in sinking to that low level." If you are not taken aback by that statement, how do you respond to this one from another authority? "Only a fool would continue to wish to be normal after he discovered what it would be like."

We generally think of normal people as average. That is to say, the great hordes out there in the world moving about their daily business are normal, while the few unfortunates—usually found in a mental hospital—are the abnormal. But this is not the case. Even Freud assures us that nobody is normal. It is, according to him, a question of the degree of deviation from the normal. Does normal then become a useless term, an obsolete word for which there is no present-day meaning?

The situation becomes still more confusing when we attempt to resolve it by resorting to experiments conducted in this area in recent years. Temerlin (1968, 1970) came up with some "hair-raising" findings that should terrify anyone who had to face a psychiatrist or clinical psychologist for diagnosis. You might be the epitome of mental health, but if a prestigious psychotherapist should cast aspersions on your normality then other psychiatrists and psychologists will damn you as mentally ill just to follow suit.

Since it is impossible to find a person in perfect mental health, Temerlin's experiment utilized an actor who feigned all the symptoms, signs, attitudes, actions, feelings, and accomplishments of a person enjoying absolute mental health—at least as healthy as one could be. He, Temerlin, had a prestigious confederate drop the remark: "A very interesting man because he looks neurotic, but actually is quite psychotic." The comment was all that the professionals needed. All twenty-five of the psychiatrists present denied that he was mentally healthy. Fifteen of them labeled the man psychotic, the rest neurotic. Only three of the clinical psychologists saw the subject as healthy, seven of them condemned him as psychotic, and another fifteen as neurotic. Actually, laypeople did better. Yet, alas, even they did poorly. It shows the immense social influence authorities carry. We lose all confidence in our own good judgment in the face of theirs.

If you think that the foregoing was not indictment enough concerning our psychiatrists and clinical psychologists, then get sick over Rosenhan's (1973) experiment. Rosenhan would caution us not to get caught in a mental hospital! If you do, then whether or not you are in perfect mental health, they will condemn you as ill. He had five men and three women disguise the fact that they were normal so as to be admitted as mental patients. Once being admitted, they behaved as their usual normal selves. Rather than the authorities seeing these pseudopatients as the healthy people they were, they perceived them in terms of their diagnosis on entering the hospital. Only the psychotics—the inmates—could tell they were faking. Still worse, if you are well outside of a mental hospital, then once you become a patient, conditions are such that you will go berserk or be seen as one who is ill. You may go for a walk out of sheer boredom, for example, but the staff will read that behavior as nervousness. Or, you may be found writing, and that will be interpreted as compulsive behavior correlated with schizophrenia. Your regimen of depersonalization alone is sufficient to create mental problems. Rosenhan's experimental findings would advise that a mental hospital is no place for a sick person—or for a well one either. It is comparable to going to a disreputable hospital and picking up all of the diseases circulating there—or becoming worse due to the incompetent staff. Rosenhan concluded that "we cannot distinguish insanity from sanity" and that "we cannot distinguish the sane from the insane in psychiatric hospitals" (1973, p. 257).

In our universities we call our courses in this field "abnormal psychology." But abnormal psychology is itself a terrible misnomer. The prefix "ab" means "away from." Hence abnormal means a deviation from the normal. If normal means the average, then our moral leaders, our scientists of distinctions, and all other enviable people would be lobbed into the abnormal heap. If on the other hand it means deviating from the norm—the standard of perfection—then I am afraid that we have all fallen short. That is to say, no one is normal.

Treating abnormality as a deviation presents another problem. It begs the question: Deviation from whom? Deviation from what? If it means deviation from what is currently in vogue in one's society, then anyone challenging his society is branded abnormal. Does not this sort of thing go on in Russia? In the Western world it might mean deviating from what a psychotherapist fancies the norm. How dangerous it would be if psychiatrists viewed their own behavior as the norm! Yet is this not the temptation among a number of us clinicians?

1.

D. L. Rosenhan

DISTINGUISHING SANITY FROM INSANITY

If sanity and insanity exist, how shall we know them?

The question is neither capricious nor itself insane. However much we may be personally convinced that we can tell the normal from the abnormal, the evidence is simply not compelling. It is commonplace, for example, to read about murder trials wherein eminent psychiatrists for the defense are contradicted by equally eminent psychiatrists for the prosecution on the matter of the defendant's sanity. More generally, there are a great deal of conflicting data on the reliability, utility, and meaning of such terms as "sanity," "insanity," "mental illness," and "schizophrenia."[1] Finally, as early as 1934, Benedict suggested that normality and abnormality are not universal.[2] What is viewed as normal in one culture may be seen as quite aberrant in another. Thus, notions of normality and abnormality may not be quite as accurate as people believe they are.

To raise questions regarding normality and abnormality is in no way to question the fact that some behaviors are deviant or odd. Murder is deviant. So, too, are hallucinations. Nor does raising such questions deny the existence of the personal anguish that is often associated with "mental illness." Anxiety and depression exist. Psychological suffering exists. But normality and abnormality, sanity and insanity, and the diagnoses that flow from

them may be less substantive than many believe them to be.

At its heart, the question of whether the sane can be distinguished from the insane (and whether degrees of insanity can be distinguished from each other) is a simple matter: do the salient characteristics that lead to diagnoses reside in the patients themselves or in the environments and contexts in which observers find them? From Bleuler, through Kretchmer, through the formulators of the recently revised *Diagnostic and Statistical Manual* of the American Psychiatric Association, the belief has been strong that patients present symptoms, that those symptoms can be categorized, and, implicitly, that the sane are distinguishable from the insane. More recently, however, this belief has been questioned. Based in part on theoretical and anthropological considerations, but also on philosophical, legal, and therapeutic ones, the view has grown that psychological categorization of mental illness is useless at best and downright harmful, misleading, and pejorative at worst. Psychiatric diagnoses, in this view, are in the minds of the observers and are not valid summaries of characteristics displayed by the observed.[3-5]

Gains can be made in deciding which of these is more nearly accurate by getting normal people (that is, people who do not have, and have never suffered, symptoms of serious psychiatric disorders) admitted to psychiatric hospitals and then determining whether they were discovered to be sane and, if so, how. If the sanity of such pseudopatients were always detected, there

From D.L. Rosenhan, *Science,* vol. 179, 19 January 1973, pp. 250–258. Copyright 1973 by the American Association for the Advancement of Science.

would be prima facie evidence that a sane individual can be distinguished from the insane context in which he is found. Normality (and presumably abnormality) is distinct enough that it can be recognized wherever it occurs, for it is carried within the person. If, on the other hand, the sanity of the pseudopatients were never discovered, serious difficulties would arise for those who support traditional modes of psychiatric diagnosis. Given that the hospital staff was not incompetent, that the pseudopatient had been behaving as sanely as he had been outside of the hospital, and that it had never been previously suggested that he belonged in a psychiatric hospital, such an unlikely outcome would support the view that psychiatric diagnosis betrays little about the patient but much about the environment in which an observer finds him.

This article describes such an experiment. Eight sane people gained secret admission to 12 different hospitals.[6] Their diagnostic experiences constitute the data of the first part of this article; the remainder is devoted to a description of their experiences in psychiatric institutions. Too few psychiatrists and psychologists, even those who have worked in such hospitals, know what the experience is like. They rarely talk about it with former patients, perhaps because they distrust information coming from the previously insane. Those who have worked in psychiatric hospitals are likely to have adapted so thoroughly to the settings that they are insensitive to the impact of that experience. And while there have been occasional reports of researchers who submitted themselves to psychiatric hospitalization,[7] these reseachers have commonly remained in the hospitals for short periods of time, often with the knowledge of the hospital staff. It is difficult to know the extent to which they were treated like patients or like research colleagues. Nevertheless, their reports about the inside of the psychiatric hospital have been valuable. This article extends those efforts.

PSEUDOPATIENTS AND THEIR SETTINGS

The eight pseudopatients were a varied group. One was a psychology graduate student in his 20s. The remaining seven were older and "established." Among them were three psychologists, a pediatrician, a psychiatrist, a painter, and a housewife. Three pseudopatients were women, five were men. All of them employed pseudonyms, lest their alleged diagnoses embarrass them later. Those who were in mental health professions alleged another occupation in order to avoid the special attentions that might be accorded by staff, as a matter of courtesy or caution, to ailing colleagues.[8] With the exception of myself (I was the first pseudopatient and my presence was known to the hospital administrator and chief psychologist and, so far as I can tell, to them alone), the presence of pseudopatients and the nature of the research program was not known to the hospital staffs.[9]

The settings were similarly varied. In order to generalize the findings, admission into a variety of hospitals was sought. The 12 hospitals in the sample were located in five different states on the East and West coasts. Some were old and shabby, some were quite new. Some were research-oriented, others not. Some had good staff-patient ratios, others were quite under-staffed. Only one was a strictly private hospital. All of the others were supported by state or federal funds or, in one instance, by university funds.

After calling the hospital for an appointment, the pseudopatient arrived at the admissions office complaining that he had been hearing voices. Asked what the voices said, he replied that they were often unclear, but as far as he could tell they said "empty," "hollow," and "thud." The voices were unfamiliar and were of the same sex as the pseudopatient. The choice of these symptoms was occasioned by their apparent similarity to existential symptoms. Such symptoms are alleged to arise from painful concerns about the perceived meaninglessness of one's life. It is as if the hallucinating person were saying, "My life is empty and hollow." The choice of these symptoms was also determined by the *absence* of a single report of existential psychoses in the literature.

Beyond alleging the symptoms and falsifying name, vocation, and employment, no further alterations of person, history, or circumstances were made. The significant events of the pseudopatient's life history were presented as they had actually occurred. Relationships with parents and siblings, with spouse and children, with people at work and in school, consistent with the aforementioned exceptions, were described as they were or had been. Frustrations and upsets were described along with joys and satisfactions. These facts are important to remember. If anything, they strongly biased the subsequent results in favor of detecting sanity, since none of their histories or current behaviors were seriously pathological in any way.

Immediately upon admission to the psychiatric ward, the pseudopatient ceased simulating *any* symptoms of abnormality. In some cases, there was a brief period of mild nervousness and anxiety, since none of the pseudopatients really believed that they would be admitted so easily. Indeed, their shared fear was that they would be immediately exposed as frauds and greatly embarrassed. Moreover, many of them had never visited a psychiatric ward; even those who had, nevertheless had some genuine fears about what might happen to them. Their nervousness, then, was quite appropriate to the novelty of the hospital setting, and it abated rapidly.

Apart from that short-lived nervousness, the pseudopatient behaved on the ward as he "normally" behaved. The pseudopatient spoke to patients and staff as he might ordinarily. Because there is uncommonly little to do on a psychiatric ward, he attempted to engage others in conversation. When asked by staff how he was feeling, he indicated that he was fine, that he no longer experienced symptoms. He responded to instructions from attendants, to calls for medication (which was not swallowed), and to dining-hall instructions. Beyond such activities as were available to him on the admissions ward, he spent his time writing down his observations about the ward, its patients, and the staff. Initially these notes were written "secretly," but as it soon became clear that no one much cared, they were subsequently written on standard tablets of paper in such public places as the dayroom. No secret was made of these activities.

The pseudopatient, very much as a true psychiatric patient, entered a hospital with no foreknowledge of when he would be discharged. Each was told that he would have to get out by his own devices, essentially by convincing the staff that he was sane. The psychological stresses associated with hospitalization were considerable, and all but one of the pseudopatients desired to be discharged almost immediately after being admitted. They were, therefore, motivated not only to behave sanely, but to be paragons of cooperation. That their behavior was in no way disruptive is confirmed by nursing reports, which have been obtained on most of the patients. These reports uniformly indicate that the patients were "friendly," "cooperative," and "exhibited no abnormal indications."

THE NORMAL ARE NOT DETECTABLY SANE

Despite their public "show" of sanity, the pseudopatients were never detected. Admitted, except in one case, with a diagnosis of schizophrenia,[10] each was discharged with a diagnosis of schizophrenia "in remission." The label "in remission" should in no way be dismissed as a formality, for at no time during any hospitalization had any question been raised about any pseudopatient's simulation. Nor are there any indications in the hospital records that the pseudopatient's status was suspect. Rather, the evidence is strong that, once labeled schizophrenic, the pseudopatient was stuck with that label. If the pseudopatient was to be discharged, he must naturally be "in remission"; but he was not sane, nor, in the institution's view, had he ever been sane.

The uniform failure to recognize sanity cannot be attributed to the quality of the hospitals, for, although there were considerable variations among them, several are considered excellent. Nor can it be alleged that there was simply not enough time to observe the pseudopatients. Length of hospitalization ranged from 7 to 52 days, with an average of 19 days. The pseudopatients were not, in fact, carefully observed, but this failure clearly speaks more to traditions within psychiatric hospitals than to lack of opportunity.

Finally, it cannot be said that the failure to recognize the pseudopatients' sanity was due to the fact that they were not behaving sanely. While there was clearly some tension present in all of them, their daily visitors could detect no serious behavioral consequences—nor, indeed, could other patients. It was quite common for the patients to "detect" the pseudopatients' sanity. During the first three hospitalizations, when accurate counts were kept, 35 of a total of 118 patients on the admissions ward voiced their suspicions, some vigorously. "You're not crazy. You're a journalist, or a professor [referring to the continual note-taking]. You're checking up on the hospital." While most of the patients were reassured by the pseudopatient's insistence that he had been sick before he came in but was fine now, some continued to believe that the pseudopatient was sane throughout his hospitalization.[11] The fact that the patients often recognized normality when staff did not raises important questions.

Failure to detect sanity during the course of hospitalization may be due to the fact that physicians operate with a strong bias toward what statisticians call the type 2 error.[5] This is to say that physicians are more inclined to call a healthy person sick (a false positive, type 2) than a sick person healthy (a false negative, type 1). The reasons for this are not hard to find: it is clearly more dangerous to misdiagnose illness than health. Better to err on the side of caution, to suspect illness even among the healthy.

But what holds for medicine does not hold equally well for psychiatry. Medical illnesses, while unfortunate, are not commonly pejorative. Psychiatric diagnoses, on the contrary, carry with them personal, legal, and social stigmas.[12] It was therefore important to see whether the tendency toward diagnosing the sane insane could be reversed. The following experiment was arranged at a research and teaching hospital whose staff had heard these findings but doubted that such an error could occur in their hospital. The staff was informed that at some time during the following 3 months, one or more pseudopatients would attempt to be admitted into the psychiatric hospital. Each staff member was asked to rate each patient who presented himself at admissions or on the ward according to the likelihood that the patient was a pseudopatient. A 10-point scale was used, with a 1 and 2 reflecting high confidence that the patient was a pseudopatient.

Judgments were obtained on 193 patients who were admitted for psychiatric treatment. All staff who had had sustained contact with or primary responsibility for the patient—attendants, nurses, psychiatrists, physicians, and psychologists—were asked to make judgments. Forty-one patients were alleged, with high confidence, to be pseudopatients by at least one member of the staff. Twenty-three were considered suspect by at least one psychiatrist. Nineteen were suspected by one psychiatrist *and* one other staff member. Actually, no genuine pseudopatient (at least from my group) presented himself during this period.

The experiment is instructive. It indicates that the tendency to designate sane people as insane can be reversed when the stakes (in this case, prestige and diagnostic acumen) are high. But what can be said of the 19 people who were suspected of being "sane" by one psychiatrist and another staff member? Were these people truly "sane," or was it rather the case that in the course of avoiding the type 2 error the staff tended to make more errors of the first sort—calling the crazy "sane"? There is no way of knowing. But one thing is certain: any diagnostic process that lends itself so readily to massive errors of this sort cannot be a very reliable one.

THE STICKINESS OF PSYCHODIAGNOSTIC LABELS

Beyond the tendency to call the healthy sick—a tendency that accounts better for diagnostic behavior on admission than it does for such behavior after a lengthy period of exposure—the data speak to the massive role of labeling in psychiatric assessment. Having once been labeled schizophrenic, there is nothing the pseudopatient can do to overcome the tag. The tag profoundly colors others' perceptions of him and his behavior.

From one viewpoint, these data are hardly surprising, for it has long been known that elements are given meaning by the context in which they occur. Gestalt psychology made this point vigorously, and Asch[13] demonstrated that there are "central" personality traits (such as "warm" versus "cold") which are so powerful that they markedly color the meaning of other information in forming an impression of a given personality.[14] "Insane," "schizophrenic," "manic-depressive," and "crazy" are probably among the most powerful of such central traits. Once a person is designated abnormal, all of his other behaviors and characteristics are colored by that label. Indeed, that label is so powerful that many of the pseudopatients' normal behaviors were overlooked entirely or profoundly misinterpreted. Some examples may clarify this issue.

Earlier I indicated that there were no changes in the pseudopatient's personal history and current status beyond those of name, employment, and, where necessary, vocation. Otherwise, a veridical description of personal history and circumstances was offered. Those circumstances were not psychotic. How were they made consonant with the diagnosis of psychosis? Or were those diagnoses modified in such a way as to bring them into accord with the circumstances of the pseudopatient's life, as described by him?

As far as I can determine, diagnoses were in no way affected by the relative health of the circumstances of a pseudopatient's life. Rather, the reverse occurred: the perception of his circumstances was shaped entirely by the diagnosis. A clear example of such translation is found in the case of a pseudopatient who had had a close relationship with his mother but was rather remote from his father during his early childhood. During adolescence and beyond, however, his father became a close friend, while his relationship with his mother cooled. His present relationship with his wife was characteristically close and warm. Apart from occasional angry exchanges, friction was minimal. The children had rarely been spanked. Surely there is nothing especially pathological about such a history. Indeed, many readers may see a similar pattern in their own experiences, with no markedly deleterious consequences. Observe, however, how such a history was translated in the psychopathological context, this from the case summary prepared after the patient was discharged.

This white 39-year-old male . . . manifests a long history of considerable ambivalence in close relationships, which begins in early childhood. A warm relationship with his mother cools during his adolescence. A distant relationship to his father is described as becoming very intense. Affective stability is absent. His attempts to control emotionality with his wife and children are punctuated by angry outbursts and, in the case of the children, spankings. And while he says that he has several good friends, one senses considerable ambivalence embedded in those relationships also. . . .

The facts of the case were unintentionally distorted by the staff to achieve consistency with a popular theory of the dynamics of a schizophrenic reaction.[15] Nothing of an ambivalent nature had been described in relations with parents, spouse, or friends. To the extent that ambivalence could be inferred, it was probably not greater than is found in all human relationships. It is true the pseudopatient's relationships with his parents changed over time, but in the ordinary context that would hardly be remarkable —indeed, it might very well be expected. Clearly, the meaning ascribed to his verbalizations (that is, ambivalence, affective instability) was determined by the diagnosis: schizophrenia. An entirely different meaning would have been ascribed if it were known that the man was "normal."

All pseudopatients took extensive notes publicly. Under ordinary circumstances, such behavior would have raised questions in the minds of observers, as, in fact, it did among patients. Indeed, it seemed so certain that the notes would elicit suspicion that elaborate precautions were taken to remove them from the ward each day. But the precautions proved needless. The closest any staff member came to questioning these notes occurred when one pseudopatient asked his physician what kind of medication he was receiving and began to write down the response. "You needn't write it," he was told gently. "If you have trouble remembering, just ask me again."

If no questions were asked of the pseudopatients, how was their writing interpreted? Nursing records for three patients indicate that the writing was seen as an aspect of their pathological behavior. "Patient engages in writing behavior" was the daily nursing comment on one of the pseudopatients who was never questioned about his writing. Given that the patient is in the hospital, he must be psychologically disturbed. And given that he is disturbed, continuous writing must be a behavioral manifestation of that disturbance, perhaps a subset of the compulsive behaviors that are sometimes correlated with schizophrenia.

One tacit characteristic of psychiatric diagnosis is that it locates the sources of aberration within the individual and only rarely within the complex of stimuli that surrounds him. Consequently, behaviors that are stimulated by the environment are commonly misattributed to the patient's disorder. For example, one kindly nurse found a pseudopatient pacing the long hospital corridors. "Nervous, Mr. X?" she asked. "No, bored," he said.

The notes kept by pseudopatients are full of patient behaviors that were misinterpreted by well-intentioned staff. Often enough, a patient would go "berserk" because he had, wittingly or unwittingly, been mistreated by, say, an attendant. A nurse coming upon the scene would rarely inquire even cursorily into the environmental stimuli of the patient's behavior. Rather, she assumed that his upset derived from his pathology, not from his present interactions with other staff members. Occasionally, the staff might assume that the patient's family (especially when they had recently visited) or other patients had stimulated the outburst. But never were the staff found to assume that one of themselves or the structure of the hospital had anything to do with a patient's behavior. One psychiatrist pointed to a group of patients who were sitting outside the cafeteria entrance half an hour before lunchtime. To a group of young residents he indicated that such behavior was characteristic of the oral-acquisitive nature of the syndrome. It seemed not to occur to him that there were very few things to anticipate in a psychiatric hospital besides eating.

A psychiatric label has a life and an influence of its own. Once the impression has been formed that the patient is schizophrenic, the expectation is that he will continue to be schizophrenic. When a sufficient amount of time has passed, during which the patient has done nothing bizarre, he is considered to be in remission and available for discharge. But the label endures beyond discharge, with the unconfirmed expectation that he will behave as a schizophrenic again. Such labels, conferred by mental health professionals, are as influential on the patient as they are on his relatives and friends, and it should not surprise anyone that the diagnosis acts on all of them as a self-fulfilling prophecy. Eventually, the patient himself accepts the diagnosis, with all of its surplus meanings and expectations, and behaves accordingly.[5]

The inferences to be made from these matters are quite simple. Much as Zigler and Phillips have demonstrated that there is enormous overlap in the symptoms presented by patients who have been variously diagnosed,[16] so there is enormous overlap in the behaviors of the sane and the insane. The sane are not "sane" all of the time. We lose our tempers "for no good reason." We are occasionally depressed or anxious, again for no good reason. And we may find it difficult to get along with one or another person—again for no reason that we can specify. Similarly, the insane are not always insane. Indeed, it was the impression of the pseudopatients while living with them that they were sane for long periods of time—that the bizarre behaviors upon which their diagnoses were allegedly predicated constituted only a small fraction of their total behavior. If it makes no sense to label ourselves permanently depressed on the basis of an occasional depression, then it takes better evidence than is presently available to label all patients insane or schizophrenic on the basis of bizarre behaviors or cognitions. It seems more useful, as Mischel[17] has pointed out, to limit our discussions to *behaviors*, the stimuli that provoke them, and their correlates.

It is not known why powerful impressions of personality traits, such as "crazy" or "insane," arise. Conceivably, when the origins of and stimuli that give rise to a behavior are remote or unknown, or when the behavior strikes us as immutable, trait labels regarding the *behaver* arise. When, on the other hand, the origins and stimuli are known and available, discourse is limited to the behavior itself. Thus, I may hallucinate because I am sleeping, or I may hallucinate because I have ingested a peculiar drug. These are termed sleep-induced hallucinations, or dreams, and drug-induced hallucinations, respectively. But when the stimuli to my hallucinations are unknown, that is called craziness, or schizophrenia—as if that inference were somehow as illuminating as the others.

THE EXPERIENCE OF PSYCHIATRIC HOSPITALIZATION

The term "mental illness" is of recent origin. It was coined by people who were humane in their inclinations and who wanted very much to raise the station of (and the public's sympathies toward) the psychologically disturbed from that of witches and "crazies" to one that was akin to the physically ill. And they were at least partially successful, for the treatment of the mentally ill *has* improved considerably over the years. But while treatment has improved, it is doubtful that people really regard the mentally ill in the same way that they view the physically ill. A broken leg is something one recovers from, but mental illness allegedly endures forever.[18] A broken leg does not threaten the observer, but a crazy schizophrenic? There is by now a host of evidence that attitudes toward the mentally ill are characterized by fear, hostility, aloofness, suspicion, and dread.[19] The mentally ill are society's lepers.

That such attitudes infect the general population is perhaps not surprising, only upsetting. But that they affect the professionals—attendants, nurses, physicians, psychologists, and social workers—who treat and deal with the mentally ill is more disconcerting, both because such attitudes are self-evidently pernicious and because they are unwitting. Most mental health professionals would insist that they are sympathetic toward the mentally ill, that they are neither avoidant nor hostile. But it is more likely that an exquisite ambivalence characterizes their relations with psychiatric patients, such that their avowed impulses are only part of their entire attitude. Negative attitudes are there too and can easily be detected. Such attitudes should not surprise us. They are the natural offspring of the labels patients wear and the places in which they are found.

Consider the structure of the typical psychiatric hospital. Staff and patients are strictly segregated. Staff have their own living space, including their dining facilities, bathrooms, and assembly places. The glassed quarters that contain the professional staff, which the pseudopatients came to call "the cage," sit out on every dayroom. The staff emerge primarily for caretaking purposes—to give medication, to conduct a therapy or group meeting, to instruct or reprimand a patient. Otherwise, staff keep to themselves, almost as if the disorder that afflicts their charges is somehow catching.

So much is patient-staff segregation the rule that, for four public hospitals in which an attempt was made to measure the degree to which staff and patients mingle, it was necessary to use "time out of the staff cage" as the operational measure. While it was not the case that all time spent out of the cage was spent mingling with patients (attendants, for example, would occasionally emerge to watch television in the dayroom), it was the only way in which one could gather reliable data on time for measuring.

The average amount of time spent by attendants outside of the cage was 11.3 percent (range, 3 to 52 percent). This figure does not represent only time spent mingling with patients, but also includes time spent on such chores as folding laundry, supervising patients while they shave, directing ward cleanup, and sending patients to off-ward activities. It was the relatively rare attendant who spent time talking with patients or playing games with them. It proved impossible to obtain a "percent mingling time" for nurses, since the amount of time they spent out of the cage was too brief. Rather, we counted instances of emergence from the cage. On the average, daytime nurses emerged from the cage 11.5 times per shift, including instances when they left the ward entirely (range, 4 to 39 times). Late afternoon and night nurses were even less available, emerging on the average 9.4 times per shift (range, 4 to 41 times). Data on early morning nurses, who arrived usually after midnight and departed at 8 a.m., are not available because patients were asleep during most of this period.

Physicians, especially psychiatrists, were even less available. They were rarely seen on the wards. Quite commonly, they would be seen only when they arrived and departed, with the remaining time being spent in their offices or in the cage. On the average, physicians emerged on the ward 6.7 times per day (range, 1 to 17 times). It proved difficult to make an accurate estimate in this regard, since physicians often maintained hours that allowed them to come and go at different times.

The hierarchical organization of the psychiatric hospital has been commented on before,[20] but the latent meaning of that kind of organization is worth noting again. Those with the most power have least to do with patients, and those with the least power are most involved with them. Recall, however, that the acquisition of role-appropriate behaviors occurs mainly through the observation of others, with the most powerful having the most influence. Consequently, it is understandable that attendants not only spend more time with patients than do any other members of the staff—that is required by their station in the hierarchy—but also, insofar as they learn from their superiors' behavior, spend as little time with patients as they can. Attendants are seen mainly in the cage, which is where the models, the action, and the power are.

I turn now to a different set of studies, these dealing with staff response to patient-initiated contact. It has long been known that the amount of time a person spends with you can be an index of your significance to him. If he initiates and maintains eye contact, there is reason to believe that he is considering your requests and needs. If he pauses to chat or actually stops and talks, there is added reason to infer that he is individuating you. In four hospitals, the pseudopatient approached the staff member with a request which took the following form: "Pardon me, Mr. [or Dr. or Mrs.] X, could you tell me when I will be eligible for grounds privileges?" (or ". . . when I will be presented at the staff meeting?" or ". . . when I am likely to be discharged?"). While the content of the question varied according to the appropriateness of the target and the pseudopatient's (apparent) current needs the form was always a courteous and relevant request for information. Care was taken never to approach a particular member of the staff more than once a day, lest the staff member become suspicious or irritated. In examining these data, remember that the behavior of the pseudopatients was neither bizarre nor disruptive. One

TABLE 1-1
Self-Initiated Contact by Pseudopatients with Psychiatrists and Nurses and Attendants,
Compared to Contact with Other Groups.

Contact	Psychiatric hospitals		University campus (nonmedical)	University medical center		
				Physicians		
	(1) Psychiatrists	(2) Nurses and attendants	(3) Faculty	(4) "Looking for a psychiatrist"	(5) "Looking for an internist"	(6) No additional comment
Responses						
Moves on, head averted (%)	71	88	0	0	0	0
Makes eye contact (%)	23	10	0	11	0	0
Pauses and chats (%)	2	2	0	11	0	10
Stops and talks	4	0.5	100	78	100	90
Mean number of questions answered (out of 6)	*	*	6	3.8	4.8	4.5
Respondents (No.)	13	47	14	18	15	10
Attempts (No.)	185	1283	14	18	15	10

* Not applicable.

could indeed engage in good conversation with them.

The data for these experiments are shown in Table 1-1, separately for psychiatrists (column 1) and for nurses and attendants (column 2). Minor differences between these four institutions were overwhelmed by the degree to which staff avoided continuing contacts that patients had initiated. By far, their most common response consisted of either a brief response to the question, offered while they were "on the move" and with head averted, or no response at all.

The encounter frequently took the following bizarre form: (pseudopatient) "Pardon me, Dr. X. Could you tell me when I am eligible for grounds privileges?" (physician) "Good morning, Dave. How are you today?" (Moves off without waiting for a response.)

It is instructive to compare these data with data recently obtained at Stanford University. It has been alleged that large and eminent universities are characterized by faculty who are so busy that they have no time for students. For this comparison, a young lady approached individual faculty members who seemed to be walking purposefully to some meeting or teaching

engagement and asked them the following six questions.

1) "Pardon me, could you direct me to Encina Hall?" (at the medical school: ". . . to the Clinical Research Center?").

2) "Do you know where Fish Annex is?" (there is no Fish Annex at Stanford).

3) "Do you teach here?"

4) "How does one apply for admission to the college?" (at the medical school: ". . . to the medical school?").

5) "Is it difficult to get in?"

6) "Is there financial aid?"

Without exception, as can be seen in Table 1-1 (column 3), all of the questions were answered. No matter how rushed they were, all respondents not only maintained eye contact, but stopped to talk. Indeed, many of the respondents went out of their way to direct or take the questioner to the office she was seeking, to try to locate "Fish Annex," or to discuss with her the possibilities of being admitted to the university.

Similar data, also shown in Table 1-1 (columns 4, 5, and 6), were obtained in the hospital. Here too, the young lady came prepared with six questions. After the first question, however, she remarked to 18 of her respondents (column 4), "I'm looking for a psychiatrist," and to 15 others (column 5), "I'm looking for an internist." Ten other respondents received no inserted comment (column 6). The general degree of cooperative responses is considerably higher for these university groups than it was for pseudopatients in psychiatric hospitals. Even so, differences are apparent within the medical school setting. Once having indicated that she was looking for a psychiatrist, the degree of cooperation elicited was less than when she sought an internist.

POWERLESSNESS AND DEPERSONALIZATION

Eye contact and verbal contact reflect concern and individuation; their absence, avoidance and depersonalization. The data I have presented do not do justice to the rich daily encounters that grew up around matters of depersonalization and avoidance. I have records of patients who were beaten by staff for the sin of having initiated verbal contact. During my own experience, for example, one patient was beaten in the presence of other patients for having approached an attendant and told him, "I like you." Occasionally, punishment meted out to patients for misdemeanors seemed so excessive that it could not be justified by the most radical interpretations of psychiatric canon. Nevertheless, they appeared to go unquestioned. Tempers were often short. A patient who had not heard a call for medication would be roundly excoriated, and the morning attendants would often wake patients with, "Come on, you m-----f-----s, out of bed!"

Neither anecdotal nor "hard" data can convey the overwhelming sense of powerlessness which invades the individual as he is continually exposed to the depersonalization of the psychiatric hospital. It hard-

ly matters *which* psychiatric hospital—the excellent public ones and the very plush private hospital were better than the rural and shabby ones in this regard, but, again, the features that psychiatric hospitals had in common overwhelmed by far their apparent differences.

Powerlessness was evident everywhere. The patient is deprived of many of his legal rights by dint of his psychiatric commitment.[21] He is shorn of credibility by virtue of his psychiatric label. His freedom of movement is restricted. He cannot initiate contact with the staff, but may only respond to such overtures as they make. Personal privacy is minimal. Patient quarters and possessions can be entered and examined by any staff member, for whatever reason. His personal history and anguish is available to any staff member (often including the "grey lady" and "candy striper" volunteer) who chooses to read his folder, regardless of their therapeutic relationship to him. His personal hygiene and waste evacuation are often monitored. The water closets may have no doors.

At times, depersonalization reached such proportions that pseudopatients had the sense that they were invisible, or at least unworthy of account. Upon being admitted, I and other pseudopatients took the initial physical examinations in a semi-public room, where staff members went about their own business as if we were not there.

On the ward, attendants delivered verbal and occasionally serious physical abuse to patients in the presence of other observing patients, some of whom (the pseudopatients) were writing it all down. Abusive behavior, on the other hand, terminated quite abruptly when other staff members were known to be coming. Staff are credible witnesses. Patients are not.

A nurse unbuttoned her uniform to

adjust her brassiere in the presence of an entire ward of viewing men. One did not have the sense that she was being seductive. Rather, she didn't notice us. A group of staff persons might point to a patient in the dayroom and discuss him animatedly, as if he were not there.

One illuminating instance of depersonalization and invisibility occurred with regard to medications. All told, the pseudopatients were administered nearly 2100 pills, including Elavil, Stelazine, Compazine, and Thorazine, to name but a few. (That such a variety of medications should have been administered to patients presenting identical symptoms is itself worthy of note.) Only two were swallowed. The rest were either pocketed or deposited in the toilet. The pseudopatients were not alone in this. Although I have no precise records on how many patients rejected their medications, the pseudopatients frequently found the medications of other patients in the toilet before they deposited their own. As long as they were cooperative, their behavior and the pseudo-patients' own in this matter, as in other important matters, went unnoticed throughout.

Reactions to such depersonalization among pseudopatients were intense. Although they had come to the hospital as participant observers and were fully aware that they did not "belong," they nevertheless found themselves caught up in and fighting the process of depersonalization. Some examples: a graduate student in psychology asked his wife to bring his textbooks to the hospital so he could "catch up on his homework"—this despite the elaborate precautions taken to conceal his professional association. The same student, who had trained for quite some time to get into the hospital, and who had looked forward to the experience, "remembered" some drag races that he had wanted to see

on the weekend and insisted that he be discharged by that time. Another pseudo-patient attempted a romance with a nurse. Subsequently, he informed the staff that he was applying for admission to graduate school in psychology and was very likely to be admitted, since a graduate professor was one of his regular hospital visitors. The same person began to engage in psychotherapy with other patients—all of this as a way of becoming a person in an impersonal environment.

THE SOURCES OF DEPERSONALIZATION

What are the origins of depersonalization? I have already mentioned two. First are attitudes held by all of us toward the mentally ill—including those who treat them—attitudes characterized by fear, distrust, and horrible expectations on the one hand, and benevolent intentions on the other. Our ambivalence leads, in this instance as in others, to avoidance.

Second, and not entirely separate, the hierarchical structure of the psychiatric hospital facilitates depersonalization. Those who are at the top have least to do with patients, and their behavior inspires the rest of the staff. Average daily contact with psychiatrists, psychologists, residents, and physicians combined ranged from 3.9 to 25.1 minutes, with an overall mean of 6.8 (six pseudopatients over a total of 129 days of hospitalization). Included in this average are time spent in the admissions interview, ward meetings in the presence of a senior staff member, group and individual psychotherapy contacts, case presentation conferences, and discharge meetings. Clearly, patients do not spend much time in interpersonal contact with doctoral staff. And doctoral staff serve as models for nurses and attendants.

There are probably other sources. Psychiatric installations are presently in serious financial straits. Staff shortages are pervasive, staff time at a premium. Something has to give, and that something is patient contact. Yet, while financial stresses are realities, too much can be made of them. I have the impression that the psychological forces that result in depersonalization are much stronger than the fiscal ones and that the addition of more staff would not correspondingly improve patient care in this regard. The incidence of staff meetings and the enormous amount of record-keeping on patients, for example, have not been as substantially reduced as has patient contact. Priorities exist, even during hard times. Patient contact is not a significant priority in the traditional psychiatric hospital, and fiscal pressures do not account for this. Avoidance and depersonalization may.

Heavy reliance upon psychotropic medication tacitly contributes to depersonalization by convincing staff that treatment is indeed being conducted and that further patient contact may not be necessary. Even here, however, caution needs to be exercised in understanding the role of psychotropic drugs. If patients were powerful rather than powerless, if they were viewed as interesting individuals rather than diagnostic entities, if they were socially significant rather than social lepers, if their anguish truly and wholly compelled our sympathies and concerns, would we not *seek* contact with them, despite the availability of medications? Perhaps for the pleasure of it all?

THE CONSEQUENCES OF LABELING AND DEPERSONALIZATION

Whenever the ratio of what is known to what needs to be known approaches zero, we tend to invent "knowledge" and assume that we understand more than we actually do. We seem unable to acknowledge that we simply don't know. The needs for diagnosis and remediation of behavioral and emotional problems are enormous. But rather than acknowledge that we are just embarking on understanding, we continue to label patients "schizophrenic," "manic-depressive," and "insane," as if in those words we had captured the essence of understanding. The facts of the matter are that we have known for a long time that diagnoses are often not useful or reliable, but we have nevertheless continued to use them. We now know that we cannot distinguish insanity from sanity. It is depressing to consider how that information will be used.

Not merely depressing, but frightening. How many people, one wonders, are sane but not recognized as such in our psychiatric institutions? How many have been needlessly stripped of their privileges of citizenship, from the right to vote and drive to that of handling their own accounts? How many have feigned insanity in order to avoid the criminal consequences of their behavior, and, conversely, how many would rather stand trial than live interminably in a psychiatric hospital —but are wrongly thought to be mentally ill? How many have been stigmatized by well-intentioned, but nevertheless erroneous, diagnoses? On the last point, recall again that a "type 2 error" in psychiatric diagnosis does not have the same consequences it does in medical diagnosis. A diagnosis of cancer that has been found to be in error is cause for celebration. But psychiatric diagnoses are rarely found to be in error. The label sticks, a mark of inadequacy forever.

Finally, how many patients might be "sane" outside the psychiatric hospital but seem insane in it—not because craziness resides in them, as it were, but because they are responding to a bizarre setting, one that may be unique to institutions which harbor nether people? Goffman[4] calls the process of socialization to such institutions "mortification"—an apt metaphor that includes the processes of depersonalization that have been described here. And while it is impossible to know whether the pseudopatients' responses to these processes are characteristic of all inmates—they were, after all, not real patients—it is difficult to believe that these processes of socialization to a psychiatric hospital provide useful attitudes or habits of response for living in the "real world."

SUMMARY AND CONCLUSIONS

It is clear that we cannot distinguish the sane from the insane in psychiatric hospitals. The hospital itself imposes a special environment in which the meanings of behavior can easily be misunderstood. The consequences to patients hospitalized in such an environment—the powerlessness, depersonalization, segregation, mortification, and self-labeling—seem undoubtedly counter-therapeutic.

I do not, even now, understand this problem well enough to perceive solutions. But two matters seem to have some promise. The first concerns the proliferation of community mental health facilities, of crisis intervention centers, of the human potential movement, and of behavior therapies that, for all of their own problems, tend to avoid psychiatric labels, to focus on specific problems and behaviors, and to retain the individual in a relatively nonpejorative environment. Clearly, to the extent that we refrain from sending the distressed to insane places, our impressions of them are less likely to be distorted. (The risk of distorted perceptions, it seems to me, is always present, since we are much more sensitive to an individual's behaviors and verbalizations than we are to the subtle contextual stimuli that often promote them. At issue here is a matter of magnitude. And, as I have shown, the magnitude of distortion is exceedingly high in the extreme context that is a psychiatric hospital.)

The second matter that might prove promising speaks to the need to increase the sensitivity of mental health workers and researchers to the *Catch 22* position of psychiatric patients. Simply reading materials in this area will be of help to some such workers and researchers. For others, directly experiencing the impact of psychiatric hospitalization will be of enormous use. Clearly, further research into the social psychology of such total institutions will both facilitate treatment and deepen understanding.

I and the other pseudopatients in the psychiatric setting had distinctly negative reactions. We do not pretend to describe the subjective experiences of true patients. Theirs may be different from ours, particularly with the passage of time and the necessary process of adaptation to one's environment. But we can and do speak to the relatively more objective indices of treatment within the hospital. It could be a mistake, and a very unfortunate one, to consider that what happened to us derived from malice or stupidity on the part of the staff. Quite the contrary, our overwhelming impression of them was of people who really cared, who were committed and who were uncommonly intelligent. Where they failed, as they sometimes did painfully, it would be more accurate to attribute those failures to the environment in which they, too, found themselves than to personal callousness. Their perceptions and behavior were controlled by the situation, rather than being motivated by a malicious disposition. In a more benign environment, one that was less attached to global diagnosis, their behaviors and judgments might have been more benign and effective.

REFERENCES AND NOTES

1. P. Ash, *J. Abnorm. Soc. Psychol.* **44**, 272 (1949); A. T. Beck, *Amer. J. Psychiat.* **119**, 210 (1962); A. T. Boisen, *Psychiatry* **2**, 233 (1938); N. Kreitman, *J. Ment. Sci.* **107**, 876 (1961); N. Kreitman, P. Sainsbury, J. Morrisey, J. Towers, J. Scrivener, *ibid.*, p. 887; H. O. Schmitt and C. P. Fonda, *J. Abnorm. Soc. Psychol.* **52**, 262 (1956); W. Seeman, *J. Nerv. Ment. Dis.* **118**, 541 (1953. For an analysis of these artifacts and summaries of the disputes, see J. Zubin, *Annu. Rev. Psychol.* **18**, 373 (1967); L. Phillips and J. G. Draguns, *ibid.* **22**, 447 (1971).

2. R. Benedict, *J. Gen. Psychol.* **10**, 59 (1934).

3. See in this regard H. Becker, *Outsiders: Studies in the Sociology of Deviance* (Free Press, New York, 1963); B. M. Braginsky, D. D. Braginsky, K. Ring, *Methods of Madness: The Mental Hospital as a Last Resort* (Holt, Rinehart & Winston, New York, 1969); G. M. Crocetti and P. V. Lemkau, *Amer. Sociol. Rev.* **30**, 577 (1965); E. Goffman, *Behavior in Public Places* (Free Press, New York, 1964); R. D. Laing, *The Divided Self: A Study of Sanity and Madness* (Quadrangle, Chicago, 1960); D. L. Phillips, *Amer. Sociol. Rev.* **28**, 963 (1963); T. R. Sarbin, *Psychol. Today* **6**, 18 (1972); E. Schur, *Amer. J. Sociol.* **75**, 309 (1969); T. Szasz, *Law, Liberty and Psychiatry* (Macmillan, New York, 1963); *The Myth of Mental Illness: Foundations of a Theory of Mental Illness* (Hoeber-Harper, New York, 1963). For a critique of some of these views, see W. R. Gove, *Amer. Sociol. Rev.* **35**, 873 (1970).

4. E. Goffman, *Asylums* (Doubleday, Garden City, N.Y., 1961).

5. T. J. Scheff, *Being Mentally Ill: A Sociological Theory* (Aldine, Chicago, 1966).

6. Data from a ninth pseudopatient are not incorporated in this report because, although his sanity went undetected, he falsified aspects of his personal history, including his marital status and parental relationships. His experimental behaviors therefore were not identical to those of the other pseudopatients.

7. A. Barry, *Bellevue Is a State of Mind* (Harcourt Brace Jovanovich, New York, 1971); I. Belknap, *Human Problems of a State Mental Hospital* (McGraw-Hill, New York, 1956); W. Caudill, F. C. Redlich, H. R. Gilmore, E. B. Brody, *Amer. J. Orthopsychiat.* **22**, 314 (1952); A. R. Goldman, R. H. Bohr, T. A. Steinberg, *Prof. Psychol.* **1**, 427 (1970); unauthored, *Roche Report* **1** (No. 13), 8 (1971).

8. Beyond the personal difficulties that the pseudopatient is likely to experience in the hospital, there are legal and social ones that, combined, require considerable attention before entry. For example, once admitted to a psychiatric institution, it is difficult, if not impossible, to be discharged on short notice, state law to the contrary notwithstanding. I was not sensitive to these difficulties at the outset of the project, nor to the personal and situational emergencies that can arise, but later a writ of habeas corpus was prepared for each of the entering pseudopatients and an attorney was kept "on call" during every hospitalization. I am grateful to John Kaplan and Robert Bartels for legal advice and assistance in these matters.

9. However distasteful such concealment is, it was a necessary first step to examining these questions. Without concealment, there would have been no way to know how valid these experiences were; nor was there any way of knowing whether whatever detections occurred were a tribute to the diagnostic acumen of the staff or to the hospital's rumor network. Obviously, since my concerns are general ones that cut across individual hospitals and staffs, I have respected their anonymity and have eliminated clues that might lead to their identification.

10. Interestingly, of the 12 admissions, 11 were diagnosed as schizophrenic and one, with

the identical symptomatology, as manic-depressive psychosis. This diagnosis has a more favorable prognosis, and it was given by the only private hospital in our sample. On the relations between social class and psychiatric diagnosis, see A. deB. Hollingshead and F. C. Redlich, *Social Class and Mental Illness: A Community Study* (Wiley, New York, 1958).

11. It is possible, of course, that patients have quite broad latitudes in diagnosis and therefore are inclined to call many people sane, even those whose behavior is patently aberrant. However, although we have no hard data on this matter, it was our distinct impression that this was not the case. In many instances, patients not only singled us out for attention, but came to imitate our behaviors and styles.

12. J. Cumming and E. Cumming, *Community Ment. Health* 1, 135 (1965); A. Farina and K. Ring, *J. Abnorm. Psychol.* 70, 47 (1965); H. E. Freeman and O. G. Simmons, *The Mental Patient Comes Home* (Wiley, New York, 1963); W. J. Johannsen, *Ment. Hygiene* 53, 218 (1969); A. S. Linsky, *Soc. Psychiat.* 5, 166 (1970).

13. S. E. Asch, *J. Abnorm. Soc. Psychol.* 41, 258 (1946); *Social Psychology* (Prentice-Hall, New York, 1952).

14. See also I. N. Mensh and J. Wishner, *J. Personality* 16, 188 (1947); J. Wishner, *Psychol. Rev.* 67, 96 (1960); J. S. Bruner and R. Tagiuri, in *Handbook of Social Psychology*, G. Lindzey, Ed. (Addison-Wesley, Cambridge, Mass., 1954), vol. 2, pp. 634-654; J. S. Bruner, D. Shapiro, R. Tagiuri, in *Person Perception and Interpersonal Behavior*, R. Tagiuri and L. Petrullo, Eds. (Stanford Univ. Press, Stanford, Calif., 1958), pp. 277-288.

15. For an example of a similar self-fulfilling prophecy, in this instance dealing with the "central" trait of intelligence, see R. Rosenthal and L. Jacobson, *Pygmalion in the Classroom* (Holt, Rinehart & Winston, New York, 1968).

16. E. Zigler and L. Phillips, *J. Abnorm. Soc. Psychol.* 63, 69 (1961). See also R. K. Freudenberg and J. P. Robertson, *A.M.A. Arch. Neurol. Psychiatr.* 76, 14 (1956).

17. W. Mischel, *Personality and Assessment* (Wiley, New York, 1968).

18. The most recent and unfortunate instance of this tenet is that of Senator Thomas Eagleton.

19. T. R. Sarbin and J. C. Mancuso, *J. Clin. Consult. Psychol.* 35, 159 (1970); T. R. Sarbin, *ibid.* 31, 447 (1967); J. C. Nunally, Jr., *Popular Conceptions of Mental Health* (Holt, Rinehart & Winston, New York, 1961).

20. A. H. Stanton and M. S. Schwartz, *The Mental Hospital: A Study of Institutional Participation in Psychiatric Illness and Treatment* (Basic, New York, 1954).

21. D. B. Wexler and S. E. Scoville, *Ariz. Law Rev.* 13, 1 (1971).

22. I thank W. Mischel, E. Orne, and M. S. Rosenhan for comments on an earlier draft of this manuscript.

2.

Maurice K. Temerlin

THE INABILITY TO DISTINGUISH NORMALITY FROM ABNORMALITY

ABSTRACT: Mental health professionals and nonprofessionals observed an interview with a healthy man after hearing a renowned mental health professional, acting as a confederate, characterize him as psychotic. Both professional and nonprofessional subjects then tended to diagnose the healthy man as mentally ill, even though his behavior was healthy by multiple criteria. The biasing effect of prestige suggestion upon diagnosis is discussed in terms of the efficacy of psychiatric diagnosis to community mental health.

The mental health professional working in a community setting interacts daily with many other members of the community: businessmen, judges, legislators, poverty workers, and city officials, as well as other mental health professionals and "indigenous nonprofessionals." In these interpersonal transactions the mental health specialist should be aware of the subtle suggestion effects his diagnostic opinions may have on both fellow professionals and nonprofessional members of the community. Paradoxically, whereas being a mental patient connotes social stigmata, a mental health professional, as an expert in a mysterious field, frequently occupies high social status. As such, he carries considerable prestige: for members of his own profession, if he is a diplomate, publisher, or distinguished practitioner, and for those members of the general public who accept mental illness as an

From Maurice K. Temerlin, "Diagnostic bias in community mental health," *Community Mental Health Journal,* vol. 6. Copyright 1970 by Human Sciences Press, Inc., 72 Fifth Avenue, New York, NY 10011.

explanation for maladaptive, deviant, or bizarre behavior. This paper describes an experiment which demonstrates the extreme degree to which the prestige of a mental health professional may bias interpersonal perception: the diagnosis of a healthy man as neurotic or psychotic.

As one part of a research program to study interpersonal influences upon psychiatric diagnosis, a mentally healthy man was introduced into both traditional and community mental health settings as if he were a prospective patient. Since judgments of mental health are often made by judges, attorneys, and juries of laymen, he also was "diagnosed" by several nonprofessional groups. Both professional and nonprofessional groups diagnosed with the expectation, created by the suggestion of a confederate with prestige, that they were observing a clinical interview with a psychotic.

CRITERIA OF COMMUNITY MENTAL HEALTH

Mental illness implies the existence of a psychological state called mental health. However, the criteria for recognizing mental health rarely are explicit. Functioning effectively in the community is inadequate by itself, because many people may perform effectively in a work setting yet experience considerable subjective distress; or they may function effectively on the job while being incapacitated in an intimate setting such as family life. "Social well being" lacks specificity and denotable criteria. Because theorists disagree—mental health is genitality to Freudians, personality integration to holists, autonomous selfhood to existentialists, self-actualization to humanists, etc.—it was assumed that, for purposes of this research, a man was healthy mentally if he: was happy and effective in his work; typically established warm, cordial, loving, and relaxed relationships with other members of the community; was happily married; enjoyed sexual intercourse free of anxiety, fear, or guilt; was self-confident, without being arrogant or grandiose; and if he was free of depression, psychosomatic symptoms, inappropriate affect, hostility, suspiciousness, delinquency, excessive drinking, and conceptual disorganization.

Recognizing the imperfectability of men, a professional actor was trained to portray a healthy man, by the above criteria, while talking about himself in a diagnostic interview with a clinician. To give him a reason for being in a clinical setting which would not automatically define him as sick, he said he was a successful, happy, and productive physical scientist and mathematician who had just read a book on psychotherapy, and wanted to talk about it. Since the "patient" thus had high social status, the design was loaded against his being diagnosed as mentally ill, since mental illness varies inversely with socioeconomic status (Hollingshead & Redlich, 1958). He appeared at a university-community clinic and was interviewed as if he were a regular client, the interviewer simply asking him to talk about himself after his initial curiosity about psychotherapy had been expressed. The interview was tape recorded (a transcription is available upon request) and subsequently was diagnosed by the following groups:

SUBJECTS

1. Clinical psychologists and psychiatrists: 25 each, selected from 3 cities on a stratified random basis from community clinics, state mental hospitals, veterans hospitals, and private practice.

2. Graduate students in clinical psychology: 45, enrolled in advanced courses in clinical psychology at 2 state universities, each with an APA-approved doctoral program.

3. Law students: 40, enrolled in a class in criminal law; 30 were seniors within a month of graduation; 10 were juniors. Law students were used because they quickly become the judges, legislators, civic officials, and businessmen whose attitudes towards mental health are so important in the community.

4. Undergraduates: 156, predominately freshmen and sophomores, enrolled in an introductory course in personality.

PROCEDURE

Because Ss were run in the clinics, classrooms, and hospitals of two Midwestern university communities, a state mental hospital, and in the offices of private practitioners, some details of the procedure varied slightly, as indicated:

1. Clinical psychologists and graduate students in clinical psychology listened to the interview as part of a diagnostic staff meeting, practicum course meeting, or inservice training program in diagnostic interviewing. In either case, the prestige confederate was a well-known psychologist with many professional honors. Shortly before the interview began he remarked: "I know the man being interviewed today. He's a very interesting man because he looks neurotic but actually is quite psychotic."

2. Psychiatrists were asked to give a diagnostic opinion to be used as a critical diagnosis against which test scores would be correlated.

They were told "two board-certified psychiatrists, one also a psychoanalyst, felt the patient looked neurotic, but actually was quite psychotic," but that "two opinions are not enough for a criterion group in a research project."

3. Law students were asked to participate as jurors in a mock sanity hearing. Their professor of criminal law was the prestige confederate. When the experimenter was out of the room, and ostensibly to encourage their cooperation in the project, he told them they would find participation interesting because they would observe a diagnostic interview with a man who "looked neurotic but actually was quite psychotic."

4. Undergraduates: After giving several lectures on mental health, the instructor agreed (after a rigged student request) to let the class listen to tape recorded interviews with mental patients. He introduced the interview with the remark that this was an interesting case because "the man looks neurotic but actually is quite psychotic."

All groups listened to the same tape recorded interview and then indicated their specific diagnosis on a data sheet which listed 30 psychiatric categories: 10 psychoses, 10 neuroses and character disorders, and 10 miscellaneous personality types, including "healthy personality." After indicating the psychiatric category which best fit the patient, Ss wrote a qualitative personality description to report the behavioral observations on which they had based their diagnosis. Ss were debriefed after all data had been collected, and Ss experience of the procedure was recorded either by the experimenter or confederates.

CONTROLS

Three matched groups, stratified for professional identity, diagnosed the same interview with no prior prestige suggestion; with the prestige suggestion reversed; and outside a clinical setting, as follows: Since simply being interviewed in a mental health setting might be interpreted as evidence of mental illness, a third control group "diagnosed" as part of a procedure for selecting scientists to work in industrial research. The clinical interview was changed into a personnel interview by deleting the first 30 seconds, in which curiosity about psychotherapy was expressed, and substituting a director of personnel for a clinician. The personnel director said that his company ". . . liked to know a man as well as possible before hiring him," and then asked the "candidate" to talk about himself in detail, and to include personal information. Otherwise the interview was unchanged. Ss listened to "a new kind of personnel interview designed to elicit the kind of personal information related to scientific productivity" and then evaluated the candidate for employment on 10 scales. The scales were responsibility, creativity, relations with colleagues, probable scientific productivity, etc.—all obviously related to employability. Embedded among these distractor scales was a mental-health scale with psychoses and health at the extremes, and neurosis in the center.

As a fourth control, a mock sanity hearing was conducted in a county courthouse. With the cooperation of the court, jurors were selected randomly from the regular jury wheel, physicians and teachers being excused, per standard procedure in the selection of jurors. The jury was told

TABLE 2-1
Diagnoses of Control Subjects

	Mental illness		Mental health
	Psychosis	Neurosis and character disorder	
No prestige suggestion (N = 21*)	0	9	12
Suggestion of mental health (N = 20*)	0	0	20
Employment interview (N = 24*)	0	7	17
Sanity hearing (N = 12)	0	0	12

* N's indicated by asterisk are totals after a replication, grouped together when no differences were found on replication.

that the court was experimenting with a new procedure for use in sanity hearings which involved their listening to the diagnostic interview itself instead of basing their decisions upon expert testimony. After listening to the same interview, jurors voted individually by secret ballot, then discussed the case and voted again.

Control data are presented in Table 2-1.

In general, control Ss diagnosed mental health correctly; none diagnosed psychosis. However, 16 Ss diagnosed some neurosis or character disorder. These Ss were asked the reasons for their diagnosis, and their answers fell within one or both of these categories: 1. They had implicitly used a personalized definition of neurosis. For example, they had considered him neurotic "because he was an agnostic, and did not attend church," or because he "openly talked about sex." These Ss felt such attitudes were sufficiently rare that they "must" reflect mental illness. 2. They had expanded the concept of mental illness to cover all human imperfection, or the existential conditions of human life: For example, "He looked healthy, but I called him neurotic as he must experience the loneliness and alienation of modern man."

TABLE 2-2
Diagnoses of Experimental Subjects

| | Mental illness | | Mental health |
	Psychosis	Neurosis and character disorder	
Psychiatrists (N=25)	15	10	0
Clinical psychologists (N=25)	7	15	3
Graduate students in clinical psychology (N=45)	5	35	5
Law students (N=40)	7	29	4
Undergraduates (N=156)	47	84	25

$x^2 = 26.65$, df $= 8$, p $< .001$

RESULTS

Diagnoses of experimental Ss are presented in Table 2-2.

A X^2 analysis of the differences between experimental and control groups indicates that all differences are significant at the .01 level, whether the differences are between specific experimental and control groups, or combined groups. Clearly, prestige suggestion affected diagnoses; in its absence, no S ever diagnosed psychosis, while when the suggestion was present, 60% of the psychiatrists, 28% of the clinical psychologists, 11% of the graduate students, 17% of the law students, and 30% of the undergraduates diagnosed psychosis.

Differences between experimental groups also were significant, suggesting a relationship between the effect of the suggestion and professional identity. Psychiatrists thus gave more diagnoses of psychosis, fewer of health, than any group. Conversely, undergraduates, law students, and graduate students in clinical psychology, having in common the fact of little or no identity as mental health professionals, gave fewer diagnoses of psychosis, and more of health, than did psychiatrists or clinical psychologists. That these results reflect an interaction between the prestige suggestion and professional identity, rather than a result of differences in training, is evidenced by the fact that psychologists, psychiatrists, and laymen did not diagnose differently in the control groups. These results obviously do not mean that professional training reduces the accuracy of diagnosis; rather, they suggest that being a mental health professional may constitute a set to perceive mental illness, and that the effect of this set may be increased by prestige suggestion. Indeed, it is logical to assume that the diagnostic opinion of a renowned psychologist or psychiatrist would carry considerable weight with other mental health professionals, and that laymen would naturally be more reluctant than professionals to diagnose mental illness, particularly psychosis.

QUALITATIVE RESULTS

Subjects who had diagnosed correctly were interviewed at length, to study the process by which they had avoided the pit into which about 90% had fallen. Paraphrasing their responses, they seemed to have diagnosed correctly for one or more of these reasons:

1. They had discarded or ignored the prestige suggestion, either because they typically were skeptical people, were negativistic towards authority, or were less "field dependent" than other Ss in arriving at diagnostic conclusions.

2. They had avoided categorization until the last minute, when the data sheets forced them to do so. They had a large capacity to keep an open mind, to take in interpersonal impressions and store them without organizing them into categories. They functioned in a manner diametrically opposed to the psychiatrist who said: "I thought he was psychotic from the moment he said he was a mathematician, since mathematicians are highly abstract and depersonalized people who live in a world of their own," and who then perceived none of the highly socialized and interpersonally effective behavior of the actor.

3. Several Ss had considered diagnosis a problem of understanding a particular person in a unique life situation, and felt that categorization occluded individuality. They had looked for a pattern of attitudes or personality characteristics which defined a unique individual in a particular life situation, lending consistency and predictability to the flux of words and interpersonal impressions coming to them over

the tape. They had categorized only when forced to do so by the data sheets, and by that time they had become aware that no psychiatric category described this particular person.

DISCUSSION

At the level of clinical practice, these results mean that community-oriented diagnosis might be improved if measures are taken to guard against suggestion effects; for example, through the judicious use of professional peers, through independent diagnosis, through creation of a democratic and scientific atmosphere in which skepticism is cherished, and by avoiding the traditional model of basing diagnoses upon "staffings" led by a director, superintendent, or expert consultant.

At a theoretical level, these results suggest that community-oriented diagnoses should avoid all labels and, instead, be a process of personality description, portraying the unique life situation and functioning in the community of each client; his assets, liabilities, joys and pains, and whether or not the agency might be of help, and how.

Szasz (1961) has argued that mental illness is a myth in the sense that psychiatric categories are not classifications of diseases, but are labels applied to disordered social behavior. While this study neither confirms nor rejects Szasz's position, it does demonstrate that a diagnosis may have a profound effect upon interpersonal perception, whether or not the diagnostic label refers to a disease which actually exists. When Ss heard the prestige figure describe the interviewee as psychotic, they also diagnosed him as mentally ill (either neurotic or psychotic) in spite of the fact that he portrayed himself on the tape as successful and productive in the community, happily married, and had a relaxed, warm, and cordial relationship with the interviewer, etc. Considering the socially stigmatizing effect of being mentally ill, it is doubtful that a community-oriented mental health should diagnose at all. (For example, no one would be surprised to read that "John Jones, a former mental patient, was arrested for the rape of a seventy-five-year-old woman," but who would believe, "John Jones, a former mental patient, was elected President of the Chamber of Commerce.") The community orientation to mental health implies a definition of mental health as socially effective functioning within the community, or social well being in general. Nonetheless, it is not unusual to find the diagnostic labels of traditional psychiatry applied in community settings with but slight modification; for example, "schizophrenic" may become "ambulatory schizophrenia" or "schizoid." This study illustrates the dangers of this practice.

For community mental health to eschew psychiatric diagnosis does not mean that it should ignore disordered social behavior. Disordered social behavior certainly occurs, and does so with greater than chance frequency in the lives of some people—those now diagnosed as mentally ill. But to label as mentally ill people who exhibit disordered social behavior helps neither to understand nor to change the behavior. Nor does it insure a more humane treatment of the person so labeled, in view of the stigmatizing connotations of the label.

As an example, consider two men, each effective in his work, but unhappily married, who finally decide to obtain a divorce. Although both wives are distraught when informed, one negotiates a settlement to protect herself and her children, and each individual reorganizes his life. This kind of interpersonal reorganization is often painful, but there is nothing about it which inherently is sick. Suppose, however, the second wife raises the question of her husband's mental health, which can always be done sanctimoniously, because the sick need help or treatment. For example: "He says he wants a divorce because he doesn't love me any more, but I think he needs help, because he's never acted this way before." Once this question is raised, subtle changes occur: personal preferences and decisions are not recognized and respected; a hypothesized internal state, which cannot be observed directly, acquires responsibility for the behavior; and divorce, basically a social problem, becomes a medical problem. If, now, a specific psychiatric label is applied (and these results suggest this could happen), socially disastrous consequences could occur; an unnecessary commitment, for example. Yet in this process nothing has been contributed to the social well being of either party, or to an understanding of the causes of the divorce.

The susceptibility of psychiatric diagnosis to distortion through prestige suggestion, in combination with the stigmatizing connotation of psychiatric diagnosis, suggests that traditional diagnostic labels should not be used; instead, the definition of mental health as social well being should be refined so that ever more precise criteria may be developed.

REFERENCES

Hollingshead, A. B., & Redlich, F. C. *Social class and mental illness: a community study.* New York: Wiley, 1958.

Szasz, T. *The myth of mental illness.* New York: Hoeber-Harper, 1961.

3.

George W. Albee

FALLACY OF REGARDING EMOTIONALLY DISTURBED PEOPLE AS SICK

Meltzer suggests that the prospect of high financial rewards for psychologists through the private sale of services will lure many marginally trained people into the field, will reduce the amount of service available to the poor and through public institutions, and will affect the style and length of intervention to maximize the income of the psychologist. He suggests a number of remedies for these problems. In two places he touches on the question that I believe ought to be the central issue for psychologists. He says, "There is also the question of whether an endeavor that is at least partly educational should be subsidized by funds that consumers are spending to protect their health" (p. 1153). Later in his paper he notes: "Third-party payments are based on the medical model, not on a preventive model" (p. 1154).

Because I think his arguments on his main points are clear and persuasive for the most part, I would like to expand briefly on the implications of alternative models for our strategy in psychology.

The greatest sin in science is to commit an error of the first kind. To reject the null hypothesis when we should accept it, and to do this consciously and deliberately for self-serving reasons, is considered by most scientists to be not only wrong but unethical and immoral as well. If we accept the position that problems of living are a result of illness or defect and at the same time we seek to get locked into a system of reimbursement for health services (treating sick patients for mental illnesses), we are guilty of this sin.

We also may be doing a disservice to the professional helpers of the future. I have a hunch that the next large group to appear on the intervention scene will be the applied philosophers. Conditions seem right for the emergence of philosophical therapy (or existential therapy, philotherapy, phenomenological analysis). The problems of a great many people who are seeing psychotherapists are concerned with a search for the meaning of existence, for purpose, identity. It seems probable that a well-trained PhD in philosophy, particularly if the philosopher is well grounded in logic, ethics, and existential phenomenology, is well prepared to become a psychotherapist. I hope this development comes soon, because I believe that large numbers of clinical philosophers would be powerful allies for psychology in attempting to throw off the domination of the sickness (or defect) model. I find it hard to imagine the philosophers accepting the designation of "health professionals."

Most psychologists (and most psychiatrists, as well) in private conversation readily admit that they are not treating conventional illnesses. A majority of clients seeking help from members of both groups are concerned with problems of bad marriages, career frustrations, role confusions, generational misunderstandings, and other emotional disturbances of an existential sort. They are not sick in any generally definable meaning of the term *sickness.* But because we have been brainwashed for so long to accept the illness model of mental disorder, because we have been taught that "mental illness is an illness like any other," there seems to be a strong possibility that the Congress, in passing a national health scheme, will include reimbursement for professional help for these mental "illnesses" as well as for more conventional physical illnesses. Psychologists have rushed to battle for their rights to be reimbursed with the argument that we are also providers of health services and that our citizens should be given freedom of choice as to which health service provider they want to reward with their problem and their insurance.

Meanwhile the psychiatrists have cooked up the phrase "medical psychotherapy," which they are now pushing with all their might. Inasmuch as there is only a small fraction of the number of psychiatrists needed to provide the amount of care that would be demanded under a national health scheme it seems clear that either (a) psychiatry does not understand the realities of supply and demand of professional people, or (b) psychiatry is more interested in control over other professionals in the field than in who does "treatment."

Professions exist to serve human needs. Surely if our purpose is to deliver helpful psychological services to the largest number, and to those with the most desperate need, we could find some other model than individual one-to-one therapy supported by third-party payments. How ironic it is that psychologists, nearly always left of center politically and mostly contemptuous of the power politics of the AMA, are becoming more and more power oriented. Once during an interview with a breathless reporter, W. C. Fields recounted his impoverished boyhood in Philadelphia where during a significant part of his childhood he lived in a packing box on the edge of a dump. He resolved at that time, he said, that when he became rich and famous he would help poor starving boys like he had been. "And have you done that?" asked the reporter. "Naw," said Fields. "When I got rich and famous, I said to hell with them." Ecce psychology.

What is going to happen? There are at least four possible resolutions to the current struggle over third-party payments, particularly if a federal health program gets established. I will start with the worst possible situation for psychology and ascend to the best possible situation for us (and society). I am not sure Dr. Meltzer will agree with my order.

The worst foreseeable situation would provide coverage for the services of psychologists treating mental patients with medical referral and under psychiatric supervision. I shudder that this indeed may be a high-probability outcome. I shudder that many of my psychological colleagues may actually accept this situation, even though it brings second-class stigmata, because it would also bring affluence. The number of psychiatrists available is so minuscule that there will be plenty of business for the ancillary paramedical professions. All we need do is swallow our pride and go back to work on the Team that is captained by psychiatry.

The second worst outcome—one that I would regard as unfortunate but quite possible—would cover the treatment services of both psychologists and psychiatrists, with freedom of choice for the client built in. Clearly this is the outcome most desired by the most vocal and active practitioners in psychology. I regard it as unfortunate because it still provides unqualified support for the sickness model of mental disturbance. It says that psychology is indeed in the business of treating sick people who are covered by national health insurance. Meltzer has warned us against many of the problems associated with this solution. I can only say that I agree with nearly all of what he says, but I want to go further.

A third possible outcome—one that I would *not* regard as a catastrophe—would provide coverage for the services of psychiatrists but not for the services of psychologists. This outcome would quickly halt the rush to private practice by the large numbers of young clinical psychologists described by Meltzer. It would give psychology time to develop alternative models and modes of intervention. It would so inundate psychiatry with people demanding help that the whole psychiatric delivery system would quickly break down and people with problems in living would have to look for more available, better, and more effective kinds of intervention. They would find their way to psychology, would encounter problems of paying for psychological services, and eventually would begin to press for some kind of national psychological service coverage (Blue Psi?) outside the medical model.

The fourth and best outcome, in my book, would be a decision by the Congress to exclude nearly all conditions presently considered under the general term *mental* or *emotional illness.* This would mean that the services of neither psychiatrists nor psychologists would be covered except in those very clearly specified (and clinically unpopular) cases involving psychosomatic, neurological, and organic conditions, and perhaps a few specified patterns requiring intensive emergency intervention. With neither psychology nor psychiatry covered for the wide variety of services now being offered in private offices, pressures would build up over time for the kind of efforts at primary prevention that offer the only long-range solution to the disturbances with which we are all concerned. Psychology would be free to compete in the marketplace without the handicap of third-party payments for psychiatric services. The situation would be consistent with the reality—emotionally disturbed people are not sick.

4.

Marie Jahoda

CRITERIA FOR POSITIVE MENTAL HEALTH

From an inspection of the diverse approaches uncovered, six major categories of concepts emerge.

1. There are several proposals suggesting that indicators of positive mental

From *Current Concepts of Positive Mental Health* by Maria Jahoda. ©1958 by Basic Books, Inc., Publishers. Reprinted by permission of the publisher.

health should be sought in the *attitudes of an individual toward his own self.* Various distinctions in the manner of perceiving oneself are regarded as demonstrating higher or lower degrees of health.

2. Another group of criteria designates the individual's style and degree of *growth, development, or self-actualization* as expressions of mental health. This group of criteria, in contrast to the first, is con-

cerned not with self-perception but with what a person does with his self over a period of time.

3. Various proposals place the emphasis on a central synthesizing psychological function, incorporating some of the suggested criteria defined in (1) and (2) above. This function will here be called *integration.*

The following three groups of criteria concentrate more exclusively than the preceding ones on the individual's relation to reality.

4. *Autonomy* singles out the individual's degree of independence from social influences as most revealing of the state of his mental health.

5. A number of proposals suggest that mental health is manifested in the adequacy of an individual's *perception of reality.*

6. Finally, there are suggestions that *environmental mastery* be regarded as a criterion for mental health.

* * *

ATTITUDES TOWARD THE SELF AS CRITERIA FOR MENTAL HEALTH

A recurring theme in many efforts to give meaning to the concept of mental health is the emphasis on certain qualities of a person's self. The mentally healthy attitude toward the self is described by terms such as self-acceptance, self-confidence, or self-reliance, each with slightly different connotations. Self-acceptance implies that a person has learned to live with himself, accepting both the limitations and possibilities he may find in himself. Self-confidence, self-esteem, and self-respect have a more positive slant; they express the judgment that in balance the

self is "good," capable, and strong. Self-reliance carries the connotation of self-confidence and, in addition, of independence from others and of initiative from within. However, the terms have become entrenched in everyday language in a manner leading to a large overlap in their connotations.

There exists also an overlap in meaning with other terms that indicate qualities of an attitude toward the self. Such terms are, for example, self-assertion, self-centeredness or egotism, and self-consciousness. These latter terms, however, have not been proposed as criteria for mental health.

A number of different dimensions of components appear to run through the various proposals. Those aspects of the self-concept that stand out most clearly are: (1) accessibility to consciousness, (2) correctness, (3) feeling about the self, and (4) sense of identity. Although not all of these components are made explicit by the writers who use attributes of the self as criteria for mental health, they are implicit in many of their contributions. Inevitably, there is a certain amount of overlap between these aspects.

* * *

GROWTH, DEVELOPMENT, AND SELF-ACTUALIZATION AS CRITERIA FOR MENTAL HEALTH

A number of authors see the essence of mental health in an ongoing process variously called self-actualization, self-realization, growth, or becoming. The idea that the organism strives permanently to realize its own potentialities is old. Fromm (1947) credits Spinoza with having seen the process of development as one of becoming what one potentially is. "A horse would be as much destroyed if it were changed into a man as if it were changed into an insect," Spinoza said. Fromm continues: "We might add that, according to Spinoza, a man would be as much destroyed if he became an angel as if he became a horse. Virtue is the unfolding of the specific potentialities of every organism; for man it is the state in which he is most human."

The term self-actualization probably originated with Goldstein (1940). He spoke about the process of self-actualization as occurring in every organism and not only in the healthy one: "There is only one motive by which human activity is set going: the tendency to actualize oneself." The idea is echoed in Sullivan's dictum, "the basic direction of the organism is forward," and it also dominates the thinking of authors such as Carl Rogers, Fromm, Maslow, and Gordon Allport. Sometimes the term is used as implying a general principle of life, holding for every organism; at other times it is applied specifically to mentally healthy functioning.

It is not always easy to distinguish these two meanings in the mental health literature. This lack of clarity probably has something to do with the controversial philosophical concept of Aristotelian teleology, to which the notion of realizing one's potentialities is related. The need for making the distinction in a discussion of mental health becomes urgent if one realizes that not only the development of civilization but also self-destruction and crime, from petty thievery to genocide, are among the unique potentialities of the human species.

Mayman (1955) is of the opinion that some of the proponents of self-actualization as a criterion of health have not succeeded in making the distinction. In a critical discussion of Rogers' use of the term, he says: "This position is insufficient in several respects: it presumes that this growth force is equally potent in all people; that if given the right of way, this force will inevitably assert itself for good; but most important of all it treats this force with almost religious awe rather than scientific curiosity. This urge to grow and be healthy is treated as an irreducible essence of life."

To make this life force an aspect of positive mental health requires that certain qualifications be introduced to distinguish its manifestations in healthy persons.

The process of self-actualization, as a rule, is described in rather global terms that make it difficult to identify constituent parts. Nonetheless, the various authors who regard it as a criterion of positive mental health seem to emphasize one or more of the following aspects: (1) self-concept (which has already been discussed and is mentioned here only to indicate the breadth of the term self-actualization); (2) motivational processes; and (3) the investment in living, referring to the achievements of the self-actualizing person as demonstrated in a high degree of differentiation, or maximum of development, of his basic equipment.

* * *

INTEGRATION AS A CRITERION FOR MENTAL HEALTH

In the proposals suggesting certain qualities of the self-concept or self-actualization, or both, as criteria for mental health, there is as a rule, implicit or explicit, another criterion; this is generally called integration of the personality. Indeed, some writers clearly treat this additional criterion as part of either the self-concept or of self-actualization. Others single it out for special treatment. In view of its great importance to some, it will be treated here as a major category in its own right.

Integration refers to the relatedness of all processes and attributes in an individual. The coherence of personality, often referred to as the unity or continuity of personality, is an axiomatic assumption in much psychological thought. Indeed, psychological treatment of mental patients as a rule is predicated on the search for a unifying principle in terms of which the apparently most bizarrely inconsistent manifestations of personality can be understood to hang together. When integration is proposed as a criterion for positive mental health, something additional or different is implied. Some authors suggest that integration as a criterion for mental health refers to the interrelation of certain areas of the psyche; others, that it lies in the individual's awareness of the unifying principle. Still others imply that there are distinctions in the degree or strength of the integrating factor. And some are silent on this point.

Integration as a criterion for mental health is treated, as a rule, with emphasis on one of the following aspects: (1) a balance of psychic forces in the individual, (2) a unifying outlook on life, emphasizing cognitive aspects of integration, and (3) resistance to stress.

* * *

AUTONOMY AS A CRITERION FOR MENTAL HEALTH

Many persons regard an individual's relation to the world as mentally healthy if it shows what is referred to variously as autonomy, self-determination, or independence. Most often, these terms connote a relation between individual and environment with regard to decision-making. In this sense, autonomy means a conscious discrimination by the individual of environmental factors he wishes to accept or reject. But occasionally autonomy is interpreted as a withdrawal from reality, as less need for the stimulation offered by the world, or as a small degree of involvement in external matters.

Expositions of the criterion of autonomy deal with one or both of two aspects: (1) The nature of the decision-making process, emphasizing the regulation of behavior from within, in accordance with internalized standards; (2) The outcome of the decision-making process in terms of independent actions.

* * *

PERCEPTION OF REALITY AS A CRITERION FOR MENTAL HEALTH

Pervading many efforts to conceptualize mental health is the idea that the way an individual perceives the world around him supplies an important criterion for his mental health. As a rule, the perception of reality is called mentally healthy when what the individual sees corresponds to what is actually there. In the mental health literature, perception is discussed invariably as social perception, meaning that the conditions under which perception occurs or the object of perception, or both, involve other human beings. This has an implication for terminology. Even if it makes sense under different conditions to speak of perception as distinguishable from other cognitive processes such as attention, judgment, and thinking, social perception cannot be so isolated. The term perception will here be used as implying various modes of cognition.

Two aspects of reality perception are suggested as criteria for mental health: perception free from need-distortion, and empathy or social sensitivity.

* * *

ENVIRONMENTAL MASTERY AS A CRITERION FOR MENTAL HEALTH

Perhaps no other area of human functioning has more frequently been selected as a criterion for mental health than the individual's reality orientation and his efforts at mastering the environment.

There are two central themes pervading the relevant literature: the theme of success and the theme of adaptation. As a rule the former is specified as achievement in some significant areas of living; the latter is a toned-down version of the former, implying appropriate functioning with the emphasis more often on the process than on its result.

In the mental health literature adaptation and environmental mastery are treated on different levels of specificity. Ordering these emphases roughly from most to least specific forms of human functioning, these aspects can be distinguished: (1) the ability to love; (2) adequacy in love, work and play; (3) adequacy in interpersonal relations; (4) efficiency in meeting situational requirements; (5) capacity for adaptation and adjustment; (6) efficiency in problem-solving.

CHAPTER II

Models for the Study of Psychopathology

Models used in the understanding of psychopathological phenomena have been growing in number in recent years, owing to their heuristic value of producing pregnant and fertile ideas for a fuller grasp of this complicated field of study. Models serve as conceptualizations or analogues, enabling the psychologist to pattern his approach to psychopathological phenomena along lines which have proved successful in other areas of study, especially disciplines which have proved productive. Hopefully, with the employment of a good model borrowed from a prosperous discipline, comparable success is sought in psychopathological study. A model worthy of emulation will furnish a set of concepts, technical terminology, and laws or generalizations which can be appropriated, or conclusions extrapolated from the findings of another successful field of endeavor.

The Medical Model and the Unitary Concept of Mental Disease

In the medical or disease model, psychopathological states are likened to ailments found in physical maladies with clusters of symptoms termed syndromes, each syndrome associated with its technical nomenclature identifying it. Research is then conducted in order to ascertain the etiology of the syndrome, since hopefully the cause of the ailment puts the researcher well on the way to detecting a cure. In the last chapter, numerous syndromes were enumerated and defined, almost exclusively from the standpoint of the medical model. Most psychiatrists, owing to their medical training, tend to view mental disorder from the medical model orientation. Much of the nosology employed in abnormal psychology consists of terms coined by psychiatrists.

In recent years the medical model has undergone a barrage of criticism initiated by Szasz (1960, 1961a, 1961b, 1963, 1976) and quickly supported by Torrey (1972, 1974) and others. While Thorne (1966) saw fit to rebut Szasz, Ausubel (1961) defended the disease model as a valid concept.

Closely related to the medical model is the *unitary concept* of mental illness, a view championed by Menninger (1959, 1960; Menninger, Ellenberger, Pruyser, & Mayman, 1958). According to the unitary concept, the various mental disorders are regarded as essentially one and the same malady, differing merely in the dimension of quantity or severity, rather than in quality or kind.

The Moral Model

Szasz repudiated the medical model as sheer myth, viewing mental disorder as a problem in living, whereas Mowrer (1960, 1967a, 1967b) identified it with *sin.* Mowrer seeks to impute a greater degree of responsibility upon the neurotic than the medical model will allow. Actually, the medical model exculpates the neurotic from all guilt.

The Dynamic Model

A model, called the *dynamic* because it seeks to explain mental phenomena in terms of the numerous psychodynamisms at work within the personality, is used extensively by the so-called "depth psychologists" or those who refer to the unconscious processes operative in the individual. The prototype of the dynamic, the Freudian or psychoanalytic (Freud, 1959, 1961, 1963a; Fromm-Reichmann, 1949), resorts to psychic energy systems entailing unconscious, preconscious, and conscious mind; id, ego, and superego structure of personality; instinctual and libidinal urges of eros and thanatos; the ego's various mechanisms of defense; oral, anal, phallic, and genital stages of development; the oedipus complex, and other dynamisms.

Other psychodynamic systems include the individual psychology of Adler (1926, 1929, 1969), the analytic psychology of Jung (1924, 1928, 1953), the interpersonal theory of psychiatry of Sullivan (1947a, 1953), the humanistic psychoanalysis of Fromm (1941, 1955), and the neo-Freudianism of Horney (1937, 1942, 1945).

Many of the current texts in abnormal psychology and psychiatry utilize the dynamic model to a greater or lesser extent, and Cameron (1963) has even subtitled his "a dynamic approach." White and Watt's *The Abnormal Personality* (1973) and Stern's *The Abnormal Person and His World* (1964) favor the dynamic approach.

Behavioral and Learning Theory Model

The learning theory model derives from those behavioral scientists who have made significant contributions in the field of psychology of learning. Principles of learning, motivation, individual differences, and so on, have been extended and extrapolated to apply to psychopathology. One text which has accomplished this application with remarkable success has been Maher's *Principles of Psychopathology: An Experimental Approach* (1966), but other texts are beginning to incorporate the learning theory model into their texts as special chapters (Buss, 1966) or as portions of chapters (Sarason, 1976; Ullmann & Krasner, 1975).

While Dollard and Miller (1950) have effectively synthesized Freud's dynamic model with that of learning theory, others have successfully related learning theory to some phase of psychopathology. Among them are: Rotter (1954, 1964), Phillips (1956; Phillips & Wiener, 1966), Eysenck (1959, 1965), and Mowrer (1953).

Statistical Model

The statistical model is yet another approach to the study of psychopathology, one employing mathematical-statistical methods of measurement for ascertaining the nature, extent, and intensity of various human traits and characteristics. By so doing, one can discern the nature and degree of mental disorder as well as correlate such traits with those of persons who are healthy. Cattell (1966) has edited a handbook entirely devoted to this approach which he terms multivariate experimental psychology and has effectually applied the method to psychopathology, especially in measuring anxiety and neuroticism (1962, 1963, 1973). Cattell's trait factor technique was successfully applied to psychosis by Lorr (1968b).

Eysenck (1952, 1960), utilizing a dimensional approach within the statistical model, measured three dimensions of personality: introversion-extraversion, neuroticism, and psychoticism. Instead of classifying mental disorder according to the syndrome model, he was able to produce continuous measurements by his statistical technique.

Still another variation of the statistical model, the *typological* or *type-factor* approach, was offered by Guertin (1952, 1961a, 1961b) and Zubin et al. (1961). These men applied factor analytic techniques to define behavior patterns and syndromes with a precision unobtainable by ordinary psychiatric methods. Zubin and his associates, interested in the prognostication of mental disorders, applied the factor-analytic model so as to identify factors that would enable one to predict the outcome of psychopathology in the light of the type of treatment employed.

The Ontoanalytic or Existential Model

According to the ontoanalytic or existential model, the singularly human characteristics of one's personality (*Dasein*) are emphasized. A person is seen as more than a human being (essence), he is seen as a human becoming (existence), that is, one exists in a state of continual process in which his innumerable possibilities are brought into existence by choice, freedom, and other peculiarly human qualities. By virtue of their freedom, persons choose themselves, decide responsibly what they are to be and then bring it into existence. Owning the ability to transcend themselves, persons acquire for themselves authentic selfhood through choice.

Originating as the philosophy of Martin Heidegger (1962) and Søren Kierkegaard (1941a), existential psychiatry and psychotherapy has penetrated deep into the field of psychopathology, even to the extent of its proponents publishing several journals.

Among the more prominent psychopathologists adhering to the existential model are Frankl (1967a, 1969), May (1959, 1967, 1976, 1981; May, Angel, & Ellenberger, 1958), Boss (1962, 1963; Condrau & Boss, 1968), Strauss (1961, 1966), and Binswanger (1963). Maddi has (1967) contributed a paper treating existential neurosis, a concept initially developed by Frankl who termed it noögenic neurosis. Thorne (1963) has constructed an existential theory of anxiety.

Biochemical and Drug Models

The average layman cannot understand why it is taking scientists so long to discover the chemical disturbance responsible for schizophrenia—if indeed there is something wrong with the chemistry of psychotics. Many people are tempted to conclude that if there are chemical imbalances in the schizophrenic, then we would certainly have hit upon them by now. Consequently, schizophrenia must be a purely psychological maladjustment, one of the many emotional problems of living, except that schizophrenics do not deal with their problems as effectively as the rest of us.

We cannot, however, draw that inference because the matter is not that simple. The problem lies in the fact that there are millions of chemical systems in each of us, consequently, tracking down the specific imbalance troubling schizophrenics has been compared to "searching for a needle in a haystack."

The Drug Model

One of the more promising advances to arise from biochemical approaches to mental disorder is the drug model. What makes the drug model so engaging is the ability of drugs to play the role of bloodhounds and lead us to the specific problem area. That is to say, certain drugs are highly specific in their effects. They target at specific symptoms, leaving others alone. Diazepam (Valium) and chlordiazepoxide (Librium), for example, are two sedatives that have a potent effect in dramatically decreasing anxiety. Yet these two drugs do nothing for the schizophrenic, despite the fact that anxiety is common in schizophrenics as well as neurotics. On the other hand, there are drugs that produce striking results on schizophrenics but are not indicated for neurotics. These drugs, the phenothiazines, are apparently zeroing in directly to the specific disturbance because they both pacify upset schizophrenics and vitalize the repressed or withdrawn ones.

The fascinating inference allowed by these facts is that neurotics and psychotics suffer from completely different disturbances. In other words, Freud was quite mistaken in assuming that psychopathology is on a continuum from the milder disturbances to the severer ones. The assumption is that a person who is neurotic is on the road to becoming psychotic since one is a continuation of the other. The drug model more than aids us in locating the source of schizophrenia; it instructs us that neurosis and psychosis are two completely different kinds of disorder. Snyder and his associates found that the sedative, phenobarbital, was not any more effective than a placebo as far as schizophrenics are concerned. Even supersedatives (Valium and Librium) were not efficacious despite their being powerful antianxiety drugs. "Indeed, since drugs such as diazepam and chlordiazepoxide are more effective than phenothiazines in relieving anxiety, one can conclude that anxiety per se is not a unique and primary feature of schizophrenia." Unlike the supersedatives, diazepam and chlordiazepoxide, phenothiazines not only "calm hyperactive patients, they also 'activate' withdrawn patients" (Snyder et al., 1974, p. 1244).

Because of the antipsychotic action of phenothiazines, that is, because they target on schizophrenics and their symptoms rather than on neurotics and their symptoms, drugs are more than telling us that the two disorders are completely different; they lead us to where the chemical action is as well as what it is.

Genetic Model

Behavior genetics, the investigation of selective breeding to ascertain its effects on human behavior, is a limited study due to laws prohibiting the control of human breeding. Consequently, blood ties, family constellations, and studies on identical and fraternal twins are made to determine what affect heredity has on causing or predisposing us to mental disorder.

While behavior is not inherited, DNA (deoxyribonucleic acid) molecules are. Self-replication is attributable to DNA, the material of heredity and foundation genetic activity.

Psychologists and other scientists interested in behavior genetics investigate *population genetics* to ascertain behavioral characteristics of large numbers of people who crossbreed. Twin studies particularly interest them because here they can compare identical twins (monozygotic pairs) and fraternal twins (dizygotic pairs). Such studies shed light on *concordance,* that is, the degree of agreement to which traits, disease, and other characteristics are shared. *Penetrance* is the term these researchers use when referring to the genetic transfer of mental illness or other characteristics.

Being cautioned by the first influential geneticist to study the transfer of schizophrenic traits by genetic transfer, some behavior geneticists heeded Kallmann's (1946) warning that other influences, such as environmental factors, could play an important role. This does not mean, however, that genetic factors are not crucial. *Diathesis-stress* theories of mental disorder are those that combine genetic explanations with environmental ones. According to diathesis-stress theories, not only must schizophrenics be predisposed constitutionally toward psychosis, they must confront a sufficiently stressful situation to blossom into schizophrenia. Proposing his two-stage process, Meehl (1962) suggested that a *schizotaxic* with the misfortune of having an obnoxious mother could succumb to schizophrenia.

Stein and Wise (1971) attributed schizophrenia to a genetic abnormality that prevents the brain's reward center from being activated. Olds and Milner (1954) discovered a pleasure center in the brain by electrically stimulating certain cranial regions. The psychoanalyst, Sandor Rado, characterized schizophrenics as *anhedonics,* as people with an inability or difficulty in experiencing pleasure. The Stein-Wise hypothesis postulates that this reward center in the brain of schizophrenics is disordered because of a genetic abnormality preventing the brain transmitter norepinephrine from activating the pleasure center. Levitt and Lonowski (1975), however, objected to Stein-Wise on the grounds that some diagnosed schizophrenics do enjoy the pleasure of food and sex. Furthermore, hallucinations in schizophrenics cannot be attributed to the pleasure center of the brain. We should hasten to add that hallucinations are only secondarily a schizophrenic disorder and that sexuality is practiced by the mild or recovering schizophrenic.

One of the puzzles left by the genetic model has to do with the survival of the fit. If schizophrenics are not reproducing on the order of the population in general, then they should be a dying breed. Yet, percentagewise, their population seems to hold. Rosenthal, troubled with this paradox, sought to explain the phenomenon. "Each generation established its own dominance hierarchy, and in each generation it is those at the lowest rungs of the ladder who have the lowest fitness. In this way there occurs a gradual weeding out—up to a point—of those who are least well equipped genetically to exist in a complex socially organized group life, and a gradual improvement of the species with respect to adaptability to group living. For each generation, the proportion of the entire group occupying the lowest rungs of the subjective or objective hierarchy is constant, and so the morbidity rate overall shows no appreciable change" (1970, p. 275). It does not seem like much of an explanation since those genes that purportedly cause schizophrenia are supposed to be steadily decreasing with succeeding generations. If this is not the case, then the theory of biological evolution and its attendant doctrine of the survival of the fit requires reexamination.

5.

Thomas S. Szasz

REPUDIATION OF THE MEDICAL MODEL

My aim in this essay is to raise the question "Is there such a thing as mental illness?" and to argue that there is not. Since the notion of mental illness is extremely widely used nowadays, inquiry into the ways in which this term is employed would seem to be especially indicated. Mental illness, of course, is not literally a "thing" —or physical object—and hence it can "exist" only in the same sort of way in which other theoretical concepts exist. Yet, familiar theories are in the habit of posing, sooner or later—at least to those who come to believe in them—as "objective truths" (or "facts"). During certain historical periods, explanatory conceptions such as deities, witches, and microorganisms appeared not only as theories but as self-evident *causes* of a vast number of events. I submit that today mental illness is widely regarded in a somewhat similar fashion, that is, as the cause of innumerable diverse happenings. As an antidote to the complacent use of the notion of mental illness—whether as a self-evident phenomenon, theory, or cause—let us ask this question: What is meant when it is asserted that someone is mentally ill?

In what follows I shall describe briefly the main uses to which the concept of mental illness has been put. I shall argue that this notion has outlived whatever usefulness it might have had and that it now functions merely as a convenient myth.

From Thomas S. Szasz, "The myth of mental illness," *American Psychologist*, vol. 15, pp. 113–118. Copyright 1960 by the American Psychological Association. Reprinted by permission of the publisher and author.

MENTAL ILLNESS AS A SIGN OF BRAIN DISEASE

The notion of mental illness derives its main support from such phenomena as syphilis of the brain or delirious conditions —intoxications, for instance—in which persons are known to manifest various peculiarities or disorders of thinking and behavior. Correctly speaking, however, these are diseases of the brain, not of the mind. According to one school of thought, *all* so-called mental illness is of this type. The assumption is made that some neurological defect, perhaps a very subtle one, will ultimately be found for all the disorders of thinking and behavior. Many contemporary psychiatrists, physicians, and other scientists hold this view. This position implies that people *cannot* have troubles—expressed in what are *now called* "mental illnesses"—because of differences in personal needs, opinions, social aspirations, values, and so on. *All problems in living* are attributed to physicochemical processes which in due time will be discovered by medical research.

"Mental illnesses" are thus regarded as basically no different than all other diseases (that is, of the body). The only difference, in this view, between mental and bodily diseases is that the former, affecting the brain, manifest themselves by means of mental symptoms; whereas the latter, affecting other organ systems (for example, the skin, liver, etc.), manifest themselves by means of symptoms referable to those parts of the body. This view rests on and expresses what are, in my opinion, two fundamental errors.

In the first place, what central nervous system symptoms would correspond to a skin eruption or a fracture? It would *not* be some emotion or complex bit of behavior. Rather, it would be blindness or a paralysis of some part of the body. The crux of the matter is that a disease of the brain, analogous to a disease of the skin or bone, is a neurological defect, and not a problem in living. For example, a *defect* in a person's visual field may be satisfactorily explained by correlating it with certain definite lesions in the nervous system. On the other hand, a person's *belief*—whether this be a belief in Christianity, in Communism, or in the idea that his internal organs are "rotting" and that his body is, in fact, already "dead"—cannot be explained by a defect or disease of the nervous system. Explanations of this sort of occurrence—assuming that one is interested in the belief itself and does not regard it simply as a "symptom" or expression of something else that is *more interesting*—must be sought along different lines.

The second error in regarding complex psychosocial behavior, consisting of communications about ourselves and the world about us, as mere symptoms of neurological functioning is *epistemological*. In other words, it is an error pertaining not to any mistakes in observation or reasoning, as such, but rather to the way in which we organize and express our knowledge. In the present case, the error lies in making a symmetrical dualism between mental and physical (or bodily) symptoms, a dualism which is merely a habit of speech and to which no known observations can be found to correspond. Let us see if this is so. In medical practice, when we speak of physical disturbances, we mean either

signs (for example, a fever) or symptoms (for example, pain). We speak of mental symptoms, on the other hand, when we refer to a patient's *communications about himself, others, and the world about him.* He might state that he is Napoleon or that he is being persecuted by the Communists. These would be considered mental symptoms *only* if the observer believed that the patient was *not* Napoleon or that he was *not* being persecuted by the Communists. This makes it apparent that the statement that *"X is a mental symptom"* involves rendering a judgment. The judgment entails, moreover, a covert comparison or matching of the patient's ideas, concepts, or beliefs with those of the observer and the society in which they live. The notion of mental symptoms is therefore inextricably tied to the *social* (including *ethical*) *context* in which it is made in much the same way as the notion of bodily symptom is tied to an *anatomical* and *genetic context* (Szasz, 1957a, 1957b).

To sum up what has been said thus far: I have tried to show that for those who regard mental symptoms as signs of brain disease, the concept of mental illness is unnecessary and misleading. For what they mean is that people so labeled suffer from diseases of the brain; and, if that is what they mean, it would seem better for the sake of clarity to say that and not something else.

MENTAL ILLNESS AS A NAME FOR PROBLEMS IN LIVING

The term "mental illness" is widely used to describe something which is very different than a disease of the brain. Many people today take it for granted that living is an arduous process. Its hardship for modern man, moreover, derives not so much from a struggle for biological survival as from the stresses and strains inherent in the social intercourse of complex human personalities. In this context, the notion of mental illness is used to identify or describe some feature of an individual's so-called personality. Mental illness—as a deformity of the personality, so to speak—is then regarded as the *cause* of the human disharmony. It is implicit in this view that social intercourse between people is regarded as something *inherently harmonious,* its disturbance being due solely to the presence of "mental illness" in many people. This is obviously fallacious reasoning, for it makes the abstraction "mental illness" into a *cause,* even though this abstraction was created in the first place to serve only as a shorthand expression for certain types of human behavior. It now becomes necessary to ask: "What kinds of behavior are regarded as indicative of mental illness, and by whom?"

The concept of illness, whether bodily or mental, implies *deviation from some clearly defined norm.* In the case of physical illness, the norm is the structural and functional integrity of the human body. Thus, although the desirability of physical health, as such, is an ethical value, what health *is* can be stated in anatomical and physiological terms. What is the norm deviation from which is regarded as mental illness? This question cannot be easily answered. But whatever this norm might be, we can be certain of only one thing: namely, that it is a norm that must be stated in terms of *psychosocial, ethical, and legal* concepts. For example, notions such as "excessive repression" or "acting out an unconscious impulse" illustrate the use of psychological concepts for judging (so-called) mental health and illness. The idea that chronic hostility, vengefulness, or divorce are indicative of mental illness would be illustrations of the use of ethical norms (that is, the desirability of love,

kindness, and a stable marriage relationship). Finally, the widespread psychiatric opinion that only a mentally ill person would commit homicide illustrates the use of a legal concept as a norm of mental health. The norm from which deviation is measured whenever one speaks of a mental illness is a *psychosocial and ethical one.* Yet, the remedy is sought in terms of *medical* measures which—it is hoped and assumed—are free from wide differences of ethical value. The definition of the disorder and the terms in which its remedy are sought are therefore at serious odds with one another. The practical significance of this covert conflict between the alleged nature of the defect and the remedy can hardly be exaggerated.

Having identified the norms used to measure deviations in cases of mental illness, we will now turn to the question: "Who defines the norms and hence the deviation?" Two basic answers may be offered: (*a*) It may be the person himself (that is, the patient) who decides that he deviates from a norm. For example, an artist may believe that he suffers from a work inhibition; and he may implement this conclusion by seeking help *for* himself from a psychotherapist. (*b*) It may be someone other than the patient who decides that the latter is deviant (for example, relatives, physicians, legal authorities, society generally, etc.). In such a case a psychiatrist may be hired by others to do something *to* the patient in order to correct the deviation.

These considerations underscore the importance of asking the question "Whose agent is the psychiatrist?" and of giving a candid answer to it (Szasz, 1956, 1958). The psychiatrist (psychologist or nonmedical psychotherapist), it now develops, may be the agent of the patient, of the relatives, of the school, of the military services, of a business organization, of a court of law, and so forth. In speaking of the psychiatrist as the agent of these persons or organizations, it is not implied that his values concerning norms, or his ideas and aims concerning the proper nature of remedial action, need to coincide exactly with those of his employer. For example, a patient in individual psychotherapy may believe that his salvation lies in a new marriage; his psychotherapist need not share this hypothesis. As the patient's agent, however, he must abstain from bringing social or legal force to bear on the patient which would prevent him from putting his beliefs into action. If his *contract* is with the patient, the psychiatrist (psychotherapist) may disagree with him or stop his treatment; but he cannot engage others to obstruct the patient's aspirations. Similarly, if a psychiatrist is engaged by a court to determine the sanity of a criminal, he need not fully share the legal authorities' values and intentions in regard to the criminal and the means available for dealing with him. But the psychiatrist is expressly barred from stating, for example, that it is not the criminal who is "insane" but the men who wrote the law on the basis of which the very actions that are being judged are regarded as "criminal." Such an opinion could be voiced, of course, but not in a courtroom, and not by a psychiatrist who makes it his practice to assist the court in performing its daily work.

To recapitulate: In actual contemporary social usage, the finding of a mental illness is made by establishing a deviance in behavior from certain psychosocial, ethical, or legal norms. The judgment may be made, as in medicine, by the patient, the physician (psychiatrist), or others. Remedial action, finally, tends to be sought in a therapeutic—or covertly medical—framework, thus creating a situation in which *psychosocial, ethical* and/or *legal devia-*

tions are claimed to be correctible by (so-called) *medical action.* Since medical action is designed to correct only medical deviations, it seems logically absurd to expect that it will help solve problems whose very existence has been defined and established on nonmedical grounds. I think that these considerations may be fruitfully applied to the present use of tranquilizers and, more generally, to what might be expected of drugs of whatever type in regard to the amelioration or solution of problems in human living.

THE ROLE OF ETHICS IN PSYCHIATRY

Anything that people *do*—in contrast to things that *happen* to them (Peters, 1958) —takes place in a context of value. In this broad sense, no human activity is devoid of ethical implications. When the values underlying certain activities are widely shared, those who participate in their pursuit may lose sight of them altogether. The discipline of medicine, both as a pure science (for example, research) and as a technology (for example, therapy), contains many ethical considerations and judgments. Unfortunately, these are often denied, minimized, or merely kept out of focus; for the ideal of the medical profession as well as of the people whom it serves seems to be having a system of medicine (allegedly) free of ethical value. This sentimental notion is expressed by such things as the doctor's willingness to treat and help patients irrespective of their religious or political beliefs, whether they are rich or poor, etc. While there may be some grounds for this belief—albeit it is a view that is not impressively true even in these regards—the fact remains that ethical considerations encompass a vast range of human affairs. Making the practice of medicine neutral in regard to some specific issues of value need not, and cannot, mean that it can be kept free from all such values. The practice of medicine is intimately tied to ethics; and the first thing that we must do, it seems to me, is to try to make this clear and explicit. I shall let this matter rest here, for it does not concern us specifically in this essay. Lest there be any vagueness, however, about how or where ethics and medicine meet, let me remind the reader of such issues as birth control, abortion, suicide, and euthanasia as only a few of the major areas of current ethico-medical controversy.

Psychiatry, I submit, is very much more intimately tied to problems of ethics than is medicine. I use the word "psychiatry" here to refer to that contemporary discipline which is concerned with *problems in living* (and not with diseases of the brain, which are problems for neurology). Problems in human relations can be analyzed, interpreted, and given meaning only within given social and ethical contexts. Accordingly, it *does* make a difference—arguments to the contrary notwithstanding—what the psychiatrist's socioethical orientations happen to be; for these will influence his ideas on what is wrong with the patient, what deserves comment or interpretation, in what possible directions change might be desirable, and so forth. Even in medicine proper, these factors play a role, as for instance, in the divergent orientations which physicians, depending on their religious affiliations, have toward such things as birth control and therapeutic abortion. Can anyone really believe that a psychotherapist's ideas concerning religious belief, slavery, or other similar issues play no role in his practical work? If they do make a difference, what are we to infer from it? Does it not seem reasonable that we ought to have different psychiatric therapies—each expressly recognized for the ethical positions which they embody—

for, say, Catholics and Jews, religious persons and agnostics, democrats and communists, white supremacists and Negroes, and so on? Indeed, if we look at how psychiatry is actually practiced today (especially in the United States), we find that people do seek psychiatric help in accordance with their social status and ethical beliefs (Hollingshead & Redlich, 1958). This should really not surprise us more than being told that practicing Catholics rarely frequent birth control clinics.

The foregoing position which holds that contemporary psychotherapists deal with problems in living, rather than with mental illnesses and their cures, stands in opposition to a currently prevalent claim, according to which mental illness is just as "real" and "objective" as bodily illness. This is a confusing claim since it is never known exactly what is meant by such words as "real" and "objective." I suspect, however, that what is intended by the proponents of this view is to create the idea in the popular mind that mental illness is some sort of disease entity, like an infection or a malignancy. If this were true, one could *catch* or *get* a "mental illness," one might *have* or *harbor* it, one might *transmit* it to others, and finally one could get *rid* of it. In my opinion, there is not a shred of evidence to support this idea. To the contrary, all the evidence is the other way and supports the view that what people now call mental illnesses are for the most part *communications* expressing unacceptable ideas, often framed, moreover, in an unusual idiom. The scope of this essay allows me to do no more than mention this alternative theoretical approach to this problem (Szasz, 1957c).

This is not the place to consider in detail the similarities and differences between bodily and mental illnesses. It shall suffice for us here to emphasize only one important difference between them: namely, that whereas bodily disease refers to public, physicochemical occurrences, the notion of mental illness is used to codify relatively more private, sociopsychological happenings of which the observer (diagnostician) forms a part. In other words, the psychiatrist does not stand *apart* from what he observes, but is, in Harry Stack Sullivan's apt words, a "participant observer." This means that he is *committed to some picture of what he considers reality*—and to what he thinks society considers reality—and he observes and judges the patient's behavior in the light of these considerations. This touches on our earlier observation that the notion of mental symptom itself implies a comparison between observer and observed, psychiatrist and patient. This is so obvious that I may be charged with belaboring trivialities. Let me therefore say once more that my aim in presenting this argument was expressly to criticize and counter a prevailing contemporary tendency to deny the moral aspects of psychiatry (and psychotherapy) and to substitute for them allegedly value-free medical considerations. Psychotherapy, for example, is being widely practiced as though it entailed nothing other than restoring the patient from a state of mental sickness to one of mental health. While it is generally accepted that mental illness has something to do with man's social (or interpersonal) relations, it is paradoxically maintained that problems of values (that is, of ethics) do not arise in this process.[1] Yet, in one

---

[1] Freud went so far as to say that: "I consider ethics to be taken for granted. Actually I have never done a mean thing" (Jones, 1957, p. 247). This surely is a strange thing to say for someone who has studied man as a social being as closely as did Freud. I mention it here to show how the notion of "illness" (in the case of psychoanalysis, "psychopathology," or "mental illness") was used by Freud—and by most of his followers—as a means for classifying certain forms of human behavior as falling within the scope of medicine, and hence (by *fiat*) outside that of ethics!

sense, much of psychotherapy may revolve around nothing other than the elucidation and weighing of goals and values—many of which may be mutually contradictory—and the means whereby they might best be harmonized, realized, or relinquished.

The diversity of human values and the methods by means of which they may be realized are so vast, and many of them remain so unacknowledged, that they cannot fail but lead to conflicts in human relations. Indeed, to say that human relations at all levels—from mother to child, through husband and wife, to nation and nation—are fraught with stress, strain, and disharmony is, once again, making the obvious explicit. Yet, what may be obvious may be also poorly understood. This I think is the case here. For it seems to me that—at least in our scientific theories of behavior—we have failed to *accept* the simple fact that human relations are inherently fraught with difficulties and that to make them even relatively harmonious requires much patience and hard work. I submit that the idea of mental illness is now being put to work to obscure certain difficulties which at present may be inherent—not that they need be unmodifiable—in the social intercourse of persons. If this is true, the concept functions as a disguise; for instead of calling attention to conflicting human needs, aspirations, and values, the notion of mental illness provides an amoral and impersonal "thing" (an "illness") as an explanation for *problems in living* (Szasz, 1959). We may recall in this connection that not so long ago it was devils and witches who were held responsible for men's problems in social living. The belief in mental illness, as something other than man's trouble in getting along with his fellow man, is the proper heir to the belief in demonology and witchcraft. Mental illness exists or is "real" in exactly the same sense in which witches existed or were "real."

CHOICE, RESPONSIBILITY, AND PSYCHIATRY

While I have argued that mental illnesses do not exist, I obviously did not imply that the social and psychological occurrences to which this label is currently being attached also do not exist. Like the personal and social troubles which people had in the Middle Ages, they are real enough. It is the labels we give them that concern us and, having labeled them, what we do about them. While I cannot go into the ramified implications of this problem here, it is worth noting that a demonologic conception of problems in living gave rise to therapy along theological lines. Today, a belief in mental illness implies—nay, requires—therapy along medical or psychotherapeutic lines.

What is implied in the line of thought set forth here is something quite different. I do not intend to offer a new conception of "psychiatric illness" nor a new form of "therapy." My aim is more modest and yet also more ambitious. It is to suggest that the phenomena now called mental illnesses be looked at afresh and more simply, that they be removed from the category of illnesses, and that they be regarded as the expressions of man's struggle with the problem of *how* he should live. The last mentioned problem is obviously a vast one, its enormity reflecting not only man's inability to cope with his environment, but even more his increasing self-reflectiveness.

By problems in living, then, I refer to that truly explosive chain reaction which began with man's fall from divine grace by partaking of the fruit of the tree of knowledge. Man's awareness of himself and of the world about him seems to be a steadily expanding one, bringing in its wake an even larger *burden of understanding* (an expression borrowed from Susanne Langer, 1953). *This burden,* then, *is to be expected and must not be misinterpreted.* Our only *rational* means for lightening it is *more understanding,* and appropriate *action* based on such understanding. The main alternative lies in acting as though the burden were not what in fact we perceive it to be and taking refuge in an outmoded theological view of man. In the latter view, man does not fashion his life and much of his world about him, but merely lives out his fate in a world created by superior beings. This may logically lead to pleading nonresponsibility in the face of seemingly unfathomable problems and difficulties. Yet, if man fails to take increasing responsibility for his actions, individually as well as collectively, it seems unlikely that some higher power or being would assume this task and carry this burden for him. Moreover, this seems hardly the proper time in human history for obscuring the issue of man's responsibility for his actions by hiding it behind the skirt of an all-explaining conception of mental illness.

CONCLUSIONS

I have tried to show that the notion of mental illness has outlived whatever usefulness it might have had and that it now functions merely as a convenient myth. As such, it is a true heir to religious myths in general, and to the belief in witchcraft in particular; the role of all these belief-systems was to act as *social tranquilizers,* thus encouraging the hope that mastery of certain specific problems may be achieved by means of substitutive (symbolic-magical) operations. The notion of mental illness thus serves mainly to obscure the everyday fact that life for most people is a continuous struggle, not for biological survival, but for a "place in the sun," "peace of mind," or some other human value. For man aware of himself and of the world about him, once the needs for preserving the body (and perhaps the race) are more or less satisfied, the problem arises as to what he should do with himself. Sustained adherence to the myth of mental illness allows people to avoid facing this problem, believing that mental health, conceived as the absence of mental illness, automatically insures the making of right and safe choices in one's conduct of life. But the facts are all the other way. It is the making of good choices in life that others regard, retrospectively, as good mental health!

The myth of mental illness encourages us, moreover, to believe in its logical corollary: that social intercourse would be harmonious, satisfying, and the secure basis of a "good life" were it not for the disrupting influences of mental illness or "psychopathology." The potentiality for universal human happiness, in this form at least, seems to me but another example of the I-wish-it-were-true type of fantasy. I do believe that human happiness or well-being on a hitherto unimaginably large scale, and not just for a select few, is possible. This goal could be achieved, however, only at the cost of many men, and not just a few being willing and able to tackle their personal, social, and ethical conflicts. This means having the courage and integrity to forego waging battles on false fronts, finding solutions for substitute problems—for instance, fighting the battle of stomach acid and chronic fatigue instead of facing up to a marital conflict.

Our adversaries are not demons, witches, fate, or mental illness. We have no enemy whom we can fight, exorcise, or dispel by "cure." What we do have are *problems in living*—whether these be biologic, economic, political, or sociopsychological. In this essay I was concerned only with problems belonging in the last mentioned category, and within this group mainly with those pertaining to moral values. The field to which modern psychiatry addresses itself is vast, and I made no effort to encompass it all. My argument was limited to the proposition that mental illness is a myth, whose function it is to disguise and thus render more palatable the bitter pill of moral conflicts in human relations.

REFERENCES

Hollingshead, A. B., & Redlich, F. C. *Social class and mental illness.* New York: Wiley, 1958.

Jones, E. *The life and work of Sigmund Freud.* Vol. III. New York: Basic Books, 1957.

Langer, S. K. *Philosophy in a new key.* New York: Mentor Books, 1953.

Peters, R. S. *The concept of motivation.* London: Routledge & Kegan Paul, 1958.

Szasz, T. S. Malingering: "Diagnosis" or social condemnation? *AMA Archives of Neurology and Psychiatry,* 1956, **76**, 432-443.

Szasz, T. S. *Pain and pleasure: A study of bodily feelings.* New York: Basic Books, 1957. (a)

Szasz, T. S. The problem of psychiatric nosology: A contribution to a situational analysis of psychiatric operations. *American Journal of Psychiatry,* 1957, **114**, 405-413. (b)

Szasz, T. S. On the theory of psychoanalytic treatment. *International Journal of Psycho-Analysis,* 1957, **38**, 166-182. (c)

Szasz, T. S. Psychiatry, ethics and the criminal law. *Columbia Law Review,* 1958, **58**, 183-198.

Szasz, T. S. Moral conflict and psychiatry. *Yale Review,* 1959.

6.

Karl Menninger

UNITARY CONCEPT OF MENTAL ILLNESS

My interest in this developed from my experiences in teaching psychiatrists, some hundreds of whom are or have been enrolled in the Menninger School of Psychiatry for varying periods of time. The concepts gained in their medical schooling are, naturally, carried over by the young doctors into the field of psychiatry, but often these concepts handicap them. They seek specific therapies instead of ways to help their psychiatric patients to better modes of living, to better social adjustment, to greater utilization of latent powers. We would have them think of the patient, not as one afflicted with a certain *disease* which they must *name* and then battle with and attempt to dispel, but rather as a human being, one somewhat isolated from his fellows, one whose interactive relationships with them have become mutually unsatisfactory and disturbing; to this he has reacted in various ways, all *intended* to salvage the situation and insure survival, even at the cost of social acceptance.

Suppose that instead of putting so much emphasis on different kinds of illness we tried to think of all mental illness as being essentially the same in quality, and differing, rather, quantitatively. This is what we mean when we say that we all have mental illness of different degrees at different times, and that sometimes some of us are much worse or much better. If one sets up a scale of well-being—in other words, a scale for the successfulness of an individual-environment adaptation—at one end of it would be health, happiness, success, achievement and the like and at the other end misery, failure, crime, delirium and so forth. On such a continuum one could mark some practical stages. We can say that some people are relatively healthy, that some are relatively sick, and that the latter are either mildly, moderately or extremely sick. These would vary, of course, depending upon the culture in which one lives and the duration of the particular episode of maladjustment and many other things.

Modern organismic theory conceives of systems and subsystems relating themselves to one another in the interests of homeostasis, the steady state of the open system, as defined by von Bertalanffy.[1] Pressures from instinctual urges, from somatic needs, from environmental threats, losses and excitations, from the culture and from the conscience *all* bear upon the ego, whose task it is to effect a reconciliation of them in order to maintain a steady state at the best possible level. The effectiveness *and* the cost of the reconciliatory efforts determine the degree of mental healthiness of the individual. Inadequate resolution of the conflicting pressures results in increased tension, a warning of danger to the organism which evokes compensatory shifts. If an imbalance continues despite these warnings and shifts, there comes reduced function, more pain, "sickness" and even death. Successful resolution, on the other hand, insures

From Karl Menninger, Henri Ellenberger, Paul Pruyser, and Martin Mayman, "The unitary concept of mental illness," *Bulletin of the Menninger Clinic,* 1958, vol. 22, pp. 4–12.

the continuation of constructive activity and organismic growth.

Mental illness, then, is seen by us as an impairment in self-regulation whereby comfort, production and growth are temporarily surrendered for the sake of survival at the best level possible, and at the cost of emergency coping devices which may be painful. Psychiatrists are apt to look upon mental illness as an indication of ego failure. But now this "failure" acquires a different meaning. Beset by a variety of stresses, the ego tries to insure survival and optimal adaptation at the least cost, and in this it has *succeeded.*

We believe it possible to construct an empirical series of the regulatory moves or efforts of the ego progressively more urgent, more adventitious, more symptomatic. Ours is a combined dynamic-economic scale. First come those mild symptoms regarded by the layman as "nervousness"; a Second Order of devices would include neurotic phenomena; the Third Order embraces episodic and explosive discharges, and the Fourth Order various syndromes of more persistent and severe disorganization. Our emphasis is on the *degree of disorganization and its course* or trend of development; the factors determining this trend are the keys to rational therapy.

Such an approach does not preclude the administrative usefulness of recognizing the well-known psychopathologic syndromes to which various conventional designations have been applied. *Of course one can describe a "manic" or a "depressed" or a "schizophrenic" constellation of symptoms, but what is most important about this constellation in each case? Not, we think, its curious external form, but rather what it indicates in regard to the process of organization, disorganization and reorganization of the personality in a state of attempted adjust-ment to environmental reality. Is the imbalance increasing or decreasing? To what is the stress related? What psychological factors are accessible to external modification? What latent capacities for satisfaction in work, play, love, creativity are discoverable for therapeutic exploitation? Is a restoration or reconstruction of adjustment patterns developing? Can this be fostered by discriminating medical intervention? This is what we conceive of as rational therapeutic planning.

In summary, reverting to the topic of classification with which we began, we believe that the natural "class" in psychiatry must be either the disturbed individual or all mankind in trouble. There are no natural mental disease entities. An ordering of clinical phenomena on the basis of the economics of adaptation such as we have proposed does justice to the essential unity of sickness and health; at the same time it leaves room for recognizing the latent potentials of every individual. It transcends the distinction between natural and artifical classification, the question raised in our opening paragraphs. The trend toward a unitary concept of mental illness is clearly apparent in psychiatric history, and it seems to us to follow modern trends in other fields of science. It spares us some grievous errors and offenses against our patients. It enables rational therapeutic programming. Hence it is our continuing aim to see the unity in diversity of psychiatric symptomatology as reflecting, from the side of the individual, the nature of an organism-environment interaction, and the basic continuity of the conditions labeled health and sickness of various degrees.

REFERENCE

1. Bertalanffy, L. von. An outline of general systems theory, *British Journal for the Philosophy of Science,* 1950, **1,** 134-165.

7.

Rollo May

EXISTENTIAL MODEL

There are several endeavors in this country to systematize psychoanalytic and psychotherapeutic theory in terms of forces, dynamisms, and energies. The existential approach is the opposite of these attempts. We do not deny dynamisms and forces; that would be nonsense. But we hold that they have meaning only in the context of the existing, living being—if I may use a technical word, only in the *ontological* context.

If we are to have a science adequate to serve as a basis for psychotherapy, several guiding principles are required. First, *the science must be relevant to the distinguishing characteristics of what we are trying to understand, in this case the human being.* It must be relevant, that is, to the distinctive qualities and characteristics that constitute the human being as *human*. These are the characteristics that constitute the self as self, without which this being would not be what he is: a human being.

A second guiding principle is in opposition to the assumption in conventional science that we explain the more complex by the more simple. This is generally taken on the model of evolution: the organisms and activities higher on the evolutionary scale are explained by those lower. But this is only half the truth. It is just as true that when a new level of complexity emerges (such as self-consciousness in man), this

level becomes decisive for our understanding of all previous levels. The principle here is, *the simpler can be understood and explained only in terms of the more complex.* This point is particularly important for psychology and is discussed more fully later in this chapter with the topic of self-consciousness.

A third guiding principle is this: our fundamental unit of study in psychotherapy is not a "problem" that the patient brings in, such as impotence; or a pattern, such as a neurotic pattern or sadomasochism or a diagnostic category of sickness, such as hysteria or phobia, ad infinitum; or a drive or pattern of drives. Our unit of study is, rather, *two-persons-existing-in-a-world, the world at the moment being represented by the consulting room of the therapist.* To be sure, the patient brings in all his problems, his "illness," his past history, and everything else simply because it is an integral part of him. But what is important is that the one datum that has reality at the time is that he creates a certain world in the consulting room, and it is in the context of this world that some understanding of him may emerge. This world and the understanding of it is something in which both persons, patient and therapist, participate. Our point here has far-reaching implications not only because it bears directly on our research and practice in psychotherapy, but also because it suggests the guiding lines of an existential approach to science.

Here is a patient, Mrs. Hutchens, who comes into my office for the first time, a

From *Existential Psychology, Second Edition,* edited by Rollo May. Copyright ©1961, 1969 by Random House, Inc. Reprinted by permission of the publisher.

suburban woman in her middle thirties. She tries to keep her expression poised and sophisticated. But no one could fail to see in her eyes something of the terror of a frightened deer or a lost child. I know, from what her neurological specialists have already told me, that her presenting problem is hysterical tenseness of the larynx, as a result of which she can talk only with a perpetual hoarseness. I have been given the hypothesis from her Rorschach that she has felt all her life, "If I say what I really feel, I'll be rejected; under these conditions it is better not to talk at all." During this first hour with her, I also get some hints of the genetic *why* of her problem as she tells me of her authoritarian relation with her mother and grandmother and of *how* she learned to guard firmly against telling any secrets at all. But if I am chiefly pondering these *why's* and *how's* of her problem, I will grasp everything except the most important fact of all, namely the living, existing person here in the room with me.

I propose, then, that we begin with the one real datum that we have in the therapeutic situation, namely, the existing person sitting in the consulting room with a therapist. Let us ask: What are the essential characteristics that constitute this patient as an existing person, that constitute this self as a self? I wish to propose six characteristics, which I shall call processes, that I find in my work as a psychotherapist. They can as well be called *ontological characteristics*. Though these are the product of a good deal of thought and experience with many cases, I shall illustrate them with episodes from the case of Mrs. Hutchens.

First, Mrs. Hutchens, like every existing person, *is centered in herself, and an attack on this center is an attack on her existence itself.* This is a characteristic that we human beings share with all living beings; it is self-evident in animals and plants. I never cease to marvel how, whenever we cut the top off a pine tree on our farm in New Hampshire, the tree sends up a new branch from heaven knows where to become a new center. But our principle has a particular relevance to human beings and gives a basis for the understanding of sickness and health, neurosis and mental health. Neurosis is not to be seen as a deviation from our particular theories of what a person should be. *Is not neurosis, rather, precisely the method the individual uses to preserve his own center, his own existence?* His symptoms are ways of shrinking the range of his world (so graphically shown in Mrs. Hutchens' inability to let herself talk) in order that the centeredness of his existence may be protected from threat, a way of blocking off aspects of the environment so that he may then be adequate to the remainder.

Mrs. Hutchens had gone to another therapist for half a dozen sessions a month before she came to me. He told her, in an apparently ill-advised effort to reassure her, that she was too proper, too controlled. She reacted with great upset and immediately broke off the treatment. Now, technically he was entirely correct; existentially he was entirely wrong. What he did not see, in my judgment, was this very properness, this overcontrol, far from being things that Mrs. Hutchens wanted to get over, were part of her desperate attempt to preserve what precarious center she had. As though she were saying, "If I opened up, if I communicated, I would lose what little space in life I have." We see here, incidentally, how inadequate is the definition of neurosis as a failure of adjustment. *An adjustment is exactly what neurosis is; and that is just its trouble.* It is a necessary adjustment by which centeredness can be preserved; a way of accepting *non-being,* if I may use this term, in order that some little *being* may be preserved. And in most cases it is a boon when this adjustment breaks down.

This is the only thing we can assume about Mrs. Hutchens, or about any patient, when she comes in: she, like all living beings, requires centeredness, and this has broken down. At a cost of considerable turmoil she has taken steps, that is, come for help. Our second process, thus, is: every existing person *has the character of self-affirmation, the need to preserve its centeredness.* The particular name we give this self-affirmation in human beings is "courage." Paul Tillich's emphasis on the "courage to be" is very important, cogent, and fertile for psychotherapy at this point. He insists that in man, being is never given automatically, as it is in plants and animals, but depends upon the individual's courage; and without courage one loses being. This makes courage itself a necessary ontological corollary. By this token, I as a therapist place great importance upon expressions of the patients that have to do with willing, decisions, choice. I never let such little remarks the patient may make as "maybe I can," "perhaps I can try" slip by without my making sure he knows I have heard him. It is only a half truth to say that the will is the product of the wish; I emphasize rather the truth that the wish can never come out in its real power except with will.

Now as Mrs. Hutchens talks hoarsely, she looks at me with an expression of mingled fear and hope. Obviously a relation not only exists between us here but has already existed in anticipation in the waiting room and ever since she thought of coming. She is struggling with the possibility of participating with me. The third process is, thus: *all existing persons have the need and possibility of going out from their centeredness to participate in other beings.* This always involves risk; if the organism goes out too far, it loses its own centeredness, its identity—a phenomenon that can easily be seen in the biological world. If the neurotic is so afraid of loss of his own conflicted center that he refuses to go out and holds back in rigidity, living in narrowed reactions and shrunken world space, his growth and development are blocked. This is the pattern in neurotic repressions and inhibitions, the common neurotic forms in Freud's day. But it may well be in our day of conformity and the outer-directed man, that the most common neurotic pattern takes the opposite form, namely, the dispersing of one's self in participation and identification with others until one's own being is emptied.

At this point we see the rightful emphasis of Martin Buber in one sense and Harry Stack Sullivan in another, that the human being cannot be understood as a self if participation is omitted. Indeed, if we are successful in our search for these ontological processes of the existing person, it should be true that the omission of any one of the six would mean that we do not then have a human being.

Our fourth principle is: *the subjective side of centeredness is awareness.* Such awareness is present in forms of life other than human; it is certainly observable in animals. Howard Liddell has pointed out how the seal in its natural habitat lifts its head every ten seconds even during sleep to survey the horizon lest an Eskimo hunter with poised bow and arrow sneak up on it. This awareness of threats to being in animals Liddell calls *vigilance,* and he identifies it as the primitive, simple counterpart in animals of what in human beings becomes anxiety.

The first four characteristic processes are shared by the existing person with all living beings; they are biological levels in which human beings participate. The fifth process refers now to a distinctively human characteristic: self-consciousness. *The uniquely human form of awareness is self-consciousness.* Awareness and consciousness should not be identified. I associate awareness, as Liddell indicates, with vigilance. This is supported by the derivation of the term "aware," coming as it does from the Anglo-Saxon *gewaer, waer,* meaning knowledge of external dangers and threats. Its cognates are *beware* and *wary.* Awareness certainly is what is going on in an individual's neurotic reaction to threat, in, for example, Mrs. Hutchens' experience in her first hours that I am also a threat to her.

Consciousness, however, is not simply my awareness of threat from the world but *my capacity to know myself as the one being threatened, my experience of myself as the subject who has a world.* Consciousness, to use Kurt Goldstein's terms, is man's capacity to transcend the immediate concrete situation, to live in terms of the possible. It underlies the wide range of possibility that man has in relating to his world, and it constitutes the foundation of psychological freedom. Thus, human freedom has its ontological base and I believe must be assumed in all psychotherapy.

In his book *The Phenomenon of Man,* the paleontologist Pierre Teilhard de Chardin brilliantly describes how awareness is present, including the form of tropism, in all forms of evolutionary life from amoeba to man. But in man a new function arises, namely self-consciousness. Teilhard de Chardin undertakes to demonstrate something that I have always believed, that when a new function emerges, the whole previous pattern of the organism changes. The total gestalt shifts; thereafter the organism can be understood only in terms of the new function. That is to say, it is only a half truth to hold that

the organism is to be understood in terms of the simpler elements below it on the evolutionary scale. The other half of the truth is more crucial for us, namely every new function forms a new complexity that reorganizes all the simpler elements in this organism. As I previously said, *the simple can be understood only in terms of the more complex.*

This is what self-consciousness does in man. All the simpler biological functions must now be understood in terms of this new function. No one would, of course, deny for a moment the old functions, or anything in biology that man shares with less complex organisms. Take sexuality, for example, which we obviously share with all mammals. Given self-consciousness, sex becomes a new gestalt, as is demonstrated in therapy all the time. Sexual impulses are then conditioned by the *person* of the partner; what we think of the other male or female, in reality or fantasy or even repressed fantasy, can never be ruled out. The fact that the subjective person of the other to whom we relate sexually makes least difference in *neurotic* sexuality, say in patterns of compulsive sex or prostitution, only proves our point the more firmly, for these situations require precisely the blocking off, the checking out, and the distorting of self-consciousness. Thus, when we discuss sexuality in terms of sexual objects, as Kinsey does, we may garner interesting and useful statistics; but we simply are not talking about human sexuality.

Nothing in what I am saying here should be taken as anti-biological in the slightest; on the contrary, I think it is only from this approach that we *can* understand human biology without distorting it. As Kierkegaard aptly put it, "The natural law is as valid as ever." I argue only against the uncritical acceptance of the assumption that the organism is to be understood only in terms of those elements below it on the evolutionary scale, an acceptance that has led us to overlook the self-evident truth that what makes a horse a horse are not the elements it shares with the dog but what constitutes distinctively, "horse." Now, *what we are dealing with in neurosis are those characteristics and functions that are distinctively human.* It is these that have gone awry in disturbed patients. The condition for these functions is self-consciousness—which accounts for what Freud rightly discovered, that the neurotic pattern is characterized by repression and blocking off of consciousness.

It is the task of the therapist, therefore, not only to help the patient become aware, but even more significantly, to help him *transmute this awareness into consciousness.* Awareness is his knowing that something is threatening from outside in his world—a condition that may, as in paranoids and their neurotic equivalents, be correlated with much acting-out behavior. But self-consciousness puts this awareness on a quite different level; it is the patient's seeing that *he is the one who is threatened,* that he is the being who stands in this world which threatens, that he is the subject who *has* a world. And this gives him the possibility of *in-sight,* of "inward sight," of seeing the world and his problems in relation to himself. And thus it gives him the possibility of doing something about his problems.

To come back to our too-long silent patient: After about twenty-five hours of therapy Mrs. Hutchens had the following dream. She was searching room by room for a baby in an unfinished house at an airport. She thought the baby belonged to someone else, but the other person might let her take it. Now it seemed that she had put the baby in a pocket of her robe (or her mother's robe), and she was seized with anxiety that it would be smothered. Much

to her joy, she found that the baby was still alive. Then she had a strange thought, "Shall I kill it?"

The house was at the airport where she, at about the age of twenty, had learned to fly solo, a very important act of self-affirmation and independence from her parents. The baby was associated with her youngest son, whom she regularly identified with herself. Permit me to omit the ample associative evidence that convinced both her and me that the baby stood for herself, and specifically for consciousness of herself. The dream is an expression of the emergence and growth of self-consciousness, a consciousness that she is not yet sure is hers and a consciousness that she considers killing in the dream.

About six years before her therapy, Mrs. Hutchens had left the religious faith of her parents, to which, by way of them, she had had a very authoritarian relation. She had then joined a church of her own belief. But she had never dared tell her parents of this. Instead, when they came to visit, she attended their church in great tension lest one of her children let the secret out. After about thirty-five sessions, when she was considering writing her parents to tell them of this change of faith, she had, over a period of two weeks, spells of partially fainting in my office. She would become suddenly weak, her face would go white, she would feel empty and "like water inside" and would have to lie down for a few moments on the couch. In retrospect, she called these spells "grasping for oblivion."

She then wrote her parents informing them once and for all of her change in faith and assuring them it would do no good to try to dominate her. The following session, she asked in considerable anxiety whether I thought she would become psychotic. I responded that whereas any-one of us might at some time have such an episode, I saw no more reason why she should than any of the rest of us; and I asked whether her fear of becoming psychotic was not rather anxiety arising out of her standing against her parents, as though genuinely being herself, she felt to be tantamount to going crazy. (I have noted several times that patients experience this anxiety at being themselves as tantamount to psychosis.) This is not surprising, for consciousness of one's own desires and affirming them involves accepting one's originality and uniqueness. It implies that one must be prepared not only to be isolated from those parental figures upon whom one has been dependent but at that instant to stand alone in the entire psychic universe as well.

We see the profound conflicts of the emergence of self-consciousness in three vivid ways in Mrs. Hutchens, whose chief symptom, interestingly enough, was the denial of that uniquely human capacity based on consciousness, talking. These conflicts are shown in (1) the temptation to kill the baby; (2) the grasping at oblivion by fainting, as though she were saying, "If only I did not have to be conscious, I would escape this terrible problem of telling my parents"; and (3) the psychosis anxiety.

This brings us to the sixth and last characteristic of the existing person: *anxiety.* Anxiety is the state of the human being in the struggle against that which would destroy his being. It is, in Tillich's phrase, the state of a being in conflict with nonbeing, a conflict that Freud mythologically pictured in his powerful and important symbol of the death instinct. One wing of this struggle will always be against something outside the self. But even more portentous and significant for psychotherapy is the inner battle, which we saw in Mrs. Hutchens; namely, the conflict within the person as he confronts the choice of whether and how far he will stand against his own being, his own potentialities.

Thus, I take very seriously, if metaphorically, this temptation to kill the baby, or kill her own consciousness, as expressed in these forms by Mrs. Hutchens. I neither water it down by calling it "neurotic" and the product merely of sickness, nor do I slough over it by reassuring her, "Okay, but you don't need to do it." If I did these, I would be helping her adjust at the price of surrendering a portion of her existence, that is, her opportunity for fuller independence. The self-confrontation that is involved in the acceptance of self-consciousness is anything but simple: it involves, to identify some of the elements, accepting of the hatred of the past, her mother's hatred of her and hers of her mother; accepting her present motives of hatred and destruction; cutting through rationalizations and illusions about her behavior and motives, and the acceptance of the responsibility and aloneness that this implies; the giving up of childhood omnipotence, and acceptance of the fact that although she can never have absolute certainty about her choices, she must choose anyway.

But all these specific points, easy enough to understand in themselves, must be seen in the light of the fact that *consciousness itself implies always the possibility of turning against one's self, denying one's self.* The tragic nature of human existence inheres in the fact that consciousness itself involves the possibility and temptation at every instant to kill itself. Dostoevsky and our other existential forebears were not indulging in poetic hyperbole or expressing the after effects of too much vodka the night before when they wrote of the agonizing burden of freedom.

I trust that the fact that existential psychotherapy places emphasis on these tragic aspects of life does not at all give the impression that it is pessimistic. Quite the contrary. The confronting of genuine tragedy is a highly cathartic experience psychically, as Aristotle and others through history have reminded us. Tragedy is inseparably connected with man's dignity and grandeur and is the accompaniment, as illustrated in such dramas as Oedipus and Orestes, of the human being's moment of great insight.

In my judgment, the analysis of characteristics of the existing being—these ontological characteristics that I have tried to point out—can give us a structural base for our psychotherapy. It can also give us a base for a science of man that will not fragmentize and destroy man's humanity as it studies him.

8.

David Rosenthal

GENETIC MODEL: DIATHESIS-STRESS THEORIES

THEORIES OF THE ETIOLOGY OF SCHIZOPHRENIA

It is not possible to summarize all the theories that men have proposed with regard to what causes schizophrenia. So many environmental, biochemical, or physiological "causes" have been postulated over the years that it is almost easier to list factors that have not been proposed than those that have. All metabolites that have been suspected and tested failed the tests. Physiological, psychophysiological, psychological, sociological, and ecological hypotheses are difficult to rule out or confirm. If, however, the theories are classified into broad groups, without specifying particular hypothesized etiological agents, it is possible to form a conceptual framework. When this is done, the myriad theories can be reduced to three main types: *monogenic-biochemical, diathesis-stress,* and *life-experience theories.*

According to monogenic-biochemical theory, a single gene leads to a specific metabolic error which causes the disease. In fact, a two-gene theory that proposes a specific genotype involving four alleles on two loci also belongs here if the theory assumes that this particular genotype produces a specific metabolic error that alone causes the illness. The multitude of studies that have searched for the twisted molecule that produces a twisted mind are all based on this theory. Diathesis-stress theory is more loosely formulated and more difficult to test, but its looseness gives it a broad cover that enables it to blanket most research findings regarding the causes of schizophrenia. In the main, it holds that it is not a particular biochemical abnormality that is inherited, but rather a *predisposition* to develop the illness. Environmental stresses of certain kinds may potentiate processes involving

From *Genetic Theory and Abnormal Behavior* by David Rosenthal. Copyright 1970 by McGraw-Hill Book Company. Reproduced with permission.

TABLE 8-1

Comparison of Three Major Classes of Theory Regarding the Etiology of Schizophrenia

Aspects of the Illness	Monogenic-Biochemical Theory	Diathesis-Stress Theory	Life-experience Theory
Biological unity	Homogeneity: one gene, dominant, recessive, or intermediate. Trait is qualitative, discontinuous.	Homogeneity or heterogeneity. Trait may be qualitative or quantitative.	Neither homogeneity nor heterogeneity. Some question whether it should be considered a disease at all. Trait is quantitative.
"What" is inherited?	A specific but as yet unknown error of metabolism due to a mutant gene.	(1) A single gene. (2) Several major genes. (3) Polygenes. In either case, a "constitutional predisposition."	No special genotype necessary. Anyone could be a potential victim if subjected to certain experiences.
Manifestation	Very high: almost everyone (67 to 86 percent) with the genotype, but some have constitutional resistance to expression.	Considerably lower than monogenic-biochemical. Depends on whether predisposed schizophrenic encounters sufficient stress and how predisposed he is.	Depends on whether an individual is overexposed to certain noxious experiences or deprived of some benign "necessary" ones.
Role of environment	No special environments needed to precipitate illness. Incidental or minimal. Proponents like to cite a constant rate of schizophrenia in all cultures.	Necessary to precipitate the illness. The stressors are seldom defined: head trauma, disease, alcohol, parturition, exhaustion, etc., but usually psychological.	All-important: usually intrapersonal or interpersonal, but also sociological and even ecological.
Clinical subtypes	Of secondary interest, usually thought to reflect other inherited or constitutional factors which influence the form in which the illness is expressed.	Usually holds that they represent different predispositions interacting with different kinds of stressors.	Represent the consequences of different kinds of conflicts or conflict resolutions, or indicate modal types of attempted communication by the patient, or different patterns of learned disordered behavior.
Severity of illness	Reflects the degree of metabolic disturbance.	Reflects the amount of inherited predisposition and the intensity of the stressor.	Reflects the intensity of the conflicts or of the configurational stimuli involved in the maladaptive learning, or of noxious response-reinforcement contingencies.
Remission	For some reason, the effects of biochemical disturbance clear, but personality defect remains.	Either the physiological aspects of the disease process are reduced or the stressors are reduced.	(1) Abatement of conflict intensity. (2) Modification of configuration of stimuli which maintain the illness, or of schedules of reinforcement.
Premorbid personality	Varies in usual ways. When aberrant, the deviations are thought to be early signs of the metabolic disturbance.	Can provide clues about the nature of the predisposition inherited, as introversive personality or high anxiety.	Reveals the kinds of early conflict or learning patterns which eventually culminate in psychosis.
Research strategy	(1) Search for the biochemical aberrancy and its corrective. (2) Estimate gene frequency in population, mutation rate, mode of inheritance, etc.	Learn about the nature of the predispositions, the stressors, and the nature of the interaction.	Elucidate the conflicts or learning patterns leading to schizophrenia and the kinds of interventions most effective in counteracting the morbid process.
Example of problems posed by previous findings	Why does the distribution of illness in kindreds vary so markedly, for example, showing dominant, recessive, or intermediate patterns?	Why does the illness continue when the ostensible stressor has been removed?	(1) Why do patients get better with drugs or physical therapies? (2) How explain the genetic findings?

the predisposition, culminating in clinical schizophrenia. With a benign environment no overt psychopathology need become manifest, and indeed, the carrier may have traits that are unusual, desirable, and adaptive. Although single-gene theories could fit here, this theory best accommodates a polygenic mode of inheritance. Life-experience theory denies any important role to specific genes. Although we believe that the mass of genetic studies presented here invalidates this type of theory, the many investigations by its proponents who attempt to elucidate environmental causes of schizophrenia could point up the kinds of stresses that may be implicated in diathesis-stress theory. Interested readers will find a more detailed discussion of the three classes of theory in *The Genain Quadruplets* (Rosenthal, 1963, section on theoretical overview). A comparative summary of the three theories' views of some different aspects of schizophrenia is presented in Table 8-1.

Models of Monogenic-Biochemical Theory

Is it possible to fit the data on schizophrenia into a theoretical model of single-gene dominance? Of course it cannot be complete dominance, since we do not find the Mendelian ratios and pedigrees that such a model implies. However, we can assume partial dominance and proceed from there. Slater (1965) has done just that. First, he makes the assumption that all individuals homozygous for the pathological gene manifest the illness, whereas only some of the heterozygotes do. He then assumes the best estimate of the population incidence of schizophrenia to be 0.8 percent. With this assumption, it is now possible to calculate the proportion of heterozygotes who manifest the illness as a function of different possible gene frequencies in the population. . . .

Slater found that Kallmann's figures for sibs and for the parents of one schizophrenic, and Elsässer's figure for the children of two schizophrenic parents agree well with expectation for a gene frequency of 0.015 and a corresponding manifestation rate of 26 percent in heterozygotes. Homozygotes account for 3 percent, and heterozygotes 97 percent, of all schizophrenics.

The elegance of the model is apparent... but it presents problems. The population incidence of 0.8 may be too low, and the risk figure for Kallmann's sibs may be too high. The borderline cases and schizoid relatives are excluded in the calculations, and Slater found it difficult to fit the known twin data into the model.

A model for a single, recessive gene is provided by Kallmann (1953). . . . Kallmann's model is illustrative only, and makes no attempt to account for specific rates of schizophrenia in the population or among relatives of different degree. It involves, in addition to the assumption of a single recessive gene, only one other variable: constitutional resistance to manifestation. For illustrative purposes, he divides this continuous variable into four degrees of intensity. Kallmann's intent is to show how different combinations of genotype and constitutional resistance can account for different degrees of illness severity—from normal to deteriorative schizophrenia. It can thus account for all cases in the schizophrenic spectrum. However, since constitutional resistance is itself presumed to be a polygenically determined trait, Kallmann offers in effect a single-gene theory with modifying polygenes. Such a theory is difficult to distinguish by test from a straightforward polygenic theory, but it provides greater encouragement for those seeking the metabolic error in schizophrenia. A major difficulty confronting the theory comes from the twin studies that find relatively low concordance rates in MZ twins, both of whom share the same modifying genes that are presumed to influence manifestation. However, Kallmann points to other factors that could contribute to reduced constitutional resistance, such as lower birth weight or weight loss, both of which may be related to increased manifestation in the sicker twin.

Mitsuda (1967) proposes a model that is both unusual and imaginative. It is based on a different approach to psychiatric genetics, one that he calls the *clinico-genetic* approach. He states that "genetic studies in the field of psychiatry have tended to resort merely to assembling huge amounts of material and pursuing complicated mathematical treatments. From the viewpoint of clinical genetics, it seems more important to collect step by step individual cases which can be studied in detail clinically as well as genetically." Based on this orientation, he has examined the pedigrees of typical, atypical, and intermediate schizophrenics to determine the mode of inheritance among them. His findings are given in Table 8-2.

Mitsuda finds that the majority of cases of typical schizophrenia are recessive, while both the recessive and dominant modes of inheritance are about equally represented in atypical schizophrenia. Based on such data and on his finding epileptic and manic-depressive psychoses among the family members of schizophrenics, he has evolved the following model of the major psychoses, which subsume a monogenic-biochemical theory for both typical and atypical schizophrenia. The model is illustrated diagrammatically . . . and relies upon what Mitsuda calls the *three-entities principle*. The three entities are schizophrenia, manic-depressive psychosis, and epilepsy. Each entity has both typical and atypical (nuclear or peripheral) forms. In the nuclear groups, there is hardly any overlap in the manifestational range, indicating complete genetic independence among them. But considerable overlap exists between the different peripheral groups. . . . The atypical psychosis takes a schizo-affective form in the overlap of typical schizophrenia and manic-depressive psychosis, a form classified as *ictal anxiety* or *ictal depression* when in the borderline area between epilepsy and manic-depressive psychosis. It is not clear how the genetics of the intermediate forms can be worked out with this model, but it does attempt to account for a wide variety of manifestations of psychosis, many of which are ignored, slighted, or simply included in one of the major diagnostic groupings, and it places a heavier emphasis on clinical analysis of cases than do most other genetic studies of the behavioral disorders. Such studies, however, demand strict methodological controls, especially with respect to the independence and reliability of the investigators' diagnoses.

Models of Diathesis-Stress Theory

One of the models best known to psychologists was first publicly presented by Meehl in his presidential address to the American Psychological Association Convention in 1962. Meehl proposes that the old European notion of an inherited "integrated neural defect" may well be correct.

TABLE 8-2
Mode of Inheritance in Typical, Atypical, and
Intermediate Schizophrenia (by Percentage)*

Proband	Mode of Inheritance			
	Dominant	Intermediate	Recessive	Combined
Typical	8.2	17.6	72.5	1.6
Intermediate	37.5	15.6	34.4	12.5
Atypical	42.2	11.8	42.2	3.9

* Data from Mitsuda, 1967.

The defect involves an aberration of some aspect of single-cell function which may or may not be manifested in the functioning of the more molar CNS systems. He calls this defect *schizotaxia*. Meehl, following Bleuler, also proposes that there are four core characteristics of schizophrenia, which he calls cognitive slippage, anhedonia, interpersonal aversiveness, and ambivalence. Though all schizophrenics have them, they are not innate. Rather, they are universally learned by schizotaxic individuals. The learning is *social* learning, and it will occur regardless of social-reinforcement regime—whether very good or very poor. Consequent to social learning, the schizotaxic individual develops a form of personality organization that Meehl calls *schizotypy*. If the individual also inherits a "low anxiety readiness, physical vigor, general resistance to stress, and the like," and if the social-reinforcement regime is favorable, he will remain a well-compensated schizotype who shows no mental disease. This is what happens to most schizotypes. But a minority, who have other constitutional weaknesses that are mostly polygenically determined and who undergo a noxious social-reinforcement regime—by schizophrenogenic mothers, for example—develop clinical schizophrenia. Meehl speculates imaginatively about the nature of the inherited defect and outlines three possibilities, but they are not essential for demonstrating the model.

The model that has been most subjected to empirical test is the one proposed by Mednick (1958). . . . It presupposes the possibility, but does not require, that the future schizophrenic inherits high-anxiety responsiveness which is slowly habituated. With respect to the question of what is inherited in schizophrenia, this is the most simplistic model of all. With respect to the environmental aspects in the theory,

namely, the process of learning that culminates initially in acute schizophrenia and subsequently in chronic conditions, it is the most elegantly formulated diathesis-stress theory of all. Experimental findings have forced Mednick to modify the role of habituation in the theory, but it is otherwise still viable and promising (Mednick and Schulsinger, 1968).

Many other researchers have suggested alternatives with regard to the nature of the inherited diathesis: an introversive personality, a characterological defect, a constricted personality, a brittle ego, a conglomeration of traits, and the like. The point we want to make here is that Meehl's theory is one in which the diathesis involves a single gene, either dominant or recessive, that leads to a specific defect in CNS neural integration. However, it is essentially a diathesis-stress theory that requires environmental stresses to produce the clinical illness. Nor does the theory suggest that a particular biochemical abnormality, apart from the misguided genetic programming of the neural integrative defect, will be found in schizophrenics, any more than it will be found in the "normal" schizotypes. Mednick's theory also reveals the accommodative breadth of diathesis-stress theory in that, although the diathesis is specific with respect to anxiety and habituation, Mednick leaves open the possibility that it could result from one gene or many genes, or that it may be produced solely by environmental factors.

Polygenic Theory. In the main, the diathesis is thought to be polygenically determined. Throughout this chapter we have discussed data where polygenic theory seemed to be most consistent with the findings. Now let us focus on polygenic theory itself and see what kinds of data are needed to fit it. We will review briefly how we can identify such multifactorial or quantitative inheritance and examine its implications for schizophrenia.

1. Traits that are determined by multiple factors, whether genetic, environmental, or both, tend to be continuously and normally distributed in the population. By definition, schizophrenia is itself not normally distributed, but schizophrenic-spectrum pathology of the types that we considered to be biologically homogeneous might be. We do not have reliable studies of this point, but they could be done. In such a model, schizophrenia and normality would comprise the opposite tails of the distribution. The continuously graded characteristics of "schizoidness" could be measured once they were defined, and we could see if they followed the normal curve.

However, we are equally concerned with whether the diathesis is itself polygenically determined. In Meehl's model, the diathesis was a single-gene effect, but he also postulated—like Kallmann and all other theorists—some polygenically determined traits that influence trait manifestation. Since there is no reliable information on what the nature of the schizophrenia diathesis might be, we cannot say anything about its distribution. But this, too, could be determined. For example, Mednick can easily determine whether the diathetic traits of anxiety responsiveness and habituation, as he measures them, are normally distributed in his index and control Ss or not, and they very probably are. The same could be done for other hypothezied diathetic traits as well.

2. In simple polygenic inheritance (where there is strict additivity of genes, that is, no dominance or recessiveness) the incidence in first-degree relatives of an index case should be approximately the square root of the trait's incidence in the general population (Edwards, 1960). We may use the data to compare the morbidity

TABLE 8-3

Comparison of Morbidity Risk for Schizophrenics' Sibs and Risk Predicted by Polygenic Theory

Study	Observed Morbidity Risk for Sibs	Predicted Risk ($\sqrt{p}$)	Morbidity Risk for the Population (p)
Brugger, 1928	10.3	12.4	1.53
Schulz, 1932	6.7	8.7	0.76
Luxenburger, 1936	7.6	9.2	0.85
Strömgren, 1938	6.7	6.9	0.48
Kallmann, 1938	7.5	5.9	0.35
Bleuler, 1941	10.4	12.4	1.53
Böök, 1953	9.7	16.9	2.85
Hallgren-Sjögren, 1959	5.7	9.1	0.83
Garrone, 1962	8.6	15.5	2.40

risk for schizophrenics' sibs with that of the population at large. The figures are shown in Table 8-3. The study that comes closest to the expected approximation is that of Strömgren. The only study in which the rate for sibs is higher than expectation, based on population incidence, is Kallmann's. Three studies are far below expectation, but the remainder do not deviate seriously from what polygenic theory predicts. Thus, the data are not entirely consistent, but six of the nine studies suggest that a simple polygenic model may be appropriate.

3. The correlation between relatives should be approximately equal to the proportion of genes they share in common. The data presented earlier in this chapter rather consistently meet this criterion.

4. In twin studies, if MZ concordance is more than two times higher than that of DZ twins, the trait is not a simple dominant; if it is more than four times higher, it is not a simple recessive. . . . The MZ-DZ ratios vary appreciably in the twin studies reported, with most occurring in the 3:1 to 6:1 range. The figures rule against simple —but not intermediate—dominance. If the differences between studies are not entirely the result of errors of various kinds, they could reflect differences in

population incidences of the pathological genes, environmental differences, or both.

5. Parental consanguinity can signify that pathological genes with additive effects are involved if we can rule out recessive inheritance. The latter can be achieved by demonstrating that the parent-offspring correlation is similar to the sib-sib correlation.

6. The mean for the offspring is halfway between the mean for the parents and the mean for the general population.

Criteria 5 and 6 require that we have a suitable measure of the core traits—or diathesis—in schizophrenia. At this time, we are not in a position to test a polygenic theory of schizophrenia against these criteria.

Models of the Diathesis-Stress Interaction. In a model such as Meehl's, the imposition of social learning—which must inevitably occur—upon the schizotaxia leads inexorably to the schizotype. Then the schizotype, if subjected to a noxious mother, develops into schizophrenia. Thus Meehl proposes a two-stage process. By and large, unless we are able to discover the biological nature of the defect that we call the diathesis, we are unable to come to grips with how it relates ultimately to the genesis of schizophrenia. Stating the point differently, we declare that we are not in a position at the present time to generate tests of first-stage hypotheses. However, prospects are brighter with respect to the second stage. If diathesis-stress theory is correct, it should be possible to identify, describe, and measure the schizotype in its various aspects and then to examine its further development under different environmental conditions. With respect to this second stage, it is possible to outline six general models of how the schizotype-stress interaction may be conceptualized. Since the term *schizotype* is now closely identified with Meehl's theory, and since

for all practical purposes the schizotype may well be equated with the diathesis, we will speak here of the diathesis-stress interaction rather than the schizotype-stress interaction.

1. *Variance analysis.* This is the model that holds out the greatest promise for immediate research. It does not aim to say what the diathesis is, but only to indicate how much of the phenotype it accounts for in a direct sense, and as a consequence of its interaction with different environmental or stress factors. To illustrate the model, let us take the two variables that have been so often proposed as causal agents in schizophrenia: the schizophrenic genotype and the rearing by schizophrenic parents. Let us assume that it is possible, for example, through adoption, to design the following study:

	Type of Rearing Parent	
Biological Parent	Schizophrenic	Normal
Schizophrenic	25	25
Normal	25	25

According to the design, we have 50 children with a biological schizophrenic parent, half of whom are reared by a schizophrenic parent, half by normal parents. We also have a matched group of 50 children whose both biological parents are normal, half of whom are reared by a schizophrenic parent and half by normal parents. Let us assume that we are interested in the four core characteristics of schizophrenia described by Meehl: cognitive slippage, anhedonia, interpersonal aversiveness, and ambivalence. We measure these traits in each of the 100 Ss, and these measures are entered in the appropriate cells. We carry out the analysis of variance with respect to each trait separately and determine how much of the variance is attributed to the genotype, how much to type of rearing, and how much to the genotype-rearing interaction. The same model may be used repeatedly, with different environmental or stress variables being substituted for the one shown in the design here. From many such studies, we may be able to infer the nature of the diathesis.

2. *Activation.* In this model, the stress serves as a trigger that sets off or activates the diathesis so that a force or process is generated that impels the individual toward schizophrenia. Meehl's schizophrenogenic mother serves as the activator in his model.

3. *Augmentation.* The diathesis and the stress are somehow cast in the same mold or dimension. They compound the same phenotype. The imposed stress simply piles up on the diathesis, in a sense providing more of the same, the overload leading to schizophrenia. In the Genain quadruplets, it was thought that the girls inherited constricted personalities, on top of which was heaped a severely constricted upbringing. The combination culminated in different degrees of schizophrenia, depending on each girl's ability to circumvent the imposed constriction.

4. *Facilitation-resistance.* This is the model usually applied by theorists advocating monogenic-biochemical theory, but it could apply to diathesis-stress theory as well. For example, in Kallmann's model and in Meehl's, constitutional factors could facilitate or impede the development of a schizophrenic reaction. Kallmann and others have reported that an athletic or mesomorphic body build provides resistance to trait manifestation, whereas a leptosomic or ectomorphic body build makes the individual with the genotype especially vulnerable. How such factors influence the diathesis is not specified.

5. *Reciprocal escalation.* This model is best exemplified by Mednick's theory.

Here the diathesis increases the stress, which increases the intrinsic diathetic reaction, which further increases the stress, and so on, the process intensifying until the schizophrenic break occurs. According to Mednick, the high anxiety leads to increased stimulus generalization, which increases the anxiety still further, the spiral continuing to the breaking point.

6. *Contradictory tendencies or opposed forces.* In this model, the diathesis predisposes toward one type of behavior, but the environment tries to impose a contradictory or opposed behavior. Depending on the nature of the diathesis and of the environmental pressure, the individual subjected to these opposing forces may develop various kinds of behavioral and psychological difficulties. A concrete illustration is provided by right- or left-handedness, which is clearly an inherited trait that does not conform to a strict Mendelian distribution. Falek (1967) believes that some behavioral deviation in left-handed children stems from parents' attitudes and behavior toward them. The children may provoke embarrassment, require special seating arrangements at the table, become the butt of unpleasant jokes, face problems in handwriting at school, be at a disadvantage regarding vocational opportunities, and so on. Some parents may resort to various degrees and types of coercion to induce a change of handedness in their children, and the consequences may involve various kinds of motoric and psychological difficulties. Presumably, an analogous confrontation of opposed pressures could be implicated in schizophrenia.

CLOSING COMMENTS

We will not discuss life-experience theories here, since they are so widely known and since they belong more appropriately in books dealing with such variables. There are many, and they are of great interest. Neither will we attempt to tie all the material we have covered in this chapter into a neat package with a cogent conclusion. The attempt would be forced at best. The reader can bring the bodies of data together in different ways to see what order he can bring to them, what research they suggest, or what new theories they generate. It should, however, be clear that the author leans toward a diathesis-stress theory of schizophrenia.

In the diathesis-stress theory, the mode of inheritance for most cases of schizophrenia is most likely to be either polygenic or a single dominant gene, with variable penetrance depending on multiple gene modifiers and environmental factors. As of now, the known data do not permit us to choose between these two competing hypotheses, but future research may help us to resolve the problem. We all have reason to desire a simpler solution to this disorder, but it is difficult to predict such a solution, given all the available data.

As a matter of fact, diathesis-stress theory may be even more complicated than implied here. The diathesis, for example, may have multiple genetic origins. This possibility is suggested by recent findings of an increased incidence of aneuploidy among schizophrenics. This finding in turn suggests that aneuploidy can either simulate the diathesis or lead directly to clinical schizophrenia without benefit of special stresses. It cannot by itself be a major factor in schizophrenia, however, because it accounts for only a tiny fraction of all cases, and because the same kinds of aneuploidy are more often found in nonschizophrenic subjects.

Diathesis-stress theory provides implications for research that may lead to important practical as well as theoretical results. Perhaps the first order of business is to determine the nature of the diathesis, both at the first-stage biological level and at the second-stage schizotypic level. Once we achieve the latter, which at the moment seems an easier task, we could conduct experiments to see what kinds of stresses interact in what ways with the diathesis to lead to pathological clinical manifestations. We could as well determine what kinds of environment lead not only to benign outcomes but to the realization of the artistic or creative potential that may be lying fallow in the diathesis. And once we know the nature of the diathesis-environmental stress interactions that lead to schizophrenia, we should be able to inaugurate rationally based therapeutic procedures in a preventive program of mental hygiene to assure that a large number of the predisposed individuals never develop schizophrenic illness at all.

REFERENCES

Cumings, J. N., & Kremer M. (Eds.) *Biochemical aspects of neurological disorders.* 2nd series. Oxford: Blackwell Scientific Publications, 1965. Pp. 271-285.

Falek, A. Methods to investigate the interaction of environmental and genetic factors in normal and deviant traits. Paper presented at the 75th annual meeting of the American Psychological Association, 1967.

Kallmann, F.J. *Heredity in health and mental disorder.* New York: W.W. Norton, 1953.

Mednick, S.A. A learning theory approach to research in schizophrenia. *Psychological Bulletin,* 1958, *55,* 315-327.

Mednick, S.A., & Schulsinger, F. Some premorbid characteristics related to breakdown in children with schizophrenic mothers. In D. Rosenthal & S.S. Kety (Eds.), *The transmission of schizophrenia.* London Pergamon Press, 1968, Pp. 267-291.

Meehl, P.E. Schizotaxia, schizotypy,

schizophrenia. *American Psychologist,* 1962, *17,* 827-838.

Mitsuda, H. A clinico-genetic study of schizophrenia. In H. Mitsuda (Ed.), *Clinical genetics in psychiatry.* Tokyo: Igaku Shoin, 1967, Pp. 49-90.

Rosenthal, D. (Ed.) *The Genain quadruplets.* New York: Basic Books, 1963.

Slater, E. Clinical aspects of genetic mental disorders. In J.N. Cummings & M. Kremer (Eds.), *Biochemical aspects of neurological disorders.* 2nd series. Oxford: Blackwell Scientific Publications, 1965. Pp. 271-285.

CHAPTER III

Anxiety Disorders, Factitious, Somatoform, and Dissociative Disorders

Neurosis lacks a common definition among psychologists. An attempt at a definition of this term often is predicated upon one's theory of neurosis, that is to say, some learning theorists regard a neurotic as merely a person who is victimized by some bad habits, while psychoanalysts view him as an early substage of the psychotic.

Despite the variety of views and the discrepancies involved in the nature and definition of neurosis, there nevertheless exists some consensus regarding the issue. However, agreement exists regarding the functional nature of neurosis, its absence of lesions or organic disease, its chief characteristic symptom being anxiety. Furthermore, the neurotic maintains conscious contact with external reality relatively free from any major falsification of it, his personality organization remaining intact, hence distinguishing him from the psychotic. Moreover, it is unlikely that the neurotic would resort to violent behavior. It is interesting to note that DSM-III has replaced the classification "neurosis" with "anxiety disorders."

Psychoanalysis

With the exception of advancements in psychosomatic medicine, progress in classical psychoanalysis has failed to keep pace in recent years at a comparable rate to that set by learning theorists and other schools of psychopathology. Psychoanalysts have not significantly advanced beyond Freud's original discoveries. Their efforts have fructified in stimulating other schools of thought to launch their own investigations. Similar observations may be made of certain offshoot schools whose founders were one-time associates of Freud, for example, that of Jung. Noteworthy new ideas of major significance (comparable to those sired by other schools of thought) are wanting in psychoanalytically oriented circles despite the prevalence of journals devoted to these schools. Psychoanalysis presented and re-presented is virtually the same position that existed 20, 30, or more years ago. It is not to be implied that these journals have lost their usefulness or that they no longer contain current articles of urgent or novel import, for they contain numerous significant contributions by "outsiders" and by those within the "camp" with worthwhile contributions in fields not strictly aligned with the purpose of the journal in question. For example, when a thinker of the magnitude of Viktor Frankl was without an organ devoted to the dissemination of contributions to logotherapy, he utilized periodicals devoted to other schools in order to keep the world abreast of his contributions.

The most comprehensive and authoritative treatment of psychoanalytical theory of neurosis was contributed by Fenichel (1945), but even that is over a half century old, yet unrivalled. A book of more than 700 pages, it is merely a reformulation of Freudianism, granting only minor concessions to the cultural or neo-Freudians. Nevertheless, novel advances in psychoanalysis have been made by the culturalists, environmentalists, and interpersonalists, such as Horney (1937, 1945, 1950), Sullivan (1953, 1956), Fromm-Reichmann (who synthesizes Freud and Sullivan, 1950), and Fromm (1941, 1947, 1955). Fromm later sought to integrate psychoanalysis with Zen Buddhism (Suzuki, Fromm, & DeMartino, 1960).

Fromm-Reichmann (1949), reporting on recent advances in psychoanalysis, cites the developments by Fromm, Horney, Kardiner, and Sullivan with respect to cultural factors; and revisions of the Oedipus complex by Boehm, Fromm, Malinowski, and Mullahy. Contrary to Freud, Fromm-Reichmann sees certain dissociative or repressed processes as desirable, for "man depends upon successful dissociations and processes of selective inattention for the mastery of his psychobiological existence" (1949, p. 323). Predicated upon this important observation, Whitaker and Malone (1953) constructed an experiential theory of psychotherapy. For the sake of enhancing the experience of reality, some psychoanalysts have relinquished the regulation which binds them to utilize the couch in therapy. Perhaps the greatest innovation in psychoanalysis is the trend toward more abbreviated forms of therapy. Another important advance has been the deep interest by some members in psychosomatic medicine and its recent illuminating experiments, especially by Alexander (1959, 1962) and his associates (1961).

Anxiety Theory of Neurosis

An anxiety theory of neurosis, viewing neurosis as the upshot of a person's struggle for security and rooted in self-preservation, is offered by R. W. White (1973). The warped outcome of the struggle is neurosis, the only assurance of safety offered the neurotic whose security is threatened. The neurotic's characteristics or symptoms are defensive measures, the purpose of which is to cope with his anxiety. The fundamental postulate of Keiser's book, *The Traumatic*

Neurosis, is that "all types of psychiatric illness may develop as a manifestation of traumatic neurosis" (1968, p. 42).

Learning Theory of Neurosis

The learning theorist view of neurosis as a functional disturbance produced through experience and learning has been championed by Dollard and Miller (1950), who see the main factors of neurosis as conflict, stupidity, and misery with symptoms. While conflict produces misery, and repression causes stupidity, symptoms reduce conflict slightly. In any case, neurosis obeys the laws of learning. For example, Freud's pleasure principle is merely the learning theorist's principle of reinforcement; repression is the inhibition of cue-producing responses; transference is generalized responses occurring in the therapeutic experience; and inhibition and restraint serve in place of repression and suppression.

Miller later (1959) postulated a gradient of avoidance explaining fear, anxiety, or conflict according to the following theory: "the tendency to avoid a feared stimulus is stronger the nearer the subject is to it." According to Miller's gradient model, "the strength of avoidance increases more rapidly with nearness than does that of approach." Furthermore, "the strength of tendencies to approach or avoid varies directly with the strength of the drive upon which they are based." In case two incompatible responses conflict, then the stronger one will take precedence.

Miller (1966) reported that since barbiturates reduce fear and since fear reduction acts as a reward, then this finding corroborates that of the clinicians that potent fear, guilt, and other aversive drives tend to heighten the probability that persons will become addicted to barbiturates. In the same report he cites how differing social conditions produce differing learned responses. Two children through social learning can acquire different types of psychosomatic responses to stress.

O. H. Mowrer, who is also committed to learning theory, seeks to revise Freudian postulates to harmonize with those of learning theory, especially his own two-factor theory of learning. According to Mowrer (1953), neurosis is a problem understood in the light of solution learning and sign learning; the id is viewed as a primary drive, the superego as the result of sign learning or social conditioning, and the ego as that aspect of the personality dealing with solution learning. Symptoms of neurosis manifest themselves as the result of habits (repressions) being devised as solutions to a conflict ensuing between primary drives (id forces) and secondary drives (fears), a conflict caused by social conditioning or discipline.

According to Mowrer (1960), the neurotic is not a person who is ill, nor is he a person who is to be excused for his behavior, but he is one who is entangled in sin. His inability to escape his predicament is due to his neurotic paradox (1948, 1952), that is, despite unfavorable consequences ensuing from the neurotic's behavior, he nevertheless perpetuates this senseless pattern, whereas a normal person or even animal would avoid behavior whose net effect is undesirable. Mowrer suggests that neurosis might better be viewed as an "identity crisis" or "sociosis," because the neurotic is not abnormal, but ab-normal, a deviant from "the established *norms* of the individual's reference group" (1966, p. 448). Accordingly, the neurotic is not superego-dominated, but a social deviant, for if he were superego-dominated as Freud contended, then he would not be neurotic, but socially well integrated and comfortably in conformity with his society (1967b). Psychotherapy based on amorality rather than curing personality disorder is likely to cause personality deviation (1961). Psychotherapy must be a social reintegration (1964), accomplished through "integrity therapy" (1966, 1967b).

Learning Theory and Factor Analysis of Neurosis

Eysenck's (1950, 1952) approach to neurosis is via learning theory and factor analysis. Isolating three factors in his dimensional approach to personality (neuroticism, psychoticism, and extraversion-introversion) and utilizing his criterion analysis, Eysenck finds the cause of neurosis in two types of anxiety, one stemming from an inherited autonomic lability and the second from a conditioned anxiety (1957).

Buss (1962, 1966) and Hamilton (1959) corroborate the findings of Eysenck to the extent that anxiety neurosis displays two patterns, somatic symptoms on the one hand, and cognitive-motor ones on the other. They found one factor dominated by autonomic reactions and one predominated by motor and cognitive aspects of anxiety. According to Eysenck, neurotic syndromes also vary according to extraversion-introversion, hysterics tending toward extraversion, and introverts toward dysthymia, that is, anxiety, obsession-compulsion, and so on.

As a learning theorist, as well as a factor analyst, Eysenck insists that neurotic symptoms are merely learning habits. Inasmuch as neurotic symptoms are unadaptive forms of learned patterns of behavior, "get rid of the symptom and you have eliminated the neurosis" (1959, 1965). The symptom *is* the neurosis; replace the maladaptive habit causing the symptom, and you have a neurotically-free individual with adaptive habits.

In America, factor analysis or multivariate experimental psychology, as it is coming to be called, has been championed by Cattell (1973), who edited a handbook in the field (1966). Cattell's interest is in measuring neuroticism and the various traits associated with the neurotic (1965). In recent years, he has been interested in measuring anxiety and neuroticism (1957, 1962, 1963; Cattell & Scheier, 1961) by means of variables that are their manifestations, and comparing them with personality factors recognized as dimensions within the normal individual.

Relativistic Theory of Neurosis

With time, neurosis had reached a point of meaninglessness. The behavior and feelings of any person who did not accord with one's own society or one's own personal responses to certain situations was dubbed neurotic. As such it deteriorated to the level of being a "wastebasket" term, a word for anything that had no strict classification.

The psychoanalyst, Franz Alexander, insisting that neurosis is merely a relative term, argued that "the same person may be well-adjusted in one situation and not in another. Neurosis is not an absolute attribute of a person," he contended, because "it has no meaning without considering the field in which the person operates" (1962, p. 22). An immigrant in his native culture, for example, can be perfectly adapted, but designated neurotic in a new and foreign environment. Or, an introverted person might be diagnosed as schizoid or neurotic in a frontier town of early America, but might be regarded as a celebrated luminary in a literary and highly cultured society. Many subcultures have marvelous adaptive value, and this might well be the reason that a number of people are attracted to them.

In the light of the relativistic theory of neurosis, psychotherapy acquires an entirely new perspective. Rather than dogmatically insisting that a patient's personality be reconstructed to suit a therapist or the prevailing society—that is, to comport with an imaginary norm—intelligence, in certain individual cases, might dictate changing or restructuring the social and impersonal environment instead. The therapist must grapple with the question of which is better— changing people or their environment. Some clients might be better off changing their jobs than altering their personalities, others divorcing their spouses than adjusting to an ill-starred marriage.

Neurosis, then, is not an absolute term, but a relative one. "A person is not necessarily neurotic per se. The diagnostic term 'neurotic,'" insists Alexander, "must be qualified by adding where and when a person is neurotic. Not only the person, but also the field in which he finds himself must be considered. The fully analyzed normal person is one of those fictions which at present is retarding the development of psychiatry" (1962, pp. 22-23).

The issue raised by Alexander soon won support from others. The neo-Freudians, those who are called the cultural psychoanalysts, were well aware of the societal role in shaping behavior that might conflict with behavioral norms of another society. In his examination of normality, Scott contends that mental health, adjustment, normality, or whatever else you choose to call it, is a value judgment rather than an absolute or objective fact—such as tooth decay, a broken leg, or malaria. "The question, 'What constitutes normality?' is best understood not as a question of fact, but rather as a question of conventional definition" (1968, p. 975). If this is the case, then a psychotherapist judging behavior comes perilously close to the moralist.

That irreverent iconoclast of psychiatry, Szasz, charges psychiatrists with calling the problems of living, "diseases." Psychiatry, he wrote disparagingly, "is the sewer into which societies in the second half of the twentieth century discharge all their unsolved moral and social problems" (1976, p. 119). What then is mental illness? A mere myth, answers Szasz. "To say that a person's mind is sick," retorts Szasz, "is like saying that the economy is sick or that a joke is sick. When metaphor is mistaken for reality and is used for social purposes, then we have the makings of myth. The concepts of mental health and mental illness are mythological concepts" (1973, p. 97). Szasz, thus, reduces mental illness to a matter of cruel falsification, a hoax played on an unsuspecting and helpless person.

The Drug Hypothesis of Neurotic Anxiety

When we suffer from anxiety are we all pained from the same kind of anxiety? That is to say, does neurotic anxiety differ qualitatively from psychotic anxiety? Or is all anxiety the same, differing merely in degree? Recent findings in psychopharmacological research seem to indicate that neurotic and psychotic anxiety differ.

Drugs seem to tell us that the anxiety endured by the neurotic is not the same as that suffered by the schizophrenic. At least the source of pain is quite different. Antianxiety tranquilizers, such as chlordiazepoxide (Librium) and diazepam (Valium), are very effective when administered to relieve neurotic anxiety but are not effective agents in treating schizophrenics. On the other hand, while phenothiazines are the wonder drugs for schizophrenics, they are poor agents for treating manifest anxiety. This being the case, can we conclude that anxiety found in the neurotic is of another species than that troubling the psychotic?

Thus, we find that drugs are selective; they seek out a specialized target and affect it. Different biochemical systems could possibly be affected for the anxiety of the neurotic and the anxiety experienced by the schizophrenic. The selectivity of the drugs gives us the basis for concluding that neurosis and psychosis are not on the same continuum but are fundamentally different disturbances.

The antischizophrenic drugs are not, as has been previously supposed by some individuals, merely sedating psychotics. These drugs directly affect the primary symptoms of schizophrenia, such as reducing overinclusive thinking, enhancing abstract thinking, and the like.

Safety-Signal Hypothesis of Anxiety

When an anxiety-evoking situation arrives as predicted, the psychological stress it causes is never as severe as when the fearful situation is unpredictable. It is for this reason that the people in London during World War II could cope reasonably well during frequent air raids. Sirens would signal danger of an air attack, alerting people both when to expect danger and when it terminated. If it were not for the reliable air-raid signals, the safety-signal hypothesis holds that the citizens of London would have been nervous wrecks—continually plagued by anxiety.

The safety-signal hypothesis, initiated by Seligman and his associates (1977), claims that "in the wake of traumatic events, people and animals will be afraid all the time, except in the presence of a stimulus that reliably predicts safety. In the absence of a safety signal, organisms remain in anxiety and chronic fear. On this view, asserted Seligman, "People and animals are safety-signal seekers: they search out predictors of unavoidable danger because such knowledge also gives them knowledge of safety" (1975, p. 113). It is for this reason that certain persons who know that they are going to die within a specified time are not as anxiety-prone as those who are never sure of it.

Anxiety is not as severe when we believe that we are in control of it. One dentist had the child to be treated monitor his actions, saying: "Although this will hurt somewhat, you tell me when to stop by raising your hand. Raising it a little means that it hurts a bit, but when the hand is raised upright, it means for me to stop. You control my actions." Children endure a great deal more pain under these conditions because they believe that there is no need for anxiety since they can bring things to a close. Geer, Davison, and Gatchel (1970) validated this finding experimentally. They found that subjects who believed that they were in control of aversive events were less anxious. In fact, even their false beliefs, as long as they thought they were controlling the situation, were sufficient to reduce anxiety.

Stress in Executives

When Brady published his sensational report on "Ulcers in 'Executive' Monkeys" (1958), it seemed well established that psychophysiological disorders were brought on by stress. Eight of Brady's monkeys, exposed to electric shock, could have turned off the current simply by depressing a bar. The first four to do so were classified as the executives of the group, and the others became yoked to them as their assistants. Thus each executive had his partner, but the yoked partner simply went along for the ride as it were, for he had absolutely no control over the matter. If a pair of monkeys were to escape shock, it was up to the executive to control the current every time it was turned on. The shocks were, however, unpredictable. Comparable to executives in the world of big business, these executive monkeys had to make the right decisions to avoid catastrophe, for they were in a position to predict and control shocks. As the experiment turned out, the executives, rather than the yoked partners, developed ulcers.

This once celebrated experiment is currently challenged. Seligman (1975) dismissed it as an artifact of Brady's experimental design. Experiments by Weiss (1968, 1970, 1971a, b, c) demonstrated that the opposite was true. The helpless associates—not the executives—suffered much severer psychophysiological stress disorders than the executives. They also endured more anxiety than subjects in control, that is, the executives. Weiss is telling us, in effect, that it is the rider (or the backseat driver) in a car that suffers the greater anxiety and stress rather than the actual driver. His experiments suggest that it is the assistants to the executives in big business that "sweat it out," endure greater stress and anxiety, and worry more about the decisions made than the top bosses.

Existential Neurosis

Existential neurosis is one of the newer psychopathologies to be recognized, and it is regarded as a concomitant of our present-day existence. Just as sexual neurosis dominated the neuroses of a few generations ago, owing to sex repression which was prevalent at the time, today existential neurosis is emerging as the disturbance emanating from our cultural and personal mode of existence.

The development of our knowledge of existential neurosis has been proposed by Frankl (1958a, b, 1959, 1962a, b, 1966, 1967a, b, 1975), but recently Maddi (1967) has lent his support. Existential neurosis, or as Frankl often refers to it "noögenic neurosis," stems from a void or "existential vacuum" (Frankl), that is, a sense of meaninglessness or "existential frustration." Existential neurosis emanates from spiritual conflicts, mental aimlessness, ennui, and ethical perplexities, a wrestling within a human being seeking for a meaningful life. Logotherapy is the most effective form of treatment for this peculiar type of neurosis. Logotherapy entails more than psychology; it includes philosophy as well (Fabry, 1968).

Maslow's (1967) contribution to the advancement of our knowledge of neurosis is in terms of neurosis as a failure of personal growth. Neurosis is the inability to achieve self-actualization, that is, to gain "full humanness"; instead, the neurotic is in a state of "human diminution" or a "not-yet-actualization of human capacities and possibilities." Inasmuch as man's psychological nature is innately good, then normal is equated with healthy and happy while interrupted growth is unhealthy (1968). Not too distant from Maslow's general attitude toward neurosis is that of Angyal's (1965) "holistic theory." For Angyal, neurosis is a way of life inherently destined to failure. Neurosis, a making of the real self, prevents the real or better self from emerging and assuming its proper role.

Kelly (1955), too, sees the neurotic in an improper role, with his personal constructs failing him. Anxiety is the result of the failure of personal construction; and threat, the upheaval of one's core structure. Guilt emerges when a person is dislodged from his role.

The social roles that a person plays and their relevancy to mental health have been scored by Adler (1939) and in recent years by the social learning theorists such as Rotter (1954, 1964). The social learning theorist sees behavior as goal directed. A person prefers behavior from which he has learned to acquire the greatest satisfaction under given situations. A person possesses "need potentials," that is, a set of behaviors that are goal-directed. By his "freedom of movement" (expectancies that his behavior leads to a set of goals), he achieves his "need value," the worth of the goals of reinforcements. Maladaptive behavior ensues from a low freedom of movement and a high need value. The ill-adapted person fails to learn how to achieve his goals; rather he is learning how to avoid failure and experiences concomitant frustration.

The superiority of the social learning theorists over the usual brand of learning theorists is the level of sophistication to which they have elevated learning theory. While ordinary learning theorists concentrate their experiments and extrapolate their information from animal behavior, social learning theorists derive their information from human beings and from qualities peculiarly human. Predicated on this distinction (which is also Rotter's, 1964), the authors favor social learning theory, interpreting neurotic behavior from that point of view. Subhuman neurosis is never quite the same as human neurosis, owing particularly to a human's higher mental processes and his inter-personal relationships or social atmosphere. Furthermore man has extra-animal needs (Fromm, 1955, p. 25) and a self-awareness that renders his neurosis much more complex and different from animal neurosis. Although experimental neurosis lends insight into human neurosis, it is only a partial explanation at best. One's sense of responsibility heightens his sense of guilt and even complicates it in such a manner as to compound the human sense of guilt. Social intercourse as such does not create guilt (as Freud supposed), but it does point the direction or cite that about which a person may sense a feeling of guilt. If I were devoid of guilt feeling, then my society could never make me feel guilty about any matter, but being constructed in a manner so that guilt is part of my constitution, then through social learning I may be directed toward that mode of behavior which issues in guilty feelings. Once I am victimized by a drive which directs me to behavior that is socially reprehensible, then both the be-havior and the sense of accompanying guilt become conditioned as part of my trait makeup. If I am conditioned to believe that punitive or catastrophic results are the outcome of guilt, then I associate guilt with anxiety, or I become anxiety-ridden with the sense of guilt (Sahakian, 1969b).

Taylor Manifest Anxiety Scale

The measurement of anxiety was also conducted by Janet Taylor (1951, 1953), producing the well-known Taylor Manifest Anxiety Scale (MAS). Consisting of factors indicative of manifest anxiety, the scale is a technique in studying human motivation relevant to anxiety. A correlation exists between internal anxiety and drive level. The relationship between the intensity of manifest anxiety of patients and anxiety-scale scores of normal persons is ascertained. K. W. Spence also shared in some of these studies with Taylor (1951, 1953) and with Farber also (1953).

Byrne Repression-Sensitization Scale

Studies in neurotic patterns of avoidance were accelerated by the introduction of Byrne's Repression-Sensitization Scale (1961). Stimulated by studies in perceptual defense by Eriksen (1954) and Lazarus (1954), Byrne arrived at a concept of behavior dimension consisting of psychological defenses from repression at one end and sensitization at the other. The R-S Scale serves as a measure of defensive behavior, as a measure of adjustment (Byrne, Golightly, & Sheffield, 1965), and as a dimension of personality (Byrne, 1964).

Neurotic Depression and Endogenous Depression

Kiloh and Garside (1963) have demonstrated a decisive difference between neurotic depression and endogenous depression, an important distinction from the standpoint of treatment as well as accurate prognostication.

Since the varieties of neuroses accompanied by their definitions have been enumerated in the pages that follow, we need not reiterate the matter here.

9.

American Psychiatric Association

FEATURES OF ANXIETY DISORDERS, FACTITIOUS DISORDERS, SOMATOFORM DISORDERS, AND DISSOCIATIVE DISORDERS

ANXIETY DISORDERS

In this group of disorders anxiety[1] is either the predominant disturbance, as in panic disorder and generalized anxiety disorder, or anxiety is experienced if the individual attempts to master the symptoms, as in confronting the dreaded object or situation in a phobic disorder or resisting the obsessions or compulsions in obsessive compulsive disorder. Diagnosis of an anxiety disorder is not made if the anxiety is due to another disorder, such as schizophrenia, an affective disorder, or an organic mental disorder.

It has been estimated that from 2 percent to 4 percent of the general population has at some time had a disorder that this manual would classify as an anxiety disorder.

Panic disorder, phobic disorders and obsessive compulsive disorder are each apparently more common among family members of individuals with each of these disorders than in the general population.

From Task Force on Nomenclature and Statistics of the American Psychiatric Association, *Diagnostic and Statistical Manual of Mental Disorders, Third Edition.* American Psychiatric Association, 1980.

[1]In other classifications, these disorders are grouped together in the neuroses or neurotic disorders.

PHOBIC DISORDERS (OR PHOBIC NEUROSES)

The essential feature is persistent and irrational fear of a specific object, activity, or situation that results in a compelling desire to avoid the dreaded object, activity, or situation (the phobic stimulus). The fear is recognized by the individual as excessive or unreasonable in proportion to the actual dangerousness of the object, activity, or situation.

Irrational avoidance of objects, activities, or situations that have an insignificant effect on life adjustment is commonplace. For example, many individuals experience some irrational fear when unable to avoid contact with harmless insects or spiders, but this has no major effect on their lives. However, when the avoidance behavior or fear is a significant source of distress to the individual or interferes with social or role functioning, a diagnosis of a phobic disorder is warranted.

The phobic disorders are subdivided into three types: agoraphobia, the most severe and pervasive form; social phobia; and simple phobia. Both social and simple phobias generally involve a circumscribed stimulus, but simple phobia tends to have an earlier onset and better prognosis. When more than one type is present, multiple diagnoses should be made.

Although anxiety related to separation from parental figures is a form of phobic reaction, it is classified as separation anxiety disorder, in the section disorders usually first evident in infancy, childhood, or adolescence. Similarly, phobic avoidance limited to sexual activities is classified as a psychosexual disorder not elsewhere classified.

Although simple phobia is the most common type of phobic disorder in the general population, agoraphobia is the most common among those seeking treatment.

Agoraphobia without Panic Attacks

The essential feature is a marked fear of being alone, or being in public places from which escape might be difficult or help not available in case of sudden incapacitation. Normal activities are increasingly constricted as the fears or avoidance behavior dominate the individual's life. The most common situations avoided involve being in crowds, such as on a busy street or in crowded stores, or being in tunnels, on bridges, on elevators, or on public transportation. Often these individuals insist that a family member or friend accompany them whenever they leave home.

The disturbance is not due to a major depressive episode, obsessive compulsive disorder, paranoid personality disorder, or schizophrenia.

Often the initial phase of the disorder consists of recurrent panic attacks. . . . The individual develops anticipatory fear of having such an attack and becomes reluctant or refuses to enter a variety of situations that are associated with these attacks. When there is a history of panic attacks (which may or may not be currently present) associated with avoidance behavior, the diagnosis of agoraphobia with panic attacks should be made. Where there is no such history (or this information

is lacking), the diagnosis of agoraphobia without panic attacks should be made.

* * *

Social Phobia

The essential feature is a persistent, irrational fear of, and compelling desire to avoid, situations in which the individual may be exposed to scrutiny by others. There is also fear that the individual may behave in a manner that will be humiliating or embarrassing. Marked anticipatory anxiety occurs if the individual is confronted with the necessity of entering into such a situation, and he or she therefore attempts to avoid it. The disturbance is a significant source of distress and is recognized by the individual as excessive or unreasonable. It is not due to any other mental disorder. Examples of social phobias are fears of speaking or performing in public, using public lavatories, eating in public, and writing in the presence of others. Generally an individual has only one social phobia.

Usually the individual is aware that the fear is that others will detect signs of anxiety in the phobic situation. For example, the individual with a fear of writing in the presence of others is concerned that others may detect a hand tremor. A vicious cycle may be created in which the irrational fear generates anxiety that impairs performance, thus providing an apparent justification for avoiding the phobic situation.

* * *

Simple Phobia

The essential feature is a persistent, irrational fear of, and compelling desire to avoid, an object or a situation other than being alone or in public places away from home (agoraphobia), or of humiliation or embarrassment in certain social situations (social phobia). Thus, this is a residual category of phobic disorder. This disturbance is a significant source of distress, and the individual recognizes that his or her fear is excessive or unreasonable. The disturbance is not due to another mental disorder.

Simple phobias are sometimes referred to as "specific" phobias. The most common simple phobias in the general population, though not necessarily among those seeking treatment, involve animals, particularly dogs, snakes, insects, and mice. Other simple phobias are claustrophobia (fear of closed spaces) and acrophobia (fear of heights).

* * *

ANXIETY STATES (OR ANXIETY NEUROSES)

Panic Disorder

The essential features are recurrent panic (anxiety) attacks that occur at times unpredictably, though certain situations, e.g., driving a car, may become associated with a panic attack. The same clinical picture occurring during marked physical exertion or a life-threatening situation is not termed a panic attack.

The panic attacks are manifested by the sudden onset of intense apprehension, fear, or terror, often associated with feelings of impending doom. The most common symptoms experienced during an attack are dyspnea; palpitations; chest pain or discomfort; choking or smothering sensations; dizziness, vertigo, or unsteady feelings; feelings of unreality (depersonalization or derealization); paresthesias; hot and cold flashes; sweating; faintness; trembling

or shaking; and fear of dying, going crazy, or doing something uncontrolled during the attack. Attacks usually last minutes; more rarely, hours.

A common complication of this disorder is the development of an anticipatory fear of helplessness or loss of control during a panic attack, so that the individual becomes reluctant to be alone or in public places away from home. When many situations of the kind are avoided the diagnosis of agoraphobia with panic attacks should be made rather than panic disorder.

* * *

Generalized Anxiety Disorder

The essential feature is generalized, persistent anxiety of at least one month's duration without the specific symptoms that characterize phobic disorders (phobias), panic disorder (panic attacks), or obsessive compulsive disorder (obsessions or compulsions). The diagnosis is not made if the disturbance is due to another physical or mental disorder, such as hyperthyroidism or major depression.

Although the specific manifestations of the anxiety vary from individual to individual, generally there are signs of motor tension, autonomic hyperactivity, apprehensive expectation, and vigilance and scanning.

1. *Motor Tension.* Shakiness, jitteriness, jumpiness, trembling, tension, muscle aches, fatigability, and inability to relax are common complaints. There may also be eyelid twitch, furrowed brow, strained face, fidgeting, restlessness, easy startle, and sighing respiration.

2. *Autonomic Hyperactivity.* There may be sweating, heart pounding or racing, cold, clammy hands, dry mouth, dizziness, light-headedness, paresthesias (tingling in

hands or feet), upset stomach, hot or cold spells, frequent urination, diarrhea, discomfort in the pit of the stomach, lump in the throat, flushing, pallor, and high resting pulse and respiration rate.

3. *Apprehensive Expectation.* The individual is generally apprehensive and continually feels anxious, worries, ruminates, and anticipates that something bad will happen to himself or herself (e.g., fear of fainting, losing control, dying) or to others (e.g., family members may become ill or injured in an accident).

4. *Vigilance and Scanning.* Apprehensive expectation may cause hyperattentiveness so that the individual feels "on edge," impatient, or irritable. There may be complaints of distractibility, difficulty in concentrating, insomnia, difficulty in falling asleep, interrupted sleep, and fatigue on awakening.

***

Obsessive Compulsive Disorder (or Obsessive Compulsive Neurosis)

The essential features are recurrent obsessions or compulsions. *Obsessions* are recurrent, persistent ideas, thoughts, images, or impulses that are egodystonic, that is, they are not experienced as voluntarily produced, but rather as thoughts that invade consciousness and are experienced as senseless or repugnant. Attempts are made to ignore or suppress them. *Compulsions* are repetitive and seemingly purposeful behaviors that are performed according to certain rules or in a stereotyped fashion. The behavior is not an end in itself, but is designed to produce or to prevent some future event or situation. However, the activity is not connected in a realistic way with what it is designed to produce or prevent, or may be clearly excessive. The act is performed with a sense of subjective compulsion coupled with a desire to resist the compulsion (at least initially). The individual generally recognizes the senselessness of the behavior (this may not be true for young children) and does not derive pleasure from carrying out the activity, although it provides a release of tension.

The most common obsessions are repetitive thoughts of violence (e.g., killing one's child), contamination (e.g., becoming infected by shaking hands), and doubt (e.g., repeatedly wondering whether one has performed some action, such as having hurt someone in a traffic accident). The most common compulsions involve handwashing, counting, checking, and touching.

When the individual attempts to resist a compulsion, there is a sense of mounting tension that can be immediately relieved by yielding to the compulsion. In the course of the illness, after repeated failure at resisting the compulsions, the individual may give in to them and no longer experience a desire to resist them.

***

Post-traumatic Stress Disorder, Chronic or Delayed

The essential feature is the development of characteristic symptoms following a psychologically traumatic event that is generally outside the range of usual human experience.

The characteristic symptoms involve reexperiencing the traumatic event; numbing of responsiveness to, or reduced involvement with, the external world; and a variety of autonomic, dysphoric, or cognitive symptoms.

The stressor producing this syndrome would evoke significant symptoms of distress in most people, and is generally outside the range of such common experiences as simple bereavement, chronic illness, business losses, or marital conflict. The trauma may be experienced alone (rape or assault) or in the company of groups of people (military combat). Stressors producing this disorder include natural disasters (floods, earthquakes), accidental man-made disasters (car accidents with serious physical injury, airplane crashes, large fires), or deliberate man-made disasters (bombing, torture, death camps). Some stressors frequently produce the disorder (e.g., torture) and others produce it only occasionally (e.g., car accidents). Frequently there is a concomitant physical component to the trauma which may even involve direct damage to the central nervous system (e.g., malnutrition, head trauma). The disorder is apparently more severe and longer lasting when the stressor is of human design. The severity of the stressor should be recorded and the specific stressor may be noted on Axis IV [not reprinted here].

The traumatic event can be reexperienced in a variety of ways. Commonly the individual has recurrent painful, intrusive recollections of the event or recurrent dreams or nightmares during which the event is reexperienced. In rare instances there are dissociativelike states, lasting from a few minutes to several hours or even days, during which components of the event are relived and the individual behaves as though experiencing the event at that moment. Such states have been reported in combat veterans. Diminished responsiveness to the external world, referred to as "psychic numbing" or "emotional anesthesia," usually begins soon after the traumatic event. A person may complain of feeling detached or estranged from other people, that he or she has lost the ability to become interested in previously enjoyed significant activities, or

that the ability to feel emotions of any type, especially those associated with intimacy, tenderness, and sexuality, is markedly decreased.

After experiencing the stressor, many develop symptoms of excessive autonomic arousal, such as hyperalertness, exaggerated startle response, and difficulty falling asleep. Recurrent nightmares during which the traumatic event is relived and which are sometimes accompanied by middle or terminal sleep disturbance may be present. Some complain of impaired memory or difficulty in concentrating or completing tasks. In the case of a life-threatening trauma shared with others, survivors often describe painful guilt feelings about surviving when many did not, or about the things they had to do in order to survive. Activities or situations that may arouse recollections of the traumatic event are often avoided. Symptoms characteristic of post-traumatic stress disorder are often intensified when the individual is exposed to situations or activities that resemble or symbolize the original trauma (e.g., cold snowy weather or uniformed guards for death-camp survivors, hot, humid weather for veterans of the South Pacific).

* * *

ADJUSTMENT DISORDER

The essential feature is a maladaptive reaction to an identifiable psychosocial stressor, that occurs within three months after the onset of the stressor. The maladaptive nature of the reaction is indicated by either impairment in social or occupational functioning or symptoms that are in excess of a normal and expected reaction to the stressor. The disturbance is not merely one instance of a pattern of overreaction to a stressor or an exacerbation of one of the mental disorders previously described. It is assumed that the disturbance will eventually remit after the stressor ceases or, if the stressor persists, when a new level of adaptation is achieved. This category should not be used if the disturbance meets the criteria for a specific disorder, such as an anxiety or affective disorder.

The stressors may be single, such as divorce, or multiple, such as marked business difficulties and marital problems. They may be recurrent, as with seasonal business crises, or continuous, as with chronic illness or residence in a deteriorating neighborhood. They can occur in a family setting, e.g., in discordant intrafamilial relationships. They may affect only the individual, e.g., the psychological reaction to a physical illness, or they may affect a group or community, e.g., a natural disaster, or persecution based on racial, social, religious, or other group affiliation. Some stressors are associated with specific developmental stages, such as going to school, leaving the parental home, getting married, becoming a parent, failing to attain occupational goals, and retirement.

The severity of the stressor and the specific stressor may be noted on Axis IV. The severity of a stressor is affected by its duration, timing, and context in a person's life. For example, the stress of losing a parent is different for a child and an adult.

The severity of the reaction is not completely predictable from the severity of the stressor. Individuals who are particularly vulnerable may have a more severe form of the disorder following only a mild or moderate stressor, whereas others may have only a mild form of the disorder in response to a marked and continuing stressor.

Types. The manifestations of the dis-order are varied. Each specific type represents a predominant clinical picture, many of which are partial syndromes of specific disorders. For example, adjustment disorder with depressed mood is manifested by an incomplete depressive syndrome in response to a psychosocial stressor.

* * *

SOMATOFORM DISORDERS

The essential features of this group of disorders are physical symptoms suggesting physical disorder (hence, somatoform) for which there are no demonstrable organic findings or known physiological mechanisms and for which there is positive evidence, or a strong presumption, that the symptoms are linked to psychological factors or conflicts. Unlike factitious disorder or malingering, the symptom production in somatoform disorders is not under voluntary control, i.e., the individual does not experience the sense of controlling the production of the symptoms. Although the symptoms of somatoform disorders are "physical," the specific pathophysiological processes involved are not demonstrable or understandable by existing laboratory procedures and are conceptualized most clearly using psychological constructs. For that reason, these disorders are not classified as "physical disorders."

The first disorder in this category is somatization disorder, a common and chronic polysymptomatic disorder that begins early in life and that was previously referred to as either hysteria or Briquet's syndrome. The second disorder is conversion disorder, which, as defined here, is relatively uncommon. This diagnosis is to be used only when conversion symptoms are the predominant disturbance and are not symptomatic of another disorder. Psychogenic pain disorder is characterized by psychologically induced pain not attributable to any other mental or physical disorder. Hypochondriasis involves preoccupation with the fear or belief of having a serious disease. Finally, atypical somatoform disorder is the term applied to physical symptoms without an organic basis that do not fit the criteria for any specific somatoform disorder.

Somatization Disorder

The essential features are recurrent and multiple somatic complaints of several years' duration for which medical attention has been sought but which are apparently not due to any physical disorder. The disorder begins before the age of 30 and has a chronic but fluctuating course.

Complaints are often presented in a dramatic, vague, or exaggerated way, or are part of a complicated medical history in which many physical diagnoses have been considered. The individuals frequently receive medical care from a number of physicians, sometimes simultaneously. (Although most people without mental disorders at various times have aches and pains and other physical complaints, they rarely bring them to medical attention.) Complaints invariably involve the following organ systems or types of symptoms: conversion or pseudoneurological (e.g., paralysis, blindness), gastrointestinal (e.g., abdominal pain), female reproductive (e.g., painful menstruation), psychosexual (e.g., sexual indifference), pain (e.g., back pain), and cardiopulmonary (e.g., dizziness).

***

Conversion Disorder (or Hysterical Neurosis, Conversion Type)

The essential feature is a clinical picture in which the predominant disturbance is a loss of or alteration in physical functioning that suggests physical disorder but which instead is apparently an expression of a psychological conflict or need. The disturbance is not under voluntary control, and after appropriate investigation cannot be explained by any physical disorder or known pathophysiological mechanism. Conversion disorder is not diagnosed when conversion symptoms are limited to pain or to a disturbance in sexual functioning or are part of somatization disorder.

The most obvious and "classic" conversion symptoms are those that suggest neurological disease, such as paralysis, aphonia, seizures, coordination disturbance, akinesia, dyskinesia, blindness, tunnel vision, anosmia, anesthesia, and paresthesia. More rarely, conversion symptoms may involve the autonomic or endocrine system. Vomiting as a conversion symptom can represent revulsion and disgust. Pseudocyesis (false pregnancy) can represent both a wish for, and a fear of, pregnancy.

The definition of this disorder is unique in this classification in that it implies specific mechanisms to account for the disturbance. Two mechanisms have been suggested to explain what the individual derives from having a conversion symptom.

In one mechanism, the individual achieves "primary gain" by keeping an internal conflict or need out of awareness. In such cases there is a temporal relationship between an environmental stimulus that is apparently related to a psychological conflict or need and the initiation or exacerbation of the symptom. For example, after an argument, inner conflict about the expression of rage may be expressed as "aphonia" or as a "paralysis" of the arm; or if the individual views a traumatic event, a conflict about acknowledging that event may be expressed as "blindness." In such cases the symptom has a symbolic value that is a representation and partial solution of the underlying psychological conflict.

In the other mechanism the individual achieves "secondary gain" by avoiding a particular activity that is noxious to him or her or by getting support from the environment that otherwise might not be forthcoming. For example, with a "paralyzed" hand a soldier can avoid firing a gun; or a person with marked dependency needs may develop "blindness" or inability to walk or stand, even though all leg movements can be performed normally (astasia-abasia), to prevent desertion by a spouse.

A conversion symptom is likely to involve a single symptom during a given episode, but may vary in site and nature if there are subsequent episodes.

* * *

Psychogenic Pain Disorder

The essential feature is a clinical picture in which the predominant feature is the complaint of pain, in the absence of adequate physical findings and in association with evidence of the etiological role of psychological factors. The disturbance is not due to any other mental disorder.

The pain symptom either is inconsistent with the anatomic distribution of the nervous system or, if it mimics a known disease entity (as in angina or sciatica), cannot be adequately accounted for by organic pathology, after extensive diagnos-

tic evaluation. Similarly, no pathophysiological mechanism accounts for the pain, as in tension headaches caused by muscle spasm.

That psychological factors are etiologically involved in the pain may be evidenced by a temporal relationship between an environmental stimulus that is apparently related to a psychological conflict or need and the initiation or exacerbation of the pain, or by the pain's permitting the individual to avoid some activity that is noxious to him or her or to get support from the environment that otherwise might not be forthcoming.

* * *

Hypochondriasis (or Hypochondriacal Neurosis)

The essential feature is a clinical picture in which the predominant disturbance is an unrealistic interpretation of physical signs or sensations as abnormal, leading to preoccupation with the fear or belief of having a serious disease. A thorough physical evaluation does not support the diagnosis of any physical disorder than can account for the physical signs or sensations or for the individual's unrealistic interpretation of them, although a coexisting physical disorder may be present. The unrealistic fear or belief of having a disease persists despite medical reassurance and causes impairment in social or occupational functioning. The disturbance is not due to any other mental disorder, such as schizophrenia, affective disorder, or somatization disorder.

* * *

DISSOCIATIVE DISORDERS

The essential feature is a sudden, temporary alteration in the normally integrative functions of consciousness, identity, or motor behavior. If the alteration occurs in consciousness, important personal events cannot be recalled. If it occurs in identity, either the individual's customary identity is temporarily forgotten and a new identity is assumed, or the customary feeling of one's own reality is lost and replaced by a feeling of unreality. If the alteration occurs in motor behavior, there is also a concurrent disturbance in consciousness or identity, as in the wandering that occurs during a psychogenic fugue.

Depersonalization disorder has been included in the dissociative disorders because the feeling of one's own reality, an important component of identity, is lost. Some, however, question this inclusion because disturbance in memory is absent.

Although sleepwalking disorder has the essential feature of a dissociative disorder, it is classified among the disorders usually first evident in infancy, childhood, or adolescence.

failure to recall all events occurring during a circumscribed period of time, usually the first few hours following a profoundly disturbing event. For example, the uninjured survivor of a car accident which killed his immediate family cannot recall anything that happened from the time of the accident until two days later. Somewhat less common is *selective* amnesia, a failure to recall some, but not all, of the events occurring during a circumscribed period of time. In the illustration above, the uninjured survivor might recall making the funeral arrangements, but not recall extensive simultaneous discussions with family members. The least common types of disturbance in recall are *generalized* amnesia, in which failure of recall encompasses the individual's entire life, and *continous* amnesia, in which the individual cannot recall events subsequent to a specific time up to and including the present.

During an ongoing amnestic episode, perplexity, disorientation, and purposeless wandering may occur. When the period of time for which there is amnesia is in the past the person is usually aware of the disturbance in recall.

* * *

Psychogenic Amnesia

The essential feature is a sudden inability to recall important personal information, an inability not due to an organic mental disorder. The extent of the disturbance is too great to be explained by ordinary forgetfulness. The diagnosis is not made if the person travels to another locale and assumes a new identity, in which case the diagnosis is psychogenic fugue.

There are four types of disturbance in recall. In *localized* (or circumscribed) amnesia, the most common type, there is

Psychogenic Fugue

The essential feature is sudden, unexpected travel away from home or customary work locale with assumption of a new identity and an inability to recall one's previous identity. Perplexity and disorientation may occur. Following recovery there is no recollection of events that took place during the fugue. The diagnosis is not made in the presence of an organic mental disorder.

In some cases the disorder may be manifested by the assumption of a completely new identity during the fugue, usually marked by more gregarious and uninhibited traits than characterized the former personality, which typically is quiet and altogether ordinary. In such instances the individual may give himself or herself a new name, take up a new residence, and engage in complex social activities that are well-integrated and do not suggest the presence of a mental disorder. In most cases, however, the fugue is less elaborate, and consists of little more than brief, apparently purposeful travel. Social contacts in these cases are minimal or even avoided; the new identity, while present, is incomplete. Occasionally there are outbursts of violence against another person or property. In all cases of fugue, however, the individual's travel and behavior must appear more purposeful than the confused wandering that may be seen in psychogenic amnesia.

* * *

Multiple Personality

The essential feature is the existence within the individual of two or more distinct personalities, each of which is dominant at a particular time. Each personality is a fully integrated and complex unit with unique memories, behavior patterns, and social relationships that determine the nature of the individual's acts when that personality is dominant. Transition from one personality to another is sudden and often associated with psychosocial stress.

Usually the original personality has no knowledge or awareness of the existence of any of the other personalities (subpersonalities). When there are more than two subpersonalities in one individual, each is aware of the others to varying degrees. The subpersonalities may not know each other or be constant companions. At any given moment one personality will interact verbally with the external environment, but none or any number of the other personalities may actively perceive (i.e., "listen in on") all that is going on.

The original personality and all of the subpersonalities are aware of lost periods of time. "They" will usually admit to this if asked, but will seldom volunteer this information.

The individual personalities are nearly always quite discrepant and frequently seem to be opposites. For example, a quiet, retiring spinster may alternate with a flamboyant, promiscuous bar habitué on certain nights. Usually one of the personalities over the course of the disorder is dominant.

* * *

Depersonalization Disorder

The essential feature is the occurrence of one or more episodes of depersonalization that cause social or occupational impairment. The diagnosis is not made when the symptom of depersonalization is secondary to any other disorder. (Mild depersonalization, without significant impairment, is estimated to occur at some time in 30 percent to 70 percent of young adults.)

The symptom of depersonalization involves an alteration in the perception or experience of the self so that the usual sense of one's own reality is temporarily lost or changed. This is manifested by a sensation of self-estrangement or unreality, which may include the feeling that one's extremities have changed in size, or the experience of seeming to perceive oneself from a distance. In addition, the individual may feel "mechanical" or as though in a dream. Various types of sensory anesthesias and a feeling of not being in complete control of one's actions, including speech, are often present. All of these feelings are egodystonic, and the individual maintains grossly intact reality testing.

The onset of depersonalization is rapid; its disappearance is more gradual.

***

FACTITIOUS DISORDERS

"Factitious" means not real, genuine, or natural. Factitious disorders are therefore characterized by physical or psychological symptoms that are produced by the individual and are under voluntary control. The sense of voluntary control is subjective, and can only be inferred by an outside observer.

The judgment that the behavior is under voluntary control is based, in part, on the patient's ability to simulate illness in such a way that he or she is not discovered. This involves decisions as to timing and concealment that require a degree of judgment and intellectual activity suggestive of voluntary control. However, these acts have a compulsive quality, in the sense that the individual is unable to refrain from a particular behavior, even if its dangers are known. They should therefore be considered "voluntary" in the sense that they are deliberate and purposeful, but not in the sense that the acts can be controlled. Thus, in factitious disorders, behavior under voluntary control is used to pursue goals that are involuntarily adopted.

The judgment that a particular behavior is under voluntary control is made by the exclusion of all other possible causes of the behavior. For example, an individual presenting with hematuria is found to have anticoagulants in his possession; he denies having taken them but blood studies are consistent with the ingestion of the anticoagulants. A reasonable inference is that the individual may have voluntarily taken the medication. A single episode of such behavior could be accidental rather than intentional. Repeated episodes would justify an inference of voluntary production of the symptoms—a factitious disorder. The presence of factitious psychological or physical symptoms does not preclude the coexistence of true psychological and physical symptoms.

Factitious disorders are distinguished from acts of malingering. In malingering, the "patient" is also in voluntary control of the symptoms, but it is for a goal that is obviously recognizable with a knowledge of the environmental circumstances, rather than of his or her psychology. For example, a claim of physical illness in order to avoid jury duty, standing trial, or conscription into the military would be classified as malingering. Similarly, for a patient in a mental hospital to simulate an exacerbation of his or her illness in order to avoid transfer to another, less desirable facility would be an act of malingering. In contrast, in a factitious disorder there is no apparent goal other than to assume the patient role. If the patient mentioned above were being transferred to an obviously more desirable facility, his or her simulated exacerbation of symptoms would be a factitious disorder. Whereas an act of malingering may, under certain circumstances, be considered adaptive, by definition a diagnosis of a factitious disorder always implies psychopathology, most often a severe personality disturbance.

In the past, some of the disorders classified here would have been subsumed within the category of hysteria.

Factitious disorders may present with psychological or physical symptoms.

Chronic factitious disorder with physical symptoms, often referred to as Munchausen syndrome, is the best known and most frequently reported of the factitious disorders. The other two categories included in this section are factitious disorder with psychological symptoms and atypical factitious disorder with physical symptoms.

Factitious Disorder with Psychological Symptoms

The essential feature is the voluntary production of severe psychological (often psychotic) symptoms, suggestive of mental disorder. The individual's goal is apparently to assume the "patient" role and is not otherwise understandable in light of the individual's environmental circumstances (as is the case in malingering). This has also been referred to as Ganser syndrome, pseudopsychosis, or pseudodementia.

This disorder is often recognized by the pan-symptomatic complex of psychological symptoms that are presented and by the fact that the symptoms are worse when the individual is aware of being observed. Such an individual may claim memory loss (recent and remote), hallucinations (auditory and visual), and dissociative and conversion symptoms, along with suicidal ideation. The same individual may be extremely suggestible and admit to many additional symptoms asked about by the examiner. Conversely, the individual may be extremely negativistic and uncooperative to further questioning. The psychological symptoms presented are usually a representation of the person's concept of mental disorder and may not conform to any of the recognized diagnostic categories.

10.

Gordon L. Paul and Douglas A. Bernstein

ANXIETY AND SYSTEMATIC DESENSITIZATION

Development and Maintenance of Anxiety

Since anxiety is a response to eliciting stimuli, understanding the nature of potential eliciting stimuli is essential in order to comprehend the clinical problems related to anxiety and the treatment procedures designed to alter them. Any condition that places strong demands for adjustment on an organism by threatening desired goals or homeostatic organismic conditions constitutes stress and may elicit an immediate anxiety response, followed by the slower GAS pattern if the stress continues

From Paul, Gordon L., Bernstein, Douglas A., *Anxiety and Clinical Problems: Systematic Desensitization and Related Techniques.* ©1973 General Learning Corporation (General Learning Press, Morristown, N.J.) Reprinted by permission of Silver Burdett Company.

over a long time. Developmentally, such responses are quite adaptive, since the organism is energized to take action to remove dangerous, possibly life-threatening conditions. Although genetic factors may provide nervous and endocrine systems more or less responsive to stress for each individual, a number of environmental conditions or events appear to function as stressors, or anxiety-eliciting stimuli, across individuals and species without benefit of prior learning (that is "unconditioned" stimuli). Such unconditioned stimuli are generally noxious or painful and thus threaten the homeostatic balance of the body. Thus wounds, physical trauma, impeded respiration, and so on all serve to elicit anxiety without prior experience. Rapid changes in physical orientation or support (falling, whirling, being thrown through the air) typically function as unconditioned stressors, although the introduction of learning contingencies may later result in relabeling the emotional experience as positive under certain conditions (an example, riding a roller coaster). In general, almost any physical stimulus—noise, heat, cold, light, pressure, shock—in high enough intensity may serve as an unconditioned, eliciting stimulus for anxiety or stress responses.

* * *

From an early point in psychological development, once a minimal learning history has been acquired, certain other stimulus conditions will elicit anxiety, more on the basis of posing a threat to desired goals than as an immediate threat to homeostatic regulation. These stimulus conditions may still be considered "unconditioned," since anxiety may occur without earlier experience with the specific conditions involved. Some of these stimulus conditions and the resulting anxiety reactions are often seen in infants and young children,

before the learning history has broadened experience and introduced more complex cognitive organization. One such set of stimulus conditions is the introduction of novel stimuli that cannot readily be assimilated with prior experience, as may be seen in the baby who cries uncontrollably when a stranger (even kindly rich old Uncle George) picks him up for the first time. Similarly, disconfirmation of positive expectancies, or the loss of customary or anticipated positive reinforcers, may be stressful in the absence of prior experience.

* * *

Any circumstance that elicits intense anxiety responses may, theoretically, provide the basis for the development of inappropriate conditioned anxiety. Therefore, an individual already under stress for some time (second stage of the GAS) is more likely to acquire inappropriate conditioned anxiety responses because of his lower tolerance for stress. Similarly, in approach-avoidance or avoidance-avoidance conflict situations, the avoidance tendency may be based on conditioned anxiety, thereby allowing for the compounding of anxiety in the presence of the same stimuli. Because of the cognitive aspects of anxiety, components of the anxiety response may function as "response-produced cues," which lead to intensification of the response. Mild anxiety may be elicited from some external or internal stimulus; the individual labels the sensations accompanying that mild response (trembling, or "butterflies in the stomach") as fear or anxiety, and then responds to the label with even more anxiety. Being aware of an increase in anxiety can itself act as a stressor, and the "feedback loop" of response-label-response may lead to progressive intensifications.

The higher symbolic processes of humans appear to make us uniquely capable of such spiral progressions of anxiety—"bootstrapping" . . . through the things we tell ourselves, increasing the probability of overgeneralization and higher-order conditioning. Semantic generalization on the basis of similarity of meaning can produce very inappropriate anxiety responses. Let us consider a young girl who grows up in an extremely rigid, puritanical environment, where sexual activity is characterized as dirty, sinful, and punishable. By the time she reaches adolescence, the girl is likely to consider even minor approximations to sex, like hand holding, as threatening behaviors. Through generalization even the word "sex" may act as a stressor and produce an anxiety response. This strong set of vicariously conditioned anxiety responses may interfere massively with her enjoyment of, or even participation in sex as an adult and would probably result in the label of "frigidity" in a clinical setting.

One may ask why a person who has at one time acquired an association between anxiety and a previously neutral stimulus continues to respond with anxiety to that stimulus even after it is inappropriate to do so. That is, why would not a frigid woman thaw out as a result of repeated experiences with sexual behavior? Why do people afraid of elevators, either as a result of direct or vicarious conditioning, not get over their fear once they have taken a few elevator rides and realize that there really is no danger?

These questions lead us directly into the third way anxiety can be related to inappropriate learning: the development or maintenance of behavior problems through reinforcement of escape or avoidance behavior. We might assume that if a person who has learned a maladaptive or irrational anxiety response exposes himself to the feared stimuli, the anxiety will disappear over time (through a process known as *extinction*). While this is a theoretically correct assumption, much maladaptive conditioned anxiety is not so relieved. Rather, when the person attempts to enter a stressful situation, he experiences anxiety and at some early point leaves (escapes) that situation before fully experiencing its harmless nature (seeing that no noxious unconditioned stimulus occurs). Because it is followed immediately by reduced anxiety, the behavior that is strengthened, and thus made more likely to occur the next time, is the escape response. As escape behaviors become stronger, they begin to occur earlier and earlier on approach to the anxiety-provoking situation, until the individual does not enter the situation at all and thus *avoids* rather than escapes it. Since avoidance of anxiety altogether is even more comfortable than escaping after it has begun, avoidance behaviors are strengthened over time and the conditioned anxiety response is maintained intact.

* * *

Appropriate "Targets" for Systematic Desensitization

The problems in which inappropriate conditioned anxiety is centrally important, for which systematic desensitization and related techniques are considered appropriate, are of five major kinds, each of which may overlap in a given individual:

1. *Conditioned anxiety of sufficient duration or intensity to cause extreme subjective distress is elicited in the absence of objective danger or threat.* This is the relatively "pure" anxiety response, which occurs in continued or intermittent exposure to eliciting stimulus conditions without means of escaping or avoiding. Typically, the clients' complaints are obviously related to anxiety. The stimuli may be either simple (in the sense of a single,

clear-cut class of stimulus events or objects) or complex (involving multiple classes of stimuli, conflict with one or more branches involving inappropriate conditioned stimuli, and/or vague, broadly generalized stimuli difficult to identify). Extreme episodes of intense anxiety ("nervous breakdowns," "acute psychotic episodes") may be involved, or lower intensity, chronic states may be typical.

2. *The response pattern of anxiety becomes sufficiently specific to produce tissue change of the sort seen in so-called psychophysiological or psychosomatic disorders.* Because of physiological response stereotypy, either continuous or intermittent anxiety over long periods of time can result in tissue change or damage in the most responsive physiological systems. Similarly, specific physiological systems become overworked in later stages of the GAS, and the interaction of intermittent periods of anxiety with biological cycles puts added stress on specific systems. Many physical problems (migraine headache, peptic ulcer, ulcerative colitis, dermatoses, high blood pressure, asthma, chronic fatigue) may have anxiety as a basis. When the anxiety is elicited by inappropriate stimuli, systematic desensitization may be the treatment of choice. When tissue damage has occurred, however, medical treatment to repair the damage is essential, and systematic desensitization may prevent reoccurrences.

3. *The current or prior intensity of conditioned anxiety results in the breakdown of efficient performance of complex behavior.* Several classes of clinical problems may be involved when inappropriate conditioned anxiety is the basis of a breakdown in performance. Nearly any cognitive or motor performance can suffer as a result of the inverted-U relationship between arousal and behavioral efficiency. A client's specific problem would therefore

be a function of the task demands placed on him by his job, family, friends, or other life circumstances. "Inability to talk at a party," "can't think straight," "can't study," "stutter," "no longer hit the basket" might be complained of or observed to occur in clients for whom task demands for complex performance coincide with the occurrence of inappropriate eliciting stimuli in which physiological arousal is elicited above the optimal level. At the other end of the dimension, nearly any cognitive or motor performance could suffer as a result of the inverted-U relationship when underarousal (below the optimal level) results as a reaction to prior intense levels of anxiety (reactive depression). Here, the breakdown in performance is likely to be nonspecific, involving tasks required during the period of fatigue or depression. Finally, sexual problems in which sympathetic enervation interferes with parasympathetic control of behavior (such as impotence, premature ejaculation, and frigidity) may result from inappropriate conditioned anxiety. In cases involving reactive underarousal, rest and absence of stress are instituted to restore normal physical functioning before systematic desensitization is undertaken. Where breakdown of performance of complex behavior is the predominant feature, anxiety may or may not be presented as an initial referral problem or complaint.

4. *Adaptive behavior in the client's repertoire is inhibited to avoid inappropriate conditioned anxiety reactions.* Clinical problems of this sort involve escape and avoidance behavior, and the individual either stops doing things he can do or actively goes out of his way to avoid specific stimulus situations. The classical phobia, in which a specific stimulus object or a specific set of stimulus conditions is actively avoided, is the most obvious problem of this kind. Someone with a phobic reaction

to airplanes may take a week to drive across the country rather than ride a few hours in a plane. A mailman "with a cat phobia" may stop delivering mail to a house with a pet cat on the porch. A "claustrophobic" may not apply for a job because the only way to get to the office is in an elevator. Since the inhibition of behavior is not openly bizarre, and infrequently occurring phobic objects can be avoided without much difficulty, individuals suffering from phobias are seldom referred for services, and they may not even be detected by observers. If the phobic object cannot be avoided, however, the resulting anxiety reaction (as in 1 above) may suffice to lead the individual to seek treatment. Also, if anxiety-eliciting stimuli are many or frequent, the inhibition of adaptive behavior may actually interfere with other aspects of the individual's life. In some cases inhibition may become so widespread that nearly all sources of external reinforcement are shut off, leading to depressive reactions. As in 2 above, the individual referred to treatment for "failing to do things" may or may not present anxiety as an initial referral problem or complaint. But behavior of this kind very often provides one branch of a conflict situation that may be quite dominant on initial referral.

5. *Maladaptive behaviors are learned and maintained to alleviate or avoid inappropriate conditioned anxiety reactions.* These problems also involve escape and avoidance behaviors, but of a nature that is itself maladaptive, either because of their bizarre nature, which is sufficiently beyond the experience of most people who react negatively, or because they violate laws, cultural standards, or work requirements so that the ultimate consequences at a given time and place are uniformly negative. In this class of anxiety-related problems are many traditional psychotic and neurotic "symptoms," such as amnesias, compulsions, delusions, tangential thought, and the like, in which a bizarre behavior may be adopted either as an immediate escape from the perception of anxiety-eliciting stimuli and maintained by avoidance of that perception, or as an activity that removes the individual from exposure to situations where anxiety-eliciting stimuli are more probable. Many sexual problems involving objects or acts that are deviant in a particular culture, such as fetishes or homosexual behavior, may involve inappropriate conditioned anxiety to the more usual and accepted stimulus objects or activities. Any habitual source of relief from anxiety may become excessive and maladaptive, particularly when multiple reinforcement is obtained. Frequent clinical problems of the latter sort occur through the use of drugs, alcohol, food (obesity), and sex (compulsive masturbation, nymphomania, satyriasis). The range of unusual stimuli to which the human organism may become conditioned, and the range of unusual behaviors that we may adopt by chance to escape or avoid resulting anxiety reactions, is nearly without limit.

* * *

SYSTEMATIC DESENSITIZATION THERAPY

Systematic desensitization thus refers to a package of treatment procedures that systematically includes: [a] training in deep relaxation to provide a state incompatible with anxiety; [b] constructing hierarchies of anxiety-eliciting stimuli to provide specific, controllable items for the client to visualize; [c] desensitization proper—suppressing anxiety through graduated presentation of the anxiety-eliciting stimuli from weakest to strongest while the client is in the relaxed state.

The procedures themselves appear deceptively simple; because of many subtle nuances of timing and other parameters, however, even experienced therapists typically require several months of supervised training to learn to apply skillfully all aspects of systematic desensitization, as it has been used in well-controlled evaluative studies and in most skilled clinical work. Most reports of systematic desensitization have based details of procedure on one of four identifiable approaches, those of Wolpe, Arnold A. Lazarus, Lang, or Paul, each of which follows the complete package but with minor variations in the timing or sequence of various aspects of treatment. . . . In general, the features of these major approaches appear sufficiently similar to allow the generalization of findings from one to the other.

Relaxation training is typically a much abbreviated version of the Jacobson technique. The major goal of relaxation training is to reduce physiological arousal and produce at least neutral, preferably positive affect. Since the autonomic and cortical activity to be reduced is not under direct voluntary control, relaxation training usually focuses on the skeletal muscles and respiration, which are partially under direct voluntary control. The client is usually asked to recline on a couch or recliner chair that provides complete physical support. The therapist instructs the client systematically to tense and hold small muscle groups, a hand and a forearm, for example, and then release them; some degree of relaxation or reduction of tonic muscle tension is naturally produced during the release. (You may get some idea of the sensation by resting your arm on a desk or chair, making a tight fist, holding it tense for seven seconds, and *abruptly* releasing your fist. The sensations of warmth and relaxation you notice during the first ten to twenty seconds after release

are a mild form of the sensations that relaxation training produces in the entire body.) By repeating this tension-release cycle several times systematically with all muscle groups in the body, and holding a deep breath concurrent with tension and releasing it for normal breathing at the same time he releases muscle tension, the client can usually produce a state of reduced physiological arousal with no detectable tension at all in one to six training sessions. Further, if the client focuses his attention on the sensations during release phases, he can passively learn to produce relaxation by simply recalling the sensations previously experienced during release phases.

The specific order in which muscle groups are taken varies among the major approaches, as does the timing of tension-release cycles. No differences in effectiveness have been reported as long as the sequence in which muscle groups are taken is systematic, tension is maintained for at least five to seven seconds, and the release phase for each group is at least twenty to thirty seconds, with progress from one group to another contingent on an absence of detectable tension in the first group. . . .

Initially, about half of each therapy session is devoted to relaxation training, and the client is asked to practice the procedures at home. Over time the number of muscle groups is systematically reduced by combining smaller groups. Eventually the client is able to produce deep relaxation in any or all parts of his body in less than four minutes without first having to tense his muscles at all, but simply by recalling previous relaxation. This ability allows the client to relax without reclining.

Relaxation may sometimes be induced by direct suggestion or hypnotic procedures, relying on prior associations to reduce physiological arousal. Direct suggestion has been effective, but requires longer to produce deep relaxation and produces less extensive effects than abbreviated relaxation training. . . . No matter how it is achieved, a deep and consistent state of relaxation is necessary to inhibit anxiety.

Anxiety hierarchies are constructed by the therapist in collaboration with the client, based on the client's reports on the specific nature and relative strength of the stimuli that elicit maladaptive anxiety. The hierarchy is simply a list of the entire range of these anxiety-eliciting stimulus conditions systematically ordered along an equal-interval scale from the weakest to the strongest. These specific conditions thus fall along a primary or secondary stimulus generalization gradient from the most severe stimulus.

The items in an anxiety hierarchy should be highly specific and concrete. Thus an item in a test anxiety hierarchy might be "sitting at your desk in your room, on the night before the final exam, reading your [some specified] text," rather than "studying for an exam." Note that the former version gives the client more cues than the latter to help him visualize the item.

In addition to constructing the anxiety hierarchy during the early treatment sessions, the therapist also collects information about important factors that might change the intensity of the items within the hierarchy. The information is very helpful during desensitization proper since it allows the therapist to reduce the potency of specific items if they appear to be too strong for their serial position or to insert items that had not been planned for originally (all hierarchies are considered tentative and subject to constant revision). With social anxiety, for example, it is important to know that the number of people in a group influences the degree of anxiety elicited. Thus, if during desensitization proper, the client has trouble visualizing

without anxiety, "you're at Jim's dinner party, sitting down at the table with Jim and eight of his friends," the therapist can change the item to ". . . six of his friends." When the new item has been mastered, the more troublesome one is likely to be easier to tolerate.

Since more than one anxiety hierarchy may be employed with a client, several items from each hierarchy may be presented in one session. Several hierarchies may also be completed sequentially over sessions. The number of items making up a hierarchy differs widely depending on the difficulty and complexity of the problem. Relatively simple problems (for example, a circumscribed phobia) may require hierarchies of only ten to fifteen items, while more complex problems (for example, major social-evaluative anxiety) in which many environmental factors qualify the strength of a given stimulus item may require fifty, sixty, or even one hundred items.

There are two basic types of anxiety stimulus hierarchies: spatial-temporal and thematic. Spatial-temporal hierarchies contain items that gradually and systematically approach a single object or event along a space or time dimension, for example, waking up on the morning of the exam, eating breakfast on the morning of the exam, walking toward the exam room, fifteen minutes before the exam. Note that the hierarchy approaches a single event in space and time; which could be a dog, a speech, a job interview, a party, or whatever.

A thematic hierarchy, on the other hand, does not usually involve the space-time dimension. Rather, its items are listed along some dimension of thematic similarity such as physical attributes, functions, or meaning. Thus a thematic hierarchy includes items that are progressively more anxiety producing but not necessarily part of the same event or object, for example, waiting for the English exam to begin, waiting for the French exam to begin, waiting for the math exam to begin. The thematic dimension employed here is the type of exam, which (for the hypothetical client) varied from the easiest to the most difficult. Thematic hierarchies may be focused on relatively simple targets such as types of exams, or types of dogs, or they may (and often do) deal with more complex themes involving mediated generalization such as rejection, criticism, and death.

In clinical practice it is rare that only a simple spatial-temporal or thematic hierarchy is used; more often, a combination is found. In combined hierarchies there is usually a major thematic dimension composed of spatial-temporal subdimensions. Thus, in our test anxiety example, a combined hierarchy might include items like waking up on the morning of the English exam, eating breakfast on the day of the English exam, walking toward the English exam room, fifteen minutes before the exam . . . waking up on the morning of the French exam, eating breakfast on the morning of the French exam. . . . The more complicated either the thematic or spatial-temporal dimensions become, the more elaborate the combined hierarchy is.

Whether the anxiety hierarchy employed in systematic desensitization is spatial-temporal, thematic, or a combination of both, its adequate construction is central to the success of the technique. To the extent that interitem steps are inappropriately large or items do not accurately represent the client's particular anxiety dimension(s), the degree of effectiveness of anxiety reduction in the *real* fear-stimulus situation is reduced. At the current state of development the identification of central stimulus dimensions and the construction of appropriate hierarchies depend more on the therapist's knowledge and clinical acumen than on his skills in either relaxation training or desensitization proper, both of which can be taught relatively quickly.

Desensitization proper can begin after hierarchies have been constructed, the client can reliably achieve a deep state of relaxation, and imagery has been tested (or trained) to assure that the client visualizes clearly, can start and stop images on request, and that visualization of anxiety-eliciting stimuli in the absence of relaxation does in fact increase anxiety. An easy and rapid communication system is established for the client to indicate when images are clear and when any anxiety, tension, or discomfort is experienced. Such indications are usually made by signaling with the left or right index finger, but may be verbal. Deep relaxation is induced, and the client reminded of the need to indicate even the slightest disruption of relaxation. He is then asked to visualize the lowest item on the anxiety hierarchy. After an appropriate exposure time with clear imagery, he is instructed to stop visualizing and focus his attention on feelings of deep relaxation. In the absence of any indication of anxiety (a "perfect" hierarchy with strong relaxation), each item is repeated until the entire hierarchy is completed. Of course, the therapist makes certain that each item has been imagined without disturbance before moving on to the next one.

If an anxiety response occurs during an item presentation, that presentation is immediately terminated and all further activity halted until the client again achieves deep relaxation, often aided by imagining a previously agreed upon neutral or pleasant scene. A diluted version of the anxiety-provoking item is then presented (dilution can be achieved by shortening the presentation or by adding a factor known to reduce the item's intensity), or in some cases a lower item is introduced. Ultimately, any item causing an anxiety response is repeated until it can be tolerated in its strongest form for a longer period than was initially required. The specific parameters of timing item duration and criteria for moving on vary some among the major approaches. Their effectiveness, however, does not appear to differ so long as a minimum criterion of two ten-second visualizations without anxiety (one twenty-second visualization for an item that previously disrupted relaxation) is maintained before moving to higher items.

Each desensitization session concludes with a successfully completed item, which is the first one presented at the next session. The number of items presented per session usually depends on how well the hierarchy was constructed and thus how much anxiety it generates. An ideal hierarchy spaces items so that an anxiety response never occurs. The number of items completed per session then depends solely on the time available. More often, however, some anxiety occurs, necessitating backtracking and item revision. The usual range is from about three to ten items per session, or until about forty-five minutes have elapsed. Over-long sessions may tire some clients; desensitization proper, however, has occasionally been conducted for as long as three hours in emergencies (producing therapist fatigue).

Obviously, progress in the visualized hierarachy should be paralleled by progress in the real-life anxiety situation. If it is not, the therapist must begin to look for defects in procedure or lapses in client cooperation, so that relevant remedial steps can be taken.

11.

Aaron T. Beck

COGNITIVE THERAPY OF ANXIETY

THE FALLACY OF "FREE-FLOATING ANXIETY"

The notion of free-floating anxiety has been derived from the viewpoint of the observer, not the afflicted. If we attempt to examine the disorder from the patient's frame of reference, do we get a picture of pure anxiety—divorced from danger? Quite the contrary. The acutely anxious patient complains to the physician that he has a sense of impending disaster—possibly that he is about to die. In fact, after the medical workup indicates no sign of life-threatening disease, the patient often realizes his fear is groundless and his anxiety subsides.

The fallibility of the concept of free-floating anxiety has also been recognized by Bowlby (1970).

Unless we know what is or has been going on in our patients' private environments we are in no position to decide "there is no recognizable threat, or the threat is, by reasonable standards, quite out of proportion to the emotion it seemingly evokes."

Clinical experience shows, indeed, that the more we know about natural fear and the more

Reprinted from Cognitive Therapy and Emotional Disorders by Aaron T. Beck. By permission of International Universities Press, Inc. Copyright 1976 by International Universities Press, Inc.

we learn about our patients' personal environments the less do the fears from which they suffer seem to lack a reasonable basis, and the less does anxiety appear free-floating. Were we therefore to confine our usage of the word anxiety to conditions in which threat is absent or judged inadequate, we might well find the word gone quietly out of use [p. 86].

Because the patient's anxiety seems so disproportionate to any possible stress, or life-threatening danger, the examining physician is prone to discount the patient's mumblings about his fear of death. In fact, the diagnostic manual of the American Psychiatric Association (1968) states that the fears are a rationalization, a displacement from "real" fear, or are simply a surface manifestation of the anxiety. This tendency to explain away the patient's manifest fears blinds the clinician to the thinking disorder in acute anxiety states. As a result, the clinician fails to recognize that the fears do seem plausible to the patient. They are based on his overinterpretation of "danger" stimuli, his distortions of the incoming stimuli, and his arbitrary inferences and overgeneralizations.

By encouraging the patient to discuss his fears, the examiner uncovers information that makes this mysterious condition quite understandable. From the *patient's* standpoint, the danger is quite real and plausible. What do we learn if we ask the patient what he is afraid of? At first, he may be so concerned with his anxiety, his peculiar feeling states, and his preoccupations, he may find it difficult to focus on the question. With a minimum of introspection, however, it is possible for the patient to provide the pertinent information. Often—but not always—the acutely anxious patient is overwhelmed by thoughts that he is dying. The fear of dying may be triggered by some unexpected or severe physical sensation. The patient interprets the physical distress as a sign of physical disease, becomes anxious, and a chain reaction is set up.

A forty-year-old man was brought into the emergency room of a general hospital in Denver in an acute state of distress. He stated that he had ridden to the top of a ski lift in the mountains a few hours previously and noticed he was short of breath. Following this, he felt very weak, sweated profusely, and thought that he was losing consciousness. A physical examination and an electrocardiogram at the hospital did not reveal any sign of physical abnormality. The patient was told that he was suffering from "an acute anxiety attack" and was given some phenobarbital for sedation.

The patient's severe anxiety continued, however, and he returned to his home in Philadelphia. When he consulted me the following day, the patient was vague, at first, in attempts to pinpoint the source of his anxiety. When he started to review the recent events, it was relatively easy to piece together pertinent information. He recalled that, when he had reached the top of the ski lift, he noticed he was short of breath (this was probably due to the rarefied atmosphere). He remembered having had the thought that his shortness of breath might be a sign of heart disease. He then thought of his brother who had had shortness of breath and had died of a coronary occlusion a few months previously. As he considered the thought of having a coronary occlusion more seriously, he became increasingly anxious. At this point, he began to feel weak, perspired a great deal, and felt faint. He had interpreted these symptoms as further evidence that he was having a heart attack and was on the verge of death. When examined at the emergency room, he was not reassured by the normal electrocardiogram because he believed "the disease might not have shown up yet on the test."

After we had established that "the free-floating anxiety" had been triggered and was being maintained by a fear of the coronary episode, we were able to deal with the patient's misconception. I explained that his initial shortness of breath was a common physiological reaction to the thin atmosphere in the mountains; his resulting fear of having a heart attack had aroused symptoms of anxiety which he had misinterpreted as a sign of impending death. The patient accepted this explanation as plausible and volunteered his considered opinion that his fear of having a heart attack was a "false alarm." Following this revised interpretation of his experience, his symptoms of anxiety disappeared and he felt "his normal healthy self" again. The rapid disappearance of his symptoms after the cause of his anxiety was explained provided additional evidence to the patient that he was not suffering from an organic disease.

The fears that trigger an acute anxiety attack do not necessarily center around the notion of some physical disaster, but may be concerned with psychosocial adversities.

A college instructor, for instance, came into the emergency room of a hospital because, "I am so panicky, I can't stand it another minute." The physician on duty made the diagnosis of "free-floating anxiety" and referred him for an emergency psychiatric consultation. As the sequence of events just preceding his panic was described, the following picture emerged. A few hours previously, the patient had been preparing to give his first lecture to a large class. He became increasingly anxious as he began to think that he would perform ineptly. As his anxiety increased, his thoughts dwelt on the possibility that he might not be able to prepare the lecture and, furthermore, that he would have a

mental block and would be unable to speak to the class. From this point he conjured up a series of catastrophic consequences: he would lose his job; he would be unable to make a living; he would end up on skid row—a social outcast and a disgrace to his family.

By unraveling the thought content that was generating his anxiety, the patient was able to gain more objectivity about his immediate problem. Alternative courses of action—such as telling the chairman of his department of his difficulty—were considered. Also, the probability that he could manage at other types of work, even if he were unsuccessful as a teacher, was discussed. As the patient attached less credence to his fears, his anxiety dissipated and he was able to prepare the lecture and teach his class successfully. A curious footnote to this case is the fact that the following year he was voted the best teacher at the college!

In both cases, the psychological factors involved in producing the anxiety were not elicited by the examining physician. With a minimum of questioning, the psychiatrist was able to ascertain the sequence of events and thought content involved in producing the "free-floating anxiety." In each instance, a fear of disaster—fear of death, in the first case, and fear of total failure as a human being, in the second—was responsible for generating anxiety. As each patient realized that his great fear was a "false alarm" his anxiety receded.

I subsequently started an investigation of acute anxiety attacks. I made arrangements to interview patients who had been diagnosed by the examining physician as having "free-floating anxiety." In 10 consecutive cases, I was able to elicit the kind of thought content described in the two illustrative cases.

Spiraling of Fear and Anxiety

Uncontrolled anxiety is unpleasant, and is in itself a dreaded experience. A person may experience anxiety, for example, prior to making a speech in public or taking an examination because of the threat of humiliation or failure. However, he knows from past experience that he has to contend not only with the possible suffering resulting from inept performance, but also with the period of anxiety prior to and during his "trial." The dread of excruciating anxiety adds to the discomfort directly aroused by the threatening situation.

Accumulations of anxiety may also be found when a person is afraid of social disparagement as a result of openly exhibiting signs that he is frightened. An adult, who was afraid of having a blood test, was especially fearful that his physician would regard this nervousness as a sign that he was weak and neurotic. His primary fear revolved around the pain of being pierced by a needle and the morbid meaning he attached to having blood removed. His secondary fear—of the physician's contempt—was even greater than his fear of the blood test and motivated him to avoid making medical appointments. Once the appointment was made, his anxiety became progressively greater. The more anxiety he felt, the greater the probability he attached to fainting in the doctor's office. This notion produced more anxiety—and the vicious cycle was intensified.

The continuous anxiety cycle may be exacerbated in another way. A businessman was told by an associate that economic conditions in his industry were getting worse. This remark made the patient worry that he would be having serious difficulties. As he viewed the potential problems as more threatening, his confidence in his ability to cope with them was reduced. As his confidence in his own abilities ebbed, the estimated size of the problems increased. Each step of the interaction between his conception of the problem and of his abilities produced more anxiety.

Another factor leading to the spiraling of anxiety is the way the patient interprets his unpleasant affective state of anxiety. His affective response is scanned, interpreted, and given meaning just as with an external stimulus. Since he associates anxiety with danger, he reads his anxiety as a danger signal. Hence, another vicious cycle is set up: Ideation with a threatening content produces anxiety. The feedback of cues of anxiety leads to further anxiety-producing ideation: The patient thinks, "I'm feeling anxious; therefore, the situation must really be threatening."

CHAPTER IV

Schizophrenic Disorders

Definition of Schizophrenia

Over a decade ago, this chapter opened with the words: "Although schizophrenia is probably the most baffling problem in psychopathology, yet the most remarkable scientific progress has been made in this area in recent decades." Ten years later, the chapter could have opened the same way. What should have been added as the next sentence, however, would be a statement to the effect that we are as ignorant about the nature, cause, and cure of schizophrenia now as ever. Are these statements contradictory? No. Are they paradoxical? Perhaps.

Hopefully, an analogy will help resolve whatever confusion arises from these statements. Our parallel is diabetes. Like schizophrenia, its onset is of an earlier and later type. Is it genetic or genetically predisposed? Or, is it caused by viral infections? What role, if any, do environmental factors play? Are the two forms hereditary, but the heritability of one differing from that of the other? Despite our being in the dark about diabetes, we nevertheless possess considerable knowledge about it. If this is the best that we can do with diabetes, a disorder that is much more objective in nature than schizophrenia, then our progress has been rather fair. The above questions relate to diabetes and schizophrenia equally.

Although it is common practice to type schizophrenia, that is, to classify it according to differing characteristic traits, no acceptable definition of the disorder exists. Ever since 1911, when Bleuler (1950) coined the term and referred to it in the plural or as a group of schizophrenias, there has been a growing tendency to view schizophrenia, not as a single disease, but as a group of disorders sharing similar patterns (Noyes & Kolb, 1963). Even when textbooks describe schizophrenics, "very few textbook schizophrenics exist" (Ullman & Krasner, 1975, p. 331). Traits that have been lumped under the category of schizophrenia have been so numerous as to be meaningless. Buss comments that the number of symptoms designated schizophrenic are "so large as to bewilder the student" (1966, p. 187). One reason for this proliferation of symptoms called schizophrenic is that the disorder is not a disease claims Torrey (1972). It is a relative term, and its content depends upon the culture in which you find yourself. According to Torrey (1973), universal schizophrenia (like universal syphilis) does not exist. In their textbook, *Modern Clinical Psychiatry,* Noyes and Kolb assert that no definition exists of schizophrenia that "has as yet received universal assent" (1963, p. 325).

Researchers at the McLean Hospital of the Harvard Medical School and the Massachusetts General Hospital use the Feighner criteria to isolate schizophrenia from other disorders such as mania and depression. A diagnosis of shizophrenia meets the following criteria:

1. The illness must be chronic, having a duration of at least six months without reverting to its premorbid level of psychosocial adjustment.
2. Difficulty in verbal communication is experienced (owing to the inability of logical organization) or hallucinations and/or delusions (unaccountable by anxiety pressures, disorientation, or significant perplexity) are present.
3. The presence of at least three of the following:
   a. Unmarried.
   b. Poor premorbid social or work adjustment.
   c. A family history of schizophrenia.
   d. Absence of drug abuse (including alcoholism) for at least one year prior to the onset of schizophrenia.
   e. Onset of schizophrenia occurring prior to the patient's 40th birthday.

Does Schizophrenia Exist?

In the past, it was widely held that schizophrenia was universal, some researchers claiming that in various countries the schizophrenic population held more or less constant at one percent of a given country. But Torrey challenges this contention as a myth, claiming that "no evidence exists upon which to base a belief in the universality of schizophrenia." He proffered the astonishing conclusion that "schizophrenia may *not* be a universal disorder" (1973, p. 53). Torrey argues that once an idea finds it way into a textbook and proliferates to other books, it seems to perpetuate itself without seriously being challenged. This is precisely what happened with respect to the belief that schizophrenia *is* universal.

Baruk, whose long career was spent working with psychotics, contends that "if you ask those who use it [schizophrenia] what it really means, it is unlikely that they will be capable of answering with any precision" (1977, p. 71). The uncritical acceptance of beliefs bequeathed by our psychological forefathers can be and often is quite damaging to certain individuals. There are people who have been "diagnosed schizophrenic largely because idiosyncratic diagnostic practices favor such a label" (Rimm & Somervill, 1977, p. 132).

The controversy surrounding schizophrenia has even encircled the concept itself. The confusion has led to challenging it as a disease. While Pruyser and Mayman (1958, 1959) repudiate schizophrenia as unidentifiable and indefinable, Szasz (1957, 1976) rejects the term as misleading and harmful. Rather than being a disease, schizophrenia is merely one of the many problems of living. Szasz dismisses mental illness as "a myth whose function is to disguise and thus render more palatable the bitter pill of moral conflicts in human relations" (1973, p. 98). To condemn *mental patients* as sick means to incarcerate and treat them for an illness against their will. The average criminal spends less time behind bars than the schizophrenic, and when he is released, his stigma is not as great as that of the schizophrenic. Consequently, many criminals prefer to be jailed rather than be sent to a "mental hospital."

Torrey (1974) rallies to the support of Szasz, reiterating the heresies of Szasz. Incidentally, both men are psychiatrists. To establish his contention that "mental disease" is not a disease, hence a misnomer, Torrey calls to our attention the fact that the greatest psychoanalysts and Freudians were not physicians: Otto Rank, Hans Sach, Theodore Reik, Anna Freud, Melanie Klein, Ernst Kris, Oscar Pfister, August Aichhorn, Erik Erikson. In fact, these people had no earned doctorates (MD or PhD). Other great leaders in psychotherapy had PhDs but no MDs. These include Carl Rogers, Albert Bandura, Albert Ellis, Rollo May, and many others. The success of these people proves the fact that we are dealing with problems of living rather than a disease. True mental disease is an organic disorder, such as brain damage. If psychiatrists want to operate under the guise of medicine, then they should restrict themselves to such diseases rather than feigning problems of living as mental illness. "To say that a person's mind is sick is like saying that the economy is sick or that a joke is sick" (Szasz, 1973, p. 97). Szasz adds: "Bodily illness is something the patient *has,* whereas mental illness is really something he *is* or *does.* If neurosis and psychosis were diseases, like pneumonia and cancer, it should be possible for a person to have *both*" (1973, p. 87). Psychiatrists and clinical psychologists never diagnose a person as both neurotic and psychotic but as one or the other. You cannot have both except in a novel or movie. Another observation that favors the view of schizophrenia as a problem of living is that there are no animal models of it. Weiner (1966) takes issue with these views, contending that the term has pragmatic value as an indicator. On the contrary, retorts Weiner, to treat the term as of diagnostic unreliability is a myth.

Dimensions of Schizophrenia

Although psychoses are often dichotomized into organic and functional, there are numerous divisions not only under these two heads, but under any of their subheads. For example, schizophrenics may be divided according to their traditional clinical subtypes of simple, hebephrenic, catatonic paranoid, schizo-affective, pseudoneurotic (Hoch & Polatin, 1949), pseudopsychopathic schizophrenia (Dunaif & Hoch, 1955), good premorbid and poor premorbid types (L. Phillips, 1953), process and reactive schizophreniz (Kantor, Wallner, & Winder, 1953); nuclear and peripheral schizophrenia (Benedict & Jacks, 1954), or according to Lorr and his associates (1962, 1963) 10 syndrome-based psychotic types (McNair et al., 1964). Wolman (1966) views schizophrenia according to the following five levels: neurotic, schizoid character, latent schizophrenia, manifest schizophrenia or vectoriasis praecox, and the terminal phase of schizophrenia which he terms dementive schizophrenia. But Bowman and Rose (1959) contend that there is no answer to the question, "What is schizophrenia?" except a description of its signs and symptoms.

Payne and Sloane (1968) recommend the utilization of four independent syndromes for the classification of psychoses, thereby obviating any necessity of employing the term schizophrenia. The syndromes are (1) moderate retardation (on motor and intellectual tasks); (2) severe retardation (typical of chronic schizophrenic patients); (3) overinclusive thinking (affecting less than 50 percent of schizophrenics); and (4) overinclusive perception (possibly a phase of over-inclusive thinking), a syndrome suggested by Craig (1965).

Lorr (1962, 1966, 1968a, 1968b; Lorr, Klett & McNair, 1963), utilizing factor analysis, has successfully isolated and measured 10 psychotic syndromes: (1) excitement; (2) hostile belligerence; (3) paranoid projection; (4) grandiose expansiveness; (5) perceptual distortions; (6) anxious intropunitiveness; (7) retardation and apathy; (8) disorientation; (9) motor disturbances; and (10) conceptual disorganization. "The syndrome scores are related to ward assignment, to prominent features of psychopathology, and to conventional diagnostic class membership. The syndromes have also been found to be sensitive to change with tranquilizer treatment and to psychopathology as measured by other measuring devices" (1968b, p. 263). Lorr (with his associates) carried out a more extensive series of investigations and reported them in his *Explorations in Typing Psychotics* (1966).

Process and Reactive Schizophrenia

Because the prognosis of certain schizophrenics was good, while for others it was poor, authorities began to suspect the two as basically different kinds of schizophrenia. Actually the notion, despite its current popularity, is not a new one. Bleuler (1924) and Jaspers (1913) were aware of the distinction early in the twentieth century.

Process schizophrenia, the one with the poor prognosis, is characterized by its gradual onset, while the reactive type seems to have erupted abruptly as the result of some traumatic experience. Principal traits of each are listed below:

Process Schizophrenia	*Reactive Schizophrenia*
Insidious, gradual onset—usually during late adolescence	Abrupt onset (with stressor evident)
Poor previous history	Good history prior to onset of schizophrenia
Poor personality integration prior to psychosis	No maturational, adjustmental, or developmental defects during childhood
Tendency toward introversion	Tendency toward extroversion

Process Schizophrenia (cont.)	*Reactive Schizophrenia (cont.)*
Inability to respond emotionally toward others. Problems at school and home	Good school and home adjustment
Absence of heterosexuality	Heterosexual relationships
Inadequate sexual, occupational, and social behavior	Adequate mental, physical, and social behavior
Indecent behavior (nudity and masturbation in public)	Containment of decency
Almost no capacity for alcohol	Sizable capacity for alcohol
Failure under pressure	Success notwithstanding adversity
Culture and environment clash	Culture and environment harmonize
Massive paranoia	Mild paranoid tendencies
Physical aggression	Aggression expressed verbally
Somatic delusions	No somatic delusions
Definite thought disturbance	Thought disorder not always present
Awareness of a change in self	No awareness of change in self
No acute precipitating cause prior to schizophrenic outbreak	Definite, understandable event precipitating the onset of psychosis
Poor prognosis	Good response to treatment
Lengthy hospitalization	Short hospital stay

In addition to process and reactive, researchers in schizophrenia have used other dichotomous couplets to identify this phenomenon. Included among them are:

Process Schizophrenia-Reactive Schizophrenia

Typical schizophrenia-Atypical schizophrenia
Chronic schizophrenia-Episodic schizophrenia
Chronic schizophrenia-Acute schizophrenia
Dementia praecox-Schizophrenia
Evolutionary schizophrenia-Reactive schizophrenia
True schizophrenia-Schizophreniform

Process and Reactive Schizophrenia as Two Different Disorders

There are those specialists who believe that it is a misnomer to call these two mental disorders schizophrenia since they are completely distinct from one another. Perusing the list of traits peculiar to each type of schizophrenia would lead one to agree. Authorities, however, have not resolved the issue (Garmezy, 1970).

Process and Reactive Schizophrenia as a Continuum of the Same Disorder

If process and reactive schizophrenia are not completely separate disorders are they at opposite ends of a pole of the same disorder? That is to say, can schizophrenia be viewed as a continuum progressing from reactive schizophrenia at one end to process schizophrenia at the other? Speed of recovery would be our criterion—ready recovery at one end and nonrecovery at the other, with varying degrees of rate of recovery in between.

There is evidence favoring this view. Schizophrenias are not easily diagnosable. Attempts to diagnose them into clear-cut types of either process or reactive do not work in all cases. There is an overlap in which some schizophrenics represent both types (King, 1958). This intermediate type might suggest that process and reactive schizophrenia are actually a continuum rather than disparate disorders.

The Somatic Cause of Process Schizophrenia and the Psychogenic Etiology of Reactive Schizophrenia

There is speculation that process schizophrenia is essentially biological with a genetic base, while reactive schizophrenia is fundamentally psychological. Thus we have an organic or physical cause of the one and a psychogenic cause or some sort of stress producing the other. While one is a physical disorder, the other is a psychological reaction to an overwhelming life situation.

Although this explanation sounds good, some theorists contend that it is a false dichotomy. That is to say, schizophrenia does not have to be caused either organically (by some chemical or genetic imbalance) or psychologically by some breaking point. It may entail both. Today, psychologists speak of a diathesis-stress theory. By it, they mean people who are constitutionally predisposed toward schizophrenia (genetically, chemically, physically) but who do not develop schizophrenia in the absence of some stressful situation sufficient to bring it on. The diathesis-stress theory does not resolve the present issue because there are schizophrenics (the process type) who lapse into schizophrenia without any apparent stressor. Consequently, the genetic model seems to favor separate types of causes for the two different kinds of schizophrenia. Malfunctioning of the genes causes the process type. A faulty genetic structure (that does not cause but lowers resistance to stress) accounts for reactive schizophrenia.

Schizophrenic Thought Disorder

Schizophrenic thinking has increasingly attracted attention of researchers. So much is this the case that the Chapmans (1973) saw fit to publish an entire book devoted to the study. Today, there are numerous investigations and in consequence of them a variety of theories have emerged.

Schizophrenic Thought as a Regression to a Childhood Stage of Development

Freud was among the first to theorize that the character of thinking manifested by schizophrenics not only resembles that of children but is actually a reversion to an earlier stage of childhood development. That is to say, the mind of a schizophrenic is that which the victim had as a child. Although we do not refer to thinking as it is manifested in children as a disorder, we do when that same kind of childlike mentality is found in adults.

The celebrated child psychologist, Piaget (1973; with Inhelder, 1969) discovered that the mind of a child is structured in such a manner that it is incapable of performing the operations of older children—much less those of an adult. Freud is not saying that the mind of the schizophrenic has never developed beyond the mind of the child, but that it has returned or regressed (as Freud would say) to that of a child. It is only in certain cognitive respects, however, that the reasoning of the schizophrenic compares with that of young children.

Why do schizophrenics regress to childhood? Some theorists speculate that it is done in order to escape anxiety. It was not only Arieti's (1974) opinion, but Mednick's (1966; with Schulsinger, 1968). Mednick, whose bias is toward behavior theory or learning theory, reasoned that the schizophrenic's reversion to disordered thought is rewarding. It is the schizophrenic's way of eluding anxiety-ridden thoughts. The more the schizophrenic finds that his disordered thinking can keep distressing thoughts at bay, the more he will be reinforced to continue. If this is the case, then behavior therapy should be effective in treating schizophrenics. But despite whatever success behavior therapists have had with schizophrenics, it was not sufficient to render them functional—much less to cure them. Another objection to Mednick's tracing schizophrenia to anxiety is that it fails to explain why the rest of us who experience intense anxiety do not end up schizophrenics. Many normal people have endured much severer forms of anxiety than schizophrenics, but without becoming schizophrenic. Furthermore, persons generally suffering from anxiety neurosis do not deteriorate to schizophrenia. Some investigators hold that the two are different disorders. Consequently, you cannot have both simultaneously. In other words, one is not a milder form of the other. Still another objection to Mednick's explanation is that, according to some authorities, schizophrenics have much less anxiety than others—even less than so-called normal persons.

The Von Domarus Principle

Rather than responding to traditional laws of logic (Aristotelian logic), schizophrenics seem to respond to a logic of their own. Von Domarus (1944) observed that schizophrenics are readily susceptible to what logicians call the fallacy of the undistributed middle term. You cannot argue that because

	John is a man
and	Henry is a man
	Therefore John is Henry.

Yet the schizophrenic finds nothing wrong with it.
Or,

Certain Indians are swift
Stags are swift
Therefore certain Indians are stags.

Merely because two things share a common quality, it does not follow that they are identical. But the schizophrenic mind identifies the two classes as the same. It should be added that the fallacy of the undistributed middle term is not that readily noticed even by the average person. Many advertisements are designed on the basis of this fallacy, because it is known that people are beguiled by it. To advertise in the media that "Men of distinction drink Calvert's whiskey" is readily put into syllogistic form by the unsuspecting victim thusly:

> Men of distinction drink Calvert's whiskey
> I drink Calvert's whiskey
> Therefore I am a man of distinction.

The error is in assuming that entering the class of Calvert whiskey drinkers automatically places one in the enviable class of men of distinction. Logically, it does not, for it can instead put you in the class of alcoholics.

Thus, what is the schizophrenic doing logically? He is committing the error of being overinclusive, including members in a class that do not belong there. Authorities have come to call this phenomenon in schizophrenics, *overinclusive thinking.*

Overinclusion, or as some learning theorists term it, overgeneralization, is common in young children. A child, observed Arieti (1974), is demonstrating Von Domarus' principle when he calls all men daddy rather than restricting it to just his own father. Because preliterate societies manifest Von Domarus' principle in action, Arieti referred to this type of schizophrenic reasoning as *paleological* instead of *paralogical.* Paleological means antiquated forms of reasoning, whereas paralogical means a false kind of thinking.

Von Domarus has been criticized for attributing the fallacy of the undistributed middle term to schizophrenics since many normal people are readily fooled by it. Most students entering a class in college logic easily fall prey to it. If college students have trouble with it, then it hardly seems fair to denigrate the schizophrenic for it. Nevertheless, the schizophrenic goes far beyond what the average person does. Schizophrenics loosely connect words and ideas that would strike the rest of us as weird.

Overinclusive Thinking

Not only is there a deficit of attention-span in schizophrenics, but they have trouble screening out irrelevant stimuli from their field of concentration. Cameron (1938), the first to introduce inclusion as a deficit in schizophrenic thought disorder, noted that schizophrenics' failure to give correct answers is attributable to their inability to restrict their attention to the task at hand. They allow irrelevant stimuli to interfere. Inability to exclude makes for their overinclusion. "We may define overinclusion," wrote Cameron, "as the result of unstable ego organization which fails to limit the number and kind of simultaneously effective excitants to a relatively few coherent ones" (1963, p. 613).

Thus, extreme forms of what the logician terms *non-sequitur* and the fallacy of irrelevance enter into schizophrenic thinking. The result is unstructured thinking because of a gross lack of coherence. When Cameron had a patient sort variously colored and shaped blocks into a specified number or grouping, the schizophrenic youth could not resist including irrelevant objects into the task, such as items from his pockets, portions of the room, a desk blotter, the experimenter himself, a man outside, and even a racial issue. The schizophrenic commented:

"I've got to pick it out of the whole room. I can't confine myself to the game. . . . Three blues—now, how about that green blotter? Put it in there too. (Green) peas you eat, you can't eat them unless you write on it (the green blotter). Like that wrist watch (experimenter's). I don't see any three meals coming off that watch. . . . White and blue (blocks) is Duke's Mixture. This (pulling out cigarette paper) is white. All this wood and Japan (pulling out match box). There's a man out there with a white tie; that's got something to do with white suits. . . . To do this trick *you'd* have to be made of wood. You've got a white shirt on, and the white blocks, you have to have them cut out of *you*! You've got a white shirt on. This (white block) will hold you and never let you go. I've got a blue shirt on; but it can't be a blue shirt and still go together. And the room's got to be the same." Contemplating a grouping of similar white and yellow blocks, he asked, "Are there any Chinese working here? (*No*). Only white ones, then you can't put them together" (1963, p. 614).

With time, overinclusion was used by psychologists to mean overinclusive thought and overinclusive responses as well as overinclusive stimuli (inappropriate stimuli). Some researchers view delusions of the schizophrenic as a type of overinclusion, hence they reckoned that it should be found in the same patients (Payne, Caird & Laverty, 1964). In a test on overinclusion administered to schizophrenics and neurotics, Payne, Matussek, and George (1959) found that schizophrenics were decidedly more overinclusive than neurotics and normals. In a study by Chapman and Taylor (1957), it was established that schizophrenics overinclude categories to such a degree that fruit extends to the inclusion of vegetables as well. Chapman (1961) supported the view that schizophrenics overexclude. They fail, for example, to include apples in the class of things that grow. That is, they exclude apples from the class of growing things. Because both fruits and vegetables are edible, schizophrenics overinclude vegetables in the category of fruit.

Abstract-Concrete Deficit

The virtual inability to cope with abstract notions is considered a major deficit of schizophrenics. Cameron traced the difficulty of schizophrenics to think abstractly to their overinclusiveness—to their including extraneous ideas that do not belong. Goldstein (1964) attributed their loss of abstract thinking to the schizophrenics' excessive response to sensory stimuli that especially impress them.

Because of their inability to respond abstractly, schizophrenics substitute concrete responses. Often, the schizophrenic cannot think hypothetically, to assume an "as-if" experience, or to make believe. Instruct a schizophrenic: Make believe that you are married. Or ask: What would you do if you were married? The reply might well be: But I'm not married!

While Goldstein (1964) noted that schizophrenics lacked the ability to proceed from concrete to abstract or from abstract to concrete, Gorham (1956a, b,c,) found that the schizophrenic's deficit to think abstractly extends to proverb interpretation. Take, for example, the proverb, "The sun shines upon all alike." Rather than offering the abstract interpretation of it meaning, "All are created equal," the schizophrenic would offer the concrete or literal interpretation: "The sun shines on everybody." Gorham concluded that the schizophrenics' deficit in proverb interpretation indicates a loss of abstract attitude as well as an excessive inclination for concrete responses.

Goldstein found that in addition to the loss of "as-if" ability, schizophrenics showed a loss in the abstract meaning of words. For them a word represents a particular object instead of a class of objects. "Man" represents a specific individual rather than the species of mankind. With his colleague Bolles, Goldstein (1938) observed an inability in schizophrenics to integrate different stimuli. They could not simultaneously hold their attention on two features of a puzzle. Confronted with a group of stimuli, schizophrenics could not manage more than one aspect, nor could they see the stimuli as an integrated whole. Furthermore, they could not abstract the common qualities among objects that were similar to ascertain in what respect they were uniform. Their concrete attitude toward things prevented them from so doing. For instance, schizophrenics were unable to state what was common in a red ball, a red screwdriver, and a red cardboard circle. Instead of selecting the common quality, *red,* the answer of one was: "This is for work (screwdriver), this for play (ball), this is a marker, a sort of target (circle)."

Broken Associative Threads

A deficit in schizophrenic thought, the defect of breaking associative threads, was first noted by Bleuler (1950). Bleuler distinguished between the fundamental and accessory symptoms of schizophrenia. While the latter symptoms can be found in nonschizophrenics, the former are peculiar to schizophrenics alone. The fundamental symptoms include (1) disorders of association and affectivity, (2) a predisposition for fantasy, (3) autism or a flight from reality, and (4) ambivalence of thoughts, impulses, and wishes. Among many secondary or accessory symptoms, he listed hallucinations, delusions, and motor disorders.

Bleuler, however, regarded the breaking of associative threads as *the* fundamental schizophrenic thought disturbance. This disorder, either temporary or of great duration, entails a disorganization of ideas—a breakdown in congruence or coherence. The schizophrenic's association of ideas—or associative threads as Bleuler termed them—lacks consistency and is marked by *non sequitur* relationships. From this fundamental thought disorder, Bleuler sought to account for all other thought disturbances of the schizophrenic. Keep in mind that while thought disorder characterizes schizophrenia, disturbances in mood or affect are the identifying features of affective psychosis.

The breaking of associative threads hypothesis serves as an explanation for "word-salad" or neologisms common to the schizophrenic. This deficit or loss for shared relations among ideas results, for example, in schizophrenics combining "steam-boat" and "sail-boat" to produce "steam-sail." Rather than seeing the two types of boats as alike, the first syllables were grouped together as synonymous.

Note that Bleuler referred to these logical relationships of the schizophrenic as associative *threads* because association of ideas was loosely held together rather than being completely broken. A complete severance would result in greater irrationality.

Loss of Major Set

A deficit studied by Shakow (1962, 1963, 1971) finds that schizophrenics are unable to establish a learning set. They fail to take advantage from past experience and relate it to the problem at hand. The average person with reasonable training will be set in readiness, having learned from his experiences. A *set* then is a state of readiness, and a *major set* readies one to respond appropriately. Learning appropriate responses is important in adaptation.

Much of our adaptive behavior is learned from prior experience. Schizophrenics, however, are deficient in this respect, having suffered a loss of major set. Unable to maintain a major set, schizophrenics inappropriately rely on minor sets or as Shakow termed them, *segmental sets.* Owing to the presence of this segmental set in schizophrenics, they tend to respond to inappropriate stimuli. Thus, the schizophrenic is never ready for life's experiences; old experiences are confronted as if they are completely novel and unpredictable. The loss of major set is comparable to losing one's ability to predict. How dreadful it must be for the schizophrenic! When the rest of us know what to expect, the schizophrenic is at a loss to know (despite his having the necessary experience to know better).

It is possible that these segmental sets (minor sets) get in the way of the schizophrenic; they may have become so primary that they have displaced major sets. That is to say, particulars have so fastened his attention that the situation as a whole (or abstract or as a principle) is lost. Shakow views the schizophrenic as having lost the forest for the trees.

THEORIES OF SCHIZOPHRENIA

Theoretical formulations of schizophrenia are in abundant supply, and may be ordered according to genetic, constitutional, biochemical, sociocultural, and psychodynamic classifications. Rosenthal (1963, 1970), however, reduces theories treating schizophrenia to essentially three types: (1) monogenic-biochemical theories, those which treat schizophrenia as an inherited disease; (2) diathesis-stress theories, those that view schizophrenia as stemming from an inherited constitutional predisposition; and (3) life-experience theories, or those hypotheses attributing schizophrenia to life experiences, especially to the early experiences of life, without implicating inherited diathesis or genes.

Genetic Hypotheses of Schizophrenia

Despite the scarcity of finding a psychopathologist who would regard schizophrenia as merely a genetic disorder, the majority of researchers tend to combine genetic predisposition with other important factors, such as stress, strained familial relationships, or biochemical factors.

It still remains a question as to whether schizophrenia results from a genetic predisposition or not, or that the predisposition is necessary before a psychic trauma later in life can effectually result in schizophrenia. Fish expresses no doubt as to the genetic basis of schizophrenia, and concludes that it "is due to genetic predisposition which may or may not be expressed, depending on the overall genetic constitution, the modifications of the constitution during childhood, and the severity of the stress to which the patient is subjected in adolescence and adult life" (1962, p. 17).

According to Kallmann's (1938, 1946, 1952a, 1952b, 1953, 1959, 1961) *recessive theory of transmission,* schizophrenia is due to a major mutant recessive gene, the probable effect of which is an enzyme deficiency. Instead of specific symptoms being affected by this metabolic deficiency, general behavioral adjustment is. "Some gene-specific metabolic deficiency is at the root of the disorganizing personality disorder which often leads to adaptive incompetence" (1959, p. 100). Various forms of the recessivity hypothesis have been offered, especially by members of the Munich school.

A contending *dominance theory* has been presented by a number of authorities, including Böök (1953a, 1953b), who argues that major gene differences are "very likely the basic prerequisites for the ignition of a chain of events which may result in a psychosis" (1960, p. 208). In the absence of specific genetical prerequisites, schizophrenia will not occur. A dominant gene, but one that is weak and variable in its manifestations, produces schizophrenia. Of the two hypotheses, recessive and dominant theories, Fuller and Thompson (1960) contend that evidence at the present time favors the former. Gregory (1960) pessimistically concludes that the possible genetic factors in schizophrenia remain uncertain, but later (Rosen & Gregory, 1965) concedes that evidence strongly favors a genetic predisposition to schizophrenia, even though its mode of transmission is not as yet known with certainty. His latest comment is that owing to intrafamilial concentration of schizophrenia, it could be due to any combination of three mechanisms: (1) inheritance of disposition or vulnerability; (2) direct nongenetic transmission of pathogenic agents; and (3) exposure of schizophrenic persons to pathogenic agents or experiences (1968, p. 447).

The *diathesis-stress theory* received its thrust from Meehl's presentation of it as the topic of his presidential address before the American Psychological Association in 1962. His topic, "Schizotaxia, Schizotypy, Schizophrenia," traced the development of schizophrenia from its genetic origin. Schizophrenics, because of their hereditary genetic defect, face the world with an inherited constitution called *schizotaxia.* Owing to their constitutional predisposition, these people, through social learning, acquire a personality type termed *schizotypy.* In the absence of good social reinforcement, these individuals, because of their "low anxiety readiness, physical vigor, general resistance to stress, and the like," are schizophrenic prone. Only a minority of schizotypes, however, become schizophrenic. This is due to a combination of constitutional defect compounded with noxious social stimuli (e.g., from schizophrenogenic mothers). The diathesis-stress model was clinically tested by Mednick (1958; Mednick & Schulsinger, 1968). While Meehl's is a monogenetic theory, Mednick and Schulsinger speculated that the disorder might possibly be polygenetic.

Gottesman and Shields (1972, 1976), who believe that the schizophrenic mystery will be resolved during our lifetime, conclude that a "genetic specific aetiology for schizophrenia means only that the gene or genes are necessary, not that they are sufficient, for the disorder to occur" (1966, p. 817). Summarizing genetic findings to date, Gottesman (1978) listed:

1. There is an absence of environmental causes (except where someone is related to a schizophrenic).

2. Schizophrenia is found in undeveloped as well as in industrial societies.

(2a) Lifetime risk in industrialized societies is (including people up to 55 years of age) approximately 1 percent.

3. There is in predisposed people in large urban communities a downward social drift.

4. Risk to genetic relatives of schizophrenics increases greatly, the closer their relationship (notwithstanding their living in the same or different social/physical environments).

5. Concordance rates for identical (monozygotic) twins sharing the disorder are approximately three times greater than fraternal (dizygotic) twins. This is at least thirty times greater than the rest of the population.

6. Although identical twins share all of their genes with each other, there is less than a 50 percent concordant rate. That is, if one twin is schizophrenic, the other twin has more than a 50 percent chance of escaping schizophrenia.

7. Despite their early rearing with others, the children of schizophrenics nevertheless have a higher rate of onset of schizophrenia than that of the general public. In some studies the rates are as high as for those living with their schizophrenic parents.

8. While the biological relatives of schizophrenics (who are adopted) have high rates of schizophrenia, those living with the adopted schizophrenic do not (Wender, Rosenthal, Kety, Schulsinger, & Welner, 1974).

9. By comparison, children born of normal parents have no increased rate of schizophrenia despite their being reared by a schizophrenic, that is, despite the parental figure coming down with schizophrenia.

10. It does not matter whether identical twins are reared together or apart from each other; their concordance rate for schizophrenia is approximately the same.

11. Except for the age of onset of schizophrenia, male or female gender is not a factor. It does not matter which parent is schizophrenic—mother or father.

12. The degree of risk to blood relatives of schizophrenics depends upon how severely affected the schizophrenic relative is.

13. Early total deafness and the communication problems arising therefrom have little to do with risk to schizophrenia increasing.

14. Close relatives of psychotics (whose schizophrenia-like symptoms resulted following head injuries) have no greater risk of becoming schizophrenic than the population at large.

15. The premorbid schizophrenic personality (a type of personality that is likely to become schizophrenic) cannot as yet be identified. This being the case, any particular model for the genetic transmission of schizophrenia must be ridden with ambiguity.

Biochemical Theories of Schizophrenia

Recently, there has been growing belief that schizophrenics (because one develops from apparently normal personalities and another from preexisting schizoid personalities) are of two types, and that at least one of these is of a physical etiology (Smythies, 1968).

The Adrenocrome Metabolite Theory

The adrenochrome-adrenolutin hypothesis, initially presented by Osmond and Smythies (1952; Smythies, 1963) and later cultivated by Osmond and Hoffer (1959, 1966; Hoffer & Osmond, 1960), reasons that a proportion of adrenaline found in tissues undergoes a conversion process becoming adrenochrome. It is readily transformed into 5:6 dihydroxy-N-methylinodole inasmuch as it is intensely reactive. Peculiarly, in the case of schizophrenics, the conversion is principally one of adrenolutin. Adrenochrome and adrenolutin, being mitotic poisons, account for schizophrenic mothers' abnormal fetuses; being antihistaminic, account for heightened histamine tolerance, but protection against allergies; being psychoses-mimicking when given to animals, account for psychotic phenomena in man. Hoffer and Osmond (1974; Hoffer, Osmond, Callbeck, & Kahan, 1957; Hoffer, 1962) used niacin and nicotinamide (vitamin B_3) in massive doses to treat schizophrenic patients. Of the 16 vitamin-treated patients, 12 (75 percent) needed no further hospital treatment, while 17 (63 percent) of 27 non-niacin patients did poorly.

Melatonin-harmine Hypothesis

Greiner and Nicolson (1965) developed a theory based on McIsaac's (1961) observation of there being a chemical relationship existing between the hallucinogenic drug harmine and a congenital defect in the pineal gland's production of the hormone melatonin, an important pathogenic factor in schizophrenia. Their reasoning is:

The synthesis of melatonin in the pineal gland is congenitally defective, because of which a hallucinogenic agent is produced instead of melatonin; as a result, there is an occurrence of hallucinations and an increased melanin production; the defective enzyme is probably an o-methyltransferase (Greiner & Nicolson, 1965, p. 1167).

The Taraxein Hypothesis

Heath (1960, 1966, 1967), who views schizophrenia as a "genetically determined inborn error of metabolism," theorizes that taraxein produces psychotic behavior by its affect on the limbic system of the brain. "The serum of schizophrenic patients contains antibody that can attach to antigenic sites of neural cell nuclei in the septal region and basal caudate nucleus of the brain. . . ." (1967, p. 1499). Schizophrenic symptoms are the result of an immune process brought on by a serum which contains antibody against the brain. A number of researchers are currently pursuing evidence substantiating the taraxein hypothesis and eliminating its weaknesses (Heath, 1963).

The Serotonin Hypothesis of Schizophrenia

Woolley and Shaw (1954, 1956; Woolley, 1958a, 1958b) postulate that schizophrenia issues from a cerebral serotonin hormone deficiency stemming from metabolic failure. Serotonin deficiency in the brain (responsible for mental disorder) is produced by those agents capable of antagonizing the action of serotonin, that is, the ergot, alkaloids, the harmala alkaloids, yohimbine, and their derivatives which operate as antimetabolites or serotonin in smooth muscle.

Kety (1965, 1969, 1972, 1973) cites five important areas of biochemical research in schizophrenia: (1) oxygen, carbohydrate, and energetics; (2) amino acids and amines; (3) the epinephrine hypothesis which traces schizophrenia to faulty metabolism of epinephrine, adrenochrome or adrenolutin, a hallucinogenic derivative of epinephrine, believed to cause symptoms of schizophrenia (the theory of Hoffer, Osmond, & Smythies, 1954; Osmond & Hoffer, 1959); (4) ceruloplasmin and taraxein, the work of Heath and others of the Tulane group; and (5) serotonin, especially the efforts of Woolley and Shaw (1954). In 1969, Kety embellished this list with additional hypotheses, including dimethoxyphenylethylamine and indoleamine theories.

The Dopamine Hypothesis

Tracing the effects drugs have on neurotransmitters (catecholamines and indoleamines), Snyder (1974) arrived at a dopamine hypothesis of schizophrenia. Phenothiazine drugs are highly specific in their action. They zero in on the primary schizophrenic symptoms and hold them at bay. "Knowing the neurochemical bases of such drug action should also help in elucidating the pathophysiology of schizophrenia" (Snyder et al., 1974, p. 1243). Catecholamines (norepinephrine and dopamine) are transmitters of certain tracts in the brain, with dopamine the transmitter of the dopamine tract. It is known that dopamine deficiency accounts for Parkinson's disease, and its restoration functions as miraculous therapy. A reciprocity exists between schizophrenia and Parkinsonism (Stevens, 1973). A blocking action of dopamine receptors results from the phenothiazine drugs, such as chlorpromazine. "It is quite tempting then to speculate that the antischizophrenic action of these drugs is mediated via blockade of dopamine receptor sites in the brain" (Snyder, 1974, p. 244).

The effect of the phenothiazine drugs is due to their creating a situation of dopamine deficiency. In fact, the side effects of these antipsychotic drugs resembles Parkinson's disease (a state of dopamine deficiency). Although antipsychotic drugs do not *cure* schizophrenics, remission of the disorder is dramatically facilitated.

Other Biochemical Hypotheses

Biochemical investigation of schizophrenia is not new. A classic study of the biology of schizophrenia involving endocrinological ramifications was offered by Hoskins (1946). Later, he added research in hormone therapy (1954). His efforts, however, serve only as pioneer studies.

The role of morphological characteristics in schizophrenia has been scored by Doust (1952a,b), who noted morphological immaturity coupled to dysplastic factors in schizophrenia, such as, "a scanty upper lip without discrete lobulation; a high interpupillary index, double jointedness, and persistent remnants of the epicanthic fold." Chronic anoxemia is also common in schizophrenics.

Utilizing conditional reflex studies, Astrup (1962) traced schizophrenic deterioration to an impairment of the higher nervous activity, reasoning that the more pronounced the schizophrenic deterioration, the severer the impairment. He explained schizophrenia in the light of Gantt's autokinesis and schizokinesis, while rejecting brain lesions and psychodynamic mechanisms (Astrup & Noreik, 1966). Although Astrup follows in the tradition of Pavlov, Russians (such as Malis, 1961) explain schizophrenia as an infectious disease, owing to the toxic properties in the blood and other physical factors. Some ongoing research in the Western world is examining the role played by viruses. Some researchers have reason to suspect viral infection. Toward this end, Torrey and Peterson (1976) explored a viral hypothesis of schizophrenia.

Vulnerability Hypothesis of Schizophrenia

Reviewing the major approaches to the etiology of schizophrenia, Zubin and Spring (1977) sought a common denominator among them. Genetic, neuropsychological, learning, developmental, ecological, and internal environmental models have one thing in common. That common denominator, they claim, is *vulnerability*. According to the vulnerability hypothesis, people possess an innate vulnerability of varying degrees. Persons who reach their degree or pass their threshold of vulnerability can, under stress, experience schizophrenic episodes. One's degree of vulnerability derives anywhere from genetic to environmental factors. Thus the two major springs of vulnerability are inborn and acquired. While genes account for the former, life events (such as traumas, family encounters, perinatal complications, peer interactions, diseases, and the like) are root causes of the latter.

Schizophrenic disorders arise when our equilibrium is disturbed to such an extent that we are unable to restore homeostasis. "The highly vulnerable person," claim Zubin and Spring, "is one for whom numerous contingencies encountered in daily living are sufficient to elicit an episode. Others have such a low degree of vulnerability that nothing short of a rare and probably catastrophic event would induce an episode, and even then only a very brief one" (1977, p. 109). Just as some persons are "accident-prone," others are "stress-prone" and their patterns of living exhibit a stressful lifestyle. Consequently, psychopathological episodes increase as stress exceeds one's threshold and decrease as stress falls below one's vulnerability threshold.

Psychoanalytic Theory of Schizophrenia

Though Freud sought to discourage the psychoanalytic treatment of schizophrenia, attempts to do so persisted. According to psychoanalysts (Freeman, 1965), two contributions have been made to research in schizophrenia: a technique of revealing the patient's subjective experiences; and the interpretation of the patient's denials or reluctance to communicate as manifestations of his anxiety.

Freud's formulation of a psychoanalytic theory of psychosis comes from his analysis of the Schreber case of paranoid schizophrenia, which he reported in 1911. He viewed the illness as a type of repression wherein libidinal cathexes are withdrawn from the external world of objects as well as from their intrapsychic representations, leaving the patient with only an incomplete capacity for retaining object cathexes. Hallucinations, topographic regressions, are interpreted as revived memory-traces experienced as genuine perceptions, but in 1916 he rejected the idea that topographic regression occurs in schizophrenia. Delusion-formation is an attempt at recovery. Freud (1915) attributed it to cathexes withdrawal from endopsychic object representation. "Paranoiacs are endowed with a *fixation at the stage of narcissism,* and . . . the amount of *regression* characteristic of paranoia is indicated by the length of *the step back from sublimated homosexuality to narcissism"* (1911). Psychosis is a regression to a state of narcissism, and its conflict centers on homosexual wish-phantasy. While neurosis is produced by a conflict between the ego and the id, psychosis results from a disturbance between ego and the outer world (environment) (Freud, 1924).

Contemporary psychoanalytic theories of schizophrenia utilize Freud's structure of the personality (id, ego, superego) originally presented by Freud in 1932, but stress only the role of ego and superego. Departing from Freud, Federn (1943, 1948, 1952) contended that ego defect was not the cause but the consequence of withdrawal from the object world. Ego insufficiency or dysfunction (ego cathexes deficiency), accounting for psychotic symptomatology, was initiated by Federn and accepted by the majority of psychoanalysts. Schizophrenic depersonalization ensues from loss of ego-boundary cathexes (1949).

Current psychoanalytic hypotheses regard schizophrenia as a regressive process and as a defense against guilt and anxiety vitalized by instinctual urges, though their mental phenomena may vary. The regressive process reverts to early childhood points of fixation. The fixation points are viewed as arrested forms of development, a failure in normal psychic development. Accordingly, a schizophrenic is mentally or emotionally a child, rather than an adult. The primitive regressive state is an escape from the unpleasant content of adult consciousness. The disdain for distasteful reality causes fragmentation (Bion, 1957). The schizophrenic does not think of his cognition as part of himself, but as part of the world of persecutors (Searles, 1959). Schizophrenic processes cause "varying degrees of splitting and projection of the ego. These processes are related to the working within the ego of destructive impulses, which are felt to be alien (split off) and therefore persecutors" (Rosenfeld, 1965). In earliest infancy the personality's psychotic elements are split off, claims Rosenfeld, and schizophrenia results when the split-off psychotic parts erupt through to the surface.

According to Melanie Klein (1948), should persecutory fear and schizoid mechanisms become too potent, then the ego becomes incapable of working through the depressive position. As a result the ego regresses to a paranoid schizoid state, thereby reinforcing earlier persecutory fears and schizoid elements.

Ladee, investigating hypochondriac psychosis from a psychoanalytic standpoint, claims that the disorder results from "an increase in the libidinous cathexis of a mentally resisted organ (function) and loss of an (ambivalently) loved object, let loose aggression which introjected in a somatized form" (1966, p. 262).

Existential Hypothesis of Schizophrenia

Kantor and Herron (1966) have developed an existentialist approach to reactive schizophrenia. According to this view, reactive schizophrenics are individuals who once having possessed freedom are devoid of it. Vulnerability to schizophrenia is contingent upon the loss of freedom, since freedom is essential to mental health. Having once been in possession of freedom and life's meaningfulness, the reactive schizophrenic has lost his will-to-meaning (Frankl, 1969), purpose in life, choice, and self-image. Psychosis, instead of being the resultant of a shattered ego, passive repressions, or obstructions in living, is the inability to find meaning for one's existence. The loss of life's meaningfulness alienates one from his own sense of humanity. The schizophrenic's symptoms must be interpreted as attempts to impute meaningful values to his existence. It is in an encounter with his present self that he finds meaningful living.

The goal of therapy, one of empathy and participation on the part of the therapist, is to note what is happening to the patient instead of the cause of its occurrence. Therapeutic communication is transverbal, one stemming from the patient's "presence" (May, 1958); and his existence is structured as being-in-the-world (Binswanger, 1963). Man, being a "socius," must have his psychotherapy keynoted with social interaction, dialogue with others, and freedom of choice, for schizophrenia is the antithesis of human freedom.

For the schizophrenic time lacks a future, hence life is devoid of purpose. He exists in the past; "it is this pervasive underlying preoccupation with what is behind one that is so striking in the schizophrenic" (Shakow, 1962, p. 15). His repetition of past actions is significant of his loss of futurity.

Phenomenological Theory of Schizophrenia

Laing (1965) refers to his approach to schizophrenia as existential-phenomenological. "Existential phenomenology," he explains, "attempts to characterize the nature of a person's experience of his world and himself" (1965, p. 17). Existential splits account for schizophrenia. Schizophrenia, Laing reminds us, literally means "broken-hearted," and this is essentially the phenomenological experience of the schizophrenic. The phenomenological world of the schizophrenic is one of despair. "Schizophrenia cannot be understood without despair" (Laing, 1965, p. 38). Sharing the schizophrenic's existential world with us, Laing relates: "The schizophrenic is desperate, is simply without hope. I have never known a schizophrenic who could say he was loved, as a man, by God the Father or by the Mother of God or by another man." He continues: "When someone says he is an unreal man or that he is dead, in all seriousness, expressing in radical terms the stark truth of his existence as he experiences it, that is—insanity" (1965, p. 38). How sad to be a schizophrenic!

However, to label the schizophrenic insane is another matter. He is far more sane than people that are esteemed and venerated. While the schizophrenic hurts no one, but is nevertheless institutionalized, dangerous persons are allowed to roam free. We regard a person as normal, for example, who declares that he would rather be dead than be a Communist. But if he says that he has lost his soul, we regard him as mad. A person who announces that "men are machines" might be thought a great scientist. But if someone should believe such a scientist and declare: "I am a machine," then he is labeled " 'depersonalized' in psychiatric jargon." To drive home his point that it is perhaps society that is insane rather than a sensitive individual, Laing remarks: "A man who says that Negroes are an inferior race may be widely respected. A man who says his whiteness is a form of cancer is certifiable" (1965, p. 12). A girl of seventeen was detained in a mental hospital because she claimed that she had an atomic bomb inside her. Yet, chiefs of state who threaten the world with their power and atomic weapons are allowed to move freely about, despite their being more dangerous and "far more estranged from 'reality' than many of the people on whom the label 'psychotic' is affixed" (1965, p. 12).

What then is schizophrenia? It is a label placed upon a person who utilizes an unusual strategy enabling him to survive in an unlivable situation. The schizophrenic mode of responding to the world arises from double-bind situations encountered during childhood familial situations. Laing borrows the double-bind hypothesis from Bateson and his associates (1956). The schizophrenic is in an "untenable position, the 'can't win' double-bind, the situation of checkmate" (Laing, 1967, p. 116). Thus, schizophrenia is not a disease, but a "social event or series of social events" (Laing, 1976, p. 139). Mezan, Laing's biographer, depicts Laing's view of schizophrenia:

Schizophrenia literally means *broken-hearted.* But the heartbreak, the feelings of terror and despair are not "caught," they are the result of terrifying experiences and desperate circumstances—of family situations, rather common ones, of a type that Laing calls "double-binds," in which without conscious malice, one person is repeatedly subjected to simultaneous, absolutely contradictory injunctions and attributions about who he is, or how he feels or what he thinks, until he can no longer tell who he is, or what he feels or thinks. This is a perfectly real persecution unto psychological death (1976, p. xlviii).

Schizophrenia might be the mind's natural healing process in which the unendurable contradictions experienced start to break down.

Rather than placing schizophrenics in mental institutions that exacerbate their condition, it might be advisable to permit them to work out their own problems without interference. Remission rates, speculates Laing, would probably be as high as 30 percent. At any rate, schizophrenia is a method of working out problems by abandoning all distinctions between what is and what is not real, present and future, self and not self.

A therapist who truly wants to be effective with schizophrenic patients must get to know them by becoming as they are. Furthermore psychotherapists must create the healing experience. The analyst, explains Laing, is not having that experience, he is that experience.

Binswanger (1963) and Mendel (1974) have attempted phenomenological formulations of schizophrenia. According to Mendel, the three primary phenomena seen in all cases of schizophrenia are: "(1) the failure of historicity; (2) the expensive and ineffective management of anxiety; and (3) the disastrously painful interpersonal transactions" (1974, p. 140). While the average person experiences life in sequential relationships and bases future relationships on incorporating life's experiences as part of his personal history, schizophrenics cannot. "In the schizophrenic existence there seems to be no remaining lived history at any one moment" (1974, p. 124).

The schizophrenic seems incapable of managing anxiety. "The schizophrenic existence expends a huge amount of energy in attempting to deal with anxiety and always it fails" (1974, p. 127). Consequently, these people are always spent. By contrast, the average person "can manage many more ergs of anxiety with one-tenth erg of anxiety-managing devices (defences)" (1974, p. 127).

Each interpersonal encounter of the schizophrenic is as if it were for the first time, despite his having a long acquaintance with an individual. Since the schizophrenic "has no history and does not have available to him the ability to anticipate the future, he must enter into each relationship with another human being, reinventing himself each day and each moment" (1974, p. 128). Consequently, each interpersonal transaction of the schizophrenic is a painful experience.

Secondary phenomenological characteristics of the schizophrenic life style include feelings of emptiness and nothingness, impaired self-esteem, the lack of a flow of time (no past or future), feelings of tiredness and exhaustion, loose association on encountering anxiety, a sense of dread and fear, fragility of adjustment, withdrawal, and a loosely integrated personality. Tertiary characteristics include autism, ambivalence, affective difficulty, hopelessness, confusion, inability to learn from experience, and being tied to the present.

Familial and Sociocultural Theories of Schizophrenia

No one has gone further than Harry Stack Sullivan (1953) in emphasizing the social factors involved in psychiatry. Defining psychiatry as the study of interpersonal relations, he asserted that "this made psychiatry the probable locus of another evolving discipline, one of the social sciences, namely, *social psychology*" (1947a, p. xi). Sullivan, who believes that the schizophrenic is alienated from social influences (1962, p. 220), claims the disorder ensues "when a person is driven by the insoluble character of his life situation" (1954, p. 206). Our sleep and a considerable portion of our childhood years are schizophrenic experiences. The essential nature of schizophrenia is the "failure of the self-system . . . to restrict the contents of consciousness to the higher referential processes that can be consensually validated" (1956, p. 182).

Psychiatry, the study of interpersonal phenomena according to Sullivan, examines phenomena occurring in interpersonal situations, configurations entailing two or more persons (1938). "Scientific psychiatry has to be defined as the study of interpersonal relations" (1948, p. 105). The therapeutic process itself must also be one of "participant observation," an interpersonal relationship of interpersonal influence affecting both patient and psychotherapist (1947a).

There are those psychiatrists who are so thoroughly convinced of the sociocultural factors of mental disorders that they are committed to social forms of therapy, that is, milieu therapy or a therapeutic community. Jones (1952, 1962) was an early pioneer in this field, but today a number of others have researched and are experimenting in this area of schizophrenia (Artiss, 1962; Sanders, Smith, & Weinman, 1967). Brown and his associates (1966) report a significant degree of severe distress on the part of relatives some time during the half year prior to hospitalization of the patient. "The number of problems, and the distress felt by relatives, were highly related to the degree of disturbed behaviour shown by the patient" (1966, p. 208).

The Double-Bind Hypothesis

Bateson and his colleagues Jackson, Haley, and Weakland (1956) and later Weakland (1960) developed a theory of schizophrenia based on communications analysis and Bertrand Russell's (1937) theory of logical types according to which a discontinuity exists between a class and its members, namely, a class can neither be a member of itself nor can any of its members constitute a class because the concept used for class is a different logical type, a different level of abstraction. This discontinuity is carried over into interpersonal relations or communications between mother and child, and breached with a resulting psychopathological outcome, schizophrenia.

Weakland (1960, pp. 374-375) cites the general characteristics of the double-bind predicament:

1. When the individual is involved in an intense relationship; that is, a relationship in which he feels it is vitally important that he discriminate accurately what sort of message is being communicated so that he may respond appropriately.
2. And, the individual is caught in a situation in which the other person in the relationship is expressing two orders of message and one of these denies the other.
3. And, the individual is unable to comment on the messages being expressed to correct his discrimination of what order of message to respond to, i.e., he cannot make a metacommunicative statement.

A child in a double-bind situation cannot win, for whatever he does will be censored; furthermore, the breakdown in communications between mother and child is recurrent.

Sampson and his group (1964) studied women and mothers who were schizophrenic and concluded that schizophrenic wives underwent severe difficulty in the transition of leaving home, marrying, and assuming parenthood. A number of them, symbiotically tied to the maternal figure, encountered conflict in marital separation, while others confronted conflict in "synthesizing childhood identifications, especially those revived by becoming like the mother" (1964, p. 119).

Disordered communication as the cause of schizophrenia collided with the findings of Liem (1974) whose research indicated no support for the notion that disordered communications of parents of schizophrenics contribute to their thought disorder. "Disordered communications of schizophrenic sons had an adverse effect not only on the parents of schizophrenic sons but on all parents who attempted to respond to them" (1974, p. 438). Actually, the communication disorder of schizophrenics had a negative effect on all parents (not merely the parents of schizophrenics) "who heard and attempted to respond to them" (1974, p. 445).

The Quadruple-Bind Hypothesis

From a study comparing schizophrenic patients with nonschizophrenic siblings, Lu (1961, 1962) uncovered a couple of sets of binds. One, the dependence-independence conflict, relates to the American culture which demands of our youth that they enter adulthood with independence and autonomy. But in the case of the preschizophrenic who has played a dependent role patterned on an authoritarian mother, independence and autonomy present a problem—a bind. Being dependent and subordinate, yet expected to seek achievement, responsibility, and independence, is the cause of the bind.

The bind ensues when the preschizophrenic vainly strives to fulfill the authoritarian mother's expectations that do not coincide with his own. The schizophrenic is engulfed in a "role pattern which is characterized by contradictory parental expectations coupled with the preschizophrenic's persistent efforts to fulfill them" (1962, p. 233).

Severe mental conflict is experienced when the desires of the preschizophrenic conflict—the desire to be independent of his mother clashes with that of desiring to remain dependent upon her. Nonschizophrenic siblings were involved in activities that took them away from home; they attended school or worked at distances from home; they married earlier; and they ignored their mother's domination. Hence, thereby they avoided both maternal control and serious mental conflicts. Kimble and Garmezy (1968; Garmezy, 1968) report that mothers of schizophrenic "patients are more deviant in their attitudes to their sons than are the mothers of good premorbid patients" (Kimble & Garmezy, 1968, p. 628). The poor premorbid group of schizophrenics (those prior to hospitalization exhibiting a poor social and sexual adjustment [Garmezy & Rodnick, 1959]) responded with sharply poorer discriminations to the critical mother, while the reactive group (good premorbids—those with successful adjustment prior to hospitalization) and sibling group were able to make adequate discriminations.

Marital Schism and Marital Skew Hypothesis

A number of studies conducted by Lidz and his associates (1957, 1958, 1965) linked the cause of schizophrenia to intrafamilial relationships. The schizophrenic is the product of a seriously disturbed family (Lidz & Lidz, 1949), involving psychopathological elements in the father as well as the mother. Such families were "either schismatic—that is, divided into two antagonistic and competing factions—or were 'skewed' in that the serious personality disturbance of one parent set the pattern of family interaction" (Lidz, Fleck, Alanen, & Cornelison, 1963, p. 3). The parents of such families, impervious and engaged in homosexual and incestuous struggles, proved detrimental to the child's ego development. The child, with only confused models for identification, relates poorly or inaccurately, and is victimized by irrational or paralogical modes of thought and communication. In schizophrenic families, there are "failures of the family to provide adequate nurturance to permit the child to develop autonomy, to achieve the essential structure required to direct the structuring of the personality, and to convey the basic adaptive techniques of the culture" (Lidz et al., 1965, p. 375), all stemming from parental personality deficiencies. Accordingly, schizophrenia, essentially a deficiency disease, is the product of the family's inability to provide what is necessary for a suitable integrated personality development, including the schizophrenic's failure to attain autonomy, a faulty family structure impeding the structuring of personality, and unsound enculturation. Beck's (1965) studies also disclosed family behaviors associated with schizophrenia.

Mednick's Learning Theory of Schizophrenia

Mednick's (1958, 1959) hypothesis, grounded on learning theory, asserts that high levels of anxiety (acting as a drive) spiral in intensity, leading to excessive stimulus generalization. Unlike the normal, schizophrenics: (1) more readily acquire conditioned responses, (2) exhibit greater stimulus generalization responsiveness, and (3) perform with difficulty in complex situations. The spiralling process of anxiety proceeds from an acute to a chronic phase of schizophrenia.

The thinking of abstracted, irrelevant thoughts may be rewarded by anxiety reduction by removing disturbing ideation from consciousness. This would increase the probability of the recurrence of these irrelevant thoughts and would be an admirable vehicle for continual anxiety reduction and transition to a chronic phase (1958, p. 316).

Tactics, such as alcohol consumption, which once were effective in alleviating anxiety-provoking situations that were once bearable are now beyond control. Schizophrenic symptoms function as anxiety reducers, as a defense against anxiety. Schizophrenic irrelevant thoughts are effective anxiety reducers, so much so that they reduce anxiety even below that of the normal individual. A similar relationship holds true in the case of depressives as well, according to Davies, who asserts that his "observations confirm the widely held view that depression protects the organism from excessive stimulation" (1964, p. 101).

Interference or Segmental Set Theory in Schizophrenia

Interference theory, a view that depicts the individual as a processing system, is championed by Shakow (1962, 1963, 1971, 1977). The well-adapted organism, while choosing and responding to relevant environmental data, ignores its irrelevant or extraneous elements. This sentence describes generalized set. A bizarre difference occurs, however, in segmental set. To the question, "Where were you yesterday evening," the schizophrenic segmentalizes "eve" from "evening" with the result that

the question may be given a different and overwhelming meaning based on associations to Adam and Eve, and further remote diversions. When the response comes, it is irrelevant for the question from the viewpoint of the observer, no matter how relevant it is for the associations the schizophrenic has made (1977, p. 131).

In proper adaptation, irrelevant aspects are filtered out by a filter mechanism (Broadbent, 1958), but the schizophrenic has "difficulty in focusing on the relevant aspects of the defined situation," and is "susceptible to the influence of the peripheral. He does not habituate readily" (Shakow, 1962, p. 10). Instead of habituating, the schizophrenic perseverates by responding to stimuli that are weak while underresponding when they are intense. His two problems are that

he reacts to old situations as if they were new ones (he fails to habituate), and to new situations as if they were recently past ones (he perseverates); and second, he overresponds when the stimulus is relatively small, and he does not respond enough when the stimulus is great. . . . There is little doubt that the schizophrenic's is an inefficient unmodulated system, full of "noise," and of indeterminate figure-ground relationships. What a confusing world must be the schizophrenic's when such basic modes of relating to the world are so seriously disturbed! (Shakow, 1963, p. 303).

When the time interval between stimulus and response is great, intervening stimuli distract the schizophrenic, and if it is brief, then he is unable to select among alternatives. Otherwise his performance may be comparable to normal individuals. In order to establish a set, the schizophrenic requires greater time and maintains it with greater difficulty. Operating under conditions of responsibility causes the schizophrenic to do poorly.

Progressive Teleological Regression Hypothesis of Schizophrenia

A theory, developed by Arieti (1959, 1967, 1974) and termed progressive teleological regression, purports that "schizophrenia results not from reduction of the psyche to a concrete level, but from a *process of active concretization,* which follows psychodynamic (or teleologic, or restitutional) trends" (1967, p. 272). In active concretization, the psyche is yet able to conceive the abstract though not sustaining it, owing to the abstract's being too anxiety-provoking or disintegrating. Schizophrenic regression, a returning to lower levels of adaptation, is purposeful in that it seeks to diminish intense anxiety and maintain equilibrium. Regression, though purposeful, is retrogressive. Failing in its purpose, regression tends toward repetition. While regressing to lower levels, the schizophrenic fails to maintain integration or organization at the regressed level, and deteriorates into still lower levels in a vain attempt to defend himself from disorganization.

If, in a situation of severe anxiety, behavior at a certain level of intellectual integration cannot take place or does not bring about the desired results, a strong tendency exists toward behavior of lower levels of integration in order to effect those results (1955, p. 191).

The prepsychotic undergoes four stages: (1) a family situation devoid of security and trust; (2) secondary process mechanisms replace the primary; (3) defenses tend to fail at puberty when undergoing contacts with the outside world; and (4) the psychotic stage commences with a regressive descent. By definition, a person is schizophrenic when his conflicts undergo progressive teleologic regression (Arieti, 1960). In a study over a period of five years, Brattemo (1968) sees as the more genuine schizophrenics those chronic patients with a poor clinical outcome despite treatment.

Multiple-Factor Psychosomatic Theory of Schizophrenia

Working toward a unified concept of schizophrenia, Bellak (1949, 1955) hypothesized in his multiple-factor psychosomatic theory that schizophrenia is a severe ego disturbance syndrome, rather than a disease entity. Ego impairment, however, may be the consequent of numerous somatogenic and psychogenic antecedents in diverse arrangements of combinations. Good and ill health, viewed as a continuum of ego strength, has normality at one end and schizophrenia occupying a range at the other, with neurosis and manic-depressive psychosis in an intermediary position. Childhood schizophrenia, a defect of or injury to the ego, may be grounded in genetics, brain damage, or a disruption of mother-child relationships occurring in the first half year of the infant's life. "The hypothesis is advanced that organic disorders and defects so often observed in childhood psychosis and in severe adult schizophrenias are also the result of severe disturbances of the mother-child relationship, which serves the underdeveloped sensorium of the infant as a necessary polarizing factor; when absent, the somatic substratum is affected" (Bellak, 1955, p. 65).

Uncommon Psychiatric Syndromes

Enoch and his associates (1967) have made a study of some uncommon psychiatric syndromes. Among them they discuss: (1) the *capgras syndrome,* that of believing a person (ordinarily one related to the patient) has been replaced by a double; (2) De Clérambault's syndrome or *psychose passionnelle* or *pure erotamania:* the patient, usually a woman, entertains the delusion that a man (generally of higher status, a celebrity and older man) is deeply in love with her; (3) the *Othello syndrome,* a morbid, sexual, psychotic jealousy in which the patient suffers from delusions of infidelity on the part of the spouse; (4) the *Ganser syndrome,* "that of giving of approximate answers to simple and familiar questions, in a setting of disturbed or clouded consciousness" (p. 41); (5) the *Couvade syndrome,* husbands, who during their wives' pregnancies, suffer that which pregnant women ordinarily suffer; (6) the *Munchausen* or *hospital addiction syndrome,* a hypochondriacoid disposition of a patient who deceives physicians with apparent illnesses and discharges himself from the hospital prematurely (usually following surgery); (7) *Gilles de la Tourette's syndrome,* that is, generalized or multiple tics with coprolalia.

To these syndromes, Arieti and Meth (1959) have added other rare, unclassifiable, and exotic syndromes, including the *autoscopic syndrome* or the delusional experience of a double (capgras syndrome); *Cotard's syndrome* or the chronic delusional state of nihilism or negation of the existence of surrounding reality; *latah syndrome* with symptoms of echolalia, echopraxia, coprolalia, and sometimes fugues; *amok* (comparable to *beserk* of the ancient Vikings), a brooding followed by violence; *koro,* a phobic feeling that the penis will recede into the abdomen, causing death; *whitico psychosis,* fear of craving human flesh followed by melancholy, withdrawal, and insomnia; and *voodoo death* or *thanatomania,* death following awareness of transgressing a taboo or fear of being bewitched.

Grinker (1968) and his associates (in a lengthy research) report on the "borderline syndrome," with characteristics of: (1) "anger affect"; (2) "defect in his affectional relationships"; and "absence of indications of consistent self-identity" (1968, p. 90).

Closely related to the notion of schizophrenia is *oneirophrenia* (Meduna, 1950), a dreamlike state submerging the personality yet without dissociating it. In simple oneirophrenia, the patient is aware of internal changes, but in deliroid oneirophrenia, the inner complications are projected to the external world as a dream, one usually complicated with hallucinations.

12.

American Psychiatric Association

FEATURES OF SCHIZOPHRENIC DISORDERS

The essential features of this group of disorders[1] are: the presence of certain psychotic features during the active phase of the illness, characteristic symptoms involving multiple psychological processes, deterioration from a previous level of functioning, onset before age 45, and a duration of at least six months. The disturbance is not due to an affective disorder or organic mental disorder. At some phase of the illness schizophrenia always involves delusions, hallucinations, or certain disturbances in the form of thought.

The limits of the concept of schizophrenia are unclear. Some approaches to defining the concept have emphasized the tendency toward a deteriorating course (Kraepelin), underlying disturbances in certain psychological processes (Bleuler), or pathognomonic symptoms (Schneider). In this manual the concept is not limited to illnesses with a deteriorating course, although a minimal duration of illness is required since the accumulated evidence suggests that illnesses of briefer duration (here called schizophreniform disorder) are likely to have different external correlates, such as family history and likelihood of recurrence. The approach taken

here excludes illnesses without overt psychotic features, which have been referred to as latent, borderline, or simple schizophrenia. Such cases are likely to be diagnosed in this manual as having a personality disorder such as schizotypal personality disorder. Illnesses with onset after mid-adult life are also excluded, and may be classified as atypical psychosis. Furthermore, individuals who develop a depressive or manic syndrome for an extended period relative to the duration of certain psychotic features or before the psychotic features appear, are not classified as having schizophrenia but rather as having either an affective or schizoaffective disorder. Thus, this manual utilizes clinical criteria that include both a minimum duration and a characteristic symptom picture to identify a group of conditions that has validity in terms of differential response to somatic therapy; presence of a familial pattern; and a tendency toward onset in early adult life, recurrence and deterioration in social and occupational functioning.

DETERIORATION FROM A PREVIOUS LEVEL OF FUNCTIONING

Schizophrenia always involves deterioration from a previous level of functioning during some phase of the illness in such areas as work, social relations, and self-care. Family and friends often observe that the person is "not the same."

From Task Force on Nomenclature and Statistics of the American Psychiatric Association, *Diagnostic and Statistical Manual of Mental Disorders, Third Edition.* American Psychiatric Association, 1980.
[1]Although schizophrenia is most likely a group of disorders of differing etiologies, common usage refers to schizophrenia, rather than the technically more accurate term, schizophrenic disorders.

CHARACTERISTIC SYMPTOMS INVOLVING MULTIPLE PSYCHOLOGICAL PROCESSES

Invariably there are characteristic disturbances in several of the following areas: content and form of thought, perception, affect, sense of self, volition, relationship to the external world, and psychomotor behavior. It should be noted that no single feature is invariably present or seen only in schizophrenia.

Content of Thought. The major disturbance in the content of thought involves delusions that are often multiple, fragmented, or bizarre (i.e., patently absurd, with no possible basis in fact). Simple persecutory delusions involving the belief that others are spying on, spreading false rumors about, or planning harm to the individual are common. Delusions of reference, in which events, objects, or other people are given particular and unusual significance, usually of a negative or pejorative nature, are also common. For example, the individual may be convinced that a television commentator is mocking him.

Certain delusions are far more common in this disorder than in other psychotic disorders. These include, for instance, the belief or experience that one's thoughts, as they occur, are broadcast from one's head to the external world so that others can hear them (thought broadcasting); that thoughts that are not one's own are inserted into one's mind (thought insertion); that thoughts have been removed from one's head (thought withdrawal); or that one's feelings, impulses, thoughts, or actions are not one's own but are imposed by some external force (delusions of being controlled). Less commonly, somatic, grandiose, religious, and nihilistic delusions are seen. Overvalued ideas may occur (e.g.,

preoccupation with the special significance of certain dietary habits), or markedly illogical thinking (e.g., thinking that contains clear internal contradictions or in which conclusions are reached that are clearly erroneous, given the initial premises).

Form of Thought. A disturbance in the form of thought is often present. This has been referred to as "formal thought disorder," and is distinguished from a disorder in the content of thought. The most common example of this is loosening of associations, in which ideas shift from one subject to another completely unrelated or only obliquely related subject, without the speaker showing any awareness that the topics are unconnected. Statements that lack a meaningful relationship may be juxtaposed, or the individual may shift idiosyncratically from one frame of reference to another. When loosening of associations is severe, incoherence may occur, that is, speech may become incomprehensible. There may also be poverty of content of speech, in which speech is adequate in amount but conveys little information because it is vague, overly abstract or overly concrete, repetitive, or stereotyped. The listener can recognize this disturbance by noting that little if any information has been conveyed although the individual has spoken at some length. Less common disturbances include neologisms, perseveration, clanging, and blocking.

Perception. The major disturbances in perception are various forms of hallucination. Although these occur in all modalities, by far the most common are auditory, frequently involving voices the individual perceives as coming from outside the head. The voices may be familiar, and often make insulting statements. The voices may be single or multiple. Voices speaking directly to the individual or commenting on his or her ongoing behavior are particularly characteristic. Command hallucinations may be obeyed, at times creating danger for the individual or others. Occasionally, the auditory hallucinations are of sounds rather than voices. Tactile hallucinations may be present, and typically involve electrical, tingling, or burning sensations. Somatic hallucinations, such as the sensation of snakes crawling inside the abdomen, are occasionally experienced. Visual, gustatory, and olfactory hallucinations also occur, but with less frequency, and, in the absence of auditory hallucinations, always raise the possibility of an organic mental disorder.

Other perceptual abnormalities include sensations of bodily change and hypersensitivity to sound, sight, and smell.

Affect. The disturbance often involves blunting, flattening, or inappropriateness of affect. In blunted affect there is severe reduction in the intensity of affective expression. In flat affect there are virtually no signs of affective expression; the voice is usually monotonous and the face, immobile. The individual may complain that he or she no longer responds with normal emotional intensity or, in extreme cases, no longer has feelings. In inappropriate affect, the affect is clearly discordant with the content of the individual's speech or ideation. For example, while discussing being tortured by electrical shocks, an individual with schizophrenia, paranoid type, laughs or smiles. Sudden and unpredictable changes in affect involving inexplicable outbursts of anger may occur.

Although these affective disturbances are almost invariably present, their usefulness in making the diagnosis is limited because their presence is often difficult to judge except when present in extreme

form. Furthermore, the antipsychotic drugs have effects that may appear similar to the affective blunting and flattening seen in schizophrenia.

Sense of Self. The sense of self that gives the normal person a feeling of individuality, uniqueness, and self-direction is frequently disturbed. This is sometimes referred to as a loss of ego boundaries and is frequently manifested by extreme perplexity about one's own identity and the meaning of existence, or by some of the specific delusions described above, particularly those involving control by an outside force.

Volition. Nearly always there is some disturbance in self-initiated, goal-directed activity, which may grossly impair work or other role functioning. This may take the form of inadequate interest or drive or inability to follow a course of action to its logical conclusion. Pronounced ambivalence regarding alternative courses of action can lead to near cessation of goal-directed activity.

Relationship to the External World. Frequently there is a tendency to withdraw from involvement with the external world and to become preoccupied with egocentric and illogical ideas and fantasies in which objective facts are obscured, distorted, or excluded. When severe, this condition has been referred to as "autism." Family members or friends frequently comment that the individual seems preoccupied, in his or her own world, and emotionally detached from others.

Psychomotor Behavior. Various disturbances in psychomotor behavior are observed, particularly in the chronically severe and acutely florid forms of the disorder. A marked decrease may occur in reactivity to the environment, with a reduction in spontaneous movements and activity. In extreme cases the individual appears unaware of the nature of the environment (as in catatonic stupor); may maintain a rigid posture resisting efforts to be moved (as in catatonic rigidity); may make apparently purposeless and stereotyped, excited motor movements not influenced by external stimuli (as in catatonic excitement); may voluntarily assume inappropriate or bizarre postures (as in catatonic posturing); or resist and actively counteract instructions or attempts to be moved (as in catatonic negativism). In addition, mannerisms, grimacing, or waxy flexibility may be present.

Diagnostic Criteria for a Schizophrenic Disorder

A. At least one of the following during a phase of the illness:

1. Bizarre delusions (content is patently absurd and has *no* possible basis in fact), such as delusions of being controlled, thought broadcasting, thought insertion, or thought withdrawal.
2. Somatic, grandiose, religious, nihilistic, or other delusions without persecutory or jealous content.
3. Delusions with persecutory or jealous content if accompanied by hallucinations of any type.
4. Auditory hallucinations in which either a voice keeps up a running commentary on the individual's behavior or thoughts, or two or more voices converse with each other.
5. Auditory hallucinations on several occasions with content of more than one or two words, having no apparent relation to depression or elation.
6. Incoherence, marked loosening of associations, markedly illogical think-

ing, or marked poverty of content of speech if associated with at least one of the following:
   a. Blunted, flat, or inappropriate affect.
   b. Delusions or hallucinations.
   c. Catatonic or other grossly disorganized behavior.

B. Deterioration from a previous level of functioning in such areas as work, social relations, and self-care.

C. Duration. Continuous signs of the illness for at least six months at some time during the person's life, with some signs of the illness at present. The six-month period must include an active phase during which there were symptoms from A, with or without a prodromal or residual phase, as defined below.

Prodromal phase: A clear deterioration in functioning before the active phase of the illness not due to a disturbance in mood or to a substance use disorder and involving at least *two* of the symptoms noted below.

Residual phase: Persistence, following the active phase of the illness, of at least *two* of the symptoms noted below, not due to a disturbance in mood or to a substance use disorder.

Prodromal or Residual Symptoms
1. Social isolation or withdrawal.
2. Marked impairment in role functioning as wage earner, student, or homemaker.
3. Markedly peculiar behavior (e.g., collecting garbage, talking to self in public, or hoarding food).
4. Marked impairment in personal hygiene and grooming.
5. Blunted, flat, or inappropriate affect.

6. Digressive, vague, overelaborate, circumstantial, or metaphorical speech.
7. Odd or bizarre ideation, or magical thinking, e.g., superstitiousness, clairvoyance, telepathy, "sixth sense," "others can feel my feelings," overvalued ideas, ideas of reference.
8. Unusual perceptual experiences, e.g., recurrent illusions, sensing the presence of a force or person not actually present.

Examples. Six months of prodromal symptoms with one week of symptoms from A; no prodromal symptoms with six months of symptoms from A; no prodromal symptoms with two weeks of symptoms from A and six months of residual symptoms; six months of symptoms from A, apparently followed by several years of complete remission, with one week of symptoms in A in current episode.

D. The full depressive or manic syndrome (criteria A and B of major depressive or manic episode), if present, developed after any psychotic symptoms, or was brief in duration relative to the duration of the psychotic symptoms in A.

E. Onset of prodromal or active phase of the illness before age 45.

F. Not due to any organic mental disorder or mental retardation.

TYPES

The types reflect cross-sectional clinical syndromes. Some are less stable over time than others, and their prognostic and treatment implications are variable. The diagnosis of a particular type should be based on the predominant clinical picture that occasioned the evaluation or admission to clinical care.

Disorganized Type

The essential features are marked incoherence and flat, incongruous, or silly affect. There are no systematized delusions although fragmentary delusions or hallucinations in which the content is not organized into a coherent theme are common. Associated features include grimaces, mannerisms, hypochondriacal complaints, extreme social withdrawal, and other oddities of behavior.

This clinical picture is usually associated with extreme social impairment, poor premorbid personality, an early and insidious onset, and a chronic course without significant remissions.

In other classifications this type is termed hebephrenic.

Diagnostic Criteria for Disorganized Type

A type of schizophrenia in which there are:

A. Frequent incoherence.
B. Absence of systematized delusions.
C. Blunted, inappropriate, or silly affect.

Catatonic Type

The essential feature is marked psychomotor disturbance, which may involve stupor, negativism, rigidity, excitement, or posturing. Sometimes there is rapid alternation between the extremes of excitement and stupor. Associated features include stereotypes, mannerisms, and waxy flexibility. Mutism is particularly common.

During catatonic stupor or excitement the individual needs careful supervision to avoid hurting self or others, and medical care may be needed because of malnutrition, exhaustion, hyperpyrexia, or self-inflicted injury.

Although this type was very common several decades ago, it is now rare in Europe and North America.

Diagnostic Criteria for Catatonic Type

A type of schizophrenia dominated by any of the following:

1. Catatonic stupor (marked decrease in reactivity to environment and/or reduction of spontaneous movements and activity) or mutism.
2. Catatonic negativism (an apparently motiveless resistance to all instructions or attempts to be moved).
3. Catatonic rigidity (maintenance of a rigid posture against efforts to be moved).
4. Catatonic excitement (excited motor activity, apparently purposeless and not influenced by external stimuli).
5. Catatonic posturing (voluntary assumption of inappropriate or bizarre posture)

Paranoid Type

The essential features are prominent persecutory or grandiose delusions, or hallucinations with a persecutory or grandiose content. In addition, delusional jealousy may be present.

Associated features include unfocused anxiety, anger, argumentativeness, and violence. In addition, there may be doubts about gender identity or fear of being thought of as a homosexual, or being approached by homosexuals.

The impairment in functioning may be minimal if the delusional material is not acted upon, since gross disorganization of behavior is relatively rare. Similarly,

affective responsiveness may be preserved. Often a stilted, formal quality, or extreme intensity in interpersonal interactions is noted.

The onset tends to be later in life than the other subtypes, and the features are more stable over time. If a biologically related family member of an individual who has this subtype also has schizophrenia, there is some evidence that the subtype of the relative will also be paranoid.

Diagnostic Criteria for Paranoid Type

A type of schizophrenia dominated by one or more of the following:

1. Persecutory delusions.
2. Grandiose delusions.
3. Delusional jealousy.
4. Hallucinations with persecutory or grandiose content.

Undifferentiated Type

The essential features are prominent psychotic symptoms that cannot be classified in any category previously listed or that meet the criteria for more than one.

Diagnostic Criteria for Undifferentiated Type

A. A type of schizophrenia in which there are: Prominent delusions, hallucinations, incoherence, or grossly disorganized behavior.

B. Does not meet the criteria for any of the previously listed types or meets the criteria for more than one.

Residual Type

This category should be used when there has been at least one episode of schizophrenia but the clinical picture that occasioned the evaluation or admission to clinical care is without prominent psychotic symptoms, though signs of the illness persist. Emotional blunting, social withdrawal, eccentric behavior, illogical thinking and loosening of associations are common. If delusions or hallucinations are present, they are not prominent and are not accompanied by strong affect.

The course of this type is either chronic or subchronic, since "acute exacerbation" by definition, involves prominent psychotic symptoms, and "in remission" implies no signs of the illness.

Diagnostic Criteria for Residual Type

A. A history of at least one previous episode of schizophrenia with prominent psychotic symptoms.

B. A clinical picture without any prominent psychotic symptoms that occasioned evaluation or admission to clinical care.

C. Continuing evidence of the illness, such as blunted or inappropriate affect, social withdrawal, eccentric behavior, illogical thinking, or loosening of associations.

Classification of Course

The course of the illness is coded in the fifth digit:

1. *Subchronic.* The time from the beginning of the illness, during which the individual began to show signs of the illness (including prodromal, active, and residual phases) more or less continuously, is less than two years but at least six months.

2. *Chronic.* Same as above, but greater than two years.

3. *Subchronic with Acute Exacerbation.* Reemergence of prominent psychotic symptoms in an individual with a subchronic course who has been in the residual phase of the illness.

4. *Chronic with Acute Exacerbation.* Reemergence of prominent psychotic symptoms in an individual with a chronic course who has been in the residual phase of the illness.

5. *In Remission.* This should be used when an individual with a history of schizophrenia, now is free of all signs of the illness (whether or not on medication). The differentiation of schizophrenia in remission from no mental disorder requires consideration of the period of time since the last period of disturbance, the total duration of the disturbance, and the need for continued evaluation or prophylactic treatment.

13.

Silvano Arieti

PROGRESSIVE TELEOLOGIC REGRESSION HYPOTHESIS AND PALEOLOGIC THOUGHT

We have already mentioned that the schizophrenic adopts different intellectual mechanisms. By that it was meant that he does not think with ordinary logic. His thought is not illogical or senseless, but follows a different system of logic which leads to deductions different from those usually reached by the healthy person. The schizophrenic is seen in a position similar to that of a man who would solve mathematical problems not with our decimal system, but with another hypothetical system, and would consequently reach different solutions. In other words, the schizophrenic seems to have a faculty of conception which is constituted differently from that of the normal man.

. . . This different faculty of conception or different logic is the same as that which is followed in dreams, in other forms of autistic thinking, and in many manifestations of men living in prehistorical and certain other cultures. It was consequently called *paleologic* to distinguish it from our usual logic, which is generally called Aristotelian, since Aristotle was the first to enunciate its laws. The laws of paleologic, especially as they are deduced from the study of schizophrenic thought and dreams, will be examined in detail in the following chapter. Here it is sufficient to emphasize again why the patient abandons the Aristotelian way of thinking and adopts a primitive type. He does so in order to escape anxiety; as long as he interprets reality with Aristotelian logic, he is aware of the unbearable truth, and a state of panic may ensue. Once he sees things in a different way, with a new logic, his anxiety will decrease. This new logic will permit him to see reality as he wants to, and will offer him a pseudo-fulfillment of his wishes. Once the patient sees things in a different way, with a new logic, no Aristotelian persuasion will convince him that he is wrong. He is right, according to his own logic.

The adoption of this paleologic way of thinking is predominant in that type of schizophrenia which has been termed hebephrenic. However, not all thinking in hebephrenics follows paleologic modes. Islands of logical thoughts remain, but they are more and more overwhelmed by the paleological way of thinking. In the paranoid type of schizophrenia a peculiar situation occurs: Aristotelian thought is preserved to a considerable extent, but, as we shall see later in detail, it is often strangely used to support the conclusions reached by paleologic thought. This situation is, to a certain degree, reminiscent of those defenses of the ego which in many neuroses protect or reinforce unconscious complexes.

Another mechanism by which the schizophrenic breaks with reality is the withdrawal from action. This mechanism is particularly pronounced in the catatonic type, following complicated processes which are connected . . . with "psychological causality."

In the simple type of schizophrenia the

From *Interpretation of Schizophrenia* by Silvano Arieti, M.D. ©1974 by Silvano Arieti, ©1955 by Robert Brunner. Reprinted by permission of Basic Books, Inc., Publishers.

mechanisms mentioned above are not present, or present only to a minimal degree. Rather than change reality, the simple schizophrenic limits reality. He narrows his horizon to a large extent, so that he will be able to make some kind of compromise with what is left of reality, without having to resort very much to paleologic or to withdrawal mechanisms. What he leaves out of his life is generally what pertains to the abstract. Since life in our present cultural environment, however, cannot be deprived of this increasingly important aspect of thought, the simple schizophrenic cannot successfully compromise. He will appear bizarre, odd and inappropriate.

Each of the mechanisms which have been mentioned, though predominantly found in one particular type of schizophrenia, may occur to a greater or lesser degree in every type of this illness. Transitional stages and different combinations of the various mechanisms are commonly found. In addition, there are two other mechanisms which are common to all types, the impairment of affect and desocialization. All of these mechanisms are, of course, interconnected, and possibly only different expressions of one process. . . . they will be considered separately for didactical reasons, but their interrelation will always be considered. This approach should not be interpreted as a return to psychological atomism. We are fully aware that the human psyche functions as a whole, but the problem under consideration is so involved that no other study of it is feasible except the examination of its parts separately. . . .

I. THE PRINCIPLE OF TELEOLOGIC REGRESSION

In this chapter the various intellectual alterations which occur in schizophrenia will be examined.

In this first section, however, it will be shown that intellectual distortions do not occur exclusively in schizophrenics, but occur in a much larger group of individuals than is generally assumed. These distortions never reach the intensity of the schizophrenic distortion, except in dreams. If we take mathematical thinking at one extreme, as the most typical example of pure logical Aristotelian thought, and schizophrenic thinking at the other extreme, we can also find all possible gradations between the two. Generally, the greater the intensity of the emotion involved, the greater may become the necessity for resorting to some kind of intellectual distortion. The amount of the distortion, however, is not proportional to the emotional need.

The most common of these distortions is what is generally called *rationalization*. Rationalizations are found in normal people and neurotics as well as psychotics, and consist of attempts to justify logically actions or ideas which in reality are directed, not by reason, but by an emotional need. These rationalizations are often not unrealistic at all from an intellectual point of view; as a matter of fact, they are supported by pure Aristotelian logic. For example, a patient was suffering from feelings of rivalry for his brother, who was a singer. The patient used to warn his brother in a paternal and affectionate tone of voice, "Don't sing so often at clubs and private parties. You will ruin your voice!" This was a correct recommendation. The singer had also been told by many experts that he should not strain his voice with too much work. Actually the motivation of the patient in repeating this recommendation was a different one: He was jealous of the consideration and honor that the brother was receiving when he sang, and wanted to prevent them.

Often the rational foundation which sustains the idea or action is less plausible.

Some element of plausibility, however, must remain. . . . The patient, Peter, justified his father's saying that he had been a hero during the first World War, although actually he had been a deserter. According to Peter, his father had to say this in order to remove all doubts about his participation in the war, and by so doing, he was saving the honor of the family. Peter's need to consider his father a venerable authority compelled him to resort to such a fantastic rationalization. His brother, Gabriel, when he was already psychotic, sold a gold watch and some other valuable objects for a few cents. When he was questioned about it, he justified himself with the following rationalization: "These things were mine. Can't I do what I want with my things?" He switched the problem from the advisability of the act to the permissibility of the act, in an attempt to justify it. Actually, the motivation was different. In a latent way he was saying to his parents: "I had to become crazy in order to assert myself. You never let me do what I wanted. Now I can."

From these examples, and from many others which could be cited, it is evident that an attempt is always made to maintain an element of plausibility or logic, even when the wish to have one's way is very strong. As was mentioned before, human beings cannot accept anything which to them seems irrational. The need for rationality is as powerful as the need to gratify the irrational emotions. If rationality is never completely abandoned, a certain *level* of rationality, however, is often lost, especially in situations of emergency, and a regression to a lower level is often resorted to, even by normal human beings. Similar regressions have occurred innumerable times in human history. For instance, if diplomatic discussions do not bring about certain results, much more primitive methods, such as wars or persecution of minorities, may be resorted to.

This regression occurs so often that this process can be defined in the form of a principle. *If, in a situation of severe anxiety, behavior at a certain level of intellectual integration cannot take place or does not bring about the desired results, a strong tendency exists toward behavior of lower levels of integration in order to effect those results.*

The reader should note that the word "tendency" is used. In other words, this principle is not like a physical law, which must operate without exceptions. There is just a propensity toward its occurrence, but it may not occur, as for instance, in cases where something unexpected intervenes. It should also be noted that a situation of severe anxiety *must* be present.

By resorting to lower levels of integration, the human mind turns again to methods which were used in the past, but which were discarded when new methods had been adopted. It is a repetition of history in reversed chronology. This happens not only to human beings, but to animals as well. Mowrer has demonstrated this principle in rats with a very ingenious experiment. . . . The animals learned to protect themselves from an electric current by sitting on their hind legs. Later, the rats learned a much better way; they discovered how to turn off the current by pressing a pedal. When this habit was well ingrained, it replaced the previous one. Later the pedal too was charged with electricity, and the rats had to face another shock, if they continued to press it. At this point they went back to the method of sitting on their hind legs. Thus, they reverted to the earlier and inferior method.

When experimental animals have learned to solve a problem with the mechanism of insight and, for some reason, can no longer solve the problem with this method, they revert to the method of trial and error. In other words, there is a tendency toward a reversed hierarchy of responses,[1] from the highest to the lowest. I propose to call this principle *the principle of teleologic regression: regression* because less advanced levels of mental integration are used; *teleologic* because this regression seems to have a purpose, namely, to avoid anxiety by bringing about the wanted results. As a matter of fact, studies in abnormal psychology have revealed innumerable instances in which the mind in distress does not necessarily follow scientific thinking (events are the effects of previous causes), but rather teleologic thinking (events have a purpose). Thus, dreams, hallucinations, symptoms, delusions, etc., seem to have a purpose, even though they themselves are the results of previous causes.

More often than not, of course, thinking which follows the principle of teleologic regression does not effect the desired results, but will decrease the anxiety, at least temporarily. Legends and myths frequently reveal the adoption of this principle. For instance, the Jews, as described in the Bible, had reached that high cultural level which permitted them to worship an abstract God. When, however, they were under the stress of anxiety caused by the sudden disappearance of their leader, Moses, they reverted to the worship of the Golden Calf. When Moses reappeared and the anxiety was relieved, they went back to the cult of the abstract God.

At this point, a question of terminology must be clarified. The reader may be confused by the use of the words "logical," "rational," "intellectual," to indicate thoughts or actions which appear irrational and illogical. These terms are used because these thoughts or actions are intel-

lectually organized . . . ; in other words, on careful examination they reveal an intellectual process or effort, even if this process does not correspond to the one used in our common logic. In a rationalization, for instance, there is an intellectual or logical effort to justify something, even though this actual intellectual process may be at fault from our common point of view.

The difficulty that some people may experience in calling these processes intellectual or logical is in a certain way similar to the difficulty that some philosophically-minded people experienced in calling the unconscious mechanisms discovered by Freud "psychological." They thought that a necessary characteristic for a psychological phenomenon was that it be conscious; without consciousness a phenomenon could not be psychological. In a similar way, we call a process intellectual if it has some kind of intellectual organization, although it may not necessarily follow the Aristotelian logic (the only one known to us, usually) and may therefore appear to us very illogical. *What may seem to us as forms of irrationality are instead archaic forms of rationality.* As a matter of fact, we shall find more and more that intellectual organization is always present. As I have mentioned above, it is as difficult to escape from some type of intellectual organization as it is to escape from emotions. Even the most nonsensical, bizarre, and irrational thoughts have some kind of intellectual organization. When we understand the type of intellectual organization and its content, we understand the meaning of the process. In other words, it is possible to translate the archaic thought into an Aristotelian thought. Even the so-called "word salad" of the schizophrenic is not just a bizarre, whimsical *sequence* of words. When we understand it, we discover that it is a *consequence*.

---

[1] The emphasis here, however, is given not to the response in a behavioristic way, but to the central process which is responsible for the response.

II. VON DOMARUS' PRINCIPLE

Paleologic to a great extent is based on a principle enunciated by Von Domarus. This author, as a result of his studies on schizophrenia, formulated a principle which, in slightly modified form, is as follows: *Whereas the normal person accepts identity only upon the basis of identical subjects, the paleologician accepts identity based upon identical predicates.* For instance, the normal person is able to conclude, "John Doe is an American citizen," if he is given the following information: "Those who are born in the United States are American citizens; John Doe was born in the United States." This normal person is able to reach this conclusion because the subject of the minor premise, "John Doe," is contained in the subject of the major premise, "those who are born in the United States."

On the other hand, suppose that the following information is given to a schizophrenic: "The President of the United States is a person who was born in the United States. John Doe is a person who was born in the United States." In certain circumstances, the schizophrenic may conclude: "John Doe is the President of the United States." This conclusion, which to a normal person appears delusional, is reached because the identity of the predicate of the two premises, "a person who was born in the United States" makes the schizophrenic accept the identity of the two subjects, "The President of the United States" and "John Doe." Of course, this schizophrenic has an emotional need to believe that John Doe is the President of the United States, a need which will arouse anxiety if it is not satisfied. He cannot think that John Doe is the President of the United States if he follows Aristotelian logic; thus, following the principle of teleologic regression, he abandons Aristotelian logic and follows Von Domarus' principle.

A patient thought that she was the Virgin Mary. Her thought process was the following: "The Virgin Mary was a virgin; I am a virgin; therefore, I am the Virgin Mary." The delusional conclusion was reached because the identity of the predicate of the two premises (the state of being virgin) made the patient accept the identity of the two subjects (the Virgin Mary and the patient). She needed to identify herself with the Virgin Mary because of the extreme closeness and spiritual kinship she felt for the Virgin Mary.

14.

Wesley C. Becker

PROCESS-REACTIVE DISTINCTION

In the search for a place to get a foothold on the problem of schizophrenia, one glaring consistency is manifested in the research of the past twenty years. Schizophrenic patients with certain kinds of backgrounds and symptom pictures tend to improve, while those with other backgrounds and symptom pictures tend not to improve. The prognostic studies of Hunt and Appel,[5] Langfeldt,[9] Kant,[6] Kantor, Wallner, and Winder,[7] Becker and McFarland,[3] Stotsky,[11] Benjamin,[4] and Wittman,[12-14] all have pointed to systematic differences in the personalities and case histories of remitting and nonremitting schizophrenics. These studies have led to a number of terms, all describing the same distinction: malignant-benign, chronic-acute, process-reactive. The significance of these studies lies in their highlighting of an important criterion variable, prognosis, and in their implications for gaining estimates of prognosis in a given case without having to wait five years to obtain follow-up data. The above mentioned work provides one with a means for scaling schizophrenic patients along a dimension from good to poor prognosis, and then permits one to use this dimension as one means for organizing heterogeneous schizophrenic populations for systematic research. Gerald King's recent paper[8] provides an example of this. Many previous studies on autonomic reactivity in schizophrenia have revealed inconsistent findings, but when autonomic reactivity is studied in relation to a prognostic dimension, clear-cut relationships do appear.

Before developing further the implications of a prognosis dimension or a dimension of severity of disorder, a brief discussion of an alternative interpretation of these same findings is needed. Some have suggested that the poor prognosis syndrome represents one kind of schizophrenia, organically based, while the good prognosis syndrome represents another kind of schizophrenia, psychologically based. The notion of two types is very appealing, because such an outcome would make everybody happy—both the physiogenic and psychogenic theorists. However, individual cases do not fall into two groups, but spread out in such a way that the process syndrome moves imperceptibly into the reactive syndrome.

Accepting for the moment the notion of a process-reactive continuum, the syndromes serving to identify the end-points of a dimension of severity, is there a further research lead to be found in the analysis of the descriptive elements defining this continuum? In a previous paper,[2] the writer has suggested that it might be profitable to consider this continuum as reflecting the level of organization reached by a given personality in its growth toward maturity. "Level of organization" is a difficult term to define precisely. It is concerned with changes in the content and structure of mental organization as the human organism develops toward maturity. A complete definition would encompass

From Wesley C. Becker, "The process-reactive distinction: A key to the problem of schizophrenia," *Journal of Nervous and Mental Disease,* vol. 129, pp. 442–443. ©1959 The Williams & Wilkins Co., Baltimore.

such factors as objectivity in perception, differentiation of needs, interests, and other aspects of personal motivation, and the degree of emotional control or adaptive functioning under stress. Lewin,[10] Baldwin,[1] and especially Werner[15] have all attempted to deal with this construct. Common to most attempts to conceptualize levels of personality is the general idea that "the development of biological forms is expressed in an increasing differentiation of parts and *increasing subordination,* or *hierarchization*" of the parts with respect to the whole.[15] This principle applies to phylogenesis as well as ontogenesis. It is appropriately applied to mental development. Werner uses such terms as syncretic-discrete, diffuse-articulated, rigid-flexible, and labile-stable in describing the progression from primitive functioning to higher levels of mental functioning.

While space does not permit an elaboration of details, there seems to be a marked parallel between the process-reactive distinction and Werner's description of levels of personality organization. At the process end of the continuum, the whole development is fixated, *for whatever reason,* at a primitive level; or it might also be that development has been very uneven and then regression has taken place easily and relatively completely. The process syndrome characterizes a person with a relative lack of personality differentiation. Interests are narrow and lack intensity. There is a rigidity of structure and a lack of internal direction. There is an inability to establish normal heterosexual relations and independence. The need for hospitalization arises when such a person is faced with the normal problems of adult living in our complex culture.

On the other hand, a person falling closer to the reactive end of the continuum seems to have reached a higher level of personality differentiation. The prepsy-chotic personality is relatively more normal. Interests are more varied and intense. Heterosexual relations are more likely to have been established, and personal motivation and direction is more apparent. More and greater environmental stresses are tolerated before a regressive break occurs. In addition, the vestiges of a higher level of development are still pronounced even in regression and provide the compensating strength to allow recovery when the stresses are removed. The struggle which is indicative of continued ego-function is apparent in the strong affective reactions characteristic of this end of the continuum.

This hypothesis relating the process-reactive continuum to levels of personality organization does not prejudge the etiological basis of schizophrenia, but it does provide a rational guide for further study of this severity dimension.

REFERENCES

1. Baldwin, A. L. *Behavior and development in childhood.* New York: Dryden, 1955.
2. Becker, W. C. A genetic approach to the interpretation and evaluation of the process-reactive distinction in schizophrenia. *Journal of Abnormal and Social Psychology,* **47,** 1956, 489-496.
3. Becker, W. C. & McFarland, R. L. A lobotomy prognosis scale. *Journal of Consulting Psychology,* 1955, **19,** 157-162.
4. Benjamin, J. D. A method for distinguishing and evaluating formal thinking disorders in schizophrenia. In Kasanin, J. S., (ed.), *Language and Thought in Schizophrenia.* Berkeley, University of California Press, 1946, pp. 66-71.
5. Hunt, R. C. & Appel, K. E. Prognosis in psychoses lying midway between schizophrenia and manic-depressive psychoses. *American Journal of Psychiatry,* 1936, **93,** 313-339.
6. Kant, O. Differential diagnosis of schizophrenia in the light of concepts of per-

sonality stratification. *American Journal of Psychiatry,* 1940, **97,** 342-357.

7. Kantor, R. E., Wallner, J. M., & Winder, C. L. Process and reactive schizophrenia. *Journal of Consulting Psychology,* 1953, **17,** 157-162.

8. King, G. F. Differential autonomic responsiveness in the process-reactive classifications of schizophrenia. *Journal of Abnormal and Social Psychology,* 1958, **56,** 160-164.

9. Langfeldt, G. Prognosis in schizophrenia and factors influencing course of disease: Catamnestic study, including individual reexaminations in 1936 with some considerations regarding diagnosis, pathogenesis and therapy. *Acta Psychiatrica et Neurologica,* 1937, Supplement 13, 1-228.

10. Lewin, K. *A dynamic theory of personality.* New York: McGraw-Hill, 1935.

11. Stotsky, B. A. A comparison of remitting and nonremitting schizophrenics on psychological tests. *Journal of Abnormal and Social Psychology,* 1952, **47,** 489-496.

12. Wittman, P. Scale for measuring prognosis in schizophrenic patients. *Elgin State Hospital Papers,* 1941, **4,** 20-33.

13. Wittman, P. Follow-up on Elgin prognosis scale results. *Illinois Psychiatric Journal,* 1944, **4,** 56-59.

14. Wittman, P. & Steinberg, D. L. Follow-up of objective evaluation. *Elgin State Hospital Papers,* 1944, **5,** 216-227.

15. Werner, H. *The comparative psychology of mental development.* (Rev. ed.) Chicago: Follet, 1948.

15.

Gregory Bateson, Don D. Jackson, Jay Haley, and John Weakland

DOUBLE-BIND HYPOTHESIS OF SCHIZOPHRENIA

Schizophrenia—its nature, etiology, and the kind of therapy to use for it—remains one of the most puzzling of the mental illnesses. The theory of schizophrenia presented here is based on communications analysis, and specifically on the Theory of Logical Types. From this theory and from observations of schizophrenic patients is derived a description, and the necessary conditions for, a situation called the "double bind"—a situation in which no matter what a person does, he "can't win." It is hypothesized that a person caught in the double bind may develop schizophrenic symptoms. How and why the double bind may arise in a family situation is discussed, together with illustrations from clinical and experimental data.

. . . We have now reached common agreement on the broad outlines of a communicational theory of the origin and nature of schizophrenia; this paper is a preliminary report on our continuing research.

THE BASE IN COMMUNICATIONS THEORY

Our approach is based on that part of communications theory which Russell has called the Theory of Logical Types.[12] The central thesis of this theory is that there is

From Gregory Bateson, Don D. Jackson, Jay Haley, and John Weakland, "Toward a theory of schizophrenia," *Behavioral Science,* 1956, vol. 1, pp. 251–258.

a discontinuity between a class and its members. The class cannot be a member of itself nor can one of the members *be* the class, since the term used for the class is of a *different level of abstraction*—a different Logical type—from terms used for members. Although in formal logic there is an attempt to maintain this discontinuity between a class and its members, we argue that in the psychology of real communications this discontinuity is continually and inevitably breached,[2] and that a priori we must expect a pathology to occur in the human organism when certain formal patterns of the breaching occur in the communication between mother and child. We shall argue that this pathology at its extreme will have symptoms whose formal characteristics would lead the pathology to be classified as a schizophrenia.

Illustrations of how human beings handle communication involving multiple Logical Types can be derived from the following fields:

1. *The Use of Various Communicational Modes in Human Communication.* Examples are play, non-play, fantasy, sacrament, metaphor, etc. Even among the lower mammals there appears to be an exchange of signals which identify certain meaningful behavior as "play," etc. These signals are evidently of higher Logical Type than the messages they classify. Among human beings this framing and labeling of messages and meaningful actions reaches considerable complexity, with the peculiarity that our vocabulary for such discrimination is still very poorly developed, and we rely preponderantly upon nonverbal media of posture, gesture, facial expression, intonation, and the context for the communication of these highly abstract, but vitally important, labels.

2. *Humor.* This seems to be a method of exploring the implicit themes in thought or in a relationship. The method of explo-

ration involves the use of messages which are characterized by a condensation of Logical Types or communicational modes. A discovery, for example, occurs when it suddenly becomes plain that a message was not only metaphoric but also more literal, or vice versa. That is to say, the explosive moment in humor is the moment when the labeling of the mode undergoes a dissolution and resynthesis. Commonly, the punch line compels a reevaluation of earlier signals which ascribed to certain messages a particular mode (e.g., literalness or fantasy). This has the peculiar effect of attributing *mode* to those signals which had previously the status of that higher Logical Type which classifies the modes.

3. *The Falsification of Mode-Identifying Signals.* Among human beings mode identifiers can be falsified, and we have the artificial laugh, the manipulative simulation of friendliness, the confidence trick, kidding, and the like. Similar falsifications have been recorded among mammals.[3,9] Among human beings we meet with a strange phenomenon—the unconscious falsification of these signals. This may occur within the self—the subject may conceal from himself his own real hostility under the guise of metaphoric play—or it may occur as an unconscious falsification of the subject's understanding of the other person's mode-identifying signals. He may mistake shyness for contempt, etc. Indeed most of the errors of self-reference fall under this head.

4. *Learning.* The simplest level of this phenomenon is exemplified by a situation in which a subject receives a message and acts appropriately on it: "I heard the clock strike and knew it was time for lunch. So I went to the table." In learning experiments the analogue of this sequence of events is observed by the experimenter and commonly treated as a single message

of a higher type. When the dog salivates between buzzer and meat powder, this sequence is accepted by the experimenter as a message indicating that "the dog has *learned* that buzzer means meat powder." But this is not the end of the hierarchy of types involved. The experimental subject may become more skilled in learning. He may *learn to learn,*[1,4,6] and it is not inconceivable that still higher orders of learning may occur in human beings.

5. *Multiple Levels of Learning and the Logical Typing of Signals.* These are two inseparable sets of phenomena—inseparable because the ability to handle the multiple types of signals is itself a *learned* skill and therefore a function of the multiple levels of learning.

According to our hypothesis, the term "ego function" (as this term is used when a schizophrenic is described as having "weak ego function") is precisely *the process of discriminating communicational modes either within the self or between the self and others.* The schizophrenic exhibits weakness in three areas of such function: (*a*) He has difficulty in assigning the correct communicational mode to the messages he receives from other persons. (*b*) He has difficulty in assigning the correct communicational mode to those messages which he himself utters or emits nonverbally. (*c*) He has difficulty in assigning the correct communicational mode to his own thoughts, sensations, and percepts.

At this point it is appropriate to compare what was said in the previous paragraph with von Domarus'[11] approach to the systematic description of schizophrenic utterance. He suggests that the messages (and thought) of the schizophrenic are deviant in syllogistic structure. In place of structures which derive from the syllogism, Barbara, the schizophrenic, according to this theory, uses structures which identify predicates. An example of such a distorted syllogism is:

> Men die.
> Grass dies.
> Men are grass.

But as we see it, von Domarus' formulation is only a more precise—and therefore valuable—way of saying that schizophrenic utterance is rich in metaphor. With that generalization we agree. But metaphor is an indispensable tool of thought and expression—a characteristic of all human communication, even of that of the scientist. The conceptual models of cybernetics and the energy theories of psychoanalysis are, after all, only labeled metaphors. The peculiarity of the schizophrenic is not that he uses metaphors, but that he uses *unlabeled* metaphors. He has special difficulty in handling signals of that class whose members assign Logical Types to other signals.

If our formal summary of the symptomatology is correct and if the schizophrenia of our hypothesis is essentially a result of family interaction, it should be possible to arrive a priori at a formal description of these sequences of experience which would induce such a symptomatology. What is known of learning theory combines with the evident fact that human beings use *context* as a guide for mode discrimination. Therefore, we must look not for some specific traumatic experience in the infantile etiology but rather for characteristic sequential patterns. The specificity for which we search is to be at an abstract or formal level. The sequences must have this characteristic: that from them the patient will acquire the mental habits which are exemplified in schizophrenic communication. That is to say, *he must live in a universe where the sequences of events are such that his unconventional communica-*

tional habits will be in some sense appropriate. The hypothesis which we offer is that sequences of this kind in the external experience of the patient are responsible for the inner conflicts of Logical Typing. For such unresolvable sequences of experiences, we use the term "double bind."

The Double Bind

The necessary ingredients for a double bind situation, as we see it, are:

1. *Two or More Persons.* Of these, we designate one, for purposes of our definition, as the "victim." We do not assume that the double bind is inflicted by the mother alone, but that it may be done either by mother alone or by some combination of mother, father, and/or siblings.

2. *Repeated Experience.* We assume that the double bind is a recurrent theme in the experience of the victim. Our hypothesis does not invoke a single traumatic experience, but such repeated experience that the double bind structure comes to be an habitual expectation.

3. *A Primary Negative Injunction.* This may have either of two forms: (*a*) "Do not do so and so, or I will punish you," or (*b*) "If you do not do so and so, I will punish you." Here we select a context of learning based on avoidance of punishment rather than a context of reward seeking. There is perhaps no formal reason for this selection. We assume that the punishment may be either the withdrawal of love or the expression of hate or anger—or most devastating—the kind of abandonment that results from the parent's expression of extreme helplessness.

4. *A Secondary Injunction Conflicting with the First at a More Abstract Level, and Like the First Enforced by Punishments or Signals Which Threaten Survival.* This secondary injunction is more difficult to describe than the primary for two reasons. First, the secondary injunction is commonly communicated to the child by nonverbal means. Posture, gesture, tone of voice, meaningful action, and the implications concealed in verbal comment may all be used to convey this more abstract message. Second, the secondary injunction may impinge upon any element of the primary prohibition. Verbalization of the secondary injunction may, therefore, include a wide variety of forms; for example: "Do not see this as punishment"; "Do not see me as the punishing agent"; "Do not submit to my prohibitions"; "Do not think of what you must not do"; "Do not question my love of which the primary prohibition is (or is not) an example"; and so on. Other examples become possible when the double bind is inflicted not by one individual but by two. For example, one parent may negate at a more abstract level the injunctions of the other.

5. *A Tertiary Negative Injunction Prohibiting the Victim from Escaping from the Field.* In a formal sense it is perhaps unnecessary to list this injunction as a separate item since the reinforcement at the other two levels involves a threat to survival, and if the double binds are imposed during infancy, escape is naturally impossible. However, it seems that in some cases the escape from the field is made impossible by certain devices which are not purely negative, e.g., capricious promises of love, and the like.

6. Finally, the complete set of ingredients is no longer necessary when the victim has learned to perceive his universe in double bind patterns. Almost any part of a double bind sequence may then be sufficient to precipitate panic or rage. The pattern of conflicting injunctions may even be taken over by hallucinatory voices.[10]

The Effect of the Double Bind

In the Eastern religion, Zen Buddhism, the goal is to achieve Enlightenment. The Zen Master attempts to bring about enlightenment in his pupil in various ways. One of the things he does is to hold a stick over the pupil's head and say fiercely, "If you say this stick is real, I will strike you with it. If you say this stick is not real, I will strike you with it. If you don't say anything, I will strike you with it." We feel that the schizophrenic finds himself continually in the same situation as the pupil, but he achieves something like disorientation rather than enlightenment. The Zen pupil might reach up and take the stick away from the Master—who might accept this response, but the schizophrenic has no such choice since with him there is no not caring about the relationship, and his mother's aims and awareness are not like the Master's.

We hypothesize that there will be a breakdown in any individual's ability to discriminate between Logical Types whenever a double bind situation occurs. The general characteristics of this situation are the following:

1. When the individual is involved in an intense relationship, that is, a relationship in which he feels it is vitally important that he discriminate accurately what sort of message is being communicated so that he may respond appropriately.

2. And, the individual is caught in a situation in which the other person in the relationship is expressing two orders of message and one of these denies the other.

3. And, the individual is unable to comment on the messages being expressed to correct his discrimination of what order of message to respond to, i.e., he cannot make a metacommunicative statement.

We have suggested that this is the sort of situation which occurs between the pre-schizophrenic and his mother, but it also occurs in normal relationships. When a person is caught in a double bind situation, he will respond defensively in a manner similar to the schizophrenic. An individual will take a metaphorical statement literally when he is in a situation where he must respond, where he is faced with contradictory messages, and when he is unable to comment on the contradictions. For example, one day an employee went home during office hours. A fellow employee called him at his home, and said lightly, "Well, how did you get *there?*" The employee replied, "By automobile." He responded literally because he was faced with a message which asked him what he was doing at home when he should have been at the office, but which denied that this question was being asked by the way it was phrased. (Since the speaker felt it wasn't really his business, he spoke metaphorically.) The relationship was intense enough so that the victim was in doubt how the information would be used, and he therefore responded literally. This is characteristic of anyone who feels "on the spot," as demonstrated by the careful literal replies of a witness on the stand in a court trial. The schizophrenic feels so terribly on the spot at all times that he habitually responds with a defensive insistence on the literal level when it is quite inappropriate, e.g., when someone is joking.

Schizophrenics also confuse the literal and metaphoric in their own utterance when they feel themselves caught in a double bind. For example, a patient may wish to criticize his therapist for being late for an appointment, but he may be unsure what sort of a message that act of being late was—particularly if the therapist has anticipated the patient's reaction and apologized for the event. The patient cannot say, "Why were you late? Is it because you don't want to see me today?" This would be an accusation, and so he shifts to a metaphorical statement. He may then say, "I knew a fellow once who missed a boat, his name was Sam and the boat almost sunk, . . . etc." Thus he develops a metaphorical story and the therapist may or may not discover in it a comment on his being late. The convenient thing about a metaphor is that it leaves it up to the therapist (or mother) to see an accusation in the statement if he chooses, or to ignore it if he chooses. Should the therapist accept the accusation in the metaphor, then the patient can accept the statement he has made about Sam as metaphorical. If the therapist points out that this doesn't sound like a true statement about Sam, as a way of avoiding the accusation in the story, the patient can argue that there really was a man named Sam. As an answer to the double bind situation, a shift to a metaphorical statement brings safety. However, it also prevents the patient from making the accusation he wants to make. But instead of getting over his accusation by indicating that this is a metaphor, the schizophrenic patient seems to try to get over the fact that it is a metaphor by making it more fantastic. If the therapist should ignore the accusation in the story about Sam, the schizophrenic may then tell a story about going to Mars in a rocket ship as a way of putting over his accusation. The indication that it is a metaphorical statement lies in the fantastic aspect of the metaphor, not in the signals which usually accompany metaphors to tell the listener that a metaphor is being used.

It is not only safer for the victim of a double bind to shift to a metaphorical order of message, but in an impossible situation it is better to shift and become somebody else, or shift and insist that he is somewhere else. Then the double bind cannot work on the victim, because it isn't

he and besides he is in a different place. In other words, the statements which show that a patient is disoriented can be interpreted as ways of defending himself against the situation he is in. The pathology enters when the victim himself either does not know that his responses are metaphorical or cannot say so. To recognize that he was speaking metaphorically he would need to be aware that he was defending himself and therefore was afraid of the other person. To him such an awareness would be an indictment of the other person and therefore provoke disaster.

If an individual has spent his life in the kind of double bind relationship described here, his way of relating to people after a psychotic break would have a systematic pattern. First, he would not share with normal people those signals which accompany messages to indicate what a person means. His metacommunicative system—the communications about communication—would have broken down, and he would not know what kind of message a message was. If a person said to him, "what would you like to do today?" he would be unable to judge accurately by the context or by the tone of voice or gesture whether he was being condemned for what he did yesterday, or being offered a sexual invitation, or just what was meant. Given this inability to judge accurately what a person really means and an excessive concern with what is really meant, an individual might defend himself by choosing one or more of several alternatives. He might, for example, assume that behind every statement there is a concealed meaning which is detrimental to his welfare. He would then be excessively concerned with hidden meanings and determined to demonstrate that he could not be deceived—as he had been all his life. If he chooses this alternative, he will be continually searching for meanings behind what people say and behind chance occurrences in the environment, and he will be characteristically suspicious and defiant.

He might choose another alternative, and tend to accept literally everything people say to him; when their tone or gesture or context contradicted what they said, he might establish a pattern of laughing off these metacommunicative signals. He would give up trying to discriminate between levels of message and treat all messages as unimportant or to be laughed at.

If he didn't become suspicious of metacommunicative messages or attempt to laugh them off, he might choose to try to ignore them. Then he would find it necessary to see and hear less and less of what went on around him, and do his utmost to avoid provoking a response in his environment. He would try to detach his interest from the external world and concentrate on his own internal processes and, therefore, give the appearance of being a withdrawn, perhaps mute, individual.

This is another way of saying that if an individual doesn't know what sort of message a message is, he may defend himself in ways which have been described as paranoid, hebephrenic, or catatonic. These three alternatives are not the only ones. The point is that he cannot choose the one alternative which would help him to discover what people mean; he cannot, without considerable help, discuss the messages of others. Without being able to do that, the human being is like any self-correcting system which has lost its governor; it spirals into never-ending, but always systematic, distortions.

A DESCRIPTION OF THE FAMILY SITUATION

The theoretical possibility of double bind situations stimulated us to look for such communicative sequences in the schizophrenic patient and in his family situation. Toward this end we have studied the written and verbal reports of psychotherapists who have treated such patients intensively; we have studied tape recordings of psychotherapeutic interviews, both of our own patients and others; we have interviewed and taped parents of schizophrenics; we have had two mothers and one father participate in intensive psychotherapy; and we have interviewed and taped parents and patients seen conjointly.

On the basis of these data we have developed a hypothesis about the family situation which ultimately leads to an individual suffering from schizophrenia. This hypothesis has not been statistically tested; it selects and emphasizes a rather simple set of interactional phenomena and does not attempt to describe comprehensively the extraordinary complexity of a family relationship.

We hypothesize that the family situation of the schizophrenic has the following general characteristics:

1. A child whose mother becomes anxious and withdraws if the child responds to her as a loving mother. That is, the child's very existence has a special meaning to the mother which arouses her anxiety and hostility when she is in danger of intimate contact with the child.

2. A mother to whom feelings of anxiety and hostility toward the child are not acceptable, and whose way of denying them is to express overt loving behavior to persuade the child to respond to her as a loving mother and to withdraw from him if he does not. "Loving behavior" does not necessarily imply "affection"; it can, for example, be set in a framework of doing the proper thing, instilling "goodness," and the like.

3. The absence of anyone in the family, such as a strong and insightful father, who

can intervene in the relationship between the mother and child and support the child in the face of the contradictions involved.

Since this is a formal description we are not specifically concerned with why the mother feels this way about the child, but we suggest that she could feel this way for various reasons. It may be that merely having a child arouses anxiety about herself and her relationships to her own family; or it may be important to her that the child is a boy or a girl, or that the child was born on the anniversary of one of her own siblings,[5] or the child may be in the same sibling position in the family that she was, or the child may be special to her for other reasons related to her own emotional problems.

Given a situation with these characteristics, we hypothesize that the mother of a schizophrenic will be simultaneously expressing at least two orders of message. (For simplicity in this presentation we shall confine ourselves to two orders.) These orders of message can be roughly characterized as (*a*) hostile or withdrawing behavior which is aroused whenever the child approaches her, and (*b*) simulated loving or approaching behavior which is aroused when the child responds to her hostile and withdrawing behavior, as a way of denying that she is withdrawing. Her problem is to control her anxiety by controlling the closeness and distance between herself and her child. To put this another way, if the mother begins to feel affectionate and close to her child, she begins to feel endangered and must withdraw from him; but she cannot accept this hostile act and to deny it must simulate affection and closeness with her child. The important point is that her loving behavior is then a comment on (since it is compensatory for) her hostile behavior and consequently it is of a different *order* of message than the hostile behavior—it is a message about a sequence of messages. Yet by its nature it denies the existence of those messages which it is about, i.e., the hostile withdrawal.

The mother uses the child's responses to affirm that her behavior is loving, and since the loving behavior is simulated, the child is placed in a position where he must not accurately interpret her communication if he is to maintain his relationship with her. In other words, he must not discriminate accurately between orders of message, in this case the difference between the expression of simulated feelings (one Logical Type) and real feelings (another Logical Type). As a result the child must systematically distort his perception of metacommunicative signals. For example, if mother begins to feel hostile (or affectionate) toward her child and also feels compelled to withdraw from him, she might say, "Go to bed, you're very tired and I want you to get your sleep." This overtly loving statement is intended to deny a feeling which could be verbalized as "Get out of my sight because I'm sick of you." If the child correctly discriminates her metacommunicative signals, he would have to face the fact that she both doesn't want him and is deceiving him by her loving behavior. He would be "punished" for learning to discriminate orders of messages accurately. He therefore would tend to accept the idea that he is tired rather than recognize his mother's deception. This means that he must deceive himself about his own internal state in order to support mother in her deception. To survive with her he must falsely discriminate his own internal messages as well as falsely discriminate the messages of others.

The problem is compounded for the child because the mother is "benevolently" defining for him how he feels; she is expressing overt maternal concern over the fact that he is tired. To put it another way, the mother is controlling the child's definitions of his own messages, as well as the definition of his responses to her (e.g., by saying, "You don't really mean to say that," if he should criticize her) by insisting that she is not concerned about herself but only about him. Consequently, the easiest path for the child is to accept mother's simulated loving behavior as real, and his desires to interpret what is going on are undermined. Yet the result is that the mother is withdrawing from him and defining this withdrawal as the way a loving relationship should be.

However, accepting mother's simulated loving behavior as real also is no solution for the child. Should he make this false discrimination, he would approach her; this move toward closeness would provoke in her feelings of fear and helplessness, and she would be compelled to withdraw. But if he then withdrew from her, she would take his withdrawal as a statement that she was not a loving mother and would either punish him for withdrawing or approach him to bring him closer. If he then approached, she would respond by putting him at a distance. *The child is punished for discriminating accurately what she is expressing, and he is punished for discriminating inaccurately—he is caught in a double bind.*

The child might try various means of escaping from this situation. He might, for example, try to lean on his father or some other member of the family. However, from our preliminary observations we think it is likely that the fathers of schizophrenics are not substantial enough to lean on. They are also in the awkward position where if they agreed with the child about the nature of mother's deceptions, they would need to recognize the nature of their own relationships to the mother,

which they could not do and remain attached to her in the *modus operandi* they have worked out.

The need of the mother to be wanted and loved also prevents the child from gaining support from some other person in the environment, a teacher, for example. A mother with these characteristics would feel threatened by any other attachment of the child and would break it up and bring the child back closer to her with consequent anxiety when the child became dependent on her.

The only way the child can really escape from the situation is to comment on the contradictory position his mother has put him in. However, if he did so, the mother would take this as an accusation that she is unloving and both punish him and insist that his perception of the situation is distorted. By preventing the child from talking about the situation, the mother forbids him using the metacommunicative level—the level we use to correct our perception of communicative behavior. The ability to communicate about communication, to comment upon the meaningful actions of oneself and others, is essential for successful social intercourse. In any normal relationship there is a constant interchange of metacommunicative messages such as "What do you mean?" or "Why did you do that?" or "Are you kidding me?" and so on. To discriminate accurately what people are really expressing we must be able to comment directly or indirectly on that expression. This metacommunicative level the schizophrenic seems unable to use successfully.[2] Given these characteristics of the mother, it is apparent why. If she is denying one order of message, then any statement about her statements endangers her and she must forbid it. Therefore, the child grows up unskilled in his ability to communicate about communication and, as a result, unskilled in determining what people really mean and unskilled in expressing what he really means, which is essential for normal relations.

In summary, then, we suggest that the double bind nature of the family situation of a schizophrenic results in placing the child in a position where if he responds to his mother's simulated affection her anxiety will be aroused and she will punish him (or insist, to protect herself, that *his* overtures are simulated, thus confusing him about the nature of his own messages) to defend herself from closeness with him. Thus the child is blocked off from intimate and secure associations with his mother. However, if he does not make overtures of affection, she will feel that this means she is not a loving mother and her anxiety will be aroused. Therefore, she will either punish him for withdrawing or make overtures toward the child to insist that he demonstrate that he loves her. If he then responds and shows her affection, she will not only feel endangered again, but she may resent the fact that she had to force him to respond. In either case in a relationship, the most important in his life and the model for all others, he is punished if he indicates love and affection and punished if he does not; and his escape routes from the situation, such as gaining support from others, are cut off. This is the basic nature of the double bind relationship between mother and child. This description has not depicted, of course, the more complicated interlocking gestalt that is the "family" of which the "mother" is one important part.[7,8]

REFERENCES

1. Bateson, G. Social planning and the concept of "deutero-learning." *Conference on Science, Philosophy, and Religion, Second Symposium.* New York: Harper, 1942.
2. Bateson, G. A theory of play and fantasy. *Psychiatric Research Reports,* 1955, **2,** 39-51.
3. Carpenter, C. R. A field study of the behavior and social relations of howling monkeys. *Comparative Psychological Monographs,* 1934, **10,** 1-168.
4. Harlow, H. F. The formation of learning sets. *Psychological Review,* 1949, **56,** 51-65.
5. Hilgard, J. R. Anniversary reactions in parents precipitated by children. *Psychiatry,* 1953, **16,** 73-80.
6. Hull, C. L., *et al. Mathematico-deductive theory of rote learning.* New Haven: Yale University Press, 1940.
7. Jackson, D. D. Some factors influencing the Oedipus complex. *Psychoanalytic Quarterly,* 1954, **23,** 566-581.
8. Jackson, D. D. The question of family homeostasis. Presented at the American Psychiatric Association Meeting, St. Louis, May 7, 1954.
9. Lorenz, K. Z. *King Solomon's ring.* New York: Crowell, 1952.
10. Perceval, J. *A narrative of the treatment experienced by a gentleman during a state of mental derangement, designed to explain the causes and nature of insanity, etc.* London: Effingham Wilson, 1836 and 1840.
11. von Domarus, E. The specific laws of logic in schizophrenia. In J. S. Kasanin (Ed.), *Language and thought in schizophrenia.* Berkeley: University of California Press, 1944.
12. Whitehead, A. N., & Russell, B. *Principia mathematica.* Cambridge: Cambridge University Press, 1910.

16.

R. D. Laing

PHENOMENOLOGICAL APPROACH TO SCHIZOPHRENIA

Jones: (*Laughs loudly, then pauses.*) I'm McDougal, myself. [This actually is not his name.]

Smith: What do you do for a living, little fellow? Work on a ranch or something?

Jones: No, I'm a civilian seaman. Supposed to be high mucka-muck society.

Smith: A singing recording machine, huh? I guess a recording machine sings sometimes. If they're adjusted right. Mm-hm. I thought that was it. My towel, mm-hm. We'll be going back to sea in about—eight or nine months though. Soon as we get our—destroyed parts repaired. (*Pause.*)

Jones: I've got lovesickness, secret love.

Smith: Secret love, huh? (*Laughs.*)

Jones: Yeah.

Smith: I ain't got any secret love.

Jones: I fell in love, but I don't feed any woo— that sits over—looks something like me —walking around over there.

Smith: My, oh, my only one, my only love is the shark. Keep out of the way of him.

Jones: Don't they know I have a life to live? (*Long pause.*)

Smith: Do you work at the air base? Hm?

Jones: You know what I think of work, I'm 33 in June, do you mind?

Smith: June?

Jones: Thirty-three years old in June. This stuff goes out the window after I live this, uh —leave this hospital. So I lay off cigarettes. I'm a spatial condition, from outer space myself, no shit.

Smith: (*Laughs.*) I'm a real space ship from across.

Jones: A lot of people talk, uh—that way, like crazy, but Believe It or Not by Ripley,

take it or leave it—alone—it's in the *Examiner*, it's in the comic section. Believe It or Not by Ripley, Robert E. Ripley. Believe It or Not, but we don't have to believe anything, unless I feel like it. (*Pause.*) Every little rosette—too much alone. (*Pause.*)

Smith: Yeah, it could be possible. (*Phrase inaudible because of airplane noise.*)

Jones: I'm a civilian seaman.

Smith: Could be possible. (*Sighs.*) I take my bath in the ocean.

Jones: Bathing stinks. You know why? 'Cause you can't quit when you feel like it. You're in the service.

Smith: I can quit whenever I feel like quitting. I can get out when I feel like getting out.

Jones: (*Talking at the same time.*) Take me, I'm a civilian, I can quit.

Smith: Civilian?

Jones: Go my—my way.

Smith: I guess we have, in port, civilian. (*Long pause.*)

Jones: What do they want with us?

Smith: Hm?

Jones: What do they want with you and me?

Smith: What do they want with you and me? How do I know what they want with you? I know what they want with me. I broke the law, so I have to pay for it. (Silence.) (Haley, J.: *Strategies of Psychotherapy.* New York: Grune & Stratton, 1963, pp. 99-100.)

This is not a conversation from a Pinter play, it is a conversation between two persons diagnosed as schizophrenic. What does this diagnosis mean?

In this article I wish to call in question the prevailing attitude in respect to schizophrenia, and to suggest an alternative point of view. Before I shall be able to put forward the alternative point of view, however, I shall have to examine some of our

From R. D. Laing, "Is schizophrenia a disease?" *International Journal of Social Psychiatry*, 1964, *10*, 184-193. A version of this paper is found in R. D. Laing, *The politics of experience*, Chap. 5, The schizophrenic experience. New York: Ballantine Books; and Pantheon Books, 1967. Reprinted by permission of The Avenue Publishing Co., London.

prevailing attitudes about normality and sanity, since the concept of schizophrenia as a form of madness implies a concept of sanity as the norm against which madness is judged.

PRESENT POSITION

Some people come to behave and to experience themselves and others in ways that are strange and incomprehensible to most people, including themselves.

If this behaviour and experience fall into certain broad categories, they will be likely to be diagnosed as subject to a condition called schizophrenia. By present calculations almost one in every hundred children born will fall into this category at some time or other before the age of forty-five, and in this country at the moment there are roughly 60,000 men and women in mental hospitals, and many more outside hospital, who are termed schizophrenic.

The most commonly held view among psychiatrists is that these persons suffer from some inherited predisposition to experience and to act in a predominantly meaningless way, and that an unknown genetic defect acts in some as yet undetermined biochemical-endocrinological-organic manner to produce a change. What we, the others, observe are the signs of this underlying process.

Psychiatrists have struggled for years to discover what those people who are diagnosed as schizophrenic have or have not in common with each other. The results are so far inconclusive.

No generally agreed objective clinical criteria for the diagnosis of "schizophrenia" have been discovered.

No consistency in pre-psychotic personality, course, duration, outcome, has been discovered.

Every conceivable view is held by authoritative people as to whether "schizophrenia" is a disease or a group of diseases; whether an identifiable organic pathology has been, or can be expected to be, found.

There are no pathological anatomical findings *post mortem*. There are no organic structural changes noted in course of the "illness." There are no physiological-pathological changes that can be correlated with these illnesses. There is no general acceptance that any form of treatment is of proven value, except perhaps sustained careful interpersonal relations and tranquillization. "Schizophrenia" runs in families, but observes no genetically clear law. It appears usually to have no adverse effect on physical health, and, given proper care by others, it does not cause death or foreshorten life. It occurs in every constitutional type. It is not associated with any known other physical malfunctions.

It is most important to recognize that the diagnosed patient is not suffering from a disease whose aetiology is unknown, unless he can prove otherwise. The American psychiatrist Thomas Szasz develops this argument to considerable effect in his book *The Myth of Mental Illness*. The schizophrenic is someone who has queer experiences and/or is acting in a queer way, from the point of view usually of his relatives and of ourselves. Whether these queer experiences and actions are constantly associated with changes in his body is still uncertain, although it is highly likely that relatively enduring biochemical changes may be the consequence of relatively enduring interpersonal situations of particular kinds.

That the diagnosed patient is suffering from a pathological process is either a fact, an hypothesis, an assumption or a judgment.

To regard it as fact is unequivocally

false. To regard it as an hypothesis is legitimate. It is unnecessary either to make the assumption or to pass the judgment.

Now, the psychiatrist adopting his clinical stance in the presence of the pre-diagnosed person, whom he is already looking at and listening to as a patient, has too often come to believe that he is in the presence of the "fact" of "schizophrenia." He acts "as if" its existence were an established fact. He then has to discover its "cause" or multiple "aetiological factors," to assess its "prognosis" and to treat its course. The heart of the "illness," all that is the outcome of process, then resides outside the agency of the person. That is, the illness, or process, is taken to be a "fact" that the person is subject to or undergoes, whether it is supposed to be genetic, constitutional, endogenous, exogenous, organic or psychological, or some mixture of them all. This, we submit, is a mistaken starting-point.

The judgment that the diagnosed patient is behaving in a biologically dysfunctional (hence pathological) way is, I believe, premature, and one that I shall hold in parenthesis.

There have been many studies of social factors in relation to schizophrenia. These include attempts to discover whether schizophrenia occurs more or less frequently in one or another ethnic group, social class, sex, ordinal position in the family, and so on. The general conclusion from all such studies has been that social factors do not play a significant role in the genesis of schizophrenia.

However, such studies do not get close enough to the relevant situation, besides posing the problem as though "schizophrenia" existed as some condition like pneumonia. If the police wish to determine whether a man has died of natural causes or has committed suicide or been murdered, they do not look up prevalence or incidence figures. They investigate the circumstances attendant upon each single case in turn. Each investigation is an original and unrepeatable research project, and it comes to an end when enough evidence has been gathered to answer the relevant questions.

My colleagues and I have been engaged in studying the actual circumstances around the social event when one person comes to become regarded as schizophrenic. We have studied over fifty cases, and without exception it seems to us that the experience and behaviour that gets labelled schizophrenic is a special sort of strategy that a person invents in order to live in an unlivable situation. In his life situation the person has come to be placed in an untenable position. He cannot make a move or make no move, without being beset by contradictory pressures both internally, from himself, and externally, from those around him. He is, as it were, in a position of checkmate. I must make it clear that this state of affairs may not be perceived as such by any of the people in it. The man at the bottom of the heap may be crushed and suffocated to death without anyone noticing, much less intending it. The situation in and around the schizophrenic is often impossible to see by studying the different people in it singly, as has always been done. Recently, however, different research groups in America have found ways of overcoming the great methodological difficulties in work of this kind, and their conclusions and our own are in substantial agreement.

Now, the diagnosis as such of schizophrenia is simply a social event. But among the heterogeneous motley of persons diagnosed, there are many who have found themselves, or rather have lost themselves, in regions of the inner world, into which they have been precipitated for reasons they do not know, and in realms of frightening or strange experience are temporarily unable to function competently at the same time in the shared so-called external world.

When a person finds himself in a total impasse, if he does not commit suicide, Nature sometimes calls upon a healing process that has been available to mankind at all times and in all places. No age, however, has so lost touch with this process as has our own. I refer to the ceremonies of initiation practised all over the world until very recently, when a person was conducted through an experience of (i) death; of (ii) journeying in the Other World; of (iii) rebirth from that Place and that Time back into this world with its here and now.

Schizophrenia is a confused attempt to conduct such a sequence. It is hardly surprising that the person in his terror may stand in curious postures to control the spirits that occupy him (counterparts to which are the Yoga positions), that he projects the inner onto the outer, and the outer onto the inner, that he tries in short to protect himself from destruction by every means that he has, by projection, splitting, denial and so on.

The anthropologist Gregory Bateson, in a brilliant introduction to a nineteenth-century autobiographical account of schizophrenia, has said this:

It would appear that once precipitated into psychosis the patient has a course to run. He is, as it were, embarked upon a voyage of discovery which is only completed by his return to the normal world, to which he comes back with insights different from those of the inhabitants who never embarked on such a voyage. Once begun, a schizophrenic episode would appear to have as definite a course as an initiation ceremony—a death and rebirth—into which the novice may have been precipitated by his family life or by adventitious circumstances, but which in its course is largely steered by endogenous process.

In terms of this picture, spontaneous remission is no problem. This is only the final and natural outcome of the total process. What needs to be explained is the failure of many who embark upon this voyage to return from it. *Do these encounter circumstances either in family life or in institutional care so grossly maladaptive that even the richest and best organized hallucinatory experience cannot save them?* (Bateson, G. (ed.). *Perceval's Narrative. A Patient's Account of His Psychosis.* Stanford, Calif.: Stanford University Press, 1961, pp. xiii-xiv; italics mine.)

I am in substantial agreement with this view.

THE CASE FOR A SHIFT OF POINT OF VIEW

To regard the conversational gambits of Smith and Jones (at the beginning of this article) as indicative of some incapacity or defect in thinking, is like saying that a man doing a hand-stand on a bicycle on a tight-rope a hundred feet up with no safety net is suffering from an inability to stand on his own two feet. We may well ask why these people have to be so brilliantly devious, elusive and incongruous, such adepts at making themselves so slickly and unremittingly incomprehensible.

Actually, records of such conversations between schizophrenics do not exist in psychiatric textbooks. The diagnosis of schizophrenia has always been made, and still is, on the basis of the person's behaviour during what is called a clinical examination.

It is only recently that the relationships between patients themselves have been studied without presuppositions. The best such study has been made by an American sociologist, Erving Goffman.

Goffman spent a year as an assistant physical therapist in a large mental hospital of some 7,000 beds, near Washington. His lowly staff status enabled him to fraternize with the patients in a way that upper echelons of the staff, notably psychiatrists, were unable to do. One of his conclusions is:

There is an old saw that no clear-cut line can be drawn between normal people and mental patients; rather there is a continuum with the well-adjusted citizen at one end and the full-fledged psychotic at the other. I must argue that after a period of acclimatization in a mental hospital the notion of a continuum seems very presumptuous. A community is a community. Just as it is bizarre to those not in it, so it is natural, even if unwanted, to those who live it from within. The system of dealings that patients have with one another does not fall at one end of anything, but rather provides one example of human association, to be avoided, no doubt, but also to be filed by the student in a circular cabinet along with all the other examples of association that he can collect. (Goffman, E.: *Asylums. Essays on the Social Situation of Mental Patients and Other Inmates.* New York: Doubleday-Anchor Books, 1961, p. 303.)

A large part of his study is devoted to a detailed documentation of how it comes about that persons can become defined as non-agents, non-responsible, non-blameable essences, be treated accordingly, and even come to regard themselves in this light.

The psychiatrist and patient is one of those fascinating couples that history throws up from time to time: guru-disciple, inquisitor-heretic, priest-confessor. The one person in the set of reciprocals that characterize their relationship is meaningless extrapolated from the context. They fit together like lock and key. Each indeed is the key to understanding the other.

A feature of the psychiatrist-patient reciprocals is that if the patient's reciprocals are extrapolated, as is the tactic in the clinical description, they can be plausibly represented as very odd, whereas the psychiatrist's responses are seen as congruent with our common-sense view of normality.

In other words, the psychiatrist seems to us in varying degrees sane, and the patient in varying degrees mad. This is because the psychiatrist's behaviour is assumed axiomatically to be the yardstick against which the abnormality of the patient is scaled.

But if one puts the clinical stance and perspective in brackets, and looks at the psychiatrist-patient couple as far as possible without presuppositions, then one may find it difficult to sustain this naive polarization of the situation.

Consider, for instance, the following interaction between Kraepelin, regarded by many as one of the great psychiatrists, and a patient (given in his words):

Gentlemen, the cases that I have to place before you today are peculiar. First of all, you see a servant-girl, aged twenty-four, upon whose features and frame traces of great emaciation can be plainly seen. In spite of this, the patient is in continual movement, going a few steps forward, and then back again; she plaits her hair, only to unloose it the next minute. *On attempting to stop her movement,* we meet with unexpectedly strong resistance; *if I place myself in front of her with my arms spread out* in order to stop her, if she cannot push me on one side, she suddenly turns and slips through under my arms, so as to continue her way. If *one takes firm hold of her,* she distorts her usually rigid, expressionless features with deplorable weeping, that only ceases so soon as one lets her have her own way. We notice besides that she holds a crushed piece of bread spasmodically clasped in the fingers of the left hand, which she absolutely *will not allow to be forced from her.* The patient does not trouble in the least about her surroundings so long as you leave her alone. If *you prick her in the forehead with a needle,* she scarcely winces or turns away, and leaves the needle quietly sticking there without letting it disturb her restless, beast-of-prey-like wandering backwards and forwards. *To questions* she answers almost nothing, at the most shaking her head. But from time to time she wails: 'O dear God! O dear God! O dear mother! O dear mother!' always repeating uniformly the same phrases. If *you try to grasp her hand* she draws it away very suddenly, and at last, if she can no longer avoid you, begins to roll it up in her apron. *Orders are of no use:* on the contrary, she resists in everything you try to do with her. But when she quickly hides her hand directly *one speaks of taking away the bread,* it becomes evident that she understands what is happening around her. (Kraepelin, E.: *Lectures on Clinical Psychiatry* (Johnstone, T., ed.). London: Baillière, Tindall & Cox, 1906, pp. 30-31; italics mine.)

Here is a man and a young girl. Because we have the fixed idea that this is a doctor examining a patient, it all immediately falls into place. He is sane, she is insane: he is rational, she is irrational. But if we take Kraepelin's actions (I have italicized them: he tries to stop her movements, stands in front of her with arms outspread, tries to force a piece of bread out of her hand, sticks a needle in her forehead, and so on) out of the context of the situation *as experienced and defined by him,* how extraordinary they are!

In studying the issues raised by "schizophrenia," we have to include experience as well as behaviour in our domain of relevance. The behaviour of the person diagnosed as schizophrenic is different because his experience is different. But we absolutely must not suppose that there is something sacrosanct about modern sane experience. Here there are certain matters of principle that we must bear in mind.

In the first place, we all experience far fewer things than the total possible spectrum of experience. There are certain types of experience that many people are not aware of at all, and there are some that are regarded with fear and mistrust. The ordinary person is almost totally amnesic for the first five years of life, and many people remember very few dreams, and then only scrappily. Compared to the Yogi, the ordinary man has only a vestigial experience of his body. Many people are unaware of experiences in the modality of what psychoanalysts call fantasy (to be distinguished

sharply from imagination), and even more, experiences that have been common among Western men and women until very recently (demons). Experiences of telepathy, clairvoyance, the impression of a life of some kind between death and birth, reincarnation, are perhaps more common than is often supposed.

If this is the case, it means that while evidence must be drawn from the realm of one's own and the other person's experience, not only from observation of behaviour, unfortunately, we cannot use our own adult experience of ourselves as an instrument of unqualified validity for such an inquiry. On the contrary, in becoming aware of ourselves and others as persons, we come to realize that we have to begin from a position wherein we are largely alienated from experience.

If we naïvely regard our norm of sanity as the measure of insanity, then we are led to precisely the point of view that is currently held about schizophrenia. But if we see our sanity as already a state of extreme alienation, then we will be less ready to suppose that the schizophrenic is more alienated than we are from the totality of reality.

Putting one of the essential realizations from the practice of psychotherapy in a non-technical idiom, we can say that by the time each of us is fifteen we are all likely to be to a large extent strangers to ourselves (to our childhoods, our minds, our bodies), and strangers to one another.

While not rejecting any human form of experience in so far as it is a phenomenon, that is, in so far as it makes its appearance to someone, whether this is a dream, a perception, an image, a vision, one must also place in parentheses any judgment as to the validity of this experience.

Psychiatrists have paid very little attention to the *experience* of the patient from the patient's point of view, tending to regard this as not the hard stuff of science. One might have hoped that psychoanalysis would step in here. But there is an abiding tendency in psychoanalysis to suppose that the schizophrenic's experiences are somehow unreal or invalid; one can make sense out of them only by interpreting them; without truth-giving interpretations the patient is enmeshed in a world of delusion and self-deception. Kaplan, an American psychologist, in an introduction to an excellent collection of self-reports on the experience of being psychotic, says very justly:

> With all virtue on his side, he [the psychiatrist or psychoanalyst] reaches through the subterfuges and distortions of the patient and exposes them to the light of reason and insight. In this encounter between the psychiatrist and patient, the efforts of the former are linked with science and medicine, with understanding and care. What the patient experiences is tied to illness and irreality, to perverseness and distortion. The process of psychotherapy consists in large part of the patient's abandoning his false subjective perspectives for the therapist's objective ones. But the essence of this conception is that the psychiatrist understands what is going on, and the patient does not. (*The Inner World of Mental Illness*. New York: Harper & Row, 1964.)

H. S. Sullivan used to say to young psychiatrists when they came to work with him, "I want you to remember that in the present state of our society, the patient is right, and you are wrong." This is an outrageous over-simplification. I mention it to loosen any fixed ideas that are no less outrageous, that we are right, and *they* are wrong. I think it is a sober estimate, however, that schizophrenics have had more to teach psychiatrists about the inner world than psychiatrists their patients.

It is necessary to admit all domains of experience into our context of relevance if we are going to understand schizophrenia.

Since natural science studies only the relation between things, we are thus in a context of relevance half outside and half inside the range of natural scientific investigation, but always within the legitimate domain of social science. We have to realize the phenomenal existence of an "inner" world, that goes beyond the realm of imagination, reveries, dreams and personal unconscious fantasy (which is already beyond what most people are aware of, and which itself frequently requires several years of psychoanalysis before a person becomes familiar with this domain). I still can think of no better word for this experiential domain that lies "beyond" the usual level of perception, thinking, imagination, dreams, fantasy, than the spiritual world— or the domain of spirits, Powers, Thrones, Principalities, Seraphim, Cherubim, the Light.

It is necessary to admit such experiences to our context of relevance because it frequently is into these reaches of experience that the schizophrenic may enter, without guide or guideline.

THERAPY

It is important to note that an increasing number of psychiatrists are becoming aware of the contradiction in fitting what is essentially a human drama intrinsically implicating a number of protagonists, into clinical terms designed to fit what goes on inside the skin of one body. It must be emphasized, moreover, that a number of very serious organic conditions, e.g. forms of epilepsy, brain tumour, may easily be mistaken for schizophrenia. Before anyone is regarded as a schizophrenic, that is, suffering from no known organic process in the present state of our knowledge, he should have been competently examined to exclude any discernible organic illness.

Once this has been excluded, therapy is another matter.

The following are a few necessarily telegrammatic remarks on therapy.

(1) A bare minimum is care and respect for the whole person. In the acute breakdown "he" or "she" is only partially in this world. Although his body is all here, "he" may be all "there." While the patient is *in absentia,* he should be treated with full human dignity.

(2) Occasionally another patient, or member of the staff, may have some understanding of the internal drama that is going on.

The psychiatrist should realize that nothing in his training as a doctor or psychiatrist gives him any special claim to understand this process. He may, however, be humble and gifted enough to sense when someone else does; and very rarely he may have an understanding of what is involved himself. The patient badly needs guidance, but he is much better not given any advice or "interpretations" made with no genuine authority.

The priest traditionally ought to know this realm, but he has almost totally lost direct experiential contact with that domain from which his own beliefs and liturgy emanate, and in which the schizophrenic is travelling, in a realm in which no one speaks his language.

(3) If the person is wearing out himself or his nurses beyond the limits of his or their stamina, then for his sake or theirs, tranquilization is indicated.

If he is subject to enthusiastic attempts to "cure" him by means of electricity, and by cutting off bits of his brain, it is quite likely that he will be cut off from his connection with heaven or hell and function once more comparatively well in this world.

(4) Preparation for the person's return to his family and community requires work with his family and other social networks before he leaves hospital, as well as thereafter. Continuity of care is required, without the existing tendency to separate, economically and organizationally, the "cure" of the "illness" from the "care of the person."

Today, most people sent to hospital as "schizophrenics" for the first time are out again in six months, but most of these are back again in another year. The discharge rate is encouraging and the relapse rate is unnecessary.

Admirable Half-way Homes, ex-patients' clubs and flexible day or night hospitals are beginning to be set up.

An increasing number of doctors, nurses and patients now feel that what is required for the treatment of the acute breakdown is a small Centre (with not more than twenty-four patients) that will be neither a mental hospital nor a psychiatric unit in a general hospital; where treatment will consist of the experience of community in a tranquil human setting, and where there will be people who have themselves been in and out of the world that the schizophrenic enters in terror, lost and confused. More people than are at present given a chance to be social therapists, possess patience, understanding, responsibility, stamina, and sometimes the capacity to act as guides.

Easy is the descent to Avernus; everyone agrees that it is the way back that is difficult.

When patients become integrated they would be able to work from the Centre. There would be no pressure on people to leave. One would keep in close touch with those patients who had left, and they would be free to return if they felt the need. Just as there would be no upper limit to the length of time a patient might stay, there would be no lower limit. Patients would be able to come and go, staying only a night or a few days at a time, as their situation dictated. One would also wish to provide an Emergency Home Visiting Service, to deal with family crises, and family treatment sessions would be held for those patients who were not resident. Such a Centre could pioneer new approaches to schizophrenia and to psychiatric theory and practice generally.

Schizophrenia used to be a new name for dementia praecox—a slow, insidious illness that was supposed to overtake young people in particular, and to be liable to go on to a terminable dementia.

Perhaps we can still retain the now old name, and read into it its original meaning: *Schiz*—broken; *Phrenos*—soul or heart.

The schizophrenic is one who is brokenhearted. But even broken hearts can mend, if we have the heart to let them.

17.

Solomon H. Snyder et al.

BIOCHEMICAL THEORY OF SCHIZOPHRENIA: THE DOPAMINE HYPOTHESIS

In searching for biochemical correlates of schizophrenia, the first thing to be determined is whether schizophrenia is a distinct entity or simply a conglomeration of more or less distinctive illnesses. When there are no defined organic pathologic disturbances, the psychiatrist is forced to make diagnoses on the basis of fairly arbitrarily selected symptoms. Accordingly, it is not surprising that from country to country and culture to culture there are great disparities in the criteria for a diagnosis of schizophrenia. Since at least some forms of schizophrenia have powerful genetic determinants,[1] investigators have been able to discern particular symptoms or histories that correlate with apparent

From Solomon H. Snyder, Shailesh P. Banergee, Henry I. Yamamura, and David Greenberg, *Science*, vol. 184, 21 June 1974, pp. 1243–1253. Copyright 1974 by the American Association for the Advancement of Science.

genetic loading. In certain of these studies, it has been found that patients with an acute onset and good premorbid history and prognosis seem to lack a genetic "taint," while genetic factors play a prominent role for those whose disturbance begins more insidiously and progresses to profound deterioration. Whether one or several different forms of the disease are genetically determined is unclear.

For patients with "classic" schizophrenia, about whose diagnosis most psychiatrists would concur, certain psychological characteristics, defined by Bleuler[2] as the "fundamental" symptoms of schizophrenia, are fairly constant. These include a peculiar thought disorder; a disturbance of emotional, or affective, responses to the environment; and autism, a withdrawal from interactions with other people. Bleuler felt that hallucinations and delusions, which are certainly among the most dramatic manifestations of schizophrenia, are only secondary symptoms, since they are not constant or essential to the disease. The schizophrenic thought disorder, abnormal affect, and autism are difficult to define and even more difficult to identify reliably and reproducibly in patients. By contrast, secondary symptoms are relatively straightforward and have provided more reliable diagnostic techniques for schizophrenia.[3] Accordingly, many authors have questioned whether Bleuler's primary symptoms are indeed primary. Still, the notion of focusing upon particular behaviors as reflecting either primary or secondary symptoms of schizophrenia might be helpful in seeking biochemical correlates. For instance, if a particular drug regularly evokes hallucinations but no other symptoms of schizophrenia, we would question its value in explaining the pathophysiology of the disease.

While confusion about diagnosis has been a major stumbling block, one must invoke other explanations for the many false hopes and subsequent disappointments in biochemical studies of schizophrenia. Innumerable "discoveries" of the biochemical abnormality in one or another body fluid of schizophrenics have relentlessly been followed by failures of confirmation in other laboratories. Reported abnormalities in parameters as diverse as carbohydrate, protein, amino acid, and lipid metabolism have been advanced, only to be shown by more careful studies to derive from factors such as drug ingestion, diet, muscular activity, and the effects of chronic hospitalization. Besides these difficulties, the discouraging experiences may also stem from a strategy that is sometimes tantamount to searching for a needle in a haystack. Of the literally millions of chemical systems in the human body, why should nature have chosen to inflict the "schizophrenic abnormality" upon whatever spe-

cific chemical the experimentalist happens to be best equipped to measure?

A less direct, but perhaps more heuristic, approach might be to follow up leads suggested by known "biochemical" features of schizophrenia. One aspect of schizophrenia with definite biochemical ramifications is the response of patients to drugs. Drugs can be useful in two ways. Phenothiazine drugs are generally acknowledged to be highly efficacious in alleviating symptoms of schizophrenia. If the actions of these drugs derive from effects on whatever is fundamentally deranged in schizophrenic brains, then understanding the mechanism of action might help elucidate purported abnormal brain functioning in schizophrenia. Another way in which drugs can be useful is in eliciting model psychoses, or intensifying schizophrenic symptoms. Certain drug-induced psychoses may be relatively accurate models of schizophrenic disturbance. In some cases, drugs exacerbate symptoms by increasing the schizophrenic pathology itself, rather than merely superimposing nonschizophrenic symptoms. Knowing the neurochemical bases of such drug action should also help in elucidating the pathophysiology of schizophrenia.

If certain drugs appear to be related to schizophrenic disturbance, then one would be justified in seeking out biochemical systems capable of synthesizing the chemicals predicted by drug action to be relevant to the disease. The most promising leads have involved neurotransmitters, especially the catecholamines and indoleamines, and those drugs with which they interact prominently.

PHENOTHIAZINES

More than anything else in the history of psychiatry, the phenothiazines and related drugs have influenced positively the fate of schizophrenic patients. They have enabled many patients, relegated in earlier days to a lifetime in mental institutions, to function normally or almost normally in society. In determining the relevance of phenothiazines to brain mechanisms in schizophrenia, we must assess whether their therapeutic action involves something fundamental to the disease or whether these drugs are merely some sort of supersedative. One way would be to compare the clinical efficacy of phenothiazines with that of standard sedatives. In large-scale, well-controlled, multihospital collaborative studies sponsored by the National Institute of Mental Health (NIMH) and the Veterans' Administration (VA), a variety of phenothiazines have been compared to sedatives, especially phenobarbital.[4] Phenobarbital was no more efficacious than the placebo in any of these studies of schizophrenia, whereas most phenothiazines were significantly more effective than either phenobarbital or placebo. One could conceivably argue that other sedatives, such as diazepam (Valium) or chlordiazepoxide (Librium), which are more powerful antianxiety agents than phenobarbital, might compete better with the phenothiazines in the treatment of schizophrenia. However, most trials of these agents have shown them to be ineffective in the treatment of schizophrenia, despite their accepted efficacy in relieving anxiety. Indeed, since drugs such as diazepam and chlordiazepoxide are more effective than phenothiazines in relieving anxiety, one can conclude that anxiety per se is not a unique and primary feature of schizophrenia. Some authorities have argued that phenothiazines can be used to "quiet down" patients. However, numerous studies have demonstrated that, while phenothiazines do calm hyperactive patients, they also "activate" withdrawn patients.[4]

The NIMH-VA studies provided another means of judging the extent to which phenothiazines exert a selectively antischizophrenic action. Since a large number of patients was rated for a variety of symptoms, one can analyze the extent to which particular clinical features were affected by the drugs. What Bleuler[2] referred to as the fundamental symptoms of schizophrenia tend to show the greatest response to drug treatment. Secondary symptoms, such as delusions and hallucinations, respond somewhat less, and nonschizophrenic symptoms, such as anxiety and depression, fail to show any specific improvement with phenothiazines. By contrast, sedatives relieve agitation with much less influence upon thought disorder or the abnormality of affective response to the environment. From data such as these, one can argue fairly convincingly that phenothiazines exert a unique therapeutic effect on schizophrenic patients. One must be cautious before concluding that the drugs directly reverse whatever is biochemically abnormal in the brains of schizophrenics. Phenothiazines might affect by way of an independent pathway emotional functions that are separately influenced by the site of disturbed activity in the brains of schizophrenics. The fact that phenothiazines, although facilitating remission, do not "cure" schizophrenic patients indicates such relatively indirect action. Indeed, failure to maintain schizophrenic patients on phenothiazines while they are in remission results in a much greater incidence of relapse.[5]

STIMULANTS

Amphetamines and related stimulants have two effects on brain mechanisms in schizophrenics. In large doses, amphetamines elicit a psychosis that can be clinically indistinguishable from acute paranoid schizophrenia. In very small doses, the stimulant can selectively exacerbate the symptoms of schizophrenic patients (see box on page 164).

Many cases of amphetamine psychosis have been misdiagnosed as acute paranoid schizophrenia until the history of drug use was obtained.[6,7] Accordingly, Kety[8] suggested that amphetamine psychosis might be a heuristic model of schizophrenia. Amphetamine psychosis is most frequently observed in addicts who have consumed enormous amounts of the drug over prolonged periods—for example, 500 to 1000 milligrams of *d*-amphetamine every day for a week or more. Patients develop a paranoid psychosis that usually resolves within a few days after they stop taking the drug. They frequently experience auditory hallucinations much like those typical of schizophrenia, including vague noises and voices and occasionally having conversations with the voices. The visual hallucinations in amphetamine psychotics tend to resemble those observed in very acute schizophrenics.[7]

One factor that has caused some confusion in relating the symptoms of amphetamine psychosis to those of schizophrenia is the fact that amphetamines can evoke more than one type of psychosis. Amphetamines can give rise to an acute "toxic" psychosis, with delirium, confusion, and disorientation that does not resemble the schizophrenia-like amphetamine psychosis. Topic amphetamine psychosis usually occurs after only one or two extremely large doses, rather than after prolonged use of the drug. Of the 42 cases of amphetamine psychosis studied by Connell,[7] visual hallucinations occurred primarily among patients who became acutely psychotic after one or a few large doses, and, hence, were presumably suffering from a toxic psychosis. By contrast, hallucinations were usually auditory in patients whose illness developed gradually, after frequent doses. The toxic amphetamine psychoses probably account for the fact that more visual hallucinations occur in amphetamine intoxication than in schizophrenia. In making comparisons with schizophrenia, one should focus primarily on the "non-toxic" amphetamine psychosis, in which patients retain their orientation to person, place, and time and which often closely resembles clinical schizophrenia.

Some authors have criticized amphetamine psychosis as a model schizophrenia, arguing that it might be related to lack of sleep, overexcitement, or precipitation of psychosis in borderline schizophrenics. However, in controlled studies in which large doses of amphetamine were administered to subjects who had no evidence of pre-existing schizophrenia or schizoid tendency, psychosis was uniformly produced within 1 to 4 days.[9,10] Thus, amphetamine psychosis is not likely to be simply a precipitation of latent schizophrenia. Since some patients became psychotic in about 24 hours, there could not have been sufficient deprivation of sleep to account for the psychosis. As for the question of overexcitement, after some initial moderate euphoria, most subjects were sullen rather than excited, although it is conceivable that there was "internal" hyperexcitement, which might not be evident to observers.

Although amphetamine addicts who have become psychotic after ingesting large amounts of the drug are often clinically indistinguishable from paranoid schizophrenics, subjects in some experimental studies of amphetamine psychosis apparently lack typically schizophrenic thought disorders or affective disturbances.[9] However, in other studies, with dosage schedules more closely mimicking the pattern of ingestion of amphetamine addicts, thought disorder, affective disturbance, and auditory hallucinations are consistently observed.[10]

One important reservation about treating amphetamine psychosis as a model schizophrenia is that it rarely resembles nonparanoid schizophrenia. It is conceivable that amphetamines possess a "pure" schizophrenia-mimicking action, but that some other effect of the drug transforms the clinical picture into a predominantly paranoid one. Perhaps such paranoid action results from the well-known alerting effects of amphetamines on the central nervous system. One might speculate that the major feature differentiating paranoid schizophrenics from other schizophrenics is a hyperalert striving to turn their bewildering array of psychotic transformations into a coherent and meaningful process.

Amphetamines and related stimulants of the central nervous system can, in small doses, exacerbate symptoms of schizophrenia[11] rather than superimpose a distinctive psychosis upon the illness. Patients themselves perceive that their illness is worsening under the influence of the drug. By contrast, when schizophrenics are treated with other psychotomimetic drugs, ·such as LSD (D-lysergic acid diethylamide), they recognize that the superimposed psychosis differs from their own mental disturbance.[12] The amphetamine analog methylphenidate (Ritalin) produces a florid exacerbation of schizophrenic symptoms when given in extremely low doses—often as rapidly as 2 minutes after an intravenous injection.[11] To control for the possibility that amphetamines exacerbate schizophrenic symptoms by a nonspecific stimulation of the central nervous system, Angrist et al.[13] administered large doses of caffeine to schizophrenic and nonschizophrenic subjects. Although all showed tremor, anxiety, and increased heart rate, none showed an increase of psychotic symptoms.

Yet another item favoring an association between amphetamine-induced mental disturbance and schizophrenia is the fact that phenothiazines and butyrophenones seem to be the best antidotes for amphetamine psychosis and can rapidly reverse amphetamine-induced intensification of schizophrenic symptoms.[10,14] By contrast, barbiturate sedatives fail to alleviate amphetamine psychosis and in some cases accentuate the symptoms.[14]

PSYCHEDELIC DRUGS

Psychiatric researchers first became interested in LSD primarily as a drug that could elicit model schizophrenia. They were impressed by the fact that LSD reproducibly evoked a psychotic state which differed from toxic drug psychoses in that subjects were always alert and reasonably well oriented to time, place, and person. However, detailed comparisons of the mental states produced by LSD and related psychedelic drugs such as mescaline, dimethyltryptamine (DMT), and psilocybin with the typical functioning of most schizophrenics in mental hospitals revealed many differences.[12] Psychedelic drugs tend to alter visual perception, with few changes in auditory perception. By contrast, although schizophrenics can experience visual hallucinations, these are much less frequent than auditory hallucinations. The psychedelic drug experience is frequently pleasurable, while for most schizophrenics their psychosis presumably is an unpleasant experience. Whether or not a typically schizophrenic disturbance of thinking and feeling takes place in psychedelic drug-induced psychosis is a matter of controversy. Moreover, unlike the case with amphetamine psychosis, individuals under the influence of drugs such as LSD can be readily distinguished from schizophrenics in mental institutions. Schizophrenics receiving psychedelic drugs report that the drug experience is unlike their endogenous psychosis; it seems like something "different" superimposed upon their fundamental disease.[12]

However, one should be cautious before rejecting out of hand any possibility of a relationship between psychedelic drug psychosis and schizophrenia. Even if a drug acted by disturbing the same site in the brain that is affected in schizophrenia, one would still not expect the effects of the drug to be identical to those displayed by schizophrenic patients. Patients with schizophrenia have been suffering from their disturbance for many years, probably long before overt symptoms were manifested, whereas the drug experience is acute and short-lived. Moreover, an individual receiving a psychedelic drug knows exactly what is happening to him and can anticipate speedy restitution to normality, while the schizophrenic is afflicted with an unknown and unpredictable long-term process. To test whether a drug truly mimics schizophrenia, one should administer the drug surreptitiously every day for several years, beginning in the subject's early childhood.

This line of reasoning suggests that one should compare drug psychosis to the clinical state displayed by schizophrenic patients during their earliest acute breakdown. There seem to be some striking similarities between the subjective states of some early schizophrenic patients and the effects of psychedelic drugs. Psychedelic drugs elicit feelings of enhanced self-awareness, awe, and ecstasy, with sensations of increased acuity and profundity of all sensory perception. Similarly, in case histories of patients suffering acute schizophrenic breakdowns, Bowers and Freedman[15] frequently encountered apparent psychedelic experiences. Perceptual modes were heightened, the patients feeling that they had broken through conventional modes of perceiving, thinking, and feeling to attain a "new creativity." Instead of the flattened affect of chronic schizophrenics, these patients experienced intense joy or dread, which is of interest since with psychedelic drugs one often sees an alternation between extremes of elation and abject terror. Although their thinking was altered, these patients often did not display the typical schizophrenic disturbance of thought or feeling. Moreover, in these acute schizophrenics, changes in visual perception were much more frequent than they were in chronic patients. Snyder and Lamparella[16] quantified the presence of various "psychedelic" behaviors in schizophrenia and observed that these were much more frequent in acute patients.

This "psychedelic" phase of schizophrenia seems not to be tolerated for long. Either the acute state subsides and normal mental function is restored, or the bewildering experience is resolved by encapsulation into fixed delusional systems, or restricted modes of interacting, including autistic behavior, altered affect, and a formal thought disorder.

PHENOTHIAZINES AND CATECHOLAMINES

Ascertaining the way in which a drug exerts its therapeutic effects is the pharmacologist's most difficult task. Most drugs elicit a myriad of biological effects, the majority of which are unrelated to the therapeutic action of the drug. Phenothiazines are highly reactive chemicals capable of pi electron donation or acceptance, hydrophobic binding, and ionic links by way of the side-chain amine; they produce biochemical effects on almost every system that has been examined.[17] How might one decide which of these effects is most relevant to therapeutic efficacy? Of the large number of phenothiazines that have been employed clinically and that are fairly similar in their chemical structure, some are highly effective in the treatment of schizophrenia, others are somewhat less efficacious clinically; while yet others are definitely ineffective. Biochemical actions that correlate with known clinical actions would be the best candidates to mediate the therapeutic actions of the drugs.

Most of the biochemical effects of the phenothiazines do not correlate with clinical potency. The best correlation is in certain effects upon catecholamines in the brain, especially dopamine; this suggests that the therapeutic action of these drugs is related in some way to a blockade of dopamine receptors in the brain (see box).

The catecholamines, norepinephrine and dopamine, are transmitters in a group of well-defined tracts in the brain. Dopamine is best known as the transmitter of a prominent dopamine tract with cell bodies in the substantia nigra and terminals in the caudate nucleus and putamen of the corpus striatum. The nigrostriatal dopamine pathway degenerates in Parkinson's disease, and the attendant dopamine deficiency appears to account, in large part, for the symptoms of the disease. Thus restoration of the depleted dopamine by treatment with L-dopa, the amino acid precursor of dopamine, has proved to be a veritable "miracle" therapy for Parkinson's disease. There are also prominent dopamine pathways with cell bodies dorsal to the interpeduncular nucleus and terminals in the nucleus accumbens and olfactory tubercle, areas of the limbic forebrain, that have been implicated in emotional behavior.[18] An extensive network of dopamine neurons has been found in the cerebral cortex.[19]

Relations between Drugs, Catecholamines, and Schizophrenia

Phenothiazines (and related antischizophrenic drugs)

Phenothiazines have true antischizophrenic actions:
    They are more effective than sedatives.
    They act best on fundamental symptoms.
Blockade of dopamine receptors by phenothiazines is closely related to their clinical efficacy.
The ability of phenothiazines to mimic the preferred catecholamine conformation predicts their therapeutic efficacy.

Amphetamines

In small doses, amphetamines specifically activate schizophrenic symptoms.
Amphetamines can evoke a psychosis that is often indistinguishable from acute paranoid schizophrenia.
Phenothiazines appear to be optimal antidotes for amphetamine psychosis.
Behavioral effects of amphetamines are presumably mediated by catecholamines in the brain.

TABLE 17-1
The Relative Affinities of Phenothiazines and Butyrophenones for Muscarinic Cholinergic Receptor Binding in the Brain Correlate Inversely with Extrapyramidal Side Effects.

Drug class	Relative affinity for muscarinic receptor	Frequency of extrapyramidal side effects (26, 27)
Dibenzodiazepine		
Clozapine	385.0	5
Piperidine phenothiazine		
Thioridazine	66.7	4
Alkylamino phenothiazine		
Promazine	15.2	3
Chlorpromazine	10.0	
Trifluopromazine	10.0	
Piperazine phenothiazine		
Acetophenazine	0.91	2
Perphenazine	0.93	
Trifluoperazine	0.91	
Fluphenazine	0.91	
Butyrophenone		
Haloperidol	0.21	1

Carlsson and Lindqvist[20] first suggested that phenothiazine drugs act by blocking dopamine receptors. They observed that chlorpromazine and related antischizophrenic agents elevated concentrations of the methoxylated metabolites of dopamine in the brain, while the antihistaminic phenothiazine, promethazine, which is not effective in treating schizophrenia, did not alter these concentrations. Haloperidol, a butyrophenone drug with antischizophrenic actions similar to, but more potent than, the phenothiazines, was correspondingly more potent in elevating the concentrations of these metabolites. Carlsson and Lindqvist speculated that the phenothiazines block catecholamine receptor sites, whereupon a message is conveyed by means of a neuronal feedback to the cell bodies: "We receptors are not receiving enough transmitter; send us more catecholamines!" Accordingly, the catecholamine neurons proceed to fire more rapidly and,

as a corollary, synthesize more catecholamines and release more metabolites. These speculations have been confirmed in studies showing that phenothiazines and butyrophenones do accelerate catecholamine synthesis in proportion to their clinical efficacy.[21] The influence of these drugs upon dopamine synthesis correlates much better with clinical effects than their actions on norepinephrine synthesis. Indeed, several extremely potent butyrophenone tranquilizers selectively accelerate dopamine turnover with negligible effects on norepinephrine. Kebabian *et al.*[22] have shown that a dopamine-sensitive adenylate cyclase in the caudate nucleus is inhibited by low concentrations of phenothiazines and butyrophenones that are clinically effective in treating schizophrenia, but not by phenothiazines that are ineffective in treating schizophrenia. Aghajanian and co-workers[23] have demonstrated an inhibitory effect of iontophoresed dopamine on olfactory tubercle cells receiving dopamine terminals. Very low doses of intravenously administered phenothiazines and butyrophenones block this effect of dopamine in proportion to their clinical efficacy in treating schizophrenia.

* * *

Besides being associated with antischizophrenic activity, dopamine receptor blockade by phenothiazines and butyrophenones may explain the prominent extrapyramidal side effects of these drugs. By blocking the dopamine receptors in the corpus striatum, these agents produce a functional deficiency of dopamine. One might speculate that, while the parkinsonism-like side effects of the phenothiazine drugs arise by blocking dopamine receptors in the corpus striatum, the antischizophrenic action of the phenothiazines may be related to effects upon dopamine receptors in other areas of the brain, such as the olfactory tubercle, nucleus accumbens, or the dopamine receptor sites in the cerebral cortex.

In most of their biochemical features, dopamine neurons in different parts of the brain and periphery behave quite similarly. Thus the reuptake process of dopamine nerve terminals, which presumably serves to inactivate synaptically released dopamine, appears to be the same in dopamine terminals of the corpus striatum, olfactory tubercle, nucleus accumbens, median eminence, and retina.[24] Drug responses of dopamine receptors in the olfactory tubercle, corpus striatum, kidney, and superior cervical ganglia are also quite similar.[24,25]

* * *

AMPHETAMINES AND CATECHOLAMINES

While the structural relationship between phenothiazines and the catecholamines was far from obvious, amphetamines, whose chemical structure closely resembles that of the catecholamines, have always been assumed by pharmacologists to act by way of these neurotransmitters. Which of the various dopamine and norepinephrine pathways in the brain mediates particular behavioral effects of amphetamines? In animals, one can make a discrete lesion in individual catecholamine pathways with 6-hydroxydopamine and examine the behavioral consequences. 6-hydroxydopamine is selectively accumulated into catecholamine neurons, whereupon it autooxidizes and destroys them.[28] After evaluating the influence of particular lesions on individual behavioral effects of amphetamines, one can make inferences about the tracts mediating the behaviors.

In relatively high doses, amphetamines elicit stereotyped compulsive behavior in animals, the exact pattern varying with different species, but often resembling a searching form of behavior. Rats, whose major means of exploring their environment is olfactory, tend to stay in one portion of the cage, sniff, lick, and especially gnaw.[29] Cats confined to their cages become involved in repetitive sniffing motions, while less confined cats develop constant, purposeless side-to-side looking movements that may be a response to fear.[30] Chimpanzees intoxicated with amphetamines display side-to-side looking patterns, as well as self-picking and self-grooming behavior.[31] These effects of amphetamines closely resemble the stereotyped compulsive behavior frequently observed in addicts who consume large amounts of the drug.[32] Amphetamine addicts have a compulsion to take objects apart, to sort the parts, and occasionally to put them back together again. Like the monkeys who, under the influence of amphetamines, constantly pick at their skin, amphetamine addicts indulge in "grooming" behavior; this behavior is generally associated with tactile hallucinations that bugs or amphetamine crystals are creeping beneath their skins. Of particular interest is a report that the stereotyped compulsive behavior appears to be an invariable concomitant of psychosis and does not occur in amphetamine addicts who do not develop psychosis.[33]

An abundance of evidence suggests that stereotyped compulsive behavior of rodents is mediated by way of dopamine pathways in the brain. Thus, making a lesion in the substantia nigra with 6-hydroxydopamine, with complete degeneration of the nigrostriatal dopamine pathway and some loss of dopamine terminals in the nucleus accumbens and olfactory turbercle, abolishes amphetamine-induced stereotyped compulsive behavior, while locomotor stimulation by the drug continues.[34] Lesions in the corpus striatum can abolish stereotyped behavioral effects of amphetamines.[35] However, since the nucleus accumbens and the olfactory tubercle are adjacent to the corpus striatum, it is possible that one or the other of these areas is involved in mediating certain components of the stereotyped behavioral syndrome.[36] Injecting dopamine or apomorphine (which is thought to stimulate dopamine receptors) into the vicinity of the corpus striatum, nucleus accumbens, and olfactory tubercle elicits stereotyped behavior in rats.[37]

***

Another dramatic behavioral effect of amphetamines is their ability to greatly facilitate hypothalamic self-stimulation. Animals with electrodes in the lateral hypothalamus will press levers at astronomical rates to obtain electrical stimulation, which suggests that these areas are pleasure centers. This action of amphetamines may be related to the euphoric effects of the drug in man.

***

Interestingly, physostigmine, which inhibits acetylcholinesterase and thus increases the effects of acetylcholine, can prevent the psychosis-worsening action of the amphetamine analog methylphenidate.[38] This suggests a balance between catecholamines and acetylcholine in modulated psychotic symptoms.

There is other evidence pointing to a primary role for dopamine in amphetamine psychosis and amphetamine exacerbation of schizophrenia. The stimulant methylphenidate is more active than amphetamine in exacerbating schizophrenic symptoms,[38] and in certain biochemical systems it seems to have a more selective effect upon dopamine, as compared to norepinephrine, neuronal disposition.[24,39] L-dopa, whose administration is followed by a considerable formation of dopamine with very little norepinephrine synthesis, exacerbates schizophrenic symptoms in a selective fashion, much like amphetamines.[40] Although L-dopa does produce psychiatric side effects in parkinsonian patients, there are few reports of anything resembling amphetamine psychosis.[41] It is conceivable that these results are related to the enormous doses of amphetamine (300 to 500 milligrams) required to elicit a psychosis in nonschizophrenic subjects. To obtain comparable catecholamine-enhancing effects with L-dopa would probably require much higher doses than are generally administered to parkinsonian patients. Cocaine, which facilitates the actions of both norepinephrine and dopamine, produces a psychosis that is virtually identical to amphetamine psychosis.[42]

CONCLUDING REMARKS

Of various biochemical approaches to the study of schizophrenia, the investigation of brain neurotransmitter interactions with psychotropic drugs has proved most productive in recent years. Analyses of the mechanism of the antischizophrenic activities of the phenothiazines and the ability of amphetamines to worsen schizophrenic symptoms and elicit a schizophrenia-like psychosis have focused attention upon dopamine in the brain. Findings of reduced platelet monoamine oxidase and brain dopamine β-hydroxylase activities in schizophrenics represent enticing but tentative data that would be consistent with a "dopamine hypothesis."

The ability of psychedelic drugs to mimic the symptoms of certain early stages of schizophrenia remains a promising lead. None of these approaches yet affords the definitive "answer" to the riddle of schizophrenia, and roles for other neurotransmitters, such as acetylcholine[38] and γ-aminobutyric acid,[43] are possible.

REFERENCES AND NOTES

1. S. S. Kety, D. Rosenthal, P. H. Wender, in *The Transmission of Schizophrenia,* D. Rosenthal and S. S. Kety, Eds. (Pergamon, New York, 1968), p. 345; L. L. Heston, *Science* **167,** 249 (1970); W. Pollin, *Arch. Gen. Psychiatr.* **27,** 29 (1972).
2. E. Bleuler, *Dementia Praecox, or the Group of Schizophrenias* (International Universities Press, New York, 1950).
3. W. T. Carpenter, J. S. Strauss, S. Mule, *Arch. Gen. Psychiatr.* **28,** 847 (1973); World Health Organization, *The International Pilot Study of Schizophrenia* (World Health Organization Press, Geneva, 1973); K. Schneider, *Clinical Psychopathology* (Grune & Stratton, New York, 1959).
4. J. M. Davis, *Arch. Gen. Psychiatr.* **13,** 552 (1965); J. O. Cole, *ibid.* **10,** 246 (1964); J. F. Casey, J. J. Lasky, C. J. Klett, L. E. Hollister, *Am. J. Psychiatr.* **117,** 97 (1960).
5. H. L. Blackburn and J. L. Allen, *J. Nerv. Ment. Dis.* **133,** 303 (1961); E. M. Caffey, L. S. Diamond, T. V. Frank, J. C. Grasberger, L. Herman, C. L. Klett, C. Rothstein, *J. Chronic Dis.* **17,** 347 (1964); L. S. Diamond and J. B. Marks, *J. Nerv. Ment. Dis.* **131,** 247 (1960); R. S. Gantz and D. P. Birkett, *Arch. Gen. Psychiatr.* **12,** 586 (1965).
6. D. S. Bell, *Br. J. Psychiatr.* **111,** 701 (1965); P. Beamish and L. G. Kiloh, *J. Ment. Sci.* **106,** 337 (1960); E. H. Ellinwood, Jr., *J. Nerv. Ment. Dis.* **144,** 273 (1967); D. S. Bell, *Arch. Gen. Psychiatr.*

7. P. H. Connell, *Amphetamine Psychosis* (Chapman & Hall, London, 1958).
8. S. S. Kety, *Science* **129,** 1528 (1959).
9. J. D. Griffith, J. Cavanaugh, J. Held, J. A. Oates, *Arch. Gen. Psychiatr.* **26,** 97 (1972).
10. B. M. Angrist and S. Gerson, *Biol. Psychiatr.* **2,** 95 (1970); B. Angrist, G. Sathananthan, S. Wilk, S. Gershon, *J. Psychiatr. Res.,* in press; B. Angrist, B., Shopsin, S. Gershon, *Nat. New Biol.* **239,** 152 (1971).
11. D. S. Janowsky, M. K. El-Yousef, J. M. Davis, *Compr. Psychiatr.* **13,** 83 (1972); _____, H. J. Sekerke, *Arch. Gen. Psychiatr.* **28,** 185 (1973).
12. L. E. Hollister, *Ann. N.Y. Acad. Sci.* **96,** 80 (1962); L. W. Chloden, A. Kurland, C. Savage, *J. Nerv. Ment. Dis.* **122,** 211 (1955).
13. B. M. Angrist, G. Sathananthan, S. Wilk, S. Gershon, in *Frontiers in Catecholamine Research,* E. Usdin and S. H. Snyder, Eds. (Pergamon, New York, 1974), p. 991.
14. B. Angrist, personal communication; J. Griffith, personal communication; J. M. Davis, personal communication.
15. M. J. Bowers, Jr., and D. X. Freedman, *Arch. Gen. Psychiatr.* **15,** 240 (1966).
16. S. H. Snyder and V. Lamparella, *Commun. Behav. Biol. Part A Orig. Artic.* **3,** 85 (1969).
17. P. S. Guth and M. A. Spirtes, *Int. Rev. Neurobiol.* **7,** 231 (1963).
18. N. A. Hillarp, K. Fuxe, A. Dahlstrom, *Pharmacol. Rev.* **18,** 727 (1966); U. Ungerstedt, *Acta Physiol. Scand. Suppl.* **367** (1971). p. 1.
19. A. M. Thierry, L. Stimus, G. Blanc, J. Glowinski, *Brain Res.* **50,** 230 (1973); A. M. Thierry and J. Glowinski, in *Frontiers in Catecholamine Research,* E. Usdin and S. H. Snyder, Eds. (Pergamon, New York, 1974), p. 649; K. Fuxe, personal communication.
20. A. Carlsson and M. Lindqvist, *Acta Pharmacol. Toxicol.* **20,** 140 (1963).
21. H. Nyback, Z. Borzecki, G. Sedvall, *Eur.*

J. Pharmacol. **4,** 395 (1968); H. Nyback, J. Schubert, G. Sedvall, *J. Pharm,. Pharmacol.* **22,** 622 (1970); D. F. Sharman, *Br. J. Pharmacol.* **28,** 153 (1966).

22. J. W. Kebabian, G. L. Petzold, P. Greengard, *Proc. Natl. Acad. Sci. U.S.A.* **69,** 2145 (1972).

23. G. K. Aghafanian and B. S. Bunney, in *Frontiers in Catecholamine Research,* E. Usdin and S. H. Snyder, Eds. (Pergamon, New York, 1974), p. 643.

24. J. T. Coyle and S. H. Snyder, *J. Pharmacol. Exp. Ther.* **170,** 221 (1969); L. L. Iversen, B. Jarrott, M. A. Simmonds, *Br. J. Pharmacol.* **43,** 845 (1971); A. C. Cuello, A. S. Horn, A. V. P. MacKay, L. L. Iversen, *Nat. New Biol.* **243,** 465 (1973); L. L. Iversen, in *Frontiers in Catecholamine Research,* E. Usdin and S. H. Snyder, Eds. (Pergamon, New York, 1974), p. 403; A. S. Horn, A. C. Cuello, R. J. Miller, *J. Neurochem.,* in press.

25. D. A. McAfee, M. Schorderet, P. Greengard, *Science* **171,** 1156 (1971); B. Libet and T. Tosaka, *Proc. Natl. Acad. Sci. U.S.A.* **67,** 667 (1970); L. I. Goldberg, *Pharmacol. Rev.* **24,** 1 (1972).

26. D. F. Klein and J. M. Davis, *Diagnosis and Drug Treatment of Psychiatric Disorders* (Williams & Wilkins, Baltimore, 1969), p. 95; S. Matthysse, *Fed. Proc.* **32,** 200 (1973).

27. D. DeMaio, *Arzneim-Forsch.* **22,** 919 (1971); H. Gross and E. Langer, *ibid.***19,** 496 (1969); J. Angst, U. Jaenicke, A. Padrutt, C. Scharfelter, *Pharmakopsychiatry* **4,** 192 (1971); J. Anst, D. Bentz, P. Berner, H. Heimann, K. Helmchen. H. Hippius, *ibid.,* p. 201; G. Stille and A. Hippius, *ibid.,* p. 182.

28. H. Thoenen, in *Perspectives in Neuropharmacology,* S. H. Snyder, Ed. (Oxford Univ. Press, New York, 1972), p. 301.

29. A. Randrup and I. Munkvad, *Psychopharmacologia* **11,** 300 (1967).

30. E. H. Ellinwood, Jr., and O. Duarte-Escalante, in *Current Concepts on Amphetamine Abuse,* E. H. Ellinwood, Jr., and S. Cohen, Eds. (National Institute of Mental Health, Rockville, Md., 1973), p. 59.

31. F. L. Fitzgerald, in *Neuropsychopharmacology,* H. Brill, Ed. (Excerpta Medica, Amsterdam, 1967), p. 1226.

32. G. Sylander, *Sven. Kakartidaenia* **63,** 4973 (1966).

33. E. H. Ellinwood, Jr., *J. Nerv. Ment. Dis.* **144,** 273 (1967).

34. I. Creese and S. D. Iversen, *Nat. New Biol.* **238,** 247 (1972); H. C. Fibiger, H. P. Fibiger, A. P. Zis, *Br. J. Pharmacol.* **47,** 683 (1973).

35. A. Randrup and I. Munkvad, *Acta Psychiatr. Scand. Suppl. 191* (1966), p. 193.

36. G. M. McKenzie, *Psychopharmacologia* **23,** 212 (1972); K. Fuxe, in *Abuse of Central Stimulants,* F. Sjoqvist and M. Tottie, Eds. (Raven, New York, 1969), p. 450.

37. A. M. Ernst and P. Smelik, *Experientia* **22,** 837 (1966); R. L. Fog, A. Randrup, H. Pakkenberg, *Psychopharmacologia* **11,** 179 (1967).

38. J. M. Davis and D. Janowsky, in *Frontiers in Catecholamine Research,* E. Usdin and S. H. Snyder, Eds. (Pergamon, New York, 1974), p. 977.

39. E. D. Hendley, S. H. Snyder, J. J. Fauley, J. B. LaPidus, *J. Pharmacol. Exp. Ther.* **183,** 103 (1972).

40. G. Sathananthan, B. M. Angrist, S. Gershon, *Biol. Psychiatr.,* in press; J. Yaryura-Tobias, B. Diamond, S. Merlis, *Curr. Ther. Res. Clin. Exp.* **12,** 528 (1970); B. Angrist, G. Sathananthan, S. Gershon, *Psychopharmacologia* **31,** 1 (1973).

41. F. H. McDowell, in *L-Dopa and Parkinsonism,* A. Barbeau and F. H. McDowell, Eds. (Davis, Philadelphia, 1970), p. 321; G. T. G. Celesia and A. N. Barr, *Arch. Neurol.* **23,** 193 (1970).

42. W. Mayer-Gross, F. Slater, M. Roth, *Clinical Psychiatry* (Williams & Wilkins, Baltimore, 1960), p. 377; E. Bleuler, *Textbook of Psychiatry* (Macmillan, New York, 1924), p. 359.

43. E. Roberts, *Neurosci. Res. Program Bull.* **10,** 468 (1972).

18.

T. J. Crow

LATER DEVELOPMENTS IN THE DOPAMINE HYPOTHESIS OF SCHIZOPHRENIA

MOLECULAR PATHOLOGY OF SCHIZOPHRENIA: MORE THAN ONE DISEASE PROCESS?

The social effects of schizophrenia may be devastating, but the nature of the disease process remains obscure. Indeed, we are not even certain that there is a single pathological process. The diagnosis is made partly by the presence of certain psychological symptoms and partly by exclusion of other syndromes and disease processes. Thus hallucinations which are not due to primary affective disturbance and for which there is no "organic" cause may well be described as schizophrenic. The use of stricter criteria, such as the presence of Schneider's first-rank symptoms (certain types of auditory hallucination, delusions of passivity and interference, thought alienation, and delusional perception), can increase the reliability of diagnosis, but it also restricts the definition of schizophrenia to a smaller group of illnesses than is implied by current usage—without improving the accuracy of prediction of outcome.

The belief that the primary disturbance in schizophrenia is chemical has long been plausible; that it is a disturbance of neurohumoral function is supported by observations that schizophrenic symptoms can be exacerbated in patients and provoked in non-psychotic individuals by drugs that act on specific transmitters. The psychosis seen in some amphetamine abusers may be indistinguishable from acute paranoid schizophrenia.[1,2] The psychotic changes, like those in schizophrenia, occur in clear consciousness (that is, in the absence of disorientation), and can include first-rank symptoms. In animals many of the behavioural effects of the amphetamines have been shown to be due to increased dopamine release from central dopamine pathways,[3] and the psychotic changes in man seem likely also to be associated with increased dopaminergic transmission.

MECHANISM OF THE ANTIPSYCHOTIC EFFECT

Both schizophrenic symptoms and those of the amphetamine psychosis are reduced by neuroleptic drugs. Carlsson and Lindqvist[1] found that these drugs increase dopamine turnover and suggested this was secondary to blockade of the dopamine receptor. Dopamine-induced activation of adenylate cyclase in the corpus striatum is inhibited by neuroleptic drugs; this inhibition correlates well with antipsychotic potency[5] for a range of drugs, though the butyrophenone compounds are somewhat less active than would be predicted from their clinical effects. Nevertheless, while blockade of the dopamine receptor is an obvious explanation of the extrapyramidal actions of neuroleptic drugs some con-

From T. J. Crow, "Molecular pathology of schizophrenia: More than one disease process?" *British Medical Journal,* 1978, vol. 280, pp. 66-68.

troversy exists about the extension of that mechanism to explain their antipsychotic effect. The principal argument to the contrary[6] is that the correlation between extrapyramidal and therapeutic effects is not perfect. Some drugs (such as thioridazine) have fewer Parkinsonian effects than would be expected from their clinical efficacy. These same drugs, however, have high anticholinergic potency[7]—in other words, they have "inbuilt" antiparkinsonian activity. When this is taken into account the relation between dopamine antagonism and therapeutic effectiveness becomes more compelling. In the corpus striatum, where there is an interaction between acetylcholine and dopamine, drugs with a low incidence of side effects have relatively weak effects on dopaminergic transmission. This interaction does not occur in the mesolimbic dopamine system (the nucleus accumbens and related structures), and here dopamine blockade correlates well with therapeutic effectiveness.[8,9] Moreover, when dopamine antagonism is assessed not in the adenylate cyclase system but as inhibition of butyrophenone binding (an assay that probably identifies a second type of dopamine receptor) the relative lack of potency of the butyrophenones disappears.[10,11] A recent clinical study[12] showed that only the *cis*- or α-isomer of the thiaxanthene flupenthixol, which blocks the dopamine receptor, is effective in treatment; the β-isomer, which is very much less potent as a dopamine antagonist, is no more active than placebo. This result is hard to explain except on the basis that dopamine antagonism is necessary for the therapeutic effect. The dopamine blockade theory of neuroleptic action has, indeed, survived stringent tests; and antagonism of dopamine receptors, particularly those located within the mesolimbic system and the subset that is specifically labelled by butyrophenones, is most probably the critical element in diminishing schizophrenic symptoms.

CHANGES IN THE DOPAMINE RECEPTOR

Is there, therefore, a primary disturbance of dopaminergic transmission in schizophrenia? Probenecid blocks the elimination of the dopamine metabolite homovanillic acid (HVA) from cerebrospinal fluid and can be used to obtain an estimate of dopamine turnover in the central nervous system. Use of this technique[13,14] has produced no evidence of an increase in HVA that could be attributed to overactivity of dopamine neurones. Indeed, within the group of schizophrenic patients poor prognosis[13] and increasing severity of symptoms[14] are associated with decreased concentrations of HVA in the cerebrospinal fluid. Post-mortem studies[15] have also shown no evidence of increased dopamine turnover—a surprising finding, since many patients coming to necropsy have been on long-term medication; presumably (as in animal experiments) the acute effects of neuroleptic drugs on dopamine turnover disappear with continued administration. These studies give no support to the view that dopamine neurones are overactive in schizophrenia (Table 18-1).

By contrast, there is evidence[15,16] that the numbers of dopamine receptors are increased in the brains of a proportion (perhaps two-thirds) of patients with schizophrenia, as shown by receptor assay techniques.[15,16] In experiments on animals the numbers of receptors have been found to increase after administration of neuroleptics; but the size of the change (around 100 percent) in schizophrenic patients is

TABLE 18-1
Neurohumoral Hypothesis of Schizophrenia

Authors	Theory	Principal Arguments	Evidence from Postmortem Studies	
			For	Against
Gaddum (1954)[19]; Woolley and Shaw (1954)[20]	Serotonin deficiency	LSD psychosis resembles schizophrenia LSD blocks serotonin receptors		Serotonin turnover not decreased[21] Serotonin receptors unchanged[17];
Randrup and Munkvad (1965)[22]	Dopamine neurone overactivity	Amphetamine psychosis resembles acute paranoid schizophrenia Amphetamines increase dopamine release Antipsychotic drugs block dopamine receptors		Dopamine turnover not increased[15]
Bowers (1974)[13]; Crow, Deakin, Johnstone, and Longden (1976)[23]	Dopamine receptor supersensitivity	As above	Dopamine receptors increased [15, 16]	
Stein and Wise (1971)[27]	Noradrenaline neurone degeneration	Reward processes are mediated by central noradrenergic systems; anhedonia is a core feature of chronic schizophrenia		Dopamine-β-hydroxylase not reduced[28]
Murphy and Wyatt (1972)[24]	Monoamine oxidase deficiency	Platelet monoamine oxidase activity is reduced in some schizophrenic patients		Monoamine oxidase activity not reduced[25]

relatively large, and there is an increase in some patients who had been free of medication for the year before death.[15] Moreover, two types of dopamine receptor can be identified by ligand-binding techniques, and only that type of receptor labelled by the butyrophenone antagonist drugs is increased in schizophrenia[17]; while receptors labelled by both antagonist and agonist compounds are increased after administration of neuroleptics.[18]

Other neurohumoral theories have been tested in postmortem studies of the brains of schizophrenics. On the basis of the LSD psychosis and the pharmacological an-tagonism of LSD of some effects of serotonin Gaddum[19] suggested that serotonergic transmission might be deficient. Tryptophan metabolism (by way of the serotonin and other pathways), however, is not abnormal in the schizophrenic brain,[21] and serotonin receptors (assessed by binding of LSD and 5-hydroxytryptamine) are unchanged.[17] Reports have been conflicting on possible changes in the monoamine oxidase activity in platelets[24] in schizophrenia, but interest in this question has been diminished by the finding[25] that enzyme activity, assessed with several different substrates, is normal in the brain of schizophrenics. Finally, there is evidence[26] that certain central noradrenergic pathways (such as the locus coeruleus innervation of the cerebral cortex) play a part in reward mechanisms; Stein and Wise[27] suggested that these pathways degenerate in schizophrenia. A deficient response to rewarding stimuli is a plausible explanation for some features of the disease, but studies[28] of the enzyme dopamine-β-hydroxylase (a marker for noradrenergic neurones) have not shown a consistent reduction in the schizophrenic brain.

At present, therefore, the only change found consistently in the postmortem studies of the schizophrenic brain is an increase in the numbers of dopamine receptors. Since such a change implies an increased and perhaps maladaptive response of the system, this finding could explain the beneficial effects of dopamine antagonists. The time course of the therapeutic effect is, however, noteworthy: benefit follows blockade of the dopamine receptors only after an interval of at least two weeks.[29] This suggests that blockade of the receptors may be necessary only to allow some other change to occur. Furthermore the therapeutic effects of blockade of dopamine receptors, and presumably of neuroleptic drugs in general, are limited to positive symptoms (delusions, hallucinations, and thought disorder).[12] These are the symptoms that are characteristic of acute schizophrenic illnesses. Negative symptoms (flattening of affect, poverty of speech, and loss of drive) are more commonly seen in chronic schizophrenia, particularly in institutionalised patients; and these patients probably benefit much less from drug treatment.[30]

TWO SYNDROMES?

Several lines of evidence support the view that the fundamental defect in some chronic illnesses may be distinct from that underlying the acute disturbance. Thus chronic schizophrenics may be relatively resistant to the effects of amphetamine-like drugs,[31] which readily exacerbate the symptoms of acute schizophrenia. Moreover, cognitive changes (such as disorientation in time) that resemble those of organic states are seen[32,33] in some institutionalised patients; and four radiological studies[34-37] have suggested that there is a group of chronic patients, probably including those with the greatest deterioration, who have structural changes of the cerebral ventricles. In the first computed tomography study,[36] increased ventricular size was correlated with negative symptoms and evidence of intellectual impairment.

It seems that two syndromes can be distinguished in those diseases currently described as schizophrenic and that each may be associated with a specific pathological process (Table 18-2). The first (the type I syndrome, equivalent to "acute schizophrenia," and characterised by the positive symptoms—delusions, hallucinations, and thought disorder) is in some way associated with a change in dopaminergic transmission; the second process (the type II syndrome, equivalent to the "defect state," and characterised by the negative symptoms—affective flattening and poverty of speech) is unrelated to dopaminergic transmission but may be associated with intellectual impairment and, perhaps, structural changes in the brain. Type I symptoms are reversible; type II symptoms, which are more difficult to define, may indicate a component of irreversibility. The former predict a potential response to neuroleptics; the latter are more closely associated with a poor long-

TABLE 18-2
Two Syndromes in Schizophrenia

	Type I	*Type II*
Characteristic symptoms	Hallucinations, delusions, thought disorder (positive symptoms)	Affective flattening, poverty of speech, loss of drive, (negative symptoms)
Type of illness in which most commonly seen	Acute schizophrenia	Chronic schizophrenia, the "defect" state
Response to neuroleptics	Good	Poor
Outcome	Reversible	? Irreversible
Intellectual impairment	Absent	Sometimes present
Postulated pathological process	Increased dopamine receptors	Cell loss and structural changes in the brain

term outcome. Episodes of type I symptoms may be followed by development of the type II syndrome, and both may be present together. Type II symptoms, however, define a group of illnesses of graver prognosis. They occasionally occur in the absence of the type I syndrome (for example, in "simple" schizophrenia), but because these symptoms are not well defined the diagnosis in these cases is difficult to establish.

The cause of schizophrenic illness remains obscure. A genetic influence is undoubted, but the facts that the onset of symptoms is often in adult life and that concordance in monozygotic twins (about 50 percent) falls short of 100 percent suggest that genes may be relevant only in predisposing to some other factor. Infection with a slow virus may be relevant.[38-40] Some neurotropic viruses (for example, polio, herpes simplex, and zoster) are selective in the cells they attack. Conceivably a slow virus infection might be associated either with a primary chemical disturbance (for example, through an affinity for a receptor site) or with a more general disturbance of higher cognitive functions.

REFERENCES

1. Connell, P. H. *Amphetamine psychosis.* London: Oxford University Press, 1958.
2. Ellinwood, E. H. *Amphetamine psychosis.* I Description of the individuals and process. J Nerv Ment Dis 1967;**144**:273-83.
3. Randrup, A., & Munkvad, I. Stereotyped activities produced by amphetamine in several animal species and man. *Psychopharmacologia* 1967;**11**:300-10.
4. Carlsson, A., & Lindqvist, M. Effect of chlorpromazine and haloperidol on formation of 3-methoxy-tyramine and normetanephrine in mouse brain. *Acta Pharmacol Toxicol* 1963;**20**:140-4.
5. Miller, R. J., Horn, A. S., & Iversen, L. L. The action of neuroleptic drugs on dopamine-stimulated adenosine cyclin 3',5'-monophosphate production in rat neostriatum and limbic forebrain. *Mol Pharmacol* 1974;**10**:759-66.
6. Crow, T. J., & Gillbe, C. Brain dopamine and behaviour. A critical analysis of the relationship between dopamine antagonism and therapeutic efficacy of neur-

oleptic drugs. J Psychiatr Res 1974;**11**: 163-72.

7. Miller, R. J., & Hiley, G. R. Antimuscarinic properties of neuroleptics and drug induced Parkinsonism. *Nature* 1974;**248**:596-7.

8. Andén, N. E. Dopamine turnover in the corpus striatum and the limbic system after treatment with neuroleptic and anti-acetylcholine drugs. J Pharm Pharmacol1972;**24**:905-6.

9. Crow, T. J., Deakin, J. F. W., & Longden, A. The nucleus accumbens—possible site of antipsychotic action of neuroleptic drugs? *Psychol Med* 1977;7:213-21.

10. Creese, I., Burt, D. R., & Snyder, S. H. Dopamine receptor binding predicts clinical and pharmacological potencies of antischizophrenic drugs. *Science* 1976;**192**:481-3.

11. Seeman, P., Lee, T., Chau-Wong, M., & Wong, K. Antipsychotic drug doses and neuroleptic dopamine receptors. *Nature* 1976;**261**:717-8.

12. Johnstone, E., Crow, T. J., Frith, C. D., Carney, M. W. P., & Price, J. S. Mechanism of the antipsychotic effect in the treatment of acute schizophrenia. *Lancet* 1978;i:848-51.

13. Bowers, M. B. Central dopamine turnover in schizophrenic syndromes. *Arch Gen Psychiatry* 1974;**31**:50-4.

14. Post, R. M., Fink, E., Carpenter, W. I., & Goodwin, F. K. Cerebrospinal fluid amine metabolites in acute schizophrenia. *Arch Gen Psychiatry* 1975;**32**:1063-9.

15. Owen, F., Cross, A. J., Crow, T. J., Longden, A., Poulter, M., & Riley, G. J. Increased dopamine-receptor sensitivity in schizophrenia. *Lancet* 1978;ii:223-5.

16. Lee, T., Seeman, P., Tourtellotte, W. W., Farley, I.J., & Hornykeiwicz, O. Binding of ³H-apomorphine in schizophrenic brains. *Nature* 1978;**274**:897-900.

17. Owen, F., Gross, A. J., Crow, T. J., Loftnouse, R., & Poulter, M. Neurotransmitter receptors in brain in schizophrenia. *Acta Psychiatr Scand (Suppl)* (in press).

18. Muller, P., & Seeman, P. Brain neurotransmitter receptors after long-term haloperidol: dopamine, acetylcholine, serotonin, χ-noradrenergic and naloxone receptors. *Life Sci* 1977;**21**:1751-8.

19. Gaddum, J. H. Drugs antagonistic to 5-hydroxytryptamine. In: Wolstenholme, G. W., ed. Ciba Foundation symposium on hypertension. Boston: Little Brown, 1954:75-7.

20. Woolley, D. W., & Shaw, E. A biochemical and pharmacological suggestion about certain mental disorders. *Proc Natl Acad Sci USA* 1954;**40**:228-31.

21. Joseph, M. H., Baker, H. F., Crow, T. J., Riley, G. J., & Risby, D. Brain tryptophan metabolism in schizophrenia: a post-mortem study of metabolites on the serotonin and kynurenine pathways in schizophrenic and control subjects. *Psychopharmacology* 1979;**62**:279-85.

22. Randrup, A., & Munkvad, I. Special antagonism of amphetamine-induced abnormal behaviour. Inhibition of stereotyped activity with increase of some normal activities. *Psychopharmacologia* 1965;7:416-22.

23. Crow, T. J., Deakin, J. F. W., Johnstone, E. C., & Longden, A. Dopamine and schizophrenia. *Lancet* 1976;ii:563-6.

24. Murphy, D. L., & Wyatt, R. J. Reduced monoamine oxidase activity in blood platelets from schizophrenic patients. *Nature* 1972;**238**:225-6.

25. Crow, T. J., Baker, H. F., & Cross, A. J., *et al.* Monoamine mechanisms in chronic schizophrenia: post-mortem neurochemical findings. *Br J Psychiatry* 1979;**134**:249-56.

26. Crow, T. J., Spear, P. J., & Arbuthnott, G. W. Intracranial self-stimulation with electrodes in the region of the locus coeruleus. *Brain Res* 1972;**36**:275-87.

27. Stein, L., & Wise, C. D. Possible etiology of schizophrenia: progressive damage to the noradrenergic reward system by 6-hydroxydopamine. *Science* 1971; **171**:1032-6.

28. Cross, A. J., Crow, T. J., Killpack, W. S., Longden, A., Owen, F., & Riley, G. J. The activities of brain dopamine-β-

hydroxylase and catechol-*o*-methyl transferase in schizophrenics and controls. *Psychopharmacology* 1978;59: 117-21.

29. Cotes, P. M., Crow, T. J., Johnstone, E. C., Bartlett, W., & Bourne, R. C. Neuroendocrine changes in acute schizophrenia as a function of clinical state and neuroleptic medication. *Psychol Med* 1978;8:657-65.

30. Letemendia, F. J. J., & Harris, A. D. Chlorpromazine and the untreated chronic schizophrenic: a long-term trial. *Br J Psychiatry* 1967;113:950-8.

31. Kornetsky, C. Hyporesponsivity of chronic schizophrenic patients to dextroamphetamine. *Arch Gen Psychiatry* 1976;33:1425-8.

32. Crow, T. J., & Mitchell, W. S. Subjective age in chronic schizophrenia: evidence for a sub-group of patients with defective learning capacity? *Br J Psychiatry* 1975;126:360-3.

33. Crow, T. J., & Stevens, M. Age disorientation in chronic schizophrenia; the nature of the cognitive deficit. *Br J Psychiatry* 1978;133:137-42.

34. Haug, J. O. Pneumoencephalographic studies in mental disease. *Acta Psychiatr Scand (suppl)* 1962;165:1-104.

35. Asano, N. Pneumoencephalographic study of schizophrenia. In: Mitsuda, H., ed. *Clinical genetics in psychiatry: problems in nosological classification*. Tokyo: Igaku-Shoin, 1967;209-19.

36. Johnstone, E. C., Crow, T. J., Frith, C. D., Stevens, M., Kreel, L., & Husband, J. The dementia of dementia praecox. *Acta Psychiatr Scand* 1978;57:305-24.

37. Weinberger, D. R., Torrey, E. F., Neophytides, A. N., & Wyatt, R. J. Lateral cerebral centricular enlargement in chronic schizophrenia. *Arch Gen Psychiatry* 1979;36:735-9.

38. Crow, T. J. Viral causes of psychiatric disease. *Postgrad Med J* 1978;54:763-7.

39. Tyrrell, D. A. J., Parry, R. P., Crow, T. J., Johnstone, E., & Ferrier, I. N. Possible virus in schizophrenia and some neurological disorders. *Lancet* 1979;i: 839-41.

40. Crow, T. J., Ferrier, I. N., & Johnstone, E. C. Characteristics of patients with schizophrenia or neurological disorder and virus-like agent in cerebrospinal fluid. *Lancet* 1979;i:842-4.

19.

Irving I. Gottesman & James Shields

GENETIC THEORIES OF SCHIZOPHRENIA

MAIN GROUNDS FOR OUR EMPHASIS ON GENETIC FACTORS

In support of the position we are proposing for genetic factors in theories about the

From I. Gottesman & J. Shields, "Genetic theorizing and schizophrenia," *The British Journal of Psychiatry*, 1973, vol. 122, pp. 15–20.

aetiology of schizophrenia, we cite the following:

1. Our species is extremely diverse genetically. It is logical to expect that this genetic variability will occasionally produce a combination of genes that results in a *phenodeviant* (Lerner, 1958) at the extreme of a distribution. The work of Lewontin (1967) on blood group antigens and

of Harris (1970) on enzymes suggests that about 30 per cent of all human loci are polymorphic, i.e. two or more alleles at a given gene locus, each with frequencies greater than .01 (hence not explainable by mutation). The findings imply that 16 per cent of the loci coding for the structure of proteins in any one person will be heterozygous; using conservative estimates for the number of such loci (50,000) we each of us have about 8,000 loci at which there are two different alleles, each locus resulting in a distinct protein. (Genes responsible for regulation and organization are excluded from consideration at this stage of our ignorance.) Harris calculated that the probability of two persons at random having the same type of enzymes at only eight loci was 1 in 200; the most commonly occurring types would be found in 1.8 per cent of the population. He called the kind of diversity already demonstrated merely the tip of an iceberg.

2. Many morphological and physiological traits are known to be under some genetic control. Behavioural traits such as intelligence, social introversion, and anxiety have an appreciable genetic component, with data for some of these traits coming from animal strain difference and selection studies as well as from work with twins and families. It would be a surprise if schizophrenia were altogether exempted from analogous genetic influences.

3. No environmental causes have been found which will invariably or even with moderate probability produce schizophrenia in subjects unrelated to a schizophrenic. When cases of *folie à deux* are examined carefully, a high prevalence of schizophrenia is found among the genetic relatives of the induced (Scharfetter, 1970), thus shifting the focus from the role of inducer as a cause to one of precipitator, and a consequent refocusing on the *predisposition* of the induced.

4. Schizophrenia is present in all countries that have been studied extensively. Table 19-1 shows that in many the incidence is about the same despite great variations in ecologies such as child rearing practices. Such observations detract from assigning 'culture' a major causal role in the aetiology of schizophrenia.

5. Within modern urban communities there is a disproportionately higher incidence and prevalence of schizophrenia in the lowest social classes compared to the highest. On the face of it, such observations provide strong support for the role of social stressors as causes of schizophrenia. Evaluation of the data (e.g. Goldberg and Morrison, 1963; Turner and Wagenfeld, 1967) suggests that downward social drift of the patient is the major explanation for the excess of schizophrenia in the lower classes; however, some genetically predisposed individuals might have remained compensated had they been in a more sheltered class. Paradoxically, social stressors can be both predisposing and precipitating at different times. Kay and Roth (1961) in their study of late paraphrenia noted that social isolation was initially the effect of the preferences of schizoid people and secondarily a cause of their decompensation in that isolation removed various resources for adjustment in old age. Fuller and Collins (1970) provided a clear experimental model for such a phenomenon in mice susceptible to audiogenic seiz-

TABLE 19-1
Expectation of Schizophrenia for the General Population (From Slater, 1968)

Date	Country	N (age-corrected)	Expectation (%)	S.E.
1931	Switzerland	899	1·23	0·368
1936	Germany	7,955·5	0·51	0·088
1942	Denmark	23,251	0·69	0·054
1942	Finland	194,000	0·91	0·021
1946	Sweden	10,705	0·81	0·087
1959	Japan	10,545	0·82	0·088
1964	Iceland	4,913	0·73	0·121

ures; sound as a stressor precipitated seizures in certain predisposed genotypes (DBA) on first exposure but not in others (C57BL); on a second trial 'sensitization-induced seizure susceptibility' was observed in 60 per cent of the C57BL mice but it was seen in even more (81 per cent) of the hybrids carrying half their genes from the DBAs. Even when the stressor predisposed the mice to seizures, it did so as a function of the genetic predisposition.

Let us try to make it clear that we would not downgrade the part played by stress—it is after all half of the diathesis-stress model. We, as well as others, are unable to deal adequately with the concept of stress as an explanatory construct or as an intervening variable. Many of the difficulties plaguing the concept are confronted by Levine and Scotch (1970) and their colleagues and by Selye (1956). The simplistic flow chart

$$Stressor \longrightarrow Stress \longrightarrow Disorder$$

is all right as a starting point, but denies the important role we wish to assign to the *'stressee'*. Events which are apperceived as stressors depend on the genotypic *and* experiential uniqueness (e.g. intrauterine environment, perinatal hazards, learning history, exposure to CNS toxins, etc.) of the stressee; so do the kind and degree of stress responses, and so do the various disordered outcomes of the stress responses. The problems of specificity are far from solved and we don't yet have the answers. But why might the results of stress vary from hypertension to ulcer to schizophrenia?—perhaps because of the specific properties of the stressee.

6. There is an increasing risk of schizophrenia to the relatives of schizophrenics as a function of the degree of genetic relatedness, as can be seen in Table 19-2. The familial distribution cannot entirely

TABLE 19-2
Expectation of Schizophrenia for Relatives of Schizophrenics (After Slater and Cowie, 1971)

Relationship	Total relatives (age-corrected)	Schizophrenic %	
		(a)	(b)
Parents	7,675	4·4	5·5
Sibs (all)	8,504·5	8·5	10·2
Sibs (neither parent schizophrenic)	7,535	8·2	9·7
Sibs (one parent schizophrenic)	674·5	13·8	17·2
Children	1,226·5	12·3	13·9
Children of mating Schiz. × Schiz.	134	36·6	46·3
Half-sibs	311	3·2	3·5
Uncles and aunts	3,376	2·0	3·6
Nephews and nieces	2,315	2·2	2·6
Grandchildren	713	2·8	3·5
First cousins	2,438·5	2·9	3·5

(a) Diagnostically certain cases only.
(b) Also including probable schizophrenics.

be due to environmental differences between families—the MZ concordance rate is higher than the DZ—or to gross differences within families such as sex or birth order. Table 19-3 presents the results of the earlier twin studies. These are simple pairwise rates without age correction and count as concordant pairs in which the co-twin had any schizophrenic-like illness.

The more recent twin studies have usually been reported by the authors themselves as showing a range of rates, depending on what conditions are included as concordant. In our Maudsley twin study (Gottesman and Shields, 1972) we employed a diagnosis for both proband and co-twin which is based on the consensus of six diagnosticians from three different countries. They reached their opinions from summaries which did not refer to the diagnosis or zygosity of the other twin. The consensus diagnosis of schizophrenia, reflecting middle-of-the-road standards, gave better MZ/DZ discrimination that at-

TABLE 19-3
The Earlier Twin Series
(After Gottesman and Shields, 1966)

Investigator	Date	MZ pairs			SS DZ pairs		
		N	C	%	N	C	%
Luxenburger	1928	19	11	58	13	0	0
Rosanoff *et al.*	1934	41	25	61	53	7	13
Essen-Möller	1941	11	7	64	27	4	15
Kallmann	1946	174	120	69	296	34	11
Slater	1953	37	24	65	58	8	14
Inouye	1961	55	33	60	11	2	18

TABLE 19-5
Concordance (Proband Method) in Recent Twin
Studies at a Level Approximating to the Consensus
Diagnosis of Schizophrenia

Investigation	MZ	DZ
Kringlen, Norway (1967)	31/69 45%	14/96 15%
Fischer *et al.*, Denmark (1969)	14/25 56%	12/45 26%
Tienari, Finland (1971)*	7/20 35%	3/23 13%
Allen *et al.*, U.S.A. (1972)*	52/121 43%	12/131 9%
Gottesman and Shields, U.K. (1972)	15/26 58%	4/34 12%
Total	119/261 46%	45/329 14%

* Male pairs exclusively.

tempts to apply very strict or very broad criteria, as Table 19-4 shows.

The sampling methods in recent twin studies permit accurate use of the proband method in calculating concordance, which was not possible in some of the older studies and is theoretically more correct (cf. Allen, Harvald and Shields, 1967). Such rates show the proportion of independently-ascertained schizophrenics who have affected co-twins, i.e. are casewise rates. Table 19-5 shows our estimate of probandwise concordance in the recent research, using a criterion which approximates to the consensus diagnosis of our own study.

7. The difference in identical vs. fraternal twin concordance rates is not due to aspects of the within-family environment that are more similar for MZ than DZ twins although there are many such aspects. Studies of MZ twins reared apart as well as adoption and fostering studies show

TABLE 19-6
Psychiatric Disorders in Foster Home Reared
Children (After Heston, 1966)

	Mother schizophrenic (N=47)	Controls (N=50)
Mean age	35•8	36•3
Schizophrenia	5	—
Mental deficiency, IQ< 70	4	—
Sociopathic personality	9	2
Neurotic personality disorder	13	7

a markedly raised incidence of schizophrenia among relatives even when they were brought up in a different home by non-relatives. Heston's data are illustrative (1966) as shown in Table 19-6.

8. Such implicitly causal constructs as schizophrenogenic mothers, double-binding, marital skew, and communication

TABLE 19-4
Concordance in Maudsley Schizophrenic Twin Study for Consensus Diagnosis and Judges with the
Most Extreme Criteria for Schizophrenia

	MZ	DZ	MZ : DZ
Judge with narrowest criteria Both twins first-choice schizophrenia	3/15 20%	3/22 14%	1•5
Consensus diagnosis of 6 judges Both twins schizophrenia, including ? schizophrenia	11/22 50%	3/33 9%	5•5
Judge with broadest criteria Both twins schizophrenia (including borderline schizophrenia) or schizotype	14/24 58%	8/33 24%	2•4

deviance, have been found wanting (by others as well as ourselves), although we would not categorically deny them a role as possible precipitators or exacerbators of schizophrenia. The offspring of male schizophrenics are as much at risk for the disorder as are the offspring of female schizophrenics. When both parents are schizophrenic the risk to their children is about 46 per cent; it is difficult to account for the absence of schizophrenia in the rest of the children on environmental grounds given such a schizophrenogenic environment; in what might be perceived as an even worse environment, one where one parent is a schizophrenic and the other is psychopathic, the risk of schizophrenia in the offspring is only 15 per cent. Both sets of data are, however, compatible with genetic theories of aetiology.

We close this section with a reminder that, paradoxically, it is the data showing that identical twins are as often discordant as concordant for schizophrenia that provide the most impressive evidence for the important role of environmental factors in schizophrenia, whatever they may be.

GENETIC MODELS FOR THE MODE OF TRANSMISSION

Once the existence of a genetic diathesis has been established, it becomes important to provide a theory for the mode of its transmission. In the first instance theories provide a scheme for systematizing diverse pieces in a jigsaw puzzle. In the second, they encourage the formation of testable and refutable hypotheses; ideally they should compete with each other in such a fashion that one theory is made more credible and another less so when subjected to a test. Different genetic models have different implications for the kinds of studies to be conducted, for the kind of molecular pathology involved and hence

the rational treatment, for possibilities of detecting premorbid cases, and for recommendations about the prevention of schizophrenia, e.g. through genetic counselling.

Models for the genetic mode of transmission in schizophrenia can be roughly classed into three categories, which can in turn be divided. The broad classes are monogenic or one major locus, genetic heterogeneity, and polygenic. Monogenic theories can be divided into recessive, requiring homozygosity or a double dose of a gene at one locus (one from each parent), and dominant, requiring only a single dose of some necessary gene (from one parent). Genes themselves are neither dominant nor recessive; the terms only have meaning with respect to a particular phenotypic characteristic. John and Lewis (1966) introduced the useful distinction between exophenotype (external phenotype) and endophenotype (internal), with the latter only knowable after aid to the naked eye, e.g. a biochemical test or a microscopic examination of chromosome morphology. As endophenotypes have become more available, the distinction between recessivity and dominance has become blurred; in a sense all genes are 'dominant' (cf. sickle-cell anaemia vs. sickling trait) when we have a way of detecting gene action molecularly. Like most inborn errors of metabolism PKU is the result of an enzyme deficiency inherited in a recessive fashion (two doses of a gene), but the heterozygote (one dose of the gene) can usually be identified. Enzyme deficiencies can also be inherited in a dominant fashion, e.g. porphyria. The difference depends on how far the normal homozygous state produces an excess of the minimal level needed for health. To quote Harris (1970, p. 252), 'Dominant inheritance of a disease due to an enzyme deficiency is most likely to occur where the enzyme in question happens to be rate limiting in the metabolic pathway in which it takes part, because the level of activity of such enzymes in the normal organism will in general be closer to the minimum required to maintain normal function'.

Dominant gene theories of schizophrenia which provide for the modifying effects on the phenotype of genes at other loci or other alleles at the same locus (cf. the G6PD polymorphism) are in practice difficult to distinguish from polygenic models; Slater's (1958; Slater and Cowie, 1971) particular model will be discussed below. A simple monogenic theory for all schizophrenic psychoses where the gene is sufficient cause for the psychosis has no advocates.

Genetic heterogeneity means different things to many people. It can mean that schizophrenia, like low grade mental deficiency, is comprised of many rare varieties of different recessive or dominant conditions with the mutation rate at each locus maintaining the genes in the population. One form of genetic heterogeneity is one we *can* agree with—the model is like that of mental deficiency throughout its range; a very small percentage of schizophrenic cases are due to different dominant and recessive loci, a further group is due to symptomatic phenocopies (e.g. epilepsy, or amphetamines, or psychic trauma), but the vast majority are segregants in a normal distribution of a liability towards schizophrenia.

Polygenic models can be divided into continuous phenotypic variation and quasi-continuous variation or threshold effect. Examples of the former are height and IQ scores where extremes of a distribution may be labelled as pathological (dwarf or retardate) at some arbitrary point in the distribution; individuals just to the other side of the point are not distinctively different. The most widely known polygenic trait models posit a large number of underlying genes all of whose effects are equal; with traits so determined we would expect the phenotypic correlation between relatives to be the same as the genetic correlation if the traits are completely heritable. We find, for example, that the parent-child and sib-sib correlations for height or fingerprint ridge count are very close to 0.50. A less well-known polygenic model of importance to our thinking about a model for schizophrenia permits the gene effects to be unequal. Thoday (1961, 1967) has shown that, although bristle number in Drosophila is under polygenic control, 87.5 per cent of the genetic difference between the means of a high and a low line could be accounted for by only five of the many genetic loci involved. The implications of such a weighted gene model for schizophrenia are to encourage searching by the usual methods of segregation analysis and linkage for some few handleable genes which may prove to mediate a large part of the genetic variation in the liability to schizophrenia.

A polygenic model for handling discontinuous phenotypic variation, so-called threshold or quasi-continuous characters, also forms an important background to our thinking about schizophrenia. This model has made analysis of such traits as schizophrenia, cleft palate, diabetes, and seizure susceptibility feasible, provided one accepts the working hypothesis that the underlying liability is continuously and normally distributed. Falconer (1965, 1967), Edwards (1969), Morton *et al.* (1970) and Smith (1970, 1971) have illustrated the methods involved, and we (Gottesman and Shields, 1967) were the first to study psychopathology with such methods. Data on the occurrence of cleft lip with or without cleft palate, CL(P), in the relatives of probands can be used to illustrate the threshold model (Carter, 1969; Woolf, 1971). Schizophrenia is not present at birth like cleft lip so the analogy

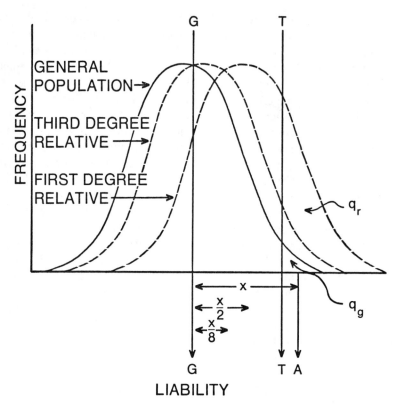

FIGURE 19-1.—Model for Polygenic Inheritance of Threshold Characters: Three Distributions of the Underlying Liability in the General Population, in First-Degree Relatives, and in Third-Degree Relatives (See Text for Symbol Definitions).

is wanting in this respect, but such elegant data for a disorder with both a variable age of onset and with the capacity for remission are not available yet.

The population incidence (q_{g}) of CL(P) can be taken as ·001 (Woolf, 1971). The risk in sibs is ·04, a low absolute value but a 40-fold increase over the population risk; in second degree relatives it is ·0065 and in third degree (first cousins), ·0036. The sharp falling off of incidence as one moves to more remote relatives is one of the tests for polygenic theory; a dominant gene theory calls for the frequency of affected relatives to decrease by ½ in each step. An important parallel between CL(P) and schizophrenia is that the risk to parents is about ½ that in sibs although both are classes of first degree relatives. In both disorders the

reduced values probably represent the effect of social selection for who become parents; different values of q_{g} will be required to evaluate the significance to genetic theorizing of lower rates in parents when such selection is probable. Fig. 19.1 shows a diagram for the hypothetical distribution of the genetic liability to CL(P) or other threshold character, for the general population as well as first and third degree relatives.

The X axis is for normal deviate values of the posited polygenically determined predisposition or liability to the threshold trait. At a point on the X axis (not drawn to scale) corresponding to a value of ·001 (q_{g}) of the general population we can erect a vertical line (T) to represent the threshold value of liability beyond which all persons are affected; such a line would cut off 4·0 per cent of the sibs (q_{r}) and only 0·36 per cent of first cousins. The distances x/2, and x/8 in the figure are the increased means of the liability distributions for first and third degree relatives and are predictable from our general knowledge about genetic correlation between relatives, once A and G, the mean liability of affected persons, and of the general population, have been determined. A sharp threshold between the liability of affected and unaffected persons is artificial; the threshold model implies an increasing likelihood of being affected as the polygenic predisposition increases (Edwards, 1969; Smith, 1970).

Support for the threshold model arises from a demonstration of a relationship between the severity of the defect in the proband and the risk to his relatives, based on the assumption that the more genes, the more severe the condition, and the more genes, the more the relatives will have when the amount is halved, quartered, etc. for CL(P) unilateral and bilateral affectation form two levels of severity; in the sibs of unilateral cases the risk is 3·83 per cent, in those of bilaterals, 6·71 per cent; and the generalization holds for other degrees of relatives. Further support for the theory comes from the demonstration that the risk to probands' relatives, say sibs, increases with the number of other relatives affected; i.e. families with two patients are more 'high risk' families than those with only one. In the case of CL(P), if no other relative is affected, the recurrence risk to a proband's sib is 2·24 per cent; if an aunt or uncle is affected, the risk rises to 9·91 per cent; finally if a parent is affected, the risk to the sib rises to 15·55 per cent. The malformation is too rare for there to have been extensive twin studies. From the available evidence Carter (1965, 1969) estimates the risk to the identical twin of a proband to be about 40 per cent.

From the above data estimates of the heritability of the underlying liability to CL(P) can be made. Heritability (h^2) is defined as the proportion of the total variability of the trait in the population that is due to genetic differences, in the absence of dominance and interaction between genes. The risks to MZ twins, sibs, and first cousins yield h^2 estimates (Smith, 1970) of 88 per cent, 92 per cent, and 100 per cent respectively, reasonably consistent values.

COMPATIBILITY BETWEEN THEORY AND DATA

We shall deal with monogenic theories first. Recessive inheritance for schizophrenia is difficult to support, since sibs are not more often affected than children. Most monogenic theories invoke a dominant gene. Slater's final version of the theory which he first proposed in 1958 fits the pooled family data best when the population life-time risk for developing schizophrenia is taken as 0.008_5 and the gene frequency as 0.03. Ninety per cent of schizophrenics will then be heterozygotes, so the trait is basically a dominant one. Only 13 per cent of heterozygotes manifest the psychosis; however, manifestation is complete in the 10 per cent of schizophrenics who have inherited the gene in double dose (Slater and Cowie, 1971). Elston and Campbell (1970) proposed a similar theory, derived from the application of rigorous mathematical methods to the data of Kallmann. According to this theory, the manifestation rate in heterozygotes is only 6 per cent or 7 per cent, even lower than the 13 per cent 'penetrance' on Slater's theory. Clearly such theories are still viable and have the merit of simplicity. They suggest that the search for a simply inherited biological error underlying all cases may not be in vain. The problem of how the abnormal gene can maintain itself in the population in view of the low fertility of schizophrenics prompts a search for compensating selective advantage, such as an increased resistance to virus infections early in life (e.g. Carter and Watts, 1971). However, no mendelizing defect has so far been identified in schizophrenia—unless it is, the theory will remain implausible for many. Anderson (1972) has pointed out that 'it is difficult to estimate the degree of penetrance unless the variations in phenotype can be identified unequivocally, and unless there is independent information establishing the mode of inheritance'. If the mode of inheritance is independently established as due to a dominant gene there is no objection in principle to invoking very low penetrances; Sewall Wright himself (1963, p. 178) cited a penetrance of 2 per cent for a gene associated with a morphological character in hybrid guinea-pigs.

To avoid invoking greatly reduced penetrance Meehl (1962, 1973) and Heston (1970) have concerned themselves with a phenotype broader than schizophrenia, the schizotype and schizoid disease respectively. Heston considers most studies to have shown about 50 per cent of the first degree relatives of schizophrenics to have some mental abnormality. The difficulty is that there is no reliable way of defining schizoid disease without reference to relatedness to a schizophrenic. If the concept is defined broadly enough to encompass abnormalities in 50 per cent of schizophrenics' parents, sibs, and children, and then generalized, the population base rate will be exaggerated and include many false positives. Nevertheless, there is certainly merit in carrying out family investigations based on borderline schizophrenics, schizoid personalities and the like in order to test a Mendelian hypothesis.

Heterogeneity theories are less well defined, so it is more difficult to say whether they are compatible with the data or not.

One class of heterogeneity theory claims that in principle schizophrenia can be divided aetiologically, though not necessarily clinically, into two groups: (1) a high-risk genetic group comprising a large number of individually rare genetic disorders, each with a very high manifestation rate and inherited as recessive (Dewey *et al.*, 1965), or as dominant traits (Erlenmeyer-Kimling, personal communication); and (2) a residual group of sporadic cases with a low risk of recurrence consisting on the one hand of fresh mutations and on the other of a group of cases of environmental or complex aetiology. Deafness, blindness, low grade retardation, and the muscular dystrophies are conditions which belong to this class. The theory avoids the *ad hoc*

assumption of low penetrance, though in practice there are few schizophrenic families in which the risk to sibs is as high as 25 per cent. If there were many recessive loci for schizophrenia (as there are for deafness), dual mating parents would be unlikely to be of the same type, hence less than 100 per cent of the children would be affected, as is the case; but the observed rate in children, 13.9 per cent, when only one parent is affected remains unaccountable. The consequences of dominant gene heterogeneity are essentially the same as those of monogenic dominance for the recurrence risk in families; however, the theory accounts better for the continuing prevalence of schizophrenia in the population without invoking either unrealistically high mutation rates, as pointed out by Erlenmeyer-Kimling and Paradowski (1966), or speculative selective advantages for the heterozygote.

There is increasing evidence (Davison and Bagley, 1969) that some cases—the symptomatic schizophrenias—develop on the basis of organic pathology, e.g. Huntington's chorea, Wilson's disease, temporal lobe epilepsy, and amphetamine intoxication. Slater *et al.* (1963) believe that the pathogenesis of such cases may give important clues to the pathogenesis of the more genetic forms of schizophrenia.

TESTS OF POLYGENIC THEORY

In this section we shall muster some of the lines of evidence which can be brought to bear on the relative merits of polygenic theory in accounting for the data on schizophrenia. One indirect approach we have favoured in the past consisted of an effort to evaluate the compatibility and consistency of independent estimates of the heritability (h^2) of the liability to schizophrenia, after assuming it could be a threshold trait (Gottesman and Shields, 1967). We now present a summary in Fig. 19-2 of an updated version of this approach. We used Smith's (1970, 1971) improvements to Falconer's method, our own consensus diagnosis pairwise MZ concordance rate (50 per cent) and DZ rate (9 per cent), and the pooled rate for sibs (10.2 per cent), offspring of dual matings (46 per cent), and second degree relatives (3.3 per cent). Six different values of q_p, the population risk, ranging from 0.85 per cent to 3.0 per cent, were used so as to show the effects on estimations of heritability values. Probandwise twin rates might have been more technically correct here, but they would not change the overall impression; the pooled probandwise rate for MZ twins in

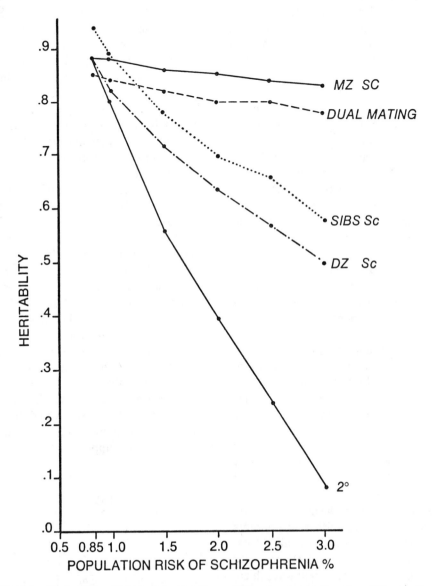

FIGURE 19-2.—Heritabilities (Smith) of the Liability to Schizophrenia as a Function of Varying Population Risks (%), Estimated from Risks in Different Classes of Probands' Relatives.

the recent studies approaches 50 per cent.

For Fig. 19-2 we have taken the rates in relatives at the level including probable schizophrenia; again the overall impression would have been little affected had we only used 'strictly' diagnosed rates. Earlier questions we and others raised about the suitability of the Falconer method for MZ twin data have been resolved by Smith's refinements; and since the child regression on midparent is the same as that for one MZ twin on his co-twin (1.0), we can calculate the h^2 from risks to dual mating offspring.

It is the consistency of the estimates rather than their absolute values which is our main concern. Fig. 19-2 shows the results of this procedure; the results are most consistent at values of population risk of about 1 per cent, yielding heritability estimates close to 85 per cent. It can be seen that the MZ and dual mating data are least sensitive to changes in q_p, while the second degree data are very much affected by changes in q_p exceeding 1 per cent.

When pooled data on the risk to parents are subjected to the procedure, we must take account of the lower value of q_p in a sample selected for mental health (cf. Mednick *et al.*, 1971); by halving a risk of 1 per cent to 0.5 per cent and entering Smith's nomograph with a risk q_r for parents of 5.5 per cent, we obtain an estimate of heritability of 72 per cent, not too much different from the values of unselected relatives at $q_p = 1$ per cent. The consistency of h^2 estimates across relatives sharing different amounts of environmental communality provides one line of evidence in favour of polygenic theory.

Risk as a function of the number of relatives already affected with schizophrenia provides a further test of polygenic theory; (a) the increase in risk to probands' sibs depending on whether a parent was schizophrenic or not and (b) to children depending on whether one or both parents were

affected. Simple monogenic theory would predict no increase in the case of sibs and a rise from 50 per cent to 75 per cent for children. However, current modifications of monogenic theory predict a considerable rise under both (a) and (b). Slater and Cowie (1971) have calculated the extent of these increases for Slater's theory. We have compared the increased risks with those predicted by polygenic theory (Smith, 1971) taking q_p at 1 per cent and H^2 at 80 per cent as the tabled values closest to our interpretation of Fig. 19-2. The risks are given in Table 19-7. For sibs, both theories are equally good at predicting the empirical risks. In the cases of children when one parent is affected the observed risks are too high for both theoretical predictions; if Kallmann's data were omitted, or if the median empirical risk (9.7 per cent) were used as a criterion, the fit with both theoretical predictions would be much improved.

Other tests not discussed here (cf. Gottesman and Shields, 1967; Slater and Cowie, 1971; Ødegaard, 1972) include: (a) the drop in risk as one moves from MZ twins, to first degree and to second degree relatives; (b) the association between severity in the proband and the risk to the relative; (c) the occurrence in relatives of disorders other than strict schizophrenia, shading off into normality; and (d) the unilateral and bilateral familial distribution of affected relatives. The data are not free from ambiguity, but the first three tests tend to support polygenic theory,

TABLE 19-7
Schizophrenia Risk as Function of Parent Status

Risk (per cent)	(a) To probands' sibs		(b) To probands' children	
No. of parents affected	0	1	1	2
Observed, Table II	9.7	17.2	13.9	46.3
Predicted, polygenic	6.5	18.5	8.3	40.9
Predicted, monogenic	9.4	13.5	8.8	37.1

while the latter is consistent with a weighted polygenic as well as a monogenic model.

We agree with Anderson (1972) that it is not too helpful to rely on evolutionary theory in deciding among genetic models; we simply do not know enough about how any human behaviour evolved (cf. Gottesman and Heston, 1972). However, data on the fertility or Darwinian fitness of schizophrenics are interesting and important in their own right. The question of how a disadvantageous genetic condition can be maintained in the population over time despite the greatly reduced fitness of both male and female schizophrenics (e.g. Slater, Hare and Price, 1971) can perhaps be answered more readily by polygenic than monogenic theory. The former would obviate the need to find a selective advantage in gene carriers hypothesized by the balanced polymorphism theory of Huxley *et al.* (1964). Response to natural selection against a polygenic trait associated with lowered marriage and fertility rates would be very slow. Genes in the system would only be eliminated from the gene pool when they were present in the rare individual at the tail end of the distribution, while those below the threshold would not be subject to negative selection. Schizophrenics could be thought of as part of the genetic load, the price paid for conserving genetic diversity. In passing, we may note that high heritabilities suggest that the traits concerned may not have been objects of directional selection pressures and so may be irrelevant to the evolution of our species.

The evidence we have adduced in favour of polygenic threshold inheritance shows that it is an equal contender with current monogenic theories. On general grounds polygenic inheritance appears more likely to us; the commonest disorder for which single gene inheritance has been established, cystic fibrosis of the pancreas, is about 20 times rarer than schizophrenia. However, there is considerable overlap between the two principal models, and the tests proposed for differentiating between them are far from efficient. As Slater and Cowie (1971) say, 'Two genetical models are available, either of which provides an adequate framework for the observations, so that the worker is entitled to choose the model which suits his purposes best.' To these we would add heterogeneity theories. Our own preference for a polygenic framework leads us to look for specific and important contributing factors on both the diathesis and the stressor sides of the model. Refutation of a polygenic theory would come about by the discovery of an endophenotype which segregated in a monogenic way in all schizophrenics.

FACTORS CONTRIBUTING TO LIABILITY

It would be both defeatist and incorrect to assume that because a trait such as the liability to schizophrenia is inherited polygenically the search for cause has ended and relevant specific genetic loci are undiscoverable in principle. The genes underlying continuous variation are not qualitatively different from those associated with discontinuous traits at the molecular level—both are subject to the same rules of inheritance because they are chromosomal and thus segregate, show dominance, epistasis, linkage, and genotype-environment interactions (cf. Penrose, 1938). From the beginning of this century geneticists have succeeded in identifying specific loci in polygenic systems and in locating them on specific chromosomes by linkage with major genes; however, the feats were accomplished with genetically tractable organisms such as wheat and *Drosophila* (Thoday, 1961, 1967). It is heuristically important to us to learn that whenever polygenic variation has been studied under *laboratory conditions* (e.g. inbreeding, backcrossing, availability of chromosome markers), 'a few handleable genes have proved to mediate a large part of the genetic variance under study' (Thoday, 1967). One locus in wheat accounted for 83 per cent of the variance in ripening date, with three others jointly accounting for 14 per cent. Such 'weighted genes' for bristle number were mentioned, but we must add the striking fact that separable components of the complex character permitted their study as more or less discontinuous variables. Wright (1934a, b) concluded that three or four major factors (genes) controlled the threshold character polydactyly in inbred lines of guinea-pigs.

Encouraged by the demonstration that the genes in polygenic inheritance need not be and often are not roughly equal in their effects on the phenotype, and bolstered by our clinical observations on what appears to be 'excess' similarity between pairs of affected relatives on the simpler equal effects assumption, we hazard the speculation that there are a few genes of large effect in the polygenic system underlying many schizophrenias. In other words, we view the aetiology of schizophrenia as being due to a weighted kind of polygenic system with a threshold effect. Some of the heuristic implications of our speculations about high value genes in the polygenic system underlying schizophrenia include a focusing on partitionable facets of the syndrome such as catatonia, paranoid features, protein polymorphisms in brain and blood, and neurophysiology, on the chance that family studies will reveal one or more of the high value genes. There are already suggestions in the human genetics literature that a gene associated with a biochemically different insulin in juvenile diabetics may be identified as one of the polygenes causing early onset diabetes (Falconer,

1967), and one facet of congenital dislocation of the hip, joint laxity, may segregate as a Mendelian trait (Wynne-Davies, 1970).

The contribution of specific genetic factors to the genetic liability to schizophrenia analogous to the specific contributors in the diabetes and hip examples above forms only part of the picture in respect to the *total* liability to schizophrenia. General genetic contributors which serve as modifiers or potentiators, together with general environmental contributors which serve as modifiers or potentiators, each define dimensions of liability which combine with the specific genetic liability to determine the net liability and the position of an individual *vis-à-vis* the threshold at a particular time.

DIATHESIS-STRESS AND THE UNFOLDING OF SCHIZOPHRENIA

A static depiction of schizophrenia is not very satisfying when it comes to communicating knowledge about the changes over time which add to or subtract from the combined genetic predisposition to schizophrenia. A dynamic picture of an individual's trajectory through life is needed to do justice to the concept of a genetic diathesis interacting with stress to produce the varieties of schizophrenic phenotypes (cf. Bleuler, 1968). Fig. 19-3 presents a trial scheme which incorporates the ideas of changes in the combined liability over time from environmental sources and from the environmental triggering of genes that had not been switched on at birth. The time axis starts with zero time at the moment of conception. Both chance (random) factors and ontogenetic constitutional changes will influence the trajectories, leading to both upward and downward inflections. Environmental stressors coming close together in time would be expected to exert a cascade effect and have more effect than the same stressors spread out in time.

G₁ is intended to indicate the trajectory of a person with a low (for schizophrenics generally) combined *genetic* liability to schizophrenia; over time environmental contributors to liability, say first the death of a spouse and then the onset of deafness, cause upward deflections of his trajectory to the threshold (T), culminating in a late-onset paraphrenia. The dashed line at the bottom of the zone of the so-called schizophrenic spectrum disorders (Kety, Rosenthal *et al.*, 1968) is intended to convey the idea of a possible need for a second threshold in our model; Wright (1934b) invoked a second threshold to account for the imperfectly formed fourth digit seen in crosses between a high and a moderate line of

guinea pigs with liabilities to polydactyly.

G₂ could be the divergent trajectories of a pair of MZ twins; only the A-twin encounters the sufficient factors over time leading to schizophrenia for a person with his genotype. The B-twin at the time of observation is discordant for schizophrenia, but close to the threshold of schizophrenic spectrum disorders. Sub-threshold values of combined liability make it clear why so many first degree relatives can have normal MMPIs (Gottesman and Shields, 1972) and why two phenotypically normal parents are typical for the vast majority of schizophrenics. The A-twin is shown to have an acute onset with an undistinguishable premorbid personality, and a remission from schizophrenia into a chronic schizoid state.

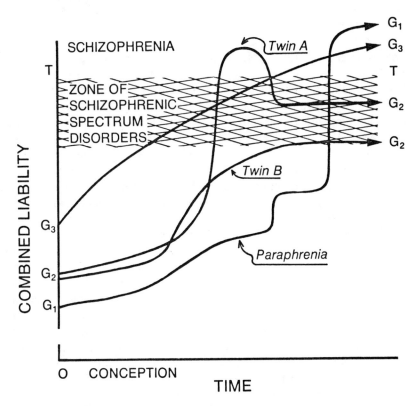

FIGURE 19-3.—Schematic Proposal for How Diathesis Interacts with Stress in the Ontogenesis of Schizophrenia.

G_3 is the posited trajectory of a person with a high genetic loading needing very little in the way of environmental contributors to make him schizoid; he is shown as having a poor premorbid personality, an insidious onset, and a deteriorating course. Many other life trajectories could have been drawn to illustrate the unfolding of schizophrenia. It is easy to see how the hospitalization data in pairs of twins and the fascinating histories of the Genain quadruplets (Rosenthal, 1963) would augment the total perspective about the pathogenesis of schizophrenia.

CONCLUSIONS

At the present time the case for a genetic basis for schizophrenia rests on the compatibility of the pattern of elevated risks to relatives with certain genetic models, together with the continued exclusion of any particular environmental factor as a sufficient cause. Ordinary Mendelian models will not do for explaining the mode of transmission for mental disorders since we find almost no families with 25 per cent or 50 per cent segregation ratios, and the population rates are so high as to make each condition 'common' by the standards for Mendelian diseases. Dominant gene models with incomplete penetrance, genetic heterogeneity models, and polygenic models are all viable contenders in the explanatory arena.

A satisfactory *corpus delicti* for the biochemical geneticist or cytogeneticist is not yet at hand. This does not mean that specific genetic factors play no part, or even that we must compare progress in the genetics of mental disorders unfavourably with that in other fields. In the first *Annual Review of Genetics* Robertson (1967) pointed out that, after years of control over such characters as milk yield in cows and egg size in poultry, we are surprisingly ignorant of the real biochemical or physiological differences between inbred lines. One of the most exciting challenges of the near future will consist of the best ways to synthesize the empirical facts about twin, family, and adoptee studies so as to lead to testable hypotheses.

Methods developed by Falconer, Edwards, and Smith permit the estimation of the heritability of the underlying predisposition or liability to developing a mental disorder, once the assumptions about the model being appropriate are accepted. Independent estimates from various classes of relatives lead to the convergence on a heritability value of about 80-90 per cent for the liability to schizophrenia. A weighted polygenic model (cf. Thoday on bristle number in *Drosophila*) offers hope that some facets of the schizophrenic phenotype will be shown to segregate or to have detectable biochemical or neurophysiological consequences.

It is important to understand the implications of finding that a trait such as the liability to schizophrenia has a high heritability. In the samples so far studied, it means that environmental factors were unimportant as causative agents of the schizophrenias. However, and this cannot be emphasized too strongly, these data do not permit the conclusion that curative or preventive measures will be ineffective. As Falconer (1965, p. 69) has pointed out, 'The environmental factors proved to be unimportant are those operating in the population sampled and these do not include special treatments or preventive measures. *No prediction can be made from a knowledge of the degree of genetic determination about the efficacy of curative or preventive treatments. All that could be said in such a case is that one will have to look outside the range of normal environments experienced by the untreated population.*' (Italics added.)

The beauty of a diathesis-stressor theory, or philosophy if you will, is that it fills the chasm between geneticism and environmentalism. Our preferred model for construing the syndrome of schizophrenia permits the clearer separation of aetiological and phenomenological considerations. It comprises a network of events connected by sequential causal arrows. A chain of consequences is set into motion by a variable, polygenically caused predisposition and culminates in a set of symptoms recognizable as schizophrenia. Feedback loops and chance have important roles in the total picture. Our construction clarifies how psychotherapy or phenothiazines or a good mother may each contribute to symptom amelioration without necessarily casting light on aetiological questions. It is our hope that a heuristic genetic theory about the aetiology of schizophrenia will hasten the day which brings it under man's control.

REFERENCES

Allen, G., Harvald, B., and Shields, J. (1967). 'Measures of twin concordance.' *Acta Genetica et Statistica Medica* (Basel), **17**, 475-81.

Allen, M. G., Cohen, S., and Pollin, W. (1972). 'Schizophrenia in veteran twins: a diagnostic review.' *American Journal of Psychiatry*, **128**, 939-45.

Anderson, V. E. (1972). 'Genetic hypotheses in schizophrenia', in *Genetic Factors in 'Schizophrenia'* (ed. Kaplan), Springfield, Ill.

Bleuler, E. (1911). *Dementia Praecox or the Group of Schizophrenias*. Translated by Joseph Zinkin. New York, 1950.

Bleuler, M. (1968). 'A 23-year longitudinal study of 208 schizophrenics and impressions in regard to the nature of schizophrenia', in *The Transmission of Schizophrenia* (eds. Rosenthal and Kety). Oxford.

Carter, C. O. (1965). 'The inheritance of common congenital malformations', in *Progress in Medical Genetics*, vol. 4 (eds. Steinberg and Bearn). New York.

_____ (1969). 'Genetics of common disorders.' *British Medical Bulletin*, **25**, 52-7.

Carter, M., and Watts, C. A. H. (1971). 'Possible biological advantages among schizophrenics' relatives.' *British Journal of Psychiatry*, **118**, 453-60.

Davison, K., and Bagley, C. R. (1969). 'Schizophrenia-like psychoses associated with organic disorders of the central nervous system: a review of the literature', in *Current Problems in Neuropsychiatry* (ed. Herrington). Ashford, Kent. (*British Journal of Psychiatry* Special Publication no. 4.)

Dewey, W. J., Barrai, I., Morton, N. E., and Mi, M. P. (1965). 'Recessive genes in severe mental defect.' *American Journal of Human Genetics*, **17**, 237-56.

Dobzhansky, T. (1968). 'On some fundamental concepts of Darwinian biology', in *Evolutionary Biology*, vol. 2 (eds. Dobzhansky, Hecht, and Steere). New York.

Edwards, J. H. (1969). 'Familial predisposition in man.' *British Medical Bulletin*, **25**, 58-64.

Elston, R. C., and Campbell, M. A. (1970). 'Schizophrenia: evidence for the major gene hypothesis.' *Behavior Genetics*, **1**, 3-10.

Erlenmeyer-Kimling, L., and Paradowski, W. (1966). 'Selection and schizophrenia.' *American Naturalist*, **100**, 651-65.

Falconer, D. S. (1965). 'The inheritance of liability to certain diseases, estimated from the incidence among relatives.' *Annals of Human Genetics*, **29**, 51-76.

_____ (1967). 'The inheritance of liability to diseases with variable age of onset, with particular reference to diabetes mellitus.' *Annals of Human Genetics*, **31**, 1-20.

Fischer, M., Harvald, B., and Hauge, M. (1969). 'A Danish twin study of schizophrenia.' *British Journal of Psychiatry*, **115**, 981-90.

Fuller, J. L., and Collins, R. L. (1970). 'Genetics of audiogenic seizures in mice: a parable for psychiatrists.' *Seminars in Psychiatry*, **2**, 75-88.

Goldberg, E. M., and Morrison, S. L. (1963). 'Schizophrenia and social class.' *British Journal of Psychiatry*, **109**, 785-802.

Gottesman, I. I., and Heston, L. L. (1972, in press). 'Human behavioral adaptations—speculations on their genesis', in *Genetic Endowment and Environment in the Determination of Behavior* (eds. Ehrman and Omenn). New York.

———— and Shields, J. (1966). 'Schizophrenia in twins: 16 years' consecutive admissions to a psychiatric clinic.' *British Journal of Psychiatry*, **112**, 809-18.

———— ———— (1967). 'A polygenic theory of schizophrenia.' *Proceedings of the National Academy of Sciences*, **58**, 199-205.

———— ———— (1972). *Schizophrenia and Genetics—a Twin Study Vantage Point*. New York.

Harris, H. (1970). *The Principles of Human Biochemical Genetics*. Amsterdam.

Heston. L. L. (1966). 'Psychiatric disorders in foster home reared children of schizophrenic mothers.' *British Journal of Psychiatry*, **112**, 819-25.

———— (1970). 'The genetics of schizophrenic and schizoid disease.' *Science*, **167**, 249-56.

Huxley, J., Mayr, E., Osmond, H., and Hoffer, A. (1964). 'Schizophrenia as a genetic morphism.' *Nature (London)*, **204**, 220-1.

John, B., and Lewis, K. R. (1966). 'Chromosome variability and geographic distribution in insects.' *Science*, **152**, 711-21.

Katz, M. M., Cole, J. O., and Barton, W. E. (eds.) (1968). *The Role and Methodology of Classification in Psychiatry and Psychopathology*. Public Health Service Publication No. 1584. Washington, D.C.: U.S. Government Printing Office.

Kay, D. W., and Roth, M. (1961). 'Environmental and hereditary factors in the schizophrenias of old age ('late paraphrenia') and their bearing on the general problem of causation in schizophrenia. *Journal of Mental Science*, **107**, 649-86.

Kety, S. S., Rosenthal, D., Wender, P. H., and Schulsinger, F. (1968). 'The types and prevalence of mental illness in the biological and adoptive families of adopted schizophrenics', in *The Transmission of Schizophrenia* (eds. Rosenthal and Kety). Oxford.

Kraepelin, E. (1896). *Psychiatrie*, 5th ed. Leipzig.

Kringlen, E. (1967). *Heredity and Environment in the Functional Psychoses*. London.

Lerner, I. M. (1958). *The Genetic Basis of Selection*. New York.

Levine, S., and Scotch, N. A. (eds.) (1970). *Social Stress*. Chicago.

Lewontin, R. C. (1967). 'An estimate of average heterozygosity in man.' *American Journal of Human Genetics*, **19**, 681-5.

Mayr, E. (1964). 'From molecules to organic diversity.' *Federation Proceedings, Federation of American Societies for Experimental Biology*, **23**, 1231-5.

Mednick, S. A., Mura, E., Schulsinger, F., and Mednick, B. (1971). 'Perinatal conditions and infant development in children with schizophrenic parents', in *Differential Reproduction in Individuals with Mental and Physical Disorders* (eds. Gottesman and Erlenmeyer-Kimling). *Social Biology*, **18** (Suppl.).

Meehl, P. E. (1962). 'Schizotaxia, schizotypy, schizophrenia.' *American Psychologist*, **17**, 827-38.

———— (1973). 'MAXCOV-HITMAX: a taxonomic search method for loose genetic syndromes', in P. E. Meehl, *Psychodiagnosis: Selected Papers*. Minneapolis. In press.

Morton, N. E., Yee, S., Elston, R. C., and Lew, R. (1970). 'Discontinuity and quasicontinuity: alternative hypotheses of multifactorial inheritance.' *Clinical Genetics*, **1**, 81-94.

Ødegaard, Ø. (1972). 'The multifactorial theory of inheritance in predisposition to schizophrenia', in *Genetic Factors in 'Schizophrenia'* (ed. Kaplan). Springfield, Ill.

Penrose, L. S. (1938). 'Genetic linkage in graded human characters.' *Annals of Human Genetics*, **8**, 233-7.

Robertson, A. (1967). 'Animal breeding', in *Annual Review of Genetics* (eds. Roman, Sandler and Stent). Palo Alto, California.

Rosenthal, D., and colleagues (1963). *The Genain Quadruplets*. New York.

Scharfetter, C. (1970). 'On the hereditary aspects of symbiotic psychoses—a contribution towards the understanding of the schizophrenia-like psychoses.' *Psychiatria Clinica (Basel)*, **3**, 145-52.

Selye, H. (1956). *The Stress of Life.* New York.

Simpson, G. G. (1964). *This View of Life.* New York.

Slater, E. (1958). 'The monogenic theory of schizophrenia.' *Acta Genetica et Statistica Medica (Basel)*, **8**, 50-6.

—— (1968). 'A review of earlier evidence on genetic factors in schizophrenia', in *The Transmission of Schizophrenia* (eds. Rosenthal and Kety). Oxford.

—— Beard, A. W., and Glithero, E. (1963). 'The schizophrenia-like psychoses of epilepsy.' *British Journal of Psychiatry*, **109**, 95-150.

—— and Cowie, V. A. (1971). *The Genetics of Mental Disorders.* London.

—— Hare, E. H., and Price, J. S. (1971). 'Marriage and fertility of psychiatric patients compared with national data', in *Differential Reproduction in Individuals with Mental and Physical Disorders* (eds. Gottesman and Erlenmeyer-Kimling). *Social Biology*, **18**, (Suppl.).

Smith, C. (1970). 'Heritability of liability and concordance in monozygous twins.' *Annals of Human Genetics*, **34**, 85-91.

—— (1971). 'Recurrence risks for multifactorial inheritance.' *American Journal of Human Genetics*, **23**, 578-88.

Thoday, J. M. (1961). 'Location of polygenes.' *Nature (London)*, **191**, 368-70.

—— (1967). 'New insights into continuous variation', in *Proceedings of the Third International Congress of Human Genetics* (eds. Crow and Neel). Baltimore.

Tienari, P. (1971). 'Schizophrenia and monozygotic twins.' *Psychiatria Fennica 1971*, 97-104.

Turner, R. J., and Wagenfeld, M. O. (1967). 'Occupational mobility and schizophrenia: an assessment of the social causation and social selection hypotheses.' *American Sociological Review*, **32**, 104-13.

Woolf, C. M. (1971). 'Congenital cleft lip: a genetic study of 496 propositi.' *Journal of Medical Genetics*, **8**, 65-83.

Wright, S. (1934a). 'An analysis of variability in number of digits in an inbred strain of guinea pigs.' *Genetics*, **19**, 506-36.

—— (1934b). 'The results of crosses between inbred strains of guinea pigs, differing in number of digits.' *Genetics*, **19**, 537-51.

—— (1963). 'Genetic interaction', in *Methodology in Mammalian Genetics* (ed. Burdette). San Francisco.

Wynne-Davies, R. (1970). 'A family study of neonatal and late-diagnosis congenital dislocation of the hip.' *Journal of Medical Genetics*, **7**, 315-33.

CHAPTER V

Paranoid and Affective Disorders

Manic-Depressive Psychosis

Manic-depressive psychosis is characterized by extreme swings in moods of mania or depression. When moods alternate, it is referred to as the circular type. Consequently, manic-depressive disorder of the circular type is marked by alternating episodes of mania interchanged with depression. But manic-depressives of the circular type (depressed) are characterized by waves of depression with mania absent. Here the individual is disturbed with cyclical relapses into moods of depression. Manic-depressive psychosis of the depressive type need not be circular, nor does the manic type need be. While recurrent depressed moods characterize the one, unwarranted episodes of unexplainable elation mark the other.

The *Diagnostic and Statistical Manual of Mental Disorders* (DSM III) of the American Psychiatric Association (1980) characterizes mania by euphoria or irritability, but at least three (four if the mood is only irritable) of the following must be present: hyperactivity, racing thoughts, grandiosity, pressure of speech, decreased sleep, excessive involvement in high-risk activities, and distractibility. Depression is marked by dysphoric moods with at least four of the following present: energy loss, sleep abnormalities, decreased sexual interest or decreased interest in activities as such; self-reproach or guilt; difficulty in concentrating or thinking; appetite disturbance or weight change; agitation or retardation; death and suicide as recurring thoughts.

In the past, the broad category of mania has been subdivided into hypomania, acute mania, delirious mania, and chronic mania. The distinction between these subdivisions was not always clear. The classification has now been changed somewhat in DSM III (American Psychiatric Association, 1980) so that major affective disorders include bipolar disorder and major depression. If there are one or more manic episodes, with or without a history of a major depressive episode, then the category bipolar is used.

The etiology of mania is unclear, although there is evidence of a genetic predisposition. Factors necessary for triggering manic episodes remain obscure. A number of pharmacological agents have been used to treat mania, including neuroleptic drugs, α-methyl-p-tyrosine, tryptophan, and physostigmine. These drugs exert their behavioral effects through many different neurotransmitter systems in the brain. Recent evidence suggests that lithium treatment may have a relatively selective therapeutic effect for mania that is not, in general, shared by the other agents. While lithium exerts a therapeutic action on mania, it may produce only limited or no improvement in other syndromes, such as schizoaffective psychosis (Goodwin & Ebert, 1973). The relative specificity of lithium in the treatment of mania is still under debate and requires further assessment (Quitkin et al., 1973). Lithium, however, is now the preferred treatment for mania (Goodwin & Ebert, 1973; Schou, 1968). It may be used in combination with a neuroleptic in an acute episode of mania. How lithium exerts a relatively specific antimanic effect is unknown, since it can produce alterations in the turnover and metabolism of several brain neurotransmitters (Schildkraut, 1973).

Arieti (1967) informs us that manic-depressive psychosis is on the wane and is no longer a serious threat; accordingly, research in this area has decreased considerably. In New York State, first admissions for manic-depressive psychosis diminished from 177 per 100,000 in 1920 to 71 in 1950 (Kolb, 1968).

Depression is one of the major concerns in the United States today. "To put it quite specifically," commented Kline, "there are fewer than 2,000 psychoanalysts in the country today, and they probably treat about 40,000 patients a year. If they were to ignore all other emotional ills and devote themselves exclusively to depression, they could see less than 1 percent of those who need immediate help" (1974, pp. 111–112).

Factor Analysis Approach to Depression

In a factor analytic approach studying the phenomena of depression, Grinker (1961, 1975; Grinker & Nunnally, 1968; Grinker, Miller, Sabskin, Nunn, & Nunnally, 1961) noted the following factors: 5 feelings and concerns, 10 current behaviors, and 4 factor patterns that combine the two sets. The characteristics of the five feelings and concerns are: (1) hopelessness, helplessness, failure, sadness, unworthiness, guilt, and internal suffering; (2) concern over material loss; (3) sense of guilt and a desire for atonement; (4) free anxiety; and (5) envy, loneliness, martyred affliction, secondary gain, gratification from illness, and instilling guilt so that the world is forced to make redress. The 10 factors acquired from the current behavior list are: (1) isolation, withdrawal, and apathy; (2) retardation, deceleration of thought processes and speech, and a disregard for personal appearance; (3) retardation of behavior and gait; (4) behavior traits of anger, provocation, and complaint; (5) somatic complaints; (6) memory impairment, confusion, concentration difficulties, and repetitive or limited thought content; (7) agitation, restlessness, and tremulousness; (8) rigidity and psychomotor retardation; (9) somatic symptoms (dry skin and hair); (10) ingratiating behavior (assisting others and expressing appreciation). The four patterns, a combination of the 15 above-listed factors, are:

Feelings	*Behavior*
1. Dismal, hopeless, loss of self-esteem, slight guilt feelings.	1. Isolated, withdrawn, apathetic, speech and thinking slowed with some cognitive disturbances.
2. Hopeless with low self-esteem, considerable guilt feelings, much anxiety.	2. Agitation and clinging demands for attention.
3. Abandonment and loss of love.	3. Agitated, demanding, hypochrondriacal.
4. Gloom, hoplessness, and anxiety.	4. Demanding, angry, provocative. (Grinker, 1961, p. 228–233)

Suicidal preoccupation was infrequent in this research. In Dublin's (1963) findings, however, it was reported that suicide rates for manic depressives and those with involutional melancholia were far above the next two categories (cerebral arteriosclerosis and dementia praecox).

Studying the characteristics of persons with depression, Silverman (1968) noted that all types of depression were invariably more common in women than in men, but with regard to suicide among depressives the practice is more common among the males. Women with hysterectomies prior to age 40 have lower rates of mental illness than their female counterparts, and a low incidence during pregnancy (suggesting pregnancy's protective effect); but in postpartum illness, depression was frequent (Paffenbarger & McCabe, 1966). Bragg (1965) records less incidence of depression in women having undergone hysterectomy than those with cholecystectomy. Reviewing children (3–14 years of age) attempting suicide, Lourie (1965) discovered the absence of depressions but the presence of situational depressions, a view confirmed by Jennings (1965).

Neurotic and Psychotic Depression

In a comparison of distinguishing characteristics of endogenous and reactive depression, Watts (1966) cites those of endogenous depression as: lacking an apparent cause, futility of psychotherapy, accompaniment by mania, presence of insomnia, stages of mood swing, disappearance without treatment (but with rapidity with E.C.T.), unaffected by environmental changes, and common in the obsessional hard-working type. Those of reactive depression are: an external cause, usefulness of psychotherapy, absence of mania, insomnia minor (though falling off to sleep may be difficult), minor mood swings, disorder alleviated with the removal of its cause, E.C.T. ineffective or detrimental, patient easily diverted from his symptom (e.g., by viewing an amusing film), patient usually the worrying type, and reporting ill (with regard to work).

Kendell (1968), utilizing factor analysis and criterion analysis of Eysenck (1950), found significant differences between psychotic and neurotic depression, and between neurotic depression and involutional melancholia. The only difference discernible between psychotic depression and involutional melancholia was merely one of a difference of age, hence the recommendation that involutional melancholia should not be retained as a diagnostic category. He further concluded that "depressive illnesses are best regarded as a single continuum extending between the traditional neurotic and psychotic stereotypes" (Kendell, 1968, p. 83). Others (Boseelman, 1964) draw dichotomous or sharp distinctions among depressions as a normal reaction, a neurosis, and a psychosis. Frazier and Carr (1964) define neurotic depression in terms of the patient's ability to test and evaluate reality as being intact, while in psychotic depression reality testing has undergone serious disruption.

Kiloh and Garside (1963), experimenting with imipramine (Tofranil), also draw a distinction between neurotic and endogenous depression. Comparing 35 clinical features entailing symptoms and personality traits of 143 patients, their factor analysis indicated the necessity of two factors in order to account adequately for the data observed. Their review cites clinical features identifiable with neurotic depression and others related to endogenous depression. Buss (1966, p. 182) listed a table of the features cited by Kiloh and Garside for neurotic and psychotic depression:

CLINICAL FEATURES OF NEUROTIC VERSUS PSYCHOTIC DEPRESSION

Feature	Neurotic Depression	Psychotic Depression
1. Quality of depression	Normal despondency	Abnormal melancholy
2. Variability of depression	Much	Little or none
3. Delusions	Absent	Sometimes present
4. Depersonalization	Absent	Present
5. Anxiety component	Strong	Weak
6. Neurotic components (hysteria, obsessive compulsiveness, etc.)	Strong	Weak
7. Diurnal variation	None	Worse in morning or evening
8. Concentration	Intact	Poor
9. Guilt	None or insincere	Intense remorse
10. Reaction to self	Pity	Pitiless
11. Weight loss	Variable	Invariable
12. Constipation	Variable	Invariable
13. Health	Usually poor	Good except during episode
14. Precipitating event	Clear and strong	Absent or weak
15. Family history of depression	Absent	Present

From *Psychopathology* by A.H. Buss. Copyright ©1966 by John Wiley & Sons. Reprinted by permission of John Wiley & Sons, Inc.

Anaclitic Depression and Separation Anxiety

Lehmann (1966) contends that depression is singularly human, absent in animals. But this contention has been seriously challenged by recent and current research and was found wanting. *Separation anxiety,* the intense distress experienced by children when compelled to become separated from their parents, results from children becoming overly dependent upon adults. Overattachment of the infant-mother relationship accounts for it (Ainsworth & Bell, 1969). The attachment bond arises from rewarding dependency behavior. Overprotectiveness is a form of reward that accounts for it (Kagan & Moss, 1962).

Bowlby (1960, 1980) traced depression to separation anxiety. Experimenting on this thesis, Seay/Hanson/Harlow (1962) found that monkeys did resist and protest violently against separation from their mothers, with symptoms of despair, withdrawal, and depression resulting. Harlow and his collaborators (1971) also found that "an infant monkey placed alone in a strange situation will typically clutch himself, huddle, and scream with fright. However, in the safe presence of his mother, real or surrogate, the same situation fails to elicit any fear at all" (1971, p. 110). In research with McKinney and Suomi, Harlow (1973) connected separation anxiety with depression.

Spitz (1946) coined the term *anaclitic depression* to identify the state of depression arising from the child's separation from his mother, symptoms of which were listlessness and withdrawal. In 1914, Freud had distinguished between two types of object-choice: anaclitic and narcissistic. The child's dependence on a person unlike himself was termed by Freud an *anaclitic object-choice*; narcissistic object-choice was reserved for individuals sharing a similarity.

Helplessness Theory of Depression

Recently there has been growing support in favor of understanding depression in terms of helplessness. The popularity of this viewpoint extends from psychodynamic theorists to experimentalists. In 1964, Mandler defined helplessness as anxiety, and soon thereafter a number of psychologists along with Melges and Bowlby (1969) began to connect helplessness and hopelessness as responsible for subsequent depressions. Bibring (1965) made helplessness central to his theory of depression, and existentialists made despair and meaninglessness their focal point. When the ego feels helpless in attaining its goal, it manifests itself in the form of depression.

Learned-Helplessness Model of Depression

Seligman's (1975; with Miller & Rosellini, 1977) theory of anxiety and depression contends that from the fertile ground of a feeling of helplessness, anxiety and depression flourish. Anxiety and depression are not accidents; they are learned. And, if learned, they must be able to be cured. The cure, too, is a learning experience. It is learning to exert a more effective control over one's life or, more specifically, one's environment. In fact, we can be immunized against depression. Immunization is accomplished in childhood. Children must learn that they can indeed influence a great number of events in their lives. The learning response operative in depressed people is that they cannot, despite whatever they do, change their unhappy situation. Much of this attitude, discovered Seligman, is learned early in life. Helplessness, if not checked, can be crucial in precipitating death.

Symptoms of learned depression are:

1. A reduction of ability to initiate voluntary responses.
2. The establishment of a negative cognitive set, that is, the acquisition of the learning set that whatever one does will be of no avail.
3. With the passing of time, helplessness dissipates.
4. A diminishing of the aggressive and competitive spirit.
5. Loss of appetite for food, sex, and companions.
6. Biochemical changes, such as a depletion of norepinephrine.

One need not wait for time to dissipate learned helplessness. "Forced exposure to the fact that responding produces reinforcement is the most effective way of breaking up learned helplessness" (1975, p. 99). Anger, a potent reinforcer, is one of the most compelling methods of disrupting depression permanently. Assertive training therapy might help in this respect, but simply harassing the depressed individual until he breaks out in a fit of anger will do nicely. Other methods of dealing with learned helplessness include electroconvulsive shock, simply waiting it out (the time cure), and the administration of drugs (possibly norepinephrine stimulants). "The central theme in successful therapy," we are advised by Miller, Rosellini, and Seligman, is "having the patient discover and come to accept that his responses produce the gratification that he desires" (1977, p. 125), in other words, helping the individual afflicted with learned helplessness to become "an effective individual."

To be sure, we must not forget that valuable weapon against depression: immunization against learned helplessness through a mastery over reinforcement. A child should never be trained to think that the desirable things of life come without initiating the necessary responses to obtain them. The good things of life are never independent of our responses. To assume otherwise is to render the child vulnerable to learned depression.

Summarizing his learned-helplessness theory of depression, Seligman enumerated the following points that contribute to the expectation that an outcome is independent of responding. Such an attitude or conditioning:

1. Reduces the motivation to control the outcome.
2. Interferes with learning that responding controls the outcome; and if the outcome is traumatic.

3. Produces fear for as long as the subject is uncertain of the uncontrollability of the outcome, and then produces depression (1975, p. 56).

Revised Version of the Learned Helplessness Hypothesis

The learned helplessness model theorizes that learning followed by adverse consequences that "are uncontrollable results in three deficits: motivational, cognitive, and emotional" (Abramson, Garber, & Seligman, 1980, p. 4). Uncontrollable events alone are insufficient to effect learned helplessness, cognitive factors such as the *expectation* that the ensuing consequences are uncontrollable are necessary to produce a sense of learned helplessness.

The initial helplessness hypothesis failed to discriminate among varieties of learned helplessness, and assumed that only one type existed. Bandura, for example, noted that "people can give up trying because they lack a sense of efficacy in achieving the required behavior, or they may be assured of their capabilities but give up trying because they expect their behavior to have no effect on an unresponsive environment" (1977, pp. 204–205). Thus a number of people in the same set of circumstances might respond quite differently. Accordingly one individual might experience learned helplessness and another be indifferent to the same situation.

Different responses to uncontrollable situations was not the only inadequacy that the hypothesis suffered. A second is a transsituational problem and a further difficulty with chronicity over time. The hypothesis as originally stated failed to account for helplessness being global at times and at other times specific or situational. With the passage of time, researchers noted, the feeling of helplessness erodes. Why? Is it due to forgetting? Is it due to retroactive or proactive inhibition? In other words, is it due to the interference theory of forgetting?

With his associates, Seligman sought to resolve the inadequacies of the helplessness hypothesis by implementing three dimensions of attribution theory: internal-external; stable-unstable; and global-specific dimensions. According to the first dimension (internal-external), persons tend to attribute consequences to themselves when they believe that they are more vulnerable than relevant others to the same set of circumstances. However, when they think that relevant others are equally susceptible then they attribute consequences to the situation (external attribution).

The stable-unstable dimension pertains to long-lived/recurrent or short-lived/intermittent consequences. According to the global dimension, attributing lack of control to global factors means that helplessness is transsituational, that it tends to occur in numerous situations or has a universal quality about it. Thus, "the dimension of internality predicts the type of helplessness (universal versus personal); the dimension of globality predicts the generality of helplessness across situations; and the dimension of stability predicts the chronicity of helplessness over time" (Abramson et al., 1980, p. 16). Individuals believing that consequences are out of their control tend to suffer low self-esteem. Values or the importance one attributes to consequences affects the intensity of loss of self-esteem. Rejection by a loved one, for example, produces more severe consequences of helplessness than failing a driver's test.

Behavioral Approaches to Depression

Ferster (1974) and Lewinsohn (1974) have attempted behavioral hypotheses of depression. While Ferster accounts for depression in terms of the loss of reinforcement in the environment, Lewinsohn attributes it to a deficiency of positive reinforcement. "The depressed person is considered to be on a prolonged extinction schedule" (1974, p. 158).

Although these two behavioral theorists work within the operant behavior framework of Skinner, others do not. The most influential model stemming from behavior theory is one already examined—the learned helplessness hypothesis of depression generated by Seligman. The work of Wolpe in behavior theory is also well known. Wolpe (1973) saw depression as the "consequence of severe and prolonged anxiety" and as "a consequence of failure to control interpersonal situations" (1973, p. 236), as well as a normal reaction to loss that has been exaggerated and prolonged. To cope with depression, Wolpe (1976) draws on a variety of therapies from systematic desensitization for deconditioning anxiety to assertive training.

According to Becker (1977), findings to date support the hypothesis of dysfunctional reinforcement mechanisms as the most common denominator in affective disorders. Summarizing progress to date he offers:

1. Dependency as a predisposer to depression
2. Learned helplessness hypothesis of depression
3. Cognitive-behavioral psychotherapy
4. Catecholamine hypothesis
5. Identification of additional subtypes of "unipolar depressives"

A *unipolar* depressive is one who has depressive episodes only as distinguished from the *bipolar,* who undergoes both manic and depressive episodes.

Biochemical Hypothesis of Depression

Information in the nervous system is transmitted by the conduction of neural impulses of an electrical nature. Most synaptic contacts involve chemical transmission, although some synapses work by direct electrical communication between neurons.

In chemical transmission, a nerve impulse or action potential arrives at the nerve terminal and initiates the release of a small amount of chemical transmitter. There are gaps between the individual neurons or nerve cells; these gaps are called synapses. The chemical transmitter or messenger diffuses across the synapse to the dendrite or cell body of the neuron with which it communicates. Dendrite is from the Greek dendron, which means tree. These trees receive messages from other neurons.

What kinds of messages are conveyed between two neurons in the central nervous system (CNS)? Depending on the areas of the brain and the chemical being transmitted, a message might be sent which excites the next neuron, and causes it to release a chemical messenger. Conversely, it might be that an inhibitory message is sent. This message is a negative one. Think of all the possibilities that this type of arrangement allows! A simple situation could exist where a neuron sends an excitatory message to another neuron which then passes an excitatory message on to a third. However, there are more complicated interactions. Suppose, for example, an inhibitory transmitter arrives at the dendrite of a second neuron (n_2), which is inhibiting a third neuron (n_3). The inhibition of inhibition leads to excitation (two negatives make a positive). In other words, if neuron, n_1, inhibits n_2, then n_3 is no longer under the inhibition of n_2.

Certain chemicals are known to be neurotransmitters in the CNS. However, many other neurotransmitters remain to be discovered. Several neurotransmitters have been implicated in the mediation or modulation of affect, as well as a variety of behaviors. The indolamine serotonin (5HT) and the catecholamines, norepinephrine (NE) and dopamine (DA), are of especial interest in terms of mood and affect. It may be that an imbalance in the relationship between these neurotransmitters in various areas of the brain induces disorders, such as mania and depression.

Ellison, for example, found that "rats with norepinephrine depletions are inactive, have hunger deficits, and model aspects of depression, while rats with serotonin depletions are hyperactive, are frightened in novel environments, and model aspects of anxiety" (1977, p. 1036). Earlier, we read that Seligman hypothesized that depression resulted from learned helplessness. Weiss and his colleagues (1970, 1974), however, challenged Seligman's hypothesis. They argued that stress arising from a condition of learned helplessness depletes norepinephrine, and this loss of norepinephrine accounts for depression.

It has been known for some time that reserpine, a drug that acts by depleting amines, produces clinical depression (pharmacological depression). This condition is

In an eclectic model of depression, Akiskal and McKinney (1973, 1975) object to equating depression with depletion of any particular transmitter. Rather, they prefer an "integrative model" of depression. According to this model, depression "represents the feedback interactions of three sets of variables at chemical, experiential, and behavioral levels—with the diencephalon serving as the field of action" (1975, p. 299). In other words, "Object losses, interpersonally induced states of frustration and helplessness, and depletion of biogenic amines ultimately result in impairment of the neurophysiological substrates of reinforcement; this impairment is manifested behaviorally as depressive phenomena" (1973, p. 21). Their claim is that not one, but many factors play a role in producing depression. (See Akiskal and Tashjian, 1983).

Cognitive Theory of Depression

Investigating orphans, Beck and his associates (1963) found that there is a larger incidence of depression among patients who lost their parents by the age of 16, and the high-depressed group comprised those cases in which orphanhood occurred before the age of four. In a number of patients, therefore, "the death of a parent in childhood may be a factor in the later development of a severe depression" (1967, p. 227).

Beck (1974) came to the realization that depressives, because of an altered cognitive function that produces erroneous conceptualizations, misconstrue reality. Their cognitions are marked by negativity, and hence they are motivated by a negative view of the world, of the self, and of the future, termed by Beck as the primary triad in depression. The depression-prone person, observes Beck, appraises "his experiences in a negative way. He overinterprets his experiences in terms of defeat or deprivation. He regards himself as deficient, inadequate, unworthy, and is prone to attribute unpleasant occurrences to a deficiency in himself. As he looks ahead, he anticipates that his present difficulties of suffering will continue indefinitely.... Since he attributes his difficulties to his own defects, he blames himself and becomes increasingly self-critical" (1976, p. 129). This cognitive frame of reference is incapacitating, rendering its victim helpless.

One's feelings mirror his thoughts. "If the patient incorrectly perceives himself as inadequate, deserted or sinful, he will experience corresponding affects such as sadness, loneliness, or guilt" (1963, p. 332). The interaction between cognition and affect spirals downward engulfing low self-evaluation, self-criticism, deprivation, exaggeration of difficulties, and the like. Such observations led Beck to the conviction that thought disorder is common to all mental disorders, particularly since depressed patients experienced distorted ideas immediately prior to the intensification of their depressive affects. Accordingly, the thesis follows that "cognitive distortions in depression result from the progressive dominance of the thought processes by idiosyncratic schemas. By superseding more appropriate schemas, the idiosyncratic schemas force the conceptualization of experience into certain rigid patterns with the consequent sacrifice of realistic and logical qualities" (1963, p. 333).

Because they are motivating, attitudes, beliefs, and assumptions (termed schemas) influence us. In depressed persons, negative conceptions of self-worth, called idiosyncratic schemas, produce an unwholesome thought content that evinces feelings of depression, such as guilt, sadness, loneliness, and pessimism. The severer the depression, the more the schemas dominate one's cognitions, and the more distorted becomes one's cognitive outlook on reality, and the steeper is the downward spiral of depression. Hence, the cognitive thesis of depression is: *"Certain idiosyncratic cognitive structures (schemas) become prepotent during depression, dominate the thought processes, and lead to cognitive distortions"* (Beck, 1964, p. 561). Consequently, if one's cognition of the world is one of threat, anxiety is aroused; if it is one of enhancement, happiness ensues; and if it is one that is personally diminishing, sadness results. It is the meaning that people attach to situations that elicits a corresponding emotion.

Accordingly, the therapy called for is one that reorients an individual's mode of self-judgment from one of deduction to that of induction, that is, from a biased subjectivity to a factual objectivity. Since cognitive distortions are the cause of psychopathological states, then the cure must be in "helping the patient form more realistic concepts in order to eliminate the cognitive distortions" (1976, p. 333).

By 1979, A. T. Beck and his associates (A. J. Rush, B. F. Shaw, and G. Emery) developed the *cognitive triad thesis,* the belief that depression arises from three errors: the manner in which a person infers, recollects, and generalizes. Such "depressogenic thoughts," as they are called, must be dislodged and uprooted. In the first element of the cognitive triad, patients acquire a negative self-image by attributing moral, psychological and other defects to themselves. Further still, depressives view themselves as devoid of the wherewithal necessary to acquire contentment or happiness. In the second element of the cognitive triad, depressives view their experiences and their world negatively. According to the third component, depressives view their future negatively, with no end in sight to their miseries, and only failures in the offing. "If the patient incorrectly *thinks* he is being rejected, he will react with the same negative affect (for example, sadness, anger) that occurs with *actual* rejection. If he erroneously believes he is a social outcast, he will feel lonely" (Beck et al., 1979). Thus negative cognitions motivate depressives, determine their outlook, and contribute to psychomotor inhibition or apathy.

Logotherapeutic and Existential Approach to Depression

The mechanism triggering depression is the loss of the meaning of one's existence. So contend the existentialists. Depression is rooted in a meaningless life. Consequently, it is necessary for the depressed person to find some meaning for living. A sense of an empty life, an "existential vacuum," as Frankl (1975) termed it, is at the base of depression. This sort of depression is referred to as a *noogenic neurosis.* It manifests itself as existential frustration; that is, as boredom and apathy. It is resolved by finding those unique meanings that have a special significance for one's life. It is not the meaning of life in general, the meaning of life that philosophers pursue, but some purpose that is personally meaningful. Being existential meanings, they cannot be taught, much less presented to an individual, they must be lived out in the individual's life and they must have some special significance in his life.

The individual life is permeated with meaning. There is meaning in everything, claims Frankl, especially in suffering. Suffering that is transformed into a meaningful experience is not only endurable but it does not terminate in depression. The tragic triad—pain, death, and guilt—can be quite depressive unless transformed into a meaningful experience (Frankl, 1969). If a situation that causes suffering cannot be changed, then one must change his attitude toward it to escape depression. Frankl cites the case of an elderly physician who was thrown into deep depression at the death of his wife. By changing the man's attitude, Frankl dissolved his depression. Frankl had transformed the physician's morose attitude by rendering it a meaningful one—meaningful for him. He made the physician aware that since one of the two had to die first, it was better that he survive his wife. Frankl said that it would not have been better that the physician die first to spare him his agony. Realizing that his wife would not be able to fend for herself, the physician thought that this was the better alternative.

He felt now that he had a mission; he was living for someone he loved; it fell upon him to be the survivor. Once his suffering assumed a meaningful turn, he was able to cope with it and gain victory over his depression.

Psychoanalytic Theories of Depression

Among the psychodynamic interpreters of depression patterning their ideas according to the adaptational or motivational model are: those who construe symptoms as a defense against drives (Freud, 1917); those who explain symptoms as the fulfillment of needs or drives (Abraham, 1916; Rado, 1928); and those who view symptoms as modes of adaptation (Adler, 1961; Davies, 1964; Rado, 1928).

Distinguishing mourning from melancholia, Freud depicts melancholia as a "regression from object-cathexis to the still narcissistic oral phase of the libido" (1917). A narcissistic type of object-choice typifies the melancholic. Transforming the loss of object into a loss of ego, and a conflict of the ego and the loved person into a cleavage between superego ("criticizing aspect of the ego") and the ego is Freud's explanation of psychotic depression. During depression—or melancholy, as he termed it—a person's "super-ego becomes over-severe, abuses the poor ego, humiliates it and ill-treats it, threatens it with the direst punishments, reproaches it for actions in the remotest past which had been taken lightly at the time—as though it had spent the whole interval in collecting accusations and had only been waiting for its present access of strength in order to bring them up and make a condemnatory judgment on their basis" (1965, p. 61). Freud, with time, grew closer to Abraham's (1911, 1916, 1924) theory of depression.

Abraham believed the root of depression to be in feelings of hatred and hostility that diminish the depressive's love ability, a state emanating from unfulfilled sex needs. Regressing to the anal-sadistic stage and even to the oral stage, the melancholic, disappointed in pre-oedipal experiences in love and associating sex with nutritive gratification, resorts to autoeroticism to counteract and diminish depression.

The Freud-Abraham hypothesis of depression came to be explained as an "aggression-turned-inward" model. "The process of introjection in the melancholiac," wrote Abraham, "is based on a radical disturbance of his libidinal relations to his object. It rests on a severe conflict of ambivalent feelings, from which he can only escape by turning against himself the hostility he originally felt towards this object" (1968, p. 438). Freud at one time saw anxiety as arising from a dammed-up libido. In a similar vein, he viewed depression as a consequence of dammed-up aggression. When the aggressive instinct reverts from its initial or intended object and turns inward toward onself, depression results. Hence depression is simply inverted hostility.

Viewing depression as a desperate cry for love, Rado (1928, 1961) saw depression as a need for oral gratification ("alimentary orgasm"). The melancholic rebels with hostility against love, the factor behind his guilt, remorse, and reproach. The depressed individual, torn in opposite directions by coercive rage and guilty fear (with guilty fear taking the upper hand), experiences rage "vented in remorseful bouts of self-reproach." Contemptuous of inability to measure up to his expectations, he resorts to self-punishment. "This deeply hidden meaning of self-punishment from retroflexed rage makes mockery of the patient's remorse and reveals the real root of his sense of unworthiness" (1954, p. 153). With the loss of self-confidence, his adaptive degradation is seen to lie at the root of his depressive spell. Interpreting his condition as a threat of starvation, the patient like a hungry infant with excessive guilty fear and retroflexed rage is driven to expiation, that is, of punishing himself in order to regain the mother's loving care and feeding breast. The disturbance in melancholia "finds clamourous expression in the patient's delusional self-accusations and self-aspersions, which we call 'the delusion of moral inferiority' " (1928, p. 421). Thus is summarized Rado's theory of intrapsychic propitiation or adaptational theory of depression.

As for other psychoanalysts, Melanie Klein (1934), following Abraham, interpreted depression in children as rooted in insufficient love. Adult depression is infantile depression reactivated. Bibring (1965) construed it as a conflict raging within the ego that originates as a loss of self-esteem rooted in childhood traumatic experiences, frustration, and lack of love. Jacobson (1953, 1954), sharing Bibring's loss of self-esteem theory, saw in the childhood of the psychotic depressive an inability to tolerate hurt, frustration, and disappointment, utilizing denial as a defense mechanism, even to the point of reality withdrawal. Zetzel (1966) attributes the predisposition to psychotic depression to the failure of achieving psychological maturity, that is, the inability to accept the facts of reality and strive for realistic goals. One must recognize, master, and have a tolerance for depression as he does for other stress situations of normal adult life as a developmental challenge. Bellak et al. (1952), comparing manic-depressive psychosis to schizophrenia, relate both disorders to extreme ego weakness; as ego weakness continues to develop, schizophrenia is the outcome. Bowlby (1960, 1980) attributed the aetiology of depression separation anxiety.

Sociogenic Theory of Depression

Role loss or loss of role status accounts for depression according to Bart (1974) and those who approach this problem from a sociopsychological perspective. People find their identity in their respective roles. When people, for example, are given the "Who am I" test, they almost invariably respond in terms of their roles in life, such as, housewife, mother, lawyer, doctor, daughter, and the like. Once identity is menaced or lost, depression becomes a threat. "One's concept of self stems from one's roles; thus, a loss of a role relationship and a loss of significant others, can result in a sense of 'mutilated self' " (1974, p. 144). Sociogenic depression, then, arises from a loss of self—a loss of identity.

Since roles are determined by the social structure, a person can, as a consequent of a change in his immediate social life, lose his role. Thus, people with careers, especially careers from which they do not have to retire, are protected from sociogenic depression. On the other hand, those with relatively brief careers, such as mothers, are the most vulnerable. Unless a mother can change her self-conceptualization, she falls easy prey to depression when her children leave home. Bart found that Jewish mothers, because of the strong mother-identity in this ethnic structure, were particular targets of sociogenic depression. Because black grandmothers often assumed the role of mother when their own daughters were forced to look for outside employment, they were the least vulnerable.

Nevertheless, any role loss whatever makes us ready prey to sociogenic depression. Bart summarized her findings accordingly:

1. Depressed women would be more likely to experience a role loss than would nondepressed women.
2. There would be a higher proportion of depressed than of nondepressed women with maternal role loss.
3. Certain roles would be structurally conducive to increasing the effect of the loss of other roles.
4. Impending role loss would also be associated with depression.
5. Depression among middle-aged women with maternal role loss would be related to the family structure and typical interactive patterns of the ethnic group to which they belong (1974, p. 147).

Integrity Hypothesis of Depression
(Promotion Depression)

Mowrer interprets *promotion depression* (depression resulting from the reception of distinction, honors, new responsibilities; Lidz, 1968, p. 462), as a threat to one's integrity rather than to his dependency. Interpreting depression as an expiation of guilt resulting from the accumulation of moral transgressions against one's moral nature (conscience), the depressive is overcome by any crisis of life causing a confrontation with his personal deficiencies.

His unresolved load of guilt comes to *exceed* his capacity for self-affirmation and approval, then ... we must once again recognize radical openness with the "significant others" in one's life, not only as the most effective means of "treatment," but also as the best form of *prevention,* as a *way of life* (Mowrer, 1964, p. 90).

What is called for is an action therapy which Mowrer terms *integrity therapy* (Drakeford, 1967), a form of behavior therapy based on the assumption that the patient has "stupidly" or mistakenly used as his personal strategy deception, denial, and "phoniness." Such a strategy must be superseded by one of honesty and openness, that is, by "sharing" and "modeling" through encouragement, persuasion, and inspiration (Mowrer, 1966). Inasmuch as guilt is a violation of one's integrity, "therapy should be aimed at exposing the *behavioral* source of guilt and encouraging its expiation" (London, 1968, p. 404).

Holistic Hypothesis of Depression

Wolpert developed a holistic approach to bipolar depressive disorder in which he regards the disturbance as a "genetically determined actual neurosis" (1975). The manifest psychological and physiological components are assumed to be "the outcome of an alternation of periodic lack of or excess of energy in the physiological as well as psychological spheres." He adds that "individual episodes of illness may be either spontaneous, due to unknown factors causing a shift in energy in the 'physiological affective system' of the central nervous system, or psychogenic, in that an external loss or an intrapsychic loss of objects triggers off the same reaction as noted in the spontaneous episode" (1977, p. 586). In agreement with Kraepelin, Wolpert holds that "permanent internal changes" are at the root of depressive disorders.

Dexamethasone Suppression Test

The *dexamethasone suppression test* (DST) is intensely debated in current research. A key article by Carroll et al. (1981) sees it as a definitive test for melancholia, and hence capable of distinguishing endogenous depression from neurotic depression (one arising from a stress reaction). Bernard Carroll of Duke University Medical School, who is credited with applying the DST test to endogenous depression, found that the plasma cortisol concentrations of melancholics altered abnormally within a 24-hour period when dexamethasone was administered.

Over the six-year period in which 438 subjects were given dexamethasone, Carroll et al. found that "with a 1-mg dose of dexamethasone, with blood samples drawn at 4 and 11 P.M., and with plasma cortisol criterion value of 5 g/dL, a sensitivity greater than 65 percent can be achieved, together with a specificity and diagnostic confidence close to 95 percent" (1981, p. 22). A synthetic glucocorticoid, dexamethasone (in normal people) suppresses endogenous adrenocorticotropic hormone and cortisol production. As early as 1960, Liddle utilized the DST for pituitary-adrenal suppression in diagnosing of Cushing's disease. If dexamethasone fails to suppress plasma cortisol, it is a sign of hypothalamic-pituitary-adrenal (HPA) overactivity. Individuals with endogenous depression seem unable to suppress plasma cortisol levels when DST is administered. Kalin et al. (1981) support Carroll's findings stating that "up to 50 percent of patients with primary depressive illness fail to suppress plasma cortisol concentrations with DST" (1981, p. 68). The editor of the Massachusetts General Hospital newsletter, Alan J. Galenberg, denegrates DST as merely indicating that the subject is under stress.

Tests for depression competing with the DST include one that measures MHPG, a brain substance; another monitors alterations in sleep patterns; and a third applies electrodes to one's fingers; the amount conducted apparently differs in the melancholic.

20.

American Psychiatric Association

**FEATURES OF PARANOID
AND AFFECTIVE DISORDERS**

PARANOID DISORDERS

The essential features are persistent persecutory delusions or delusional jealousy, not due to any other mental disorder, such as a schizophrenic, schizophreniform, affective, or organic mental disorder. The paranoid disorders include paranoia, shared paranoid disorder, and acute paranoid disorder.

The boundaries of this group of disorders and their differentiation from such other disorders as severe paranoid personality disorder and schizophrenia, paranoid type, are unclear.

The persecutory delusions may be simple or elaborate and usually involve a single theme or series of connected themes, such as being conspired against, cheated, spied upon, followed, poisoned or drugged, maliciously maligned, harassed, or obstructed in the pursuit of long-term goals. Small slights may be exaggerated and become the focus of a delusional system.

There may be only delusional jealousy ("conjugal paranoia"), in which an individual may become convinced without due cause, that his or her mate is unfaithful. Small bits of "evidence," such as disarrayed clothing or spots on the sheets, may be collected and used to justify the delusion.

* * *

From Task Force on Nomenclature and Statistics of the American Psychiatric Association. *Diagnostic and Statistical Manual of Mental Disorders, Third Edition.* American Psychiatric Association, 1980.

297.10 Paranoia

The essential feature is the insidious development of a paranoid disorder with a permanent and unshakable delusional system accompanied by preservation of clear and orderly thinking. Frequently the individual considers himself or herself endowed with unique and superior abilities. Chronic forms of "conjugal paranoia" and involutional paranoid state should be classified here.

* * *

297.30 Shared Paranoid Disorder

The essential feature is a persecutory delusional system that develops as a result of a close relationship with another person who already has a disorder with persecutory delusions. The delusions are at least partly shared. Usually, if the relationship with the other person is interrupted, the delusional beliefs will diminish or disappear. In the past this disorder has been termed *folie à deux,* although in rare cases, more than two persons may be involved.

* * *

298.30 Acute Paranoid Disorder

The essential feature is a paranoid disorder of less than six months' duration. It is most commonly seen in individuals who have experienced drastic changes in their environment, such as immigrants, refugees, prisoners of war, inductees into military services, or people leaving home for the first time. The onset is usually relatively sudden and the condition rarely becomes chronic.

* * *

AFFECTIVE DISORDERS

The essential feature of this group of disorders is a disturbance of mood, accompanied by a full or partial manic or depressive syndrome, that is not due to any other physical or mental disorder. Mood refers to a prolonged emotion that colors the whole psychic life; it generally involves either depression or elation. The manic and depressive syndromes each consist of characteristic symptoms that tend to occur together.

In other classifications these disorders are grouped in various categories, including affective, personality, and neurotic disorders.

MAJOR AFFECTIVE DISORDERS

The essential feature is an illness involving either a manic episode (see below) or a major depressive episode. These major affective episodes are not diagnosed if the affective disturbance is due to an organic mental disorder or if it is superimposed on schizophrenia.

Manic Episode

The essential feature is a distinct period when the predominant mood is either elevated, expansive, or irritable and when there are associated symptoms of the manic syndrome. These symptoms include hyperactivity, pressure of speech, flight of ideas, inflated self-esteem, decreased need for sleep, distractibility, and excessive involvement in activities that have a high potential for painful consequences, which is not recognized.

The elevated mood may be described as euphoric, unusually good, cheerful, or high; often has an infectious quality for the uninvolved observer; but is recognized as excessive by those who know the individual well. The expansive quality of the mood disturbance is characterized by unceasing and unselective enthusiasm for interacting with people and seeking involvement with other aspects of the environment. Although elevated mood is considered the prototypical symptom, the predominant mood disturbance may be irritability, which may be most apparent when the individual is thwarted.

The hyperactivity often involves excessive planning of and participation in multiple activities (e.g., sexual, occupational, political, religious). Almost invariably there is increased sociability, which includes efforts to renew old acquaintanceships and calling friends at all hours of the night. The intrusive, domineering, and demanding nature of these interactions is not recognized by the individual. Frequently, expansiveness, unwarranted optimism, grandiosity, and lack of judgment lead to such activities as buying sprees, reckless driving, foolish business investments, and sexual behavior unusual for the individual. Often the activities have a disorganized, flamboyant, or bizarre quality, for example, dressing in colorful or strange garments, wearing excessive, poorly applied make-up, or distributing candy, money, or advice to passing strangers.

Manic speech is typically loud, rapid, and difficult to interrupt. Often it is full of jokes, puns, plays on words, and amusing irrelevancies. It may become theatrical, with dramatic mannerisms and singing. Sounds rather than meaningful conceptual relationships may govern word choice (clanging). If the mood is more irritable than expansive, there may be complaints, hostile comments, and angry tirades.

Frequently there is flight of ideas, i.e., a nearly continuous flow of accelerated speech with abrupt changes from topic to topic, usually based on understandable associations, distracting stimuli, or plays on words. When flight of ideas is severe, the speech may be disorganized and incoherent. However, loosening of associations and incoherence may occur even when there is no flight of ideas, particularly if the individual is on medication.

Distractibility is usually present and manifests itself as rapid changes in speech or activity as a result of responding to various irrelevant external stimuli, such as background noise or signs or pictures on the wall.

Characteristically, there is inflated self-esteem, ranging from uncritical self-confidence to marked grandiosity, which may be delusional. For instance, advice may be given on matters about which the individual has no special knowledge, such as how to run a mental hospital or the United Nations. Despite a lack of any particular talent, a novel may be started, music composed, or publicity sought for some impractical invention. Grandiose delusions involving a special relationship to God or some well-known figure from the political, religious, or entertainment world are common.

Almost invariably there is a decreased need for sleep; the individual awakens several hours before the usual time, full of energy. When the sleep disturbance is severe, the individual may go for days without any sleep at all and yet not feel tired.

The term "hypomania" is used to describe a clinical syndrome that is similar to, but not as severe as, that described by the term "mania" or "manic episode."

***

Major Depressive Episode

The essential feature is either a dysphoric mood, usually depression, or loss of interest or pleasure in all or almost all usual activities and pastimes. This disturbance is prominent, relatively persistent, and associated with other symptoms of the depressive syndrome. These symptoms include appetite disturbance, change in weight, sleep disturbance, psychomotor agitation or retardation, decreased energy, feelings of worthlessness or guilt, difficulty concentrating or thinking, and thoughts of death or suicide or suicidal attempts.

An individual with a depressive syndrome will usually describe his or her mood as depressed, sad, hopeless, discouraged, down in the dumps, or in terms of some other colloquial variant. Sometimes, however, the mood disturbance may not be expressed as a synonym for depressive mood but rather as a complaint of "not caring anymore," or as a painful inability to experience pleasure. In a child with a depressive syndrome there may not be complaints of any dysphoric mood, but its existence may be inferred from a persistently sad facial expression.

Loss of interest or pleasure is probably always present in a major depressive episode to some degree, but the individual may not complain of this or even be aware of the loss, although family members may notice it. Withdrawal from friends and family and neglect of avocations that were previously a source of pleasure are common.

Appetite is frequently disturbed, usually with loss of appetite, but occasionally with increased appetite. When loss of appetite is severe, there may be significant weight loss or, in the case of children, failure to make expected weight gains. When appetite is markedly increased there may be significant weight gain.

Sleep is commonly disturbed, more frequently with insomnia present, but sometimes with hypersomnia. The insomnia may involve difficulty falling asleep (initial insomnia), waking up during sleep and then returning to sleep only with difficulty (middle insomnia), or early morning awakening (terminal insomnia).

Psychomotor agitation takes the form of inability to sit still, pacing, handwringing, pulling or rubbing of hair, skin, clothing, or other objects, outbursts of complaining or shouting, or pressure of speech. Psychomotor retardation may take the form of slowed speech, increased pauses before answering, low or monotonous speech, slowed body movements, a markedly decreased amount of speech (poverty of speech), or muteness. (In children there may be hypoactivity rather than psychomotor retardation.) A decrease in energy level is almost invariably present, and is experienced as sustained fatigue even in the absence of physical exertion. The smallest task may seem difficult or impossible to accomplish.

The sense of worthlessness varies from feelings of inadequacy to completely unrealistic negative evaluations of one's worth. The individual may reproach himself or herself for minor failings that are exaggerated and search the environment for cues confirming the negative self-evaluation. Guilt may be expressed as an excessive reaction to either current or past failings or as exaggerated responsibility for some untoward or tragic event. The sense of worthlessness or guilt may be of delusional proportions.

Difficulty in concentrating, slowed thinking, and indecisiveness are frequent. The individual may complain of memory difficulty and appear easily distracted.

Thoughts of death or suicide are common. There may be fear of dying, the belief that the individual or others would be better off dead, wishes to die, or suicidal plans or attempts.

* * *

OTHER SPECIFIC AFFECTIVE DISORDERS

The essential feature is a long-standing illness of at least two years' duration, with either sustained or intermittent disturbance in mood, and associated symptoms. A full affective syndrome is not present, and there are no psychotic features. These disorders usually begin in early adult life, without a clear onset. This category contains two disorders: Cyclothymic disorder and dysthymic disorder. Other terms for these disorders are cyclothymic and depressive personality disorders.

301.13 Cyclothymic Disorder

The essential feature is a chronic mood disturbance of at least two years' duration, involving numerous periods of depression and hypomania, but not of sufficient severity and duration to meet the criteria for a major depressive or a manic episode (full affective syndrome).

The depressive periods and hypomanic periods may be separated by periods of normal mood lasting as long as several months at a time. In other cases the two types of periods are intermixed or alternate.

During the affective periods there are signs of depression (depressed mood or loss of interest or pleasure in all, or almost all, usual activities and pastimes) and hypomania. In addition, during the affective periods there are paired sets of symptoms (see criterion C below). The following pairs of symptoms are particularly common: feelings of inadequacy (during depressed periods) and inflated self-esteem (during hypomanic periods); social withdrawal and uninhibited people-seeking; sleeping too much and decreased need for sleep; diminished productivity at work and increased productivity, often associated with unusual and self-imposed working hours; decreased attention or concentration and sharpened and unusually creative thinking.

***

Diagnostic Criteria for Cyclothymic Disorder

A. During the past two years, numerous periods during which some symptoms characteristic of both the depressive and the manic syndromes were present, but were not of sufficient severity and duration to meet the criteria for a major depressive or manic episode.

B. The depressive periods and hypomanic periods may be separated by periods of normal mood lasting as long as months at a time, they may be intermixed, or they may alternate.

C. During depressive periods there is depressed mood or loss of interest or pleasure in all or almost all, usual activities and pastimes, and at least three of the following:

1. Insomnia or hypersomnia.
2. Low energy or chronic fatigue.
3. Feelings of inadequacy.
4. Decreased effectiveness or productivity at school, work, or home.
5. Decreased attention, concentration, or ability to think clearly.
6. Social withdrawal.
7. Loss of interest in or enjoyment of sex.
8. Restriction of involvement in pleasurable activities; guilt over past activities.

9. Feeling slowed down.
10. Less talkative than usual.
11. Pessimistic attitude toward the future, or brooding about past events.
12. Tearfulness or crying.

During **hypomanic** periods there is an elevated, expansive, or irritable mood and at least three of the following:

1. Decreased need for sleep.
2. More energy than usual.
3. Inflated self-esteem.
4. Increased productivity, often associated with unusual and self-imposed working hours.
5. Sharpened and unusually creative thinking.
6. Uninhibited people-seeking (extreme gregariousness).
7. Hypersexuality without recognition of possibility of painful consequences.
8. Excessive involvement in pleasurable activities with lack of concern for the high potential for painful consequences, e.g., buying sprees, foolish business investments, reckless driving.
9. Physical restlessness.
10. More talkative than usual.
11. Overoptimism or exaggeration of past achievements.
12. Inappropriate laughing, joking, punning.

D. Absence of psychotic features such as delusions, hallucinations, incoherence, or loosening of associations.

E. Not due to any other mental disorder, such as partial remission of bipolar disorder. However, cyclothymic disorder may precede bipolar disorder.

300.40 Dysthymic Disorder (or Depressive Neurosis)

The essential feature is a chronic disturbance of mood involving either depressed mood or loss of interest or pleasure in all, or almost all, usual activities and pastimes, and associated symptoms, but not of sufficient severity and duration to meet the criteria for a major depressive episode (full affective syndrome).

For adults, two years' duration is required; for children and adolescents, one year is sufficient.

The depressed mood may be characterized by the individual as feeling sad, blue, down in the dumps, or low. The depressed mood or loss of interest or pleasure may be either relatively persistent or intermittent and separated by periods of normal mood, interest, and pleasure. These normal periods may last a few days to a few weeks. The diagnosis should not be made if an apparently chronic course has been interrupted by a period of normal mood lasting more than a few months.

21.

Aaron T. Beck

COGNITIVE THEORY OF DEPRESSION

DEFINITION OF DEPRESSION

Depression may be defined in terms of the following attributes:

1. A specific alteration in mood: sadness, loneliness, apathy.

2. A negative self-concept associated with self-reproaches and self-blame.

3. Regressive and self-punitive wishes: desires to escape, hide, or die.

4. Vegetative changes: anorexia, insomnia, loss of libido.

5. Change in activity level: retardation or agitation.

From Beck, A. T. *Depression: Causes and Treatment.* Philadelphia: University of Pennsylvania Press, 1970.

SYMPTOMS OF DEPRESSION

TABLE 21-1

Cognitive and Motivational Manifestations: Frequency among Depressed and Nondepressed Patients

	Depth of depression			
Manifestation	None (%) (n = 224)	Mild (%) (n = 288)	Moderate (%) (n = 377)	Severe (%) (n = 86)
Low self-evaluation	38	60	78	81
Negative expectation	22	55	72	87
Self-blame and self-criticism	43	67	80	80
Indecisiveness	23	48	67	76
Distorted self-image	12	33	50	66
Loss of motivation	33	65	83	86
Suicidal wishes	12	31	53	74

n = No. of patients.

TABLE 21-2

Frequency of Clinical Features of Patients Varying in Depth of Depression ($n = 486$)

	Depth of depression			
Clinical feature	None (%)	Mild (%)	Moderate (%)	Severe (%)
Sad faces	18	72	94	98
Stooped posture	6	32	70	87
Crying in interview	3	11	29	28
Speech: slow, etc.	25	53	72	75
Low mood	16	72	94	94
Diurnal variation of mood	6	13	37	37
Suicidal wishes	13	47	73	94
Indecisiveness	18	42	68	83
Hopelessness	14	58	85	86
Feeling inadequate	25	56	75	90
Conscious guilt	27	46	64	60
Loss of interest	14	56	83	92
Loss of motivation	23	54	88	88
Fatigability	39	62	89	84
Sleep disturbance	31	55	73	88
Loss of appetite	17	33	61	88
Constipation	19	26	38	52

n = No. of patients.

From *Depression: Causes and Treatment* by Aaron T. Beck. Copyright, 1967, Aaron T. Beck. Used with permission of University of Pennsylvania.

COURSE AND PROGNOSIS OF DEPRESSION

1. Complete recovery from an episode of depression occurs in 70-95 percent of the cases. About 95 percent of the younger patients recover completely.

2. The median duration of the attacks is approximately 6.3 months among inpatients and approximately 3 months among outpatients. The more severe cases (i.e., those requiring hospitalization), therefore, have a longer duration than the milder cases.

3. When the initial attack occurs before age 30, it tends to be shorter than when it occurs after 30. Acute onset also favors shorter duration.

4. Contrary to prevalent opinion, there is *not* a trend towards prolongation of the attacks with each recurrence, the later attacks lasting about as long as the earlier attacks.

5. After an initial attack of depression, 47-79 percent of the patients will have a recurrence at some time in their lives. The correct figure is probably closer to 79 percent, because this is based on a longer follow-up period.

6. The likelihood of frequent recurrences is greater in the biphasic cases than in cases of depression without a manic phase.

7. After the first attack of depression, most patients have a symptom-free interval of more than three years before the next attack.

8. Although the duration of multiple episodes remains about the same, the symptom-free interval tends to decrease with each successive attack. In the biphasic cases the intervals are consistently shorter than in the simple depressions.

9. Whether any of the cases of pure depression have a schizophrenic outcome cannot be determined as yet, because of the relatively high percentage of incorrect diagnoses at the time of the initial episode. At most, only 5 percent become schizophrenic after repeated attacks.

10. Approximately 5 percent of hospitalized manic-depressive patients subsequently commit suicide. The suicide risk is especially high on weekend leaves from the hospital and during the month following hospitalization and remains high for six months after discharge.

11. The notion that a person who threatens suicide will not carry out the threat is fallacious. The communication of suicidal intent is the best single predictor of a successful suicidal attempt. Previously unsuccessful suicidal attempts are followed by successful suicides in a substantial proportion of the cases.

DIFFERENTIAL DIAGNOSIS

In trying to make a distinction between neurotic and psychotic depression, the best guide is to designate as psychotic depressive all cases that show definite signs of psychosis, such as loss of reality, delusions and hallucinations.

Foulds (1960) conducted a systematic study to determine what symptoms differentiated neurotic and psychotic depressives. He administered an inventory of 86 items to 20 neurotic depressives and 20 psychotic depressives, all under 60 years of age. He found that 14 items occurred at least 25 percent more frequently among the psychotic than among the neurotic group. Using those 14 items as a scale, he was able to sort out correctly 90 percent of the patients diagnosed clinically as psychotic depressives and 80 percent of the neurotic depressives. In the list below, the frequency among the psychotics is stated first in the parentheses after each item and that among neurotics is second.

1. He is an unworthy person in his own eyes (12-3).

2. He is a condemned person because of his sins (12-3).

3. People are talking about him and criticizing him because of things he has done wrong (10-1).

4. He is afraid to go out alone (13-4).

5. He has said things that have injured others (9-2).

6. He is so "worked-up" that he paces about wringing his hands (11-4).

7. He cannot communicate with others because he doesn't seem to be on the same "wave-length" (10-3).

8. There is something unusual about his body, with one side being different

TABLE 21-3
Frequency of Clinical Features in Neurotic Depressive Reaction (NDR)
and Psychotic Depressive Reaction (PDR)

	Feature present		Present to severe degree	
Clinical feature	*NDR (%)* *(n = 50)*	*PDR (%)* *(n = 50)*	*NDR (%)* *(n = 50)*	*PDR (%)* *(n = 50)*
Sad faces	86	94	4	24
Stooped posture	58	76	4	20
Speech: slow, etc.	66	70	8	22
Low mood	84	80	8	44
Diurnal variation of mood	22	48	2	10
Hopelessness	78	68	6	34
Conscious guilt	64	44	6	12
Feeling inadequate	68	70	10	42
Somatic preoccupation	58	66	6	24
Suicidal wishes	58	76	14	40
Indecisiveness	56	70	6	28
Loss of motivation	70	82	8	48
Loss of interest	64	78	10	44
Fatigability	80	74	8	48
Loss of appetite	48	76	2	40
Sleep disturbance	66	80	12	52
Constipation	28	56	2	16

n = No. of patients.

from the other, or meaning something different (6-0).

9. The future is pointless (12-7).

10. He might do away with himself because he is no longer able to cope with his difficulties (8-3).

11. Other people regard him as very odd (8-3).

12. He is often bothered with pains over his heart, in his chest, or in his back (8-3).

13. He is so low in spirits that he just sits for hours on end (12-7).

14. When he goes to bed, he wouldn't care if he "never woke up again" (10-5).

Ideas or delusions relevant to being unworthy, condemned, and criticized, and the delusion of being physically altered, are the best differentiators between the two groups.

Aside from delusions, the typical signs and symptoms of depression are found in a large proportion of both neurotic and psychotic depressives. As shown in Table 21-3, the features appear with relatively

high frequency in both conditions. This frequency distribution was obtained by abstracting the ratings and diagnoses made by our psychiatrists on a random sample of psychiatric inpatients and outpatients.... Each clinical feature was rated according to its severity as: absent, mild, moderate, or severe. The records of 50 patients diagnosed as psychotic depressive reaction and of 50 diagnosed as neurotic depressive reaction were used in this analysis.

* * *

SCHEMAS IN DEPRESSION

A depressed person's ideation is tinged with certain typically depressive themes. His interpretation of his experiences, his explanation for their occurrence, and his outlook for the future, show respectively, themes of personal deficiency, of self-blame, and of negative expectations. These idiosyncratic themes pervade not only his interpretations of immediate environmen-

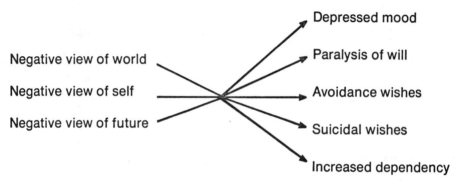

The Effect of Cognitive Patterns on Affects and Motivations in Depression

tal situations but also his free associations, his ruminations, and his reflections.

As the depression deepens, his thought content becomes increasingly saturated with depressive ideas. Almost any external stimulus is capable of evoking a depressive thought. There may be no logical connection between the interpretation and the actual situation. The patient reaches negative conclusions about himself based on the most scanty data, and shapes his judgments and interpretations according to his idiosyncratic preconceptions. As his distortion and misinterpretation of reality increases, his self-objectivity decreases.

This cognitive impairment may be analyzed in terms of the proposition that in depression specific idiosyncratic schemas assume a dominant role in shaping the thought process. These schemas, relatively inactive during the nondepressed period, become progressively more potent as the depression develops. Their influence is reflected in characteristic disturbances in the patient's thinking.

* * *

During the developmental period the depression-prone individual acquires certain negative attitudes regarding himself, the outside world, and his future. As a result of these attitudes, he becomes especially sensitive to certain specific stresses such as being deprived, thwarted, or rejected. When exposed to such stresses he responds disproportionately with ideas of personal deficiency, with self-blame, and with pessimism.

The idiosyncratic attitudes represent persistent cognitive patterns, designated as schemas. The schemas influence the way an individual orients himself to a situation, recognizes and labels the salient features, and conceptualizes the experience.

The idiosyncratic schemas in depression consist of negative conceptions of the individual's worth, personal characteristics, performance or health, and of nihilistic expectations. When these schemas are evoked, they mold the thought content and lead to the typical depressive feelings of sadness, guilt, loneliness, and pessimism. The schemas may be largely inactive during the asymptomatic periods but become activated with the onset of depression. As the depression deepens, these schemas increasingly dominate the cognitive processes and not only displace the more appropriate schemas but also disrupt the cognitive processes involved in attaining self-objectivity and reality testing.

It is suggested that the affective reactions

may facilitate the activity of these idiosyncratic schemas and, consequently, enhance the downward spiral in depression. The relative absence of anger in depression is attributed to the displacement of schemas relevant to blaming others by schemas of self-blame.

REFERENCE

Foulds, G. A. Psychotic depression and age. *Journal of Mental Science,* 1960, *106,* 1394.

22.

Martin E. P. Seligman et al.

LEARNED HELPLESSNESS: REVISION AND CRITIQUE

The learned helplessness hypothesis is criticized and reformulated. The old hypothesis, when applied to learned helplessness in humans, has two major problems: (*a*) It does not distinguish between cases in which outcomes are uncontrollable for all people and cases in which they are uncontrollable only for some people (universal vs. personal helplessness), and (*b*) it does not explain when helplessness is general and when specific, or when chronic and when acute. A reformulation based on a revision of attribution theory is proposed to resolve these inadequacies. According to the reformulation, once people perceive noncontingency, they attribute their helplessness to a cause. This cause can be stable or unstable, global or specific, and internal or external. The attribution chosen influences whether expectation of future helplessness will be chronic or acute, broad or narrow, and whether helplessness will lower self-esteem or not. The implications of this reformulation of human helplessness for the learned helplessness model of depression are outlined.

* * *

The cornerstone of the hypothesis is that learning that outcomes are uncontrollable results in three deficits: motivational, cognitive and emotional. The hypothesis is "cognitive" in that it postulates that mere exposure to uncontrollability is not sufficient to render an organism helpless; rather, the organism must come to expect that outcomes are uncontrollable in order to exhibit helplessness. In brief, the motivational deficit consists of retarded initiation of voluntary responses and is seen as a consequence of the expectation that outcomes are uncontrollable. If the organism expects that its responses will not affect some outcome, then the likelihood of

From Lyn Y. Abramson, Martin E. P. Seligman, & John D. Teasdale, "Learned helplessness in humans: Critique and reformulation," *Journal of Abnormal Psychology,* vol. 87, pp. 50-70. Copyright 1978 by the American Psychological Association. Reprinted by permission of the publisher and author.

Ivan Miller (Note 1) has proposed an almost identical reformulation. We believe this work to have been done independently of ours, and it should be so treated.

emitting such responses decreases. Second, the learned helplessness hypothesis argues that learning that an outcome is uncontrollable results in a cognitive deficit since such learning makes it difficult to later learn that responses produce that outcome. Finally, the learned helplessness hypothesis claims that depressed affect is a consequence of learning that outcomes are uncontrollable.

Historically, the learned helplessness hypothesis was formulated with human subjects. In the main, early studies of human helplessness attempted to reproduce the animal findings in humans and were rather less concerned with theory building. Recently, however, investigators of human helplessness (e.g., Blaney, 1977; Golin & Terrell, 1977; Wortman & Brehm, 1975; Roth & Kilpatrick-Tabak, Note 2) have become increasingly disenchanted with the adequacy of theoretical constructs originating in animal helplessness for understanding helplessness in humans. And so have we. We now present an attributional framework that resolves several theoretical controversies about the effects of uncontrollability in humans. We do not know whether these considerations apply to infra-humans. In brief, we argue that when a person finds that he is helpless, he asks *why* he is helpless. The causal attribution he makes then determines the generality and chronicity of his helplessness deficits as well as his later self-esteem. In developing the attributional framework, we find it necessary to refine attribution theory (cf. Heider, 1958; Weiner, 1972, 1974). Finally, we discuss the implications of the reformulation for the helplessness model of depression (Seligman, 1972, 1975; Seligman, Klein, & Miller, 1976).

PERSONAL HELPLESSNESS VERSUS UNIVERSAL HELPLESSNESS

Inadequacy 1 of the Old Theory

Several examples highlight a conceptual problem encountered by the existing learned helplessness hypothesis when applied to human helplessness. Consider a subject in Hiroto's experiment (1974) who is assigned to the group that received uncontrollable noise. The experimenter tells the subject there is something he can do to turn off the noise. Since the noise is actually uncontrollable, the subject is unable to find a way to turn off the noise. After repeated unsuccessful attempts, the subject may come to believe the problem is unsolvable; that is, neither he nor any other subject can control noise termination. Alternatively, the subject may believe that the problem is solvable but that he lacks the ability to solve it; that is, although he can't control noise termination, other subjects could successfully control the noise. The old helplessness hypothesis does not distinguish these two states, either of which could be engendered by the procedure of presenting uncontrollable outcomes.

In a recent publication, Bandura (1977) discussed a similar distinction:

Theorizing and experimentation on learned helplessness might well consider the conceptual distinction between efficacy and outcome expectations. People can give up trying because they lack a sense of efficacy in achieving the required behavior, or they may be assured of their capabilities but give up trying because they expect their behavior to have no effect on an unresponsive environment or to be consistently punished. These two separable expectancy sources of futility have quite different antecedents and remedial implications. To alter efficacy-based futility requires development of competencies and expectations of personal effectivness. By contrast, to change outcome-based futility necessitates changes in prevailing environmental contingencies that restore the instrumental value of the competencies that people already possess. (pp. 204–205)

A final way of illustrating this inadequacy concerns the relation between helplessness and external locus of control. Early perspectives of learned helplessness (Hiroto, 1974; Miller & Seligman, 1973; Seligman, Maier, & Geer, 1968) emphasized an apparent similarity between the helplessness concept of learning that outcomes are uncontrollable and Rotter's (1966) concept of external control. Rotter argued that people's beliefs about causality can be arrayed along the dimension of locus of control, with "internals" tending to believe outcomes are caused by their own responding and "externals" tending to believe outcomes are not caused by their own responding but by luck, chance, or fate. Support for this proposed conceptual similarity of externals and helpless individuals was provided by studies of verbalized expectancies for success in tasks of skill (Klein & Seligman, 1976; Miller & Seligman, 1975). Helpless subjects gave small expectancy changes, which suggests a belief in external control, whereas subjects not made helpless gave large expectancy changes, which suggests a belief in internal control. These findings indicated that helpless subjects perceived tasks of skill as if they were tasks of chance. A puzzling finding, however, was consistently obtained in these studies. On postexperimental questionnaires, helpless and nonhelpless subjects rated skill as playing the same large role in a person's performance on the skill task. Both helpless and nonhelpless subjects said they viewed the skill task as a skill task. Thus, the relation between the concepts of external control and uncontrollability may be more complex than implied by the old hypothesis.

Taken together, these examples point to one conceptual problem concerning the notions of uncontrollability and helplessness. Recall the distinction made by the old helplessness hypothesis between controllable and uncontrollable outcomes. An outcome is said to be uncontrollable for an individual when the occurrence of the outcome is not related to his responding. That is, if the probability of an outcome is the same whether or not a given response occurs, then the outcome is independent of that response. When this is true of all voluntary responses, the outcome is said to be uncontrollable for the individual (Seligman, 1975; Seligman, Maier, & Solomon, 1971). Conversely, if the probability of the outcome when some response is made is different from the probability of the outcome when the response is not made, then the outcome is dependent on that response: The outcome is controllable. The early definition, then, makes no distinction between cases in which an individual lacks requisite controlling responses that are available to other people and cases in which the individual as well as all other individuals do not possess controlling responses. These three examples all illustrate the same inadequacy. In the next section we outline a framework that resolves this inadequacy, and we discuss the implications of this framework.

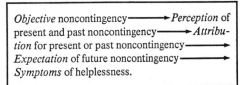

Objective noncontingency⟶*Perception* of present and past noncontingency⟶*Attribution* for present or past noncontingency⟶ *Expectation* of future noncontingency⟶ *Symptoms* of helplessness.

FIGURE 22-1. Flow of events leading to symptoms of helplessness.

Resolution of Inadequacy 1

Suppose a child contracts leukemia and the father bends all his resources to save the child's life. Nothing he does, however, improves the child's health. Eventually he comes to believe there is nothing he can do. Nor is there anything anyone else can do since leukemia is incurable. He subsequently gives up trying to save the child's life and exhibits signs of behavioral helplessness as well as depressed affect. This example fits the specifications of the old learned helplessness hypothesis. The parent believed the course of the child's disease was independent of all of his responses as well as the responses of other people. We term this situation *universal helplessness.*

Suppose a person tries very hard in school. He studies endlessly, takes remedial courses, hires tutors. But he fails anyway. The person comes to believe he is stupid and gives up trying to pass. This is not a clear case of uncontrollability according to the old model, since the person believed there existed responses that would contingently produce passing grades although he did not possess them. Regardless of any voluntary response the person made, however, the probability of his obtaining good grades was not altered. We term this situation *personal helplessness.*

Before discussing the distinction between universal and personal helplessness, it is useful to spell out the flow of events leading to symptoms of helplessness in both examples. First, the person perceived that all of his acts were noncontingently related to the desired outcome; regardless of what the father did, the child's illness did not improve, and the student continued to do poorly no matter how hard he tried. The person then made an attribution for the perceived noncontingency between his acts and the outcome; the father came to believe leukemia was incurable and the student came to believe he was stupid. In each case, the attribution led to an expectancy of noncontingency between future acts of the individual and the outcome. Finally, the symptoms of helplessness were a consequence of the person's expectancy that his future responses would be futile in obtaining the outcome. The usual sequence of events leading from objective noncontingency to the helplessness is diagrammed in Figure 22–1.

Both the old and reformulated hypotheses hold the expectation of noncontingency to be the crucial determinant of the symptoms of learned helplessness. Objective noncontingency is predicted to lead to symptoms of helplessness only if the expectation of noncontingency is present (Seligman, 1975, pp. 47–48). The old model, however, was vague in specifying the conditions under which a perception that events are noncontingent (past or present oriented) was transformed into an expectation that events will be noncontingent (future oriented). Our reformulation regards the attribution the individual makes for noncontingency between his acts and outcomes in the here and now as a determinant of his subsequent expectations for future noncontingency. These expectations, in turn, determine the generality, chronicity, and type of his helplessness symptoms. In the context of this general account of the role of attribution in the production of symptoms, the distinction between universal and personal helplessness can now be clarified.

Table 22–1 explicates the distinction between universal helplessness and personal helplessness and ultimately serves to define our usage of the attributional dimension of internality. We take the self–other dichotomy as the criterion of internality. When people believe that outcomes are more likely or less likely to happen to themselves than to relevant others, they attribute these outcomes to internal factors. Alternatively, persons make external attribution for outcomes that they believe are as likely to happen to themselves as to relevant others.

In the table, the x-axis represents the person's expectations about the relation between the desired outcome and the responses in his repertoire.[1] The person expects the outcome either to be contingent on some response in his repertoire or not to be contingent on any response in his repertoire. The y-axis represents his expectations about the relation between the desired outcome and the responses in the repertoires of relevant others. The person expects the outcome to be either contingent on at least one response in at least one relevant other's repertoire or not contin-

gent on any response in any relevant other's repertoire. Cell 4 represents the universal helplessness case and includes the leukemia example, and Cell 3 represents the personal helplessness case and includes the school failure example. Because the person does not believe he is helpless in Cells 1 and 2, these cells are not relevant here and are not discussed. It should be pointed out, however, that a person in Cell 2 would be more likely to make an internal attribution for his perceived control than would a person in Cell 1.

In Table 22–1, the y-axis represents the person's expectations about whether someone else, a relevant other, had the controlling response in his repertoire. The following example makes it clear why we use a "relevant other" rather than a "random other" or "any other": It is of no solace to a floundering graduate student in mathematics that "random others" are unable to do topological transformations. Crucial to the student's self-evaluation is his belief that his peers, "relevant others," have a high probability of being able to do topological transformations. Nor is it self-esteem damaging for a grade school student to fail to solve mathematical

[1]For the purpose of exposition, dichotomies rather than continua are used. The person expects that the controlling response is or is not available to him and that the controlling response is or is not available to others. These two dichotomies allow for four possible belief states. Strictly speaking, however, the x-axis is a continuum. At the far right, the person expects there is a zero probability that the desired outcome is contingent on any response in his repertoire. Conversely, on the far left he expects there is a probability of one that the desired outcome is contingent on a response in his repertoire. Similar considerations apply to the y-axis as a continuum.

TABLE 22-1.
Personal Helplessness and Universal Helplessness

	Self	
Other	The person expects the outcome is contingent on a response in his repertoire.	The person expects the outcome is not contingent on any response in his repertoire.
The person expects the outcome is contingent on a response in the repertoire of a relevant other.	1	Personal helplessness 3 (Internal attribution)
The person expects the outcome is not contingent on a response in the repertoire of any relevant other.	2	Universal helplessness 4 (External attribution)

problems that only professional mathematicians can solve, although he may have low self-esteem if his peers can solve them. Therefore, the y-axis is best viewed as representing the person's expectations about the relation between the desired outcome and the responses in the repertoires of relevant others.[2]

Implications

The distinction between universal and personal helplessness resolves the set of inadequacies with which we began the

---

[2]Our formulation of "internal" and "external" attributions resembles other attributional frameworks. Heider (1958), who is generally considered the founder of attribution theory, made a basic distinction between "factors within the person" and "factors within the environment" as perceived determinants of outcomes. Similarly, in the locus of control literature, Rotter (1966) distinguished between outcomes that subjects perceive as causally related to their own responses and personal characteristics and outcomes that subjects perceive as caused by external forces such as fate. Unlike these previous formulations that ask whether a factor resides "within the skin" or "outside the skin" to determine whether it is internal or external, we define the self-other dichotomy as the criterion of internality. Although these two formulations may appear to be at odds, analysis reveals strong similarities. For example, Heider (1958) argued that in making a causal attribution, individuals hold a condition responsible for an outcome if that condition is present when the outcome is present and absent when the outcome is absent. Likewise, Kelley (1967) suggested that the procedure individuals use in determining the cause of events is similar to an analysis of variance procedure employed by scientists. The factor that consistently covaries with an outcome is considered to be its cause.

Let us examine the leukemic child and the school failure examples from the perspective of Kelley and Heider. The responses of no person are consistently associated with improvement of the leukemic child's disease. If the father performed Kelley or Heider's causal analysis, he would conclude that his failure was due to some external factor (e.g., leukemia is incurable). Alternatively, in the school example, failing is consistently associated with the student and not associated with his peers. Here, the student would conclude that some internal factor (e.g., stupidity) was the cause of his failure. Thus, Heider and Kelley also rely on social comparison as a major determinant of internality.

article. Situations in which subjects believe they cannot solve solvable problems are instances of personal helplessness according to the reformulated hypothesis. Alternatively, situations in which subjects believe that neither they nor relevant others can solve the problem are instances of universal helplessness. Similarly, Bandura's (1977) conceptual distinction between efficacy and outcome expectancies relates to the reformulation in the following way: Personal helplessness entails a low efficacy expectation coupled with a high outcome expectation (the response producing the outcome is unavailable to the person), whereas universal helplessness entails a low outcome expectation (no response produces the outcome). Finally, the reformulation regards "external locus of control" and "helplessness" as orthogonal. One can be either internally or externally helpless. Universally helpless individuals make external attributions for failures, whereas personally helpless individuals make internal attributions. The experimental finding that helpless individuals view skill tasks as skill tasks, not as chance, is no longer puzzling. The task is one of skill (relevant others can solve it), but they do not have the relevant skill. These subjects view themselves as personally rather than universally helpless.

The distinction between universal helplessness and personal helplessness also clarifies the relation of uncontrollability to failure. In the literature these two terms have often been used synonymously. Tennen (Note 3), arguing from an attributional stance, suggested that the terms are redundant and that we abandon the concept of uncontrollability for the simpler concept of failure. We believe this suggestion is misguided both from the point of view of attribution theory and from common usage of the term *failure*.

In current attribution theories (e.g., Weiner, 1972) success and failure refer to outcomes. Success refers to obtaining a desired outcome and failure to not obtaining a desired outcome. According to this framework, then, the term *failure* does not embrace all cases of uncontrollability. Thus, from a strict attributional point of view, failure and uncontrollability are not synonymous: Failure is a subset of uncontrollability involving bad outcomes. Early theoretical accounts of helplessness suggested that good things received independently of responding should lead to helplessness deficits. Recent evidence bears this out: Uncontrollable positive events produce the motivational and cognitive deficits in animals (Goodkin, 1976; Welker, 1976) and in humans (Griffiths, 1977; Eisenberger, Mauriello, Carlson, Frank, & Park, Note 4; Hirsch, Note 5; Nugent, Note 6; but see Benson & Kennelly, 1976, for contrary evidence) but probably do not produce sad affect. Similarly Cohen, Rothbart, and Phillips (1976) produced helplessness effects in the absence of perceived failure. In the future, such studies should measure perception of noncontingency as well as performance, since Alloy and Abramson (Note 7) found that noncontingency is more difficult to perceive when one is winning than when one is losing. So the notion of uncontrollability means more than just failure, and it makes predictions concerning both failure and noncontingent success.

In ordinary language, failure means more than merely the occurrence of a bad outcome. People say they have failed when they have tried unsuccessfully to reach a goal and attribute this to some internal factor. Obtaining poor grades in school is considered failure, but being caught in a flash flood is generally considered misfortune. The concepts of trying and personal helplessness are both necessary to analyze failure in the ordinary language sense. According to the reformulated model, then, failure, seen from the individual's point of view, means the subset of personal helplessness involving unsuccessful trying.

The final ramification of the distinction between universal and personal helplessness is that it deduces a fourth deficit of human helplessness—low self-esteem. A major determinant of attitudes toward the self is comparison with others (Clark & Clark, 1939; Festinger, 1954; Morse & Gergen, 1970; Rosenberg, 1965). Our analysis suggests that individuals who believe that desired outcomes are not contingent on acts in their repertoires but are contingent on acts in the repertoires of relevant others, will show lower self-esteem than individuals who believe that desired outcomes are neither contingent on acts in their repertoires nor contingent on acts in the repertoires of relevant others. That is, an unintelligent student who fails an exam his peers pass will have lower self-esteem than a student who fails an exam that all of his peers fail as well.

The dichotomy between universal and personal helplessness determines cases of helplessness (and depression, see below) with and without low self-esteem. But it is neutral with regard to the cognitive and motivational deficits in helplessness. It is important to emphasize that the cognitive and motivational deficits occur in both personal and universal helplessness. Abramson (1977) has demonstrated this empirically while showing that lowered self-esteem occurs only in personal helplessness. According to both the old and the new hypotheses, the expectation that outcomes are noncontingently related to one's own responses is a sufficient condition for motivational and cognitive deficits.

We now turn to the second set of inadequacies. The old hypothesis was vague about when helplessness would be general across situations and when specific, and when it would be chronic and when acute. We now formulate this inadequacy and develop an attributional framework that resolves it.

GENERALITY AND CHRONICITY OF HELPLESSNESS

Inadequacy 2 of the Old Theory

A second set of examples point to the other inadequacy of the old helplessness hypothesis. Consider debriefing in a typical human helplessness study: The subject is presented with an unsolvable problem, tested on a second solvable task, and finally debriefed. The subject is told that the first problem was actually unsolvable and therefore no one could have solved it. Experimenters in human helplessness studies seem to believe that telling a subject that no one could solve the problem will cause helplessness deficits to go away. The prior discussion suggests that convincing a subject that his helplessness is universal rather than personal will remove self-esteem deficits suffered in the experiment. Neither the old nor the new hypothesis, however, predicts that such debriefing will remove the cognitive and motivational deficits. What does debriefing undo and why?

A second way of illustrating this inadequacy is the following: A number of investigators (Hanusa & Schulz, 1977; Tennen & Eller, 1977; Wortman & Brehm, 1975) have emphasized those cases of learned helplessness in which a person inappropriately generalizes the expectation of noncontingency to a new, controllable situation. It is important to point out that the old hypothesis does not require an inappropriate generalization for helplessness. Helplessness exists when a person shows motivational and cognitive deficits as a consequence of an expectation of uncontrollability. The veridicality of the

belief and the range of situations over which it occurs are irrelevant to demonstrating helplessness. But the old hypothesis does not specify where and when a person who expects outcomes to be uncontrollable will show deficits. In keeping with the resolution of the first inadequacy, an attributional framework is now presented to resolve the second inadequacy by explaining the generality and chronicity of deficits associated with helplessness.

A Resolution: The Attributional Dimensions of Stability and Generality

Helplessness deficits are sometimes highly general and sometimes quite specific. An accountant, fired from his job, may function poorly in a broad range of situations: he cannot get started on his income tax, he fails to look for a new job, he becomes impotent, he neglects his children, and he avoids social gatherings. In contrast, his helplessness may be situation specific: He does not do his income tax and fails to look for a new job, but he remains an adequate lover, father, and party-goer. When helplessness deficits occur in a broad range of situations, we call them *global*; when the deficits occur in a narrow range of situations, we call them *specific*.

The time course of helplessness (and depression, see below) also varies from individual to individual. Some helplessness deficits may last only minutes and others may last years. Helplessness is called *chronic* when it is either long-lived or recurrent and *transient* when short-lived and nonrecurrent.

The old hypothesis was vague about generality and chronicity. The helpless person had learned in a particular situation that certain responses and outcomes were independent. The deficits resulting could crop up in new situations if either the responses called for or the outcomes desired were similar to the responses and outcomes about which original learning had occurred. Helplessness was global when it depressed responses highly dissimilar to those about which original learning had occurred or when it extended to stimuli highly dissimilar to those about which original learning had occurred. No account was given about why helplessness was sometimes specific and sometimes global.

When helplessness dissipated in time, forgetting produced by interference from prior or later learning was invoked (e.g., Seligman, 1975, pp. 67–68). Forgetting of helplessness could be caused either by earlier mastery learning or by subsequent mastery learning. Again, the explanation was largely post hoc. Helplessness that dissipated rapidly was assumed to have strong proactive or retroactive interference; that which persisted was not.

The reformulated hypothesis makes a major new set of predictions about this topic: The helpless individual first finds out that certain outcomes and responses are independent, then he makes an attribution about the cause. This attribution affects his expectations about future response–outcome relations and thereby determines, as we shall see, the chronicity, generality, and to some degree, the intensity of the deficits. Some attributions have global, others only specific, implications. Some attributions have chronic, others transient, implications. Consider an example: You submit a paper to a journal and it is scathingly rejected by a consulting editor. Consider two possible attributions you might make: "I am stupid" and "The consulting editor is stupid." The first, "I am stupid," has much more disastrous implications for your future paper-submitting than the second. If "I am stupid" is true, future papers are likely to be rejected as well. If "The editor is stupid" is true, future papers stand a better chance of being accepted as long as you do not

happen on the same consulting editor. Since "I" is something I have to carry around with me, attributing the cause of helplessness internally often but not always (see below) implies a grimmer future than attributing the cause externally, since external circumstances are usually but not always in greater flux than internal factors.

Recent attribution theorists have refined the possible attribution for outcomes by suggesting that the dimension "stable-unstable" is orthogonal to "internal-external" (Weiner, 1974; Weiner, Frieze Kukla, Reed, Rest, & Rosenbaum, 1971). Stable factors are thought of as long-lived or recurrent, whereas unstable factors are short-lived or intermittent. When a bad outcome occurs, an individual can attribute it to (a) lack of ability (an internal–stable factor), (b) lack of effort (an internal–unstable factor), (c) the task's being too difficult (an external–stable factor), or (d) lack of luck (an external–unstable factor).

While we applaud this refinement, we believe that further refinement is necessary to specify the attributions that are made when an individual finds himself helpless. In particular, we suggest that there is a third dimension—"global-specific"—orthogonal to internality and stability, that characterizes the attributions of people. Global factors affect a wide variety of outcomes, but specific factors do not.[3] A

---

[3]In principle, there are a large number of dimensions on which attributions can be specified. Weiner (Note 8) suggested that the criterion for a dimension, as opposed to a mere property, of attribution be that we can sensibly ask, Does it apply to all the causes that we assign to behavior? So stable–unstable is a dimension because we can sensibly ask, Is ability a factor that persists stably over time? Is patience a factor that persists stably?, and so on. Similarly, global–specific qualifies as a dimension since we can ask sensibly, Is ability a factor that affects many situations or only few? Is patience a factor that affects many situations?, and so on.

global attribution implies that helplessness will occur across situations, whereas a specific attribution implies helplessness only in the original situation. This dimension (like those of stability and internality) is a continuum, not a dichotomy; for the sake of simplicity, however, we treat it here as a dichotomy.

Consider a student taking graduate record examinations (GREs) measuring mathematical and verbal skills. He just took the math test and believes he did very poorly. Within the three dimensions, there are eight kinds of attribution he can make about the cause of his low score (Internal–External × Stable–Unstable × Global–Specific). These attributions have strikingly different implications for how he believes he will perform in the next hour on

the verbal test (generality of the helplessness deficit across situations) and for how he believes he will do on future math tests when he retakes the GRE some months hence (chronicity of the deficit over time in the same situation). Table 22-2 describes the formal characteristics of the attributions and exemplifies them. Table 22-1 relates to Table 22-2 in the following way: Table 22-2 uses the attributional dimensions of stability and generality to further subdivide the cases of personal helplessness (Cell 3—internal attribution) and universal helplessness (Cell 4—external attribution) in Table 22-1.

According to the reformulated hypothesis, if the individual makes any of the four global attributions for a low math score, the deficits observed will be far-reaching:

TABLE 22-2
Formal Characteristics of Attribution and Some Examples

Dimension	Internal		External	
	Stable	*Unstable*	*Stable*	*Unstable*
Global Failing student	Lack of intelligence	Exhaustion	ETS gives unfair tests.	Today is Friday the 13th.
	(Laziness)	(Having a cold, which makes me stupid)	(People are usually unlucky on the GRE.)	(ETS gave experimental tests this time which were too hard for everyone.)
Rejected woman	I'm unattractive to men.	My conversation sometimes bores men.	Men are overly competitive with intelligent women.	Men get into rejecting moods.
Specific Failing student	Lack of mathematical ability.	Fed up with math problems.	ETS gives unfair math tests.	The math test was from No. 13.
	(Math always bores me.)	(Having a cold, which ruins my arithmetic)	(People are usually unlucky on math tests.)	(Everyone's copy of the math test was blurred.)
Rejected woman	I'm unattractive to him.	My conversation bores him.	He's overly competitive with women.	He was in a rejecting mood.

Note: ETS = Educational Testing Service, the maker of graduate record examinations (GRE).

Global attributions imply to the individual that when he confronts new situations the outcome will again be independent of his responses. So, if he decides that his poor score was caused by his lack of intelligence (internal, stable, global) or his exhausted condition (internal, unstable, global) or that the Educational Testing Service (ETS; the creator of GREs) gives unfair tests (external, stable, global) or that it is an unlucky day (external, unstable, global), when he confronts the verbal test in a few minutes, he will expect that here, as well, outcomes will be independent of his response, and the helplessness deficits will ensue. If the individual makes any of the four specific attributions for a low math score, helplessness deficits will not necessarily appear during the verbal test: i.e., lack of mathematical ability (internal, stable, specific) or being fed up with math problems (internal, unstable, specific) or that ETS asks unfair math questions (external, stable, specific) or being unlucky on that particular math test (external, unstable, specific).

In a parallel manner, chronicity of the deficits follows from the stability dimension. Chronic deficits (he will be helpless on the next math GRE when he retakes it at a later time) will ensue if the attribution is to stable factors: lack of intelligence, lack of mathematical ability, ETS gives unfair tests, ETS gives unfair math tests. Attribution to stable factors leads to chronic deficits because they imply to the individual that he will lack the controlling response in the future as well as now. If the attribution is to an unstable factor—exhaustion, fed up with the math problems, unlucky day, or unlucky on the math tests—he will not necessarily be helpless on the next math GRE. If he makes any of the internal attributions—lack of intelligence, lack of math ability, exhaustion, or fed up with math problems—the self-esteem deficits will occur. In contrast, none of the external attributions will produce self-esteem deficits.[4]

Because so much real-life helplessness stems from social inadequacy and rejection, Table 22-2 illustrates a social example. Here a woman is rejected by a man she loves. Her attribution for failure will determine whether she shows deficits in situations involving most other men (global) and whether she shows deficits in the future with this particular man or with other men (chronic). She might select any of four types of global attributions: I'm unattractive to men (internal, stable, global); my conversation sometimes bores men (internal, unstable, global); men are overly competitive with intelligent women (external, stable, global); men get into rejecting moods (external, unstable, global). All four of these attributions will produce helplessness deficits in new situations with most other men. The four specific attributions will produce deficits

---

[4] A critical remark is in order on the adequacy of ability, effort, task difficulty, and luck as embodying, respectively, internal–stable, internal–unstable, external–stable, external–unstable attributions (Weiner et al., 1971). While we find the orthogonality of internality and stability dimensions useful and important, we do not believe that the ability–effort/task difficulty–luck distinctions map into these dimensions. Table 22–2 presents (in parentheses) attributions that systematically violate the mapping. An internal–stable attribution for helplessness need not be to lack of ability; it can be to lack of effort: laziness (global), math always bores me (specific). An internal–unstable attribution need not be to lack of effort, it can be to (temporary) inabilities: I have a cold, which makes me stupid (global); I have a cold, which ruins my arithmetic ability (specific). An external–stable attribution need not be to task difficulty; it can be to lack of luck: Some people are always unlucky on tests (global); people are always unlucky on math tests (specific). An external–unstable attribution need not be to bad luck: it can be to task difficulty: ETS gave experimental tests this time that were difficult for everyone (global); everyone's copy of the math test was blurred (specific). So, ability and effort are logically orthogonal to internal–stable and internal–unstable attributions, and luck and task difficulty are orthogonal to external–stable and external–unstable attributions.

only with this particular man: I'm unattractive to him (internal, stable, specific); my conversation sometimes bores him (internal, unstable, specific); he is overly competitive with intelligent women (external, stable, specific); he was in a rejecting mood (external, unstable, specific). Any of the four stable attributions will produce chronic deficits either with that man (if specific) or with most men (if global); the four unstable attributions will produce transient deficits. The four internal attributions will produce self-esteem deficits; the four external attributions will not.

Having stated what we believe are the determinants of the chronicity and generality of helplessness deficits, a word about intensity or severity is in order. Severity is logically independent of chronicity and generality; it refers to how strong a given deficit is at any one time in a particular situation. We believe that the intensity of the motivational and cognitive deficits increases with the strength or certainty of the expectation of noncontingency. We speculate that intensity of self-esteem loss and affective changes (see Implications of the Reformulated Model for the Helplessness Model of Depression below) will increase with both certainty and importance of the event the person is helpless about. We also speculate that if the attribution is global or stable, the individual will expect to be helpless in the distant future (both across areas of his life and across time) as well as in the immediate future. The future will look black. This expectation will increase the intensity of the self-esteem and affective deficits. If the attribution is internal, this may also tend to make these deficits more severe, since internal attributions are often stable and global.

Attribution and Expectancy

In general, the properties of the attribu-

tion predict in what new situations and across what span of time the expectation of helplessness will be likely to recur. An attribution to global factors predicts that the expectation will recur even when the situation changes, whereas an attribution to specific factors predicts that the expectation need not recur when the situation changes. An attribution to stable factors predicts that the expectation need not recur after a lapse of time. Whether or not the expectation recurs across situations and with elapsed time determines whether or not the helplessness deficits recur in the new situation or with elapsed time. Notice that the attribution merely *predicts* the recurrence of the expectations but the expectation *determines* the occurrence of the helplessness deficits. New evidence may intervene between the initial selection of an attribution and the new and subsequent situation and change the expectation. So the person may find out by intervening successes that he was not as stupid as he thought, or he may gather evidence that everyone obtained low scores on the math GRE and so now ETS is under new management. In such cases, the expectation need not be present across situations and time. On the other hand, if the expectation is present, then helplessness deficits must occur (see Weiner, 1972, for a related discussion of achievement motivation).

Implications

The attributional account of the chronicity and generality of the symptoms of helplessness explains why debriefing ensures that deficits are not carried outside the laboratory. The debriefing presumably changes the attribution from a global (and potentially harmful outside the laboratory) and possibly internal (e.g., I'm stupid) one to a more specific and external one (e.g., psychologists are nasty: They give unsolvable problems to experimental subjects).

Since the attribution for helplessness is to a specific factor, the expectation of uncontrollability will not recur outside the laboratory anymore than it would have without the experimental evidence.

These attributional dimensions are also relevant to explaining when inappropriate, broad generalization of the expectation of noncontingency will occur. Broad transfer of helplessness will be observed when subjects attribute their helplessness in the training phase to very global and stable factors. Alternatively, attributing helplessness to very specific and unstable factors predicts very little transfer of helplessness.

A final question concerns the determinants of what particular attribution people make for their helplessness. Attribution theorists (e.g., Heider, 1958; Kelley, 1967; Weiner, 1974) have discussed situational factors that influence the sort of attribution people make. In addition, Heider and Kelley pointed to systematic biases and errors in the formation of attributions. Later, we discuss an "attributional style" that may characterize depressed people.

VALIDITY OF THE REFORMULATED MODEL

The validity of the new hypothesis must ultimately be assessed by its ability to generate novel predictions that survive attempts at experimental disconfirmation. As it is a new hypothesis, no results from such attempts are yet available. However, a minimum requirement is that this hypothesis should be consistent with the available experimental evidence. Although such consistency can lend only limited support to the hypothesis (as the available evidence has been one factor shaping the hypothesis), inconsistency might seriously embarrass the hypothesis.

Is the Reformulated Hypothesis Consistent with the Experimental Evidence on Learned Helplessness in Humans?

Three basic classes of evidence are covered: (a) deficits produced by learned helplessness, (b) attributional evidence, and (c) skill/chance evidence.

Deficits Produced by Learned Helplessness. Nondepressed students given inescapable noise or unsolvable discrimination problems fail to escape noise (Glass, Reim, & Singer, 1971; Hiroto & Seligman, 1975; Klein & Seligman, 1976; Miller & Seligman, 1976), fail to solve anagrams (Benson & Kennelly, 1976; Gatchel & Proctor, 1976; Hiroto & Seligman, 1975; Klein et al., 1976), and fail to see patterns in anagrams (Hiroto & Seligman, 1975; Klein et al., 1976). Escapable noise, solvable discrimination problems, or no treatment does not produce these deficits. Both the old and the reformulated hypotheses explain these deficits by stating that subjects expect that outcomes and responses are independent in the test situation. This expectation produces the motivational deficit (failure to escape noise and failure to solve anagrams) and the cognitive deficit (failure to see patterns). The reformulated hypothesis adds an explanation of why the expectation for the inescapability of the noise or the unsolvability of the discrimination problems must have been global enough to transfer across situations (e.g., I'm unintelligent; problems in this laboratory are impossible) and stable enough to survive the brief time interval between tests. The data are ambiguous about whether the global, stable attribution is internal (e.g., I'm stupid) or external (e.g., laboratory problems are impossible); self-esteem changes would have been relevant to this determination. Nondepressed students who escape noise, solve problems, or receive nothing as pretreatment do not perceive response–outcome independence and do not, of course, make any attribution about such independence.

For a control procedure, subjects have been told to listen to noise (which is inescapable) but not to try to do anything about it (Hiroto & Seligman, 1975); similarly, subjects have been given a panic button that "will escape noise if pressed" but have been successfully discouraged from pressing ("I'd rather you didn't, but it's up to you"); (Glass & Singer, 1972). These subjects do not become helpless. Both the old and reformulated hypotheses hold that these subjects do not perceive noncontingency (in this latter case, they perceive potential response–outcome contingency; in the first case, they have no relevant perception) and so do not form the relevant expectations and attributions.

A number of studies on human helplessness have obtained findings that are difficult to explain with the old helplessness hypothesis. Examination of these studies suggests that investigators may have tapped into the attributional dimensions of generality and stability. For example, Roth and Kubal (1975) tested helplessness across very different situations: Subjects signed up for two separate experiments that happened to be on the same day in the same building. They failed on the task in Experiment 1 (pretraining) and then wandered off to Experiment 2 (the test task). When subjects were told in Experiment 1 that they had failed a test that was a "really good predictor of grades in college" (important), they showed deficits on the cognitive problem of Experiment 2. When told that Experiment 1 was merely "an experiment in learning" (unimportant), they did better on Experiment 2. In the case of "good predictor of grades," subjects probably made a more global, internal, and possibly more stable attribution (e.g., I'm stupid enough to do badly on

this, therefore on college exams as well). The expectation therefore recurred in the new situation, producing deficits. In the unimportant condition, subjects probably made a more specific and less stable attribution, so the expectation of failure was not present in Experiment 2. (See Cole and Coyne, 1977, for another way of inducing a specific, rather than a global, attribution for failure.)

Similarly, Douglas and Anisman (1975) found that failure on simple tasks produced later cognitive deficits but that failure on complex tasks did not. It seems reasonable that failure on simple tasks should produce a more global and internal attribution (e.g., I'm stupid) whereas failure on the complex tasks could be attributed to external and more specific factors (e.g., these problems are too difficult).

An important advantage of the reformulation is that it better explains the effects of therapy and immunization than does the old hypothesis. The key here is the attributional dimension of generality. Helplessness can be reversed and prevented by experience with success. Klein and Seligman (1976) gave nondepressed people inescapable noise and then did "therapy," using 4 or 12 cognitive problems, which the subjects solved. (Therapy was also performed on depressed people given no noise.) Therapy worked: The subjects (both depressed and nondepressed) escaped noise and showed normal expectancy changes after success and failure. Following inescapable noise the subjects presumably made an attribution to a relatively global factor (e.g., I'm incompetent, or laboratory tasks are unsolvable), which was revised to a more specific one after success on the next task (e.g., I'm incompetent in only some laboratory situations, or, only some laboratory tasks are difficult). The new test task, therefore, did not evoke the expectation of uncontrollability. Teasdale (1978) found that real success experiences and recalling similar past successes were equally effective in shifting attribution for initial failure from internal to external factors. Only real success, however, reversed helplessness performance deficits. This suggests success does not have its effect by shifting attribution along the internal–external dimension. Although the relevant data were not collected, it is likely that real, but not recalled, success modifies attribution along the global–specific dimension. Immunization (Thornton & Powell, 1974; Dyck & Breen, Note 9) is explained similarly: Initial success experience should make the attribution for helplessness less global and therefore less likely to recur in the new test situation.

A number of human helplessness studies have actually shown facilitation in subjects exposed to uncontrollable events (Hanusa & Schulz, 1977; Roth & Kubal, 1975; Tennen & Eller, 1977; Wortman et al., 1976). While such facilitation is not well understood (see Wortman & Brehm, 1975; Roth & Kilpatrick-Tabak, Note 2, for hypotheses), it seems reasonable that compensatory attempts to reassert control might follow helplessness experiences, once the person leaves the situations in which he believes himself helpless (see Solomon & Corbit, 1973, for a relevant rebound theory). Such compensatory rebound might be expected to dissipate in time and be less strong in situations very far removed from the original helplessness training. When the "facilitation" effect of helplessness is brought under replicable, experimental control, the compensatory rebound hypothesis can be tested. People may also show facilitation of performance in uncontrollable situations when they cannot find a controlling response but have not yet concluded that they are helpless.

The reformulated hypothesis accounts for the basic helplessness results better than does the old hypothesis. The explanations given by the reformulated hypothesis are

necessarily post hoc, however. Relevant measures of the generality, stability, and internality of attribution were not made. Helplessness studies can, in principle, test the hypothesis either by measuring the attributions and correlating them with the deficits that occur or by inducing the attributions and predicting deficits. We now turn to the few studies of helplessness that have induced or measured attribution.

Attributional Evidence. Dweck and her associates (Dweck, 1975; Dweck & Reppucci, 1973; Dweck, Davidson, Nelson, & Enna, Note 10; Dweck, Goetz, & Strauss, Note 11) have demonstrated the differential effects of attribution for failure to lack of ability versus lack of effort. When fourth-grade girls fail, they attribute their failure to lack of ability (consonant with their teachers' natural classroom criticisms of girls) and perform badly on a subsequent cognitive test. Lack of ability is a global attribution (as well as internal and stable) and implies failure expectation for the new task. Fourth-grade boys, on the other hand, attribute failure to lack of effort or bad conduct (also consonant with the teacher's natural classroom criticisms of boys) and do well on the subsequent test. Lack of effort is unstable and probably more specific (but also internal). Boys, having failed and attributed failure to lack of effort, put out more effort on the test task and do adequately. Similarly, when students are told to attribute failure on math problems to not trying hard enough, they also do better than if they attribute it to lack of ability (Dweck, 1975).

Effort is not only "unstable," but it is readily controllable by the subject himself, unlike being bored, for example, which is also unstable, specific, and internal, or unlike lack of ability. It should be noted that the dimension of controllability is logically orthogonal to the Internal $\times$ Global $\times$ Stable dimensions (although it is empirically more frequent in the internal and unstable attribution), and as such it is a candidate for a $2 \times 2 \times 2 \times 2$ table of attributions. While we do not detail such an analysis here, we note that the phenomena of self-blame, self-criticism, and guilt (a subclass of the self-esteem deficits) in helplessness (and depression) follow from attribution of failure to factors that are controllable. Lack of effort as the cause of failure probably produces more self-blame than does boredom, although both are internal and unstable attributions. Similarly, a failure caused by not speaking Spanish attributed to lack of ability to speak Spanish, which might have been corrected by taking a Berlitz course, probably causes more self-blame than a less correctable lack of ability, such as ineptitude for foreign languages, even though both are internal and stable.

According to the reformulation, performance deficits should occur in cases of both universal and personal helplessness. In both cases people expect that outcomes are independent of their responses. In addition, attribution of helplessness to specific or unstable factors should be less likely to lead to performance deficits than attribution to stable or global factors. To date, four studies have manipulated attribution for helplessness in adults. In line with the reformulation, Klein et al. (1976) found that relative to groups receiving solvable problems or no problems at all, nondepressed students did poorly on an anagrams task following experience with unsolvable discrimination problems regardless of whether they attributed their helplessness to internal factors (personal helplessness) or external factors (universal helplessness).

Tennen and Eller (1977) attempted to manipulate attribution by giving subjects unsolvable discrimination problems that were labeled either progressively "easier" or progressively "harder." The authors reasoned that failure on easy problems should produce attribution to lack of ability (internal, stable, and more global) whereas failure on hard problems should allow attribution to task difficulty (external, unstable, and more specific). Subjects then went to what they believed was a second, unrelated experiment (see Roth & Kubal, 1975) and tried to solve anagrams. In line with the reformulation, attribution to inability (easy problems) produced deficits. Attribution to task difficulty (hard problems) resulted in facilitation of anagram solving. The most likely explanation for lack of performance deficits in the task-difficulty group is that their attributions for helplessness were too specific to produce an expectation of noncontingency in the test task.

Finally, two studies (Hanusa & Schulz, 1977; Wortman et al., 1976) found that relative to a group exposed to contingent events, neither a group instructed to believe they were personally helpless nor a group instructed to believe they were universally helpless on a training task showed subsequent performance deficits on a test task. While the results appear contrary to the reformulation, they are difficult to interpret. The problem is that in both studies, the typical helplessness group (a group exposed to noncontingent events in the training task but given no explicit attribution) did not show performance deficits on the test task. Thus, the test task may not have been sensitive to helplessness deficits. (For a discussion of the relative sensitivity of tasks to helplessness in animals, see Maier and Seligman, 1976). It is interesting that Wortman et al. (1976) found that personally helpless subjects showed more emotional distress than universally helpless subjects.

Overall, then, the few helplessness studies directly assessing and manipulating attribution provide some support for the reformulation. Because of the methodological problems in some of these studies, future research that manipulates attribution is necessary. Care must be taken to ensure that one attributional dimension is not confounded with another. Past studies, for example, have confounded externality with specificity and internality with generality.

Helpless Subjects Show Dampened Expectancy Changes in Skill Tasks. In skill tasks, expectancy for future success increases less following success and/or decreases less following failure for helpless subjects than for subjects not made helpless (Klein & Seligman, 1976; Miller & Seligman, 1976; Miller, Seligman, & Kurlander, 1975; see also Miller & Seligman, 1973, and Abramson, Garber, Edwards & Seligman, 1978, for parallel evidence in depression). The old hypothesis interpreted these results as a general tendency of helpless subjects to perceive responding and outcomes on skill tasks as independent, and it was assumed that this index measured the central helplessness deficit directly. In other words, it had been suggested that such subjects perceive skill tasks as if they were chance tasks. The rationale for this interpretation was derived from the work of Rotter and his colleagues (James, 1957; James & Rotter, 1958; Phares, 1957; Rotter, Liverant, & Crowne, 1961). These investigators argued that reinforcements on previous trials have a greater effect on expectancies for future success when the subject perceives reinforcement as skill determined than when he perceives it as chance determined. According to this logic, subjects will show large expectancy changes when they believe outcomes are chance determined.

Recent developments in attribution theory suggest that expectancy changes are not a direct index of people's expectations about response–outcome contingencies. Weiner and his colleagues (1971) argued that the attributional dimension of stability rather than locus of control is the primary determinant of expectancy changes. According to Weiner (Weiner, 1974; Weiner, Heckhausen, Meyer, & Cook, 1972) people give small expectancy changes when they attribute outcomes to unstable factors and large expectancy changes when they attribute outcomes to stable factors. The logic is that past outcomes are good predictors of future outcomes only when they are caused by stable factors.

In the absence of knowledge about individual attributions, the reformulated helplessness hypothesis cannot make clear-cut predictions about expectancy changes and helplessness, since belief in response–outcome dependence or independence is orthogonal to stable–unstable. For example, suppose a person makes an internal attribution to lack of ability for his helplessness, i.e., he believes in response–outcome independence for himself. When confronted with the skill task, he may show very large expectancy changes after failure since he believes he lacks the stable factor of ability for the task. Alternatively, when confronted with the 50 percent success rate typically used in helplessness studies, he may maintain his belief that he lacks the stable factor of ability but conclude that ability is not necessary for success on the task. After all, he succeeded sometimes in spite of his perceived lack of ability. Under such conditions, the person will believe outcomes are a matter of chance (unstable factor) for himself but not for others. Accordingly, he will give small expectancy changes. Moreover, a nonhelpless person (who perceives response-outcome dependency) may believe unstable factors, such as effort, cause his outcomes and show little expectancy change; alternatively, if he believes a stable factor is responsible for response–outcome dependence, he will show large shifts.

Rizley (1978) similarly argued that expectancy changes on chance and skill tasks do not directly test the learned helplessness model of depression. We agree. As argued in the previous paragraph, small expectancy changes need not imply belief in independence between responses and outcomes, and large expectancy changes need not imply belief in dependence between responses and outcomes. Nor does belief in response–outcome independence imply small expectancy changes, or belief in dependence imply large changes. The fact that depressives often show smaller expectancy changes than nondepressed people (Abramson et al., 1978; Klein & Seligman, 1976; Miller & Seligman, 1973, 1976; Miller et al., 1975) is intriguing but provides only limited support for the learned helplessness model. In order for expectancy changes to be used as a way of inferring perception of response–outcome independence, the particular attribution and its stability must also be known. None of the studies to date that measured expectancy shifts also measured the relevant attributions, so these studies do not tell us unambiguously that helpless (or depressed) people perceive response–outcome independence. They support the model only in as far as these two groups show the same pattern of shifts, but the pattern itself cannot be predicted in the absence of knowledge about the accompanying attribution.

To conclude this section, examination of expectancy changes on chance and skill tasks is not a direct way of testing helplessness, since such changes are sensitive to the attributional dimension of stability and not to expectations about response–outcome contingencies. Recent failures to obtain small expectancy changes in depressed people (McNitt & Thornton, 1978; Willis & Blaney, 1978) are disturbing empirically, but less so theoretically, since both depressed and helpless subjects show the same pattern, albeit a different pattern from the one usually found.

IMPLICATIONS OF THE REFORMULATED MODEL FOR THE HELPLESSNESS MODEL OF DEPRESSION

This reformulation of human helplessness has direct implications for the helplessness model of depression. The cornerstone of previous statements of the learned helplessness model of depression is that learning that outcomes are uncontrollable results in the motivation, cognitive, and emotional components of depression (Seligman, 1975; Seligman et al., 1976). The motivational deficit consists of retarded initiation of voluntary responses, and it is reflected in passivity, intellectual slowness, and social impairment in naturally occurring depression. According to the old model, deficits in voluntary responding follow directly from expectations of response–outcome independence. The cognitive deficit consists of difficulty in learning that responses produce outcomes and is also seen as a consequence of expecting response–outcome independence. In the clinic, "negative cognitive set" is displayed in depressives' beliefs that their actions are doomed to failure. Finally, the model asserts that depressed affect is a consequence of learning that outcomes are uncontrollable. It is important to emphasize that the model regards expectation of response–outcome independence as a sufficient, not a necessary, condition for depression. Thus, physiological states, postpartum conditions, hormonal states, loss of interest in reinforcers, chemical depletions, and so on may produce depression in the absence of the expectation of uncontrollability. According to the model, then, there exists a subset of depression— helplessness depressions—that is caused by expectation of response–outcome independence and displays the symptoms of passivity, negative cognitive set, and depressed affect.

We believe that the original formulation of the learned helplessness model of depression is inadequate on four different grounds: (*a*) Expectation of uncontrollability per se is not sufficient for depressed *affect* since there are many outcomes in life that are uncontrollable but do not sadden us. Rather, only those uncontrollable outcomes in which the estimated probability of the occurrence of a desired outcome is low or the estimated probability of the occurrence of an aversive outcome is high are sufficient for depressed affect. (*b*) Lowered self-esteem, as a symptom of the syndrome of depression, is not explained. (*c*) The tendency of depressed people to make internal attributions for failure is not explained. (*d*) Variations in generality, chronicity, and intensity of depression are not explained. All but the first of these shortcomings are directly remedied by the reformulation of human helplessness in an attributional framework.

Inadequacy 1: Expectation of Uncontrollability Is Not Sufficient for Depressed Affect

We view depression as a syndrome, to be made up of four classes of deficits: (*a*) motivational, (*b*) cognitive, (*c*) self-esteem, and (*d*) affective (but see Blaney, 1977, for a review that contends that only affective changes are relevant to depression). Whereas the first three deficits are the result of uncontrollability, we believe the affective changes result from the expectation that bad outcomes will occur, not from their expected uncontrollability.

Everyday observation suggests that an expectation that good events will occur with a high frequency but independently of one's responses is not a sufficient condition for depressed affect (see Seligman, 1975 (p. 98), versus Maier & Seligman, 1976 (p. 17), for previous inconsistent accounts). People do not become sad when they receive $1,000 each month from a trust fund, even though the money comes regardless of what they do. In this case, people may learn they have no control over the money's arrival, become passive with respect to trying to stop the money from arriving (motivational deficit), have trouble relearning should the money actually become response contingent (cognitive deficit), but they do not show dysphoria. Thus, only those cases in which the expectation of response—outcome independence is about the loss of a highly desired outcome[5] or about the occurrence of a highly aversive outcome are sufficient for the emotional component of depression. It follows, then, that depressed affect may occur in cases of either universal or personal helplessness, since either can involve expectations of uncontrollable, important outcomes.

At least three factors determine the intensity of the emotional component of depression. Intensity of affect (and self-esteem deficits) increases without desirability of the unobtainable outcome or

---

[5] One problem remains. It is a "highly desired" outcome for us that the editor of this journal give us each $1 million, and we believe this to have a very low probability and to be uncontrollable. Yet, we do not have depressed affect upon realizing this. Some notion, like Klinger's (1975) "current concerns," is needed to supplement our account. We feel depressed about the nonoccurrence of highly desired outcomes that we are helpless to obtain only when they are "on our mind," "in the realm of possibility," "troubling us now," and so on. Incidentally, the motivational and cognitive deficits do not need current concerns, only the affective deficit. We take this inadequacy to be general not only to the theory stated here but to much of the entire psychology of motivation, which focuses on behavior, and we do not attempt to remedy it here. We find Klinger's concept heuristic but in need of somewhat better definition. We, therefore, use the notion of "loss of a highly desired outcome" rather than "nonoccurrence." Loss implies that it will probably be a current concern. Since this is only part of a sufficiency condition, we do not deny that nonoccurrence can also produce depressed affect.

with the aversiveness of the unavoidable outcome, and with the strength or certainty of the expectation of uncontrollability. In addition, intensity of depressed affect may depend on whether the person views his helplessness as universal or personal. Weiner (1974) suggested that failure attributed to internal factors, such as lack of ability, produces greater negative affect than failure attributed to external factors, such as task difficulty. The intensity of cognitive and motivational components of depression, however, does not depend on whether helplessness is universal or personal, or, we speculate, on the importance of the event.

Perhaps the expectation that one is receiving positive events noncontingently contributes indirectly to vulnerability to depressed affect. Suppose a person has repeatedly learned that positive events arrive independently of his actions. If the perception or expectation of response–outcome independence in future situations involving loss is facilitated by such a set, then heightened vulnerability to depression will occur.

Inadequacy 2: Lowered Self-esteem as a Symptom of Depression

A number of theoretical perspectives (Beck, 1967, 1976; Bibring, 1953; Freud, 1917/1957) regard low self-esteem as a hallmark symptom of depression. Freud has written, "The melancholic displays something else besides which is lacking in mourning—an extraordinary diminution in his self-regard, an impoverishment of his ego on a grand scale" (p. 246). A major shortcoming of the old model of depression is that it does not explain the depressive's low opinion of himself. Our analysis of universal and personal helplessness suggests that depressed individuals who believe their helplessness is personal show lower self-esteem than individuals who

believe their helplessness is universal. Suppose two individuals are depressed because they expect that regardless of how hard they try they will remain unemployed. The depression of the person who believes that his own incompetence is causing his failure to find work will feel low self-regard and worthlessness. The person who believes that nationwide economic crisis is causing his failure to find work will not think less of himself. Both depressions, however, will show passivity, negative cognitive set, and sadness, the other three depressive deficits, since both individuals expect that the probability of the desired outcome is very low and that it is not contingent on any responses in their repertoire.

It is interesting that psychoanalytic writers have argued that there are at least two types of depression, which differ clinically as well as theoretically (Bibring, 1953). Although both types of depression share motivational, cognitive, and affective characteristics, only the second involves low self-regard. Further paralleling our account of two types of depression is recent empirical work (Blatt, D'Afflitti, & Quinlan, 1976) suggesting that depression can be characterized in terms of two dimensions: dependency and feelings of deprivation, and low self-esteem and excessively high standards and morality.

Inadequacy 3: Depressives Believe They Cause Their Own Failures

Recently, Blaney (1977) and Rizley (1978) have construed the finding that depressives attribute their failures to internal factors, such as lack of ability, as disconfirming the learned helplessness model of depression. Similarly, aware that depressives often blame themselves for bad outcomes, Abramson and Sackeim (1977) asked how individuals can possibly blame themselves for outcomes about which they believe they can do nothing. Although the reformulation does not articulate the relation between blame or guilt and helplessness, it clearly removes any contradiction between being a cause and being helpless. Depressed individuals who believe they are personally helpless make internal attributions for failure, and depressed individuals who believe they are universally helpless make external attributions for failure. A personally helpless individual believes that the cause of the failure is internal (e.g., I'm stupid) but that he is helpless (No response I could make would help me pass the exam).

What are the naturally occurring attributions of depressives? Do they tend to attribute failure to internal, global, and stable factors, and success to external, specific, and unstable factors?[6]

Hammen and Krantz (1976) looked at cognitive distortion in depressed and nondepressed women. When responding to a story containing "being alone on a Friday night," depressed women selected more depressed–distorted cognitions ("upsets me and makes me start to imagine endless days and nights by myself"), and nondepressed women selected more nondepressed–nondistorted cognitions ("doesn't bother me because one Friday night alone isn't that important; probably everyone has spent nights alone"). Depressed people seem to make more global and stable attributions for negative events. When depressed women were exposed to failure on an interpersonal judgment task, they lowered their self-rating more than did

nondepressed women. This indicates that the depressed women are systematically generating more internal as well as global and stable attributions for failure.[7]

Rizley (1978) caused depressed and nondepressed students to either succeed or fail on a cognitive task and then asked them to make attributions about the cause. Depressed students attributed failures to incompetence (internal, global, stable), whereas nondepressed students attributed their failures to task difficulty (external, specific, stable). Similarly, depressed students attributed success to the ease of the task (external, specific, stable), whereas nondepressed students attributed their success to ability (internal, global, stable). Although inconsistent with the old model, Rizley's results are highly consistent with the reformulation.

Klein et al. (1976) assessed the attribution depressed and nondepressed college students made for failure on discrimination problems. Whereas depressed students tended to attribute failure to internal factors, nondepressed students tended to attribute failure to external factors. These findings parallel those of Rizley on attribution in achievement settings.

Garber and Hollon (Note 12) asked depressed and nondepressed subjects to make predictions concerning their own future success as well as the success of

---

[6]The literature on the relation between internal locus of control and depression might be expected to yield direct information about internal attribution in depression. It is, however, too conflicting at this stage to be very useful. Externality, as measured by the Rotter scale, correlates weakly (.25–.30) with depression (Abramowitz, 1969; Miller & Seligman, 1973), but the external items are also rated more dysphoric and the correlation may be an artifact (Lamont, 1972).

[7]Alloy and Abramson (Note 7) also examined distortion, not in attributions but in perception of contingency between depressed and nondepressed students. The subjects were exposed to different relations between button pushing and the onset of a green light and were asked to judge the contingency between the outcome and the response. Depressed students judged both contingency and noncontingency accurately. In contrast, nondepressed students distorted: When the light was noncontingently related to responding but occurred with a high frequency, they believed they had control. So there was a net difference in perception of contingency by depressed and nondepressed subjects, but the distortion occurred in the nondepressed, who picked up noncontingency less readily (see also Jenkins & Ward, 1965).

another person in the skill/chance situation. The depressed subjects showed small expectancy changes in relation to their own skilled actions; however, when they predicted the results of the skilled actions of others, they showed large expectancy changes, like those of nondepressives rating themselves. These results suggest that depressives believe they lack the ability for the skill task but believe others possess the ability, the internal attribution of personal helplessness.

Taken together, the studies examining depressives' attributions for success and failure suggest that depressives often make internal, global, and stable attributions for failure and may make external, specific, and perhaps less stable attributions for their success. Future research that manipulates and measures attributions and attributional styles in depression and helplessness is necessary from the standpoint of our reformulated hypothesis.

Inadequacy: Generality and Chronicity of Depression

The time course of depression varies greatly from individual to individual. Some depressions last for hours and others last for years. "Normal" mourning lasts for days or weeks; many severe depressions last for months or years. Similarly, depressive deficits are sometimes highly general across situations and sometimes quite specific. The reformulated helplessness hypothesis suggests that the chronicity and generality of deficits in helplessness depressions follow from the stability and globality of the attribution a depressed person makes for his helplessness. The same logic we used to explain the chronicity and generality of helplessness deficits above applies here.

The reformulation also sheds light on the continuity of miniature helplessness depressions created in the laboratory and of real-life depression. The attributions subjects make for helplessness in the laboratory are presumably less global and less stable than attributions made by depressed people for failure outside the laboratory. Thus, the laboratory-induced depressions are less chronic and less global and are capable of being reversed by debriefing, but, we hypothesize, they are not different in kind from naturally occurring helplessness depressions. They differ only quantitatively, not qualitatively, that is, they are mere "analogs" to real helplessness depressions.

Do depressive deficits occur in situations that have nothing to do with the expectation of noncontingency? After failing a math GRE, the student goes home, burns his dinner, cries, has depressive dreams, and feels suicidal. If this is so, there are two ways our reformulation might explain this: (*a*) He is still in the presence of the relevant cues and expectations, for even at home the expectation that he will not get into graduate school is on his mind, and (*b*) the expectation, present earlier but absent now, has set off endogenous processes (e.g., loss of interest in the world, catecholamine changes) that must run their course. Remember that expectations of helplessness are held to be sufficient, not necessary, conditions of depression.

Finally, does the attributional reformulation of helplessness make depression look too "rational"? The chronicity, generality, and intensity of depression follow inexorably, "rationally" from the attribution made and the importance of the outcome. But there is room elsewhere for the irrationality implicit in depression as a form of psychopathology. The particular attribution that depressed people choose for failure is probably irrationally distorted toward global, stable, and internal factors and, for success, possibly toward specific, unstable, and external factors. It is also possible that the distortion resides not in attributional styles but in readiness to perceive helplessness, as Alloy and Abramson (Note 7) have shown: Depressed people perceive noncontingency more readily than do nondepressed people.

In summary, here is an explicit statement of the reformulated model of depression:

1. Depression consists of four classes of deficits: motivational, cognitive, self-esteem, and affective.

2. When highly desired outcomes are believed improbable or highly aversive outcomes are believed probable, and the individual expects that no response in his repertoire will change their likelihood, (helplessness) depression results.

3. The generality of the depressive deficits will depend on the globality of the attribution for helplessness, the chronicity of the depression deficits will depend on the stability of the attribution for helplessness, and whether self-esteem is lowered will depend on the internality of the attribution for helplessness.

4. The intensity of the deficits depends on the strength, or certainty, of the expectation of uncontrollability and, in the case of the affective and self-esteem deficits, on the importance of the outcome.

We suggest that the attributional framework proposed to resolve the problems of human helplessness experiments also resolves some salient inadequacies of the helplessness model of depression.

VULNERABILITY, THERAPY, AND PREVENTION

Individual differences probably exist in attributional style. Those people who typically tend to attribute failure to global, stable, and internal factors should be most prone to general and chronic helplessness depressions with low self-esteem. By the reformulated hypothesis, such a style predisposes depression. Beck (1967) argued

similarly that the premorbid depressive is an individual who makes logical errors in interpreting reality. For example, the depression-prone individual overgeneralizes; a student regards his poor performance in a single class on one particular day as final proof of his stupidity. We believe that our framework provides a systematic framework for approaching such overgeneralization: It is an attribution to a global, stable, and internal factor. Our model predicts that attributional style will produce depression proneness, perhaps the depressive personality. In light of the finding that women are from 2 to 10 times more likely than men to have depression (Radloff, Note 13), it may be important that boys and girls have been found to differ in attributional styles, with girls attributing helplessness to lack of ability (global, stable) and boys to lack of effort (specific, unstable; Dweck, 1976).

The therapeutic implications of the reformulated hypothesis can now be schematized. Depression is most far-reaching when (a) the estimated probability of a positive outcome is low or the estimated probability of an aversive outcome is high, (b) the outcome is highly positive or aversive, (c) the outcome is expected to be uncontrollable, (d) the attribution for this uncontrollability is to a global, stable, internal factor. Each of these four aspects corresponds to four therapeutic strategies.

1. Change the estimated probability of the outcome. Change the environment by reducing the likelihood of aversive outcomes and increasing the likelihood of desired outcomes.

2. Make the highly preferred outcomes less preferred by reducing the aversiveness of unrelievable outcomes or the desirability of unobtainable outcomes.

3. Change the expectation from uncontrollability to controllability when the outcomes are attainable. When the re-

TABLE 22-3

Treatment, Strategies, and Tactics Implied by the Reformulated Hypothesis

A. Change the estimated probability of the relevant event's occurrence: Reduce estimated likelihood for aversive outcomes and increase estimated likelihood for desired outcomes.

   a. Environmental manipulation by social agencies to remove aversive outcomes or provide desired outcomes, for example, rehousing, job placement, financial assistance, provision of nursery care for children.

   b. Provision of better medical care to relieve pain, correct handicaps, for example, prescription of analgesics, provision of artificial limbs and other prostheses.

B. Make the highly preferred outcomes less preferred.

   a. Reduce the aversiveness of highly aversive outcomes.

      1. Provide more realistic goals and norms, for example, failing to be top of your class is not the end of the world — you can still be a competent teacher and lead a satisfying life.

      2. Attentional training and/or reinterpretation to modify the significance of outcomes perceived as aversive, for example, you are not the most unattractive person in the world. "Consider the counterevidence" (Beck, 1976; Ellis, 1962).

      3. Assist acceptance and resignation.

   b. Reduce the desirability of highly desired outcomes.

      1. Assist the attainment of alternative available desired outcomes, for example, encourage the disappointed lover to find another boy or girl friend.

      2. Assist reevaluation of unattainable goals.

      3. Assist renunciation and relinquishment of unattainable goals.

C. Change the expectation from uncontrollability to controllability.

   a. When responses are not yet within the person's repertoire but can be, train the necessary skills, for example, social skills, child management skills, skills of resolving marital differences, problem-solving skills, and depression-management skills.

   b. When responses are within the person's repertoire, modify the distorted expectation that the responses will fail.

      1. Prompt performance of relevant, successful responses, for example, graded task assignment (Burgess, 1968).

      2. Generalized changes in response–outcome expectation resulting from successful performance of other responses, for example, prompt general increase in activity; teach more appropriate goalsetting and self-reinforcement; help to find employment.

      3. Change attributions for failure from inadequate ability to inadequate effort (Dweck, 1975), causing more successful responding.

      4. Imaginal and miniaturized rehearsal of successful response–outcome sequences: Assertive training, decision-making training, and role playing.

D. Change unrealistic attributions for failure toward external, unstable, specific; change unrealistic attributions for success toward internal, stable, global.

   a. For failure

      1. External: for example, "The system minimized the opportunities of women. It is not that you are incompetent."

      2. Unstable: for example, "The system is changing. Opportunities that you can snatch are opening at a great rate."

      3. Specific: for example, "Marketing jobs are still relatively closed to women, but publishing jobs are not" (correct overgeneralization).

   b. For success

      1. Internal: for example, "He loves you because you are nurturant not because he is insecure."

      2. Stable: for example, "Your nurturance is an enduring trait."

      3. Global: for example, "Your nurturance pervades much of what you do and is appreciated by everyone around you."

sponses are not yet in the individual's repertoire but can be, train the appropriate skills. When the responses are already in the individual's repertoire but cannot be made because of distorted expectation of response–outcome independence, modify the distorted expectation. When the outcomes are unattainable, Strategy 3 does not apply.

4. Change unrealistic attributions for failure toward external, unstable, specific factors, and change unrealistic attributions for success toward internal, stable, global factors. The model predicts that depression will be most far-reaching and produce the most symptoms when a failure is attributed to stable, global, and internal factors, since the patient now expects that many future outcomes will be noncontingently related to his responses. Getting the patient to make an external, unstable, and specific attribution for failure should reduce the depression in cases in which the original attribution is unrealistic. The logic, of course, is that an external attribution for failure raises self-esteem, an unstable one cuts the deficits short, and a specific one makes the deficits less general.

Table 22–3 schematizes these four treatment strategies.

Although not specifically designed to test the therapeutic implications of the reformulated model of depression, two studies have examined the effectiveness of therapies that appear to modify the depressive's cognitive style. One study found that forcing a depressive to modify his cognitive style was more effective in alleviating depressive symptoms than was antidepressant medication (Rush, Beck, Kovacs, & Hollon, 1977). A second study found cognitive modification more effective than behavior therapy, no treatment, or an attention–placebo therapy in reducing depressive symptomatology (Shaw, 1977). Future research that directly tests the therapeutic implications of the reformulation is necessary.

The reformulation has parallel preventive implications. Populations at high risk for depression—people who tend to make stable, global, and internal attributions for failure—may be identifiable before onset of depression. Preventive strategies that force the person to criticize and perhaps change his attributional style might be instituted. Other factors that produce vulnerability are situations in which highly aversive outcomes are highly probable and highly desirable outcomes unlikely; here environmental change to less pernicious circumstances would probably be necessary for more optimistic expectations. A third general factor producing vulnerability to depression is a tendency to exaggerate the aversiveness or desirability of outcomes. Reducing individuals' "catastrophizing" about uncontrollable outcomes might reduce the intensity of future depressions. Finally, a set to expect outcomes to be uncontrollable—learned helplessness—makes individuals more prone to depression. A life history that biases individuals to expect that they will be able to control the sources of suffering and nurturance in their life should immunize against depression.

REFERENCE NOTES

1. Miller, I. *Learned helplessness in humans: A review and attribution theory model.* Unpublished manuscript, Brown University, 1978.
2. Roth, A., & Kilpatrick-Tabak, B. *Development in the study of learned helplessness in humans: A critical review.* Unpublished manuscript, Duke University, 1977.
3. Tennen, H. A. *Learned helplessness and the perception of reinforcement in depression: A case of investigator misattribution.* Unpublished manuscript,

State University of New York at Albany, 1977.

4. Eisenberger, R., Mauriello, J., Carlson, J., Frank, M., and Park, D. C. *Learned helplessness and industriousness produced by positive reinforcement.* Unpublished manuscript, State University of New York at Albany, 1976.

5. Hirsch, Kenneth A. *An extension of the learned helplessness phenomenon to potentially negatively punishing and potentially positively reinforcing stimuli non-contingent upon behavior.* Unpublished manuscript, 1976. (Available from K. A. Hirsch, Galesburg Mental Health Center, Galesburg, Illinois.)

6. Nugent, J. *Variations in non-contingent experiences and test tasks in the generation of learned helplessness.* Unpublished manuscript, University of Massachusetts.

7. Alloy, L. B., & Abramson, L. Y. *Judgment of contingency in depressed and nondepressed students: A nondepressive distortion.* Unpublished manuscript, University of Pennsylvania, 1977.

8. Weiner, B. Personal communication to M. E. P. Seligman, 1977.

9. Dyck, D. G., & Breen, L. J. *Learned helplessness, immunization and task importance in humans.* Unpublished manuscript, University of Manitoba, 1976.

10. Dweck, C. S., Davidson, W., Nelson, S., & Enna, B. *Sex differences in learned helplessness: (II) The contingencies of evaluative feedback in the classroom and (III) An experimental analysis.* Unpublished manuscript, University of Illinois at Urbana-Champaign, 1976.

11. Dweck, C. S., Goetz, T., & Strauss, N. *Sex differences in learned helplessness: IV. An experimental and naturalistic study of failure generalization and its mediators.* Unpublished manuscript, University of Illinois at Urbana-Champaign, 1977.

12. Garber, J., & Hollon, S. *Depression and the expectancy of success for self and for others.* Unpublished manuscript, University of Minnesota, 1977.

13. Radloff, L. S. *Sex differences in helplessness—with implication for depression.* Unpublished manuscript, Center for Epidemiologic Studies, National Institute of Mental Health, 1976.

REFERENCES

Abramowitz, S. I. Locus of control and self-reported depression among college students. *Psychological Reports,* 1969, *25,* 149–150.

Abramson, L. *Universal versus personal helplessness: An experimental test of the reformulated theory of learned helplessness and depression.* Unpublished doctoral dissertation, University of Pennsylvania, 1977.

Abramson, L. Y., Garber, J., Edwards, N. B., & Seligman, M. E. P. Expectancy changes in depression and schizophrenia. *Journal of Abnormal Psychology,* 1978, *87,* 102–109.

Abramson, L. Y., & Sackeim, H. A. A paradox in depression: Uncontrollability and self-blame. *Psychological Bulletin,* 1977, *84,* 838–851.

Bandura, A. Self-efficacy: Toward a unifying theory of behavioral change. *Psychological Review,* 1977, *84,* 191–215.

Beck, A. T. *Depression: Clinical, experimental and theoretical aspects.* New York: Hoeber, 1967.

Beck, A. T. *Cognitive therapy and emotional disorders.* New York: International Universities Press, 1976.

Benson, J. S., & Kennelly, K. J. Learned helplessness: The result of uncontrollable reinforcements or uncontrollable aversive stimuli? *Journal of Personality and Social Psychology,* 1976, *34,* 138–145.

Bibring, E. The mechanism of depression. In P. Greenacre (Ed.), *Affective disorders: Psychoanalytic contributions to their study.* New York: International Universities Press, 1953.

Blaney, P. H. Contemporary theories of depression: Critique and comparison. *Journal of Abnormal Psychology,* 1977, *86,* 203–223.

Blatt, S. J., D'Afflitti, J. P., & Quinlan, D. M. Experiences of depression in normal young adults. *Journal of Abnormal Psychology,* 1976, *85,* 383–389.

Burgess, E. P. The modification of depressive behaviors. In R. D. Rubin & C. M. Franks (Eds.), *Advances in behavior therapy.* New York: Academic Press, 1968.

Clark, K. B., & Clark, M. P. The development of consciousness of self and the emergence of racial identification in Negro preschool children. *Journal of Social Psychology,* 1939, *10,* 591–599.

Cohen, S., Rothbart, M., & Phillips, S. Locus of control and the generality of learned helplessness in humans. *Journal of Personality and Social Psychology,* 1976, *34,* 1049–1056.

Cole, C. S., & Coyne, J. C. Situational specificity of laboratory-induced learned helplessness. *Journal of Abnormal Psychology,* 1977, *86,* 615–623.

Douglas, D., & Anisman, H. Helplessness or expectation incongruency: Effects of aversive stimulation on subsequent performance. *Journal of Experimental Psychology: Human Perception and Performance,* 1975, *1,* 411–417.

Dweck, C. S. The role of expectations and attributions in the alleviation of learned helplessness. *Journal of Personality and Social Psychology,* 1975, *31,* 674–685.

Dweck, C. S. Children's interpretation of evaluative feedback: The effect of social cues on learned helplessness. In C. S. Dweck, K. T. Hill, W. H. Reed, W. M. Steihman, & R. D. Parke. The impact of social cues on children's behavior. *Merrill-Palmer Quarterly,* 1976, *22,* 83–123.

Dweck, C. S., & Reppucci, N. D. Learned helplessness and reinforcement responsibility in children. *Journal of Personality and Social Psychology,* 1973, *25,* 109–116.

Ellis. A. *Reason and emotion in psychotherapy.* New York: Lyle Stuart, 1962.

Festinger, L. A theory of social comparison processes. *Human Relations,* 1954, *7,* 117–140.

Freud, S. Mourning and melancholia. In J. Strachey (Ed. and trans.), *Standard edition of the complete psychological works of Sigmund Freud* (Vol. 14). London: Hogarth Press, 1957. (Originally published, 1917.)

Gatchel, R. J., & Proctor, J. D. Physiological correlates of learned helplessness in man. *Journal of Abnormal Psychology,* 1976, *85,* 27–34.

Glass, D. C., Reim, B., & Singer, J. R. Behavioral consequences of adaptation to controllable and uncontrollable noise. *Journal of Experimental Social Psychology,* 1971, *7,* 244–257.

Glass, D. C., & Singer, J. E. *Urban stress: Experiments on noise and social stressors.* New York: Academic Press, 1972.

Golin, S., & Terrell, F. Motivational and associative aspects of mild depression in skill and chance. *Journal of Abnormal Psychology,* 1977, *86,* 389–401.

Goodkin, F. Rats learn the relationship between responding and environmental events: An expansion of the learned helplessness hypothesis. *Learning and Motivation,* 1976, *7,* 382–393.

Griffiths, M. Effects of noncontingent success and failure on mood and performance. *Journal of Personality,* 1977, *45,* 442–457.

Hammen, C. L., & Krantz, S. Effect of success and failure on depressive cognitions. *Journal of Abnormal Psychology,* 1976, *85,* 577–586.

Hanusa, B. H., & Schulz, R. Attributional mediators of learned helplessness. *Journal of Personality and Social Psychology,* 1977, *35,* 602–611.

Heider, F. *The psychology of interpersonal relations.* New York: Wiley, 1958.

Hiroto, D. S. Locus of control and learned helplessness. *Journal of Experimental Psychology,* 1974, *102,* 187–193.

Hiroto, D. S. & Seligman, M. E. P. Generality of learned helplessness in man. *Journal of Personality and Social Psychology,* 1975, *31,* 311–327.

James, W. H. *Internal versus external control of reinforcement as a basic variable in learning theory.* Unpublished doctoral dissertation, Ohio State University, 1957.

James, W. H., & Rotter, J. B. Partial and one hundred percent reinforcement under chance and skill conditions. *Journal of*

Experimental Psychology, 1958, *55,* 397–403.

Jenkins, H. M., & Ward, W. C. Judgment of contingency between responses and outcomes. *Psychological Monographs,* 1965 *79* (1, Whole No. 594).

Kelley, H. H. Attribution theory in social psychology. In D. Levine (Ed.), *Nebraska Symposium on Motivation* (Vol. 15). Lincoln: University of Nebraska Press, 1967.

Klein, D. C., Fencil-Morse, E., & Seligman, M. E. P. Learned helplessness, depression, and the attribution of failure. *Journal of Personality and Social Psychology,* 1976, *33,* 508–516.

Klein, D. C., & Seligman, M. E. P. Reversal of performance deficits in learned helplessness and depression. *Journal of Abnormal Psychology,* 1976, *85,* 11–26.

Klinger, E. Consequences of commitment to and disengagement from incentives. *Psychological Review,* 1975, *82,* 1–25.

Krantz, D. S., Glass, D. C., & Snyder, M. L. Helplessness, stress level, and the coronary prone behavior pattern. *Journal of Experimental Social Psychology,* 1974, *10,* 284–300.

Lamont, J. Depression, locus of control, and mood response set. *Journal of Clinical Psychology,* 1972, *28,* 342–345.

Maier, S. F., Albin, R. W., & Testa, T. J. Failure to learn to escape in rats previously exposed to inescapable shock depends on nature of escape response. *Journal of Comparative and Physiological Psychology,* 1973, *85,* 581–592.

Maier, S. F., & Seligman, M. E. P. Learned helplessness: Theory and evidence. *Journal of Experimental Psychology: General,* 1976, *105,* 3–46.

McNitt, P. C., & Thornton, D. W. Depression and perceived reinforcement: A reconsideration. *Journal of Abnormal Psychology,* 1978, *87,* 137–140.

Miller, W. R., & Seligman, M. E. P. Depression and the perception of reinforcement. *Journal of Abnormal Psychology,* 1973, *82,* 62–73.

Miller, W. R., & Seligman, M. E. P. Depression and learned helplessness in man. *Journal of Abnormal Psychology,* 1975, *84,* 228–238.

Miller, W. R., & Seligman, M. E. P. Learned helplessness, depression, and the perception of reinforcement. *Behaviour Research and Therapy,* 1976, *14,* 7–17.

Miller, W. R., Seligman, M. E. P., & Kurlander, H. M. Learned helplessness, depression and anxiety. *Journal of Nervous and Mental Disease,* 1975, *161,* 347–357.

Morse, S., & Gergen, K. J. Social comparison, self-consistency, and the concept of self. *Journal of Personality and Social Psychology,* 1970, *16,* 148–156.

Phares, E. J. Expectancy change in chance and skill situations. *Journal of Abnormal and Social Psychology,* 1957, *54,* 339–342.

Rizley, R. Depression and distortion in the attribution of causality. *Journal of Abnormal Psychology,* 1978, *87,* 32–48.

Rosenberg, M. *Society and the adolescent self-image.* Princeton, N.J.: Princeton University Press, 1965.

Roth, S., & Kubal, L. Effects of noncontingent reinforcement on tasks of differing importance: Facilitation and learned helplessness. *Journal of Personality and Social Psychology,* 1975, *32,* 680–691.

Rotter, J. B. Generalized expectancies for internal versus external control of reinforcement. *Psychological Monographs,* 1966, *80* (1, Whole No. 609).

Rotter, J. B., Liverant, S., & Crowne, D. P. The growth and extinction of expectancies in chance controlled and skilled tasks. *Journal of Psychology,* 1961, *52,* 161–177.

Rush, A. J., Beck, A. T., Kovacs, M., & Hollon, S. Comparative efficacy of cognitive therapy and pharmacotherapy in the treatment of depressed outpatients. *Cognitive Therapy and Research,* 1977, *1,* 17–37.

Seligman, M. E. P. Learned helplessness. *Annual Review of Medicine,* 1972, *23,* 407–412.

Seligman, M. E. P. *Helplessness: On depression, development, and death.* San Francisco: Freeman, 1975.

Seligman, M. E. P., & Beagley, G. Learned

helplessness in the rat. *Journal of Comparative and Physiological Psychology*, 1975, *88*, 534–541.

Seligman, M. E. P., Klein, D. C., & Miller, W. R. Depression. In H. Leitenberg (Ed.) *Handbook of behavior modification and behavior therapy.* Englewood Cliffs, N.J.: Prentice-Hall, 1976.

Seligman, M. E. P., Maier, S. F., & Geer, J. The alleviation of learned helplessness in the dog. *Journal of Abnormal and Social Psychology*, 1968, *73*, 256–262.

Seligman, M. E. P., Maier, S. F., & Solomon, R. L. Unpredictable and uncontrollable aversive events. In F. R. Brush (Ed.), *Aversive conditioning and learning.* New York: Academic Press, 1971.

Shaw, B. F. Comparison of cognitive therapy and behavior therapy in the treatment of depression. *Journal of Consulting and Clinical Psychology*, 1977, *45*, 543–551.

Solomon, R. L., & Corbit, J. D. An opponent-process theory of motivation: II. Cigarette addiction. *Journal of Abnormal Psychology*, 1973, *81*, 158–171.

Teasdale, J. D. Effects of real and recalled success on learned helplessness and depression. *Journal of Abnormal Psychology*, 1978, *87*, 155–164.

Tennen, H., & Eller, S. J. Attributional components of learned helplessness and facilitation. *Journal of Personality and Social Psychology*, 1977, *35*, 265–271.

Thornton, J. W., & Powell, G. D. Immunization and alleviation of learned helplessness in man. *American Journal of Psychology*, 1974, *87*, 351–367.

Weiner, B. *Theories of motivation: From mechanism to cognition.* Chicago: Rand McNally, 1972.

Weiner, B. (Ed.). *Achievement motivation and attribution theory.* Morristown, N.J.: General Learning Press, 1974.

Weiner, B., Frieze, I., Kukla, A., Reed, L., Rest, S., & Rosenbaum, R. M. *Perceiving the causes of success and failure.* Morristown, N.J.: General Learning Press, 1971.

Weiner, B., Heckhausen, H., Meyer, W., & Cook, R. E. Causal ascriptions and achievement behavior: A conceptual analysis of locus of control. *Journal of Personality and Social Psychology*, 1972, *21*, 239–248.

Welker, R. L. Acquisition of a free operant appetitive response in pigeons as a function of prior experience with response-independent food. *Learning and Motivation*, 1976, *7*, 394–405.

Willis, M. H., & Blaney, P. H. Three tests of the learned helplessness model of depression. *Journal of Abnormal Psychology*, 1978, *87*, 131–136.

Wortman, C. N., & Brehm, J. W. Responses to uncontrollable outcomes: An integration of reactance theory and the learned helplessness model. In L. Berkowitz (Ed.), *Advances in experimental social psychology* (Vol. 8). New York: Academic Press, 1975.

Wortman, C. B., Panciera, L., Shusterman, L., & Hibscher, J. Attributions of causality and reactions to uncontrollable outcomes. *Journal of Experimental Social Psychology*, 1976, *12*, 301–316.

23.

Hagop S. Akiskal and
William T. McKinney, Jr.

DEPRESSIVE DISORDERS: TOWARD A UNIFIED HYPOTHESIS

Clinical, experimental, genetic, biochemical, and neurophysiological data are integrated.

Depressive disorders are perhaps the most distressful, and certainly among the most common, maladies that afflict mankind. Although man has known and experienced melancholic states since antiquity, it is only during the past decade or so that we have begun to develop scientific insights into the basic mechanisms involved.

Unfortunately, the literature on depressive disorders, like that on other psychiatric disorders, is composed of isolated research reports, with few attempts at systematically integrating them.[1] Different schools of thought utilize dissimilar dialects, thereby hindering communication, while ethical considerations often preclude direct testing of hypotheses in human subjects. Studies are being carried out in an attempt to create experimental animal models of depression—models that would simulate the central features of human depressions. This article reviews these studies, as well as other formulations, both clinical and metapsychological, that derive from different frames of reference. We present evidence that depression in animals is sufficiently analogous to human depression to offer insights into the human condition. A comprehensive hypothesis of depression, incorporating and synthesizing findings from different schools, is proposed.

DEPRESSION AS A FINAL COMMON PATHWAY

Several models of depression, reflecting diverse theoretical orientations, have been formulated.

1) The "aggression–turned–inward" model, originally proposed by Abraham and later elaborated by Freud, sees depression as hostility turned inward upon the loss of an ambivalently loved person.[2] Although this is the most widely quoted psychological theory of depression, there is no systematic evidence to substantiate it.[3] Indeed, this theory does not lend itself easily to empirical verification because it is expressed in metapsychological terms.

2) The "object loss" model, which also has its roots in psychoanalysis,[4,5] views depression as a reaction to the loss of a loved object. Although the loss may involve symbolic possessions, such as one's values, status, and self–esteem,[6] object loss generally refers to traumatic separation from a loved person—that is, the disruption of an attachment bond.

3) The "reinforcement" model, which utilizes behavioral concepts, postulates that depression is the name given to behaviors that result from the loss of major sources of reinforcement, followed by

From Hagop S. Akiskal and William T. McKinney, Jr., *Science*, vol. 182, 5 October 1973, pp. 20–29.

operant conditioning in the form of attention and sympathy.[7] Depression is equated with chronic frustration stemming from environmental stresses that are beyond the coping ability of the individual, who views himself as being helpless and finds relief in the rewards of the "sick role."

4) Finally, the "biogenic amine" model, which focuses on biochemical derangements, hypothesizes a state of the central nervous system characterized by depletion of biogenic amines.[8] These neurotransmitters are concentrated in the areas of the brain that mediate arousal, sleep, appetite, sex drive, and psychomotor activity,[9] functions impaired in depression.

We examine the interrelations among these models and propose a biological final common pathway for depression. Specifically, we argue that depressive behaviors must be understood as occurring on several levels simultaneously rather than as having a one-to-one, direct relationship with a single chemical event in the brain, and that a multiplicity of genetic, developmental, pharmacological, and interpersonal factors converge in the midbrain and lead to a reversible, functional derangement of the mechanisms of reinforcement. According to our hypothesis, then, object losses, interpersonally induced states of frustration and helplessness, and depletion of biogenic amines ultimately result in impairment of the neurophysiological substrates of reinforcement; this impairment is manifested behaviorally as depressive phenomena.

HETEROGENEITY IN CLINICAL DEPRESSION

Defining and classifying depressive disorders are crucial for research. As Klerman suggests,[10] some of the confusion in research reports may derive from divergent concepts of what constitutes depressive behaviors and from patient population that are diagnostically heterogeneous.

Depression has been used to denote a variety of conditions, including (i) a normal mood state—for example, grief; (ii) a symptom synonymous with sadness that is seen in many psychiatric disorders; and (iii) a syndrome characterized by psychomotor retardation or agitation, dejection, hopelessness, self-derogation, suicidal preoccupations, insomnia, loss of appetite (anorexia), and loss of libido. To avoid unnecessary confusion, Whybrow proposes the use of "depression" for mood states, while reserving "melancholia" for the syndrome.[11] A sustained state of deep dejection (melancholia) is a psychobiological final common pathway; once attained, the state becomes autonomous and assumes the dimensions of illness—that is, morbidity, course, prognosis, and response to pharmacological therapies. It should, therefore, be distinguished from the ubiquitous, transient, and minor changes in affective responses which occur as part of everyday living.

The American Psychiatric Association, in the latest edition (1980) of its diagnostic and statistical manual,[12] classifies depressions into two broad categories: (i) those characterized by antecedent psychosocial conditions—"neurotic depression" and "psychotic depressive reaction"—that are presumably "reactive" to life events and, therefore, are more or less psychogenic and (ii) "involutional melancholia" and "manic–depressive illness," where "the onset of the mood does not seem to be related directly to a precipitating life experience" (hence "endogenous," or coming from within), with the implication that they are biological in origin.

The major problem with this system of classification is that an etiological index—presence or absence of precipitating psychosocial events—is used in defining disorders whose etiology is largely unknown. Moreover, studies have demonstrated[13] that the lack of psychosocial precipitants, thought to be characteristic of the "endogenous" depressive, results from *nonreporting*. The severely depressed patient is too disturbed to appraise fully the psychosocial context within which the illness manifests itself; upon clinical recovery, the frequency and type of stressful events, revealed by careful questioning, are no different from those in the "reactive" group. Depressive phenomena are neither inherently psychosocial nor biological.[1,14] As a final common pathway, they are the culmination of processes that can be described in many frames of reference. Our hypothesis is an attempt to build conceptual bridges between these various frames of reference.

Robins and Guze propose a system of classification that would exclude etiological considerations.[15] The label "secondary depression" refers to depressed patients with a history of a definite psychiatric illness other than affective disorder. Currently, little is known about secondary depression, because there are no large-scale systematic studies of it.[16] On the other hand, "primary affective illness," which is reserved for patients with no psychiatric disorder other than depression and mania, has received great attention from researchers during the past decade. It has been subdivided into two groups: unipolar affective disease, single or recurrent depressions; and bipolar affective disease, characterized by manic attacks in the subject or in his close biological relatives. Clinical,[17] genetic,[18] biochemical,[19] pharmacological,[20] and neurophysiological[21] differences have been described to further substantiate the unipolar-bipolar dichotomy. For instance, bipolar depressives, as compared with unipolars, are characteristically retarded in psychomotor activity;[22] have high genetic loading for affective illness, suggesting dominant transmission;[18] are more likely to have postpartum affective episodes;[23] will switch to mania upon treatment with sympathomimetic drugs;[19] and their brain waves (average evoked potentials) exhibit neurophysiological overreaction (augumentation responses) when presented with visual stimuli—these responses can be corrected by administering lithium carbonate.[21] The bipolar type is clinically manifested in affective episodes only (manias and depressions), and the vulnerability might be transmitted autosomally or by X–linkage.[24] Unipolar depressions, on the other hand, are clinically heterogeneous and apparently are manifested in forms other than depression, such as alcoholism, as suggested by the work of Winokur *et al.*;[25] the mode of inheritance is uncertain, with some suggestion that it is polygenic.[18]

The heterogeneity of depressive disorders encountered in clinical practice can be understood as interactions among biological, psychological, and sociological factors.[26] In view of the evidence for genetic heterogeneity, it is probable that there is more than one biochemical form of depression. On the other hand, little attention has been paid to the possibility that certain forms of depression result from interpersonal factors that secondarily induce biochemical changes in those areas of the brain that modulate affect. Despite the clinical and biological differences described for the various categories of depression (secondary, bipolar, unipolar), many symptoms that constitute the syndrome of depression (psychomotor and vegetative dysfunction, dysphoria, hopelessness, suicidal preoccupation) are common to the entire group of depressive disorders. This uniformity of symptoms is consistent with the hypothesis that a neurophysiological final common pathway underlies all types of depressive illness (see Fig. 23–1).

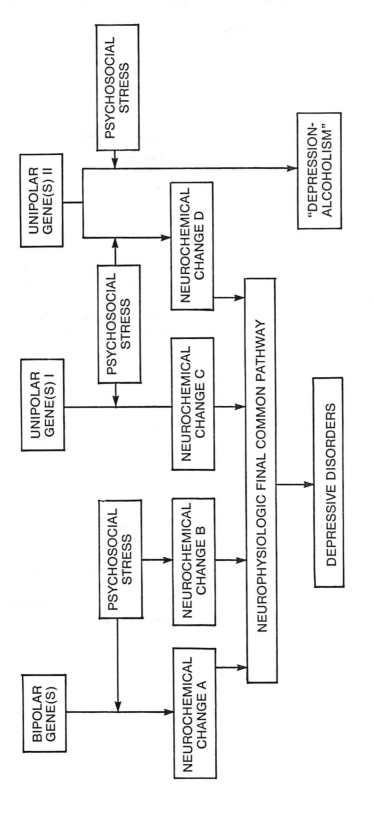

FIGURE 23.1—Hypothetical model of genetic-environmental interaction in depressive disorders.

OBJECT LOSS IN PRIMATES

The interaction of genetic and environmental factors in the genesis of human depressions is complex. To study the psychosocial conditions that permit the expression of depressive behaviors in a given individual, who may or may not have a depressive genetic diathesis, one should investigate each of the psychosocial factors. For instance, to state that separation from a loved person might precipitate a depressive condition is not very revealing. One must, for example, specify the age at which separation occurs; the object from whom separation takes place; the nature of the relationship between the two before the separation; the manner in which separation is achieved; and, finally, the length of separation required to cause depression. In other words, one has to define the concept of separation in a system where other factors are kept constant. Obviously this can be achieved most readily at the animal level. Such experimental paradigms would permit rigorous investigation of the behavioral, developmental, and biochemical variables involved. One can do the same with the concept of chronic frustration and helplessness or any other psychosocial factor thought to enter into the pathogenesis of depressive phenomena.

The modeling of certain aspects of the psychopathology of human depressions at the animal level had to await the establishment of objective criteria for the evaluation of nonhuman psychopathology[27,28] and the production of stable behavioral syndromes. Otherwise, the situation would have been similar to clinical psychiatric research, where confusion in the classification of disorders has often prevented generalization of findings from one study to another.

The nature and variety of reactions to separation have been studied extensively in nonhuman primates because these animals form very strong attachment bonds. These experiments were stimulated by clinical research undertaken by child psychoanalysts.

Spitz[4] reported a deprivational reaction in human infants separated from their mothers in the second half of their first year. The reaction was characterized by: (i) apprehension and crying; (ii) withdrawal; (iii) gross retardation of development, retardation of reaction to stimuli, slowness of movement, dejection, and stupor; and (iv) anorexia, weight loss, and insomnia. This syndrome, called anaclitic depression, could, unless reversed by providing a substitute mother, result in death from inanition and superimposed infection. It is interesting that only 15 percent of the infants suffered anaclitic depression. According to Spitz, those infants who had enjoyed a gratifying relationship with their mothers were the ones most susceptible to the trauma of separation. Yet one should also consider the possible interaction of genetic vulnerability with loss of the mother at a critical age.

A similar reaction was described in older children by Robertson and Bowlby.[5] It had three distinct phases: a "protest" phase, during which the child exhibited restlessness and tearfulness in search for the mother; a "despair" phase, in which the behavior of the child was characterized by apathetic withdrawal; and a final "detachment" phase, in which the child rejected the mother upon reunion.

These investigations stimulated research in infrahuman primates, with the purpose of creating animal models of anaclitic depression. Starting in the late 1950's, many experiments were designed at the Wisconsin Primate Laboratory to study the differential effects of maternal separation and social isolation on rhesus monkeys (*Macaca mulatta*) at different ages.[29]

Separation from the mother during infancy provided the best parallel to human anaclitic depression.[30] Monkeys (5 to 7 months old) that were separated from their mothers but still living with their peers in their original playpen, went through a predictable course of agitation in search for their mothers to almost total lack of interaction with their peers and their environment. This was a rather stable behavioral syndrome, reproduced and amplified by other investigators.[31] These stages of separation are illustrated in Fig. 23–2.

In one of the Kaufman-Rosenblum experiments,[32] four pigtail (*Macaca nemestrina*) infants (4 to 5 months old) that had been reared in a laboratory pen in a group living situation with their feral mothers were separated from their mothers for a period of 4 weeks. The mothers were removed from the original pen, leaving the four infants together. The first 24 to 36 hours were marked by "acute distress" (protest phase): loud screams, searching head movements, pacing, and restlessness. During the next 5 to 6 days, the infants were described as "depressed" (despair phase): they "sat hunched over, almost rolled into a ball," with the head down between the legs, and indulged in self–mouthing: their behavior was generally withdrawn, with only occasional reference to inanimate objects and almost no interaction with peers.

Anaclitic depression is complicated by the fact that, in addition to the disruption of a strong attachment bond, the loss of the relationship with the mother could markedly interfere with the infant's adaptive responses and, ultimately, survival. Studies of infants separated from their peers[33] circumvent this problem, because separation from peers interferes almost exclusively with the attachment bond. The experimental paradigm consisted of either

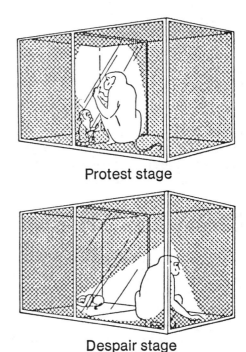

Protest stage

Despair stage

FIGURE 23.2—Illustration of typical protest and despair stages following separation from the mother.

a single, protracted separation or multiple, short separations of a group of four infant macaques that had been reared together since birth. During separation, they went through a protest phase, with excessive vocalization and random locomotion, followed by a despair phase, with marked increase in self–clasping and huddling and marked decrease in locomotion and exploration. One can conclude that the disruption of an attachment bond, whether infant–mother or infant–infant, is a powerful inducer of psychopathology of the "depressive" type.

The age at which separation takes place and prior experience with separation seem to be important factors in determining the form that reactions to separation take. Juvenile monkeys (3 to 4 years old) ordinarily react to separation only with behavior characteristic of the protest phase.[34] Hence, great caution should be exercised in viewing anaclitic depression as the prototype for adult depressions. On the other hand, a Wisconsin study[35] found that juvenile monkeys that had undergone traumatic separation during infancy responded to separation in a manner reminiscent of the despair phase. This suggests that early breaks in attachment bonds could predispose one to adult depression.

PHARMACOLOGICAL "DEPRESSION"

Chemically induced psychopathological states in primates provide further parallels with human depression. Consistent with the biogenic amine hypothesis is the fact that reserpine, a depletor of biogenic amines, precipitates depression in 15 to 20 percent of hypertensive human patients when given in doses of more than 0.5 milligram per day.[36] In a third of these patients, the depression is serious enough to require psychiatric hospitalization and electroconvulsive therapy. For this reason, the reactions of primates to reserpine have been tested. Rhesus monkeys fed reserpine for 81 days exhibited significant decreases in locomotion and visual exploration and an increase in huddling behavior.[37] The resemblance to the despair phase of both human and primate infants is apparent. It would be interesting to compare the effect of reserpine on normally reared adult monkeys with its effect on adult monkeys with a history of traumatic separation. This would more closely parallel the reserpine story in man, since severe depression is induced most readily in persons with a history of depressive illness or a family history of such illness.[36]

Alpha-methylparatyrosine (AMPT), a selective depletor of dopamine and norepinephrine,[38] was administered to adult stump-tail monkeys (*Macaca speciosa*) by Redmond *et al.* at the Illinois State Psychiatric Institute.[39] The animals (which exhibited no signs of toxicity at the end of the study) displayed marked changes in behavior 5 to 6 weeks after treatment with AMPT was begun: (i) decreased total social interactions; (ii) decreased social initiative; (iii) changes in posture and facial expression, suggesting withdrawal and lack of concern with the environment; and (iv) retarded motor activity, without evidence of extrapyramidal reactions. The Wisconsin group found similar results with AMPT.[40] Both the Illinois[41] and Wisconsin[40] investigators, however, found no appreciable effects on the behavior of monkeys treated with parachlorphenylalanine, the selective depletor of serotonin.[42] Monkeys treated with AMPT, despite their "retarded" motor appearance and behavior, exhibited electroencephalographic evidence of arousal. This is consistent with studies in man; contrary to classical notions, evidence for hyperarousal has been found in depressed individuals.[43]

When injected into the central nervous system, 6-hydroxydopamine (6-OHDA) causes permanent destruction of central catecholamine fibers, while leaving the peripheral sympathetic system, and both the central and peripheral serotonergic systems, intact.[44] Stein and Wise[45,46] have hypothesized that 6-OHDA is somehow involved in the etiology of schizophrenia (and perhaps also of manic-depressive illness). Whether or not this is found to be true, it is now established that 6-OHDA given intraventricularly to rats and rhesus monkeys produces significant changes in behavior. In the adult rat, there is a temporary diminution in activity and in eating and drinking, a reduction in the rate of self-stimulation in the brain, and failure to learn to avoid unpleasant events in active avoidance tasks.[47] In rhesus monkeys, there is a dramatic decrease in locomotion and social interaction and increased passivity.[48] These changes in behavior occur after each injection of 6-OHDA; they are temporary, however, despite a permanent depletion of norepinephrine in the brain. This phenomenon requires further investigation, but is generally consistent with the hypothesis presented here. The data from studies of monkeys support the notion that depression is a final common pathway, rather than a specific chemical event, and that it represents the response of the central nervous system to multiple stresses that could be described in interpersonal or biochemical language.

HELPLESSNESS AND DEPRESSION

Is it possible to induce helplessness in animals—that is, a state in which the animal can no longer cope with the frustrations in its environment and simply gives up? For many clinicians, hopelessness and helplessness represent the central feature of human depression.[49] For instance, Beck and his associates[50] found that "negative cognitive set," the perception of oneself as being helpless and hopeless and having no control over one's fate, correlates best with the depth of depression and suicidal behavior.

"Learned helplessness" is an operational construct which Seligman *et al.*[51] use to refer to a stable behavioral pattern characterized by failure to initiate responses to escape traumatic events and failure to learn that one's own responses could be instrumental in terminating noxious stimuli. Dogs were subjected to repeated, inescapable electric shock while strapped in a Pavlovian harness; when these dogs later received electric shock in a shuttlebox, they failed to cross the barrier, thereby "pas-

sively" accepting the highly traumatic shock experience. This behavior was in remarkable contrast to that of dogs which had not been previously exposed to inescapable shock; during shuttlebox training, they immediately learned that their response—to jump the barrier—ended the shock. Learned helplessness was reversed by forcibly dragging the dog to the other side of the shuttlebox; apparently the dog learned that its own responses could bring relief from noxious stimulation.

In Seligman's view,[28] learned helplessness parallels clinical depressions in which the individual loses control over the reinforcers in the environment. Negative expectations about the effectiveness of one's efforts in bringing the environment under one's control (hopelessness, helplessness, powerlessness) lead to passivity and diminished initiation of responses (retardation of psychomotor activity and thought processes, seen clinically).

Such clinical states of helplessness and passivity do not seem to indicate actual deficiencies in the behavioral repertoire of the patients. Some studies have found that depressed patients actively attempt to manipulate their environments;[52] others have found no evidence of objective deficiencies in actual performance when patients were coerced into engaging in the task at hand.[53] One is led to conclude that depressed patients have an underlying disorder of motivation and that their ability to derive reinforcement from their environments is impaired.

What interpersonal situations lead to such maladaptive patterns of behavior?

For those in the Wolpian tradition,[54] chronic aversive stimulation—that is, chronic failure in one's attempts to have the upper hand in interpersonal relationships—culminates in chronic anxiety and inability to reduce anxiety by means of one's usual behavioral repertoire.

The clinical picture of such maladaptive behavior, characterized by passivity and hopelessness, is somewhat similar to that of Seligman's dogs. It is claimed that systematic desensitization, aimed at reducing the anxiety, or assertive training, designed to help the individual gain control over interpersonal contingencies, are successful in treating such "neurotic depressions."

Lewinshon *et al.*,[55] who utilize a Skinnerian frame of reference, state that a low rate of positive reinforcement is the antecedent of depression, which is further maintained by positive reinforcement in the form of sympathy and attention. Lack of "social skill," defined as behaviors that are seldom positively reinforced by others, is viewed as the central behavioral deficit. This concept is useful because it emphasizes the fact that it is not passivity per se which characterizes the depressive, but behaviors that do not reinforce him, no matter how "active" he is. Observations of both the patient and his family at home provide a powerful tool in manipulating interpersonal contingencies that elicit or maintain depressive behaviors. Indeed, managing interpersonal contingencies has proved successful in treating depressed individuals.[56] Positive reinforcement is provided for active behaviors that take the place of the lost source of reinforcement; such reinforcement, coupled with selective inattention to depressive behaviors, leads to their extinction.

In summary, chronic aversive stimulation, loss of reinforcement, and loss of control over reinforcement are overlapping concepts that describe a state of hopelessness and helplessness deriving from interpersonal relations. A variety of techniques, deriving from both classical and instrumental conditioning, could be utilized to alleviate such depressive states, but apparently these techniques are useful in the milder, so-called neurotic, depressions and that the more severe depressions usually require antidepressant drugs or electroconvulsive therapy.[54] There are two possible explanations for this phenomenon: (i) no matter what interpersonal factors elicit or maintain depressive behaviors, once these behaviors assume severe proportions they become biologically autonomous—the stage of melancholia[11]—and, consequently, require somatic therapies; (ii) severe depressions have underlying biochemical predispositions and, therefore, would not respond to any appreciable degree to verbal therapy.

BIOGENIC AMINES AND DEPRESSION

Disturbances in both classes of biogenic amines, the catecholamines (dopamine and noradrenaline) and the indoleamines (serotonin and tryptamine), have been hypothesized to cause affective disorders.[8] The catecholamine hypothesis, the first biogenic amine hypothesis to be formulated explicitly, states that depression is associated with a deficiency of catecholamines, particularly norepinephrine, in the central nervous system, and mania with an excess of catecholamine. The possible role of impaired biogenic amine function in these disorders was first inferred from pharmacological evidence.[57] It was known, for instance, that a syndrome resembling naturally occuring depressions would develop in hypersensitive patients being given large doses of reserpine and alpha–methyl–dopa over a period of, on the average, 3 months. Both drugs are biogenic amine depletors. It now appears, however, that reserpine is more of a chemical trigger, which upsets a vulnerable biochemical–neurophysiological system, than a primary cause of depression.[36] As for the pharmacological therapies effective in depression, they are known to raise the level of free amines in the brain.[57] Tricyclic antidepressants such as imipramine and amitriptyline prevent the reuptake of biogenic amines released from the presynaptic stores, thereby causing a net increase in these transmitters at the postsynaptic junction. Monoamine oxidase inhibitors such as tranylcypromine and phenelzine prevent the oxidative deamination of these amines at the presynaptic stores, again increasing their availability at the receptor sites on the postsynaptic membrane.

Because the effects of reserpine and the antidepressant drugs on biogenic amine metabolism, storage, and release are nonspecific, the pharmacological evidence thus far reviewed does not distinguish between the role of indoleamines and that of catecholamines. Depressed patients have been given the metabolic precursors of these amines in an attempt to discriminate between their respective effects. A collaboration between U.S. and British researchers[58] has strengthened the earlier British claims that L-tryptophan, the amino acid precursor of serotonin, has antidepressant properties, especially when coupled with a monoamine oxidase inhibitor.[59] The catecholamine precursor, L-dopa, on the other hand, has been a failure in therapy, except for a small subgroup of retarded depressives.[60] The precursor loading strategy, therefore, lends support to the hypothesis that a deficiency of indoleamines in the central nervous system plays an important etiological role in the pathogenesis of depressive disorders[61]. It also suggests that retarded psychomotor activity, a behavioral correlate of catecholaminergic deficiency in the central nervous system, could be of etiological significance in some depressed patients.[62] Yet, if optimal states of mood and psychomotor functioning depend on the harmonious functioning of serotoner-

gic and catecholaminergic systems in the diencephalon, then the negative results with L-dopa could perhaps be explained by the decreased serotonin synthesis that has been observed in depressed patients receiving L-dopa.[63]

Definitive evidence for the biogenic amine hypotheses has to await the demonstration of significant alterations of monoamines in the brains of depressed patients. Although 5-hydroxyindoleacetic acid (5-HIAA), the major metabolite of serotonin, and 5-hydroxytryptamine have been found in low concentrations in the hindbrain of depressive suicides,[64] one must remember that postmortem neurochemical determinations are beset with methodological problems. However, analysis of the cerebrospinal fluid from depressed patients—and, interestingly, from manic patients—has revealed low concentrations of 5-HIAA,[65] which, at least in depression, persist with clinical recovery.[61] Since concentrations of 5-HIAA in cerebrospinal fluid are affected by peripheral (gastrointestinal) sources of indoleamines, the probenecid technique of preventing the active transport of organic acids across the blood-brain barrier has been introduced into clinical research; the results obtained with the probenecid modification, however, have been largely inconclusive, with some suggestion that both dopamine and serotonin metabolites are lowered in concentration.[66]

As for noradrenaline, about 30 percent of the 3-methoxy-4-hydroxyphenylethylene glycol (MHPG) in the urine is thought to come from the metabolic degradation of noradrenaline in the central nervous system.[67] This metabolite has been found in subnormal concentrations in depressed patients, returning to normal after treatment with imipramine.[68] However, it is not clear at present whether low concentrations of MHPG, and low concentrations of metabolites of other biogenic amines correlate best with retarded psychomotor function or with depressed mood.[69]

In summary, the available data on biogenic amines and depressive disorders do not distinguish between one biogenic amine and another. Although it is possible that distinct groups of depressed patients suffer depletion of a particular biogenic amine, a depletion model based on one biogenic amine is probably an oversimplification. One should perhaps consider the possibility of inefficient interactions of these amines or substitution by faulty neurotransmitters.[70] The failure of indoleamines to return to normal after the patient's clinical recovery from depression has led to the hypothesis that serotonergic deficiency in the central nervous system determines the patient's predisposition to depressive (and manic) illness; while the depressive episode is triggered by catecholamine depletion (and mania is triggered by an increase in catecholamines). In this view, depression and mania are on a continuum, sharing the same basic dysfunction, rather than being polar opposites, with mania representing a more severe deviation from normal mood.[71] Bunney, Goodwin, and Murphy have suggested that the available data point to the role of catecholamine excess in exacerbations of manic episodes, but that the underlying dysfunction in both mania and depressions of the bipolar variety probably involves a basic instability of the presynaptic neuronal membrane; such dysfunction is perhaps partially correctable by imipramine or lithium carbonate, or both.[72] Another hypothesis, postulated by Janowsky, El-Yousef, and Davis, attributes depression to a shift in the balance of norepinephrine and acetylcholine in the diencephalon toward the cholinergic side.[73] Finally, the work of Prange *et al.* suggests impaired sensitivity of the postsynaptic

monoaminergic receptor,[74] a condition that can be partially corrected by administering thyroid hormone or thyroid-stimulating hormone on top of the tricyclic antidepressant regimen.[75] This is an important consideration, since synaptic transmission is determined jointly by presynaptic changes in biogenic amines and by postsynaptic receptor sensitivity. With impaired receptor sensitivity present, it is possible that depression could exist with normal or high levels of catecholamines.

ATTACHMENT, REINFORCEMENT, AND BIOGENIC AMINES

The original psychoanalytic model, paraphrased by Spitz[4] and by Robertson and Bowlby[5] as a reaction to the loss of the love object, can also be conceived of in terms of disruption of an attachment bond, as suggested by primatologists.[76]

Learning theorists like Dollard and Miller[77] regard the love of the infant for its mother as a learned "secondary dependency drive" derived from the reinforcement of nursing.[78] However, the Harlows have demonstrated that the affection of the infant for its mother is independent of feeding and that attachment is a powerful "primary drive" in its own right, just as feeding and sex are.[79] The attachment of one human being to another, be that infant–mother or peer–peer, is a powerful reinforcer, and its loss can lead to serious psychopathology. This fact gives psychoanalytic, ethological, and behavioral theories a common denominator: depression is associated with the loss of significant reinforcers. Although the behavioral formulation is a broader one, it is a common clinical observation that human depression is usually a reaction to withdrawal of reinforcement from significant others. In primate species, including man, object losses in the form of disrupted attachment bonds are probably the most traumatic examples of loss of reinforcement. Seligman's formulation is even broader, because it views loss of reinforcement as a special instance of loss of control over reinforcement. In conclusion, loss of reinforcement, however achieved, seems to be antecedent to a perception of oneself as having lost one's ability to exercise future control over such reinforcers.

Is it possible to reconcile this behavioral–ethological formulation with the biochemical point of view? Stein's work[80] links the pharmacology of depression with the neurophysiological substrates of motivation and reward. Thus amphetamines, euphoriant agents, when injected through permanently implanted electrodes into the "reward centers," increase self-stimulation. Imipramine, an antidepressant, augments the action of amphetamines. Reserpine and AMPT, which are known to precipitate a depression–like syndrome, decrease the action of amphetamines.

Extensive studies of the neurophysiological substrates of reinforcement have elucidated the biology of reward and punishment.[80,81] The medial forebrain bundle (MFG), the anatomical substrate for the "reward system," originates in the locus coerulus and the adjacent reticular formation and forms noradrenergic synapses in the lateral hypothalamus, at higher levels in the limbic system, and in the frontal cortex. The periventricular system (PVS), the anatomical substrate for the "punishment system," arising in the dorso–medial region of the midbrain, forms cholinergic synapses in the medial hypothalamus and elsewhere in the limbic system. It appears that noradrenaline exercises inhibitory control over behavior–suppressant cell groups in the forebrain, while acetylcholine

facilitates the activity of these nuclei. It should be noted that stimulation of certain portions of the noradrenergic system enhances sexual activity; whereas lesions in this system (for example, in the lateral hypothalamus) produce anorexia. Stimulation of the PVS results in behavioral reactions usually associated with pain, such as jumping, biting, and screaming. Finally, simulation along the punishment and reward pathways is analogous to the action of primary reinforcers, in that neutral stimuli, presented just before stimulation, acquire secondary reinforcing properties.

Thus "one may think of the noradrenergic medial forebrain bundle fibers as part of a behavior–facilitating or 'go' mechanism [that] . . . initiates facilitatory feedback [and] . . . increases the probability that the behavior will run off to completion."[46] The MFB contains serotonergic fibers too.[82]

TOWARD A UNIFIED HYPOTHESIS

From the foregoing information one can predict that impairment of biogenic amine function would result in diminished initiation of responses, decreased activity, and disturbances in appetite, sex drive,[9] and sleep.[83] It also provides a conceptual bridge between the behavioral and the biological models of depression. Loss of reinforcement influences the behavior of the organism through its effects on the diencephalic mechanisms of reward and punishment. For instance, conventional reinforcers have no effect on behavior when the anatomical or chemical integrity of the self–stimulation system of the diencephalon is disrupted.[84]

If depressive behaviors elicited by a variety of mechanisms have as their neurophysiological final common pathway a reversible, functional derangement in the diencephalic mechanisms of reinforcement, as we have hypothesized, then chemical, genetic, developmental, and interpersonal–experiential factors should all impinge on the diencephalic centers of reward, as shown in Fig. 23–3.

1) *Chemical.* Certain drugs or metabolic disorders can suppress or interfere with the neurotransmitters of this system—for example, reserpine and alphamethyldopa in man, reserpine and alphamethylparatyrosine in infrahuman primates; and "borderline hypothyroidism" which could chemically interfere with the sensitivity of the monoaminergic receptor.

2) *Genetic.* These factors must act by means of their effects on the chemistry of reinforcement, because chemistry is the only language into which genes translate their message in controlling organismic function. There is substantial evidence for the contribution of heredity in some, if not all, forms of primary affective illnesses.[18] However, the specific enzymatic defects that lead to the chemical derangements are unknown. If instability of the neuronal membrane is the underlying dysfunction in affective illness,[72] then one possible enzymatic defect might be in the mechanism that controls sodium extrusion from the neuron—that is, a derangement in neuronal membrane adenosine triphosphatase. The work of Coppen and his associates provides evidence that there may be, in depression, an accumulation of intraneuronal sodium.[85] It is also known that an increase in intraneuronal sodium results in extraneuronal leakage of biogenic amines.[86] This hypothetical chain of events can be summarized as follows: Abnormal gene $\rightarrow$ (periodic) adenosine triphosphatase deficiency $\rightarrow$ increased intraneuronal sodium $\rightarrow$ biogenic amine depletion $\rightarrow$ derangement of diencephalic mechanisms of reinforcement $\rightarrow$ failure to respond to reinforcement $\rightarrow$ depressive behaviors.[87] As indicated earlier, there are most likely several distinct genetic defects that could lead to various patterns of impairment in the functional level or activity of biogenic amines in the diencephalon. Relative insensitivity of the monoaminergic receptors,[74] which could be caused by a genetically transmitted, defective structural lipo–protein of the postsynaptic membrane, is another possibility. According to the scheme presented here, and irrespective of the individual lesions, they would all result in a decrease in the functional capacity of the reward system; or a predominance of the punishment system—that is, cholinergic dominance,[73,80,82] to phrase it in neurophysiological terms.

3) *Interpersonal.* The occurrence of anaclitic depression in human and primate infants deprived of or separated from their mothers can be readily understood if one remembers the work of the Harlows, which showed attachment behavior to be a primary drive.[79] Its neurophysiological substrate probably resides in the diencephalon, as is true of other primary drives. As noted earlier, depressions in human adults are often preceded by the withdrawal of reinforcement from significant others, usually in the form of breaks in attachment bonds. Such a state of affairs could conceivably lead to (reversible) derangements in the diencephalon, which would in turn lead to the dominance of the periventricular punishment system.

But is there any evidence that experiential factors lead to derangements of the biological substrates of reinforcements? Weiss *et al.*[88] demonstrated that norepinephrine is depleted in the brain of animals exposed to aversive stimuli beyond their coping ability; these animals also suffered anorexia and weight loss. On the other hand, those animals that could cope with or avoid the aversive stimulus did not exhibit such chemical and somatic derangements. To extrapolate to human

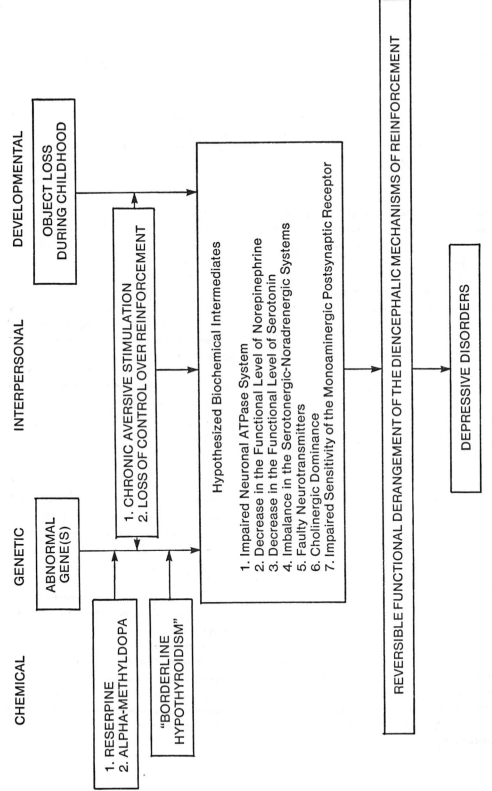

CHEMICAL   GENETIC   INTERPERSONAL   DEVELOPMENTAL

ABNORMAL GENE(S)

OBJECT LOSS DURING CHILDHOOD

1. RESERPINE
2. ALPHA-METHYLDOPA

"BORDERLINE HYPOTHYROIDISM"

1. CHRONIC AVERSIVE STIMULATION
2. LOSS OF CONTROL OVER REINFORCEMENT

Hypothesized Biochemical Intermediates

1. Impaired Neuronal ATPase System
2. Decrease in the Functional Level of Norepinephrine
3. Decrease in the Functional Level of Serotonin
4. Imbalance in the Serotonergic-Noradrenergic Systems
5. Faulty Neurotransmitters
6. Cholinergic Dominance
7. Impaired Sensitivity of the Monoaminergic Postsynaptic Receptor

REVERSIBLE FUNCTIONAL DERANGEMENT OF THE DIENCEPHALIC MECHANISMS OF REINFORCEMENT

DEPRESSIVE DISORDERS

FIGURE 23.3.—A multidisciplinary model of the pathogenesis of depressive disorders.

beings, interpersonally induced states of helplessness, whether from chronic aversive stimulation or loss of control over reinforcement contingencies, could result in alterations of biogenic amines.

4) *Developmental.* Psychoanalysts claim that bereavement in childhood predisposes one to depression in adulthood. Epidemiological evidence for this hypothesis has been generally negative or inconclusive.[89] It is possible, however, that if the bereavement occurs at certain critical ages it can predispose to adult depression. Furthermore, a good parental substitute might prevent the adverse effects of childhood bereavement. On the other hand, both childhood bereavement and adult depression might be caused by the same factor (for example, genetic vulnerability to depression), since it has been demonstrated that mortality in bipolar illness, both from suicide and other causes, is very high.[18] Therefore, one would expect patients from families with bipolar illness to suffer bereavement during childhood and depression during adult life. Future epidemiological work should control for these variables. Primate models of depression may help clarify this issue. In a recent study,[35] 2–year–old monkeys were shown to respond differently to separation, depending on whether or not they had undergone traumatic separation during infancy; those with a history of separation responded with increased self–directed behaviors and social withdrawal, as compared to control subjects. As to the way in which childhood bereavement operates, in terms of the model presented here, one can hypothesize that early breaks in attachment bonds stunt the maturational potential of the brain mechanisms that subserve reinforcement, making them more vulnerable to adult disappointment and frustration—that is, the individual has a "fragile reward system," one which can be easily upset.

5) *Genetic–interpersonal.* Probably genetic predisposition in the form of a "labile diencephalic reinforcement system" (neuronal membrane instability? impaired sensitivity of monoaminergic receptors?) renders 10 to 15 percent of the population[18] extremely vulnerable to the effects of interpersonal conflicts or events that result in a decrease in positive reinforcement. That reinforcing events from the environment coverage and interact with the reward centers of the hypothalamus has been demonstrated in infrahuman animals;[84] and there is no reason to believe that man has two separate systems of reinforcement, or that interpersonally defined reinforcement bypasses the diencephalon.

One might raise the question of why genetic vulnerability to depression most commonly manifests itself in middle age and later. Two possibilities suggest themselves: (i) the stresses of late adulthood are such that they result in substantial decrease in positive reinforcement or loss of control over one's destiny—for example, physical decline, chronic illnesses, retirement, financial troubles, loss of children through marriage, and loss of friends through death; and (ii) if an optimally functioning diencephalic reward system depends on adequate levels of monamine neurotransmitters, then a decrease of such amines with age—which would be expected from the finding that concentrations of the enzyme monoamine oxidase in the brain increase with age[90]—might provide another answer to the increased vulnerability of the elderly to depression.

Melancholia,[11] then, can be looked upon as a psychobiological state that is the final common pathway of processes involving interpersonally induced states of mind in which the individual sees himself as losing control over his fate (hopelessness); increased psychic turmoil; increased neuronal excitability and hyperarousal; disturbance of genetically vulnerable neuronal circuits in the diencephalon; depletion of biogenic amines; impairment of the neurophysiological substrates of reinforcement; further decrements in coping mechanisms; and a vicious cycle of more hopelessness, psychic turmoil, and hyper-arousal.

SUMMARY

Our scientific understanding of psychiatric syndromes, including the phenomena of depression, has been hampered because of: (i) the use of metapsychological concepts that are difficult to test; (ii) methodological and linguistic barriers that prevent communication among psychoanalysts, behaviorists, experimental psychologists, and psychiatrists; and (iii) the reluctance of psychiatrists to accept animal models as possible approximations of certain aspects of human psychopathology.

We have attempted to demonstrate that the animal models simulate some of the central features of clinical depression (for example, helplessness and object loss), thereby allowing one to rigorously investigate them from developmental behavioral, and biochemical perspectives.

The object loss model, as a concrete version of a metapsychological-psychoanalytic concept, has enabled primatologists to study the disruption of an attachment bond. The behavioral model accommodates this concept to a broader generalization: loss of reinforcement or loss of control over reinforcement. We have reviewed the evidence that these processes involve the diencephalic centers of reward or reinforcement, thereby permitting integration of the psychoanalytical and behavioral formulations with the biochemical hypotheses. Also, we have presented data strongly suggesting that the breaking of an attachment bond in the primate represents significant loss of reinforcement that induces helplessness and disrupts motivated behavior.

Finally, we have argued that the depressive syndrome could be caused by interactions of genetic, chemical, developmental, and interpersonal factors, all of which impinge on the diencephalic centers of reinforcement.

REFERENCES AND NOTES

1. H. Akiskal and W. McKinney, *Arch. Gen. Psychiat.* **28**, 367 (1973).
2. K. Abraham, in *Selected Papers of Karl Abraham* (Hogarth, London, 1948), p. 137; S. Freud, in *Collected Papers,* J. Strachey, Ed. (Hogarth, London, 1956), vol. 4, p. 152.
3. M. Weisman, E. Paykel, G. Klerman, *Amer. J. Psychiat.* **128**, 261 (1971); Y. Cohen, in *Social Structure and Personality,* Y. Cohen, Ed. (Holt, Rinehart & Winston, New York, 1961), p. 477.
4. R. Spitz, *Psychoanal. Study Child* **2**, 213 (1946); *ibid.* **1**, 53 (1945).
5. J. Robertson and J. Bowlby, *Cour. Cent. Int. Enfant* **2**, 131 (1952); J. Bowlby, *Int. J. Psychoanal.* **41**, 89 (1960); *ibid.* **42**, 317 (1961).
6. E. Bibring, in *Affective Disorders,* P. Greenacre, Ed. (International University Press, New York, 1953), p. 13; W. Gaylin, in *The Meaning of Despair,* W. Gaylin, Ed. (Science House, New York, 1968), p. 3.
7. L. Ullman and L. Krasner, *A Psychological Approach to Abnormal Behavior* (Prentice-Hall, Englewood Cliffs, N.J., 1969), p. 414; P. Liberman and D. Raskin, *Arch. Gen. Psychiat.* **24**, 515 (1971).
8. A. Prange, *Dis. Nerv. Syst.* **25**, 217 (1964); J. Schildkraut, *Amer. J. Psychiat.* **122**, 509 (1965); W. Bunney and J. Davis, *Arch. Gen. Psychiat.* **13**, 483 (1965); A. Coppen, *Brit. J. Psychiat.* **113**, 1237 (1967).
9. P. McGreer, *Amer. Sci.* **59**, 221 (1971).
10. G. Klerman, *Arch. Gen. Psychiat.* **24**, 305 (1971).
11. P. Whybrow, unpublished manuscript.

12. American Psychiatric Association, *Diagnostic and Statistical Manual* (American Psychiatric Association, Washington, D.C., ed. 3, 1980), p. 205.
13. M. Leff, J. Roatch, W. Bunney, *Psychiatry* 33, 293 (1970); E. Paykel, J. Myers, M. Dienelt, G. Klerman, *Arch. Gen. Psychiat.* 21, 753 (1969).
14. D. Graham, *Psychosom. Med.* 29, 52 (1967); A. Lazare, *N. Engl. J. Med.* 288, 345 (1973).
15. E. Robins and S. Guze, in *Recent Advances in the Psychobiology of Depressive Illness,* T. Williams, M. Katz, J. Shields, Eds. (Government Printing Office, Washington, D.C., 1972), p. 283.
16. S. Guze, R. Woodruff, P. Clayton, *Psychol. Med.* 1, 426 (1971); G. Winokur, *Dis. Nerv. Syst.* 33, 94 (1972).
17. G. Lundquist, *Acta Psychiat. Neurol. Scand. Suppl.* 35, 1 (1945); C. Perris, *Acta Psychiat. Scand.* 44, 238 (1968).
18. C. Perris, *Acta Psychiat. Scand. Suppl.* 42 (No. 194), 7 (1966); G. Winokur, P. Clayton, T. Reich, *Manic–Depressive Illness* (Mosby, St. Louis, 1969); R. Cadoret, G. Winokur, P. Clayton, *Brit. J. Psychiat.* 116, 625 (1970); E. Gershon, D. Dunner, F. Goodwin, *Arch. Gen. Psychiat.* 25, 1 (1971); R. Cadoret and G. Winokur, *Int. J. Ment. Health* 1, 159 (1972).
19. W. Bunney, D. Murphy, F. Goodwin, *Lancet* 1970-II, 1022 (1970); D. Murphy, H. Brodie, F. Goodwin, W. Bunney, *Nature* 229, 135 (1971).
20. F. Goodwin, D. Murphy, D. Dunner, W. Bunney, *Amer. J. Psychiat.* 129, 44 (1972).
21. M. Buchsbaum, F. Goodwin, D. Murphy, G. Borge, *ibid.* 128, 25 (1971); F. Borge, M. Buchsbaum, F. Goodwin, D. Murphy, J. Silverman, *Arch. Gen. Psychiat.* 24, 501 (1971).
22. A. Beigel and D. Murphy, *Arch. Gen. Psychiat.* 24, 215 (1971).
23. T. Reich and G. Winokur, *J. Nerv. Ment. Dis.* 151, 60 (1970).
24. T. Reich, P. Clayton, G. Winokur, *Amer. J. Psychiat.* 125, 1358 (1969); G. Winokur and V. Tana, *Dis. Nerv. Syst.* 30, 89 (1969); J. Mendlewicz, J. Fleiss, R. Fieve,

J. Amer. Med. Assoc. 222, 1624 (1972); R. Green, V. Goetzl, P. Whybrow, R. Jackson, *ibid.* 223, 1289 (1973).
25. G. Winokur, R. Cadoret, J. Dorzab, M. Baker, *Arch. Gen. Psychiat.* 24, 135 (1971); G. Winokur, T. Reich, J. Rimmer, F. Pitts, *ibid.* 23, 104 (1970).
26. M. Blumenthal, *ibid.* 24, 524 (1971).
27. W. McKinney and W. Bunney, *ibid.* 21, 240 (1969).
28. M. Seligman, in *The Psychology of Depression: Contemporary Theory and Research,* R. Friedman and M. Katz, Eds., in press. A shorter version appeared in *Psychol. Today* 7, 43 (1973).
29. W. Seay, E. Hansen, H. Harlow, *J. Child Psychol. Psychiat.* 3, 123 (1962); W. Seay and H. Harlow, *J. Nerv. Ment. Dis.* 140, 434 (1965).
30. H. Harlow and W. McKinney, *J. Autism Child. Schiz.* 1, 368 (1971).
31. G. Jensen and C. Toleman, *J. Comp. Physiol. Psychol.* 55, 131 (1962); R. Hinde, Y. Spencer-Booth, M. Bruce, *Nature* 210, 1021 (1966); G. Mitchell, H. Harlow, G. Moller, *Psychonomic Sci.* 8, 197 (1967).
32. I. Kaufman and L. Rosenblum, *Science* 155, 1030 (1967); *Psychosom. Med.* 29, 648 (1967).
33. W. McKinney, S. Suomi, H. Harlow, *Amer. J. Psychiat.* 127, 1313 (1971); S. Suomi, H. Harlow, C. Domek. *J. Abnorm. Psychol.* 76, 161 (1970).
34. W. McKinney, S. Suomi, H. Harlow, *Arch. Gen. Psychiat.* 27, 200 (1972).
35. L. Young, S. Suomi, H. Harlow, W. McKinney, *Amer. J. Psychiat.* 130, 400 (1973).
36. F. Goodwin and W. Bunney, *Semin. Psychiatry* 3, 435 (1971).
37. W. McKinney, R. Eising, E. Moran, S. Suomi, H. Harlow, *Dis. Nerv. Syst.* 32, 735 (1971).
38. S. Spector, A. Sjoerdsma, S. Udenfriend, *J. Pharmacol. Exp. Ther.* 147, 69 (1965).
39. D. Redmond, J. Maas, A. Kling, H. Dekirmenjian, *Psychosom. Med.* 33, 97 (1971).
40. W. McKinney, S. Suomi, I. Mirsky, R. Miller, in preparation.

41. D. Redmond, J. Maas, A. Kling, C. Graham, H. Dekirmenjian, *Science* **174**, 428 (1971).
42. B. Koe and A. Weisman, *J. Pharmacol. Exp. Ther.* **154**, 499 (1966).
43. P. Whybrow and J. Mendels, *Amer. J. Psychiat.* **125**, 1491 (1969).
44. G. Breese and P. Traylor, *J. Pharmacol. Exp. Ther.* **174**, 413 (1970); *Brit. J. Pharmacol.* **42**, 88 (1971); N. Uretsky and L. Iverson, *J. Neurochem.* **17**, 269 (1970).
45. L. Stein and C. Wise, *Science* **171**, 1032 (1971).
46. L. Stein, *J. Psychiat. Res.* **8**, 354 (1971).
47. J. Howard, L. Grant, G. Breese, *Pharmacologist* **13**, 233 (1971); G. Breese, J. Howard, J. Leahy, *Brit. J. Pharmacol.* **43**, 255 (1971).
48. G. Breese, A. Prange, J. Howard, M. Lipton, W. McKinney, R. Bowman, P. Bushnell, *Nature* **240**, 286 (1972).
49. R. Grinker, *The Phenomena of Depression* (Hoeber, New York, 1961); I Melges and J. Bowlby, *Arch. Gen. Psychiat.* **20**, 690 (1969).
50. A. Beck, *Depression: Causes and Treatment* (Univ. of Pennsylvania Press, Philadelphia, 1967), p. 23; K. Minkoff, E. Bergman, A. Beck, R. Beck, *Amer. J. Psychiat.* **130**, 455 (1973).
51. M. Seligman and S. Maier, *J. Exp. Psychol.* **74**, 1 (1967); J. Overmier and M. Seligman, *J. Comp. Physiol. Psychol.* **63**, 28 (1967); M. Seligman, S. Maier, J. Geer, *J. Abnorm. Soc. Psychol.* **73**, 256 (1968); M. Seligman and D. Groves, *Psychonomic Sci.* **19**, 191 (1970).
52. W. Bonime, in *American Handbook of Psychiatry*, S. Arieti, Ed. (Basic Books, New York, 1966), vol. 3, p. 239; A. Lazare and G. Klerman, *Amer. J. Psychiat.* **124** (Suppl.), 48 (1968).
53. A. Friedman, *J. Abnorm. Soc. Psychol.* **69**, 237 (1964); A. Loeb, A. Beck, S. Feshbach, in *Proceedings of the 75th Annual Convention of the American Psychological Association* (American Psychological Association, Washington, D.C., 1967), p. 193.
54. C. Ferster, in *Research in Behavior Modification*, L. Krasner and L. Ullman, Eds. (Holt, Rinehart & Winston, New York, 1965), p. 6; A. Lazarus, *Behav. Res. Ther.* **6**, 83 (1968); J. Wolpe, *Amer. J. Psychother.* **25**, 362 (1971).
55. P. Lewinsohn and M. Shaffer, *J. Consult. Clin. Psychol.* **37**, 87 (1971); P. Lewinsohn and D. Shaw, *Psychother. Psychosom.* **17**, 82 (1969).
56. E. Burgess, in *Advances in Behavior Therapy*, R. Rubin and C. Franks, Eds. (Academic Press, New York, 1969), p. 53.
57. J. Schildkraut, *N. Engl. J. Med.* **281**, 197, 248, 302 (1969).
58. A. Coppen, P. Whybrow, R. Noguera, R. Maggs, A. Prange, *Arch. Gen. Psychiat.* **26**, 234 (1972).
59. A. Coppen, D. Shaw, M. Harrel, *Lancet* **1963-II**, 527 (1963); C. Pare, *ibid.,* p. 527; A. Coppen, D. Shaw, B. Hertzberg, *ibid.* **1967-II**, 1178 (1967); A. Glassman and S. Platman, *J. Psychiat. Res.* **7**, 83 (1969).
60. G. Klerman, J. Schildkraut, J. Hassenbush, *J. Psychiat. Res.* **1**, 289 (1963); F. Goodwin, D. Murphy, H. Brodie, W. Bunney, *Biol. Psychiat.* **2**, 341 (1970).
61. A. Coppen, A. Prange, P. Whybrow, R. Noguera, *Arch. Gen. Psychiat.* **26**, **474** (1972); A. Coppen, *J. Psychiat. Res.* **9**, 1963 (1972).
62. F. Goodwin, *Semin. Psychiatry* **3**, 477 (1971).
63. ——, D. Dunner, E. Gershon, *Life Sci.* **10**, 751 (1971); D. Dunner and F. Goodwin, *Arch. Gen. Psychiat.* **26**, 364 (1972).
64. D. Shaw, F. Camps, E. Eccleston, *Brit. J. Psychiat.* **113**, 1407 (1967); H. Bourne, W. Bunney, R. Colburn, J. Davis, J. Davis, *Lancet* **1968-II**, 805 (1968); C. Pare, D. Yeung, K. Price, R. Stacy, *ibid.* **1969-II**, 133 (1969).
65. G. Ashcroft, T. Crawford, E. Eccleston, *Lancet* **1966-II**, 1049 (1966); S. Dencker, V. Malm, B. Roos, B. Werdinius, *J. Neurochem.* **13**, 1545 (1966).
66. H. Van Praag, J. Korf, J. Puite, *Nature* **225**, 1259 (1970); F. Goodwin, R. Post, D. Dunner, *Amer. J. Psychiat.* **130**, 73 (1973); H. Van Praag, J. Korf, D. Schut, *Arch. Gen. Psychiat.* **28**, 827 (1973).

67. J. Maas and D. Landis, *J. Pharmacol. Exp. Ther.* **163**, 147 (1968); S. Schanberg, J. Schildkraut, I. Kopin, *Biochem. Pharmacol.* **17**, 247 (1968); J. Maas and D. Landis, *Psychosom. Med.* **28**, 247 (1966).

68. J. Fawcett, J. Maas, H. Dekirmenjian, *Arch. Gen. Psychiat.* **26**, 246 (1972).

69. M. Ebert, R. Post, F. Goodwin, *Lancet* **1972-II**, 766 (1972); R. Post, E. Gordon, F. Goodwin, W. Bunney, *Science* **179**, 1002 (1973); R. Post, J. Kotin, F. Goodwin, E. Gordon, *Amer. J. Psychiat.* **130**, 73 (1973).

70. D. Murphy, *Amer. J. Psychiat.* **129**, 141 (1972); J. Axelrod, *Semin. Psychiatry* **4**, 199 (1972).

71. A. Prange, paper presented at National Institute of Mental Health Conference on serotonin and behavior, organized by Stanford University and held in Palo Alto, California, January 1972; J. Court, *Brit. J. Psychiat.* **120**, 133 (1972).

72. W. Bunney, F. Goodwin, D. Murphy, *Arch. Gen. Psychiat.* **27**, 312 (1972); *J. Psychiat. Res.* **9**, 207 (1972).

73. D. Janowsky, M. El-Yousef, J. Davis, *Lancet* **1972-II**, 632 (1972).

74. A. Prange, I. Wilson, A. Knox, *J. Psychiat. Res.* **9**, 187 (1972).

75. A. Prange, I. Wilson, A. Rabon, M. Lipton, *Amer. J. Psychiat.* **126**, 457 (1969); A. Prange, I. Wilson, A. Knox, T. McClane, M. Lipton, *ibid.* **127**, 191 (1970); D. Wheatley, *Arch. Gen. Psychiat.* **26**, 229 (1972); A. Coppen, P. Whybrow, R. Noguera, R. Maggs, A. Prange, *ibid.*, p. 234.

76. M. Harlow and H. Harlow, *Discovery* **27**, 11 (1966).

77. J. Dollard and N. Miller, *Personality and Psychotherapy* (McGraw-Hill, New York, 1950), p. 132.

78. For a comprehensive review of object relations, attachment, and love, see M. Ainsworth, *Child Develop.* **40**, 969 (1969).

79. H. Harlow, *Amer. Psychol.* **13**, 673 (1958); ____ and M. Harlow, *Amer. Sci.* **54**, 244 (1966).

80. L. Stein, in *Recent Advances in Biological Psychiatry,* J. Wortis, Ed. (Plenum, New York, 1962), vol. 4, p. 288; L. Stein, in *Psychopharmacology: A Review of Progress, 1957–1967,* D. Efron, Ed. (Government Printing Office, Washington, D.C., 1968), p. 105.

81. J. Olds and P. Milner, *J. Comp. Physiol. Psychol.* **47**, 419 (1954); J. Delgado, W. Roberts, N. Miller, *Amer. J. Physiol.* **179**, 587 (1954); R. Heath, Ed. *The Role of Pleasure in Behavior* (Hoeber, New York, 1964).

82. C. Wise, B. Berger, L. Stein, *Biol. Psychiat.* **6**, 3 (1973). Stein and his associates have postulated that the biochemical etiology of all the major psychiatric disorders is to be found in derangements in MFB and PVS (*45, 46, 80*).

83. M. Jouvet, *Science* **163**, 32 (1969).

84. B. Poschell, *Physiol. Behav.* **3**, 53 (1967).

85. A. Coppen and D. Shaw, *Brit. Med. J.* **2**, 1439 (1963).

86. D. Bogdanski and B. Brodie, *Life Sci.* **5**, 1563 (1966).

87. For a discussion of mineral metabolism, catecholamines, and depression, see J. Maas, *J. Psychiat. Res.* **9**, 227 (1972).

88. J. Weiss, *J. Comp. Physiol. Psychol.* **65**, 251 (1968); ____, E. Stone, N. Harrel, *ibid.* **72**, 153 (1970).

89. K. L. Granville-Grossman, in *Recent Developments in Affective Disorders,* A. Coppen and A. Walk, Eds. (Headley, Ashford, England, 1968), p. 65.

90. D. Robinson, J. Davis, A. Nies, C. Ravaris, D. Sylvester, *Arch. Gen. Psychiat.* **24**, 536 (1971).

91. We thank L. Benjamin, P. Lang, and J. Westman (University of Wisconsin) and E. Brown, G. Aivazian, J. Beard, and B. Kulig (University of Tennessee) for their critical comments on earlier versions of the manuscript. This work was supported, in part, by research grants MH-18070 and MH-21892 and research scientist development award MH-47353 (W.T.M.), all from the National Institute of Mental Health.

24.

Edwin S. Shneidman

SUICIDAL LOGIC

No one really knows why human beings commit suicide. Indeed, the very person who takes his own life may be least aware at the moment of decision of the essence (much less the totality) of his reasons and emotions for doing so. At the outset, it can be said that a dozen individuals can kill themselves and "do" (or commit) 12 psychologically different deeds. Understanding suicide—like understanding any other complicated human act such as drug or alcohol misuse or antisocial behaviour—involves insights drawn from many fields that touch on man's entire psychological and social life.

DEFINITION OF SUICIDE

In this article the definition of suicide will be treated in two ways: first, a definition is put forward and, then, some of the difficulties and complexities involved in defining the term are discussed. Briefly defined, suicide is the human act of self-inflicted, self-intentioned cessation.

Suicide is not a disease (although there are those who think so); it is not, in the view of the most detached observers, an immorality (although, as noted below, it has often been so treated in Western and other cultures); and, finally, it is unlikely that any one theory will ever explain phenomena as varied and as complicated as human self-destructive behaviours. In general, it is probably accurate to say that

Reprinted with permission from *Encyclopaedia Britannica,* 14th edition, ©1973 by Encyclopaedia Britannica, Inc.

suicide always involves an individual's tortured and tunneled logic in a state of inner-felt, intolerable emotion. In addition, this mixture of constricted thinking and unbearable anguish is infused with that individual's conscious and unconscious psychodynamics (of hate, dependency, hope, etc.), playing themselves out within a social and cultural context, which itself imposes various degrees of restraint on, or facilitation of, the suicidal act.

* * *

MAIN THREADS OF SUICIDAL STUDY

The modern era of the study of suicide began around the turn of the 20th century, with two main threads of investigation, the sociological and the psychological, associated with the names of Émile Durkheim (1858-1917) and Sigmund Freud (1856-1939), respectively. Much earlier, during classical Greek times, suicide was viewed in various ways, but in classical Rome, in the centuries just before the Christian era, life was held rather cheaply and suicide was viewed either neutrally or even positively. The Roman Stoic Seneca said: "Living is not good, but living well. The wise man, therefore, lives as well as he should, not as long as he can. . . . He will always think of life in terms of quality not quantity. . . . Dying early or late is of no relevance, dying well or ill is . . . even if it is true that while there is life there is hope, life is not to be bought at any cost."

Historically it seems that the excessive martyrdom and penchant toward suicide of the early Christians frightened the church elders sufficiently for them to introduce a serious deterrent. That constraint was to relate suicide to crime and the sin associated with crime. A major change occurred in the 4th century with a categorical rejection of suicide by St. Augustine (354-430). Suicide was considered a crime, because it precluded the possibility of repentance and because it violated the Sixth Commandment relating to killing. Suicide was a greater sin than any sin one might wish to avoid. This view was elaborated by St. Thomas Aquinas (1225-74), who emphasized that suicide was a mortal sin in that it usurped God's power over man's life and death. Although neither the Old nor the New Testament directly forbids suicide, by 693 the Council of Toledo proclaimed that an individual who attempted suicide was to be excommunicated. The notion of suicide as sin took firm hold and for hundreds of years played an important part in Western man's view of self-destruction.

The Christian injunctions against suicide seemed paradoxically to rest on a respect for life (especially the life of the soul in the hereafter) and were a reaction to the light way in which life was held by the Romans. If those were the church's original motivations, however, they went awry and the results were excessive and counterproductive, and resulted in degrading, defaming, impoverishing, torturing, and persecuting individuals (who had attempted suicide, committed suicide, or were the survivors) whom they had originally tried to protect and succor.

The French philosopher Jean Jacques Rousseau (1712-78), by emphasizing the natural state of man, transferred sin from man to society, making man generally good (and innocent) and asserting that it is society that makes him bad. The disputation as to the locus of blame—whether in man or in society—is a major theme that dominates the history of suicidal thought. David Hume (1711-76) was one of the first major Western philosophers to discuss suicide in the absence of the concept of sin. His famous essay "On Suicide," published in 1777, a year after his death, was promptly suppressed. That well-reasoned essay is a statement of the Enlightenment position on suicide. The burden of the essay is to refute the view that suicide is a crime; it does so by arguing that suicide is not a transgression of our duties to God, to our fellow citizens, or to ourselves. He states that ". . . prudence and courage should engage us to rid ourselves at once of existence when it becomes a burden. . . . If it be no crime in me to divert the Nile or Danube from its course, were I able to effect such purposes, where then is the crime in turning a few ounces of blood from their natural channel?"

Whereas Hume tried to decriminalize suicide, Rousseau turned the blame from man to society. In the 20th century, the two giants of suicidal theorizing played rather different roles: Durkheim focused on society's inimical effects on the individual, while Freud—eschewing the notions of either sin or crime—gave suicide back to man but put the locus of action in man's unconscious.

Durkheim's best-known work, *Le Suicide* (1897), established a model for sociological investigations of suicide. There have been many subsequent studies of this genre. The monographs and books by R. S. Cavan on suicide in Chicago (1926), of Calvin F. Schmid on suicide in Seattle (1928) and Minneapolis (1933), of Peter Sainsbury on suicide in London (1955), of Louis I. Dublin and Bessie Bunzel (1933), and of Andrew F. Henry and James F. Short, Jr., on suicide in the U.S. (1954) all fall within the sociological tradition of taking a plot of ground—a city or a country—and figuratively or literally reproducing its map several times to show its socially shady (and topographically shaded) areas and their differential relationships to suicide rates.

According to Durkheim suicide is the result of society's strength or weakness of control over the individual. He posited three basic types of suicide, each a result of man's relationship to his society. In one instance, the "altruistic" suicide is literally required by society. Here, the customs or rules of the group demand suicide under certain circumstances. Hara-kiri and suttee are examples of altruistic suicides. In such instances, however, the persons had little choice. Self-inflicted death was honourable; continuing to live was ignominious. Society dictated their action and, as individuals, they were not strong enough to defy custom.

Most suicides in the United States are "egoistic"—Durkheim's second category. Contrary to the circumstances of an altruistic suicide, egoistic suicide occurs when the individual has too few ties with his community. Demands, in this case to live, do not reach him. Thus, proportionately, more individuals, especially men, who are on their own kill themselves than do church or family members.

Finally, Durkheim called "anomic" those suicides that occur when the accustomed relationship between an individual and his society is suddenly shattered. The shocking, immediate loss of a job, a close friend, or a fortune is thought sufficient to precipitate anomic suicides; or, conversely, poor men surprised by sudden wealth also have been shocked into anomic suicide.

The students and followers of Durkheim include Maurice Halbwachs in France and Ronald W. Maris and Jack D. Douglas in the United States. Douglas, especially, has argued that Durkheim's constructs came not so much from the facts of life and death as from official statistics, which themselves may distort the very facts they are supposed to report.

As Durkheim detailed the sociology of suicide, so Freud fathered psychological explanations. To him, suicide was essentially within the mind. Since men ambivalently identify with the objects of their own love, when they are frustrated the aggressive side of the ambivalence will be directed against the internalized person. The main psychoanalytical position on suicide was that it represented unconscious hostility directed toward the introjected (ambivalently viewed) love object. For example, one killed oneself in order to murder the image of one's loved-hated father within one's breast. Psychodynamically, suicide was seen as murder in the 180th degree.

In an important exegesis of Freud's thoughts on suicide by Robert E. Litman (1967, 1970), he traces the development of Freud's thoughts on the subject, taking into account Freud's clinical experiences and his changing theoretical positions from 1881 to 1939. It is evident from Litman's analysis that there is more to the psychodynamics of suicide than hostility. These factors include the general features of human condition in Western civilization, specifically, suicide-prone mechanisms involving rage, guilt, anxiety, dependency, and a great number of specifically predisposing conditions. The feelings of helplessness, hopelessness, and abandonment are very important.

Psychodynamic explanations of suicide theory did not move too much from the time of Freud to that of Karl Menninger. In his important book *Man Against Himself* (1938), Menninger (in captivating ordinary language) delineates the psychodynamics of hostility and asserts that the hostile drive in suicide is made up of three skeins: (1) the wish to kill, (2) the wish to be killed, and (3) the wish to die. Gregory Zilboorg refined this psychoanalytic hypothesis and stated that every suicidal case contained strong, unconscious hostility combined with an unusual lack of capacity to love others. He extended the concern from solely intrapsychic dynamics to the external world and maintained that the role of a broken home in suicidal proneness demonstrated that suicide has both intrapsychic and external etiological elements.

In addition to the sociological and psychological approaches to the study of suicide, there is a third main contemporary thrust that might be called the philosophical or existential. Albert Camus, in his essay *The Myth of Sisyphus,* begins by saying: "There is but one serious philosophic problem and that is suicide." The principal task of man is to respond to life's apparent meaninglessness, despair, and its absurd quality. Ludwig Wittgenstein also states that the main ethical issue for man is suicide. To Camus, Wittgenstein, and other philosophers, however, their ruminations were never meant as prescriptions for action. Arthur Schopenhauer (1788-1860), the philosopher of pessimism, lived to a fairly ripe age and died of natural causes.

PSYCHOLOGICAL CHARACTERISTICS OF SUICIDE

Suicide has been related to many emotions: hostility, despair, shame, guilt, dependency, hopelessness, ennui. The traditional psychoanalytic position, first stated by Wilhelm Stekel at a meeting in Vienna in 1910, is that "no one kills himself who has not wanted to kill another or at least wished the death of another." This thought became translated into the psychoanalytic formulation that suicide represented hostility toward the introjected (ambivalently identified) love object. Currently, even psychodynamically oriented suicidologists believe that although hostility can be an important psychological component in some suicides, other emotional states—especially frustrated dependency and hopelessness and helplessness—often play the dominant role in the psychological drama of suicide. If there is one general psychological state commonly assumed to be associated with suicide it is a state of intolerable emotion (or unbearable or "unrepeatable despair")—what Herman Melville, in his masterpiece on self-destruction, *Moby Dick,* called "insufferable anguish."

Over and above the emotional states related to suicide, there are three important general psychological characteristics of suicide:

(1) The first is that the acute suicidal crisis (or period of high and dangerous lethality) is an interval of relatively short duration—to be counted, typically, in hours or days, not usually in months or years. An individual is at a peak of self-destructiveness for a brief time and is either helped, cools off, or is dead. Although one can live for years at a chronically elevated self-destructive level, one cannot have a loaded gun to one's head for too long before either bullet or emotion is discharged.

(2) The second concept is ambivalence. Few persons now dispute that Freud's major insights relating to the role of unconscious motivation (and the workings of what is called the unconscious mind) have been one of the giant concepts of this century in revolutionizing our view of man. The notion of ambivalence is a critical concept in 20th-century, psychodynamically-oriented psychiatry and psychology. The dualities, complications, concomitant contradictory feelings, attitudes, and thrusts toward essentially the same person

or introjected image are recognized hallmarks of psychological life. The dualities of the mind's flow constitute a cardinal feature of man's inner life. One can no longer ask in a simple Aristotelian way, "Make up your mind." To such a question a sophisticated respondent ought to say: "But that is precisely the point. I am at least of two, perhaps several, minds on this subject." A law has equal force whether it is passed in the Senate by a 100-0 or a 51-49 vote; so has a bullet. The paradigm of suicide is not the simplistic one of wanting to or not wanting to. The prototypical psychological picture of a person on the brink of suicide is one who wants to and does not want to. He makes plans for self-destruction and at the same time entertains fantasies of rescue and intervention. It is possible—indeed probably prototypical—for a suicidal individual to cut his throat and to cry for help at the same time.

(3) Most suicidal events are dyadic events, that is, two-person events. Actually this dyadic aspect of suicide has two phases: the first during the prevention of suicide when one must deal with the "significant other," and the second in the aftermath in the case of a committed suicide in which one must deal with the survivor-victim. Although it is obvious that the suicidal drama takes place within an individual's head, it is also true that most suicidal tensions are between two people keenly known to each other: spouse and spouse, parent and child, lover and lover. In addition, death itself is an extremely dyadic event.

The cold sociological truth is that some modes of death are more stigmatizing to the survivors than are other modes of death and that, generally speaking, suicide imposes the greatest stigma of all upon its survivors. The British physician John Hinton deals with this in his book *Dying* (1967). Hinton also comments that the notes left by the suicidal subject often cause further anguish.

Suicide notes provide an unusual window into the thoughts and feelings of a suicidal person. Various surveys in different places indicate that about 15% of individuals who commit suicide leave suicide notes—although the actual range is from 2 to 20%. By the 1970s fewer than 20 systematic studies of suicide notes had been completed. One of the first scientific studies of suicide notes was by W. Morgenthaler (1945) in a monograph that reported 47 suicide notes (in German) from Bern, Switzerland. The best-known reports in the United States are by Edwin S. Shneidman and Norman L. Farberow (1947, 1970) in their studies of genuine suicide notes and elicited matched notes written by nonsuicidal persons. Suicide notes have been subjected to a number of types of analyses: by emotional states, logical styles, "reasons" stated or implied, death wishes, language characteristics, relations to persons, and by computer count of key "tag words." In general these analyses indicate that (1) it is possible to distinguish between genuine and simulated suicide notes, and, more importantly, (2) genuine suicide notes are characterized by dichotomous logic, greater amount of hostility and self-blame, use of very specific names and instructions to the survivor, more decisiveness, less evidence of thinking about thinking, and more use of the various meanings of the word "love."

The Two Fundamental Aspects of Death and Suicide. Twentieth-century philosophers, especially Percy Bridgman (1938), pointed out that there is an epistemological characteristic unique to death, specifically that there are two fundamental aspects of death: the private aspect, as an individual lives it himself (my death); and the public aspect, as one can experience, in reality, the death of another (your death). In death (and suicide) there is a key difference between the principal actor and the observer. One major implication of this key difference is that I can observe and experience your death (just as you can observe and experience my death), but I can never experience my own death for if I could, I should still be alive.

Some of this kind of thinking operates in suicide, especially when it is seen as a psychologically magical act. Just as Melville wrote that "All evil, to crazy Ahab, were visibly personified and made practically assailable in Moby Dick," so to the suicidal mind, using this same tortured logic, the whole world is "made practically assailable" and can be thought to be expunged by destroying oneself.

The fantasies of one's own suicide can represent the greatest possible combination of omnipotence and potential realization of effectiveness—greater even than one's fantasies of the assassination of another, group revenge, mass murder, or even genocide. Any "average" individual can say: "From my point of view, suicide destroys all"—and it can be done.

These inferred psychodynamics of suicide (relating to delusions of annihilation) are thought by psychoanalysts to have their origins in the earliest notions of an individual's infantile omnipotence. The literature of suicide in Western man, however, continually emphasizes that suicide can be an individual's final act, his final escape hatch, his final revenge—often misconstrued as a final "right." This unique epistemological dual characteristic of death (the difference between my death and your death) is fundamental to an understanding of suicide.

ATTEMPTED SUICIDE

Although it is obvious that one has to "attempt" suicide in order to commit it, it is equally clear that often the event of "attempting suicide" does not have death (cessation) as its objective. It is an acknowledged fact that often the goal of "attempted suicide" (such as cutting oneself or ingesting harmful substances) is to change one's life (or to change the "significant others" around one) rather than to end it. On the other hand, sometimes death is intended and only fortuitously avoided. After that, one's life—what has been called "a bonus life"—is forever somewhat different. Alfred Alvarez, who himself made a serious suicide attempt, said that survivors have a changed life, with entirely different standards.

Erwin Stengel, a student of attempted suicide, in his arguments and statistical presentations, seems to suggest, in the main, that persons who attempt suicide and those who commit suicide represent essentially two different "populations"— with admittedly some overflow from the first to the second. It is useful to think of two sets of overlapping populations: (1) a group of those who attempt suicide, few of whom go on to commit it, and (2) a group of those who commit suicide, many of whom have previously attempted it. A great deal has to do with the lethality of the event. Lethality is roughly synonymous with the "deathfulness" of the act and is an important dimension in understanding any potentially suicidal person. Avery D. Weisman in 1972 distinguished three aspects of lethality: that of intention (ideation and involvement); that of implementation (risk and rescue); and that of intercession (resources, relief, and reorientation). The ratio between suicide attempts and commits is about 8 to 1—1 committed suicide for every 8 attempts.

Suicide attempts have many meanings and, whatever their level of lethality, ought to be taken seriously. A person who attempts suicide because he believes that there is no use living may not necessarily mean that he wants to die but that he has exhausted the potential for being someone who matters.

PARTIAL DEATH AND SUBSTITUTES FOR SUICIDE

Sometimes the very life-style of an individual seems to truncate and demean his life so that he is as good as dead. Often alcoholism, drug addiction, mismanagement of physical disease (such as diabetes or Buerger's disease), and masochistic behaviour can be seen in this light. A study of gifted individuals (with IQ's over 140) indicated that conspicuous failure in adult life—a kind of "partial death"—was sometimes the "price" for life as a substitute for overt suicide.

The chief theorist of the concept of partial death is Karl Menninger. Much of his conception is explicated in *Man Against Himself*. Menninger writes of (1) chronic suicide, including asceticism, martyrdom, neurotic invalidism, alcohol addiction, antisocial behaviour, and psychosis; (2) focal suicide—focused on a limited part of the body—including self mutilations, malingering, multiple surgery, purposive accidents, impotence, and frigidity; and (3) organic suicide, focusing on the psychological factors in organic disease, especially the self-punishing, aggressive, and erotic components. In the 1970s, the focus was on concepts such as indirect self-destructive behaviour. There have been many studies of alcoholism and drug addiction and diabetes and on aspects of homicide (on both the murderer and the victim) as suicidal equivalents. In relation to the role of the homicidal victim in his own death, the work of Marvin Wolfgang (1958) has been particularly interesting.

A related concept is that of "subintentioned death." That concept asserts that there are many deaths that are neither clearly suicidal nor clearly accidental or natural but are deaths in which the decedent has played some covert or unconscious role in "permitting" his death to occur, sort of "accidentally," or by "inviting" homicide, or, by unconsciously disregarding what could be life-extending medical regimen, and thus dying sooner than "necessary." Losing the "will to live" and so-called voodoo deaths—as well as many deaths in ordinary society—can be viewed as subintentional deaths. Obviously, this view of death changes the nature and statistics of suicide dramatically.

This concept of a reduced level of life as a substitute (or psychological "trade") for suicide itself presents fascinating philosophic, social, psychological, and moral questions that relate to whether or not there actually is an irreducible suicide rate among human beings. Is there a price for civilization? Indeed, a price for life? Litman, reflecting on Freud's work, agrees with Freud's general schematic view and that there is a suicidal trend in everyone. This self-destructiveness is controlled through constructive habits of living and loving, but when they break down, the individual may easily be forced into a suicidal crisis. To keep alive one must keep his thoughts, feelings, and aspirations in a vital balance.

SUICIDE AND RELIGION

In the Western world it has been traditionally said that the suicide rate is higher among Protestants than among Catholics or Jews and that the latter group shows significantly low suicidal figures. By the 1970s it was known, however, that the role of religion in relation to suicide is more complicated and that religious affiliation serves both to inhibit and, at other times, to facilitate suicide. At the outset it is important to distinguish between religious beliefs and religious (social) affiliation. Durkheim not unexpectedly emphasized the sociological aspects of religion. He stated: "If religion protects one from the desire for self-destruction, it is not because it preaches to him, with elements of religious origin, respect for one's person; it is because it forms a social group." A nationwide study in the United States indicated that the pro rata suicide rate among veterans—a fairly representative group of U.S. citizenry—for Catholics and Protestants was about equal to the numbers (and percentages) of Protestants and Catholics in the country generally. Much more important than nominal religious affiliation would be a number of subtleties of religious belief: the feeling of group belongingness, belief in an omnipotent God, belief in the efficacy of prayer, belief in a hereafter or existence after death, and other issues relating to death in general. Results of a national U.S. survey of 30,000 persons reported by Shneidman in 1970 indicated that a sizable percentage (57%) of individuals of all religious backgrounds (and with a variety of intensities of religious belief) did not believe in any life after death and that over one-third indicated that religion had played either a relatively minor role or no role at all in the development of their attitudes toward death (and toward suicide). Just as in the 20th century there has been an enormous "secularization" of death—the physician and hospital in many ways replacing the clergyman and the church in relation to the anxieties surrounding death—so too has there been a secularization of suicide. Few of the current debates about suicide are on primary religious grounds; when the ethics of suicide are debated, those usually are in terms of such concepts as "freedom" and "life," *i.e.,* how free an individual should be to take his own life

and how far "benign intervention" should go in an attempt to save an individual's life before the intervention is intrusive and robs him of more than his life is worth.

When Durkheim spoke of religion as a source of social organization (holding individuals together with common beliefs and practices), he was not only speaking of social integration but he was also, from a psychological point of view, referring to personal identification. Walter T. Martin and Jack P. Gibbs (1964) proposed a theory relating status integration with suicide and Henry and Short (1954) discussed the positive relationship between suicide and status and the negative relation between suicide and the strength of a relational source. In general it appears that a person who is uneasy in his religion (or in his irreligion) or changes his religion several times (like a person who is uneasy in his marriage or has several marriages) is more likely to commit suicide, not so much on purely religious (or marital) grounds but because of his general perturbation and lack of good self-concept, which underlie his uneasy search for certainty and stability in his life.

SUICIDE AND THE LAW

Not surprisingly, the history of suicide and the law closely parallel and reflect— often with significant lags—the major cultural and philosophic attitudes toward suicide. Probably the most important single legal change was the passage of the Suicide Act in England in 1961 that (1) finally abolished criminal penalties for committing suicide—considering that in the 19th century (as late as 1823), a London citizen who committed suicide was buried at a crossroads in Chelsea with a stake pounded through his heart; (2) no longer made survivors of suicide attempts liable to criminal prosecution; and (3) as a kind of quid pro quo for the liberalization of the first two measures, increased the penalties (up to 14 years' imprisonment) for aiding and abetting a suicidal act. Earlier, the Homicide Act of 1957 changed the charge against a survivor of a suicide pact from murder to manslaughter.

In the United States, most aspects of suicide are not against the law. As of the early 1970s a comparatively small number of states (9) listed suicide as a crime, although no penalties (such as mutilation of bodies or forfeiture of estates) were exacted. In such states suicide attempts are either felonies or misdemeanours and could result in jail sentences, although such laws are selectively or indifferently enforced. Two states (Nevada and New York) repealed such laws, stating in effect that although suicide is "a grave social wrong" there is no way to punish it. Eighteen states—Alaska, Arkansas, California, Florida, Kansas, Louisiana, Michigan, Massachusetts, Minnesota, Mississippi, Missouri, Montana, Nevada, New Mexico, New York, Oregon, Wisconsin, and Wyoming—have no laws against either suicide or suicide attempts but specify that to aid, advise, or encourage another person to commit suicide is a felony. In the more than 20 other states, there are no penal statutes referring to suicide.

In the early 1970s, especially in Great Britain, there was some movement (among some eminent lawyers, theologians, philosophers, and physicians) toward the legalization of voluntary euthanasia; proposals were to repeal the aiding and abetting aspect of suicide laws, so that a physician might, on a patient's request, assist him to his own voluntary death.

SOME ODDITIES OF SUICIDE

The lore about suicide contains a large number of interesting and esoteric items about various cultures. Suicide was thought, for example, to be absent among so-called primitive cultures, but it is evident that this is not so. Studies were made of suicide in Africa (Paul Bohannan, 1960), India (Verrier Elwin, 1943; Upendra Thakur, 1963), Hong Kong (Yap Powmeng, 1958), and Japan (Ohara, 1961). Practically every popular article on suicide routinely contains a statement about the kamikaze pilots who flew and died for Japan in World War II. Also, in relation to Japan, one often reads of the practice of hara kiri or seppuku, which is the ritual act of disemboweling oneself and was limited to the samurai warrior and noble classes. General Tojo, who attempted hara kiri at the end of World War II, was saved by U.S. doctors, only to be hanged later by a military tribunal. In 1970 the well-known Japanese author Mishima Yukio (*q.v.*) committed seppuku (with ritual self-disemboweling and decapitation) at the age of 45. In general, however, suicide in contemporary Japan is more "Western" than otherwise—often done with barbiturates. In a discussion of suicide in 19th-century India one finds references to suttee, the custom in which Hindu widows threw themselves onto the funeral pyres of their husbands.

Six suicides are recorded in the Old Testament: Abimelech, Samson, Saul, Saul's armour bearer, Ahithophel, and Zimri. The most famous and among the most frequently cited suicides perhaps, are Socrates' drinking hemlock and Cato's throwing himself upon his sword. The apocryphal stories of Bismarck's contemplating suicide, Napoleon's attempting suicide, Washington's despondency, and Lincoln's depression keep reappearing in articles on suicide—including this one.

Myths of Suicide. Following is a summary of some of the more outstanding misconceptions of suicide:

Fable: Persons who talk about suicide do not commit suicide. *Fact:* Of any ten persons who will themselves commit it, eight have given definite warnings of their suicidal intentions.

Fable: Suicide happens without warning. *Fact:* Studies reveal that the suicidal person gives many clues and warnings regarding his suicidal intentions.

Fable: Suicidal persons are fully intent on dying. *Fact:* Most suicidal persons are undecided about living or dying, and they "gamble with death," leaving it to others to save them. Almost no one commits suicide without letting others know how he is feeling.

Fable: Once a person is suicidal, he is suicidal forever. *Fact:* Individuals who wish to kill themselves are suicidal only for a limited period of time.

Fable: Improvement following a suicidal crisis means that the suicidal risk is over. *Fact:* Most suicides occur within about three months following the beginning of "improvement," when the individual has the energy to put his morbid thoughts and feelings into effect.

Fable: Suicide strikes much more often among the rich, or, conversely, it occurs almost exclusively among the poor. *Fact:* Suicide is neither the rich man's disease nor the poor man's curse. Suicide is represented proportionately among all levels of society.

Fable: Suicide is inherited or "runs in the family." *Fact:* It follows individual patterns.

Fable: All suicidal individuals are mentally ill, and suicide always is the act of a psychotic person. *Fact:* Studies of hundreds of genuine suicide notes indicate that although the suicidal person is extremely unhappy, he is not necessarily mentally ill.

Romantic Suicide and the Artist. Since at least the 16th century, specifically in the Italian commedia dell'arte, there has been a character named Harlequin who typically wears a multi-coloured suit and a black mask—and has a connection with death. Indeed to be loved by Harlequin was to be married to death. This is the idea of death as a lover; it relates to the romanticization of death itself. As a refinement of this idea, suicide has historically been thought to be a romantic kind of death. One specific myth is that suicide is caused by unrequited love. Suicide pacts (portrayed romantically in *Mayerling* and in *Elvira Madigan*) are depicted as the essence of intense love. One result of this mystique is a belief that especially sensitive people, artists—poets, painters, and writers—are unusually prone to commit suicide and, indeed, add to their reputations as artists by committing suicide. Perhaps the best-known novel of this genre is Goethe's *The Sorrows of Young Werther,* published in 1774 when the author was 24 years old and credited, in the mythology of suicide, with having created a veritable epidemic of romantic suicides throughout Europe. By the 1970s the list of suicides of artists was sufficiently long and vivid to persuade an uncritical student of suicide that the sensitivity of the artist is somehow related to the special nature of a romantic suicidal death. The list includes Van Gogh, Virginia Woolf, Hart Crane, the Italian writer Cesare Pavese, Randall Jarrell, Modigliani, Jackson Pollock, Mark Rothko, Ernest Hemingway, John Berryman, Sylvia Plath, Mishima, and Kawabata Yasunari. Perhaps the best description and analysis of suicide and the creative literary artist is by the English poetry editor and critic Alfred Alvarez in his book *The Savage God: a Study of Suicide* (1971). Maksim Gorki attempted suicide when he was 19. One of the most romanticized suicides in Western literature is that of the English poet Thomas Chatterton (1752-70), who took poison at the age of 17. This particular death illustrates the notion (or myth) "that those with more life and passion go soon"—that the best die young. It reminds one of those who have died "too young"—Byron, Shelley, Keats, Mozart—and the particular poignancy of an untimely death of an especially beautiful or gifted person. We tend to be essentially undemocratic about death and suicide—because we tend to believe that some deaths level (or elevate) certain people more than others.

STATISTICS ON SUICIDE

The demographic use of statistics on suicide perhaps were given their greatest impetus by John Graunt and Johann Peter Süssmilch. Graunt was a London tradesman who, in 1662, published a small book of observations on the London bills of mortality. He separated various bits of information contained in these rolls of names of the dead into separate categories and organized the information systematically, finally constructing mortality tables —the first attempt to organize data in that manner. Of great significance was his success in demonstrating the regularities that can be found between medical and social phenomena when one deals with large numbers. He demonstrated how an analysis of the mortality statistics could be used to the advantage of physicians, businessmen and government.

Much of what is known today as statistical information came into existence with the work of Süssmilch, a Prussian clergyman who in 1741 in his analyses of vital data from church registers created political arithmetic, or what is now called vital statistics. It is important to keep in mind that statistics, particularly statistics on suicide, are in part socially manufactured data—mostly by coroners and physicians. Suicidal deaths are notoriously underrep-

resented and obviously vary from country to country dependent not only on the number of suicides that in fact occur in each country but also on deeply ingrained cultural folkways relating to the social, cultural, and religious attitudes of that country.

There are several sources of suicide statistics. Louis Dublin's text, *Suicide* (1963), is a standard source; the World Health Organization (WHO) booklet, *The Prevention of Suicide* (1968), is another. *Suicide in the United States, 1950-1964* (1967) and *The Facts of Life and Death* (1970), both published by the U.S. Department of Health, Education, and Welfare, are standard sources in the United States. In general, the reported suicide rate for the United States is between 10 and 12 per 100,000, which places the United States about in the middle of the countries that report to the United Nations. Austria, West Germany, Hungary, Japan, Czechoslovakia, Denmark, Finland, Sweden, and Switzerland report rates of over 25 per 100,000 population, and Italy, the Netherlands, and Spain report rates under 10 per 100,000. The number of suicides in the United States per year is given at about 22,000 but many experts believe the actual number to be at least twice as high.

In any discussion of the statistics of suicide—keeping in mind their tenuous character—it is important to distinguish among rank, rate, and number. Currently, in the United States, suicide is ranked among the first five causes of death for white males from 10 to 55. For example, suicide is the second-ranked cause of death for white males age 15-19, but one must appreciate that the first leading cause of death, accidents, yields 627 chances in 100,000 of the individual's dying from that cause, while suicide yields (only) 88 chances in 100,000. Generally, in the early ages when suicide is high, it occupies that rank because the other killers like heart disease, malignant neoplasms (cancer), vascular lesions of the central nervous system (stroke), and cirrhosis of the liver are not then common.

In general, statistics on suicide in the 19th and 20th centuries indicate that more men than women commit suicide (about 3 to 1) and that more women than men attempt suicide (again about 3 to 1). In the early 1970s there was evidence that the ratio for committed suicide seemed to be changing, moving toward (but not yet achieving) an equal proportion between the sexes. Statistics relating to race and ethnic origin seem to be undergoing changes, probably reflecting general changes in attitude toward the concept of race and ethnicity. In the United States it was reported for years that Caucasian suicides far outnumbered Negro suicides, but the rate for Negroes seems to be changing, moving closer to that for Caucasians. Whether this reflects the effects of urban ghetto living, the effects of identifying with "the white man's problems," or simply better and more accurate record-keeping are all issues for further study. Some studies (conducted in England and Australia) that followed individuals who emigrated either to the United States or to Australia seem to indicate that the suicide rates of specific groups such as Hungarians, Italians, Poles, and Irish appear, for a generation or so, to be closer to the rates of the homeland than to the rates of the adopted country. In these data, there are many methodological issues that are also yet to be resolved.

In relation to suicide statistics, a standard textbook on sociology published in 1972 reported that sociologists still made continuous reference to the work of Durkheim. Rates derived from Durkheim's studies show that suicide rates for Protestants have been consistently higher than those for Jews or Catholics. In the early part of the 20th century the Jewish rate in the Netherlands was higher than the Protestant, and during the depression, in Toronto, Canada, Catholic rates also were higher than Protestant. The inference is that the time, the place, and the social circumstances are all important factors.

In the matter of comparative national statistics, Alvarez points out that U.S. Pres. Dwight D. Eisenhower blamed the high Swedish suicide rate on what too much social welfare can do. But the present rate in Sweden, Alvarez notes, is about the same as it was in 1910, before comprehensive social welfare programs were begun and is actually ranked ninth on a table published by WHO. The countries of Central Europe show the highest rates: Hungary has the highest national rate; Austria and Czechoslovakia are third and fourth. The highest suicide rate in the world is that of West Berlin; its rate is more than twice that of West Germany as a whole. The city, it has been suggested, is a model of what Durkheim called anomie—alienated not only geographically but also in cultural, social, and political aspects. Countries like Ireland and Egypt, where suicide is considered by many a mortal sin, have rates among the lowest in the world, bearing out Stengel's conclusion that highly industrialized and prosperous countries tend to have comparatively high suicide rates. Alvarez concludes that official statistics reflect only a fraction of the true figures, which a number of authorities reckon to be anywhere from a quarter to a half again as large. Because of religious and bureaucratic prejudices, family sensitivity, differences in the proceedings of coroners' hearings and postmortem examinations, the shadowy distinctions between suicides and accidents—in short, the unwillingness to recognize the act for what it is—knowledge of the extent to which suicide pervades modern society is diminished and distorted.

A certain sizable percentage of deaths that are certified by coroners or medical examiners—estimated to be between 10 and 15%—are equivocal as to what the actual mode of death ought to be; this uncertainty usually lies between suicide or accident. A procedure, called the psychological autopsy, has been developed to deal with these equivocal deaths. Essentially, the psychological autopsy involves the use of social and behavioural scientists (psychologists, psychiatrists, social workers, and other trained personnel) who interview relatives and friends of the decedent with the goal of developing information about the decedent's intention vis-à-vis his own death in the days just before the death. Clues—verbal ("You won't be seeing me around"); behavioural (*e.g.,* giving away prized possessions or marked changes in patterns of eating, sexuality, interests); or situational (*e.g.,* the loss of a loved one)—are deemed to point more to suicide than to accident. In the absence of such clues, a recommendation for a non-suicidal or "undetermined" mode of death should be made to the certifying official.

SUICIDE VENTION (PREVENTION, INTERVENTION, POSTVENTION)

The Latin word *venire* means "to come" or "to do." In relation to any event (*e.g.,* suicide) one can act before, during, or after—corresponding to prevention, intervention, and postvention. These terms also correspond roughly to the public health concepts of primary, secondary, and tertiary prevention.

Prevention. If, as this article has suggested, suicidal phenomena are existential-social-psychological-dyadic events, then obviously primary prevention is enormously complicated—almost tantamount to preventing human unhappiness. Some students of human nature believe that the urge toward self-destruction is ubiquitous and that a certain amount of it is an inevitable and constant price of civilization, if not of life itself. Primarily, prevention would relate to the principles of good mental hygiene in general.

Intervention. Intervention relates to the treatment and care of suicidal crisis or suicidal problems. On this score, suicide prevention centres could be more accurately labeled suicide intervention centres. A great deal has been learned about practical techniques for effective suicide intervention. There is a vast literature on therapy and treatment of suicidal persons in various settings—in the community, in suicide prevention and crisis intervention centres, in poison-control centres, in outpatient offices, and in both medical and mental hospitals. In general, most of the suggestions for care have in common the stressing of good rapport, working with the "significant others" in the suicidal person's life, using the available community resources for referral (for emotional support, legal aid, financial help, employment, individual and group psychotherapy, hospitalization), and focusing on the reduction of the person's "lethality" during the period of suicidal crisis. Much of the suicide prevention work borrows from the theory of crisis intervention developed by Erich Lindemann (1944) and Gerald Caplan (1964). In the United States, the theoretical and empirical work of the Los Angeles Suicide Prevention Center, established in 1955, and in Great Britain, the work of the Samaritans, established in 1953, has been widely emulated.

In 1960 there were fewer than a half-dozen suicide prevention centres in the United States; a decade later there were over 200. Typically they are telephone-answering centres; maintaining 24-hour service, they serve as short-term resources, are theoretically modeled in terms of the concept of crisis intervention, and use both professional and lay volunteer staff.

Suicide is best understood as a socio-psychological, existential human event that calls for compassionate response to an individual in an emotional and philosophic crisis. Obviously suicide is not solely a medical problem and many kinds of persons including volunteers—provided they are carefully selected, well-trained, and continuously supervised—can serve as life-saving agents in the prevention of suicide. The lay volunteer has been described as probably the most important single discovery in the history of suicide prevention. Nonetheless, professionally trained persons—psychologists, psychiatrists, social workers—continue to play the primary roles in suicide prevention and especially in research.

Postvention. A term introduced by Shneidman in 1971, refers to those things done after the dire event has occurred that serve to mollify the aftereffects of the event in a person who has attempted suicide, or to deal with the adverse effects on the survivor-victims of a person who has committed suicide. It is offering psychological services to the bereaved survivors. It includes work with the surviving children, parents, and spouses. Much of postventive work has been focused on widows. Studies show that survivors are apt to have a higher morbidity and mortality rate in the year following the death of their loved one than comparable persons who are not survivors of such a death. It may well be that the major public mental-health challenge in suicide lies in offering postventive help to the survivor-victims. The development of postvention is part of the current new view of the special psychological needs relating to death.

BIBLIOGRAPHY

Alvarez, A. *The Savage God: A Study of Suicide.* New York: Random House, 1970.

Choron, Jacques. *Suicide.* New York: Charles Scribner's Sons, 1972.

Douglas, Jack D. *The Social Meanings of Suicide.* Princeton, N.J.: Princeton University Press, 1967.

Dublin, Louis I. *Suicide: A Sociological and Statistical Study.* New York: Ronald Press, 1963.

Durkheim, Émile. *Suicide.* Eng. trans. by J. R. Spaulding and G. Simpson. New York: Free Press, 1951. (Originally printed in 1897.)

Farberow, N. L. *Bibliography on Suicide and Suicide Prevention,* 1897–1970. Washington, D.C.: U.S. Department of Health, Education and Welfare (HSM) 72-9080, 1972/1969.

Farberow, Norman L., & Shneidman, E. S. (Eds.). *The Cry of Help.* New York: McGraw-Hill, 1961.

Freud, Sigmund. "Mourning and Melancholia." In the *Standard Edition of The Complete Psychological Works.* Vol. 14. New York: Macmillan, 1959.

Friedman, Paul (Ed.). *On Suicide: With Particular Reference to Suicide among Young Students.* New York: International Universities Press, 1967.

Litman, Robert E. "Sigmund Freud and Suicide." In E. S. Shneidman (Ed.). *Essays in Self-Destruction.* New York: Jason Aronson, 1967.

Menninger, Karl A. *Man against Himself.* New York: Harcourt Brace Jovanovich, 1938.

Murray, Henry A. "Dead to the World." In E. S. Shneidman (Ed.), *Essays in Self-Destruction.* New York: Jason Aronson, 1967.

Public Health Papers. *Prevention of Suicide,* Series no. 35. New York: World Health Organization, 1968.

Shneidman, E. S. (Ed.). *On the Nature of Suicide.* San Francisco: Jossey-Bass, 1969.

Shneidman, Edwin S. "Suicide, Lethality, and the Psychological Autopsy." In E. S. Shneidman and M. Ortega (Eds.), *Aspects of Depression.* Boston: Little, Brown, 1969.

Shneidman, Edwin S., and Farberow, Norman L. (Eds.). *Clues to Suicide.* New York: McGraw-Hill, 1957.

Shneidman, E. S., Farberow, N. L., and Litman, R. E. *The Psychology of Suicide.* New York: Jason Aronson, 1970.

Stengel, Erwin. *Suicide and Attempted Suicide.* New York: Penguin Books, 1964. Rev. Ed. New York: Aronson, 1974.

Toynbee, Arnold, et al. *Man's Concern with Death.* New York: McGraw-Hill, 1969.

U.S. Public Health Service. *Suicide in the United States, 1950–1964.* Washington D.C.: U.S. Government Printing Office, 1967.

Williams, Glanville. *The Sanctity of Life and Criminal Law.* New York: Alfred A. Knopf, 1957.

CHAPTER **VI**

Childhood and Adolescent Disorders

What Is Infantile Autism?

Description and History

What is infantile autism? How can we prevent it, and how can we cure it? These are three questions with which psychiatrists, research workers, and parents of autistic children have been struggling ever since the syndrome was first clearly described and coined *early infantile autism* by Kanner (1943, 1944) in the early 1940s.

Kanner's papers, "Autistic Disturbances of Affective Contact" (1943), reported observations on 11 children with an inability to display appropriate social feelings with people. Some do not even care to be touched by their parents! In Kanner's paper, 11 cases of autistic children accumulated since 1938 are carefully detailed. Symptoms that Kanner regarded as key features of the syndrome include:

1. An extreme autistic aloneness.
2. Obsessive insistence on sameness.
3. An excellent rote memory.
4. Stereotyped speech and motor movement.

Behavior strikingly characteristic of these children includes their lack of appropriate responses to affection shown them. Indeed, unless they themselves initiate body contact, to show them affection may upset autistic children even to the extent of provoking violent outbursts. Autistic children are known to approach an individual and initiate or request bodily contact, but it is often ambiguous whether this is for their own personal emotional satisfaction or merely for some impersonal tactile stimulation.

Often autistic children are found to repeat actions (stereotypy) such as executing tasks that do not vary one iota from the one initially performed. In fact, they may insist that others adhere to their bizarre repetitive sameness as well. Failure to comply with their demand provokes outbursts of crying, destructiveness, or other forms of aggressive behavior. An example is found in Kanner's patient, Donald T., who, when threading buttons, invariably arranged them in precisely the same pattern that his father by chance happened to use when he first demonstrated it to Donald.

These children, moreover, engage in stereotyped motor movements and speech (stereotypies). Body rocking, hand flapping, and head shaking (movement of the head from side to side) are common forms of stereotyped behavior found in autistic children. Some autistics are known to go on endlessly repeating a word or phrase. Some of their ordinary eating, bedtime, and other activities have acquired weird "verbal rituals." Some seem to insist on performing these peculiar "verbal rituals" during their daily routine activities.

Relationship of Infantile Autism to Schizophrenia in Childhood

The relationship of autism to schizophrenia has been debated (Bender, 1947; Kanner, 1973; Rimland, 1964; M. Rutter, 1977; Wing, 1976a). Kanner described autism as a distinct syndrome, having unique features, yet appropriately classified among childhood schizophrenias. The observation that schizophrenia is not any more frequent in families of autistic children is suggestive evidence that autism is not connected with schizophrenia (American Psychiatric Association, 1980). In the *Diagnostic and Statistical Manual of Mental Disorders* (DSM-III) (American Psychiatric Association, 1980), the two—autism and schizophrenia—are classified separately. The distinct category of childhood schizophrenia has not been included in DSM-III.

Cantor and colleagues (1982) have argued that the DSM-III has failed to account for a particular group of psychotic children. They say that even though most infantile psychoses do not later resemble schizophrenia, there is nevertheless a group of children with an onset of psychoses prior to 30 months of age who later share characteristics resembling adult-type schizophrenia. However, deterioration in functioning necessary for the diagnosis to be classed as schizophrenia is not apparent.

Children with incoherence, loosening of associations, hallucinations, or delusions may be classed as schizophrenic disorders occurring in childhood. Conversely, these symptoms are not found in autistic children. Even as adults, autistic children do not tend to have hallucinations or delusional thinking (Rutter, 1977). Furthermore, the course of autism tends to fluctuate less than that of schizophrenia.

What Causes Autism?

Etiology of Autism

The frequency of autism in the population has been reported from two to five or more cases per 10,000 people (American Psychiatric Association, 1980; Lotter, 1966; Schopler, 1982). It is three to four times more prevalent in males than in females. Its cause is still unknown (Ritvo, 1976b; Wing, 1976a). Kanner attributed it to a kind of social isolation; to a lack of personal or parental interaction that is crucial to wholesome development; to an infant's lack of love. Kanner's hypothesis gained the support of a number of authorities, most notably that of Bettelheim (1967) and Goldfarb (1945, 1961, 1964).

According to Rutter (1968, 1983), a basic cognitive deficit exists in autistic children that extends to abnormalities in language, in addition to difficulties in abstraction, sequencing, and coding. This cognitive deficit is not due to, but rather the root of, other abnormal characteristics of autism. Rutter regards the impairment of receptive language alone as an inadequate explanation of the autistic disorder, and also repudiates a general perceptual cognition abnormality as an etiologic factor. He prefers to explain social inadequacies as secondary to an impairment in handling stimuli with affective or social connotations, rather than a defect in processing information from a specific sensory modality.

Organic hypotheses, implicating genetic factors in the cause of autism, have also been explored. Consonant with a genetic component, the disorder is found 50 times more frequently in brothers and sisters of autistic children (American Psychiatric Association, 1980). While these epidemiological data are suggestive, a genetic hypothesis has yet to be validated by more substantive evidence (Ornitz, 1973; Rutter, 1967). Although perinatal complications as a causative factor also require additional supporting evidence (Wing, 1976a), a review of literature (Fish & Ritvo, 1979) found pregnancy complications to be two to three times more frequent in children with early onset psychosis compared with those who develop psychosis later in childhood. Among illnesses linked to this disorder are maternal rubella, celiac disease, tuberous sclerosis, encephalitis, meningitis, and phenylketonuria (American Psychiatric Association, 1980; Schopler, 1982).

Abnormal electroencephalograms (EEG) appear more frequently in autistic children (Rutter, 1977). More than one fourth of autistic individuals have a seizure disorder since adolescence (Rutter, 1977; Schopler, 1982). Such findings led to neurophysiological and neurochemical hypotheses of autism. Hutt and Hutt, for instance, implicated the reticular activating system in autism. Basing their results on EEG patterns, they hypothesized that autistic children are constantly in a state of hyperarousal (1970, p. 193). Other evidence involves changes in the brain neurotransmitter, serotonin. Heeley and Roberts (1965) adduced evidence for suspecting abnormal tryptophan metabolism in autistic children. With his associates, Yuwiler (1976) initially found higher blood serotonin, higher platelet counts, and somewhat higher serotonin levels per platelet in autistic children than in age-matched nonautistic children. Others have replicated the finding of increased blood serotonin levels in about ⅓ of autistic individuals (Young, Kavanaugh, Anderson, Shaywitz & Cohen, 1982); however, more recent findings suggest that this hyperserotonemia in autistic patients is probably not due to increased platelet counts but rather to higher levels of serotonin per platelet (Ritvo, Freeman, Geller, & Yuwiler, 1983).

Preliminary neuroendrocrine research involving the thyroid system has implicated the possibility of hypothalamic disease being associated with autism (Campbell, Hollander, Fern, & Greene, 1978).

Based on observations of stereotyped behavior characteristic of autistic children and the use of dopamine receptor blocking agents in the treatment of autism, Sahakian postulates that autism results from an increase in functional activity of the brain's dopamine systems (B. J. Sahakian, Svendsen, & Klove, in press). A related hypothesis, one offered by Snyder (1974), proposes a primary role for dopamine in the neurochemical basis of schizophrenia.

What Is the Best Treatment for an Autistic Child?

Treatment

The increasing acceptance that autism is not an emotional disturbance due to faulty parental interactions but a developmental disorder has led to some advances being made in treatment approaches (Schopler, 1982). The main trend has been toward behavior modification and special education in a structured setting, and a departure from insight-oriented psychotherapy (Rutter, 1977; Schopler, 1982). Measures should be implemented to promote generalization of improvement. Also recommended are casework approaches and parental training in behavioral methods.

The most effective chemotherapeutic agents for the treatment of autism are the antipsychotic drugs, with the most frequently used being the less sedating ones such as haloperidol, a dopamine receptor blocking agent (Campbell, 1978; Fish, 1976). For some time, it has been known that these drugs may reduce some symptoms, including stereotyped behavior. However, in a recent study by Campbell, haloperidol was recognized to have an additional effect when used in combination with a behavioral approach; it improved speech imitation (Campbell, Cohen, & Anderson, 1981). Fenfluramine, a drug found to lower blood serotonin levels in autistic patients, is currently being studied with some promising findings reported (Ritvo, Freeman, Geller & Yuwiler, 1983).

Prognosis

Rutter (1977) reviewed literature indicating that approximately one sixth of autistic children as they grow older seem to manage socially, and obtain employment despite not being totally symptom-free. However, the majority of autistic children (60 percent) remain significantly impaired when adults. Autistic children's intelligence is the primary prognostic indicator. Mentally retarded autistic children, constituting approximately 75 percent of the autistic population, tend to perform most poorly, and have a greater likelihood of developing seizures. Autistic children of normal intelligence, while more likely to progress well, do not necessarily do so. Other prognostic indicators are the acquisition of useful speech by age five, which is a positive sign, and the inability to play constructively, which is a sign of a poor prognosis (Rutter, 1977; Shapiro & Sherman, 1983).

Is There Hope for a Cure in the Future?

Future Research

Although a better understanding of autism has developed in recent years, progress is slow. Nevertheless, some advance has been made with respect to early detection and treatment. But further research is sorely needed regarding its cause and cure. In the meantime it is necessary to determine which variables exacerbate autistic behavior and which promote improvement.

Information of this nature should enhance the autistic child's chance of learning and the ability to function independent of institutional care. Pertinent to this discussion, Lovaas and his associates (1971) have evidence that autistic children are less responsive to their environment during periods of stereotyped behavior. In support of this thesis, Koegel and Covert (1972) found that stereotyped behavior can significantly impair performance on discrimination tasks. What replaces stereotyped behavior after its disruption? With his research team, Koegel et al. (1974) observed marked increases in play behavior when eliminating stereotyped behavior. It appears that disruption of stereotypy through environmental manipulation or by some other means might contribute to establishing personal contact with autistic children and thereby increase their learning potential. The results of Campbell and colleagues (1981) may support this suggestion since they propose that enhanced speech imitation may have resulted from a reduction in both stereotyped and withdrawal behavior, which they regarded as interfering with the learning process. If by interrupting stereotyped behavior the ability to learn is enhanced, then techniques which successfully interrupt stereotyped behavior can be employed in programs designed for autistic children to assist them in reaching their full educational potential.

Eating Disorders: Anorexia Nervosa and Bulimia

Diagnosis and Prevalence of Anorexia Nervosa

The disorder anorexia nervosa is diagnosed by the criterion of self-induced weight loss (which may be so severe as to result in amenorrhea in female patients). Additional criteria include a morbid fear of becoming fat accompanied by the relentless pursuit of thinness (Bruch, 1973; Crisp, 1974; G. F. M. Russell, 1970). There also exists a marked disturbance of body image, such that anorexics, who may be painfully thin, perceive themselves as overweight (American Psychiatric Association, 1980, pp. 67–68). Associated features include a denial of hunger feelings and a heightened energy expenditure through physical activity, which may be so intense that it terminates in exhaustion.

Most commonly, anorexia occurs in middle social-class females, although it has been reported to occur in males also (Hay & Leonard, 1979). The disorder generally develops during adolescence, but occasionally it occurs earlier or sometimes during adulthood.

In young women, the incidence of anorexia nervosa has been estimated to range between 1–4 percent in Britain (Crisp, Palmer, & Kalucy, 1976; J. A. O. Russell, 1972). Failure to treat the disorder successfully can prove fatal, the mortality rate running from 10 to 21 percent (American Psychiatric Association, 1980; Minuchin, Rosman, & Baker, 1978).

The popular belief that anorexia nervosa is a disorder of recent origin, occurring only within the past 10 to 15 years is a myth since physicians of the 17th and 19th centuries had already described the disturbance (Gull, 1888; Lasegue, 1873; Morton, 1694).

Diagnosis and Prevalence of Bulimia

The related disorder, bulimia, is considerably less familiar to people than anorexia. The failure to identify this disorder early may have been partly due to the embarrassment of bulimics to admit their symptoms, and in some measure due to many bulimics escaping notice because of normal body weight.

Only in recent years has bulimia been differentiated from anorexia with its own distinct characteristics (Boskind-Lodahl & Sirlin, 1977; G. Russell, 1979). Like anorexics, bulimics have a distorted perception of their body size, are obsessed with their body weight, and possess an intense fear of becoming "fat." However, bulimics experience an overwhelming desire to consume huge quantities of food during a single meal. Following this phenomenon of "binge" eating, bulimics resort to self-induced vomiting, the abuse of laxatives, diuretics, or a combination of these tactics to prevent the undesired consequences of gaining weight from the ingested food. Before the consumed food has had time to be digested and absorbed, bulimics induce vomiting immediately following bingeing.

The pervasiveness of bulimia is currently in the process of being assessed, and statistics of its prevalence are somewhat at odds. One survey (Halmi, Falk, & Schwartz, 1981) reports that possibly 19 percent of the female students at a suburban campus of the State University of New York manifested this disorder (*as it would have been diagnosed clinically*). Fairburn, however, places the incidence of bulimia in adult women between 1 and 2 percent, reasoning that the New York study's inflated value is due to its use of an unrepresentative population of women, that of college students (Cooper & Fairburn, 1983).

Because bulimics tend generally to maintain normal weight (more or less) because of their bizarre methods of weight control, many of them have never undergone treatment for their disorder. Unlike the emaciated, almost skeletal-like anorexic, whose disorder is evident to others, bulimics can go years with the disorder undetected, even escaping discovery by family and friends.

Most bulimics induce vomiting by thrusting their fingers into their throats, thereby activating the gagging reflex. This technique can cause callouses along the dorsum of the hand, produced by the hand's rubbing against the upper teeth

(See Figure 1 of Russell, 1979). Some bulimics have actually conditioned their behavior to such an extent that they can induce vomiting without requiring the use of their fingers to elicit gagging and vomiting. Food is heaved up as they merely bend over the toilet bowl. Obsessive thoughts about food and body weight are accompanied by compulsive behavior in regard to food. Some bulimics, for example, show as many as 20 or 30 incidents of bingeing and vomiting in a span of 24 hours (Fairburn, 1981; Russell, 1979; B. J. Sahakian, unpublished data).

The quantity of energy ingested during frequent binges has been measured by B. J. Sahakian, Bingham, Murgatroyd, Lean, and James (1981), who discovered that a bulimic may eat as much as 26 megaJoules (approximately 6,214 kilocalories) each day. Obviously much of this energy would never be absorbed by the body because the partly digested food would be expelled by vomiting immediately following the binge. It was found that women with no history of eating disorders and with comparable indices of body weight (as determined by a measure relating weight in kilograms to height in meters, $\frac{\text{Weight}}{\text{Height}^2}$; with normal values ranging from 21 to 24) were eating under 15 megaJoules per day (approximately 2,585 kilocalories).

Etiology

To date, the etiology of either anorexia nervosa or bulimia is unknown. There is no convincing evidence for either a hereditary or biological determining factors. Precipitating factors in these disorders have been presented by clinicians and researchers alike. Psychodynamically, anorexia nervosa has been explained (1) as a struggle toward a self-respecting identity (Bruch, 1977), and (2) as a "defensive, biologically-regressed" attitude assumed in response to pressures (especially sexual ones) experienced in puberty (Crisp, 1977, 1978). The etiology has also been viewed in social terms as an attempt to realize society's prevailing view of the ideal feminine figure as "sylphlike" (M. G. Thompson & Schwartz, 1982). This latter view is paralleled by Boskind-Lodahl and White's (1978) contention that bulimia is associated with the attempt to attain the stereotyped perception of the female: perfectly beautiful, yet helpless and dependent.

Treatment of Anorexia Nervosa and Bulimia

Although both anorexia nervosa and bulimia are resistant to treatment, prognosis for bulimia is the less favorable of the two (Russell, 1979). Bulimic behavior may result in severe physical complications, such as potassium depletion and renal damage. Moreover, there is a considerable risk of suicide.

Drug Treatment. By and large, drugs used to treat anorexia nervosa and bulimia effect their behavioral action through the central monoamine and opiate neurotransmitter systems. Some of these drugs have proved effective in treating psychiatric and neurological disorders. For example, chlorpromazine, which is used in treating schizophrenia and which appears to have some success in reducing compulsive behavior, has been tried in the treatment of patients with anorexia and bulimia (Crisp, 1977; B. J. Sahakian, et al., 1981). Tricyclic antidepressants, including amitriptyline, clomipramine, and imipramine, have also been tried in the treatment of anorexic and bulimic patients (Agras & Kraemer, 1983; Mills, 1976; Needleman & Waber, 1977; Pope & Hudson, 1982).

Due to the small number of subjects studied and the failure to use double-blind control procedures, the results of many of these pharmacological trials are inconclusive. In the relatively few studies utilizing double-blind methods, drug treatment has not been established as effective, with the possible exception of imipramine. Hudson and colleagues (1983) showed significant reduction of symptoms following imipramine treatment in 19 bulimic patients. Results of a study by Johnson and Larson (1982) indicated that bulimics experienced significantly more dysphoric and fluctuating moods than normal controls.

Final conclusions on the efficacy of antidepressants in treating these disorders must await the outcome of further controlled studies.

Psychological and Dietary Management. Dally (1977) found that 80 percent of anorexics require inpatient treatment. Patients usually regain weight when separated from their families; however, this process was not easy. Combining psychotherapy with capable nursing, and (in approximately 50 percent of the cases) the administration of chlorpromazine produces successful results. Most patients responded to treatment between one and five years. Their weight was stabilized at a reasonable level, their anxiety over increased weight alleviated, and their recovery reasonably assured.

A "cognitive behavioral" technique developed by Fairburn (1981) for treating bulimics focuses on increasing the patient's control of eating, eliminating food avoidance, and changing maladaptive attitudes. Fairburn reports considerable success employing this method.

Sahakian and associates employed an approach resembling Fairburn's. These researchers (B. J. Sahakian, Bingham, Murgatroyed, Lean, & James, unpublished results) determine the bulimic patients metabolic rate by means of whole-body calorimetry, so that patients can then be placed on a calorie-controlled diet which allows them to control their weight at an acceptable level while on a balanced diet. Foods rich in carbohydrate, normally avoided by bulimics, are included in the diet. This dietary regimen is employed in conjunction with behavior modification techniques and cognitive and self-control strategies. While behavior therapy aids in the normalization of the patients' eating patterns, cognitive techniques enable patients to focus on positive and creative dimensions of living and away from ruminations on food and body weight.

The success of eclectic approaches, combining dietary, cognitive, and behavioral techniques appears promising. However, additional studies with larger populations of bulimic patients than have been used to date are required before final conclusions on the efficacy of these new multifarious approaches in treating bulimia can be made.

25.

American Psychiatric Association

DISORDERS USUALLY FIRST EVIDENT IN INFANCY, CHILDHOOD, OR ADOLESCENCE

MENTAL RETARDATION

The essential features are: (1) significantly subaverage general intellectual functioning, (2) resulting in, or associated with, deficits or impairments in adaptive behavior, (3) with onset before the age of 18. The diagnosis is made regardless of whether or not there is a coexisting mental or physical disorder.

General intellectual functioning is defined as an intelligence quotient (IQ) obtained by assessment with one or more of the individually administered general intelligence tests. Significantly subaverage intellectual functioning is defined as an IQ of 70 or below on an individually administered IQ test. Since any measurement is fallible, an IQ score is generally thought to involve an error of measurement of approximately five points; hence, an IQ of 70 is considered to represent a band or zone of 65 to 75. Treating the IQ with some flexibility permits the inclusion in the mental retardation category of individuals with IQs somewhat higher than 70 who truly need special education or other programs. It also permits exclusion from the diagnosis of those with IQs somewhat lower than 70 if the clinical judgment is that there are no significant deficits or impairment in adaptive functioning.

Adaptive behavior refers to the effectiveness with which an individual meets

From Task Force on Nomenclature and Statistics of the American Psychiatric Association, *Diagnostic and Statistical Manual of Mental Disorders, Third Edition.* American Psychiatric Association, 1980.

the standards of personal independence and social responsibility expected of his or her age and cultural group. There are scales designed to quantify adaptive behavior, but none is considered sufficiently reliable and valid to be used alone to evaluate this aspect of functioning. Therefore, clinical judgment is necessary for the assessment of general adaptation, the individual's age being taken into consideration. The IQ level of 70 was chosen as the upper limit for mental retardation because most people with IQs below 70 are so limited in their adaptive functioning that they require special services and protection, particularly during the school-age years.

The arbitrary IQ ceiling values are based on data indicating a positive association between intelligence (as measured by IQ score) and adaptive behavior. This association declines at the upper levels of mild retardation. Some individuals with an IQ near but below 70 may not have the impairment in adaptive behavior required for a diagnosis of mental retardation.

When the clinical picture develops for the first time after the age of 18, the syndrome is a dementia, not mental retardation, and is coded within the organic mental disorders section of the classification. When the clinical picture develops before the age of 18 in an individual who previously had normal intelligence, mental retardation and dementia should *both* be diagnosed.

Etiologic factors may be primarily biological, psychosocial, or an interaction of both. When a known biological factor is present, the specific biological condition should be noted on Axis III.

***

ATTENTION DEFICIT DISORDER

The essential features are signs of developmentally inappropriate inattention and impulsivity. In the past a variety of names have been attached to this disorder including: hyperkinetic reaction of childhood, hyperkinetic syndrome, hyperactive child syndrome, minimal brain damage, minimal brain dysfunction, minimal cerebral dysfunction, and minor cerebral dysfunction. In this manual attention deficit is the name given to this disorder, since attentional difficulties are prominent and virtually always present among children with these diagnoses. In addition, though excess motor activity frequently diminishes in adolescence, in children who have the disorder, difficulties in attention often persist.

There are two subtypes of the active disorder, attention deficit disorder with hyperactivity, and attention deficit disorder without hyperactivity, although it is not known whether they are two forms of a single disorder or represent two distinct disorders. Finally, there is a residual subtype for individuals once diagnosed as having attention deficit disorder with hyperactivity in which hyperactivity is no longer present, but other signs of the disorder persist.

314.01 Attention Deficit Disorder with Hyperactivity

The essential features are signs of developmentally inappropriate inattention, impulsivity, and hyperactivity. In the classroom, attentional difficulties and impulsivity are evidenced by the child's not staying with tasks and having difficulty

organizing and completing work. The children often give the impression that they are not listening or that they have not heard what they have been told. Their work is sloppy and is performed in an impulsive fashion. On individually administered tests, careless, impulsive errors are often present. Performance may be characterized by oversights, such as omissions or insertions, or misinterpretations of easy items even when the child is well motivated, not just in situations that hold little intrinsic interest. Group situations are particularly difficult for the child, and attentional difficulties are exaggerated when the child is in the classroom, where sustained attention is expected.

At home, attentional problems are shown by a failure to follow through on parental requests and instructions and by the inability to stick to activities, including play, for periods of time appropriate for the child's age.

Hyperactivity in young children is manifested by gross motor activity, such as excessive running or climbing. The child is often described as being on the go, "running like a motor," and having difficulty sitting still. Older children and adolescents may be extremely restless and fidgety. Often it is the quality of the motor behavior that distinguishes this disorder from ordinary overactivity in that hyperactivity tends to be haphazard, poorly organized, and not goal-directed.

In situations in which high levels of motor activity are expected and appropriate, such as on the playground, the hyperactivity seen in children with this disorder may not be obvious.

Typically, the symptoms of this disorder in any given child vary with situation and time. A child's behavior may be well-organized and appropriate on a one-to-one basis but become dysregulated in a group situation or in the classroom; or home adjustment may be satisfactory and difficulties may emerge only in school. It is the rare child who displays signs of the disorder in all settings or even in the same setting at all times.

***

CONDUCT DISORDER

The essential feature is a repetitive and persistent pattern of conduct in which either the basic rights of others or major age-appropriate societal norms or rules are violated. The conduct is more serious than the ordinary mischief and pranks of children and adolecents.

Four specific subtypes are included: undersocialized, aggressive; undersocialized, nonaggressive; socialized, aggressive; and socialized, nonaggressive. These subtypes are based on the presence or absence of adequate social bonds and the presence or absence of a pattern of aggressive antisocial behavior. The validity of these diagnostic subtypes within the category of conduct disorder is controversial. Some investigators believe that a more useful distinction would be on the basis of the variety, frequency, and seriousness of the antisocial behavior rather than the type of disturbance, whereas others believe that the undersocialized and socialized types represent distinct disorders.

The *undersocialized* types are characterized by a failure to establish a normal degree of affection, empathy, or bond with others. Peer relationships are generally lacking, although the youngster may have superficial relationships with other youngsters. Characteristically the child does not extend himself or herself for others unless there is an obvious immediate advantage. Egocentrism is shown by readiness to manipulate others for favors without any effort to reciprocate. There is generally a lack of concern for the feelings, wishes, and well-being of others, as shown by callous behavior. Appropriate feelings of guilt or remorse are generally absent. Such a child may readily inform on his or her companions, and try to place blame on them.

The *socialized* types show evidence of social attachment to others, but may be similarly callous or manipulative toward persons to whom they are not attached and lack guilt when these "outsiders" are made to suffer.

The *aggressive* types are characterized by a repetitive and persistent pattern of aggressive conduct in which the rights of others are violated, by either physical violence against persons, or thefts outside the home involving confrontation with a victim. The physical violence may take the form of rape, mugging, assault, or, in rare cases, homicide. In some cases, the physical violence may be directed against parents. Thefts outside the home may involve extortion, pursesnatching, or holdup of a store.

The *nonaggressive* types are characterized by the *absence* of physical violence against persons and of robbery outside the home involving confrontation with a victim. However, there is a persistent pattern of conduct in conflict with norms for their age, which may take the form of: chronic violations of a variety of important rules that are reasonable and age-appropriate for the child at home or at school, such as persistent truancy and substance abuse; running away from home overnight while living in the parental home; persistent serious lying in and out of the home; vandalism or fire-setting; or stealing (not involving confrontation of a victim).

***

ANXIETY DISORDERS OF CHILDHOOD OR ADOLESCENCE

This subclass includes three disorders in which anxiety is the predominant clinical feature. In the first two categories, separation anxiety disorder and avoidant disorder of childhood or adolescence, the anxiety is focused on specific situations. In the third category, overanxious disorder, the anxiety is generalized to a variety of situations.

309.21 Separation Anxiety Disorder

The essential feature is a clinical picture in which the predominant disturbance is excessive anxiety on separation from major attachment figures or from home or other familiar surroundings. When separation occurs, the child may experience anxiety to the point of panic. The reaction is beyond that expected at the child's developmental level.

Children with separation anxiety disorder are uncomfortable when they travel independently away from the house or from familiar areas. They may refuse to visit or sleep at friends' homes, to go on errands, or to attend camp or school. They may be unable to stay in a room by themselves, and may display clinging behavior, staying close to the parent, "shadowing" the parent around the house. Physical complaints, such as stomachaches, headaches, nausea, and vomiting, are common when separation is anticipated or occurs. Cardiovascular symptoms such as palpitations, dizziness, and faintness are rare in younger children, but may occur in adolescents.

When separated from significant others to whom they are attached, these children are often preoccupied with morbid fears that accidents or illness will befall their parents or themselves. They often express fear of getting lost and never being reunited with their parents. The exact nature of the fantasized mishaps varies. In general, young children have less specific, more amorphous concerns. As the child gets older, the fears may become systematized around identifiable potential dangers. Such

concerns vary greatly; and many children, even some older ones, do not report fears of definite threats, but only pervasive anxiety about ill-defined dangers or death. In addition, children typically exhibit anticipatory anxiety when separation is threatened or impending. In young children, whose immature cognitive development precludes the formation of well-defined morbid worries, the mechanism of anticipatory anxiety has not yet developed, and there is distress only when separation actually occurs.

Children with this disorder often have fears of animals, monsters, and situations that are perceived as presenting danger to the integrity of the family or themselves; consequently, they have exaggerated fears of muggers, burglars, kidnappers, car accidents, or plane travel. Concerns about dying are common.

These children often have difficulty going to sleep, and may require that someone stay with them until they fall asleep. They may make their way to their parents' bed (or that of another significant person, such as a sibling); if entry to the parental bedroom is barred, they may sleep outside the parents' door. Nightmares, whose content expresses the child's morbid fears, may occur.

Some children do not show morbid apprehension about possible harm befalling them or those close to them, but instead experience acute homesickness and feel uncomfortable to the point of misery and even panic when away from home. These children yearn to return home, and are preoccupied with reunion fantasies.

Children may refuse to see former friends or relatives to avoid accounting for their difficulties while in school or their absence from school. On occasion a child may become violent toward an individual who is forcing separation.

Adolescents with this disorder, especially boys, may deny overconcern about their mother or the wish to be with her; yet their behavior reflects anxiety about separation. Thus, they are reluctant or unable to leave the home or the parent and feel comfortable only in situations in which no separation is demanded.

Although the disorder represents a form of phobia, it is not included among the phobic disorders because it has unique features and is characteristically associated with childhood.

* * *

EATING DISORDERS

This subclass of disorders is characterized by gross disturbances in eating behavior; it includes anorexia nervosa, bulimia, pica, rumination disorder of infancy, and atypical eating disorder. Bulimia usually has a chronic, remitting course, whereas the other three specific disorders commonly are limited to a single episode. Two of these, anorexia nervosa and rumination disorder of infancy, may have an unremitting course that progresses to death.

Simple obesity is included in ICD-9-CM as a physical disorder and is not in this section since it is not generally associated with any distinct psychological or behavioral syndrome. However, when there is evidence that psychological factors are of importance in the etiology or course of a particular case of obesity, this can be indicated by noting psychological factors affecting physical condition.

307.10 Anorexia Nervosa

The essential features are intense fear of becoming obese, disturbance of body image, significant weight loss, refusal to maintain a minimal normal body weight and amenorrhea (in females). The disturbance cannot be accounted for by a known physical disorder. (The term "anorexia" is a misnomer, since loss of appetite is usually rare until late in the illness.)

Individuals with this disorder say they "feel fat" when they are of normal weight or even emaciated. They are preoccupied with their body size and often gaze at themselves in a mirror. At least 25 percent of their original body weight is lost, and a minimal normal weight for age and height is not maintained.

The weight loss is usually accomplished by a reduction in total food intake, with a disproportionate decrease in high carbohydrate- and fat-containing foods, self-induced vomiting, use of laxatives or diuretics, and extensive exercising.

The individual usually comes to medical attention when weight loss becomes significant. When it becomes profound, physical signs such as hypothermia, dependent edema, bradycardia, hypotension, lanugo (neonatal-like hair), and a variety of metabolic changes occur. Amenorrhea often appears before noticeable weight loss has occurred.

* * *

307.51 Bulimia

The essential features are episodic binge eating accompanied by an awareness that the eating pattern is abnormal, fear of not being able to stop eating voluntarily, and depressed mood and self-deprecating thoughts following the eating binges. The bulimic episodes are not due to anorexia nervosa or any known physical disorder.

Eating binges may be planned. The food consumed during a binge often has a high caloric content, a sweet taste, and a texture that facilitates rapid eating. The food is usually eaten as inconspicuously as possible, or secretly. The food is usually gobbled down quite rapidly, with little chewing. Once eating has begun, additional food may be sought to continue the binge, and often there is a feeling of loss of control or inability to stop eating. A binge is usually terminated by abdominal pain, sleep, social interruption, or induced vomiting. Vomiting decreases the physical pain of abdominal distention, allowing either continued eating or termination of the binge, and often reduces post-binge anguish. Although eating binges may be pleasurable, disparaging self-criticism and a depressed mood follow.

Individuals with bulimia usually exhibit great concern about their weight and make repeated attempts to control it by dieting, vomiting, or the use of cathartics or diuretics. Frequent weight fluctuations due to alternating binges and fasts are common. Often these individuals feel that their life is dominated by conflicts about eating.

***

STEREOTYPED MOVEMENT DISORDERS

The essential feature of disorders in this subclass is an abnormality of gross motor movement. The specific stereotyped movement disorders all involve tics and include transient tic disorder, chronic motor tic disorder, and Tourette's disorder. It is unknown whether the three tic disorders represent distinct conditions or a continuum of severity.

***

307.60 Functional Enuresis

The essential feature is repeated involuntary voiding of urine during the day or at night, after an age at which continence is expected, that is not due to any physical disorder. The disorder is somewhat arbitrarily defined as involuntary voiding of urine at least twice a month for children

between the ages of five and six and once a month for older children.

Functional enuresis is often referred to as *primary* if it has not been preceded by a period of urinary continence for at least one year, and *secondary* if it has been preceded by a period of urinary continence for at least one year. Either of the above types may be *nocturnal* (most common), defined as the passage of urine during sleep time only, *diurnal,* defined as the passage of urine during waking hours, or *both* diurnal and nocturnal. There is no provision for coding these distinctions.

In most cases of nocturnal functional enuresis, the child awakens with no memory of a dream and no memory of having urinated because typically the disturbance occurs during the first third of the night, during non-REM sleep. However, in a few cases the voiding takes place during the rapid eye movement (REM) stage of sleep, and in such cases the child may recall a dream that involved the act of urinating.

***

307.70 Functional Encopresis

The essential feature is repeated voluntary or involuntary passage of feces of normal or near-normal consistency into places not appropriate for that purpose in the individual's own sociocultural setting, not due to any physical disorder.

Functional encopresis is generally referred to as *primary* if it occurs after the child has reached the age of four and has not been preceded by fecal continence for at least one year and *secondary* if it has been preceded by fecal continence for at least one year. There is no provision for recording the primary-secondary distinction. When the passage of feces in functional encopresis is involuntary rather than deliberate, it is often related to constipation, impaction, or retention with subsequent overflow. In such cases there often is soiling of clothes shortly after bathing because of reflex stimulation.

* * *

299.0x Infantile Autism

The essential features are a lack of responsiveness to other people (autism), gross impairment in communicative skills, and bizarre responses to various aspects of the environment, all developing within the first 30 months of age. Infantile autism may be associated with known organic conditions, such as maternal rubella or phenylketonuria. In such cases the behavioral syndrome infantile autism should be recorded on Axis I, and the physical disorder, on Axis III.

The relationship of this category to schizophrenia is controversial. Some believe that infantile autism is the earliest form of schizophrenia, whereas others believe that they are two distinct conditions. However, there is apparently no increased incidence of schizophrenia in the families of children with infantile autism, which supports the hypothesis that the two disorders are unrelated.

The failure to develop interpersonal relationships is characterized by a lack of responsiveness to and a lack of interest in people, with a concomitant failure to develop normal attachment behavior. In infancy these deficiencies may be manifested by a failure to cuddle, by lack of eye contact and facial responsiveness, and by indifference or aversion to affection and physical contact. As a result, parents often suspect that the child is deaf. Adults may be treated as interchangeable, or the child may cling mechanically to a specific individual.

In early childhood there is invariably failure to develop cooperative play and friendships; but, as the children grow older, greater awareness of and attachment to parents and other familiar adults often develop. Some of the least handicapped may eventually reach a stage where they can become passively involved in other children's games or physical play such as running with other children. This apparent sociability is superficial, however, and can be a source of diagnostic confusion if mistaken for social relatedness when the diagnosis is made retrospectively.

Impairment in communication includes both verbal and nonverbal skills. Language may be totally absent. When it develops, it is often characterized by: immature grammatical structure, delayed or immediate echolalia, pronominal reversals (use of the pronoun "you" when "I" is the intended meaning), nominal aphasia (inability to name objects), inability to use abstract terms, metaphorical language (utterances whose usage is idiosyncratic and whose meaning is not clear), and abnormal speech melody, such as questionlike rises at ends of statements. Appropriate nonverbal communication, such as socially appropriate facial expressions and gestures, is often lacking.

Bizarre responses to the environment may take several forms. There may be resistance and even catastrophic reactions to minor changes in the environment, e.g., the child may scream when his or her place at the dinner table is changed. There is often attachment to odd objects, e.g., child insists on always carrying a string or rubber band. Ritualistic behavior may involve motor acts, such as hand clapping or repetitive peculiar hand movements, or insisting that fixed sequences of events precede going to bed. The fascination with movement may be exemplified by staring at fans, and the child may display inordinate interest in spinning objects. Music of all kinds may hold a special interest for the child. The child may be extremely interested in buttons, parts of the body, playing with water, or peculiar rote topics such as train schedules or historical dates. Tasks involving long-term memory, for example, recall of the exact words of songs heard years before, may be performed remarkably well.

* * *

SPECIFIC DEVELOPMENTAL DISORDERS (AXIS II)

This subclass is for disorders of specific areas of development not due to another disorder. For example, a delay in language development in an otherwise normal child would be classified as a specific developmental disorder whereas a delay in language development in a child with infantile autism would be attributed to the infantile autism and therefore would not be classified as a specific developmental disorder. Similarly, an individual with general delays in development would receive a diagnosis of mental retardation, not a specific developmental disorder.

Each aspect of development noted here is related to biological maturation. However, there is no assumption regarding the primacy of biological etiological factors, and nonbiological factors are clearly involved in these disorders.

The inclusion of these categories in a classification of "mental disorders" is controversial, since many of the children with these disorders have no other signs of psychopathology, and the detection and treatment of the most common category, developmental reading disorder, take place mainly within the educational system rather than the mental health system. Nevertheless, these conditions fall within the DSM-III concept of mental disorder; moreover, they are included in the mental disorders section of ICD-9.

Because specific developmental disorders occur so frequently in conjunction with other disorders, they are coded on a separate axis (Axis II) to ensure that they are not overlooked. Thus, in the case of a child with conduct disorder and developmental reading disorder, the conduct disorder will be coded on Axis I, and the reading disorder on Axis II. A particular child may have more than one specific developmental disorder; all should be diagnosed.

Although most of the clinical features seen in specific developmental disorders represent functional levels that are normal for very young children (e.g., inability to do arithmetic), there is no implication that children with these disorders are simply at a lower end of a normal continuum and that they will "catch up" with time. In fact, children with these disorders frequently continue to show signs of the disturbance as adolescents or as adults; and the relevant diagnosis should be noted when an adult still has clinically significant signs of the disorder.

* * *

26.

Michael Rutter

COGNITIVE DEFICITS IN AUTISM

In summary, the findings showed that autism was associated with both language abnormalities and a cognitive deficit that was more severe, more widespread and somewhat different in pattern from that found in developmental "dysphasia." The cognitive abnormalities were indeed of a kind linked with language (it was striking that visuo-spatial and perceptual deficits were not associated with autism), but they extended well beyond spoken language; moreover, it appeared to be language deviance as much as language delay that was characteristic of autism.

IS THIS COGNITIVE DEFICIT BASIC TO AUTISM?

We must now return to the question of whether this cognitive deficit is basic to autism. Several pieces of evidence suggest that it may be. To begin with, it appears that the deficit is present in virtually all cases of autism. The possible exception is provided by some cases of so-called autistic psychopathy (Wing, 1981b), in which there is no appreciable language delay or deviance. Whether these constitute mild cases of autism or some rather different condition is not yet clear.

Secondly, there is a close association between the cognitive abnormalities and the social/behavioural features of autism. Discriminant function analysis based on Bartak's comparison of autistic and

'dysphasic' children showed that autism could be diagnosed almost as well on the basis of cognitive test performance as on behavioural or linguistic grounds (Bartak et al., 1977).

Thirdly, follow-up studies have shown the very considerable prognostic importance of language measures. In our own follow-up study (Rutter et al., 1967) both a marked lack of response to sounds during the pre-school years and the failure to acquire useful speech by five years proved to be among the most powerful predictors of social adjustment in adolescence. Other studies have confirmed that apart from IQ, language features constitute the best predictors of psychosocial outcome (Lotter, 1978).

Fourthly, Howlin and Hemsley's intensive behavioural treatment study (Hemsley et al., 1978; Rutter, 1980c; Howlin, 1981) showed that in both the short-term and long-term, the experimental home-based treatment group had a better outcome than their matched controls dealt with on the more conventional and less intensive outpatient basis. But, strikingly, the features least influenced by treatment were IQ and language competence. This marked resistance to treatment strongly suggests that the cognitive deficit is intrinsic and perhaps central to the autistic child's basic biological handicap.

The fifth set of findings stem from Folstein's twin study of autistic individuals (Folstein & Rutter, 1977). This was designed to examine genetic factors rather than the cognitive features, but, incidentally, it provided powerful evidence on the links between autism and cognitive deficits. Two results from Folstein's study are relevant on this issue. Firstly, it was found that whereas none of the dizygotic pairs was concordant for autism, 4 of the 11 monozygotic pairs were concordant. This difference pointed to the importance of hereditary factors. However, the second question that had to follow that finding was "what is inherited?" To answer that query it was necessary to determine whether any of the non-autistic co-twins showed any abnormalities other than autism. It was found that few often did in the DZ pairs, but most of the MZ pairs of co-twins showed cognitive problems. Altogether, 9 out of the 11 MZ pairs were concordant for some form of cognitive disorder, compared with only 1 of the 10 DZ pairs. The findings both strengthened the suggestion of genetic determination and indicated that what is inherited is some form of cognitive abnormality, that includes but is not restricted to autism. The cognitive abnormalities linked with autism were rather varied in type, but most involved some form of language impairment.

Folstein's conclusions on the importance of a genetic determination that applied to a broader form of cognitive deficit, of which autism is but one part, have recently been supported by a study from Iowa. August and his colleagues (1981) found that compared with the siblings of Down's syndrome individuals, the siblings of autistic probands showed a significant family clustering of cognitive disabilities. Some 15 percent of the sibs of autistic children, compared with 3 percent in the Down's syndrome group, had some form of language disorder, learning disability or mental retardation.

All of these findings are consistent in pointing to the presence of a basic cognitive deficit in autism—a deficit that is closely linked with the social and behavioural features of the condition. However, there are a few other findings that emphasize that much remains unexplained. Let me note just two of these. Among the language characteristics that I have mentioned is the autistic child's relative failure to use language for social communication. Autistic individuals may learn to talk fluently and, indeed, some autistic adults develop considerable language fluency and talk almost excessively. But still they tend to bombard their conversational partners with rather stereotyped statements and questions rather than converse in the reciprocal responsive fashion that is typical of the language interchanges of even very young normal children. It is not obvious why a cognitive deficit involving language, coding, sequencing, and abstraction should lead to this lack of a social component in the use of language. The other finding is that long after autistic individuals gain fluent language and cease to show the gross cognitive deficits that characterized them when younger, they remain obviously abnormal in their social interactions (Rutter, 1970). The implication is that there is a need to focus research more explicitly on the characteristics of autistic children's social impairments and on the possible cognitive deficits that might underlie them.

* * *

Putting these findings together, we are forced to the conclusion that autistic children's social abnormalities probably do stem from some kind of "cognitive" deficit, if by that one means a deficit in dealing with social and emotional cues. But equally, the data suggest that the deficit does not lie in the processing of stimuli of any particular sensory modality or, indeed, of stimuli that are defined in terms of any particular sensory qualities. Rather, it appears that the stimuli that pose difficulties for autistic children are those that carry emotional or social "meaning." As yet it is not clear just what that might reflect in terms of brain functions or neurophysiological processes, but at least one key area that needs further systematic research has been identified.

* * *

CONCLUSIONS

In concluding, I need to return to the issue with which I started—cognitive deficits in the pathogenesis of autistic behaviour. The research findings I have considered leave no doubt that autistic children do indeed suffer from crucial cognitive deficits—that much may be regarded as established. Moreover, there is every reason to believe that these cognitive deficits are basic in the dual sense that they are not secondary to other autistic features and that they underlie many of the important handicaps of autistic children. However, the recent research findings emphasize how much remains to be explained. Clearly there are fundamental connections between the abnormalities of cognition, conation and affect found in autism, but we remain ignorant of just what those connections are and, especially, we lack knowledge about the nature of the symptoms of autism that gives the name to the syndrome. In my introductory remarks I drew attention to developmental issues and I have done so again in considering the social anomalies of autistic children. These are important, of course, for theoretical reasons, but they are also crucial for therapeutic concerns. A dozen years ago, when Sussenwein and I (Rutter & Sussenwein, 1971) discussed the rationale for the treatment of young autistic children, we emphasized that one of the prime goals must be the fostering of normal development. In that paper we sought to draw lessons from a combination of what was known about the nature of autism and what was known about normal development. It is evident that this linkage continues to pose difficulties in therapeutic planning. We have learned an enormous amount about how to modify the behaviour of autistic children and there is little doubt that these gains in knowledge have led to improved treatment programmes with real benefits for the children in them. Nevertheless the most crucial aspect of treatment—the facilitation of normal development—continues to wait on the solution of the riddle of the nature of the disordered cognitive processes in autism.

REFERENCES

August, G. J., Stewart, M. A., & Tsai, L. (1981) The incidence of cognitive disabilities in the siblings of autistic children. *Br. J. Psychiat.* **138**, 416–422.

Bartak, L., Rutter, M., & Cox, A. (1977) A comparative study of infantile autism and specific developmental receptive language disorders, III. Discriminant function analysis. *J. Autism Child Schizophr.* **7**, 383–396.

Folstein, S., & Rutter, M. (1977) Infantile autism: a genetic study of 21 twin pairs. *J. Child Psychol. Psychiat.* **18**, 297–321.

Hemsley, R., Howlin, P., Berger, M., Hersov, L., Holbrook, D., Ritter, M., & Yule, W. (1978) Training autistic children in a family context. In *Autism: A Reappraisal of Concepts and Treatment* (Edited by Ritter, M., and Schopler, E.), pp. 379–411. Plenum, New York.

Howlin, P. (1981) The effectiveness of operant language training with autistic children. *J. Autism Dev. Dis.* **11**, 89–106.

Lotter, V. (1978) Follow-up studies. In *Autism: A Reappraisal of Concepts and Treatment* (Edited by Rutter, M., and Schopler, E.), pp. 475–495. Plenum, New York.

Rutter, M. (1970) Autistic children, infancy to adulthood. *Semin. Psychiat.* **2**, 435–450.

Rutter, M. (1980c) Language training with

autistic children: how does it work and what does it achieve? In *Language and Language Disorders in Childhood* (Edited by Hersov, L. A. and Berger, M.), pp. 147–172. Pergamon, Oxford.

Rutter, M., Greenfeld, D., & Lockyer, L. (1967) A five to fifteen year follow-up study of infantile psychosis, II. Social and behavioural outcome. *Br. J. Psychiat.* **113**, 1183–1199.

Rutter, M., & Sussenwein, F. (1971) A developmental and behavioral approach to the treatment of pre-school autistic children. *J. Autism Childh. Schizophr.* **1**, 376–397.

Wing, L. (1981*b*) Asperger's syndrome: a clinical account. *Psychol. Med.* **11**, 115–130.

27.

Bernard Rimland

AUTISM AS AN ABNORMALITY OF PHYSIOLOGICAL AROUSAL

AUTISM AS COGNITIVE DYSFUNCTION

Baffling and paradoxical though early infantile autism has been considered to be, it is possible to trace its diversity of symptoms and manifestations to a single critical disability: *The child with early infantile autism is grossly impaired in a function basic to all cognition: the ability to relate new stimuli to remembered experience.* The vital connections between sensation and memory can be made only with difficulty. New sensation can be related only to sharply limited fragments of memory. The child is thus virtually divested of the means for deriving meaning from his experience. This impairment has two readily observable and interdependent consequences: (1) the child cannot understand relationships nor think in terms of concepts, symbols, analogies or abstractions; (2) he cannot integrate his sensations

From Bernard Rimland, *Infantile Autism*, pp. 79, 87–90. Copyright © 1964 by Bernard Rimland.

into a comprehensible whole—his perception of the world is vague and obscure.

Relationship between the Cognitive Dysfunction in Autism and the Reticular Formation of the Brain Stem: An Hypothesis

In some very real way, memories, thoughts, and ideas are somehow locked into separate compartments of the autistic child's brain. They may be evoked by certain very specifically associated stimuli, but never in useful combination with other ideas, which themselves would appear to be similarly remembered only as isolated and unintegrated fragments of experience.

Where in the brain do incoming stimuli interact with previously stored experience to provide meaning to the former and exercise the *raison d'être* for the latter? In terms of our mechanical analogy, where can we find the sidings and switches whose absence, in fact or in effect, would produce the closed-loop, in-and-out-unchanged memory which characterizes so much of the behavior of the autistic child?

The academically correct and scientifically most defensible response to these questions is that nobody knows. And at least partly because the thought-mechanisms involved and the questions themselves have not heretofore been formulated in this specific way, no one, to the present writer's knowledge, has addressed himself to this problem. But a good deal of relevant controversy and speculation has taken place in recent years concerning the functions of a small but highly complex network of nerve cells in the brain stem — the reticular formation.

We will consider some of the laboratory and clinical research on the functions of the reticular formation which have led several investigators to consider it as a possible site for the higher mental functions, despite its location in a phylogenetically ancient part of the brain. As will be demonstrated, certain research on these functions of the reticular formation tends to support our proposition that malfunction in this part of the brain may be the direct cause of the syndrome of infantile autism. For the present, we wish merely to point out that *anatomically* the reticular formation fits very well the requirements of the site of dysfunction in our mechanical model of autism.

The pivotal anatomical position of the reticular formation of the brain stem within the central nervous system may be understood by visualizing a slender arm with the fist enclosed in a rather large boxing glove. The cortex and its associated structures would roughly correspond to the glove, the brain stem and spinal cord to the flesh of the hand and arm, and the reticular formation to the bones of the hand and fingers. Like these bones, the reticular formation is actually composed of a series

of identifiable but highly integrated substructures. But here the analogy ends.

Unlike the above depiction, the elements of the reticular formation are intertwined and interrelated to an extent which is quite beyond imagining. It has been referred to as a "thicket" of neurons, which are intermeshed not only with each other, but with all parts of the cortex. Clark has provided an excellent description of the reticular formation:

> ... It can be visualized as a sort of central core composed of scatterings of nerve cells entangled in an irregular and closely meshed network of nerve fibres, and extending up from the spinal cord through the brain stem to run into continuity with the intralaminar nuclei of the thalamus. As is now well known, the whole system is linked up indirectly with the cerebral cortex and by circuitous routes is capable of influencing and profoundly modifying cortical activity as a whole. Into the reticular formation stretching through the spinal cord and brain stem there stream numerous collaterals from the incoming sensory fibres of peripheral nerves, as well as a continuous succession of collaterals from many (perhaps all) of the ascending tracts of the specific sensory pathways (1958, p. 10).

Like most who describe the reticular system, Clark has emphasized the ascending nerve tracts and consequently the effects of the reticular formation upon the cortex. It will be of importance to our discussion that the cortex may similarly exert descending influences on the reticular formation.

In terms of its anatomical location within the brain, in terms of its intricate numerous neural connections to the sense organs and cortex, the reticular formation seems admirably well suited to supply the collaterals and interconnections within the normal brain whose functional absence in cases of autism could result in thought impairment of the type we have described.

The reticular formation has in fact been referred to by some writers as the "communications-center," "central relay station" or "master switchboard" of the brain. While the concept of reticular function we wish to invoke is somewhat similar, it should be emphasized that such imaginative descriptions do not reflect the majority opinion concerning the role the reticular formation plays in mental functioning.

Ivanitskiy (1960) has discussed the problem of higher functions in his review of the world literature on the reticular formation. He emphasizes that its primary function is believed to consist in maintaining the tone of the cortex and of other parts of the brain at "the level optimum for the given moment." This is the widely accepted "arousal function," resulting from the so-called diffuse, non-specific effects of reticular stimulation. According to Ivanitskiy, "Attempts at creating a theory relegating the main role in carrying out the functions of consciousness to a nonspecific system (theory of the centrencephalic system), has not been widely recognized by the majority of research workers" (p. 10).

Ivanitskiy admits, however, that "the idea of the diffuseness, 'nonspecificity' influences exerted by the reticular formation are being subjected to criticism on a progressively greater scale at the present time" (p. 7), and cites works by Olszewski, Brodal, Narikashvili, and Moruzzi as supplying evidence in support of the view that the reticular formation may serve purposes in addition to, or apart from, its maintenance and regulatory roles.

The role ascribed here to the reticular formation, that of providing a site for the linking of sensory input (real or symbolic) with the prior content of the brain is admittedly highly speculative. It should be made clear that the general theory of autism offered in this paper is not contingent upon the correctness of this hypothesis. Nor is our theory of autism dependent upon the reticular formation as the actual site of the localized brain impairment which the theory does assume. Nevertheless, in the face of both supporting and contradictory evidence, we choose for the present to refer to the reticular formation as the site of the impairment. The advantages of being specific on this point appear to outweigh the risks entailed in being wrong.

REFERENCES

Clark, W. LeG. Sensory experience and brain structure. *Journal of Mental Science*, 1958, *104*, 1–13.

Ivanitskiy, A. M. *The functions of the reticular formation of the brain stem.* Office of Technical Services, U.S. Dept. of Commerce: JPRS Report 2935, August 15, 1960.

28.

O. Ivar Lovaas

STIMULUS OVERSELECTIVITY HYPOTHESIS

STIMULUS OVERSELECTIVITY AS THE PSYCHOLOGICAL DEFICIT OF AUTISTIC CHILDREN

Certain recent studies in our laboratory on perceptual deviations in autistics may provide some clues as to why autistic children encounter such great difficulty in discrimination learning. The main focus of this research centers on our finding (Lovaas et al., 1971) of what we referred to as "stimulus overselectivity" or "overselective attention." In that study three groups of children (autistic, retarded, and normal) were reinforced for responding to a complex stimulus involving the simultaneous presentation of auditory, visual, and tactile cues. Once this discrimination was established, elements of the complex were presented separately to assess which aspects of the complex stimulus had acquired control over the child's behavior. We found that: (a) The autistics responded primarily to only one of the cues, the normals responded uniformly to all three cues, and the retardates functioned between these two extremes. (b) Conditions could be arranged such that a cue which had remained nonfunctional when presented in association with other cues could be established as functional when trained separately. The data failed to support notions that any one sense modality is impaired in autistic children. Rather, when presented with a stimulus complex, their attention was overselective.

Shortly thereafter, we replicated this

Reprinted with permission from Irvington Publishers, Inc., New York.

finding in a two-stimulus situation (Lovaas & Schreibman, 1971) in which autistic Ss again showed overselective attention by responding to only one of the two stimulus components, while normal Ss tended to respond to both.

We also found (Schreibman & Lovaas, 1973) that when autistic children were taught to discriminate between two life-like boy and girl figures, they made this discrimination on the basis of only one or a peculiar combination of components of these figures. For example, one child discriminated the figures on the basis of their shoes; when the shoes were removed, he could no longer tell the boy and girl figures apart.

We hypothesized from these findings that autistic children would encounter difficulties in learning situations requiring *shifts in stimulus* control over behavior. There are at least three such shifts (substitutions) which are basic to normal functioning. In each of the following three situations the organism receives two stimulus inputs, roughly simultaneously: (1) In classical conditioning, behavior elicited by a particular stimulus (the US) comes under the control of contiguously presented, previously neutral (the CS) stimuli. Many consider that classical conditioning underlies the acquisition of appropriate *affect* and the acquisition of *secondary* (symbolic) *reinforcers*. The autistic child appears to have problems in both kinds of acquisitions. (2) Stimulus overselectivity should lead to problems in the acquisition of environmental contexts that underlie meaningful speech. One can argue that speech exists without meaning to the extent that it has an impoverished context. The acquisition of a context for speech probably involves shifts and extensions in stimulus control to simultaneous presentations of auditory, visual, tactile, and other cues. Much autistic speech (e.g., "echolalia") appears to be contextually impoverished. (3) Stimulus overselectivity should also seriously interfere with learning when prompt and prompt fading procedures are employed. In most teaching situations, the teacher "helps" the child to the correct response by some form of "guidance," "aid," or "suggestion," as in prompt fading techniques. This, of course, involves added cues which should interfere with the autistics' learning.

The first study to investigate problems with shifts in stimulus control was conducted by Koegel (1971), who raised the question of whether autistic children would learn a discrimination more easily if there were *no prompts* available and also whether between-modality or within-modality transfers affected learning. Briefly, this is what he did. Two groups of children (autistic and normal) were pretrained in a color discrimination task. The intent was to use the color cues as prompts subsequently for more difficult training stimuli. Once the children had mastered the color discriminations the colors were presented simultaneously with training stimuli in a prompt-fading procedure which was used to train four different discriminations. The results were as follows: First, autistic *S*s failed to transfer from the color prompt to the training stimuli more often than normal *S*s. Second, gradually fading the prompt generally produced a transfer for normal *S*s but not for autistic *S*s. Third, those autistic and normal *S*s who did not transfer to the training stimuli continued to respond correctly to the faded color cue, and autistic *S*s discriminated differences in the color (prompt) discrimination that were as small as those the normal *S*s discriminated. In other words, they were capable of making extremely fine discriminations, but they had particular difficulty in shifting from one cue to another.

REFERENCES

Koegel, R. *Selective attention to prompt stimuli by autistic and normal children.* Unpublished doctoral dissertation. University of California, Los Angeles, 1971.

Lovaas, O. I., Litrownik, A., & Mann, R. Response latencies to auditory stimuli in autistic children engaged in self-stimulatory behavior. *Behaviour Research and Therapy,* 1971, **9**, 39–49.

Lovaas, O. I., & Schreibman, L. Stimulus overselectivity of autistic chldren in a two-stimulus situation. *Behaviour Research and Therapy,* 1971, **9**, 305–310.

Schreibman, L., & Lovaas, O. I. Overselective response to social stimuli by autistic children. *Journal of Abnormal Child Psychology,* 1973, **1** (2), 152–168.

29.

C. G. Fairburn

COGNITIVE-BEHAVIORAL APPROACH TO THE TREATMENT OF BULIMIA

Before starting treatment, the therapist describes the nature of the program and the likelihood of improvement. He stresses that the patient will retain responsibility for her behavior and, as a consequence, the outcome reflects the strength of her commitment to change. He provides reassurance that the progress made during treatment tends to be maintained. However, he also explains that she will not be "cured" in the conventional sense of the word. Instead, she may well be liable to transitory relapses at times of stress, her eating problem remaining an Achilles' heel.

Three stages in the treatment may be identified. The first is a sustained attempt to disrupt the habitual overeating and vomiting that characterizes the more severe cases of bulimia nervosa. During this stage, the patient requires intensive support with appointments two or three times each week. At first she is simply asked to monitor the food she eats (either just before its consumption or immediately afterward) and when and where it is eaten. She is asked to identify which eating episodes were planned meals over which she felt she had control and which signified a loss of control. At this stage some patients may be unable to distinguish between controlled and uncontrolled eating, or they may describe episodes of overeating that were intentional but nevertheless followed by depression and self-condemnation.

Once self-monitoring is established the patient is instructed to restrict her eating to three or four planned meals each day regardless of her degree of hunger. She is advised that her hunger sensations are likely to have been disturbed by her irregular eating habits and that they are therefore an unsatisfactory guide to when and what she should eat. No restrictions are set on the foods she eats; the emphasis is solely on establishing a controlled and regular eating pattern. Neither are there attempts to restrict the self-induced vomiting; this ceases once eating is under control. She is reassured that these changes in her behavior will not result in weight gain, and, so that she can check this, she is advised to weigh herself once or twice a month.

Each interview focuses on the patient's attempts to control her eating. The therapist and patient scrutinize the daily monitoring sheets: success is praised, and periods of low control are explored with the intention of finding ways of preventing their reoccurrence. Various means of enhancing self-control may be suggested: the most useful appear to be stimulus control measures, especially those that directly or indirectly reduce the availability of food (Stuart & Davis, 1972; Mahoney & Mahoney, 1976). In addition, the patient may find it helpful to engage in incompatible behavior (such as exercise or meeting friends) at times she senses her control is poor.

From C. G. Fairburn, "The place of a cognitive behavioral approach in the management of bulimia." In P. L. Darby, *Anorexia Nervosa: Recent Developments in Research.* Alan R. Liss, Inc., 1983.

Some patients' eating habits are so disturbed that it is unrealistic to expect them immediately to confine their eating to mealtimes. In these cases the therapist identifies the times of day at which control is at its greatest and encourages the patient to focus on these times and increase their duration. For example, if control is worst in the evening, the initial emphasis is on establishing control during the day. Only when this has been achieved are attempts made to deal with the evenings. In particularly severe cases, one or two weeks of daily contact with the therapist are necessary if the habitual overeating and vomiting are to be overcome.

Many individuals with bulimia nervosa live away from the parental home, and a significant number are married (Fairburn & Cooper, 1982). Interviews with the parents of these patients are therefore not a routine part of treatment. However, it appears essential to arrange occasional joint interviews with the people with whom the patient lives and shares her meals. These interviews serve two functions: first, by bringing the problem into the open, the patient's guilt over her secrecy is assuaged; second, by explaining the principles of treatment, and in particular the importance of *self*-control, the friends or relatives can be encouraged to provide an environment which facilitates the patient's own efforts to overcome the problem. Although most patients prefer to keep their monitoring sheets private, it should be possible for cohabitees to inquire about the patient's progress without provoking a hostile or evasive response. Means of doing this may be usefully discussed. In addition, the therapist may emphasize the value of reacting sensitively to requests by the patient for help or distraction at times when her control is low.

This intensive therapeutic input usually has dramatic effects. Within four-six weeks most patients are overeating and vomiting on an intermittent basis, perhaps once a week or less. However, it is often apparent that though the eating pattern has improved the diet is highly selective with "fattening" foods being avoided.

In the second stage of treatment appointments are weekly. The emphasis on self-control is maintained and interviews open with a review of the previous week's eating. Episodes of loss of control are examined and almost invariably it is evident that they are in response to stressful events. Ways of increasing control at such times are discussed, and in addition more adaptive means of coping with these events are explored using the problem-solving approach of Goldfried and Goldfried (1975). It is interesting to note that at assessment many of these patients insist they have no problems other than their eating disorder. This apparent denial may stem in part from the intensity of their preoccupation with food and eating since once this has diminished problems begin to emerge that had not been identified earlier. In addition, it is common for patients to recognize that some episodes of eating had served in the past to distract them from thinking about other difficulties.

Certain other strategies may be introduced in order to deal with related problem areas. As binge eating may result from excessive dietary restraint (Wardle & Beinart, 1981), patients are encouraged to eat "banned foods" at times of satisfactory control. The intention is that they should relax control over the content of their diet while continuing to restrict eating to predetermined mealtimes.

In addition, it may be necessary to

help the patient identify thoughts that are proving an obstacle to behavior change. Often these can be traced to irrational concerns regarding body shape and weight. Patients can be taught to challenge and replace such thoughts using the methods of Beck (1976) or Meichenbaum (1977). Small experiments can promote this process. For example, if the patient insists that she is "fat" on some days and "thin" on others, the basis for this belief can be tested by asking her to weigh herself and measure her waistline each morning. In the author's experience, although fluctuations in these measures may occur, they fail to parallel the "shape" of the day; instead, it becomes apparent that day-to-day problems are the cause of her feeling fat or thin.

With the flexible and individualized use of these strategies progress usually continues. Overeating and vomiting become infrequent, preoccupation with food and eating diminishes in intensity, and abnormal attitudes tend to become progressively less salient. In the majority of cases the patient's weight remains stable and is of little concern. However, if the patient is significantly underweight, she is urged to gain weight gradually to a mutually agreed level. Such encouragement is best delayed until the eating pattern has been satisfactorily controlled.

In the final stage of treatment, appointments are at monthly or twice-monthly intervals and the focus is on the maintenance of change. Patients are told to expect episodes of poor conrol, particularly when under stress, and they are encouraged to prepare a written plan for use at such times. In most cases their plan includes reestablishing monitoring and stimulus control, getting help from friends and relatives, and, of course, identifying and tackling current areas of difficulty. All these skills will have been learnt during treatment. The hope is that if the patient is prepared for difficulties in the future the frequency and severity of lapses will be diminished.

REFERENCES

Beck, A. T. *Cognitive therapy and the emotional disorders.* New York: International Universities Press, 1976.

Fairburn, C. G., & Cooper, P. J. Self-induced vomiting and bulimia nervosa: An undetected problem. *British Medical Journal,* 1982, *284,* 1153–1155.

Goldfried, M. R., & Goldfried, A. P. Cognitive change methods, In F. H. Kanfer & A. P. Goldstein (Eds.), *Helping people change.* New York: Pergamon, 1975.

Mahoney, M. L., & Mahoney, K. *Permanent weight control.* New York: W. W. Norton, 1976.

Meichenbaum, D. *Cognitive behaviour modification.* New York: Plenum, 1977.

Stuart, R. B., & Davis, B. *Slim chance in a fat world: Behavioral control of obesity.* Champaign, Ill.: Research Press, 1972.

Wardle, J., & Beinart, H. Binge-eating: A theoretical review. *British Journal of Clinical Psychology,* 1981, *20,* 97–109.

CHAPTER VII

Personality Disorders

Psychopathy and Sociopathy

Psychopathy as a psychological concept is a controversial one, not even found in the *Diagnostic and Statistical Manual of Mental Disorders* of the American Psychiatric Association (1980). Mathis (1968) and his associates identified the term as obsolete, and replaced it by "character and behavioral disorders."

McCord and McCord define the psychopath as an "asocial, aggressive, highly impulsive person, who feels little or no guilt and is unable to form lasting bonds of affection with other human beings" (1964, p. 3). Maher summarizes the primary psychopath as having a "behavior pattern marked by poor acquisition of a conditioned response to noxious stimulation, poor development of adaptive response in an avoidance learning task, little sign of any manifest anxiety, poor or shortened future time perspective, and a history of antisocial behavior" (1966, pp. 221–222).

In a study conducted by Albert, Brigante, and Chase (1959), these researchers concluded from an analysis involving 70 articles and books that there is considerable consensus regarding the concept, with disagreement entailing etiology of psychopathy.

Cleckley, who favors the term *psychopath* and uses it interchangeably with *sociopath*, hypothesizes that it is a serious and "subtle disorder at deep levels disturbing the integration and normal appreciation of experience and resulting in pathology that might, in analogy with Henry Head's classifications of the aphasias, be described as semantic" (1976, p. 388). Cleckley's (1959, 1976) diagnostic criteria of psychopathic states include: unexplained failure; undisturbed technical intelligence; absence of neurotic anxiety; persistent and inadequately motivated antisocial behavior; irresponsibility; peculiar inability to distinguish between truth and falsehood; inability to accept blame; failure to learn by experience; incapacity for love; inappropriate or fantastic reactions to alcohol; lack of insight; shallow and impersonal responses to sexual life; persistent pattern of self-defeat; and the rare execution of suicides. Maher (1966) characterizes psychopaths by (1) impulsive antisocial behavior; (2) inability for forming lasting, genuine emotional attachments; and (3) vanity concerning appearance, social importance, etc.

Frankenstein (1959) cites 11 criteria of psychopathy under a dichotomous division of extraversion and introversion, with the morally indolent psychopath common to both groups. The other five characterizing the extravert are: (1) brutal destructiveness; (2) egocentric incorporation of the nonego, owing to the need to regain security and a fear of the void; (3) oscillating psychopathy (with contradictory reality elements); (4) shallow-attachment variety of oscillation; and (5) imposter and swindler type. Characteristics of the introvert are (1) explosiveness (fantasies of destructive mastery over a hostile world); (2) paranoid who sees his identity as a negated one; (3) drifting psychopath (addict, sex pervert); (4) unstable psychopath (imitates another's behavior); and (5) owner of absolute truth (eccentricity, peculiar saint).

Buss (1966) ascribes three characteristics to the psychopathic personality: (1) a hollow, isolated person; (2) lacking any fundamental identity of his own; and (3) inability to bind time. Concerning the problem of time in relation to psychopathy, Siegman (1961), and Brock and Del Giudice (1963) found a shorter time perspective among delinquents, suggesting an inability of psychopaths to adapt behavior in the light of future adverse consequences. The question arises as to their time perspective respecting the future.

In a British study conducted by Craft (1965), he found the following clinical features of psychopathy, with the only negative ones being the "absence of psychosis" and "severe dullness": (1) emotional instability; need to act impulsively (thus preventing the psychopaths the time or opportunity of considering the consequences of their actions); (2) lovelessness; inability to feel affection for another; to think in terms of another, self-centeredness, coldness, hostility, and desire for destructiveness terminating in (3) antisocial behavior that is not deterred by (4) shame, guilt, or punishment (qualities lacking in psychopaths); and (5) rationality remaining intact. Craft inferred a concomitant relationship existing between the severity of personality disturbance and the frequency of early adverse childhood influences, that is, an adverse parental relationship.

Primary psychopaths are often distinguished from neurotics by their lack of anxiety, while some authorities recognize *secondary psychopaths* who do show some manifestations of anxiety, hence complicate their condition with neurosis. Measuring anxiety by the Taylor Manifest Anxiety Scale, Fairweather (1954) found that psychopaths obtained the lowest scores. Using the Heineman (1953) form of the Taylor Manifest Anxiety Scale, Lykken (1957) obtained an AI (Anxiety Index) calculated by Welsh's (1952) formula of 49 psychopaths identified by Cleckley's criteria, and discovered that primary psychopaths displayed less anxiety while the neurotic psychopaths showed significantly higher scores on the Taylor Anxiety Scale and Welsh Anxiety Scale. In the employment of the Psychopathic Deviate Scale of the Minnesota Multiphase

Personality Inventory, Hetherington and Klinger (1964) found psychopathy to be associated with "deficient passive avoidance" learning under punishment; that is, psychopathic subjects learned at slower rates when punished for incorrect responses, but at the same rate when rewarded for correct ones.

In her study regarding conscience in the psychopath, Greenacre ascertained a faulty structural development of the conscience of psychopaths or those personalities "characterized by impulsiveness and marked irresponsibility, intense but labile emotional states, and generally quixotic and superficial love relationships" (1945, p. 495). She does not find them to be deliberate offenders, but rather persons who lie and steal impulsively, particularly when under pressure.

Stern (1964) differentiates between sociopathy and "character neurosis"; while both come into conflict with their society, the latter (on the increase) are neurotics who "manifest themselves mainly in pathological distortions of patterns of behavior and conduct" (p. 134). He also recognizes a subtype of sociopath, the psychopath who is "morally colorblind." Approaching the subject matter from the standpoint of a clinician, Schneider, however, rejects the prevailing view that psychopathy is a study of the asocial or delinquent personality. Psychopaths are those individuals "who either suffer personally because of their own abnormality or make the community suffer because of it" (1958, p. 3).

According to Maher's (1966) subcultural hypothesis of criminal behavior, criminality has been acquired through a subculture, one of criminal environment in which the criminal is not a psychological deviant per se, since he is the product of reinforcements conducive to his subculture. Accordingly he should be regarded as subcultural rather than criminal. Related to Maher's hypothesis is "differential association" of Sutherland and Cressey (1960) that relates criminality to frequency, priority, duration, and intensity of association with other criminals.

Employing a learning theory approach to psychopathy, Eysenck recommends the treatment of "children with a sufficient degree of severity to achieve conditioning required by society, but not to treat them so severely that they fall prey to neurotic disorders" (1964, p. 159), the introverted child requiring less severe discipline than the extravert.

30.

American Psychiatric Association

FEATURES OF PERSONALITY DISORDERS

The personality disorders have been grouped into three clusters. The first cluster includes paranoid, schizoid, and schizotypal personality disorders. Individuals with these disorders often appear "odd" or eccentric. The second cluster includes histrionic, narcissistic, antisocial, and borderline personality disorders. Individuals with these disorders often appear dramatic, emotional, or erratic. The third cluster includes avoidant, dependent, compulsive, and passive-aggressive personality disorders. Individuals with these disorders often appear anxious or fearful. Finally, there is a residual category, atypical, mixed or other personality disorder, that can be used for other specific personality disorders or for conditions that do not qualify as any of the specific personality disorders described in this manual.

301.00 Paranoid Personality Disorder

The essential feature is a personality disorder in which there is a pervasive and unwarranted suspiciousness and mistrust of people, hypersensitivity, and restricted affectivity not due to another mental disorder, such as schizophrenia, or a paranoid disorder.

An attitude of suspicion is not only justified but is adaptive in many difficult life situations. A person without signs of mental disorder is willing in such a situa-

tion to abandon suspicions when presented with convincing contradictory evidence, but one with paranoid personality disorder ignores such evidence, and may even become suspicious of someone who challenges his or her suspicious ideas. Individuals with this disorder are typically hypervigilant and take precautions against any perceived threat. They tend to avoid blame even when it is warranted. They are often viewed by others as guarded, secretive, devious, and scheming. They may question the loyalty of others, always expecting trickery. For this reason, there may be pathological jealousy.

When individuals with this disorder find themselves in a new situation, they intensely and narrowly search for confirmation of their expectations, with no appreciation of the total context. Their final conclusion is usually precisely what they expected in the first place. They are concerned with hidden motives and special meanings. Often, transient ideas of reference occur; e.g., that others are taking special notice of them, or saying vulgar things about them.

Individuals with this disorder are usually argumentative and exaggerate difficulties by "making mountains out of molehills." They often find it difficult to relax, usually appear tense, and show a tendency to counterattack when they perceive any threat. Though they are critical of others, and often litigious, they have great difficulty accepting criticism themselves.

These individuals' affectivity is restricted, and they may appear "cold" to others. They have no true sense of humor and are usually serious. They may pride themselves on always being objective, rational,

From Task Force on Nomenclature and Statistics of the American Psychiatric Association, *Diagnostic and Statistical Manual of Mental Disorders, Third Edition.* American Psychiatric Association, 1980.

and unemotional. They usually lack passive, soft, sentimental, and tender feelings.

* * *

301.20 Schizoid Personality Disorder

The essential feature is a personality disorder in which there is a defect in the capacity to form social relationships, evidenced by the absence of warm, tender feelings for others and indifference to praise, criticism, and the feelings of others. The diagnosis is not made if eccentricities of speech, behavior, or thought characteristic of schizotypal personality disorder are present or if the disturbance is due to a psychotic disorder such as schizophrenia.

Individuals with this disorder show little or no desire for social involvement, usually prefer to be "loners," and have few, if any, close friends. They appear reserved, withdrawn, and seclusive and usually pursue solitary interests or hobbies. Individuals with this disorder are usually humorless or dull and without affect in situations in which an emotional response would be appropriate. They usually appear "cold" and aloof.

* * *

301.22 Schizotypal Personality Disorder

The essential feature is a personality disorder in which there are various oddities of thought, perception, speech, and behavior that are not severe enough to meet the criteria for schizophrenia. No single feature is invariably present. The disturbance in the content of thought may include magical thinking (or in children, bizarre fantasies or preoccupations), ideas of reference, or paranoid ideation. Perceptual disturbances may include recurrent illusions, depersonalization, or derealization (not associated with panic attacks). Often, speech shows marked peculiarities: concepts may be expressed unclearly or

oddly or words used deviantly, but never to the point of loosening of associations or incoherence. Frequently, but not invariably, the behavioral manifestations include social isolation and constricted or inappropriate affect that interferes with rapport in face-to-face interaction.

* * *

301.50 Histrionic Personality Disorder

The essential feature is a personality disorder in which there are overly dramatic, reactive, and intensely expressed behavior and characteristic disturbances in interpersonal relationships.

Individuals with this disorder are lively and dramatic and are always drawing attention to themselves. They are prone to exaggeration and often act out a role, such as the "victim" or the "princess," without being aware of it.

Behavior is overly reactive and intensely expressed. Minor stimuli give rise to emotional excitability, such as irrational, angry outbursts or tantrums. Individuals with this disorder crave novelty, stimulation, and excitement and quickly become bored with normal routines.

Interpersonal relationships show characteristic disturbances. Initially, people with this disorder are frequently perceived as shallow and lacking genuineness, though superficially charming and appealing. They are often quick to form friendships; but once a relationship is established they can become demanding, egocentric, and inconsiderate; manipulative suicidal threats, gestures, or attempts may be made; there may be a constant demand for reassurance because of feelings of helplessness and dependency. In some cases both patterns are present in the same relationship. These people's actions are frequently inconsistent, and may be misinterpreted by others.

Such individuals are typically attractive and seductive. They attempt to control the opposite sex or enter into a dependent relationship. Flights into romantic fantasy are common; in both sexes overt behavior often is a caricature of femininity. The actual quality of their sexual relationships is variable. Some individuals are promiscuous; others, naïve and sexually unresponsive; but still others have apparently normal sexual adjustment.

In other classifications this category is termed hysterical personality.

***

301.81 Narcissistic Personality Disorder

The essential feature is a personality disorder in which there are a grandiose sense of self-importance or uniqueness; preoccupation with fantasies of unlimited success; exhibitionistic need for constant attention and admiration; characteristic responses to threats to self-esteem; and characteristic disturbances in interpersonal relationships, such as feelings of entitlement, interpersonal exploitativeness, relationships that alternate between the extremes of overidealization and devaluation, and lack of empathy.

The exaggerated sense of self-importance may be manifested as extreme self-centeredness and self-absorption. Abilities and achievements tend to be unrealistically overestimated. Frequently the sense of self-importance alternates with feelings of special unworthiness. For example, a student who ordinarily expects an A and receives an A minus may at that moment express the view that he or she, more than any other student, is revealed to all as a failure.

Fantasies involving unrealistic goals may involve achieving unlimited ability, power, wealth, brilliance, beauty, or ideal love. Although these fantasies frequently substitute for realistic activity, when these goals are actually pursued, it is often with a "driven," pleasureless quality, and an ambition that cannot be satisfied.

Individuals with this disorder are constantly seeking admiration and attention, and are more concerned with appearances than with substance. For example, there might be more concern about being seen with the "right" people than having close friends.

Self-esteem is often fragile; the individual may be preoccupied with how well he or she is doing and how well he or she is regarded by others. In response to criticism, defeat, or disappointment, there is either a cool indifference or marked feelings of rage, inferiority, shame, humiliation, or emptiness.

Interpersonal relationships are invariably disturbed. A lack of empathy (inability to recognize and experience how others feel) is common. For example, annoyance and surprise may be expressed when a friend who is seriously ill has to cancel a date.

Entitlement, the expectation of special favors without assuming reciprocal responsibilities, is usually present. For example, surprise and anger are felt because others will not do what is wanted; more is expected from people than is reasonable.

Interpersonal exploitativeness, in which others are taken advantage of in order to indulge one's own desires or for self-aggrandizement, is common; and the personal integrity and rights of others are disregarded. For example, a writer might plagiarize the ideas of someone befriended for that purpose.

Relations with others lack sustained, positive regard. Close relationships tend to alternate between idealization and devaluation ("splitting"). For example, a man repeatedly becomes involved with women whom he alternately adores and despises.

***

301.70 Antisocial Personality Disorder

The essential feature is a personality disorder in which there is a history of continuous and chronic antisocial behavior in which the rights of others are violated, persistence into adult life, or a pattern of antisocial behavior that began before the age of 15, and failure to sustain good job performance over a period of several years (although this may not be evident in individuals who are self-employed or who have not been in a position to demonstrate this feature; e.g., students or housewives). The antisocial behavior is not due to either severe mental retardation, schizophrenia, or manic episodes.

Lying, stealing, fighting, truancy, and resisting authority are typical early childhood signs. In adolescence, unusually early or aggressive sexual behavior, excessive drinking, and use of illicit drugs are frequent. In adulthood, these kinds of behavior continue, with the addition of inability to sustain consistent work performance or to function as a responsible parent and failure to accept social norms with respect to lawful behavior. After age 30 the more flagrant aspects may diminish, particularly sexual promiscuity, fighting, criminality, and vagrancy.

* * *

301.82   Avoidant Personality Disorder

The essential feature is a personality disorder in which there are hypersensitivity to potential rejection, humiliation, or shame; an unwillingness to enter into relationships unless given unusually strong guarantees of uncritical acceptance; social withdrawal in spite of a desire for affection and acceptance; and low self-esteem.

Individuals with this disorder are exquisitely sensitive to rejection, humiliation, or shame. Most people are somewhat concerned about how others assess them, but these individuals are devastated by the slightest hint of disapproval. Consequently, they withdraw from opportunities for developing close relationships because of a fearful expectation of being belittled or humiliated. They may have one or two close friends, but these relationships are contingent on unconditional approval.

Unlike individuals with schizoid personality disorder, who are socially isolated but have no desire for social relations, those with avoidant personality disorder yearn for affection and acceptance. They are distressed by their lack of ability to relate comfortably to others and suffer from low self-esteem.

* * *

301.60   Dependent Personality Disorder

The essential feature is a personality disorder in which the individual passively allows others to assume responsibility for major areas of his or her life because of a lack of self-confidence and an inability to function independently; the individual subordinates his or her own needs to those of others on whom he or she is dependent in order to avoid any possibility of having to be self-reliant.

Such individuals leave major decisions to others. For example, an adult with this disorder will typically assume a passive role and allow his or her spouse to decide where they should live, what kind of job he or she should have, and with which neighbors they should be friendly. A child or adolescent with this disorder may allow his or her parents to decide what he or she should wear, with whom to associate, and how to spend free time.

Generally individuals with this disorder are unwilling to make demands on the people they depend on for fear of jeopardizing the relationships and being forced to rely on themselves. For example, a wife with this disorder may tolerate a physically abusive husband for fear that he will leave her.

Individuals with this disorder invariably lack self-confidence. They tend to belittle their abilities and assets. For example, an individual with this disorder may constantly refer to himself or herself as "stupid."

***

301.40   Compulsive Personality Disorder

The essential feature is a personality disorder in which there generally are restricted ability to express warm and tender emotions; perfectionism that interferes with the ability to grasp "the big picture"; insistence that others submit to his or her way of doing things; excessive devotion to work and productivity to the exclusion of pleasure; and indecisiveness.

Individuals with this disorder are stingy with their emotions and material possessions. For example, they rarely give compliments or gifts. Everyday relationships have a conventional, formal, and serious quality. Others often perceive these individuals as stilted and "stiff."

Preoccupation with rules, efficiency, trivial details, procedures, or form interferes with the ability to take a broad view of things. For example, such an individual, having misplaced a list of things to be done, will spend an inordinate amount of time looking for the list rather than spend a few moments to recreate the list from memory and proceed with accomplishing the activities. Time is poorly allocated, the most important tasks being left to the last moment. Although efficiency and perfection are idealized, they are rarely attained.

Individuals with this disorder are always mindful of their relative status in dominance-submission relationships. Although they resist the authority of others, they stubbornly insist that people conform to their way of doing things. They are unaware of the feelings of resentment or hurt that this behavior evokes in others. For example, a husband may insist that his wife complete errands for him regardless of her plans.

Work and productivity are prized to the exclusion of pleasure and the value of interpersonal relationships. When pleasure is considered, it is something to be planned and worked for. However, the individual usually keeps postponing the pleasurable activity, such as a vacation, so that it may never occur.

Decision making is avoided, postponed, or protracted, perhaps because of an inordinate fear of making a mistake. For example, assignments cannot be completed on time because the individual is ruminating about priorities.

***

301.84   Passive-Aggressive Personality Disorder

The essential feature is a personality disorder in which there is resistance to demands for adequate performance in both occupational and social functioning; the resistance is expressed indirectly rather than directly. The consequence is pervasive and persistent social or occupational ineffectiveness, even when more self-assertive and effective behavior is possible. The name of the disorder is based on the assumption that such individuals are passively expressing covert aggression.

Individuals with this disorder habitually resent and oppose demands to increase or maintain a given level of functioning. This occurs most clearly in work situations, but is also evident in social functioning. The resistance is expressed indirectly, through such maneuvers as procrastination, dawdling, stubbornness, intentional inefficiency, and "forgetfulness." For example, when an executive gives a subordinate some material to review for a meeting the next morning, rather than complain that he or she has no time to do the work, the subordinate may misplace or misfile the material and thus attain his or her goal by passively resisting the demand on him or her. Similarly, when an individual always comes late to appointments, promises to help make arrangements for particular events but never does, and keeps "forgetting" to bring important documents to club meetings, he or she is passively resisting demands made on him or her by others.

The individual is ineffective both socially and occupationally because of the passive-resistant behavior. For example, job promotions are not offered because of the individual's intentional inefficiency. A housewife with the disorder fails to do the laundry or to stock the kitchen with food because of procrastination and dawdling.

***

DISORDERS OF IMPULSE CONTROL

This is a residual diagnostic class for disorders of impulse control that are not classified in other categories; e.g., as a substance use disorder or paraphilia.

The essential features of disorders of impulse control are:

1. Failure to resist an impulse, drive, or temptation to perform some act that is harmful to the individual or others. There may or may not be conscious resistance to the impulse. The act may or may not be premeditated or planned.

2. An increasing sense of tension before committing the act.

3. An experience of either pleasure, gratification, or release at the time of committing the act. The act is ego-syntonic in that it is consonant with the immediate conscious wish of the individual. Immediately following the act there may or may not be genuine regret, self-reproach, or guilt.

This class contains five specific categories: pathological gambling, kleptomania, pyromania, intermittent explosive disorder, and isolated explosive disorder. Finally, there is a residual category, atypical impulse control disorder.

312.31 Pathological Gambling

The essential features are a chronic and progressive failure to resist impulses to gamble and gambling behavior that compromises, disrupts, or damages personal, family or vocational pursuits. The gambling preoccupation, urge, and activity increase during periods of stress. Problems that arise as a result of the gambling lead to an intensification of the gambling behavior. Characteristic problems include loss of work due to absences in order to gamble, defaulting on debts and other financial responsibilities, disrupted family relationships, borrowing money from illegal sources, forgery, fraud, embezzlement, and income tax evasion.

Commonly these individuals have the attitude that money causes and is also the solution to all their problems. As the gambling increases, the individual is usually forced to lie in order to obtain money and to continue gambling, but hides the extent of the gambling. There is no serious attempt to budget or save money. When borrowing resources are strained, antisocial behavior in order to obtain money for more gambling is likely. Any criminal behavior—e.g., forgery, embezzlement, or fraud—is typically nonviolent. There is a conscious intent to return or repay the money.

* * *

312.32 Kleptomania

The essential feature is a recurrent failure to resist impulses to steal objects that are not for immediate use or their monetary value; the objects taken are either given away, returned surreptitiously, or kept and hidden. Almost invariably the individual has enough money to pay for the stolen objects. The individual experiences an increasing sense of tension before committing the act and intense gratification while committing it. Although the theft does not occur when immediate arrest is probable (e.g., in full view of a policeman), it is not preplanned, and the chances of apprehension are not fully taken into account. The stealing is done without long-term planning and without assistance from, or collaboration with, others.

The diagnosis is not made if the stealing is due to conduct disorder or antisocial personality disorder.

* * *

312.23 Pyromania

The essential features are recurrent failure to resist impulses to set fires and intense fascination with setting fires and seeing them burn. Before setting the fire, the individual experiences a buildup of tension; and once the fire is underway, he or she experiences intense pleasure or release. Although the fire-setting results from a failure to resist an impulse, there may be considerable advance preparation for starting the fire, and the individual may leave obvious clues.

The diagnosis is not made when fire-setting is due to conduct disorder, anti-

social personality disorder, schizophrenia, or an organic mental disorder.

Individuals with the disorder are often recognized as regular "watchers" at fires in their neighborhoods, frequently set off false alarms, and show interest in fire-fighting paraphernalia. They may be indifferent to the consequences of the fire or property, or they may get satisfaction from the resulting destruction.

* * *

312.34 Intermittent Explosive Disorder

The essential features are several discrete episodes of loss of control of aggressive impulses that result in serious assault or destruction of property. For example, with no or little provocation the individual may suddenly start to hit strangers and throw furniture. The degree of aggressivity expressed during an episode is grossly out of proportion to any precipitating psychosocial stressor. The individual may describe the episodes as "spells" or "attacks." The symptoms appear within minutes or hours and, regardless of duration, remit almost as quickly. Genuine regret or self-reproach at the consequences of the action and the inability to control the aggressive impulse may follow each episode. There are no signs of generalized impulsivity or aggressiveness between the episodes.

The diagnosis is not made if the loss of control is due to schizophrenia, antisocial personality disorder, or conduct disorder. Mild forms of this disorder have, in the past, been called explosive personality.

Prodromal affective or autonomic symptoms may signal an impending episode. During the episode there may be subtle changes in sensorium; and following the episode there may be partial or spotty amnesia. The behavior is usually a surprise to those in the individual's milieu, and even the afflicted individual is often startled by his or her own behavior, sometimes describing the events as resulting from a compelling force beyond his or her control, even though he or she is willing to accept responsibility for his or her actions.

***

312.35   Isolated Explosive Disorder

The essential feature is a single, discrete episode of failure to resist an impulse that led to a single, violent, externally directed act, which had a catastrophic impact on others and for which the available information does not justify the diagnosis of schizophrenia, antisocial personality disorder, or conduct disorder. An ex would be an individual who for no apparent reason suddenly began shooting at total strangers in a fit of rage and then shot himself. In the past this disorder was referred to as "catathymic crisis."

In some cases additional information indicates an underlying psychosis, such as schizophrenia, paranoid type, which would then preempt this diagnosis. As with intermittent explosive disorder, this category is defined behaviorally. In those rare instances in which an underlying organic etiology is revealed, such as a brain tumor, this would be an additional diagnosis, coded on Axis III.

Other features of this disorder are similar to those of intermittent explosive disorder.

31.

David T. Lykken

ANXIETY IN PSYCHOPATHS (SOCIOPATHS)

The concept of the psychopathic personality includes so heterogeneous a group of behavior disorders as to be at least two steps removed from the level of useful psychiatric diagnosis. Sociopathic personality is a more recent designation (1) which refers to a subgroup of these disorders in which the pathognomic characteristics are impulsiveness, antisocial tendencies, immorality, and a seemingly self-destructive failure to modify this pattern of behavior in spite of repeated painful consequences. This category may be regarded as a genus composed of phenotypically similar, but etiologically distinct, subtypes such as the dissocial and the neurotic sociopaths.

A third species has been described (3, 12, 13, 14, 17), which may be called *primary sociopathy,* in which neither neurotic motivations, hereditary taint, nor dissocial nurture seem to be determining factors. Cleckley (3) has reported the chief clinical characteristic of this group as a lack of the normal affective accompaniments of experience. If this observation is correct, it would point the way toward accurate diagnostic isolation of primary sociopathy as well as guiding research into the question of its etiology. Classification according to the presence or absence of defective emotional reactivity, therefore,

From David T. Lykken, "A study of anxiety on the sociopathic personality," *Journal of Abnormal and Social Psychology,* vol. 55, pp. 6–10. Copyright 1957 by the American Psychological Association. Reprinted by permission of the publisher and author.

satisfies one criterion of useful diagnosis in that it shows promise of relationship to the as yet unknown origins of the disorders to be distinguished.

The other requirement for useful diagnosis is that the criteria of classification must be objective. Clinical assessment of the "normality of the affective accompaniments of experience" is subjective and unreliable. In consequence, Cleckley's work has had as yet little real impact on psychiatric practice. By expressing this putative defect of the primary sociopath in terms of the anxiety construct of experimental psychology (18, 19, 20, 21, 22), it becomes susceptible to quantification and empirical test.

An experimental hypothesis may now be formulated. Among persons conventionally diagnosed as psychopathic personality, those who closely resemble the syndrome described by Cleckley are (*a*) clearly defective as compared to normals in their ability to develop (i.e., *condition*) anxiety, in the sense of an anticipatory emotional response to warning signals previously associated with nociceptive stimulation. Persons with such a defect would also be expected to show (*b*) abnormally little *manifest anxiety* in life situations normally conducive to this response, and to be (*c*) relativly incapable of *avoidance learning* under circumstances where such learning can only be effected through the mediation of the anxiety response.

METHOD

The Sample

The extreme heterogeneity, even on the crudest descriptive level, of persons diagnosed as psychopathic personalities in various clinical or institutional settings complicated the selection of an appropriate experimental sample. The institution psychologists were given a list of 14 criteria drawn from Cleckley (3, pp. 355-392) and were asked to compare against these criteria those inmates diagnosed as psychopathic personality. Inmates who, in their opinion, best fitted the Cleckley prototype were listed as candidates for experimental Group I, the primary sociopathic group. Inmates who they felt did *not* meet the criteria in important respects were listed as candidates for experimental Group II, designated as the neurotic sociopathic group. In this selection process, the psychologists were asked to reaffirm the original diagnosis, discarding from consideration for either group those inmates who, in their present opinion, would not be diagnosed as psychopathic personality at all.

A control Group III of 15 "normals," roughly comparable in age, intelligence, and socioeconomic background, was selected from the University General College and a local high school.

Group I, composed of 12 males and 7 females, had a mean age of 21.6 years (*SD* = 4.3), and a mean IQ of 109.2 (*SD* = 10.7). Group II included 13 males and 7 females, had a mean age of 24.5 years (*SD* = 5.4), and a mean IQ of 104.5 (*SD* = 8.8). For the 10 male and 5 female normals, the mean age was 19.07 (*SD* = 3.2), and the mean IQ 100.4 (*SD* = 10.2). None of these group differences were significant.

The Measures and Testing Procedure

It was necessary to do the testing at the several institutions under varying conditions. In all cases, however, the apparatus was arranged on a large table, the experimenter on one side and the subject (*S*) seated comfortably opposite. The *S* was told that he was assisting in a psychological experiment having no bearing on his personal record and that his performance would be treated with strict anonymity. An attempt was made throughout to keep the testing on an informal basis.

As an indicant of manifest anxiety as referred to in hypothesis *b,* an "Anxiety Scale" was constructed expressly for this study to supplement the Taylor scale and Anxiety Index which appear to be more strongly loaded on a factor of neurotic self-description. In this new scale, each of the thirty-three items involves two statements of activities or occurrences, matched for general unpleasantness or undesirability according to a modified Thurstone scaling procedure utilizing 15 college student judges. One activity of each pair is unpleasant, presumably because of its frightening or embarrassing character (e.g., "making a parachute jump" or "knocking over a glass in a restaurant"). The paired activity is intended to be onerous but not frightening (e.g., "digging a big rubbish pit" or "cleaning up a spilled bottle of syrup"). The *S* is required to choose that member of each pair which he would prefer as a lesser of evils. The degree to which the "frightening" alternatives are rejected as interpreted as an index of the extent to which anxiety determines behavior choices within the range of life situations sampled by this test.

The booklet form of the MMPI was used and the answer sheets scored and *K*-corrected in the usual way (10). The Anxiety Index, or AI, was calculated according to the formula given by Welsh (23). The Heineman form (11) of the Taylor scale was given and scored by subtracting the number of "anxiety" items rejected as "least applies to me" from the number endorsed as "most applies to me."

An avoidance learning test was given to determine whether there were group differences in capacity to learn on the basis of anxiety reduction (hypothesis *c*). It involved an elaborate, electrically operated mental maze which the *S* was given 20 trials to learn (the "manifest task"). At each of the 20 choice points in this maze, choice of one of the 4 possible alternatives (always an error alternative) gave an electric shock. It was intended that social and ego rewards should reinforce performance in the manifest task. Performance on the "latent task," which was to avoid the shocked alternatives—to err instead on the unshocked alternatives—was presumably reinforced only through anxiety reduction.

The measure of anxiety conditionability (hypothesis *a*) employed the GSR as the dependent variable. A shocking electrode was attached to *S*'s nondominant hand, the GSR electrodes being already in place on the dominant hand. The *S* was told that after the blindfold had been replaced, he was to sit as quietly as possible for the next 30 to 40 minutes, during which time he would periodically hear a buzzer (which was then demonstrated) and occasionally receive a brief electric shock. When the *S* was seated comfortably and relaxed insofar as possible, the recording apparatus was started and the conditioning series (CS) begun.

Two buzzers were used which were distinguishably different in timbre rather than in pitch, the difference being one not easily labeled (to minimize verbal mediation of a discrimination between them). Buzzer No. 1 was used as the CS and was the only one reinforced; buzzer No. 2 was used to test for generalization effects. In all cases, stimuli of the conditioning series were presented as soon as GSR activity from preceding stimuli had subsided, the intertrial interval being therefore not constant within or between *S*s, but averaging between 20 and 60 seconds. (This method of stimulus timing automatically eliminates temporal conditioning.) When turned on, the buzzers sounded for a period of 5 seconds, controlled by an automatic timer.

The reinforcing stimulus or UnCS was an electric shock from a 700-volt AC supply through two 68,000-ohm series resistors, presented automatically for about 100 milliseconds just before the termination of the CS (buzzer No. 1). The shock was applied between an electrode on the palm of one hand and the GSR *ground* electrode on the palmar tip of the middle finger of the opposite hand. The shock sensation was felt mainly on the richly innervated finger tip and was a decidedly unpleasant stimulus, producing in most cases a pronounced startle reaction and in all cases a strong GSR.

The sequence of trials or stimulus presentations was as follows:

1. To permit the adaptation of unconditioned GSR, to the buzzers themselves, stimuli were first presented without shock reinforcement for a total of 10 trials in the order 2, 1, 2, 1, S, 2, 2, 1, 1, 1, 1. A single preliminary shock was given in the series at the point S, separated by at least 30 seconds from the buzzers occurring before and after it.

2. Seven consecutive shock-reinforced presentations of the CS were given as the conditioning series, followed by four more reinforcements interspersed with four unreinforced trials with buzzer No. 2 in the order 1, 1, 1, 1, 1, 1, 1, 2, 1, 2, 2, 1, 2, 1, 1.

3. A total of 24 extinction trials was then given, the two buzzer stimuli being presented in the order 1, 2, 1, 1, 2, 1, 2, 1, 1, 2, 1, 1, 1, 1, 2, 2, 1, 2, 1, 1, 2, 1, 1, 1. Considering only the CS buzzer No. 1, the series therefore consisted of 6 prereinforcement trials, 11 reinforced conditioning trials, and 16 extinction trials.

Skin resistance was measured by a modification of a circuit suggested by Flanders (6) which passed an electronically regulated constant DC current of 40 microamperes through *S*. The electrodes were curved discs of Monel metal, 15 mm. in diameter, applied to the palmar surface of the distal phalange of the first, second, and third fingers of the same hand. The skin surface was first scrubbed with alcohol and then coated with Sanborn electrode paste. The exosomatic current was applied between the first and third fingers, which were also connected to the push-pull input grids of a Sanborn Model 126 DC amplifier, driving a Sanborn Model 127 recording milliameter. The electrode on the second finger was connected to amplifier and external ground. The instrument was calibrated before each use and provided a linear record of resistance and resistance change, accurate to less than $\pm$ 50 ohms.

All GSRs were recorded in terms of resistance change. A variety of transformations was then applied and tested against the usual criteria of normality of distribution, correlation with basal resistance, and homogeneity of variance across people with respect to several test stimuli (2, 8, 9, 16). The result of this analysis was that each resistance change was expressed as the logarithm of the ratio of the change to the mean resistance change produced by the first six electric shocks. This unit expresses the galvanic CR as a proportion of the individual's UnCR and, for a conditioning study, seems quite appropriate for individual comparisons.

Three GSR indices were derived from the protocols of the conditioning series: (*a*) GSR Reactivity, which is the mean GSR to the CS during the fourth through seventh conditioning trials; (*b*) GSR Conditioning, which is equal to (*a*) minus the mean GSR to the last three preconditioning trials and the last three extinction trials (this index measures essentially the slope of the conditioning curve or the increment actually produced by the reinforced trials); (*c*) GSR Generalization, the ratio of the mean GSR to buzzer No. 2 during early extinction trials 18, 20, 21, 23 to the mean GSR to buzzer No. 1 during trials 17, 19, 22, 24.

The testing sequence was as follows: (*a*) Anxiety scale; (*b*) GSR Conditioning series; (*c*) Avoidance Learning test; (*d*) MMPI (given during the week following the foregoing individual testing); (*e*) Taylor Manifest Anxiety Scale, forced-choice form given later with the MMPI.

RESULTS AND DISCUSSION

Scores on all measures were converted for easier comparison to a standard score form with each distribution having a grand mean of 500 and a standard deviation of

TABLE 31-1
Group Means on All Measures: Significance Tests*

Measure	Group			d-Test prob.†
	I	II	III	
Taylor Scale	471	556	462	.01
Anxiety Index	472	557	464	.01
Anxiety Scale	470	511	529	.05
MMPI *Pd*-Scale	532	547	395	.05
Avoidance Learning	461	501	558	.01
GSR Reactivity	498	494	534	.05
GSR Conditioning	478	483	551	.05
Generalization	473	542	490	—

* All measures converted to a scale having an over-all mean of 500 and *SD* of 100.

† Probabilities given are for significance of largest difference [e.g., III-I for GSR Conditioning]. Significance test was Festinger's distribution-free '*d*' test (5).

100. Group means on all measures, together with significance test results, are given in Table 31-1.

It would clearly be too much to expect of the judgments based upon the Cleckley criteria that they should have perfectly separated the psychopathic sample into a "primary" species in Group I, and a neurotic or dissocial species in Group II. That the separation was reasonably good, however, is supported by the finding that Group II scored significantly higher than the normals on the Taylor scale, a great deal of evidence having accumulated (4, 7, 15) to indicate that this scale is primarily a measure of neurotic maladjustment or neuroticism rather than of anxiety level or anxiety reactivity *per se.* On the MMPI Anxiety Index, which like the Taylor scale is unquestionably polydimensional with a

heavy loading on neuroticism, Group II again has the highest mean, with Group I again only slightly higher than Group III.

In contrast, the Anxiety scale, which was designed for this study and which is not loaded on neuroticism and only negligibly correlated with the Taylor scale or the AI, separated the groups in a different order. On this test, the primary types of Group I show the least anxiety reactivity, significantly less than the normals, with Group II falling in between but rather nearer to the Group III mean. This result appears to support hypothesis *b* of this study, that the subset of primary sociopaths shows abnormally little manifest anxiety, i.e., anxiety reactivity to the real-life anxiety stimuli referred to in the questionnaire.

Both sociopathic groups scored significantly higher than the normals on the *Pd* scale of the MMPI, but this measure, which differentiates at the phenotypic or genus level, does not distinguish between the types or species of sociopathy represented in Groups I and II.

Schedule difficulties unfortunately led to a reduction in the number of *S*s to whom the avoidance learning test could be given. With nearly half of the total group, the available testing time was too short to cover all of the procedures; in such cases the avoidance test, requiring nearly an hour to give, was passed over. Even on the residual sample of 34 *S*s, however, rather clear-cut differences exist. As a crude, overall index of avoidance learning, the avoidance scores (shock errors divided by unshocked errors) were averaged for all but the first of the 20 trials; this is the basis of the mean scores entered under "avoidance" in Table 31-1. The distribution was reversed to make high values represent greater avoidance of the shock. It is impossible, of course, to summarize adequately a complex learning process by a single numerical index of this sort, but in spite of these limitations, it is striking that Group I (primaries) shows the least avoidance as expected, Group II (neurotics) next, and Group III (normals) the most. The Group I versus Group III, and Group II versus Group III differences are significant by Festinger's *d*-test (5), and the actual distribution of scores shows the groups to be remarkably well separated (only 17 per cent overlap between Groups I and III). This result supports hypothesis *c* of this study, that the primary sociopath demonstrates defective avoidance learning.

Results of the GSR Conditioning Series

Of all the tests employed here, principal emphasis should be laid on GSR conditioning. The various difficulties attending the interpretation of GSR data are well known, but one fact stands out with relative certainty: given certain necessary conditions, if an *S* does *not* produce a GSR to a stimulus, one can be sure that he has not "reacted emotionally" to that stimulus.

The two numerical indices which were derived as alternative ways of representing in a single value the conditioning indicated by the GSR protocols (anticipatory GSR to the buzzer after several pairings with shock) have already been described. As shown in Table 31-1, the group means are in the expected order on both indicants, with Group I significantly lower than Group III on GSR Reactivity and GSR Conditioning (.05 level, *d*-test).

A somewhat more meaningful comparison is obtained by contrasting the reactivity by trials for the three groups. Group I shows the least GSR reaction to CS in 14 out of the 16 double trials. Group II is significantly higher (.02 level) than Group I at the end of the extinction trials. The positions of Group II and Group III interchange during the series with Group II beginning to show greater reactivity during the extinction trials, suggesting a perseveration (failure of extinction) of the anxiety response in the neurotic group. This trend was tested for statistical reliability by correlating the differences between Group II and Group III with the ordinal position in the conditioning series at which the difference was taken. The quadrant sign test (24) shows this association to be significant at the .01 level: This result supports hypothesis *a* of this study, that the primary sociopath is defective in his ability to condition the anxiety response.

The generalization scores were leptokurtically distributed, the group differences being determined by a few deviant *S*s. Group II shows the highest mean generalization score, but the differences are not significant.

SUMMARY

Forty-nine diagnosed psychopaths were divided into two groups according to the descriptive criteria of Cleckley. Fifteen normals served as controls. A battery of tests related to anxiety reactivity or anxiety conditionability were administered. As compared with normals, the Cleckley, or "primary" sociopaths, showed significantly less "anxiety" on a questionnaire device, less GSR reactivity to a "conditioned" stimulus associated with shock, and less avoidance of punished responses on a test of avoidance learning. The "neurotic" sociopaths scored significantly higher on the Taylor Anxiety Scale and on the Welsh Anxiety Index.

REFERENCES

1. American Psychiatric Association. *Diagnostic and statistical manual: mental disorders.* Washington, D.C.: A.P.A., 1952.
2. Bitterman, M. E., & Holtzman, W. H. Development of psychiatric screening of flying personnel. III. Conditioning and extinction of the GSR in relation to clinical evi-

dence of anxiety. *USAF School of Aviation Medicine,* 1952, Proj. No. 21-37-002, Rep. No. 3, N. 232 p.

3. Cleckley, H. *The mask of sanity.* (2nd ed.) St. Louis: C. V. Mosby, 1950.

4. Eriksen, C. W., & Davids, A. The meaning and clinical validity of the Taylor Anxiety Scale and the hysteria-psychasthenia scales from the MMPI. *Journal of Abnormal and Social Psychology,* 1955, **50,** 135-137.

5. Festinger, L. The significance of the difference between means without reference to the frequency distribution function. *Psychometrika,* 1945, **11,** 97-105.

6. Flanders, N. A. A circuit for the continuous measurement of palmar resistance. *American Journal of Psychology,* 1953, **66,** 295-299.

7. Franks, C. Conditioning and personality: a study of normal and neurotic subjects. *Journal of Abnormal and Social Psychology,* 1956, **52,** 143-150.

8. Haggard, E. A. Experimental studies in affective processes. II. On the quantification and evaluation of "measured" changes in skin resistance. *Journal of Experimental Psychology,* 1945, **33,** 45-56.

9. Haggard, E. A. On the application of analysis of variance to GSR data. I. The selection of an appropriate measure. *Journal of Experimental Psychology,* 1949, **39,** 378-392.

10. Hathaway, S. R. *Supplementary manual for the MMPI. Part I, the K scale and its use.* New York: Psychological Corp., 1946.

11. Heineman, C. E. A forced choice form of the Taylor Anxiety Scale. *Journal of Consulting Psychology,* 1953, **17,** 447-454.

12. Karpman, B. Psychopathic types: the symptomatic and the ideopathic. *Journal of Criminal Psychopathology,* 1941, **3,** 112-124.

13. Karpman, B. The myth of the psychopathic personality. *American Journal of Psychiatry,* 1948, **104,** 523-534.

14. Karpman, B. Conscience in the psychopath: another version. *American Journal of Orthopsychiatry,* 1948, **18,** 455-491.

15. Kerrick, Jean S. Some correlates of the Taylor Manifest Anxiety Scale. *Journal of Abnormal Social Psychology,* 1955, **50,** 75-77.

16. Lacey, O. L., & Siegel, P. S. An analysis of the unit of measurement of the galvanic skin responses. *Journal of Experimental Psychology,* 1949, **39,** 122-123.

17. Lipman, H. S. Psychopathic behavior in infants and children: a critical survey of existing concepts. *American Journal of Orthopsychiatry,* 1951, **21,** 227-231.

18. May, M. A. Experimentally acquired drives. *Journal of Experimental Psychology,* 1948, **38,** 66-77.

19. Miller, N. E. Studies of fear as an acquirable drive. I. Fear as motivation and fear-reduction as reinforcement in the learning of new responses. *Journal of Experimental Psychology,* 1948, **38,** 89-101.

20. Miller, N. E. Learnable drives and rewards. In S. S. Stevens (Ed.), *Handbook of experimental psychology.* New York: Wiley, 1951. Pp. 435-472.

21. Mowrer, O. H. A stimulus-response analysis of anxiety. *Psychological Review,* 1939, **46,** 553-565.

22. Mowrer, O. H. Anxiety reduction and learning. *Journal of Experimental Psychology,* 1940, **27,** 497-516.

23. Welsh, G. S. An anxiety index and an internalization ratio for the MMPI. *Journal of Consulting Psychology,* 1952, **16,** 65-72.

24. Wilcoxon, F. *Some rapid approximate statistical procedures.* New York: American Cyanamid Co., 1949.

32.

Hervey M. Cleckley

CHARACTERISTICS OF PSYCHOPATHY

We shall list the characteristic points that have emerged. . . .

1. Superficial charm and good "intelligence"
2. Absence of delusions and other signs of irrational thinking.
3. Absence of "nervousness" or psychoneurotic manifestations
4. Unreliability
5. Untruthfulness and insincerity
6. Lack of remorse or shame
7. Inadequately motivated antisocial behavior
8. Poor judgment and failure to learn by experience
9. Pathologic egocentricity and incapacity for love
10. General poverty in major affective reactions
11. Specific loss of insight
12. Unresponsiveness in general interpersonal relations
13. Fantastic and uninviting behavior with drink and sometimes without
14. Suicide rarely carried out
15. Sex life impersonal, trivial, and poorly integrated
16. Failure to follow any life plan

From Cleckley, Hervey: *The Mask of Sanity,* ed. 5, St. Louis, 1976, The C.V. Mosby Co.

Reprinted from *International Encyclopedia of Social Sciences,* Vol. 13, pp. 113-114; 118. New York: The Macmillan Company and The Free Press, 1968.

CHARACTERISTICS OF THE PSYCHOPATH

The psychopath does not give the impression, even on careful examination, of being mentally ill, handicapped, or emotionally disturbed. Nor does he, typically, show any attitude or outlook that would indicate he lacked conscience or had chosen rebellious or antisocial aims. His reasoning is excellent. What he tells of his allegiances, aims, and understanding indicates that he is normal, reliable, and utterly sincere. Despite this, his past conduct and what will emerge in the future are very likely to bear out the truth of Lindner's statement that here we encounter "the most expensive and most destructive of all known forms of aberrant behavior."

The typical psychopath is a person who appears to have at least average, and often unusual, ability and who seems to be clearly aware of the amenities and to affirm the moral code. Frequently he demonstrates superior intelligence and other assets and is likely to succeed brilliantly for a time in work, in studies, and in all his human relations. But inevitably, and repeatedly, he fails, losing his job, alienating his friends, perhaps losing his wife, and children. It is difficult to account for these failures. Seldom can one find adequate motivation to explain why a person has, in the midst of success, grossly shirked his immediate responsibilities, and perhaps abandoned his work, at the behest of impulses that seem to the observer no more compelling than a trivial whim. However effective he may show himself to be over a limited period, when given sufficient time, he proves himself inadequate. His failures deprive him of what he tells us are his chief objectives and also bring hardship, shame, and disaster to his wife, children, parents, and all those closely connected with him (Cleckley 1941).

In addition to such relatively passive types of failure most fully developed psychopaths also commit aggressive antisocial acts. They forge checks, swindle, steal repeatedly, lightly indulge in bigamy, and show little or 'no compunction about their sexual behavior, regardless of the consequences. Some psychopaths who have attracted wide public attention committed murder or other shocking felonies, usually with little or no provocation, often without comprehensible motivation (Cleckley 1941). The majority, despite many conflicts with the law, appear to avoid crimes sufficiently grave to result in their removal from society for long prison terms. The psychopath may repeatedly receive punishment that would be likely to cause an ordinary person to mend his ways. But he appears to learn nothing important from experience. He is quite familiar with the correct ethical criteria, claims allegiance to such criteria, and can formulate in words excellent rules and plans for himself to follow. He does not seem to be lying as simply as the ordinary liar, whose motives are usually comprehensible. Sometimes the psychopath does not seem to be aware that he is lying or even to grasp emotionally the essence of falsehood and how falsehood differs from truth. Sometimes such people seem to mean for the moment to do what they promise so convincingly, but the resolution passes almost as the words are spoken.

The psychopath expresses normal reactions (love, loyalty, gratitude, etc.) with a most impressive appearance of sincerity and depth, but the emotional ties and the attitudes he professes fail to deter him from deeds that continually contradict his verbal claims. There appears to be in him a strange lack of insight or, perhaps more accurately, a total lack of one of the dimensions that constitute insight. After innumerable lies that he knows have been detected, he still speaks confidently of giving his word of honor, apparently assured that this will settle the issue immediately and absolutely. Although he may demonstrate, over considerable periods, adequate general abilities, or even extraordinary talent, he always throws away what he has gained, what he insists are his chief objectives. No adequate motivation can be found or even imagined to account for his conduct. Conceivable temptations are often extremely trivial, but they inevitably evoke actions that lead to the loss of fortune and the respect of friends, the destruction of marriage, and imprisonment or confinement in a psychiatric institution. The psychopath seems to be almost totally immune to real remorse or deep feelings of guilt or shame.

Etiology: Masked Personality Disorder. Is there some defect or disorder within the psychopath that causes him to lack the capacity to feel guilt? If so, this hypothetical deficiency seems also to interfere with his reacting to, and pursuing consistently, the normal goals of life. And he seems to lack the ability to participate adequately in the major emotional experiences of life.

The typical psychopath's excellent intellectual abilities and his freedom from the manifestations of ordinary psychiatric disorder make it difficult to believe that deep within him may be concealed a deficiency that leads not to conflict or unconscious guilt but, instead, makes him incapable of feeling normal remorse and of appreciating adequately the major emotional experiences of human life (Cleckley 1941).

The outer characteristics of the psychopath strongly indicate warmth of feeling, kindness, sincerity, pride, courage, a deep sense of honor, and genuine capacities for love and loyalty. Such an outer appearance could be the result of excellent peripheral function in the organism, which gives strong and convincing promise of robust health within and makes it difficult to suspect that there may be a central and very serious inner defect. The psychopath's conduct, however, is consistent with a serious defect in the very qualities for which his superficial aspect and verbal performance give such rich promise. The peripheral mechanisms, one might say, of his functional entity are undamaged and operate well. They demonstrate technical intelligence and convincingly mimic the expression of normal inner experience. But the implied inner experience, the glowingly promised emotional participation in life, is not there.

If we compare speech disorders with personality disorders, an analogy emerges that may be helpful in conveying this concept. When the outer physiologic apparatus involved in the production of speech is damaged, the disability is overt, and its cause is usually easy to understand. When the tongue is mutilated or its motor nerve damaged, there is likely to be gross difficulty in enunciating words and perhaps even in moving the tongue itself. Efforts to speak may give rise only to inarticulate sounds that communicate nothing. The inner use of language, however, and its meaning to the person who has suffered the injury, is preserved intact. In contrast with dysarthria, in which the peripheral apparatus of speech is affected, let us consider the aphasias which are caused by lesions more centrally located in the brain. In these the outer mechanisms of speech are preserved.

Let us consider particularly semantic aphasia as described by Henry Head (1926). In this very deep-seated disorder of speech, words are clearly and accurately enunciated, and often complete and grammatical sentences are fluently spoken. These utterances, however, have little or no meaning. They are not related, within the person, to ideas or feelings that they seem to indicate and seem intended to convey. The words of this ostensible communication are, in a very important sense, not really words but only a mimicry of words, produced mechanically by the peripheral mechanisms of speech that have become isolated from the inner source that gives rise to thought, feeling, and intention. Despite this more or less reflex simulation of real speech, a deep loss has occurred that prevents the person from using language inwardly to think.

If the psychopath has a profound and centrally located defect that prevents him from participating significantly in man's deepest fulfillments and joys, is it not possible that this inability to participate might contribute to restlessness and boredom? And might this not in turn prompt him to indulge in unprofitable or damaging indiscretions and destructive behavior that would not be particularly tempting to others who are devoting their attention to major goals and responding to major fulfillments? This hypothesis—of an extremely serious central pathology or a biological deficit concealed by misleading peripheral functions, by what one might call an impressive "mask of sanity"—cannot be established by objective evidence at present but is, in many important respects, consistent with the psychopath's behavior (Cleckley 1941).

REFERENCES

Cleckley, H. *The mask of sanity.* St. Louis: C. V. Mosby, 1941, 5th ed., 1976.

Head, H. *Aphasia and kindred disorders of speech.* 2 Vols. Cambridge: Cambridge University Press, 1926.

33.

Robert D. Hare

RESEARCH IN PSYCHOPATHY

PSYCHOMETRIC STUDIES OF PSYCHOPATHY

While psychopaths as a group receive at least average scores on global measures of intelligence, more research is needed in which the dimensions of intellect are tapped.

A variety of psychometric devices has been used to study the personality of the psychopath. In general, the results have been reasonably consistent with clinical accounts of psychopathy.

* * *

CORTICAL CORRELATES OF PSYCHOPATHY

In spite of their limitations, the EEG studies of psychopathy have produced rather consistent results. One finding, that the widespread slow-wave activity often found in psychopaths bears a certain resemblance to the EEG patterns usually found in children, has led to a *cortical immaturity* hypothesis of psychopathy. A second hypothesis, based on the presence of localized EEG abnormalities, is that psychopathy is associated with a defect or malfunction of certain brain mechanisms concerned with emotional activity and the regulation of behavior. Finally, it has been suggested that psychopathy may be related to a lowered state of cortical excitability

---

From *Psychopathy: Theory and Research* by Robert D. Hare. Copyright ©1970 John Wiley & Sons, Inc., Publishers. Reprinted by permission of John Wiley & Sons, Inc.

and to the attenuation of sensory input, particularly input that would ordinarily have disturbing consequences.

* * *

AUTONOMIC CORRELATES OF PSYCHOPATHY

Although the number of relevant studies is not very large, several tentative conclusions about the relationship between psychopathy and autonomic functioning are possible.

During periods of relative quiescence psychopathic subjects tend to be hypoactive on several indices of autonomic activity, including resting level of skin conductance and autonomic variability ("spontaneous" fluctuations in electrodermal and cardiac activity). Although these findings must be interpreted with caution, they are at least consistent with most clinical statements about the psychopath's general lack of anxiety, guilt, and emotional "tension."

The situation with respect to autonomic responsibility is more complex. Nevertheless, it appears that psychopaths may give relatively small electrodermal responses to "lie detection" situations and to situations that would ordinarily be considered stressful. They may also exhibit rapid electrodermal recovery at the termination of stressful situations.

Finally, there is some evidence (although scant) that psychopaths give a blood pressure response to injection of mecholyl that is indicative of rapid homeostatic recovery and a tendency to become aggressive under stress.

* * *

PSYCHOPATHY AND THE CONCEPT OF AROUSAL

Several lines of research and theory suggest that psychopathy is related to cortical underarousal. As a result, the psychopath actively seeks stimulation with arousing or "exciting" qualities. In the process, however, he may be unaware of, or inattentive to, many of the subtle cues required for the guidance of behavior and for adequate social functioning.

* * *

PSYCHOPATHY AND LEARNING

It appears that psychopaths do not develop conditioned fear responses readily. As a result, they find it difficult to learn responses that are motivated by fear and reinforced by fear reduction. The fact that their behavior appears to be neither motivated nor guided by the possibility of unpleasant consequences, particularly when the temporal relationship between behavior and its consequences is relatively great, might be interpreted in this way. There is some evidence that psychopaths are also less influenced than are normal persons by the relationship between past events and the consequences of their present behavior.

Psychopaths perform well on verbal conditioning and rote-learning tasks, as well as on tasks that are not dependent on acquired fear. Any differences between their performance and that of normal persons on these tasks probably result from a lack of motivation and from the use of inappropriate incentives instead of from an inability to learn the task. Several considerations lead to the prediction that when these tasks are complex, involving many competing responses, or when they must be performed under stressful conditions, psychopaths may actually perform them better than would normal individuals.

* * *

PSYCHOPATHY AND SOCIALIZATION

Although many psychopaths come from broken, impoverished homes and have experienced some form of parental loss and rejection, it appears that one of the best predictors of adult psychopathy is having a father who was himself psychopathic, alcoholic, or antisocial.

Several theorists have suggested that the psychopath is pathologically unable to role-play and that his early experiences lead him to learn a social facade with no moral or emotional constraints other than what looks good to others.

The psychopath's apparent lack of guilt for transgressions and his low resistance to temptation are interpreted as the result of parental discipline and punishment that are considerably delayed and perhaps administered inconsistently.

It has also been suggested that the psychopath's inability to delay gratification may be related to a family background in which impulse-control training was generally poor and in which parental models themselves displayed little capacity to delay.

* * *

THE MODIFICATION OF PSYCHOPATHIC BEHAVIOR

The traditional therapeutic procedures have not been effective in changing the behavior of psychopaths. A possible exception to this generally pessimistic outcome is the use of some sort of "therapeutic community" in which an attempt is made to improve the psychopath's interpersonal relations and to restructure his social environment. Evidence also exists that the apparent persistence and immutability of the psychopath's behavior may be somewhat overemphasized, and that, in some cases, a gradual reduction in the severity of antisocial behavior occurs with age.

CHAPTER VIII

Substance Use Disorders

Addiction
Alcoholism: Definition and Research

The American Medical Association's *Manual on Alcoholism* defines alcoholism as *"an illness characterized by preoccupation with alcohol and loss of control over its consumption such as to lead usually to intoxication if drinking is begun; by chronicity; by progression; and by tendency toward relapse. It is typically associated with physical disability and impaired emotional, occupational, and/or social adjustments as a direct consequence of persistent and excessive use"* (1967, p. 6). Keller's definition of alcoholism is "a chronic disease manifested by repeated implicative drinking so as to cause injury to the drinker's health or to his social or economic functioning" (1960, p. 133).

The etiology of alcoholism is unknown, but consensus favors a multiple-cause theory (Alexander, 1963), linking it to one or a number of the following possibilities: biological, psychological, and social factors, with the psychological considered as of primary importance. As a progressive disease that is chronic in nature, alcoholism is associated with liver, kidney, stomach, nervous, and mental disorders, including brain damage. Alcohol, as a drug, with its direct action "on the individual nerve cell seems to be narcotic in nature with consequent depression of its function" (Courville, 1966, p. 85). The narcotic effects compare with those of anoxia, the need for oxygen. But according to Forbes and Duncan (1957), alcohol is also a stressing agent.

According to the U. S. Department of Health, Education, and Welfare (1966), using the Jellinek Estimation Formula, 4½ percent of Americans 21 years of age and over are alcoholic. Holmes, reporting for the National Council on Alcoholism, Inc. (1962), estimates 258,000 alcoholics in New York City. Lindesmith (1968), citing statistics from the Federal Bureau of Investigation in the *Uniform Crime Reports* for the year 1966, notes that drug arrests have increased from 3,400 in 1947 to 60,000 in 1966.

The addictive alcoholics, those persons psychologically and physically dependent upon alcohol as a drug, represent a large percentage of alcoholics according to Catanzaro (1968); the same is true of nonaddictive alcoholics, that is, those dependent upon alcohol as a drug psychologically but who lack a physical dependence and experience no withdrawal symptoms. With time, however, they too may become addictive alcoholics.

Bowman and Jellinek (1942) also have drawn distinctions between primary and secondary addiction, secondary addiction being the physical dependence upon the drug, while primary addiction is considered as the immediate, psychological dependence devoid of the physiological component. Thompson (1956) rejects the concept of primary alcoholism. Furthermore, Jellinek (1960) identifies four species of alcoholism: (*a*) *alpha,* the "purely psychological *continual* dependence or reliance upon the effect of alcohol to relieve bodily or emotional pain"; (*b*) *beta,* that form of alcoholism resulting in polyneuropathy, gastritis and cirrhosis of the liver, yet without physical or psychological alcoholic dependence; (*c*) *gamma,* that species of alcoholism wherein is found: "(1) acquired increased tissue tolerance to alcohol, (2) adaptive cell metabolism . . . , (3) withdrawal symptoms and 'craving,' that is, physical dependence, and (4) loss of control" (1960, p. 37); (*d*) *delta,* the inability to abstain added to the previous three species of alcoholism.

In an earlier study on alcoholism, Jellinek (1952) cites four phases of alcohol addiction: (1) *prealcoholic symptomatic phase:* social drinking experienced as a rewarding relief of tension; (2) *prodromal phase:* characterized by blackouts, alcoholic palimpsests, surreptitious drinking, preoccupation with alcohol, avid drinking, guilt feelings associated with drink-induced behavior, heavy drinking; (3) *crucial phase:* identified by loss of control (or physical need) of the drug, rationalization of behavior, loss of self-esteem, grandiose behavior, withdrawal from society, aggressive behavior, persistent remorse, periods of total abstinence, changing patterns of drink, dropping of friends and jobs, loss of outside interests, reinterpretation of interpersonal relations, self-pity, change of family habits, resentment, neglect of proper nutrition, decrease in sexual desire, alcoholic jealousy, habitual matutinal drinking, intensive evening drinking; and (4) *chronic phase:* ethical deterioration, thought impairment, alcoholic psychoses, drinking with social inferiors, resorting to substitutes (bay rum, rubbing alcohol), loss of tolerance for alcohol, fears (indefinable), tremors, psychomotor inhibition, obsessive drinking, development of vague religious ideas, failure of the rationalization system.

Researching alcoholic psychoses in New York state, Malzberg (1960) found it rare in the under 20-year-old bracket, and rising in males to a rate of first admissions of 27.8 at ages 45 to 49; for females to 8.9 at ages 40 to 44. The male rate (11.6) not only exceeds the female (3.3) rate of first admissions, but also increases with age. Education is also a factor, rates being highest for those lacking any education (14.4) or with only a secondary education (14.5), and lowest for the college educated (4.0).

On a twin study project regarding heredity factors underlying the use of alcohol, Partanen and his associates found that "normal drinking as well as abstinence and heavy use show considerable heredity variation. . . . On the other hand, the social consequences and arrests for drunkenness . . . do not show any hereditary determination" (1966, p. 19).

In the classic experiments of the influence of alcohol on experimentally induced neuroses in cats, Masserman and Yum (1946) report a preference for alcohol in drinking water by neurotic cats. To varying degrees, adaptive patterns were disintegrated, especially the more recent and complex one, whereas normal cats on recovery from intoxication showed complete functional restitution with but little alcoholic habituation and no preference for the drug, the inference of the experiments being that under conflict situations, alcohol has a drive reducing effect, alleviating the drive of anxiety.

Experimenting on the effect of stress on the consumption of alcohol and reserpine on rats, Casey's (1960) findings supported those of Masserman and Yum. Casey favors a "reinforcement theory interpretation in terms of a stress produced anxiety drive which is reduced by the effect of consumed alcohol, thereby reinforcing alcohol-drinking behavior" (1960, pp. 213-214). With the continued absence of stress, behavior (based on the drive of anxiety) is eventually extinguished.

Personality of Alcoholics

In her research on alcoholic personalities from the orientation of intelligence, Pollmer (1965) found the lower the intelligence of a given group of alcoholics, the more numerous were their stable personality characteristics, the same holding true of parental home environment. "The higher the intelligence of subjects, the more pronounced and, compared to the total environment, the more exclusively similar their problem areas seemed to be. . . . The lower the intelligence of subjects, the more their total home environments seemed to be alike, and the more diffuse the border of their particular problem area" (1965, p. 154). Furthermore, alcoholics of higher intelligence had a higher rate of cure as well as treatment of a relatively shorter duration. Moreover, they blamed others for their predicament.

Fox (1967) notes that alcoholism tends to run in families, with 52 percent of alcoholics with at least one parent an alcoholic. She thinks this fact may reflect an inadequate family life with poor models with whom to identify. In his study of the alcoholic personality, Tähkä (1966) found that subjects' mothers had a tendency to insecurity concerning their roles as women, and married men over whom they could feel superior. They narcissistically used their sons by way of overcompensation for inferiority regarding their sex. Subjects were submissive to and ambivalently dependent upon the mother who was the dominant parent.

On a comparison of male with female cases of alcoholism, Karpman (1957) noted that males report alcohol as a secondary factor (emotional maladjustment being the primary) while females attribute their alcoholism to external circumstances, unaware of their emotional maladjustment. Hence the male's insight as to his alcoholic problem is markedly greater than the female's. Females deplore their weakness in succumbing to alcohol, while men accept their weakness. Women compensate for this deficiency by resorting to culture and aesthetic interests.

Therapy

As yet, no cure of alcoholism is known though a variety of approaches are helpful. Among some common ones are: (1) *disulfiram* (Antabuse) and calcium carbimide (Temposil), drugs which interfere with alcohol metabolism, making the individual sick; (2) *hypnosis,* used to alter attitude toward alcohol; (3) *conditioned reflex therapy,* used to create an aversion to drink; (4) *Alcoholics Anonymous,* a social-spiritual approach; (5) *group therapy* and *psychodrama,* for gaining self-insight; (6) *psychoanalysis and psychotherapy* (*individual*), valuable only after sobriety for gaining a better perspective of self; (7) *team psychotherapy and counseling* entailing psychologists, psychiatrists, psychiatric social workers and clergy working conjointly where possible; and (8) *"halfway" houses.*

In addition to endorsing Alcoholics Anonymous as a successful mode of therapy, Williams (1959) recommends a nutritional approach to therapy, one consisting of good amounts of high quality protein (plus vitamins and minerals but avoidance of refined foods) so that the alcoholic's improved physical condition will enhance his ability to cope with the problem of abstinence. Tracing alcoholism to the immaturity of personality, Thompson sees Alcoholics Anonymous as an excellent vehicle for building character in the alcoholic. Even Cain, whose hostile attitude toward A.A. is uninhibited, recommends: "To *anyone* who is having trouble with alcohol I say: try A.A. first; it's the answer for most people" (1964, p. 72).

The most desirable approach to alcoholism is preventive treatment (Block, 1967); however, in the case of alcoholism, when signs of diagnostic significance manifest themselves, the disorder is already in an advanced state. According to Hayman (1966), only 5 to 10 percent of alcoholics are in a psychiatric condition that is amenable to recovery. Conducting experimental research on 178 alcoholic patients at Winter VA Hospital, Wallerstein and his colleagues (1957) report that Antabuse precipitated psychotic reactions in borderline schizophrenia and depressed patients, whereas the same type patients benefited from milieu therapy owing to increased personal relationships with their therapists. Although the schizoid type responded to hypnotherapy, he failed to improve on hospital discharge. For the masochistic individual, conditioned reflex therapy was contraindicated, while the oppressed patient responded to it. Mullan and Sanguiliano (1966) found the most satisfactory therapy to consist of a separate treatment unit, group treatment, vocational counseling, and rehabilitation.

Following the lead of Hollingshead and Redlich (1958), Schmidt and his collaborators (1968) corroborate the findings of the former in regard to alcoholics, their hypothesis being that a patient's "social class is related to all aspects of treatment for alcoholics, that is, to sources of referral, diagnoses, prognoses, and types and duration of treatment including treatment personnel involved" (1968, p. 19).

Theories of Alcoholism and Drug Addiction

Levy (1958), whose neo-Freudian views identify the function of alcohol as residing in its toxic effect, theorizes that it consists of "discharge" and "narcotizing" functions, and the toxic effects possess symbolic meaning. The list of functions are: (1) *discharge* (cathartic value; blocks anxiety, guilt, and shame); (2) *narcotizing* (sleep value in dealing with tensions); (3) *symbolic;* (4) *infantomimetic* (orally gratifying); (5) *masochistic;* (6) *hostility* (release of rage); (7) *homosexuality* (discharge, sublimation, and denial of homosexual strivings); (8) *identification* and *identity* (parental identification).

Button (1956) proceeding also from neo-Freudian principles, seeks to isolate dynamic variables peculiar to alcoholics, and presents a schematic outline giving a theoretical basis of the genesis and development of alcoholism.

Conger (1951) and Kingham (1958) developed learning theory approaches to alcoholism. The former, applying Dollard and Miller views on drive and reinforcement, concluded that the alleviation of anxiety through alcohol consumption acts as a reinforcement and eventually becomes habit forming. The latter hypothesizes that alcoholism develops from predisposing conditions: (1) desire to escape reality; (2) uncontrollable blitz drinking pattern; and (3) drive-cue-response-reinforcement learning paradigm enacted with the "blitz drinking pattern reducing the disturbance in psychological homeostasis." More than resolving unconscious conflicts is needed for successful treatment; total abstinence is necessary to extinguish the blitz drinking pattern.

Storm and Smart (1965), building on the findings of Overton (1964) and Otis (1964) that animals acquiring habits when drugged fail to show a transfer to a nondrugged state (the inverse also being true), verified this hypothesis in reference to alcohol. They found that the longer the span of intoxication, the greater the dissociation (difference) between the intoxicated and sober condition. Accordingly, the sober-state learned behavior fails to generalize to states of inebriation. Thus learning theory rather than physiological response accounts for loss of control and "blackouts" (dissociation). These findings imply that "if dissociation is important, then treatment should be given to alcoholics while alcohol is present in the organism and be directed to conditioning the patient to respond to the cues of increased intoxication by not drinking" (p. 115).

According to Hebb (1966), addiction is theorized as an *artificial hunger* and as a *homeostatic process* that occurs in two stages: an intermediate stage of "physiological dependence," followed by "addiction proper." The two may occur concurrently, but usually happen consecutively. The first stage, the physiological modification of physical tissues, leads to the need for the drug in order to maintain stable, homeostatic functioning; while the second results from a learning process.

Devoting many years to the study of opiate addiction, Lindesmith (1965, 1968) defines addiction as "that behavior which is distinguished primarily by an intense, conscious desire for the drug, and by a tendency to relapse, evidently caused by the persistence of attitudes established in the early stages of addiction" (1968, p. 64). Lindesmith attributes drug addiction, not to the pleasure or euphoria derived from the use of it, but from the recognition and identification of it with withdrawal distress. Relief from withdrawal distress (once physical distress has been established) accounts for addiction.

Convinced of multiple causality in drug addiction, Ausubel (1958, 1961) hypothesizes that both internal factors such as hereditary susceptibility and external factors such as the social environment conducive to the use of the drug and its availability explain narcotic addiction. Inasmuch as physiological addiction and withdrawal symptoms can be readily eliminated by a hospital stay for a relatively brief period of time, and inasmuch as addicts return to the drug soon on release from a hospital cure of physical dependence, more than an explanation of physical addiction is necessary. Two important types of addiction are (1) maturational deficiency, the failure of the personality to mature and actualize himself (motivationally, vocationally, etc.); and (2) reactive addiction, the need for an outlet (especially to rebel and defy the norms of conventional society). A third or miscellaneous type is an escape from anxiety or depression.

34.

American Psychiatric Association

FEATURES OF SUBSTANCE USE DISORDERS

CLASSES OF SUBSTANCES

Five classes of substances are associated with both abuse and dependence: alcohol, barbiturates or similarly acting sedatives or hypnotics, opioids, amphetamines or similarly acting sympathomimetics, and cannabis. Some of these substances are used medically, such as the amphetamines, barbiturates, and opioids. Three classes of substances are associated only with abuse because physiological dependence has not been demonstrated: cocaine, phencyclidine (PCP) or similarly acting arylcyclohexylamines, and hallucinogens. Finally, one substance, tobacco, is associated only with dependence, since heavy use of tobacco itself is not associated with impairment in social or occupational functioning (though the reaction of others to the tobacco use may cause difficulties).

* * *

SUBSTANCE-INDUCED ORGANIC MENTAL DISORDERS

This section of the classification deals with the various organic brain syndromes caused by the direct effects on the nervous system of various substances. They are distinguished from the substance use disorders that refer to the behavior associated with taking substances that affect the central nervous system. In most cases the diagnosis of these organic mental

From Task Force on Nomenclature and Statistics of the American Psychiatric Association, *Diagnostic and Statistical Manual of Mental Disorders, Third Edition.* American Psychiatric Association, 1980.

disorders will be made in individuals who also have a substance use disorder.

This section includes those substance-induced organic mental disorders caused by the ten classes of substances that most commonly are taken nonmedicinally to alter mood or behavior: alcohol, barbiturates or similarly acting sedatives or hypnotics, opioids, cocaine, amphetamines or similarly acting sympathomimetics, phencyclidine (PCP) or similarly acting arylcyclohexylamines, hallucinogens, cannabis, tobacco, and caffeine. Although some of these substances also have a legitimate medicinal purpose, they may under unsupervised circumstances cause organic mental disorders. In addition, there is a residual class for organic mental disorders caused by other or unknown substance.

* * *

ALCOHOL ORGANIC MENTAL DISORDERS

This section includes the following organic mental disorders attributed to the ingestion of alcohol: alcohol intoxication, alcohol idiosyncratic intoxication, alcohol withdrawal, alcohol withdrawal delirium, alcohol hallucinosis, alcohol amnestic disorder, and dementia associated with alcoholism.

Although ICD-9-CM has a category for alcoholic jealousy, the literature does not provide sufficient evidence to support the existence of this syndrome as an independent entity. The concept "alcoholic jealousy" can be expressed in DSM-III terms by a diagnosis of alcohol dependence and an additional diagnosis of a paranoid disorder.

303.00 Alcohol Intoxication

The essential feature is maladaptive behavior due to the recent ingestion of alcohol. This may include aggressiveness, impaired judgment, and other manifestations of impaired social or occupational functioning. Characteristic physiological signs include flushed face, slurred speech, unsteady gait, nystagmus, and incoordination. Characteristic psychological signs include loquacity, impaired attention, irritability, euphoria, depression, and emotional lability.

The diagnosis is not made when there is evidence that the amount of alcohol ingested was insufficient to cause intoxication in most people, as in alcohol idiosyncratic intoxication.

Associated Features. The individual's usual behavior may be accentuated or altered. For example, an individual who tends to be somewhat suspicious may, under the influence of alcohol, become markedly paranoid. On the other hand, individuals who are ordinarily withdrawn and uncomfortable in social situations may become exceptionally convivial.

Alcohol intoxication is sometimes associated with an amnesia for the events that occurred during the course of the intoxication ("blackouts").

* * *

291.40 Alcohol Idiosyncratic Intoxication

The essential feature is a marked behavioral change—usually to aggressiveness—that is due to the recent ingestion of an amount of alcohol insufficient to induce intoxication in most people. There is usually subsequent amnesia for the period of intoxication. The behavior is atypical of

the person when not drinking—for example, a shy, retiring, mild-mannered person may, after one weak drink, become belligerent and assaultive. During the episode the individual seems out of contact with others.

This disorder has also been called "pathological intoxication."

* * *

291.80 Alcohol Withdrawal

The essential features are certain characteristic symptoms such as a coarse tremor of the hands, tongue, and eyelids, nausea and vomiting, malaise or weakness, autonomic hyperactivity (such as tachycardia, sweating, and elevated blood pressure), anxiety, depressed mood or irritability, and orthostatic hypotension, that follow within several hours cessation of or reduction in alcohol ingestion by an individual who has been drinking alcohol for several days or longer. The diagnosis is not made if the disturbance is alcohol withdrawal delirium.

* * *

291.00 Alcohol Withdrawal Delirium

The essential feature is a delirium that is due to recent cessation of or reduction in alcohol consumption. Autonomic hyperactivity, such as tachycardia and sweating, and elevated blood pressure, is present. Delusions, vivid hallucinations, and agitated behavior usually occur. Hallucinations, when present, are usually visual, but may occur in other sensory modalities.

This disorder has been called "delirium tremens."

* * *

291.30 Alcohol Hallucinosis

The essential feature is an organic hallucinosis with vivid auditory hallucinations following cessation of or reduction in alcohol ingestion by an individual who apparently has alcohol dependence. The hallucinations are usually voices, and less commonly unformed sounds such as hissing or buzzing. Onset may accompany a gradual decrease in blood alcohol levels toward the end of an extended period of intoxication; but it most often occurs soon after cessation of drinking, usually within the first 48 hours, although occasionally somewhat later.

In the majority of cases, the content of the hallucinations is unpleasant and disturbing. However, the hallucinatory content may be benign, leaving the individual undisturbed. The voices may address the individual directly, but more often they discuss him or her in the third person. When the voices are threatening, the individual may act to defend himself or herself by calling on the police for protection, or arming against invaders. The actions of the individual are practically never the result of the hallucinations' commanding the individual to act in a certain way, but rather are motivated by the desire to avoid disgrace, injury, or other consequences of what the voices threaten.

* * *

BARBITURATE OR SIMILARLY ACTING SEDATIVE OR HYPNOTIC ORGANIC MENTAL DISORDERS

Included in this classification are disorders induced by barbiturates and similarly acting sedatives and hypnotics.

The common minor tranquilizers are the benzodiazepines, such as chlordiazepoxide, diazepam, and oxazepam. Common hypnotics include ethchlorvynol, flurazepam, glutethimide, methyprylon, chlo-

ral hydrate, paraldehyde, and methaqualone.

Although these substances differ widely in their rates of absorption, metabolism, distribution in the body, and likelihood of producing intoxication and withdrawal, at some dose and at some duration of use they are all capable of producing signs and symptoms of intoxication and withdrawal that are essentially the same as those produced by the barbiturates. For this reason the barbiturates are the prototype for this group of substances.

Substances in this class are usually taken orally in the form of pills or capsules.

Because of the great pharmacological differences in the substances covered in this section and of the wide individual variation in responses to them, specific doses for specific withdrawal syndromes are not listed.

* * *

305.40 Barbiturate or Similarly Acting Sedative or Hypnotic Intoxication

The essential and associated features are virtually identical with those of alcohol intoxication. The only exception is that there is no syndrome of idiosyncratic intoxication. Differences that may occur between alcohol intoxication and intoxication by this class of substances are most likely due to differences in the personalities of the individuals who become intoxicated and in the settings in which the intoxications occur. For example, the settings in which alcohol intoxication is apt to occur probably account for the greater likelihood that it will be accompanied by displays of aggression or violence, compared with intoxication by this class of substances.

* * *

OPIOID ORGANIC MENTAL DISORDERS

This group includes natural opioids, such as heroin and morphine, and synthetics with morphine-like action, such as meperidine and methadone. These substances are taken either orally, intravenously, intranasally, or subcutaneously ("skin popping").

Although methadone is included in this class, individuals properly supervised in a methadone maintenance program should not develop any of the opioid organic mental disorders. When they do meet the criteria for this diagnosis, this indicates that there has been nonmedical use of methadone, in which case the appropriate diagnosis should be made.

305.50   Opioid intoxication

The essential features are specific neurological and psychological signs and maladaptive behavioral effects due to the recent use of an opioid.

Psychological signs commonly present include euphoria or dysphoria, apathy, and psychomotor retardation.

Pupillary constriction is always present (or dilation due to anoxia from a severe overdose). Other neurological signs commonly observed are drowsiness, slurred speech, and impairment in attention and memory.

The maladaptive behavioral effects may include impaired judgment, interference with social or occupational functioning, and failure to meet responsibilities.

***

COCAINE ORGANIC MENTAL DISORDER

Cocaine is usually applied to the mucous membrane of the nose by sniffing the crystalline flakes or powder. Intravenous administration is sometimes preferred, most commonly by opioid users who mix cocaine with heroin, a combination referred to as "speedball." Cocaine "base" is smoked in pipes or cigarettes, and has effects similar to cocaine taken intravenously.

There is apparently no withdrawal syndrome.

305.60   Cocaine Intoxication

The essential features are specific psychological and physical symptoms and maladaptive behavioral effects due to the recent use of cocaine. The psychological symptoms typically include a sense of well-being and confidence, with heightened awareness of sensory input. There may be psychomotor agitation, elation, grandiosity, loquacity, pacing about, and pressured speech. The physical symptoms include tachycardia, pupillary dilation, elevated blood pressure, perspiration or chills, nausea and vomiting, anorexia, and insomnia. The psychological and physical symptoms begin no longer than one hour after administration, and may occur within a few minutes.

The maladaptive behavioral effects may include fighting, impaired judgment, and interference with social or occupational functioning.

***

AMPHETAMINE OR SIMILARLY ACTING SYMPATHOMIMETIC ORGANIC MENTAL DISORDERS

This group includes all of the substances of the substituted phenylethylamine structure, such as amphetamine, dextroamphetamine, and methamphetamine ("speed"), and those with structures differing from the substituted phenylethylamine that have amphetamine-like action, such as methylphenidate or some substances used as appetite suppressants ("diet pills"). These substances are taken orally or intravenously.

305.70 Amphetamine or Similarly Acting Sympathomimetic Intoxication

The essential features are specific psychological and physical symptoms and maladaptive behavioral effects due to the recent use of amphetamine or similarly acting sympathomimetic substances.

All of the features (essential, associated, course, complications, and differential diagnosis) are virtually identical with those of cocaine intoxication. One exception is that delusions or hallucinations are always transient in cocaine intoxication, whereas in the intoxication due to amphetamine or similarly acting sympathomimetic substances, they may persist beyond the time of direct substance effect. When this occurs, the syndrome is then referred to as an amphetamine or similarly acting sympathomimetic delusional disorder. The other exception is that on occasion an intoxication from this class of substances may develop into a delirium.

***

PHENCYCLIDINE (PCP) OR SIMILARLY ACTING ARYLCYCLOHEXYLAMINE ORGANIC MENTAL DISORDERS

This group of substances includes phencyclidine and similarly acting compounds such as ketamine (Ketalar) and the thiophene analogue of phencyclidne (TCP). These substances can be taken orally or parenterally or can be smoked or inhaled. Within this class of substances, phencyclidine is the most commonly used. It is sold on the street under a variety of names, the most common of which are PCP, PeaCe Pill, angel dust, THC, and crystal.

305.90 Phencyclidine or Similarly Acting Arylcyclohexylamine Intoxication

The essential features are specific physical and psychological symptoms associated with maladaptive behavioral effects due to the recent use of phencyclidine or a similarly acting arylcyclohexylamine. The symptoms begin within one hour of oral ingestion of the substance; if smoked, insufflated, or taken intravenously, onset may be within five minutes. The physical symptoms include vertical and horizontal nystagmus, elevated blood pressure, numbness or diminished responsiveness to pain, ataxia, dysarthria, and diaphoresis or increased salivation. Psychological symptoms include euphoria, psychomotor agitation, anxiety, emotional lability, grandiosity, a sensation of slowed time, and synesthesias (e.g., seeing colors when a loud sound occurs).

The effects of this class of substance are generally dose related, although there is great variability among individuals. The effects usually range from a mild, "floaty" euphoria and numbness after ingesting less than 5 mg of phencyclidine, to muscle rigidity, hypertension, and a noncommunicative state following a dose of 5-10 mg, and coma, convulsions, and possible death after a dose of 20 mg or more of phencyclidine.

***

HALLUCINOGEN ORGANIC MENTAL DISORDERS

This group includes two types of substances, both of which have hallucinogenic properties: substances structurally related to 5-hydroxytryptamine (e.g., lysergic acid diethylamine [LSD] and dimethyltryptamine [DMT]), and substances related to catecholamine (e.g., mescaline). These substances are taken orally.

305.30 Hallucinogen Hallucinosis

The essential features are characteristic perceptual changes, physical symptoms, and maladaptive behavioral effects due to recent hallucinogen ingestion. The perceptual changes include subjective intensification of perceptions, depersonalization, derealization, illusions, hallucinations, or synthesias (e.g., seeing colors when a loud sound occurs). These occur in a state of full wakefulness and alertness. There may be hyperacusis and overattention to detail. The illusions may involve distortions of the individual's body image. The hallucinations are usually visual, often of geometric forms and figures, sometimes of persons and objects. More rarely, auditory and tactile hallucinations are experienced.

Physical symptoms include pupillary dilation, tachycardia, sweating, palpitations, blurring of vision, tremors, and incoordination.

The maladaptive behavioral effects may take the form of marked anxiety or depression, fear of losing one's mind, ideas of reference, paranoid ideation, impaired judgment, interference with social or occupational functioning, or failure to meet responsibilities.

This category is called an hallucinosis even though it is recognized that frequently, with low doses, the perceptual changes do not include hallucinations.

***

CANNABIS ORGANIC MENTAL DISORDERS

This group includes all substances with psychoactive properties from the cannabis plant as well as chemically similar synthetic substances. In the United States the most commonly used substances are marijuana, hashish, and, occasionally, purified delta-9-tetrahydrocannabinol (THC). These substances are smoked or taken orally in a number of forms, including mixed with food.

305.20 Cannabis Intoxication

The essential features are specific psychological and physical symptoms and maladaptive behavioral effects due to the recent use of cannabis.

The psychological symptoms include euphoria, subjective intensification of perceptions, the sensation of slowed time (five minutes may seem like an hour), preoccupation with auditory or visual stimuli, and apathy. The euphoria may be expressed as a marked sense of well-being and relaxation. The individual may be indifferent to his or her surroundings.

Tachycardia is invariably present, although it is not as prominent when the individual is a chronic user of cannabis. Conjunctival injection is almost always present. Other physical symptoms include increased appetite, often for "junk food," and a dry mouth.

Maladaptive behavioral effects include paranoid ideation, panic attacks, and dysphoric affects. The individual may believe that he or she is dying or going crazy. (Some believe that adverse reactions are more likely to occur in individuals with rigid personalities, in individuals with a history of having had a psychotic disorder, or in circumstances considered to be threatening, such as the possibility of a police raid.) Other maladaptive behavioral effects include impaired judgment and interference with social or occupational functioning.

***

TOBACCO ORGANIC MENTAL DISORDER

292.00   Tobacco Withdrawal

The essential feature is a characteristic withdrawal syndrome due to recent cessation of or reduction in tobacco use that has been at least moderate in duration and amount. The syndrome includes craving for tobacco, irritability, anxiety, difficulty concentrating, restlessness, headache, drowsiness, and gastrointestinal disturbances. It is assumed that this syndrome is caused by nicotine withdrawal, since nicotine is the major pharmacologically active ingredient in tobacco.

Withdrawal does not occur with all smokers; but in many heavy cigarette smokers, changes in mood and performance that are probably related to withdrawal can be detected within 2 hours after the last cigarette. The sense of craving appears to reach a peak within the first 24 hours after the last cigarette, thereafter gradually declining over a few days to several weeks. In any given case it is difficult to distinguish between a withdrawal effect and the emergence of psychological traits that were suppressed, controlled, or altered by the effects of nicotine.

***

CAFFEINE ORGANIC MENTAL DISORDER

The consumption of caffeine, especially in the form of coffee, tea, cola, chocolate, and cocoa, is ubiquitous in the United States. Other common sources of caffeine are over-the-counter analgesics, "cold" preparations, and stimulants.

305.90   Caffeine Intoxication

The essential features are such characteristic effects of the recent use of caffeine-containing substances as restlessness, nervousness, excitement, insomnia, flushed face, diuresis, and gastrointestinal complaints. These symptoms appear in some individuals following ingestion of as little as 250 mg of caffeine per day, whereas others require much larger doses. At levels of more than 1 g/day there may be muscle twitchings, periods of inexhaustibility, psychomotor agitation, rambling flow of thought and speech, and cardiac arrhythmia. Mild sensory disturbances such as ringing in the ears and flashes of light have been reported at higher doses. With doses exceeding 10 g of caffeine, grand mal seizures and respiratory failure may result in death.

This disorder has been called caffeinism.

A rough guide to calculating caffeine intake follows: coffee contains 100-150 mg of caffeine per cup; tea is about half as strong; a glass of cola is about a third as strong. Most caffeine-containing prescriptions and over-the-counter medications are one-third to one-half the strength of a cup of coffee. Two notable exceptions are migraine medications and over-the-counter stimulants that contain 100 mg per tablet.

Complications. Complications include developing or aggravating gastrointestinal and heart disease. Caffeine can produce epigastric distress and, occasionally, peptic ulcer and hematemesis. In addition to arrhythmia with extremely high dosages, the substance can cause marked hypotension and circulatory failure.

Differential diagnosis. Manic episodes, panic disorder or generalized anxiety disorder can cause a clinical picture similar to that of caffeine intoxication. The temporal relationship of the symptoms to caffeine use establishes the diagnosis.

35.

Elvin Morton Jellinek

PHASES OF ALCOHOL ADDICTION

THE CHART OF ALCOHOL ADDICTION

The course of alcohol addiction is represented graphically in Figure 35-1. The diagram is based on an analysis of more than two thousand drinking histories of male alcohol addicts. Not all symptoms shown in the diagram occur necessarily in all alcohol addicts, nor do they occur in every addict in the same sequence. The "phases" and the sequences of symptoms within the phases are characteristic, however, of the great majority of alcohol addicts and represent what may be called the average trend.

For alcoholic women the "phases" are not as clear-cut as in men and the development is frequently more rapid.

The "phases" vary in their duration according to individual characteristics and environmental factors. The "lengths" of the different phases on the diagram do not indicate differences in duration, but are determined by the number of symptoms which have to be shown in any given phases.

The chart of the phases of alcohol addiction serves as the basis of description, and the differences between addictive and nonaddictive alcoholics are indicated in the text.

The Prealcoholic Symptomatic Phase

The very beginning of the use of alcoholic beverages is always socially moti-

Reprinted by permission from *Quarterly Journal of Studies on Alcohol,* **13,** 673-684, 1952. Copyright by Journal of Studies on Alcohol, Inc., New Brunswick, N.J.

vated in the prospective addictive and non-addictive alcoholic. In contrast to the average social drinker, however, the prospective alcoholic (together with the occasional symptomatic excessive drinker) soon experiences a rewarding relief in the drinking situation. The relief is strongly marked in his case because either his tensions are much greater than in other members of his social circle, or he has not learned to handle those tensions as others do.

Initially this drinker ascribes his relief to the situation rather than to the drinking and he seeks therefore those situations in which incidental drinking will occur. Sooner or later, of course, he becomes aware of the contingency between relief and drinking.

In the beginning he seeks this relief occasionally only, but in the course of 6 months to 2 years his tolerance for tension decreases to such a degree that he takes recourse to alcoholic relief practically daily.

Nevertheless his drinking does not result in overt intoxication, but he reaches toward the evening a stage of surcease from emotional stress. Even in the absence of intoxication this involves fairly heavy drinking, particularly in comparison to the use of alcoholic beverages by other members of his circle. The drinking is, nevertheless, not conspicuous either to his associates or to himself.

After a certain time an increase in alcohol tolerance may be noticed, i.e., the drinker requires a somewhat larger amount of alcohol than formerly in order to reach the desired stage of sedation.

This type of drinking behavior may last

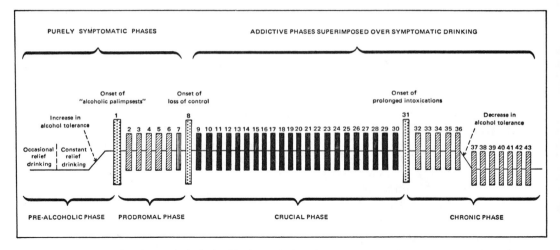

FIGURE 35-1.—*The Phases of Alcohol Addiction*. (The large bars denote the onset of major symptoms which initiate phases. The short bars denote the onset of symptoms within a phase. Reference to the numbering of the symptoms is made in the text.)

from several months to 2 years according to circumstances and may be designated as the prealcoholic phase, which is divided into stages of occasional relief-drinking and constant relief-drinking.

The Prodromal Phase

The sudden onset of behavior resembling the "blackouts" in anoxemia marks the beginning of the prodromal phase of alcohol addiction. The drinker who may have had not more than 50 to 60 g. of absolute alcohol and who is not showing any signs of intoxication may carry on a reasonable conversation or may go through quite elaborate activities without a trace of memory the next day, although sometimes one or two minor details may be hazily remembered. This amnesia, which is not connected with loss of consciousness, has been called by Bonhoeffer the "alcoholic palimpsests," with reference to old Roman manuscripts superimposed over an incompletely erased manuscript.

"Alcoholic palimpsests" (1)[1] may occur on rare occasions in an average drinker when he drinks intoxicating amounts in a state of physical or emotional exhaustion. Nonaddictive alcoholics, of course, also may experience "palimpsests," but infrequently and only following rather marked intoxication. Thus, the frequency of "palimpsests" and their occurrence after medium alcohol intake are characteristic of the prospective alcohol addict.

This would suggest heightened susceptibility to alcohol in the prospective addict. Such a susceptibility may be psychologically or physiologically determined. The analogy with the "blackouts" of anoxemia is tempting. Of course, an insufficient oxygen supply cannot be assumed, but a malutilization of oxygen may be involved. The present status of the knowledge of alcoholism does not permit of more than vague conjectures which, nevertheless, may constitute bases for experimental hypotheses.

The onset of "alcoholic palimpsests" is followed (in some instances preceded) by the onset of drinking behaviors which indicate that, for this drinker, beer, wine and

---

[1] The italicized figures in parentheses following the designations of the individual symptoms represent their order as given in Figure 35-1.

spirits have practically ceased to be beverages and have become sources of a drug which he "needs." Some of these behaviors imply that this drinker has some vague realization that he drinks differently from others.

Surreptitious drinking (2) is one of these behaviors. At social gatherings the drinker seeks occasions for having a few drinks unknown to others, as he fears that if it were known that he drinks more than the others he would be misjudged: those to whom drinking is only a custom or a small pleasure would not understand that because he is different from them alcohol is for him a necessity, although he is not a drunkard.

Preoccupation with alcohol (3) is further evidence of this "need." When he prepares to go to a social gathering his first thought is whether there will be sufficient alcohol for his requirements, and he has several drinks in anticipation of a possible shortage.

Because of this increasing dependence upon alcohol, the onset of *avid drinking* (4) (gulping of the first or first two drinks) occurs at this time.

As the drinker realizes, at last vaguely, that his drinking is outside of the ordinary, he develops *guilt feelings about his drinking behavior* (5) and because of this he begins to *avoid reference to alcohol* (6) in conversation.

These behaviors, together with an *increasing frequency of "alcoholic palimpsests"* (7), foreshadow the development of alcohol addiction; they are premonitory signs, and this period may be called the prodromal phase of alcohol addiction.

The consumption of alcoholic beverages in the prodromal phase is "heavy," but not conspicuous, as it does not lead to marked, overt intoxications. The effect is that the prospective addict reaches towards evening a state which may be designated as emotional anesthesia.

Nevertheless, this condition requires drinking well beyond the ordinary usage. The drinking is on a level which may begin to interfere with metabolic and nervous processes as evidenced by the frequent "alcoholic palimpsests."

The "covering-up" which is shown by the drinker in this stage is the first sign that his drinking might separate him from society, although initially the drinking may have served as a technique to overcome some lack of social integration.

As in the prodromal phase rationalizations of the drinking behavior are not strong and there is some insight as well as fear of possible consequences, it is feasible to intercept incipient alcohol addiction at this stage. In the United States of America, the publicity given to the prodromal symptoms begins to bring prospective alcoholics to clinics as well as to groups of Alcoholics Anonymous.

It goes without saying that even at this stage the only possible modus for this type of drinker is total abstinence.

The prodromal period may last anywhere from 6 months to 4 or 5 years according to the physical and psychological make-up of the drinker, his family ties, vocational relations, general interests, and so forth. The prodromal phase ends and the crucial or acute phase begins with the onset of loss of control, which is the critical symptom of alcohol addiction.

The Crucial Phase

Loss of control (8) means that any drinking of alcohol starts a chain reaction which is felt by the drinker as a physical demand for alcohol. This state, possibly a conversion phenomenon, may take hours or weeks for its full development; it lasts until the drinker is too intoxicated or too sick to ingest more alcohol. The physical discomfort following this drinking behavior is contrary to the object of the drinker, which is merely to feel "different." As a matter of fact, the bout may not even be started by any individual need of the moment, but by a "social drink."

After recovery from the intoxication, it is not the "loss of control"—i.e., the physical demand, apparent or real—which leads to a new bout after several days or several weeks; the renewal of drinking is set off by the original psychological conflicts or by a simple social situation which involves drinking.

The "loss of control" is effective after the individual has started drinking, but it does not give rise to the beginning of a new drinking bout. The drinker has lost the ability to control the quantity once he has started, but he still can control whether he will drink on any given occasion or not. This is evidenced in the fact that after the onset of "loss of control" the drinker can go through a period of voluntary abstinence ("going on the water wagon").

The question of why the drinker returns to drinking after repeated disastrous experiences is often raised. Although he will not admit it, the alcohol addict believes that he has lost his will power and that he can and must regain it. He is not aware that he has undergone a process which makes it impossible for him to control his alcohol intake. To "master his will" becomes a matter of the greatest importance to him. When tensions rise, "a drink" is the natural remedy for him and he is convinced that this time it will be one or two drinks only.

Practically simultaneously with the onset of "loss of control" the alcohol addict begins to *rationalize his drinking behavior* (9): he produces the well-known alcoholic "alibis." He finds explanations which convince him that he did not lose control, but that he had a good reason to get intoxicated and that in the absence of such reasons he is able to handle alcohol as well as anybody else. These rationalizations are needed primarily for himself and only secondarily for his family and associates. The rationalizations make it possible for him to continue with his drinking, and this is of the greatest importance to him as he knows no alternative for handling his problems.

This is the beginning of an entire "system of rationalizations" which progressively spreads to every aspect of his life. While this system largely originates in inner needs, it also serves to counter *social pressures* (10) which arise at the time of the "loss of control." At this time, of course, the drinking behavior becomes conspicuous, and the parents, wife, friends and employer may begin to reprove and warn the drinker.

In spite of all the rationalizations there is a marked loss of self-esteem, and this of course demands compensations which in a certain sense are also rationalizations. One way of compensation is the *grandiose behavior* (11) which the addict begins to display at this time. Extravagant expenditures and grandiloquence convince him that he is not as bad as he had thought at times.

The rationalization system gives rise to another system, namely the "system of isolation." The rationalizations quite naturally lead to the idea that the fault lies not within himself but in others, and this results in a progressive withdrawal from the social environment. The first sign of this attitude is a *marked aggressive behavior* (12).

Inevitably, this latter behavior generates prodromal guilt. While even in the prodromal period remorse about the drinking arose from time to time, now *persistent remorse* (13) arises, and this added tension is a further source of drinking.

In compliance with social pressures the addict now goes on *periods of total abstinence* (14). There is, however, another modus of control of drinking which arises out of the rationalizations of the addict. He believes that his trouble arises from his not drinking the right kind of beverages or not in the right way. He now attempts to control his troubles by *changing the pattern of his drinking (15)*, by setting up rules about not drinking before a certain hour of the day, in certain places only, and so forth.

The strain of the struggle increases his hostility towards his environment and he begins to *drop friends (16)* and *quit jobs (17)*. It goes without saying that some associates drop him and that he loses some jobs, but more frequently he takes the initiative as an anticipatory defense.

The isolation becomes more pronounced as his entire *behavior becomes alcohol-centered (18)*, i.e., he begins to be concerned about how activities might interfere with his drinking instead of how his drinking may affect his activities. This, of course, involves a more marked egocentric outlook which leads to more rationalizations and more isolation. There ensues a *loss of outside interests (19)* and a *reinterpretation of interpersonal relations (20)* coupled with *marked self-pity (21)*. The isolation and rationalizations have increased by this time in intensity and find their expression either in contemplated or actual *geographic escape (22)*.

Under the impact of these events, a *change in family habits (23)* occurs. The wife and children, who may have had good social activities, may withdraw for fear of embarrassment or, quite contrarily, they may suddenly begin intensive outside activities in order to escape from the home environment. This and other events lead to the onset of *unreasonable resentments (24)* in the alcohol addict.

The predominance of concern with alcohol induces the addict to *protect his supply (25)*, i.e., to lay in a large stock of alcoholic beverages, hidden in the most unthought-of places. A fear of being deprived of the most necessary substance for his living is expressed in this behavior.

Neglect of proper nutrition (26) aggravates the beginnings of the effects of heavy drinking on the organism, and frequently the *first hospitalization (27)* for some alcoholic complaint occurs at this time.

One of the frequent organic effects is a *decrease of the sexual drive (28)* which increases hostility towards the wife and is rationalized into her extramarital sex activities, which gives rise to the well-known *alcoholic jealousy (29)*.

By this time remorse, resentment, struggle between alcoholic needs and duties, loss of self-esteem, and doubts and false reassurance have so disorganized the addict that he cannot start the day without steadying himself with alcohol immediately after arising or even before getting out of bed. This is the beginning of *regular matutinal drinking (30)*, which previously had occurred on rare occasions only.

This behavior terminates the crucial phase and foreshadows the beginnings of the chronic phase.

During the crucial phase intoxication is the rule, but it is limited to the evening hours. For the most part of this phase drinking begins sometime in the afternoon and by the evening intoxication is reached. It should be noted that the "physical demand" involved in the "loss of control" results in continual rather than continuous drinking. Particularly the "matutinal drink" which occurs toward the end of the crucial phase shows the continual pattern. The first drink at rising, let us say at 7 a.m., if followed by another drink at 10 or 11 a.m., and another drink around 1 p.m., while the more intensive drinking hardly starts before 5 p.m.

Throughout, the crucial phase presents a great struggle of the addict against the complete loss of social footing. Occasionally the aftereffects of the evening's intoxication cause some loss of time, but generally the addict succeeds in looking after his job, although he neglects his family. He makes a particularly strong effort to avoid intoxication during the day. Progressively, however, his social motivations weaken more and more, and the "morning drink" jeopardizes his effort to comply with his vocational duties as this effort involves a conscious resistance against the apparent or real "physical demand" for alcohol.

The onset of the "loss of control" is the beginning of the "disease process" of alcohol addiction which is superimposed over the excessive symptomatic drinking. Progressively, this disease process undermines the morale and the physical resistance of the addict.

The Chronic Phase

The increasingly dominating role of alcohol, and the struggle against the "demand" set up by matutinal drinking, at last break down the resistance of the addict and he finds himself for the first time intoxicated in the daytime and on a weekday and continues in that state for several days until he is entirely incapacitated. This is the onset of *prolonged intoxications (31)*, referred to in the vernacular as "benders."

This latter drink behavior meets with such unanimous social rejection that it involves a grave social risk. Only an originally psychopathic personality or a person who has later in life undergone a psychopathological process would expose himself to that risk.

These long-drawn-out bouts commonly bring about *marked ethical deterioration (32)* and *impairment of thinking (33)* which, however, are not irreversible. True *alcoholic psychoses (34)* may occur at this time, but in not more than 10 per cent of all alcoholics.

The loss of morale is so heightened that the addict *drinks with persons far below his social level (35)* in preference to his usual associates—perhaps as an opportunity to appear superior—and, if nothing else is available, he will *take recourse to "technical products" (36)* such as bay rum or rubbing alcohol.

A *loss of alcohol tolerance (37)* is commonly noted at this time. Half of the previously required amount of alcohol may be sufficient to bring about a stuporous state.

Indefinable fears (38) and *tremors (39)* become persistent. Sporadically these symptoms occur also during the crucial phase, but in the chronic phase they are present as soon as alcohol disappears from the organism. In consequence the addict "controls" the symptoms through alcohol. The same is true of *psychomotor inhibition (40)*, the inability to initiate a simple mechanical act—such as winding a watch—in the absence of alcohol.

The need to control these symptoms of drinking exceeds the need of relieving the original underlying symptoms of the personality conflict, and the *drinking takes on an obsessive character (41)*.

In many addicts, approximately 60 per cent, some *vague religious desires develop (42)* as the rationalizations become weaker. Finally, in the course of the frequently prolonged intoxications, the rationalizations become so frequently and so mercilessly tested against reality that the entire *rationalization system fails (43)* and the addict admits defeat. He now becomes spontaneously accessible to treatment. Nevertheless, his obsessive drinking continues as he does not see a way out.

Formerly it was thought that the addict must reach this stage of utter defeat in order to be treated successfully. Clinical experience has shown, however, that this "defeat" can be induced long before it would occur of itself and that even incipient alcoholism can be intercepted. As the latter can be easily recognized it is possible to tackle the problem from the preventive angle.

THE "ALCOHOLIC PERSONALITY"

The aggressions, feelings of guilt, remorse, resentments, withdrawal, etc., which develop in the phases of alcohol addiction, are largely consequences of the excessive drinking, but at the same time they constitute sources of more excessive drinking.

In addition to relieving, through alcohol, symptoms of an underlying personality conflict, the addict now tends to relieve, through further drinking, the stresses created by his drinking behavior.

By and large, these reactions to excessive drinking—which have quite a neurotic appearance—give the impression of an "alcoholic personality," although they are secondary behaviors superimposed over a large variety of personality types which have a few traits in common, in particular a low capacity for coping with tensions. There does not emerge, however, any specific personality trait or physical characteristic which inevitably would lead to excessive symptomatic drinking. Apart from psychological and possibly physical liabilities, there must be a constellation of social and economic factors which facilitate the development of addictive and nonaddictive alcoholism in a susceptible terrain.

THE NONADDICTIVE ALCOHOLIC

Some differences between the nonaddictive alcoholic and the alcohol addict have been stated passim. These differences may be recapitulated and elaborated, and additional differential features may be considered.

The main difference may be readily visualized by erasing the large bars of the diagram (see Figure 35-1). This results in a diagram which suggests a progressive exacerbation of the use of alcohol for symptom relief and of the social and health conse-

quences incumbent upon such use, but without any clear-cut phases.

The prealcoholic phase is the same for the nonaddictive alcoholic as for the alcohol addict, i.e., he progresses from occasional to constant relief of individual symptoms through alcohol.

The behaviors which denote that alcohol has become a drug rather than an ingredient of a beverage (symptoms 2 to 6) occur also in the nonaddictive drinker, but, as mentioned before, the "alcoholic palimpsests" occur rarely and only after overt intoxication.

"Loss of control" is not experienced by the nonaddictive alcoholic; and this is the main differentiating criterion between the two categories of alcoholics. Initially, of course, it could not be said whether the drinker had yet reached the crucial phase, but after 10 or 12 years of heavy drinking without "loss of control," while symptoms 2 to 6 were persistent and "palimpsests" were rare and did not occur after medium alcohol intake, the differential diagnosis is rather safe.

The absence of "loss of control" has many involvements. First of all, as there is no inability to stop drinking within a given situation there is no need to rationalize the inability. Nevertheless, rationalizations are developed for justifying the excessive use of alcohol and some neglect of the family attendant upon such use. Likewise, there is no need to change the pattern of drinking, which in the addict is an attempt to overcome the "loss of control." Periods of total abstinence, however, occur as a response to social pressure.

On the other hand, there is the same tendency toward isolation as in the addict, but the social repercussions are much less marked as the nonaddictive alcoholic can avoid drunken behavior whenever the social situation requires it.

The effects of prolonged heavy drinking on the organism may occur in the nonaddictive alcoholic too; even delirium tremens may develop. The libido may be diminished and "alcoholic jealousy" may result.

Generally, there is a tendency toward a progressive dominance of alcohol resulting in greater psychological and bodily effects. In the absence of any grave initial psychopathy, however, the symptoms of the chronic phase as seen in addicts do not develop in the nonaddictive alcoholic. In the presence of grave underlying psychopathies a deteriorative process is speeded up by habitual alcoholic excess, and such a nonaddictive drinker may slide to the bottom of society.

TYPES OF ALCOHOLISM

Alpha alcoholism represents a *purely* psychological *continual* dependence or reliance upon the effect of alcohol to relieve bodily or emotional pain. The drinking is "undisciplined" in the sense that it contravenes such rules as society tacitly agrees upon—such as time, occasion, locale, amount and effect of drinking—*but does not lead to "loss of control" or "inability to abstain."* The damage caused by this species of alcoholism may be restricted to the disturbance of interpersonal relations. There may also be interference with the family budget, occasional absenteeism from work and decreased productivity, and some of the nutritional deficiencies of alcoholism, but not the disturbances due to withdrawal of alcohol. *Nor are there any signs of a progressive process.*

The relief of bodily pain or emotional disturbance implies an underlying illness and thus the "undisciplined" use of alcoholic beverages may be regarded as a symptom of the pathological conditions which it relieves. This species of alcoholism cannot be regarded as an illness per se.

Of course, it is quite possible that in many instances alpha alcoholism may develop into gamma alcoholism, i.e., that it may often be a developmental stage. On the other hand, it is well known that this species of alcoholism may be seen in a drinking career of 30 or 40 years without any signs of progression. When we speak here of alpha alcoholism we mean this latter "pure culture" but not the developmental stage of gamma alcoholism.

Alpha alcoholism as described here is sometimes called problem drinking, but that expression just as frequently includes physical dependence upon alcohol. The terms problem drinking and problem drinker will not be used in the present study.

Beta alcoholism is that species of alcoholism in which such alcoholic complications as polyneuropathy, gastritis and cirrhosis of the liver may occur without either physical or psychological dependence upon alcohol. The incentive to the heavy drinking that leads to such complications may be the custom of a certain social group in conjunction with poor nutritional habits. The damage in this instance is of course the nutritional deficiency diseases, but impaired family budget and lowered productivity as well as a curtailed life span may also occur. Withdrawal symptoms, on the other hand, do not emerge.

Beta alcoholism too may develop into gamma or delta alcoholism, but such a transition is less likely than in the instance of alpha alcoholism.

Gamma alcoholism means that species of alcoholism in which (*1*) acquired increased tissue tolerance to alcohol, (*2*) adaptive cell metabolism (see below), (*3*) withdrawal symptoms and "craving," i.e.,

---

From Elvin Morton Jellinek, *The disease concept of alcoholism.* New Haven: Hillhouse Press, 1960. Pp. 36-39. Reprinted by permission.

physical dependence, and (4) loss of control are involved. In gamma alcoholism there is a definite progression from psychological to physical dependence and marked behavior changes such as have been described previously (Jellinek, 1946 and 1952). Alpha and beta alcoholism, as already noted, may develop under given conditions into gamma alcoholism.

This species produces the greatest and most serious kinds of damage. The loss of control, of course, impairs interpersonal relations to the highest degree. The damage to health in general and to financial and social standing are also more prominent than in other species of alcoholism.

Gamma alcoholism is apparently (but not with certainty) the *predominating* species of alcoholism in the United States and Canada, as well as in other Anglo-Saxon countries. It is what members of Alcoholics Anonymous recognize as alcoholism to the exclusion of all other species. Of course they use loss of control and "craving" as the criteria par excellence but these necessarily involve the other characteristics of gamma alcoholism mentioned above. As I have said before, Alcoholics Anonymous have naturally created the picture of alcoholism in their own image, although at least 10 to 15 per cent of their membership are probably specimens of alpha alcoholism who conform in their language to the A.A. standards. I base this statement on the fact that in a sample of slightly over 2,000 A.A. members I have found 13 per cent who never experienced loss of control. More likely than not only a small percentage of those with alpha alcoholism would seek the help of Alcoholics Anonymous, and almost none of those with beta alcoholism. The latter may be seen most frequently in general hospitals.

In spite of the respect and admiration to which Alcoholics Anonymous have a claim on account of their great achievements, there is every reason why the student of alcoholism should emancipate himself from accepting the exclusiveness of the picture of alcoholism as propounded by Alcoholics Anonymous.

Delta alcoholism shows the first three characteristics of gamma alcoholism as well as a less marked form of the fourth characteristic—that is, instead of loss of control there is inability to abstain. In contrast to gamma alcoholism, there is no ability to "go on the water wagon" for even a day or two without the manifestation of withdrawal symptoms; the ability to control the amount of intake on any given occasion, however, remains intact. The incentive to high intake may be found in the general acceptance of the society to which the drinker belongs, while pre-alcoholic psychological vulnerability, more often than not, may be of a low degree. This species of alcoholism and its underlying drinking pattern have been sufficiently described in connection with the *predominant* species of alcoholism ("inveterate drinking") in France and some other countries with a large wine consumption. For reasons discussed in that chapter, delta alcoholism would rarely be seen in Alcoholics Anonymous, since the alcoholic afflicted with this species of alcoholism does not go through the distressing social and psychological experiences of the gamma alcoholic and manifests only a few of the behavior changes of the latter.

There are, of course, many other species of alcoholism—if it is defined as any drinking that causes any damage—and all the remaining 19 letters of the Greek and if necessary other alphabets are available for labeling them.

Among these other species is periodic alcoholism, which in Europe and Latin America is designated as dipsomania, a term in disuse in North America. We may denote it as *Epsilon alcoholism* but it will be neither described nor defined here, as it seems to be the least known species of alcoholism. In the course of their periodic bouts, epsilon alcoholics may cause serious damage. I should like to point out that in the last 20 or 25 years a phenomenon which may be called pseudoperiodic alcoholism has turned up. It would appear that some gamma alcoholics who have not benefited to the full extent from the A.A. program or from therapy in clinics or by private psychiatrists are able to resist drinking for 3, 6 or 12 months, but then find no other solution than intoxication, after which they remorsefully return to "sobriety."

Other species of alcoholism (accepting the criterion of damage through drinking) are, of course, "explosive drinking" as well as what the French call "alcoolisation," i.e., the undermining of health and curtailing of the life span (to the exclusion of other "alcoholic complications" and physical or psychological dependence).

Then there is the excessive weekend drinking which follows a cultural pattern and causes damage through rowdiness, absenteeism and impairment of the family budget. Still other species cause damage, for instance, "fiesta drinking" and occasional drinking that causes accidents. I do not propose to list, describe or discuss all these species of alcoholism, but should like to point out that the student of the problems of alcohol cannot afford to overlook these behaviors, whether or not he is inclined to designate them as species of alcoholism.

REFERENCES

Jellinek, E. M. Phases in the drinking history of alcoholics. *Quarterly Journal of Studies on Alcohol,* 1946, **7**, 1-88.

Jellinek, E. M. Phases of alcohol addiction. *Quarterly Journal of Studies on Alcohol,* 1952, **13**, 673-684.

36.

William McCord and Joan McCord

CAUSES OF ALCOHOLISM

We have pointed to numerous conditions that appear to compose the causes of alcoholism. In attempting to make a coherent theory out of the many significant relationships we have found, we have centered on three types of external pressures: family background, cultural pressure, and the adult situation. The interaction of these environmental pressures with personality structure can perhaps best be summarized in the model presented in this reading.

_____

From *Origins of Alcoholism* by William McCord and Joan McCord. Copyright, 1960, Leland Stanford Junior University. Used with permission of Stanford University Press.

Three qualifications to this model must be stated. First, it may well be that future research will uncover a set of variables even more directly relevant to alcoholism. An investigation of the very first years of life, for example, might demonstrate that various experiences are of critical importance; or, perhaps, more subtle metabolic tests might reveal some type of biochemical deficiency that is related to the causation of addiction. We cannot maintain, therefore, that the model exhausts the theoretical possibilities. Second, it is clear that the factors summarized in the following pages are not necessarily independent.

Certain negative factors "go together"— ambivalent mothers, for example, were often deviant in behavior, were often married to rejecting husbands, and were often involved in intense familial conflicts. To treat these factors as independent "causes" of alcoholism is, to some extent, arbitrary. Third, some of the elements in this model are frankly speculative—we lack information on the unconscious needs of the prealcoholic in childhood and we lack information on his adult experiences and responses. Thus, while the model seems to be a reasonable extrapolation of our empirical results, it goes beyond the material and attempts to explain why certain childhood experiences are statistically associated with adult behavior.

Let us now examine the reasons for including these factors in the theoretical scheme:

1. *Family Background: General Stress.* The potential alcoholic had undergone a variety of frustrating experiences: he was more likely to have suffered from various neurological disorders; more likely to have been raised in a family disrupted by a high degree of conflict and basic disagreement; and more likely to have been reared in a family characterized by incest and illegitimacy. We can assume that these influences create a high level of stress and insecurity in a child and lead to a basic unsureness about his proper role in life. This stress can be expressed in many ways, not necessarily in alcoholism.

2. *Family Background: Erratic Satisfaction of Dependency Needs.* The major force which seemed to lead a person under high stress to express his anxiety in alcoholism was the erratic frustration of his dependency desires. The prealcoholic often came from an environment in which his desire to be loved was satisfied and then frustrated in a strikingly erratic fashion. Typically, he had been raised by a mother who alternated between loving indulgence

and overt rejection, who was likely to see herself as a "martyr" whose own interests she had begrudgingly sacrificed to the interests of her family, who also tended to react to crises in an escapist manner and to participate in various kinds of deviant behavior. An intense degree of parental antagonism also distinguished the alcoholic's family from the nondeviant's. In addition, the potential alcoholic's father tended to regard the boy's mother with low esteem.

3. *Resultant Personality: Conflict Over Heightened Dependency Desires.* We reasoned that these influences had two major effects: (1) boys raised in such environments underwent an intensification of their need for love; and (2) they felt great anxiety about the satisfaction of this heightened need. We are unable to present direct empirical evidence for these two deductions. From a variety of experimental studies, nevertheless, comes evidence that erratic satisfaction of any drive leads to an intensification of the need. Moreover, it seems reasonable to assume that conflict would be generated whenever a person is alternately rewarded and then punished for the same kind of behavior. The prealcoholic was raised, on the one hand, by a mother who sometimes indulged him, who talked constantly of her sacrifices, who titillated him with various examples of sexual deviance. On the other hand, the same mother would, at times, berate the child and fail to come to his aid in critical situations. In the background, the boy's father talked disparagingly of the mother's failings. This strange combination of rewarding and punishing the child's need for love and maternal care would, it seems reasonable to suppose, cause extreme dependency conflict in the child.

4. *Family Background: Inadequate Specification of the Male Role.* The potential alcoholic was not offered a clear, specific image of manhood. His father

Model of Alcoholism

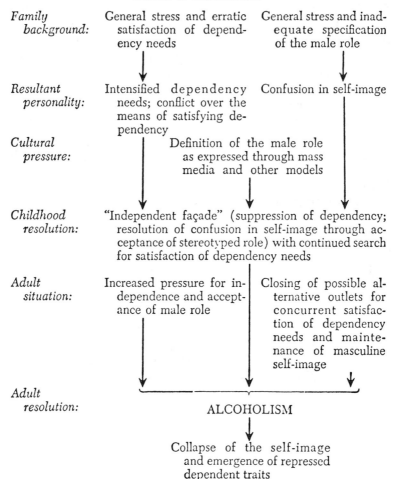

Family background:	General stress and erratic satisfaction of dependency needs	General stress and inadequate specification of the male role
Resultant personality:	Intensified dependency needs; conflict over the means of satisfying dependency	Confusion in self-image
Cultural pressure:		Definition of the male role as expressed through mass media and other models
Childhood resolution:	"Independent façade" (suppression of dependency; resolution of confusion in self-image through acceptance of stereotyped role) with continued search for satisfaction of dependency needs	
Adult situation:	Increased pressure for independence and acceptance of male role	Closing of possible alternative outlets for concurrent satisfaction of dependency needs and maintenance of masculine self-image
Adult resolution:	ALCOHOLISM	

Collapse of the self-image
and emergence of repressed
dependent traits

tended to be antagonistic and tried to escape from the pressures of critical situations. The prealcoholic's parents did not enforce high demands that he accept responsibility. In short, such children were raised in environments in which the responsibilities of the male role were neither exemplified nor enforced.

5. *Resultant Personality: Confusion in Self-image.* One major result of these experiences was confusion in the child's self-image. The typical alcoholic lacked specific definitions of the male role. He was commonly exposed to highly erratic experiences—at times, his parents might ap-

prove a certain action; at other times, they might ignore or actually punish him for the same thing. In many ways, his father's behavior contradicted the usual stereotype of the male's role in American society. Radio, the newspapers, his teachers, the movies, all picture the typical male as being responsible, courageous, law-abiding, and loving. The alcoholic's parents, particularly his father, tended to be the opposite: cowardly, rejecting, and often deviant. It seems likely, therefore, that the child raised under the influence of such contradictory examples would be confused over his role in life.

6. *Childhood Resolution: Creation of an Independent Façade.* The person who has been subjected to these experiences often seeks to resolve his various conflicts behind a façade that can satisfy his dependency conflict, end his confusion about his self-image, and ensure the approval of his society. The evidence has indicated that the typical prealcoholic creates an independent, super-masculine façade. He tends to be aggressive, outwardly self-confident, highly independent. In other words, the potential alcoholic accepts the American stereotype of masculinity and then plays this role to the hilt. We would assume that his choice of an independent self-image involved the suppression of dependency desires. Thus, by becoming a highly independent male, he achieves a temporary resolution of his disturbing conflicts.

Underneath his façade of self-reliant manhood, the typical alcoholic, we have proposed, continues to feel anxious, to suffer conflict, and to be desirous of dependent relationships. If one assumes that his traumatic early experiences produce a permanently heightened desire for dependency, then it follows that his conscious attempt at suppressing these desires is doomed to failure. Outwardly, he might attempt to maintain a façade of independence; inwardly, he would long for supporting, maternal care. Consequently, he would attempt to satisfy these forbidden urges in various vicarious ways; simultaneously he would strive to protect and defend his self-image and to assure vicarious satisfaction of his repressed dependent needs. This search for vicarious satisfaction might take him down a number of different channels; he might try to find a wife who would serve as a pseudo-mother, he might join social organizations that would offer him a sense of belonging and of camaraderie, or he might choose an occupation where he could be under the care of comforting figures.

7. *Adult Situation: Closing Possible Alternative Outlets for Expression of Dependency.* As an adult, the typical prealcoholic would involve himself in a quixotic quest to satisfy his dual desires to be independent and dependent. Because of his background, certain outlets would be closed to him. As we have shown in the previous chapters, the alcoholic was raised by parents who were nominally religious, but not deeply committed to their faith. Raised in such an environment, it is likely that the prealcoholic, too, would not put much reliance on the church. Thus, one major outlet for his conflicts—submergence in a strong religious faith—would be denied him. Unlike the strongly religious person, the prealcoholic would tend to withdraw from the comforts of a church; he could not express his dependent longings by seeking direction from God, the priest, the minister, or the elders. He could not find, in the church, the sure direction and guidance that he lacked in his early life.

In addition to the religious channel, other outlets are denied the typical middle-class male (among whom we found a significantly higher proportion of alcoholics). Such possible outlets as professional prize-fighting (with the manager taking over the "maternal" role) or soldiering as careers are largely taboo for the middle class. Unless he wrenched himself from his entire ideological background, the prealcoholic would thus be denied certain satisfactions available to lower-class males. Simultaneously, the middle-class values of achievement and success would press the prealcoholic toward accepting the role of independent masculinity.

8. *The Function of Alcoholism.* Alcohol would be a major outlet available to such a person. When intoxicated, he could achieve feelings of warmth, comfort, and omnipotence. His strong desires to be dependent would be satisfied. At the same

time, he could maintain his image of independence and self-reliance. The hard drinker in American society is pictured as tough, extroverted, and manly—exactly the masculine virtues the alcoholic strives to incorporate into his own self-image.

With his basic psychological make-up, together with the social pressures, the absence of alternative resolutions, and the lack of strong proscriptions against imbibing, such a person would be likely to succumb to alcohol.

9. *Collapse of the Self-image.* The reports on the lives of adult alcoholics indicate that the severe effects of alcoholism do not become manifest until middle age. Typically, the alcoholic begins drinking only at parties, then on week-end binges, then every day. He moves from drinking only at night to drinking in the evening, then to drinking at lunch and in the morning. He finds that he is "blacking-out" after sessions of heavy drinking, that he must sneak drinks at parties. Finally, his life becomes oriented around securing his daily supply of alcohol.

We believe that the confirmed alcoholic increases his intake of alcohol because intoxication satisfies his dependency urges and obliterates reminders of his own inadequacies. We assume that his character is organized around a quest for dependency; in alcohol he finds a permanent, easily available, and, at first, non-threatening method of satisfaction.

The alcoholic's almost continuous state of intoxication naturally interferes with many other aspects of his life. His occupational efficiency falters, he loses his role as the "rock" of the family, his image of himself as an independent male is undermined in various ways. The evidence indicates that he is usually a social outcast and that he finds himself in profound conflict with his wife and family.

Research also indicates that unless the alcoholic finds some resolution of his conflicts (e.g., by membership in Alcoholics Anonymous), his repressed traits of dependency, inferiority, and passivity become openly manifested; his attempt to maintain a façade of independent manliness collapses.

CHAPTER IX

Psychosexual Disorders

Sexual Deviance
The Problem of Defining Sexual Perversion

Sexual deviance does not admit of a simple definition, inasmuch as what one society would allow as normal, another may condemn as a perversion. For example, in the American society mouth to mouth kissing is considered quite normal, even with persons with whom one is hardly acquainted. But when the Thonga first observed kissing among the Europeans, they ridiculed them saying: "Look at them—they eat each other's saliva and dirt" (Ford & Beach, 1951, p. 49).

The problem of defining sexual perversion is clearly seen in the matter of voyeurism. In the *Psychiatric Dictionary* of Hinsie and Shatsky (1953), "voyeur" is defined as "sexual pervert. . . . One who obtains sexual gratification by looking at the genitals of another. . . . A scopophiliac" (p. 549). They define scopophilia as "sexual pleasure derived from contemplation or looking" (p. 476). According to this definition (which is widely used) virtually all persons are sexual perverts. In the light of such encompassing definitions, Gebhard and his colleagues comment:

Thus, a lounger on the street watching passing girls, or a person watching a strip-tease act could qualify as a voyeur, or so could the peruser of "cheesecake" magazines. One might say that a peeper is a voyeur who has no legal right to be at the location from whence he observes, but even this definition is imperfect since a man has a right to be on a public street at night, but is liable to arrest if he stands on the sidewalk looking into the window of the adjacent apartment house. . . . All males have voyeuristic and peeping tendencies (1965, pp. 358-359).

Another problem confronting psychopathologists regarding sexual normality and deviation is the social strictures prohibiting experimentation with humans.

However, Masters and Johnson (1966) were remarkably successful in conducting experiments on human sexual activity.

Homosexuality

Of the great variety of sexual offenses, more attention and research has been allocated in recent years to homosexuality than any other form of deviation.

Buss (1966), differentiating between two types of homosexuality, seems to imply that one is normal and the second a deviation. The first, "appropriate sexual activity," is "sexual behavior consistent with the gender of the participant," that is, the male plays the role normally undertaken by males in heterosexual activity; but in the second, "sexual inversion," the male homosexual assumes the female role, and this is considered the more abnormal. Neustatter (1968) draws a distinction between psychopathic homosexuals and those that are not; the psychopathic are identified by the lack of a sense of conscience or scruples regarding their behavior.

According to Bergler (1956), there are "statistically induced homosexuals," those who read books citing the widespread practice of homosexuality, thus assume it to be normal and yield to experimentation. Although there are healthy heterosexuals, Bergler claims that there are "no healthy homosexuals."

Neither Kinsey and his associates (1948, 1953) nor Allen (1958) found glandular factors accounting for homosexuality. Allen is adamant in his stand regarding the absence of discernible differences in physique between homo- and heterosexuals. Despite the increase in premarital, extramarital, and masturbatory sex practices in individuals born subsequent to 1920, Kinsey found no increase in homosexuality in comparing the 1920 plus figures with those prior to the year 1910. Although homosexuality is not on the increase, the Committee on Public Health of the New York Academy of Medicine (1964) has found it to be "more open and obtrusive." The Committee cites two goals of present-day homosexuals: (1) acceptance, rather than mere toleration; and (2) to be regarded as desirable, noble, and a preferable way of life, rather than merely an acceptable mode of existence. Suggs (1966), in an elaborate study of Marquesan sexual behavior, reports that homosexuality is rare among them and considered unnatural.

Studies on homosexuality by Westwood (1960) revealed the following sequence: from 13 to 15 years of age sexual play among boys was a matter of curiosity rather than "homosexuality," followed by an experimental phase and a latent period; from 16 to 19 years of age was a time of conflict of guilt and shame coupled with a determined effort to resist homosexual feelings; and by the early twenties the homosexual finds self-acceptance and pursues his unmistakable homosexual inclinations.

Concluding from a limited sampling, Schofield (1965a) suggests that 1 in 7 boys succumbs to homosexuality, but only 1 in 10 girls. He also found that one third of the boys are introduced to heterosexual intercourse by a partner older than himself, as against two thirds of the girls. A hearsay report is recorded by Ellis to the effect that "a Catholic confessor, a friend tells me, informed him that for one man who acknowledges homosexual practices there are three women" (1963, p. 195).

Homosexuality and Psychopathology

The official view of the American Psychiatric Association being that homosexuals are not mentally ill, researchers regard their condition as neutral when assessing them in psychopathological studies. In one such study by Saghir and Robins (1973), very few personality differences were found distinguishing male homosexuals from their heterosexual counterparts. Homosexual men did, however, have a tendency to feel hurt more readily. Homosexuals, whose behavior was feminine, exhibited an "exaggerated femininity and a caricature of a woman's manifest behavior" (1973, p. 108). These people described themselves as "sissies" during childhood. Three-fourths of the homosexuals claimed that external appearance was sufficient in assessing masculinity. And the same percentage held that "effeminacy in males is a genuine part of the individual's behavior" (1973, p. 106). Yet, 60 percent of them saw themselves as masculine, assuming the gender role, and not being different from heterosexual males. Male homosexuals had only a minor tendency, in comparison to their counterparts, to drink more heavily or have alcoholic problems. Actually, the vast majority were mild drinkers or did not drink at all. The same was true of their heterosexual counterparts. Suicide, whenever it was attempted, usually had some direct or indirect bearing on homosexuality, such as disagreeable disputes with parents, disappointment in love, and the like.

In a questionnaire study correlating homosexuality and race, Weinberg and Williams (1974) found that Blacks "expect less negative reaction to their homosexuality and anticipate less discrimination from other people on account of it" (p. 262). Blacks showed less concern in passing as homosexuals.

In a more recent report by the psychologist and sociologist Bell and Weinberg (1978), it was found that homosexuals vary considerably. They found five major types: (1) "close-coupled" homosexuals. Comparable to their happily married heterosexual counterparts, their sexual problems were minor, they shared a close circle of friends, and limited their sex to this single partnership. (2) "Open-coupled" homosexuals looked elsewhere for their sex in addition to the partner with which they lived. They also regretted their homosexuality more. (3) "Functional" homosexuals had a multiplicity of partners, living with none of them. These confident and gregarious individuals frequented homosexual bars for novel contacts. They neither worried nor had problems about sex. (4) "Dysfunctional" homosexuals lacked confidence about their sexuality as well as about themselves, had greater regrets about their homosexuality, remained single though they had many partners, and surprisingly, were considerably more educated. (5) "Asexual" homosexuals were those with a low sexual activity level, socially insecure, lonely, older, and with definite regrets about their homosexuality.

Other facts the Bell and Weinberg research disclosed included virtually a fifth of homosexuals seriously contemplated suicide in consequence of their homosexuality (guilt or loss of lover). The tendency of this group was to fall into the dysfunctional or asexual categories. By comparison with their heterosexual counterparts, male homosexuals were found to be lonelier, more depressed and worried, and less accepting of themselves. Although some lesbians regretted their homosexuality, especially with respect to not having children, they differed less from their heterosexual counterparts than did the males.

These researchers concur with the American Psychiatric Association with respect to homosexuality not being an illness. But this can be a dangerous conclusion. If it is not an illness, some will argue, then it is a moral issue and should be dealt with accordingly. We may revert to the days when homosexuals will be fired from their jobs, incarcerated, and ostracized from society. We must not forget the many years that alcoholism was considered a moral (not a medical) issue, with the result that alcoholics were unsympathetically rejected from family, jobs, and society.

Theories of Homosexuality

In a series of papers on homosexuality, Saghir (1969a, 1969b) and his associates reported the majority of male homosexuals became such in preadolescence. Unlike female homosexuals, males tend to be more of the "one-night stand" type, with little concern for fidelity, and significantly more casual. The majority of male homosexuals

were unfaithful even in their prolonged relationships. They made their contact impersonally and early and most often the goal was apparently sexual release. All masturbated, and their mean sexual outlets through homosexual practices were over twice that of the women (1969b, p. 229).

Least reported sexual fantasies were of a heterosexual nature, and beyond 19 years of age they became still fewer. Both male and female homosexuals acquire similar psychological responses to their own sex and at relatively the same age bracket. Of the females, 80 percent formed emotional attachments prior to age 14, whereas only 15 percent had heterosexual attachments during the same age range.

Homosexual women tended to be relatively stable in their relationships. About two-thirds of them reported having less than a total of 8 partners, and about one-third, 3 partners or less (1969a, p. 201).

Saghir's study had a population of 89 homosexual males and 57 lesbians.

Viewing homosexuality from a genetic orientation, Kallmann (1952a, 1952b, 1953) found post-adolescent overt homosexual behavior in the entire series of 44 one-egg pairs of twins. More than merely being concordant, the majority of the one-egg pairs displayed a tendency toward similarity in the roles they assumed in their individual sexual activities in addition to their femininity both as to appearance and behavior. Kallmann found in identical twins twice the incidence of homosexuality than that which occurred in the two-egg group.

Theorizing as to the etiology of sexuality, Ollendorff (1966) asserts that homosexuality is found only in "sex-negating societies," and absent in sex-permissive ones, or at the most is regarded as a childish deviation which has no place in the normal sexually mature personality.

The causes of homosexuality, as induced in childhood by the sex-negating patterns of upbringing, grow to promote a fixed neurotic illness in the predisposed, especially by the mass occurrence of mutual masturbation and homosexual play in adolescence.... Homosexuality is a neurotic illness of great strength caused by two factors: a predisposed neurotic personality and the impact of sex-negating and prohibitive elements of conventional upbringing (1966, p. 116-117).

He believes that overt or constitutional homosexuals number approximately 3 percent of the male population.

According to psychoanalytic theory, Freud (1946) assumed a polymorphous perversity in childhood that may (through improper psychosexual development) reach a stage of arrested development—homosexuality. Stekel (1948) conjectures that homosexuality results when a child experiences a deep sense of rejection by the parent of the opposite sex so that the parent of the same sex wins his love and affection.

Kurt Adler (1967), following in the tradition of his father, postulates that a person's style of life determines his sexual behavior. Impaired "gender-identity" or "gender-role" in childhood issues in a "fear of the opposite sex, or fear of inadequacy in one's proper sex role, or both" (1967, p. 77), hence is responsible for homosexuality.

A theory resulting from the research of homosexuals convicted of the crime was advanced by Schofield (1965b). Although homosexuality affects personality development slightly, the attitude of nonhomosexuals toward the homosexual produces a stress that does have profound effects upon the homosexual, resulting in "character deterioration," preventing suitable social integration. While some homosexuals can cope with society's hostility, others, becoming social casualties, end in prisons or clinics. Accordingly, not homosexuality per se, but accompanying social pressures associated with it create the attending psychopathological consequences.

37.

American Psychiatric Association

FEATURES OF PSYCHOSEXUAL DISORDERS

The psychosexual disorders are divided into four groups. The gender identity disorders are characterized by the individual's feelings of discomfort and inappropriateness about his or her anatomic sex and by persistent behaviors generally associated with the other sex. The paraphilias are characterized by arousal in response to sexual objects or situations that are not part of normative arousal-activity patterns and that in varying degrees may interfere with the capacity for reciprocal affectionate sexual activity. The psychosexual dysfunctions are characterized by inhibitions in sexual activity. The psychosexual dysfunctions are characterized by inhibitions in sexual desire or the psychophysiological changes that characterize the sexual response cycle. Finally, there is a residual class of other psychosexual disorders that has two categories: egodystonic homosexuality and a final residual category, psychosexual disorders not elsewhere classified.

GENDER IDENTITY DISORDERS

The essential feature of the disorders included in this subclass is an incongruence between anatomic sex and gender identity. Gender identity is the sense of knowing to which sex one belongs, that is, the awareness that "I am a male," or "I am a female." Gender identity is the private

experience of gender role, and gender role is the public expression of gender identity. Gender role can be defined as everything that one says and does, including sexual arousal, to indicate to others or to the self the degree to which one is male or female.

Disturbance in gender identity is rare, and should not be confused with the far more common phenomena of feelings of inadequacy in fulfilling the expectations associated with one's gender role. An example would be an individual who perceives himself or herself as being sexually unattractive yet experiences himself or herself unambiguously as a man or woman in accordance with his or her anatomic sex.

302.5x Transsexualism

The essential features of this heterogeneous disorder are a persistent sense of discomfort and inappropriateness about one's anatomic sex and a persistent wish to be rid of one's genitals and to live as a member of the other sex. The diagnosis is made only if the disturbance has been continuous (not limited to periods of stress) for at least two years, is not due to another mental disorder, such as schizophrenia, and is not associated with physical intersex or genetic abnormality.

Individuals with this disorder usually complain that they are uncomfortable wearing the clothes of their own anatomic sex; frequently this discomfort leads to cross-dressing (dressing in clothes of the other sex). Often they choose to engage in activities that in our culture tend to be

From Task Force on Nomenclature and Statistics of the American Psychiatric Association, *Diagnostic and Statistical Manual of Mental Disorders, Third Edition.* American Psychiatric Association, 1980.

associated with the other sex. These individuals often find their genitals repugnant, which may lead to persistent requests for sex reassignment by surgical or hormonal means.

To varying degrees, the behavior, dress, and mannerisms are those of the other sex. With cross-dressing, hormonal treatment, and electrolysis, a few males with the disorder will appear relatively indistinguishable from members of the other sex. However, the anatomic sex of most males and females with the disorder is quite apparent to the alert observer.

***

302.60 Gender Identity Disorder of Childhood

The essential features are a persistent feeling of discomfort and inappropriateness in a child about his or her anatomic sex and the desire to be, or insistence that he or she is, of the other sex. In addition, there is a persistent repudiation of the individual's own anatomic attributes. This is not merely the rejection of stereotypical sex role behavior as, for example, in "tomboyishness" in girls or "sissyish" behavior in boys, but rather a profound disturbance of the normal sense of maleness and femaleness.

Girls with this disorder regularly have male peer groups, an avid interest in sports and rough-and-tumble play, and a lack of interest in playing with dolls or playing "house" (unless playing the father or another male role). More rarely, a girl with this disorder claims that she will grow up to become a man (not merely in role), that she is biologically unable to become pregnant, that she will not develop breasts, or that she has, or will grow, a penis.

Boys with this disorder invariably are preoccupied with female stereotypical activities. They may have a preference for dressing in girls' or women's clothes, or

may improvise such items from available material when genuine articles are unavailable. (The cross-dressing never causes sexual excitement.) They often have a compelling desire to participate in the games and pastimes of girls. Dolls are often the favorite toy, and girls are regularly the preferred playmates. When playing "house," the role of a female is typically adopted. Rough-and-tumble play or sports are regularly avoided. Gestures and actions are often judged against a standard of cultural stereotype to be feminine, and the boy is invariably subjected to male peer group teasing and rejection, which rarely occurs among girls until adolescence. In rare cases a boy with this disorder claims that his penis or testes are disgusting or will disappear, or that it would be better not to have a penis or testes.

Some children refuse to attend school because of teasing or pressure to dress in attire stereotypical of their sex. Most children with this disorder deny being disturbed by it except as it brings them into conflict with the expectations of their family or peers.

***

PARAPHILIAS

The essential feature of disorders in this subclass is that unusual or bizarre imagery or acts are necessary for sexual excitement. Such imagery or acts tend to be insistently and involuntarily repetitive and generally involve either: (1) preference for use of a nonhuman object for sexual arousal, (2) repetitive sexual activity with humans involving real or simulated suffering or humiliation, or (3) repetitive sexual activity with nonconsenting partners. In other classifications these disorders are referred to as sexual deviations. The term paraphilia is preferable because it correctly emphasizes that the deviation (para) is in that to which the individual is attracted (philia).

The imagery in a paraphilia, such as simulated bondage, may be playful and harmless and acted out with a mutually consenting partner. More likely it is not reciprocated by the partner, who consequently feels erotically excluded or superfluous to some degree. In more extreme form, paraphiliac imagery is acted out with a nonconsenting partner, and is noxious and injurious to the partner (as in severe sexual sadism) or to the self (as in sexual masochism).

Since paraphiliac imagery is necessary for erotic arousal, it must be included in masturbatory or coital fantasies, if not actually acted out alone or with a partner and supporting cast or paraphernalia. In the absence of paraphiliac imagery there is no relief from nonerotic tension, and sexual excitement or orgasm is not attained.

The imagery in a paraphiliac fantasy or the object of sexual excitement in a paraphilia is frequently the stimulus for sexual excitement in individuals without a psychosexual disorder. For example, women's undergarments and imagery of sexual coercion are sexually exciting for many men; they are paraphiliac only when they become necessary for sexual excitement.

The paraphilias included here are, by and large, conditions that traditionally have been specifically identified by previous classifications. Some of them are extremely rare; others are relatively common. Because some of these disorders are associated with nonconsenting partners, they are of legal and social significance. Individuals with these disorders tend not to regard themselves as ill, and usually come to the attention of mental health professionals only when their behavior has brought them into conflict with society.

The specific paraphilias described here are: (1) fetishism, (2) transvestism, (3) zoophilia, (4) pedophilia, (5) exhibitionism, (6) voyeurism, (7) sexual masochism, and (8) sexual sadism. Finally, there is a residual category, atypical paraphilia, for noting the many other paraphilias that exist but that have not been sufficiently described to date to warrant inclusion as specific categories.

Paraphilias may be multiple or may coexist with other mental disorders, such as schizophrenia or various personality disorders. In such cases multiple diagnoses should be made.

* * *

302.30 Transvestism

The essential feature is recurrent and persistent cross-dressing by a heterosexual male that during at least the initial phase of the illness is for the purpose of sexual excitement. Interference with the cross-dressing results in intense frustration. This diagnosis is not made in those rare instances in which the disturbance has evolved into transsexualism.

Transvestic phenomena range from occasional solitary wearing of female clothes to extensive involvement in a transvestic subculture. Usually more than one article of women's clothing is involved, and the man may dress entirely as a woman. The degree to which the cross-dressed individual appears as a woman varies, depending on mannerisms, body habitus, and cross-dressing skill. When not cross-dressed, he is usually unremarkably masculine. Although the basic preference is heterosexual, rarely has the individual had sexual experience with several women, and occasional homosexual acts may occur.

* * *

302.81 Fetishism

The essential feature is the use of nonliving objects (fetishes) as a repeatedly preferred or exclusive method of achieving sexual excitement. The diagnosis is not made when the fetishes are limited to articles of female clothing used in cross-dressing, as in transvestism, or when the object is sexually stimulating because it has been designed for that purpose, e.g., a vibrator.

Sexual activity may involve the fetish alone, such as masturbation into a shoe, or the fetish may be integrated into sexual activities with a human partner. In the latter situation the fetish is required or strongly preferred for sexual excitement, and in its absence there may be erectile failure in males.

Fetishes tend to be articles of clothing, such as female undergarments, shoes, and boots, or, more rarely, parts of the human body, such as hair or nails. The fetish is often associated with someone with whom the individual was intimately involved during childhood, most often a caretaker.

***

302.10 Zoophilia

The essential feature is the use of animals as a repeatedly preferred or exclusive method of achieving sexual excitement. The animal may be the object of intercourse or may be trained to sexually excite the human partner by licking or rubbing. Usually the preferred animal is one with which the individual had contact during childhood, such as a household pet or farm animal. The animal is preferred no matter what other forms of sexual outlet are available.

***

302.20 Pedophilia

The essential feature is the act or fantasy of engaging in sexual activity with prepubertal children as a repeatedly preferred or exclusive method of achieving sexual excitement. The difference in age between the adult with this disorder and prepubertal child is arbitrarily set at 10 years or more. For late adolescents with the disorder, no precise age difference is specified; and clinical judgment must be used, the sexual maturity of the child as well as the age difference being taken into account.

Adults with the disorder are oriented toward children of the other sex twice as often as toward children of the same sex. The sexual behavior of these two groups is different. Heterosexually oriented males tend to prefer eight-to-ten year-old girls, the desired sexual activity usually being limited to looking or touching. Most incidents are initiated by adults who are in the intimate interpersonal environment of the child. Homosexually oriented males tend to prefer slightly older children. The percentage of couples in this group who know each other only casually is higher than in the heterosexually oriented group. Individuals with undifferentiated sexual object preference tend to prefer younger children than either of the other two groups.

Most individuals oriented homosexually have not been married, whereas most individuals oriented heterosexually either have been or are married.

***

302.40 Exhibitionism

The essential feature is repetitive acts of exposing the genitals to an unsuspecting stranger for the purpose of achieving sexual excitement, with no attempt at further sexual activity with the stranger. The wish to surprise or shock the observer is often consciously perceived or close to conscious awareness, but these individuals are usually not physically dangerous to the victim. Sometimes the individual masturbates while exposing himself. The condition apparently occurs only in males, and the victims are female children or adults.

* * *

302.82   Voyeurism

The essential feature is repetitive looking at unsuspecting people, usually strangers, who are either naked, in the act of disrobing, or engaging in sexual activity, as the repeatedly preferred or exclusive method of achieving sexual excitement. The act of looking ("peeping") is for the purpose of achieving sexual excitement, and no sexual activity with the person is sought. Orgasm, usually produced by masturbation, may occur during the voyeuristic activity, or later in response to the memory of what the individual has witnessed. Often these individuals enjoy thinking about the observed individuals' being helpless and feeling humiliated if they knew they were being seen. In its severe form, peeping constitutes the exclusive form of sexual activity.

* * *

302.83   Sexual Masochism

The essential feature is sexual excitement produced in an individual by his or her own suffering. The diagnosis of sexual masochism is warranted under either of two conditions:

(1)   A preferred or exclusive mode of producing sexual excitement is to

be humiliated, bound, beaten, or otherwise made to suffer.

(2)   The individual has intentionally participated in an activity in which he or she was physically harmed or his or her life was threatened in order to produce sexual excitement, which did occur. A single well-documented episode is sufficient to make the diagnosis.

* * *

302.84   Sexual Sadism

The essential feature is the infliction of physical or psychological suffering on another person in order to achieve sexual excitement.

The diagnosis of sexual sadism is warranted under any of three different conditions:

(1)   On a nonconsenting partner, the individual has repeatedly and intentionally inflicted psychological or physical suffering in order to achieve sexual excitement.

(2)   With a consenting partner a repeatedly preferred or exclusive mode of achieving sexual excitement combines humiliation with simulated or mildly injurious bodily suffering.

(3)   On a consenting partner bodily injury that is extensive, permanent, or possibly mortal is inflicted in order to achieve sexual excitement.

* * *

PSYCHOSEXUAL DYSFUNCTIONS

The essential feature is inhibition in the appetitive or psychophysiological changes that characterize the complete sexual response cycle. Ordinarily this diagnostic category will be applied only when the disturbance is a major part of the clinical picture, although it may not be part of the chief complaint. The diagnosis is not made if the sexual dysfunction is attributed entirely to organic factors, such as a physical disorder or a medication, or if it is due to another Axis I mental disorder.

The complete sexual response cycle can be divided into the following phases:

1. *Appetitive.* This consists of fantasies about sexual activity and a desire to have sexual activity.

2. *Excitement.* This consists of a subjective sense of sexual pleasure and accompanying physiological changes. The major change in the male consists of penile tumescence leading to erection. In addition, there is the appearance of Cowper's gland secretion. The major changes in the female consist of vasocongestion generalized in the pelvis with vaginal lubrication and swelling of the external genitalia. In addition there are the development of the orgasmic platform, which is the narrowing of the outer third of the vagina by increased pubococcygeal muscle tension and vasocongestion; vasocongestion of the labia minora; breast tumescence; and lengthening and widening of the inner two-thirds of the vagina.

3. *Orgasm.* This consists of a peaking of sexual pleasure, with release of sexual tension and rhythmic contraction of the perineal muscles and pelvic reproductive organs. In the male there is the sensation of ejaculatory inevitability, which is followed by emission of semen, caused by contractions of the prostate, seminal vesicles, and urethra. In the female there are contractions, not always subjectively experienced as such, of the wall of the outer third of the vagina. In both the male and the female there is often generalized muscular tension

or contractions, such as involuntary pelvic thrusting.

4. *Resolution.* This consists of a sense of general relaxation, well-being, and muscular relaxation. During this phase men are physiologically refractory to further erection and orgasm for a period of time. In contrast, women may be able to respond to additional stimulation almost immediately.

Inhibitions in the response cycle may occur at one or more of these phases, although inhibition in the resolution phase is rarely of primary clinical significance. Whenever more than one psychosexual dysfunction is present, they should all be recorded, in the order of clinical significance.

The particular manifestations of each of the psychosexual dysfunctions are noted in the diagnostic criteria. In most instances there will be a disturbance in both the subjective sense of pleasure or desire and objective performance. More rarely there may be subjective disturbance alone, without any objective signs of dysfunction, or, conversely, inhibition in performance without any acknowledged subjective distress.

In specifying diagnostic criteria, no attempt is made to require a minimum proportion or type of sexual encounter in which the dysfunction must occur to warrant a diagnosis. This judgment has to be made by the clinician, who must take into account various factors such as frequency, chronicity, subjective distress, and effect on other areas of functioning. The phrase "recurrent and persistent" in the diagnostic criteria is a shorthand method of designating the need for such a clinical judgment.

All of the dysfunctions may be lifelong or acquired (developing after a period of normal functioning), generalized or situational (limited to certain situations or with certain partners), and total or partial (degree or frequency of disturbance). Although in most instances the dysfunctions occur during sexual activity with a partner, in some cases it may be appropriate to identify dysfunctions that occur during masturbation.

* * *

OTHER PSYCHOSEXUAL DISORDERS

302.00 Ego-dystonic Homosexuality

The essential features are a desire to acquire or increase heterosexual arousal so that heterosexual relationships can be initiated or maintained, and a sustained pattern of overt homosexual arousal that the individual explicitly states has been unwanted and a persistent source of distress.

This category is reserved for those homosexuals for whom changing sexual orientations is a persistent concern, and should be avoided in cases where the desire to change sexual orientations may be a brief, temporary manifestation of an individual's difficulty in adjusting to a new awareness of his or her homosexual impulses.

Individuals with this disorder may have either no or very weak heterosexual arousal. Typically there is a history of unsuccessful attempts at initiating or sustaining heterosexual relationships. In some cases no attempt has been made to initiate a heterosexual relationship because of the expectation of lack of sexual responsiveness. In other cases the individual has been able to have short-lived heterosexual relationships, but complains that the heterosexual impulses are too weak to sustain such relationships. When the disorder is present in an adult, usually there is a strong desire to be able to have children and family life.

Generally individuals with this disorder have had homosexual relationships, but often the physical satisfaction is accompanied by emotional upset because of strong negative feelings regarding homosexuality. In some cases the negative feelings are so strong that the homosexual arousal has been confined to fantasy.

38.

William H. Masters and Virginia E. Johnson

PSYCHOSEXUAL DYSFUNCTIONS

PREMATURE EJACULATION

From a clinical point of view it is extremely difficult to define the syndrome of

premature ejaculation. Most definitions refer specifically to the duration of intravaginal containment of the penis. For teaching purposes a genitourinary service in a medical center has described a premature ejaculator as a man who cannot control his ejaculatory process for at least the first 30 seconds after penetration. In similar vein a hospital psychiatric service

From William H. Masters and Virginia E. Johnson, *Human Sexual Inadequacy*. Little, Brown & Co., 1970, pp. 92, 116, 137, 157, 227, 150-1.

has described the premature ejaculator as a man who cannot repress his ejaculatory demand for one full minute of intravaginal containment.

More realistically, a definition of premature ejaculation should reflect sociocultural orientation together with consideration of the prevailing requirements of sexual partners rather than an arbitrarily specific period of time. On occasion, 30 to 60 seconds of intravaginal containment is quite sufficient to satisfy a woman, if she has been highly excited during precoital sex play and is fully ready for orgasmic release with the initial thrusts of the penis. However, during most coital opportunity, the same woman may require variably longer periods of penile containment before attaining full release of sexual tension.

While readily admitting the inadequacies of the definition, the Foundation considers a man a premature ejaculator if he cannot control his ejaculatory process for a sufficient length of time during intravaginal containment to satisfy his partner in at least 50 percent of their coital connections. If the female partner is persistently non-orgasmic for reasons other than rapidity of the male's ejaculatory process, there is no validity to the definition. At least this definition does move away from the "stopwatch" concept.

EJACULATORY INCOMPETENCE

Ejaculatory incompetence is a specific form of male sexual dysfunction that can be considered either primary or secondary in character. From diagnostic and therapeutic points of view, it is easier and psychophysiologically more accurate to consider this form of sexual inadequacy as a clinical entity entirely separate from the classical concepts of impotence. In the spectrum of male sexual inadequacy, symptoms of ejaculatory incompetence should be assessed clinically as the reverse of premature ejaculation.

A man with ejaculatory incompetence rarely has difficulty in achieving or maintaining an erection quality sufficient for successful coital connection. Clinical evidence of sexual dysfunction arises when the afflicted individual cannot ejaculate during intravaginal containment. Frequently this inability to ejaculate intravaginally occurs with first coital experience and continues unresolved through subsequent coital encounters. Some men contending with the dysfunction of ejaculatory incompetence experience such pressures of sexual performance that they may develop the complication of secondary impotence. If this natural progression in dysfunctional status occurs, the man with ejaculatory incompetence parallels the man with premature ejaculation.

PRIMARY IMPOTENCE

For clinical purposes the primarily impotent man *arbitrarily* has been defined as a male never able to achieve and/or maintain an erection quality sufficient to accomplish successful coital connection. If erection is established and then lost under the influence of real or imagined distractions relating to coital opportunity, the erection usually is dissipated without accompanying ejaculatory response. No man is considered primarily impotent if he has been successful in any attempt at intromission in either heterosexual or homosexual opportunity.

* * *

SECONDARY IMPOTENCE

Definition of secondary impotence depends upon acceptance of the concept of primary impotence. . . . Primary impotence arbitrarily has been defined as the inability to achieve and/or maintain an erection quality sufficient to accomplish coital connection. If erection is established and then lost from real or imagined distractions related to the coital opportunity, the erection usually is dissipated without an accompanying ejaculatory response. If diagnosed as primarily impotent, a man not only evidences erective inadequacy during his initial coital encounter but the dysfunction also is present with every subsequent opportunity.

If a man is to be judged secondarily impotent, there must be the clinical landmark of at least one instance of successful intromission, either during the initial coital opportunity or in a later episode. The usual pattern of the secondarily impotent male is success with the initial coital opportunity and continued effective performance with the first fifty, hundred, or even thousand or more coital encounters. Finally, an episode of failure at effective coital connection is recorded.

When the first erective failure occurs, the involved man certainly should not immediately be judged secondarily impotent. Many men have occasional episodes of erective failure, particularly when fatigued or distracted. However, an initial failure at coital connection may become a harbinger, and, as apprehension increases during episodes of erection, a pattern of erective failure subsequently may be established. Finally, erective inadequacy may become a relatively constant companion to opportunities for sexual connection. When an individual male's rate of failure at successful coital connection approaches 25 percent of his opportunities, the clinical diagnosis of secondary impotence must be accepted.

* * *

PRIMARY ORGASMIC DYSFUNCTION

In order to be diagnosed as having primary orgasmic dysfunction, a woman must report lack of orgasmic attainment during her entire lifespan. There is no definition of male sexual dysfunction that parallels in this severity of exclusion. If a male is judged primarily impotent, the definition means simply that he has never been able to achieve intromission in either homosexual or heterosexual opportunity. However, he might, and usually does, masturbate with some regularity or enjoy occasions of partner manipulation to ejaculation. For the primarily nonorgasmic woman, however, the definition demands a standard of total inorgasmic responsivity.

The edict of lifetime nonorgasmic return in the Foundation's definition of primary orgasmic dysfunction includes a history of consistent nonorgasmic response to all attempts at physical stimulation, such as masturbation or partner (male or female) manipulation, oral-genital contact, and vaginal or rectal intercourse. In short, every possible physical approach to sexual stimulation initiated by self or received from any partner has been totally unsuccessful in developing an orgasmic experience for the particular woman diagnosed as primarily nonorgasmic.

If a woman is orgasmic in dreams or in fantasy alone, she still would be considered primarily nonorgasmic. Foundation personnel have encountered two women who provided a positive history of an occasional dream sequence with orgasmic return and a negative history of physically initiated orgasmic release. However, no woman has been encountered to date that described the ability to fantasy to orgasm without providing a concomitant history of successful orgasmic return from a variety of physically stimulative measures.

* * *

VAGINISMUS

Vaginismus is a psychophysiological syndrome affecting woman's freedom of sexual response by severely, if not totally, impeding coital function. Anatomically this clinical entity involves all components of the pelvic musculature investing the perineum and outer third of the vagina. . . . Physiologically, these muscle groups contract spastically as opposed to their rhythmic contractural response to orgasmic experience. This spastic contraction of the vaginal outlet is a completely involuntary reflex stimulated by imagined, anticipated, or real attempts at vaginal penetration. Thus, vaginismus is a classic example of a psychosomatic illness.

Vaginismus is one of the few elements in the wide pattern of female sexual dysfunctions that cannot be unreservedly diagnosed by any established interrogative technique. Regardless of the psychotherapist's high level of clinical suspicion, a secure diagnosis of vaginismus cannot be established without the specific clinical support that only direct pelvic examination can provide. Without confirmatory pelvic examination, women have been treated for vaginismus when the syndrome has not been present. Conversely, there have been cases of vaginismus diagnosed by pelvic examination when the clinical existence of the syndrome had not been anticipated by therapists.

The clinical existence of vaginismus is delineated when vaginal examination constitutes a routine part of the required complete physical examination. The presence of involuntary muscular spasm in the outer third of the vaginal barrel, with the resultant severe constriction of the vaginal orifice, is obvious. The literature has remarked on an unusual physical response pattern of a woman afflicted with vaginismus. She reacts in an established pattern to psychological stress during a routine pelvic examination that includes observation of the external genitalia and manual vaginal exploration. The patient usually attempts to escape the examiner's approach by withdrawing toward the head of the table, even raising her legs from the stirrups, and/or constricting her thighs in the midline to avoid the implied threat of the impending vaginal examination. Frequently this reaction pattern can be elicited by the woman's mere anticipation of the examiner's physical approach to pelvic examination rather than the actual act of manual pelvic investigation.

When vaginismus is a fully developed clinical entity, constriction of the vaginal outlet is so severe that penile penetration is impossible. Frequently, manual examination can be accomplished only by employing severe force, an approach to be decried, for little is accomplished from such a forced pelvic investigation, and the resultant psychosexual trauma can make the therapeutic reversal of the syndrome more difficult. The diagnosis of vaginismus can easily be established by a one-finger pelvic examination. If a nontraumatic pelvic exploration is conducted, and a markedly apprehensive woman somewhat reassured in the process, the first step has been taken in therapeutic reversal of the involuntary spasm of the vaginal outlet.

Vaginismus may be of such severity that a marriage cannot be consummated. Medical consultants frequently have mistaken unrecognized involuntary vaginal spasm for the presence of a pressure-resistant hymen. As the result of this clinical confusion, surgical excision of the presumed resistant hymen has been recommended and conducted on many occasions without providing the patient and her husband with the expected relief from physical obstruction to effective coital connection. The possibility of coexistent vaginismus should be explored in depth by means of an accurate psychosexual-social history as well as a definitive, but not forced, pelvic examination before surgical excision of a presumed all-resistant hymen is conducted.

CHAPTER X

Organic Mental Disorders

Organic brain disorders affecting thought, emotion, and behavior may be classified in several ways, one order (Gregory, 1968; Rosen & Gregory, 1965) being a dichotomous one as to whether the brain impairment is acute (temporary and reversible) or chronic (permanent and irreversible). Both forms exhibit at least five primary symptoms of intellectual dysfunction: (1) orientation (particularly for time, but also for place and person); (2) memory (especially for recent events, but also for remote ones); (3) intellectual dysfunction, including ideational; (4) impairment of judgment, including conscience and planning ability; (5) shallowness, lability, or affective responses (emotional responses).

The following tables (10.1; 10.2) by Gregory (1968, pp. 564, 566) cite the relationship of acute or reversible to chronic or irreversible brain disorders; and the main acute and chronic brain syndromes.

Brain disorders consist of a variety of types and subtypes. Kolb (1968) lists (1) *disorders that are caused by or are associated with impairment of brain tissue function:* meningococcal (epidemic) meningitis; tuberculous meningitis; acute (Sydenham's) chorea; epidemic encephalitis; deliria; (2) *brain syndromes stemming from drug or poison intoxication:* barbiturates and other tranquilizers; sympathomimetic amines (amphetamines); hallucinogenic agents (LSD-25 and mescaline); bromides; cortisone and ACTH; isoniazid; sulfonamides; thiocyanates; lead; mercury; manganese; carbon monoxide; carbon disulfide; (3) *acute brain syndromes associated with metabolic disturbances:* hyperthyroidism; hypocalcemia; Cushing's syndrome; adrenogenital syndrome; hypoglycemia; acute pancreatitis; acute vitamin deficiency syndrome; exhaustion delirium; postoperative neuroses and psychoses; (4) *chronic brain disorders:* syphilitic meningoencephalitis; syphilitic meningitis; (5) *brain syndromes associated with chronic arteriosclerosis;* (6) *senile psychoses;* (7) *brain syndromes associated with convulsive disorders* (*epilepsy*): grand mal; petit mal; cerebral dysrhythmias; narcolepsy; cataplexy; epileptic personality; epileptic deterioration; (8) *chronic brain syndrome associated with intracranial neoplasm;* (9) *chronic brain syndromes associated with disturbance of metabolism, growth, or nutrition:* Alzheimer's disease; vitamin deficiency syndromes; Wernicke syndrome; psychoses with pellagra; mental syndromes associated with pernicious anemia; porphyria; hepatolenticular degeneration; myxedema; acromegaloid personality; (10) *chronic brain syndromes associated with diseases of doubtful causes:* demyelinating diseases (multiple sclerosis; diffuse sclerosis); paralysis agitans; Huntington's chorea; Pick's disease; lupus erythematosus.

To this list may be added those that fall under *mental retardation,* such as *those due to infection:* cytomegalic inclusion body disease, congenital rubella, influenza, congenital syphilis, toxoplasmosis; *those due to intoxication:* bilirubin encephalopathy (kernicterus) and other encephalopathies; *those due to disorders of nutrition, growth or metabolism:* lipoidoses (sphingolipoidoses), including Tay-Sach disease, Niemann-Pick disease, Gaucher disease, metachromatic leukodystrophy; aminoacidurias, including phenylketonuria, maple syrup urine disease; *defects of carbohydrate metabolism,* including galactosemia, gargoylism, hypothyroidism; *those due to new growths:* tuberous

TABLE 10-1
Characteristics of Acute (Reversible) and Chronic (Irreversible) Brain Disorders*

Acute Reversible Brain Disorders	*Chronic Irreversible Brain Disorders*
Usual clinical syndrome delirium (sometimes stupor or coma).	Usual clinical syndrome dementia.
Primary impairment of orientation, memory, all intellectual functions, judgment, and affective response.	Primary impairment of orientation, memory, all intellectual functions, judgment, and affective response.
Usually associated with disordered perception (especially visual illusions and hallucinations), consciousness (e.g., stupor), and psychomotor activity (excitement or retardation).	May be prominent secondary "functional" manifestations due to release or accentuation of latent personality characteristics—psychotic, neurotic, or behavioral (e.g., depressed, paranoid, anxious, or antisocial behavior).
Due to temporary, reversible changes in brain cell function, or "biochemical lesions."	Due to permanent, irreversible damage to brain structure, or "morphological lesions."
Frequently "symptomatic" of generalized toxic, infective or metabolic disorder, also affecting other parts of the body.	May result from all the same pathogenic agents as acute (reversible) disorders; but also from insidious, localized intracranial lesion or degenerative process (sometimes hereditary).
Commonly encountered on general medical and surgical, pediatric, or obstetric wards of general hospitals.	Commonly encountered on neurological services of general hospitals or in mental hospitals.
Course brief, and may terminate in (1) death, (2) complete remission, (3) chronic (irreversible) brain disorders.	Course may be (1) chronic, or (2) progressive (with fatal termination).

* From I. Gregory. *Fundamentals of psychiatry* (2nd ed.). Philadelphia: W. B. Saunders, 1968, p. 564. Reprinted by permission of the publisher and the author.

sclerosis; *those due to chromosomal aberrations:* mongolism, Klinefelter's syndrome, Turner's syndrome; *those due to unknown prenatal influence:* craniostenosis, including hydrocephalus and hypertelorism.

The term "mental retardation" is used interchangeably with "mental deficiency" (and sometimes with "feeblemindedness"), though some authors prefer to draw distinctions between them (Sarason, 1966), yet these diagnostic labels refer to a heterogeneous group of individuals (Sarason & Doris, 1969). Ellis (1963) also concurs with the view that mental deficiency is not a unitary state, but a collection of numerous and varying conditions. Mental retardation, as is true of other areas of psychopathology (e.g., psychopharmacology), should not be viewed as the exclusive province of any single discipline (Philips, 1966).

TABLE 10-2
The Main Acute and Chronic Brain Syndromes*

I. *Chronic brain syndromes associated with congenital cranial anomaly, congenital spastic paraplegia, mongolism, prenatal maternal infectious disease, birth trauma*
Consists of all congenital brain disorders producing secondary or "pathological" mental deficiency.

II. *Acute and chronic brain syndromes associated with infection*
  A. Intracranial infections such as encephalitis, meningitis, brain abscess, and central nervous system syphilis.
  B. Systemic infections such as pneumonia, typhoid fever, rheumatic fever, and malaria.

III. *Acute and chronic brain syndromes associated with intoxication*
  A. Drugs (and withdrawal of drugs) generally used in medical practice, such as hypnotics and narcotics, stimulants, antibiotics, and analgesics, antihistamines, and hormones.
  B. Poisons not ordinarily used in medical practice, such as lead and other metals, carbon monoxide and other gases, and methyl alcohol ("wood alcohol or rubbing alcohol").
  C. Alcohol (ethyl alcohol) and associated vitamin deficiencies.

IV. *Acute and chronic brain syndromes associated with trauma*
Any physical brain injury, including that caused by surgical operations.

V. *Acute and chronic brain syndromes associated with circulatory disturbances*
  A. High blood pressure, heart and kidney diseases.
  B. Cerebral arteriosclerosis.

VI. *Acute and chronic brain syndromes associated with conculsive disorder*
Due to uncontrolled seizures caused by primary or "idiopathic" epilepsy.

VII. *Acute and chronic brain syndromes associated with disorders of metabolism*
  A. With recognized metabolic disorders, such as anoxia, anemia, vitamin deficiencies, and disorders of the thyroid or other endocrine glands.
  B. With presumed disorders of metabolism, as in senile brain disease and Alzheimer's presenile dementia.

VIII. *Acute and chronic brain syndromes associated with intracranial neoplasm*
  A. Primary tumors, originating with the skull, may be invasive (malignant) or localized (benign).
  B. Secondary (metastatic) tumors from primary cancer elsewhere in the body.

IX. *Acute and chronic brain syndromes associated with diseases of unknown or uncertain cause*
These are usually chronic degenerative diseases of the brain and nervous system whose causation is only partly established, such as multiple sclerosis, Huntington's chorea, and Pick's presenile dementia.

* From I. Gregory. *Fundamentals of psychiatry* (2nd ed.). Philadelphia: W. B. Saunders, 1968, p. 566. Reprinted by permission of the publisher and the author.

Theories of Brain Pathology

Goldstein's Organismic and Holistic Theory of Brain Pathology

According to Goldstein (1939, 1940, 1952), the personality with but a single drive strives to actualize itself and to "come to terms" with its environment. But in certain cases of brain damage, a "catastrophic reaction" of anxiety prevails that inhibits the individual from coming to suitable terms with the world. Brain-damaged patients find their ability to think abstractly impaired, with other portions of the brain striving to undertake the function of the impaired area. Brain-damaged patients "have lost initiative and the capacity to look forward to something and to make plans and decisions; they lack phantasy and inspiration; their perceptions, thoughts, and ideas are reduced; they have lost the capacity for real contact with others, and they are therefore incapable of real friendship" (Goldstein, 1952, p. 255). The brain-damaged patient, being in a catastrophic condition characterized by anxiety, cannot achieve self-realization. Such persons seek to achieve self-realization by exhibiting fanatical orderliness and preferring familiar surroundings. Their inability to cope with change creates within them a state of anxious excitement.

Penfield's Theory of the Memory Mechanism

Penfield, in experiments with Rasmussen (1950) that entailed the frontal lobes of monkeys, found that these lobes are involved in memory information storage. In surgical operations on epileptics, Penfield (1952, 1959; Penfield & Milner, 1958; Penfield & Roberts, 1959) found that the electrical stimulation of the temporal cortex evoked memories of both a visual and auditory character. Occasionally, and while the patient is yet conscious, the stimulation of the same or an adjacent area on the cortex at a later date could reproduce the same recollection, the assumption being that the reactivation of the brain patterns in question was part of the original experience. At times, stimulation of the same area produces a quite different response; on these occasions, the patient "has somehow changed his own interpretation of what he is seeing at the moment, or hearing or thinking" (Penfield, 1959, p. 1720). Penfield concluded that the interpretive cortex contains a mechanism capable of reactivating instantly and in detail one's past record in memory. In addition it possesses mechanization capable of producing interpretive signals.

Recent Brain Phenomena

Electrical Stimulation of the Brain (ESB)

Electrical stimulation of the brain and its resulting phenomena have commanded considerable interest in recent years. By stimulating various brain centers, researchers relieved subjects of anxiety, depression, and epileptic seizures. When Yale's Delgado halted a charging bull about to attack him by stimulating electrodes implanted in its brain, two Boston researchers followed through Delgado's experiment with humans. By remote control, Delgado transmitted signals to the bull's brain and thereby controlled its aggression. The charging bull was stopped in its tracks. Vernon Mark at Boston City Hospital and Frank Ervin (1970) at Massachusetts General Hospital employed Delgado's technique to control violence in patients. One spectacular result was to control violence brought on by epileptic seizures. They report the case of a 21-year-old girl who attacked an innocent girl while the two were in a ladies powder room. The details are in the text.

Split-Brain Phenomena

Another stupendous development in brain research, arising from the efforts of Cal Tech's Roger Sperry, is split-brain phenomena. The contralateral nature of the brain has long been known, that is, the left hemisphere of the brain controls the right side of the body and vice versa. But what is new is that humans, unlike animals, can function despite the severance of the two hemispheres. Following Sperry's lead, Vogel and Bogen severed the corpus collosum that links the two hemispheres together in an epileptic patient, resulting in the control of convulsive seizures. Since the brain waves (believed to be involved in epileptic seizures) could no longer be transferred from one hemisphere to the other (via the corpus collosum), the difficulty was brought under control.

39.

American Psychiatric Association

FEATURES OF ORGANIC MENTAL DISORDERS

The essential feature of all these disorders is a psychological or behavioral abnormality associated with transient or permanent dysfunction of the brain. Organic mental disorders are diagnosed (*a*) by recognizing the presence of one of the organic brain syndromes, as described below, and (*b*) by demonstrating by means of the history, physical examination, or laboratory tests, the presence of a specific organic factor judged to be etiologically related to the abnormal mental state. Under certain circumstances, however, a reasonable inference of an organic factor can be made from the clinical features alone, in which case only step (*a*) may be necessary for diagnosis.

Organic mental disorders are a heterogeneous group; therefore, no single description can characterize them all. The differences in clinical presentation reflect differences in the localization, mode of onset, progression, duration, and nature of the underlying pathophysiological process.

Differentiation of organic mental disorders as a separate class does not imply that nonorganic ("functional") mental disorders are somehow independent of brain processes. On the contrary, it is assumed that all psychological processes, normal and abnormal, depend on brain function. Limitations in our knowledge, however, sometimes make it impossible to determine whether a given mental disorder in a given individual should be considered an organic mental disorder (because it is due to brain dysfunction of *known* organic etiology) or whether it should be diagnosed as other than an organic mental disorder (because it is more adequately accounted for as a response to psychological or social factors [as in adjustment disorder] or because the presence of a specific organic factor has not been established [as in schizophrenia]).

The organic factor responsible for an organic mental disorder may be a primary disease of the brain or a systemic illness that secondarily affects the brain. It may also be a substance or toxic agent that is either currently disturbing brain function or has left some long-lasting effect. Withdrawal of a substance on which an individual has become physiologically dependent is another cause of organic mental disorder.

The most common organic brain syndromes are delirium, dementia, intoxication, and withdrawal. These syndromes display great variability among individuals and in the same individual over time. More than one organic brain syndrome may be present in an individual simultaneously (e.g., delirium superimposed upon dementia), and one organic brain syndrome may succeed another (e.g., thiamine-deficiency delirium [Wernicke's encephalopathy] followed by alcohol amnestic disorder [Korsakoff's disease]).

From Task Force on Nomenclature and Statistics of the American Psychiatric Association, *Diagnostic and Statistical Manual of Mental Disorders, Third Edition.* American Psychiatric Association, 1980.

* * *

DELIRIUM

The essential feature is a clouded state of consciousness, that is, a reduction in the clarity of awareness of the environment. This is manifested by difficulty in sustaining attention to both external and internal stimuli, sensory misperception, and a disordered stream of thought. In addition, disturbances of sleep-wakefulness and psychomotor activity are present. The onset is relatively rapid, and the course typically fluctuates. The total duration is usually brief.

In DSM-I this syndrome was called "acute brain syndrome." It has also been termed "acute exogenous reaction type," "acute confusional state," "toxic psychosis," and "metabolic encephalopathy." Furthermore, some reserve the term "delirium" for a particular, agitated variety of confusional state with vivid visual hallucinations. In this manual, however, delirium is intended to include the broad spectrum of clinical states having in common the essential features described above.

In delirium there is difficulty shifting, focusing, and sustaining attention. The individual is easily distracted by irrelevant stimuli. It may be difficult, or impossible, to engage him or her in conversation because attention wanders.

Perceptual disturbances are common and result in various misinterpretations, illusions, and hallucinations. For example, the banging of a door may be mistaken for a pistol shot (misinterpretation); the folds of the bedclothes may appear to be animate objects (illusion); or the individual may "see" a group of people hovering over the bed when no one is actually there (hallucination). Although sensory misperceptions and hallucinations are most commonly visual, they may occur in other sensory modalities as well. Misperceptions range from simple and uniform to highly complex. There are often both a delusional conviction of the reality of hallucinations and an emotional and behavioral response in keeping with their content.

The individual with delirium cannot maintain a coherent stream of thought. Thinking loses its usual clarity and direction toward a goal; it appears fragmented and disjointed. In mild delirium, this may be manifested by acceleration or slowing of thought; in severe delirium, thinking may be totally disorganized. This disturbance is reflected in speech that, in some cases, is limited and sparse, and in others, pressured and incoherent, with unpredictable switching from subject to subject. It is also reflected in defective reasoning and impaired goal-directed behavior. Perseveration of speech and behavior may appear. Although other cognitive disturbances, particularly disorientation and memory impairment, are also present in delirium, the person may be so inattentive and incoherent that these mental functions cannot be meaningfully assessed.

The sleep-wakefulness cycle is almost invariably disturbed. This frequently involves some depression in the level of consciousness, ranging from simple drowsiness, through increasing stages of torpor, to stupor or semicoma. On the other hand, some individuals with delirium are hypervigilant and have difficulty in falling asleep. Fluctuations from hypersomnolence to insomnia and reversals of the customary sleep-waking cycle may also be present. Vivid dreams and nightmares are common, and may merge with hallucinations.

Psychomotor activity is also disturbed. Many individuals are restless and hyperactive. Groping or picking at the bedclothes, attempting to get out of bed, striking out at nonexistent objects, and sudden changes of position are manifestations of increased psychomotor activity. On the other hand, there may be decreased psychomotor activity, with sluggishness and even certain features resembling catatonic stupor. Psychomotor activity often shifts abruptly from one of these extremes to another.

* * *

DEMENTIA

The essential feature is a loss of intellectual abilities of sufficient severity to interfere with social or occupational functioning. The deficit is multifaceted and involves memory, judgment, abstract thought, and a variety of other higher cortical functions. Changes in personality and behavior also occur. The diagnosis is not made if these features are due to clouding of consciousness, as in delirium. However, delirium and dementia may coexist.

As with all organic brain syndromes, an underlying causative organic factor is always assumed. In certain clinical states, e.g., primary degenerative dementia, however, it may be impossible to show a *specific* organic factor as the definitive cause of the disturbance. These conditions may nevertheless be diagnosed as dementia if (*a*) the impairment is a multifaceted loss of intellectual ability, (*b*) there is no evidence for a diagnosis other than an organic mental disorder, and (*c*) a diligent search has failed to reveal a specific organic etiologic factor.

In the past, the term dementia often implied a progressive or irreversible course. The definition of dementia in this manual, however, is based on clinical symptoms alone, and carries no connotation as to prognosis. Dementia may be progressive, static, or remitting. The reversibility of a dementia is a function of the underlying pathology and of the availability and timely application of effective treatment.

Memory impairment is usually the most prominent symptom. In mild dementia there is forgetfulness in daily life and a need to have statements repeated several times to facilitate remembering. On examination there may only be a certain hesitancy in response to questions. In more severe memory impairment, the individual may forget names, telephone numbers, directions, conversations, and events of the day. He or she may leave tasks unfinished because of forgetting to return after an interruption. This may cause a person to leave the water running in the sink or to neglect turning off the stove. In advanced forms of dementia, memory impairment is often so severe that the person forgets the names of close relatives, his or her own occupation, schooling, birthday, or, occasionally, even his or her own name. Memory disturbance may be formally documented by demonstrating difficulty in learning new information (short-term memory deficit) and in recalling material that was known in the past (long-term memory deficit). The former is tested by asking the individual to memorize the names of several unrelated objects, or a brief sentence, and then to repeat them after a few minutes of distraction; the latter is tested by asking about events that happened in the past.

Impairment of abstract thinking takes many forms. The individual has trouble coping with novel tasks, especially if pressed for time. He or she may try to avoid situations and tasks that require the processing of new and complex information. This deficit is sometimes formally assessed by asking the individual to interpret proverbs or to perform such tasks as finding similarities or differences between related words. The individual with dementia interprets proverbs concretely and has difficulty in finding similarities or differences.

Impaired judgment and impulse control are also commonly observed. Coarse language, inappropriate jokes, neglect of personal appearance and hygiene, and a general disregard for the conventional rules of social conduct are evidence of bad judgment and poor impulse control. A previously cautious businesswoman may embark on a reckless business venture. An elderly spinster may make sexual advances to strangers. A retiree may shoplift without considering the consequences. Marked impairment of judgment and impulse control is particularly characteristic of certain dementias that affect primarily the frontal lobes.

Dementia also involves a variety of disturbances of higher cortical function.

Although language is unaffected by some neurological disorders that cause dementia, in others it is abnormal. It may appear vague, stereotyped, and imprecise, with long circumlocutory phrases; or there may be specific signs of aphasia, such as difficulty naming objects. In severe forms of dementia, the individual may be virtually mute. So-called "constructional ability" is nearly always disturbed, and can be demonstrated by having the individual copy three-dimensional figures, assemble blocks, or arrange sticks in specific designs. Agnosias (failure to recognize or identify objects despite intact sensory function) and apraxias (inability to carry out motor activities despite intact comprehension and motor function) may also be present.

Personality change is almost invariably present in dementia, and may involve either an alteration or an accentuation or premorbid traits. A common pattern is for a normally active individual to become increasingly apathetic and withdrawn. The range of social involvement narrows. The personality loses its sparkle, and the individual is described by others as "not himself (or herself)." Another pattern of change is for a previously neat and meticulous person to become slovenly and unconcerned about appearances. On the other hand, some individuals display an accentuation of preexisting compulsive, histrionic, impulsive, or paranoid traits. Irritability and cantankerousness are also common features of dementia.

***

AMNESTIC SYNDROME

The essential feature is impairment in short- and long-term memory occurring in a normal state of consciousness (i.e., not clouded). The disturbance is attributed to a specific organic factor. Amnestic syndrome is not diagnosed if memory impairment exists in the context of clouded consciousness (delirium) or in association with a more general loss of intellectual abilities (dementia).

The individual with an amnestic syndrome has both an ongoing inability to learn new material (short-term memory deficit; anterograde amnesia) and an inability to recall material that was known in the past (long-term memory deficit; retrograde amnesia). The former is conventionally assessed by requiring the individual to remember several unrelated words or a short paragraph after a brief (usually 5-15-minute) interval of distraction. The latter is tested by asking questions about events of the past such as birthplace, family, schooling, vocation, major historical events, the names of recent presidents, etc. The individual with an amnestic syndrome has difficulty with both of these operations of memory. Events of the very remote past, however, are often better recalled than more recent events. For example, an individual may remember in vivid detail a hospital stay that took place a decade before examination, but may have no idea that he or she is currently in the hospital. So-called "immediate memory" (e.g., digit span), however, is *not* impaired in amnestic syndrome.

ORGANIC HALLUCINOSIS

The essential feature is the presence of persistent or recurrent hallucinations that occur in a normal state of consciousness and that are attributable to a specific organic factor. Therefore, the diagnosis is not made if hallucinations occur in a clouded state of consciousness, as in delirium, with significant loss of intellectual abilities, as in dementia, if there is a major disturbance of mood, as in organic affective syndrome, or if delusions predominate, as in organic delusional syndrome.

Hallucinations may occur in any modality, but certain organic factors tend to produce hallucinations of a particular type. For example, hallucinogens most commonly cause visual hallucinations, whereas alcohol tends to induce auditory hallucinations. Individuals who are blind as a result of cataracts may develop visual hallucinations; those who are deaf as a result of otosclerosis will have auditory hallucinations. Hallucinations vary from very simple and unformed to highly complex and organized.

The individual may be aware that the hallucinations are not real, or may have a firm delusional conviction of their reality. Delusions, however, are not the major feature of this syndrome, and are restricted to the content of the hallucinations or to the belief that the hallucinations are real. Further elaboration of delusional material (for example, the development of systematized persecutory delusions to account for the hallucinations, or delusions not related to the hallucinations) suggests an organic delusional syndrome.

* * *

ORGANIC AFFECTIVE SYNDROME

The essential feature is a disturbance in mood, resembling either a manic episode or a major depressive episode, that is due to a specific organic factor. The diagnosis is not made if the disturbance in mood occurs in a clouded state of consciousness, as in delirium; if it is accompanied by a significant loss of intellectual abilities, as in dementia, or persistent or recurrent hallucinations, as in organic hallucinosis; or if delusions predominate, as in organic delusional syndrome.

The clinical phenomenology of this syndrome is the same as that of a manic or major depressive episode. The severity of the disturbance may range from mild to severe. If delusions or hallucinations are present, they are similar to those described under affective disorders.

* * *

ORGANIC PERSONALITY SYNDROME

The essential feature is a marked change in personality that is due to a specific organic factor but that is not due to any other organic brain syndrome. Organic personality syndrome in a young child may occur before the development of an enduring style of relating to the environment (personality). In such cases, the syndrome is recognized by significant changes in the child's usual behavior patterns.

The clinical syndrome in a given individual depends principally on the nature and localization of the pathological process. A common pattern is characterized by emotional lability and impairment in impulse control or social judgment. The individual may be belligerent or have temper outbursts and sudden bouts of crying with little or no provocation. Socially inappropriate actions, such as sexual

...ocretions, may be engaged in with little concern for the consequences. Another pattern is characterized by marked apathy and indifference. The individual may have no interest in his or her usual hobbies and appear unconcerned with events occurring in the immediate environment. (Both of these patterns may be associated with damage to the frontal lobes, and for this reason are sometimes referred to as "frontal lobe syndromes.") Another recognized pattern, seen in some individuals with temporal lobe epilepsy, is a marked tendency to humorless verbosity in both writing and speech, religiosity, and, occasionally, exaggerated aggressiveness.

The major personality change may be the development of suspiciousness or paranoid ideation.

***

DEMENTIAS ARISING IN THE SENIUM AND PRESENIUM

The dementias associated with Alzheimer's and Pick's diseases have been referred to as senile and presenile dementias, the former arbitrarily signifying an age at onset over 65. Since nearly all cases of these dementias are associated with Alz-

heimer's disease and the identification of Alzheimer's and Pick's diseases is largely or entirely dependent on histopathological data, it seems more useful to have in a clinical classification of mental disorders a single category that encompasses the syndrome of primary degenerative dementia. This category is subtyped according to the age at onset, for the purpose of historical continuity and to maintain comparability with ICD-9-CM. The clinician will rarely be in a position to identify the specific associated neurological disorder. When such information is available, it should be noted on Axis III.

In DSM-II, the dementia associated with vascular disease was called psychosis with cerebral arteriosclerosis. However, the severity of the disorder appears to be related to repeated infarcts of the brain rather than to the extent of cerebral arteriosclerosis. At autopsy the brain shows multiple infarcts of various ages. For this reason, this category is here termed multi-infarct dementia.

When a dementia is due to some other known disease, such as a brain tumor, Huntington's chorea, or vitamin B-12 deficiency, the specific disease should be noted on Axis III, and the presence of a dementia, on Axis I.

40.

Vernon H. Mark and Frank R. Ervin

CONTROLLING RAGE BY ELECTRICAL BRAIN STIMULATION

We had perfected new techniques for identifying abnormal areas of electrical discharge in the brain. In addition, we

From Vernon H. Mark & Frank R. Ervin, *Violence and the Brain*. Harper & Row Publishers, Inc., 1970, pp. 97-9, 107-8, 111.

were able to use the "stimoceiver"—the same telemetered device used to send signals and receive information from orbiting astronauts. Its application to clinical work was pioneered by Jose Delgado of Yale, who made the stimoceiver available to us.

The tools designed by Dr. Jose Delgado for remote stimulation and recording in patients with inlying depth electrodes make it possible both to stimulate and to record deep focal areas of the brain without direct wire connections between the tiny instrument attached to the electrode in the patient's head and the stationary electronic stimulating and recording device. The instrument consists of two parts: the first is the stimulator, which in turn consists of two parts: (a) radiofrequency transmitter, which is not attached to the patient and which has the circuitry for controlling the repetition rate, the duration, and the intensity of the stimulating pulse, and (b) the receiver, which is attached to the electrode on the patient's head, and measures $3.7 \times 3 \times 1.4$ cm. and weighs 20 gm. The receiver contains solid-state circuitry which enables it to detect the radiofrequency signal and demodulate it into the ordinary stimulating current. A constant circuit transistor in the output circuit makes the pulse intensity independent of biological impedance changes over a wide range. Three channels of stimulation are available, and the operating range is up to 100 feet.

The second part of the instrument capsule is used for recording the brain activity generated around the depth electrodes. It consists of a miniature FM amplifier FM transmitter combination, and the telemetering receiver. The transmitting circuitry carried by the patient consists of this amplifier with a gain of 100 and input impedance of 2 megaohms; it has a frequency response from 2 to 200 cycles per second and a voltage control oscillator for each of 3 recording channels. The miniaturized radiofrequency transmitter operates at 216 megacycles and its range is 50 to 200 feet, depending on the environment. The size of this 3 channel unit including the battery is $4.5 \times 4.5 \times 1.5$ cm and it weighs 50 gm. It sends a radiofrequency signal to a unit which demodulates this into telemetered analog information, which can be delivered into the input of a regular brain wave machine amplifier. In our case, these analog signals were fed to the inputs of a brain wave machine and a magnetic tape recorder. The entire instrument, weighing 70 gm, can be taped into the patient's head bandage.

Attaching the stimoceiver to implanted electrodes makes it possible to record or stimulate points deep within the brain touching the electrodes, from a distance of up to 100 feet without the use of connecting wires; and because the patient is unrestricted, this stimulation and recording can be carried out over a long period of time.

In Ellen's case, the relationship between brain disease and violent behavior was very clear. Her history of brain disease went back to the time when, before the age of 2, she had a severe attack of encephalitis following mumps. When she was 10, she began to have epileptic seizures; occasionally these attacks were grand mal seizures. Most of the time, they consisted of brief lapses of consciousness, staring, lip smacking, and chewing. Often after such a seizure she would be overcome by panic and run off as fast as she could without caring about destination. Her behavior between seizures was marked by severe temper tantrums followed by extreme remorse. Four of these depressions ended in serious suicide attempts. The daughter of a professional man, she looked much younger than her age of 21.

On twelve occasions, Ellen had seriously assaulted other people without any apparent provocation. By far the most serious attack had occurred when she was 18. She was at a movie with her parents when she felt a wave of terror pass over her body. She told her father that she was going to have another one of her "racing spells" and agreed to wait for her parents in the ladies' lounge. As she went to it, she automatically took a small knife out of her hand bag. She had gotten into the habit of carrying this knife for protection because her "racing spells" often took her into dangerous neighborhoods where she would come out of her fuguelike state to find herself helpless, alone, and confused. When she got to the lounge, she looked in the mirror and perceived the left side of her face and trunk (including the left arm) as shriveled, disfigured, and "evil." At the same time, she noticed a drawing sensation in her face and hands. Just then another girl entered the lounge and inadvertently bumped against Ellen's left arm and hand. Ellen, in a panic, struck quickly with her knife, penetrating the other girl's heart and then screamed loudly. Fortunately, help arrived in time to save the life of her victim.

The next serious attack occurred inside the mental hospital to which Ellen had been sent. Ellen's nurse was writing a report, and when Ellen said "I feel another spell coming on, please help me," the nurse replied, "I'll be with you in just a minute." Ellen dragged a pair of scissors out of the nurse's pocket and drove the point into the unfortunate woman's lungs. Luckily, the nurse recovered.

Ellen's case clearly illustrates the point that violent behavior caused by brain dysfunction cannot be modified except by treating the dysfunction itself. She had had extensive medical care, and years of psychotherapy. She had taken

consecutively and in combination all the known antiseizure medications, as well as the entire range of drugs used to help emotionally disturbed patients. She had been treated in three of the major medical centers of North America with no sign of improvement. As a last resort, she had been given over sixty electroshock treatments, without any change in her seizures or in the pattern of her violence and rage.

The neurological examination made in our hospital showed Ellen's ability to assimilate newly learned material was impaired, and because of her shock treatments, she had a severe deficiency in both recent and remote memory. A brain wave examination disclosed a typical epileptic seizure pattern with spikes in both temporal regions, in addition to widespread abnormality over the rest of the brain. A special x-ray film of her brain disclosed some shrinkage of the tissue in the right temporal area.

Electrodes were placed sterotactically into both temporal lobes, and after she had recovered from the surgical procedure, we recorded epileptic electrical activity from both amygdalas. Electrical stimulation of either amygdala produced symptoms characteristic of the beginning of her seizures. These symptoms were more easily elicited by stimulating her left amygdala, and therefore, a destructive lesion was made in the left temporal lobe in the region of the amygdala and all electrodes were withdrawn. However, her symptoms and seizures persisted and changed to include signs that indicated a small portion of her brain was firing abnormally, and that this area was related to the movement of her left arm (the one brushed against by the girl she stabbed). As the motor tract crosses over from one side of the brain to the opposite side of the body, this suggested that her persistent seizures and attack behavior were initiated in her right temporal lobe. Therefore, we again placed electrodes in her right amygdala.

By the time of this second operation, Dr. Delgado's "stimoceiver" had become available to us, and we attached one to Ellen's right temporal electrode. This device made it possible to record the electrical activity in her right amygdala and hippocampus from 100 feet away, while she moved around with others in her ward. We were thus able to observe the interactions between brain stimulations and environmental cues. We could also stimulate a selected target in her brain, from the same distance. Because there are no wires involved, we could try to reproduce her violent symptoms without fear that she might hurt herself by pulling out the electrodes, and we were also able to record the activity inside her brain continuously for up to 24 to 36 hours.

The following records were made from this patient in a hospital room with the cooperation of Dr. Delgado. Both Ellen and her parents knew that sometime during the day her brain was going to be recorded from and stimulated, but they had no idea when we were going to do it. Before we had done any stimulating, but while we were recording, the electrical activity recorded from the leads in Ellen's amygdaloid nucleus showed a typical epileptic seizure pattern.... The behavior that accompanied this change in Ellen's brain waves involved her getting up and running over to the wall of her bedroom. Once there, she narrowed

her eyes, bared her teeth, and clenched her fists—that is, she exhibited all the signs of being on the verge of making a physical attack.

The point we wish to make in this description of Ellen's case is twofold. First: electrical stimulation of the amygdala initiated rage and violence; second: this behavior was preceded by the development of local electrical epileptic seizures. We are not maintaining that the amygdala—nor, indeed, the limbic system—is the only part of the brain involved in violent behavior. Our strands of electrodes are able to give us only a limited view of activity within the central nervous system, and other (perhaps many) areas of the brain must have been involved to produce such well-organized behavioral patterns. However, there can be no doubt that the electrical stimulation of and the abnormal seizure activity from the amygdala preceded and was directly related to Ellen's violence. To our knowledge, this is the first time that rage behavior was artificially produced by electrical stimulation in an abnormal brain and used to diagnose the proper placement for a therapeutic lesion.

In summary, then, trigger areas exist in the human brain that can, *in susceptible individuals,* initiate violence if stimulated with a weak electric current. We also have evidence that the stimulation of neighboring points can inhibit violence—even when it has been initiated by stimulation.

41.

Edgar Miller

MANAGING DEMENTIA

A number of conclusions can be drawn from this evidence, some of which are more soundly based than the others. The main point is that there is now good evidence that even elderly demented patients are capable of showing a beneficial response to environmental manipulations. Regardless of how important this conclusion is from a purely scientific view there can be no doubt that it is of some practical importance because many of those who come into contact with disturbed elderly individuals (including psychologists) act as if this were not the case. Once this conclusion is accepted a number of more detailed questions emerge and here the answers are not always clear although some indications can be obtained.

All the investigations described have as a common feature an increase in stimulation and by far the most commonly reported benefits are in social behaviour. There is little evidence as to what the most effective forms of intervention might be or whether improvements in other types of behaviour can be obtained. One study, that of Brook et al. (1975), clearly indicates that enhanced stimulation is not enough for sustained gains for which the patient's active involvement in the situation is necessary. The implication of the Philadelphia study by Brody and her colleagues is that various types of "excess

From Edgar Miller, "The management of dementia: A review of some possibilities," *British Journal of Social and Clinical Psychology,* 1977, vol. 16, pp. 80–83.

disability" did respond but the reports do not specify in detail what these were.

It would also be useful to know the characteristics of patients most likely to respond. Again there is no hard information although there are clues. Brook et al. (1975) noted a tendency for the less advanced cases to show the best response to reality orientation. This impression is consistent with *a priori* expectations and also with Barnes' (1974) failure to show any measurable improvements in advanced cases. As part of the Philadelphia study Brody and her colleagues obtained personality ratings on the subjects. It was found that ratings of "aggressiveness" correlated with a positive response to the treatment programme (Kleban et al. 1971). This finding needs replication before it can be considered to be of value in view of the general inadequacy of measures of personality traits as predictors of other aspects of behaviour.

One so far universal finding is that where the effects of intervention have been assessed some time after the termination of a special programme the benefits have dissipated. At first encounter this is very discouraging but it need not be so. What is probably required is an alteration in the philosophy of intervention with the demented elderly. The usual pattern of therapeutic intervention practiced by psychologists is to apply a procedure (behaviour therapy, psychotherapy, etc.) which will induce a change in the subject. This therapeutic activity is then terminated when the desired change has been achieved. This type of approach may still be valid under some circumstances in dementia but the common failure of therapeutic gains to be maintained suggests that the main thrust should be towards manipulating the environment to suit the patient. Induced changes will then be seen as permanent arrangements and not as time-limited therapeutic interventions to be discontinued as soon as a goal is reached. Of course any gains in functioning are likely to be lost eventually as the disease progresses but this does not mean that all improvements must necessarily fail to withstand rapid erosion.

Although there is minimal information as to what procedures might be particularly effective some suggestions and speculations can be made. A number of methods of management suggested as being suitable for use with the elderly in general have been reviewed by Barns et al. (1973) and some of these might be useful with demented patients. The only specific technique that has obtained empirical support is that of reality orientation.

Reality orientation has been described by Taulbee & Folsom (1966) and by Folsom (1967, 1968). In essence its aim is to ensure that the patient relearns if necessary, and then continually uses, essential information relating to his orientation for time, place, and person. Knowing the names and uses of commonly encountered objects and environmental features is usually included in this. It involves two aspects. There are formal daily classes in which the therapist rehearses patients in the specified types of information. The informal aspects go on all the time and involve all members of staff who come into contact with the patient stressing basic information relating to orientation. For example, the night nurse approaching a restless patient in the early hours of the morning might normally ask, "Is anything the matter?" If she is working in a reality-orientation setting she would say something like, "It is 2 o'clock in the morning. Is anything the matter, Mrs. Smith?"

As indicated above these procedures can be of some benefit (Brook et al., 1975) and the findings suggest that patients respond best when they are not just the passive recipients of information but are forced to interact, and presumably use, this information. Other than this it is not clear whether it is the forced interaction between patient and staff that is beneficial or if the content of what the staff attempts to impart is crucial. Reality orientation is based on the idea that certain types of basic information are essential if the demented patient is to function at a reasonable level but the implicit assumption is that what constitutes this essential information is obvious. This need not be so and the issue needs to be explored.

Behaviour modification is one set of principles of obvious relevance in this context. Behaviour modification has proved useful with a wide range of other severely handicapped groups (e.g., Kazdin, 1975) and has been used successfully with non-demented geriatric patients (e.g., Hoyer, 1973; Hoyer, Kafer, Simpson & Hoyer, 1974). Specific applications to demented subjects are difficult to locate. Mueller & Atlas (1972) did apparently successfully use reinforcement principles to increase verbal interaction in a discussion group and Libb & Clements (1969) have claimed that the use of tokens as reinforcers enhanced activity in an exercise situation in a small group of demented subjects. Behaviour modification might be particularly applicable in the case of "excess disabilities" where the patient may show functional incapacities in excess of those warranted by his physical state. An example is where an elderly patient may develop a urinary tract infection and become incontinent. Often continence is not recovered as the infection clears up despite the fact that a dementing illness is not advanced enough to make incontinence inevitable. In this situation behaviour modification principles judiciously applied might be effective in reinstating more adaptive behaviour.

In view of the indication that effective management may require a permanent reorganization and redesigning of the environment an obvious tool would be the techniques of ergonomics. Lindsley (1964) has commented upon the need to alter everyday equipment and features of the environment to take into account common limitations among elderly populations (e.g., making buttons on electrical equipment larger and requiring a firmer press to activate so that inaccurate and tremulous movements are not so likely to hit the wrong button or to trigger it if they do). Occupational therapists and others have devised some special equipment for the infirm elderly and some psychogeriatric units incorporate special design features (e.g., a series of coloured stripes running along the floor of rooms and corridors so that the confused old gentleman who wishes to micturate only has to remember to follow the blue line to arrive at the right place). Ideas like these could be extended and refined by the use of ergonomic and related techniques.

So far discussion has largely assumed that the managment of the demented elderly takes place in an institution. This is not necessarily so and the Newcastle surveys (Kay, Beamish & Roth, 1964) have shown that a substantial proportion of the demented elderly remain in the community and these are not always the least advanced cases. It is possible that more could survive in the community, or stay for longer, and those who already do so manage better, if ideas similar to those discussed were applied outside the hospital. There are of course other limitations on therapeutic intervention in the community but it is unfortunate that no one has yet tackled the problem of the demented elderly individual in the community in the ways that have started to be employed in hospitals.

Finally a comment needs to be made about the moral issues involved. Some might wish to argue that the mentally impaired aged are best cared for in a humane and comfortable environment where they are not subjected to external manipulations and can function, or fail to function, as they wish. This attitude is understandable but may well not be correct. In work with handicapped individuals, of any type or age and in the absence of contrary evidence, it must be assumed that they will enjoy the best quality of life when they approach as near as is possible to the kind of life they would have lived if they had not suffered their handicaps. There is evidence that normal, elderly people still retain a need for some active involvement and participation in life (Havighurst, Neurgarten & Tobin, 1968; Maddox & Eisdorfer, 1962) and none that they are happiest when totally abdicating their independence to an institution. The assumption must therefore be that the handicapped elderly, whatever the nature of their handicaps, will attain the highest possible quality of life when they get closest to functioning in an adequate and normal manner.

REFERENCES

Barnes, J. A. (1974). Effects of reality orientation classroom on memory loss, confusion and disorientation in geriatric patients. *Gerontologist,* **14,** 138–142.

Barns, E. K., Sack, A., & Shore, H. (1973). Guidelines to treatment approaches: modalities and methods for use with the aged. *Gerontologist,* **13,** 513–527.

Brook, P., Degun, G., & Mather, M. (1975). Reality orientation, a therapy for psychogeriatric patients: a controlled study. *British Journal of Psychiatry,* **127,** 42–45.

Havighurst, R. J., Neurgarten, B. L., & Tobin, S. S. (1968). Disengagement and patterns of aging in B. L. Neurgarten (ed.), *Middle Age and Aging: A Reader in Social Psychology.* Chicago: University of Chicago Press.

Hoyer, W. J. (1973). Application of operant techniques to the modification of elderly behavior. *Gerontologist,* **13,** 18–22.

Hoyer, W. J., Kafer, R. A., Simpson, S. C., & Hoyer, F. W. (1974). Reinstatement of verbal behavior in elderly patients using operant procedures. *Gerontologist,* **14,** 149–152.

Kay, D. W. K., Beamish, P., & Roth, M. (1964). Old age mental disorders in Newcastle upon Tyne. I. A study of prevalence. *British Journal of Psychiatry,* **110,** 668–682.

Kazdin, A. E. (1975). *Behaviour Modification in Applied Settings.* Homewood, Ill.: Dorsey Press.

Kleban, M. H., Brody, E. M., & Lawton, M. P. (1971). Personality traits in the mentally impaired aged and their relationship to improvements in current functioning. *Gerontologist,* **11,** 134–140.

Libb, J. W., & Clements, C. B. (1969). Token reinforcement in an exercise program for hospitalized geriatric patients. *Perception and Motor Skills,* **28,** 957–958.

Lindsley, O. R. (1964). Geriatric behavioral prosthetics. In R. Kastenbaum (ed.), *New Thoughts on Old Age.* New York: Springer.

Maddox, G., & Eisdorfer, C. (1962). Some correlates of activity and morale among the elderly. *Social Processing,* **40,** 228–238.

Mueller, D. J., & Atlas, L. (1972). Resocialization of regressed elderly residents: A behavioural management approach. *Journal of Gerontology,* **27,** 361–363.

Taulbee, L. R., & Folsom, J. C. (1966). Reality orientation for geriatric patients. *Hospital and Community Psychiatry,* **17,** 133–135.

CHAPTER XI

Psychotherapy

Reviewing the effectiveness of psychotherapy, which they identify as a "heterogeneous collection of ingredients or psychological conditions that produce varying degrees of both positive and deteriorative personality change in patients," Truax and Carkhuff (1967, p. 21) concluded that while certain unspecified types of psychotherapy are effective, that under particular unspecified conditions, "therapy and control patients show equivalent average outcomes, but those treated by psychotherapy show greater variability in outcome than those in control conditions" (1967, p. 21). They draw the further inference that ineffective psychotherapists result from the majority of approaches currently employed in training. Psychotherapy must be more than merely two individuals affecting each other (Beier, 1966); it must yield sources of gain (Berenson & Carkhuff, 1967), though occasionally this is not the case. Psychotherapy must channel a person's behavior into more constructive patterns (Hadley, 1958).

Demoralization Hypothesis

According to the *demoralization hypothesis*, any system of psychotherapy that uplifts the morale of the patient will prove effective. The effectiveness of all forms of psychotherapy lies in their ability to alleviate demoralization. It is for this reason that all forms of therapy are effective and that "all cohorts of patients improve on the average over time" (Frank, 1972, p. 27). Except with respect to phobias (Bandura, 1977), no convincing evidence is found to prove that one form of psychotherapy is better than another (Frank, 1979).

What then are the healing elements shared by all psychotherapies? Frank lists four:

1. "A confiding, emotionally charged relationship between the patient and a help-giving individual or group."
2. "A special setting containing symbols of healing."
3. "A rationale."
4. "A set of activities prescribed by the rationale involving both patient and therapist" (1972, p. 31).

Patients with a desire to be helped, an ability to communicate, and an optimistic attitude are headed for improvement, and a psychotherapist drawing this type of patient is destined for success. On the other hand a therapist's qualities also contribute to success, characteristics such as warmth, empathy, genuineness, zealousness, and active participativeness. New therapies seem to be effective due to the zeal with which psychotherapists throw themselves into the therapeutic encounter.

Therapy vs. Patient/Therapist Relationship Controversy. Telch (1981) takes exception to Frank, arguing for the inherent strength of psychotherapeutic techniques, despite the quality of the existing patient-therapist relationship. But Frank, citing Kazdin and Wilcoxon (1976) for support, remains adamant that psychotherapeutic techniques are not where effectiveness of therapy is to be found. Bandura (1977) sees efficacy in therapy in the creating and strengthening of expectations. Orlinsky and Howard (1980) cast their lot with Frank, arguing for patient-therapist interactions as the locus of effective therapy. Frank, however, does agree that "the more important the therapy, the less important the personal qualities of patient and therapist" (1981, p. 477).

Frank believes that the psychotherapist's resistance to his position is due to the therapist's reluctance to change his own personality to accord with successful therapy. It is considerably easier to switch techniques than alter one's own personality. Ultimately, the patient-therapist combination that proves most effective, Frank maintains, is "the one that best mobilizes the patient's hopes, enhances his or her self-efficacy, and so on" (1981, p. 477).

Enhancing Morale as the Key to Effective Therapy. Patients are driven to therapy because they are demoralized. Anxiety, depression, and other unpleasant states are secondary. It is the inability to deal with these states that demoralizes them, hence driving them to therapy. Restoring the patient's morale is the sign of successful therapy. Once demoralization is overcome, patients may no longer feel the need for therapy despite the persistence of symptoms.

Psychotherapies restore morale because they provide:

1. A supportive and confiding relationship.
2. A rationale for the patient's symptoms.
3. A special setting.
4. A prescribed procedure.

"The essence of psychological healing," writes Frank, "is the restoration of morale" (1972, p. 41). Religious conversion attests to it, for conversion is the outcome of an intense state of demoralization.

Psychoanalytic and Related Therapies

More than an understanding of psychopathological phenomena, Freud's (1916–17) major contribution was a psychotherapeutic system free from the use of drugs and other physiological devices. Freud traced, as the root of mental disorder, faulty libidinal development which makes for arrested personality development, fixation, and regression. Unearthing and accepting the contents of the unconscious through dream analysis and interpretation (Freud, 1900), and through recall by free association issuing in abreaction with its accompanying cathartic effect (Breuer & Freud, 1895), Freud found it to lead to a satisfactory transference relationship with the therapist, delivering one from neurosis, provided that successful personality development (integration of id, ego, and superego; and a strong ego) is achieved through psychoanalysis (Freud, 1940).

Variations from Freudian Psychoanalysis

Numerous variations of the Freudian system are prevalent today: Stekel's (1950) short-term *active analytic psychotherapy* de-emphasizes the patient's past, while accenting the personality of the analyst, intuitive listening, and intuitive analysis. Ferenczi's (1950, 1952) *active therapy* or *relaxation therapy,* one of permissiveness, allows the patient to play games and talk as if he were a child. Believing in the curative effect of love and permissiveness, the therapist provides both love and acceptance. By active therapy Ferenczi "meant the use of prohibitions and commands by an analyst for the purpose of mobilizing the patient's resistances and affects" (Bernstein, 1965, p. 1185).

Reich's (1972, 1973a, b) *orgastic psychotherapy, orgone therapy,* and *character analysis* attempt to combat character resistances, a patient's characterological "armor." Mental illness stems from sexual repression, and therapy must "enable the human animal to accept nature within himself" and enjoy it, for "psychic health depends upon orgastic potency." Orgastic impotence, the damming up of biological energy, is the source of irrational behavior. The objective of analytic therapy is to establish orgastic potency or "the ability to discharge an amount of sexual energy equal to that accumulated" (1948, p. 67).

Rank's (1945, 1968, 1969) *will therapy,* emphasizing the role of choice or will, is predicated on: (*a*) the therapeutic situation being a present experience instead of a mere reliving of the past as in psychoanalysis; (*b*) the nonsexual nature of the transference relationship which he regarded as a reinstituting of the maternal tie; and (*c*) the establishment of a therapeutic control by setting a time for the termination of treatment (W. S. Sahakian, 1977b, p. 118).

According to Federn's (1952) *ego psychology therapy,* neurosis is regarded as a loss of cathexis, whereas psychosis is a disease of the ego. Psychotherapy's aim is the restoration of the lost cathexis to the psychotic ego, but a reduction of hypercathexis to the neurotic ego. In psychosis the weakened ego, experiencing a loss of ego boundary, must have as its therapeutic goal, re-repression.

Klein (1948b, 1960) adds the following modifications to Freudian analysis: the ego's existence originating at birth; and good and bad emotions stemming from the infant's relationship with his mother, who constitutes the external world.

Introjection and projection, two processes appearing with the development of the infantile ego, are fundamental to the infant's outlook on the world. Healthy development enhances reality testing, while anxiety, guilt, and destructive impulses split the ego in a paranoid-schizoid state, eventuating in depression. The *object relations theory of personality* developed by Fairbairn (1952) shows the influence of his British compatriot Klein. Bad infant experiences cause splitting of the ego that at birth is a unity. The psyche's primary life drive, the libido, makes for good ego relations and growth, but with the loss of ego unity, ego splitting occurs.

The *Chicago School,* championed by Alexander and French (1946), sought corrective emotional experiences, interpretation of resistances, examination of character or total behavior of the patient; and a flexibility respecting the frequency of interview, the use of the couch, and interruptions in the therapeutic relationship.

The *direct analysis* technique of Rosen (1953) calls for therapist-participation in the patient's psychosis or world of fantasy as a figure in the psychosis by accepting his psychotic reality, thereby accompanying or assisting him in returning to reality. Utilizing the "governing principle" (therapist as a "loving, omnipotent protector and provider for the patient") and direct interpretation, insight (a vital ingredient for recovery) is achieved. Other tactics employed in direct analysis are: attacking the patient's mother; promising help, care, and cure; informing the patient of his insanity; enhancing positive transference; feigning sexual seduction; attacking the superego parental image; adopting the patient; entering into the psychosis; agreeing with megalomanic claims; love toward the patient; and interpreting delusions (English, 1961).

Other forms of psychotherapy are Deutsch's (Deutsch & Murphy, 1955) *sector therapy* wherein association with key words and phrases, taken from the patient's autobiographic social history, offer understanding of symptoms and conflicts; and Karpman's (1957) *direct psychotherapy,* adopting a similar technique.

Jung's (1966, 1969) *analytical psychotherapy,* a dialectical procedure containing the individuation process, endeavors to integrate the patient to wholeness by coordinating conscious and unconscious mind into a unity, a transcendent function.

Variations of Freudian Psychoanalysis: The Cultural School

Adler's (1929, 1939) *individual psychology* applied a therapy of social usefulness, creative selfhood, self-transcendence, and broadening of the patient's social interest, thereby eliminating inferiority feelings, egoism, and social indigency. The therapist, conveying a social feeling (transference) to his patient, who assumes a face-to-face position with him, cultivates altruism in his patient as well as a renewal of a role or position in society.

Sullivan's (1953, 1954, 1964) *interpersonal theory of psychiatry* depicts the therapist as a participant observer engaged in an interpersonal relationship with his patient. The dissipation of anxiety, tension, or the establishment of a sense of equilibrium, euphoria, or security is the goal of therapy. The processes of socialization issue in satisfactions or fulfillment of needs, and as such are conducive to becoming a person. Empathy, emotional communication, or contagion is at the disposal of the therapist for an effective (or damaging) psychiatric interview.

A synthesis of Sullivan's interpersonal approach and Freud's concepts was developed by Fromm-Reichmann (1943, 1950), the outcome being *intensive psychotherapy.* Its goal is "gaining insight into an understanding of the unconscious roots of patients' problems, the genetics and dynamics, on the part of both patient and psychiatrist, whereby such understanding and insight may frequently promote changes in the dynamic structure of the patient's personality" (1950, p. x).

Horney's (1950) *character analysis therapy,* like Sullivan's, strives for the diminution of anxiety, reducing it to levels that will free the neurotic from his behavior patterns, thereby restoring his autonomy. Neurotic self-idealization must yield to self-actualization, and the ideal self (pride-system) to the real self.

Existential, Phenomenological, and Related Psychotherapies

Existential psychologists trace their philosophical antecedents to the thought of Heidegger (1962) and Kierkegaard (1941a, 1941b, 1941c, 1957), while phenomenological psychologists are in closer affiliation with Scheler (1966), Husserl (1931), and Brentano (1874, 1968). Key emphases in the thinking of existentialists are the priority of a person's existence over his essence; the power of a person to respond with deliberation, decision, or choice; an individual viewed as in the process of becoming human; an individual's psychological dimension, that is, self-awareness; a person's becoming a person by encounter with others; and the human as a being-in-the-world, that is, only human potentially has a world whereas other beings merely have an environment.

The three existential anxieties (anxiety of having to die, the anxiety of having to become guilty, and the anxiety of lacking a meaning in life [Tillich, 1961]) have their corresponding neurotic anxieties; but unlike neurotic anxieties, no psychotherapist can remove existential or ontological anxieties. Frankl's (1967a, 1967b) *logotherapy,* predicated on one's will to meaning (1969), developed a psychotherapeutic technique to combat existential or noögenic neurosis, that is, a neurosis generated by meaninglessness in one's life rather than a sexual neurosis.

Another existential psychotherapist treating neurosis is May (1959, 1967; May, Angel, & Ellenberger, 1958). Salient features of his system include: presence; transference as "an event occurring in a real relationship between two people"; the aim of therapy being the patient's experiencing his existence as real; commitment, that is, a decisive orientation toward life or existence since insight follows decision; being as indivisible, that is, the conscious and unconscious are one.

Binswanger (1956, 1958a, 1958b, 1963) incorporates five major principles in his existential-analytic system: (1) the investigation of the patient's life history as a modification of his total structure as a being-in-the-world; (2) viewing the patient as failing in the realization of the fullness of his humanity (and seeing that he "experiences" it as such); (3) standing on the plane of common existence or the same plane with his patient, an *encounter* of relatedness and love, of "being-with-others in genuine presence"; (4) interpretation of dreams in the light of the whole man in a specific world and specific mode of existence; (5) "opening up to the sick fellow man an understanding of the structure of human existence, and [allowing] him to find his way back from his neurotic or psychotic, lost, erring, perforated or twisted mode of existence and world, into the freedom of being able to utilize his own capacities for existence" (1956, p. 148).

A synthesis of psychoanalysis and Daseinsanalysis was sought by Boss (1963) but with time Daseinsanalysis became liberated from psychoanalysis (Condrau & Boss, 1968). Daseinsanalysis is a psychotherapeutic theory that relies considerably upon the philosophical premises of Kierkegaard (1941a, 1941b, 1941c) and Heidegger (1962), especially the concepts of "therapeutic intervention" and of "anticipatory care" derived from the latter. A system that is based on the analysis of Dasein and of comprehending man as a "being-in-the-world," becomes the vehicle by which a therapist will adequately understand the "being-human."

Those psychotherapists leaning toward the phenomenological approach for understanding personality both neurotic and normal are Frankl (Fabry, 1968) and Rogers (1951, 1965). Ansbacher (1965) regards contemporary Adlerian or individual psychology as phenomenological. Kantor and Herron (1966) apply Frankl's *logotherapy* to schizophrenia. Logotherapy (Sahakian, 1979) has several important and strikingly new features to commend it: (1) will to meaning, i.e., search for life's unique meanings, an effective objective in both existential neurosis (Frankl, 1959) and schizophrenia (Kantor & Herron, 1966); (2) paradoxical intention, a desirable technique for treating phobias and obsessional neurosis (comparable to Dunlap's [1932] method of negative practice); (3) de-reflection, a valuable method in somatic preoccupations, functional sexual disturbances, and insomnia (Kaczanowski, 1967); and (4) a psychotherapy for treating suffering by offering values and meaningfulness to be found therein (Weisskopf-Joelson, 1955; Frankl, 1961, 1978).

Nondirective counseling or the *client-centered therapy* of Rogers (1942, 1951, 1959), a nonauthoritarian approach based on client permissiveness, moves from the client's state of incongruence or anxiety to congruence, insight, self-scrutiny, positive self-regard, and self-actualization. This is accomplished with the assistance of the therapist whose empathetic understanding, positive regard for, and congruent relationship with the client functions as a catalyst in the reorganization of the self-structure of the client in his achievement of reintegration and maturity. Accurate empathetic understanding is the primary task of the therapist (W. S. Sahakian, 1977b). Concentration is upon the client's phenomenological experiences, the world as he perceives it, rather than upon objective factual data. A person, innately good with a self-actualizing tendency or behavior that is purposive and goal-directed, effects changes in his personality himself by self-discovery, with the therapist establishing conditions under which the client can be effective in growing to a fully functioning person from one with merely the "existing capacity" of a "fully competent individual."

Laing (1965) sought a synthesis of the existential-phenomenological as a foundation for understanding psychosis, interpreting psychotherapy as *"an obstinate attempt of two people to recover the wholeness of being human through the relationship* between them" (1967, p. 53).

The *psychotherapy of Zen,* examined by Watts (1961) and Fromm (1963) attempts attainment of *satori* (enlightenment) by searching or "seeing" within one's being in order to achieve freedom, and the liberation of stored energies requiring channelization and activity, thereby preventing one from crippling mental disorders and enhancing one's faculty for happiness and love (Suzuki, 1949).

Behavior Therapies and Related Learning Theory Techniques

Despite their current popularity, behavior therapies are not new, dating back to the rise of learning theory. Occasionally learning theory (classical conditioning of Pavlov [1927]; instrumental learning theory of Thorndike [1911]; and Hull's theory [1943]) is synthesized with Freudian concepts to produce a psychotherapeutic system as Dollard and Miller (1950) achieved, but ordinarily the behavior therapies are free from or even antagonistic (Salter, 1949) to psychoanalysis. Behavior therapy has been used interchangeably with conditioning therapy and learning theory therapy (Wolpe, Salter & Reyna, 1964). Yates (1970) considers behavior therapy as popular as psychoanalysis.

Shoben (1948, 1949), constructing a learning theory therapy premised on Mowrer's (1947, 1953) two-factor learning theory, proposes three processes:

first, the lifting of repression and development of insight through the symbolic reinstating of the stimuli for anxiety; second, the diminution of anxiety by counter-conditioning through the attachment of the stimuli for anxiety to the comfort reaction made to the therapeutic relationship; and third, the process of reeducation through the therapist's helping the patient to formulate rational goals and behavioral methods for attaining them (1949, p. 390).

Behavior therapies are committed to the view that neurosis is merely a habit requiring attention (Dollard & Miller, 1950; Eysenck & Rachman, 1965; Schaefer & Martin, 1969; Wolpe, 1969, 1973). What distinguishes neurotic habits from others is their resistance to extinction despite their disvalue from the standpoint of reward or unadaptiveness (Wolpe, 1976; Lazarus, 1971), hence resulting in a neurotic paradox (Mowrer, 1950). Behavior therapy's aim, according to Wolpe's (1958, 1973) *psychotherapy by reciprocal inhibition,* is the alteration or removal of habits considered undesirable by counterconditioning, positive reconditioning, and experimental extinction. By systematic desensitization, a piecemeal erosion of neurotic anxiety-response habits, anxiety-evoking stimuli are diminished through training in relaxation and the construction of anxiety hierarchies.

Mowrer evaluates three basic types of behavior therapy: Type-I, Wolpe's, traces neurosis to the traumatic learning of unrealistic fears, and eliminates them by associating, in imagination, the thing or situation feared with a relaxed state.... In Type-II, Skinnerian behavior therapy, the assumption is not that the individual has learned false fears but that he has *failed to learn* effective and socially acceptable overt behavior; and change is sought through altered "reinforcement contingencies," namely, the structure of rewards and punishments, in the subject's environment. In Type-III (integrity) therapy the assumption is that the subject has mistakenly ("stupidly") decided that deception, denial, "phoniness" is a good personal strategy; and here the greatest "help" another can give is to encourage, persuade, "inspire" ... that person, by means of "sharing" and "modeling," to try honesty and openness as an alternative personal strategy (Mowrer, 1966, p. 455–456).

Integrity therapy, endorsed by Mowrer and inherent in existential psychotherapy, is enunciated by Drakeford (1967).

One form of behavior technique, *implosive therapy,* utilizes the *flooding method.* That is, instead of gradually desensitizing an individual's anxiety, implosive therapy or the flooding technique requires that the client visualize in his imagination the worst fear-provoking situation until the mental scenes are no longer distressing. According to the developers of this system, Stampfl and Levis, "the essence of the procedure is to force repeated exposures to the aversive stimuli that underlie the patient's difficulties" (1976, p. 98). Theoretically, extinction of the feared or aversive stimuli ensues. It is comparable to laughing at a joke, which eventually is no longer funny. Although a fear is at first most terrifying, the situation cannot maintain the emotion at that height perpetually. Eventually, distressing emotions, like happy ones, must subside.

Social learning theorists regard abnormal behavior "not as a symptom of a hidden illness but as a problem of 'social learning,' and can be treated directly by methods that are derived from principles of learning" (Bandura, 1967, p. 78). According to Rotter, maladaptive behavior arises when an individual's expectations of achieving desirable gratification are low, i.e., "when freedom of movement is low and need value is high" (1964, p. 82), resulting in avoidance learning or the frustration of failing to achieve one's goals. Social learning therapy employs flexible techniques suitable for the particular patient in question, and the cultivation of problem-solving skills, especially offering alternative courses for the patient's achievement of goals. The therapist, assuming an active role, interprets so that optimal behavior is acquired through reinforcement and reward, and valuable and satisfying life goals are achieved. Furthermore, social, physical, vocational, and environmental changes are effected as a way of altering personality. The therapist, however, possesses no special characteristic (Rotter, 1954) except to be warmly concerned or interested and to guide the learning process. Modeling psychotherapy is a form of social learning theory developed by Bandura (1971).

Today, considerable varieties of psychotherapy related to learning theory are prevalent. Among them are: an *assertioned-structured therapy* based on interference theory developed by Phillips (1956) and revised with the assistance of Weiner (1966), the goal of which is behavior alteration by restructuring the patient's behavior on a suitable set of probabilities and assumptions; *constructive alternativism psychotherapy* based on the personal construct psychology of Kelly (1955, 1969) which has the client experiment with new constructs as if he were playing a role, the therapist's responsibility being that of exchanging undesirable constructs for wholesome new ones; the *reinforcement theory* of Pepinsky and Pepinsky (1954), based on a modified Hullian learning theory, attempts the reduction of anxiety as an undesirable drive that deters the patient from eliciting fitting responses, and prediction of behavioral changes expected to occur under given conditions of treatment. Reduction of anxiety augments discriminatory ability regarding anxiety-arousing stimuli, as well as other behavioral changes such as the acquisition of new and suitable patterns of stimulus-response. In recent years, Bandura (1968a, 1969), has been espousing a modeling theory of psychotherapy, a technique utilizing "observational learning," by which new response patterns are established through modeling, emotional responses through vicarious conditioning, and extinction established vicariously. Behavior patterns are modified through observing the behavior of others. "Performance of observationally learned responses is largely regulated by reinforcing outcomes that may be externally applied, self-administered, or vicariously experienced" (Bandura, 1969, p. 202). Emotional behavior is vicariously extinguished through modeling therapy by exposing the observer to feared objects without their producing adverse effects. After the client's observation of another he undergoes the feared experience without unpleasant effects.

Beier's (1966) *silent language psychotherapy,* a synthesis of the Freudian unconscious with Skinner's principle of reinforcement by reward, aims at the social reinforcement of unconscious processes.

Cognitive Therapies

In recent years cognitive therapies have been on the increase, some psychotherapists believing that in clinical settings they have actually surpassed conditioning therapies. Others have even referred to this situation as a *cognitive revolution in psychology* (Beck et al., 1979). Beck and his associates believe that behavior therapy actually contributed to the development of cognitive therapy.

Because the chapter on depression deals with Beck's view of the psychotherapy of depression, it would be redundant to review it here, except to say that his mode of "cognitive therapy consists of all the approaches that alleviate psychological distress through the medium of correcting faulty conceptions and self-signals" (1976, p. 214). By correcting misleading and erroneous beliefs, Beck claims that one can diminish or alter undesirable emotional responses. He resorts to a triad of approaches: *(1) intellectual, (2) experiential,* and *(3) behavioral;* the intellectual identifies jaundiced thinking, the experiential exposes the client to it and helps the patient avoid such thinking, while the behavioral leads to the behavior necessary to exchange defective for effective responses.

Rational-Emotive Therapy. Albert Ellis (1962, 1967, 1976, 1983, 1984) developed a cognitive therapy, termed *rational-emotive psychotherapy.* Believing that neurotic behavior arises from those emotions grounded on irrational philosophies, Ellis utilizes therapy to restructure the patient's thoughts rationally, thereby freeing those blocked rational behavior patterns. Essentially, it is a therapy suitable for patients who are appreciably free from psychosis.

Speaking of the A, B, Cs of his system, Ellis explains that "when a highly charged emotional consequence *(C)* follows a significant activating event *(A), A* may seem to, but actually does not, cause *C*. Instead, emotional consequences are largely created by *B*—the individual's belief system" (1984, p. 196). Certain anxieties and unwanted emotional responses arise from irrational beliefs. To dispute *(D)* these beliefs effectively removes the undesired emotional behavior.

Philosophical Psychotherapy. Another form of cognitive therapy, *philosophical psychotherapy* (W. S. Sahakian, 1976a, 1976b, 1980a, 1980b), seeks to alter attitudes and behavior patterns by restructuring a person's beliefs and intellectual outlook (philosophy of life or *Weltanschauung*). Individuals cope with emotional problems better by assuming appropriate philosophical attitudes, beliefs capable of coloring or reshaping their emotional tenor. Doing so considerably alleviates emotional pressure, and reduces tension.

The effectiveness of philosophical psychotherapy is seen in its elimination of tension, the driving force of emotional or psychological problems. If you cannot eliminate your problem then alter your attitude toward it. Thereby you often effectively cope with two disturbing elements: the problem itself and the emotional tension exerted in fighting it. Personality change and a person's beliefs are interdependent, as evidenced by religious conversions changing one's personality. An individual's philosophical beliefs and outlook "affect overt behavior and affective responses" (W. S. Sahakian, 1984). Certain pessimistic philosophies and beliefs, for example, can predispose an individual toward depression. By contrast, however, optimistic beliefs and thoughts can lead to more confident responses and attitudes.

The reason why philosophical psychotherapy works is that "our beliefs, intellectual viewpoint, and perspective on life affect our personalities as much as our physical environment or the external stimuli to which we respond" (W. S. Sahakian, 1980b, p. 37). Although philosophical psychotherapy has been an effective psychotherapeutic tool for ages, it has only recently been seriously and clinically applied to mental problems (W. S. Sahakian, 1982).

Nonrational and Reality Psychotherapies

Turning to the other side of the coin, Whitaker and Malone (1953; Malone, Whitaker, Warkentin, & Felder, 1961) developed an *experiential* or *nonrational psychotherapy* emphasizing the patient's feeling of experience rather than his intellect. Proper unconscious functioning is scored in the sense that certain of our makeup was intended by nature to operate below the level of awareness, such as the heart's operation, and when physical and psychic functions intended for subconscious operation are constantly held in awareness, then they fail to behave normally. Hence re-repression is an important objective in therapy, in addition to personal growth, and autonomous choice spontaneously and unconsciously executed.

Whitaker and his associates (1956) have introduced a system of *multiple therapy,* entailing two or more psychotherapists comprising a therapeutic team that interviews the patient jointly from the initial contact to the termination of treatment, with each therapist utilizing his own preferred technique. Though costly, it is valuable particularly in difficult cases.

A system termed *reality therapy* has been developed by Glasser, which he defined as "a therapy that leads all patients toward reality, toward grappling successfully with the tangible and intangible aspects of the real world ... a therapy toward reality" (1965, p. 6). Reality therapy strives for the fulfillment of the individual's needs in the real world, as well as the acceptance of the real world. It entails an intense personal involvement, responsible modes of behavior, and learning more desirable modes of behavior in addition to confronting reality. Drakeford (1967), summarizing his *integrity therapy,* adds the need for confession to what Mowrer terms the "three R's," of Glasser's therapy: responsibility, reality, right and wrong.

Holistic and Gestalt Psychotherapies

Gestalt therapy, espoused by Perls (1966a, 1966b; Perls, Hefferline & Goodman, 1965), attempts a process of integration by supporting the patient's genuine interests, needs, desires, and the achievement of maturity through a "transition from environmental support to self-support" (1966b), thereby developing his own potential, while increasing his frustration tolerance.

Goldstein (1959) also has offered an organismic psychotherapy constructed upon the principles of gestalt psychology, and aiming at self-realization by enabling the patient to make the right choices, despite conflicts with fear, by the therapist's creation of an environment conducive to an experience of communion and transference.

Psychobiologic therapy, the system of Meyer (1948, 1951), attempts to treat the patient as a whole in action, both mind and body. However, the patient is not regarded as diseased, but poorly adjusted. Therapy, a cooperative endeavor, utilizes specificity or the patient's personal history in order to investigate irrational and immature behavior patterns so as to replace them with objective and realistic responses to life that are within one's reach of choices and resources.

Eclectic Techniques of Psychotherapy

Rather than remaining loyal to a particular system of psychotherapy, therapists tend to utilize whatever technique works at the moment in the case of a particular patient. Consequently, eclectic forms of psychotherapy are emerging, a leading one being multimodal therapy proposed by Arnold A. Lazarus in a paper published in 1973 and expanded to book length form in 1981.

Multimodal Therapy

Multimodal therapy was designed to tailor therapy to suit the patient's needs. Furthermore, it entails not merely treating the individual but involving the entire family when necessary. Therapy is not merely a question of what works, but what works for whom. Recognizing that disorders rarely have a single cause, Lazarus looks to a multiplicity of therapies to resolve the problem. Consequently, a battery of therapies are employed called the BASIC I.D.: B for behavior; A for affect; S for sensation; I for imagery; C for cognition; I for interpersonal relationships; and D for drugs and or biological factors. These seven modalities need not be used independent of each other, for they are both interactive and interdependent. Take, for example, the situation: Mr. Smith's headaches concern him to a point of becoming a hypochondriac.

When Mr. Smith has a headache, he becomes quiet and withdrawn (behavior), starts feeling anxious (affect), experiences the pain as "an internal hammer with hot spikes driven into the skull" (sensation), and pictures himself dying of a brain tumor (imagery) while convincing himself that the doctors have probably missed something seriously wrong (cognition). During these episodes, he talks monosyllabically while his wife fusses over him (interpersonal) and resorts to aspirins and other pain killers (biological) (Lazarus, 1981, p. 14).

Such is Lazarus' application of multimodal therapy.

Group Psychotherapy

The *raison d'être* of group psychotherapy is that the group itself is virtually the therapeutic agent, and not (as so many persons mistakenly believe) that it simply alleviates the congestion of patients waiting for a psychotherapeutic session (Mullan & Rosenbaum, 1962).

Analytic Group Psychotherapy

Utilizing many psychoanalytic principles, Slavson (1964, 1965a, 1965b) developed a variety of group techniques: (*a*) In *play group psychotherapy,* primarily for children from 7 to 12 years of age, the children act out through free activity their impulses, fantasies, tensions, and conflicts in respect to their surrounding environment, both the social and physical. (*b*) In *activity-interview group psychotherapy,* for those in their latency period, the psychotherapist interprets, poses leading questions, and allows the members of the group to do likewise to the end that insight and understanding are achieved. (*c*) In *interview group psychotherapy,* for adolescents and adults, the setting transpires around a circular table. The participants are encouraged to speak freely, assured that their utterances are held in strictest confidence. The group functions on its own initiative. The psychodynamics operative in these three types of analytic groups are relationship or transference, catharsis, insight, ego strengthening, reality testing, and sublimation. Another variation is *para-analytic group psychotherapy* which consists of "the fusing of analytic group psychotherapy with guidance, counseling, advice and 'teaching,' as indicated" (Slavson, 1965b, p. 328).

Group Focal-Conflict Theory and Other Systems

Foulkes (1948), and in collaboration with Anthony (1957), regarding the group as a "dynamic field of experience" and the analyst as a participant-observer, strove for spontaneous contributions from members of the group. Bion (1961), influenced by Melanie Klein, viewed the group as a series of emotional states or as cultures, with its members reacting to or accepting the cultures as they move along a series of valences from one emotional culture to others. The therapist's task is the interpretation of the group's behavior as a unit. Interested in Bion's system, Thelen (Stock & Thelen, 1958) studied group interaction in terms of its emotional factors, functional process, and relationship between individual and group. Prompted by these studies, a *group focal-conflict theory of psychotherapy* was developed by three of Thelen's students (Whitaker, Stock & Lieberman, 1964) based on French's ideas (1952-1954).

Psychodrama

Group psychotherapy (1953, 1966a, 1970), especially in the form of psychodrama (1966b, 1972), has been developed by Moreno to whom therapy must be "living and doing." Motivated by spontaneity and creativity to combat anxiety, the patient acts out on a stage, living space, situations personally meaningful to him. Aided by therapists who function as directors and auxiliary egos who confront patients with significant stimulus conditions, the patient through role-playing gains insight respecting his conflict, and emotional release through catharsis.

Transactional Analysis

Utilizing the ideas of psychoanalysis, especially those of Eduardo Weiss and Paul Federn's ego psychology, Berne (1961, 1963, 1964) offered his version which he terms transactional analysis, that is, the analysis of single transactions (a unit of social action) of interpersonal relationships or various ego states. "The objective of transactional analysis in group therapy is to carry each patient through the progressive stages of structural analysis, transactional analysis proper, game analysis, and script analysis, until he attains social control" (1961, p. 165). Structural analysis, the analysis of ego states, makes for reality testing, thus leading to transactional analysis, the goal of which is social control or controlling one's own tendency to manipulate others destructively and responding without insight. Archaic ego states are segregated, while archaic conflicts and distortions are resolved.

Milieu Therapy: The Therapeutic Community

Drawing upon the social and cultural atmosphere itself as a therapeutic agent, Jones (1953, 1956, 1962) developed (and Rapoport [1960, 1968] articulated) the concept of a therapeutic community. Milieu therapy, a form of social psychiatry, employs the following concepts and tactics: (1) the holistic view wherein the entire hospital is considered a therapeutic community, a wholesome society with which patients would choose to identify; (2) permissiveness in contrast to the traditional restrictive environment of mental institutions; (3) patient participation in the conduct and affairs of their institutions; (4) broadening the base of therapy by extending the range of activities, relationships, and environment; and (5) rehabilitation through rehearsing social roles in a hospital whose social setting and operation is a replica of the world at large, hence creating a therapeutic atmosphere.

Kraft (1966) cites seven difficulties facing the therapeutic community: (1) the lack of clear, conceptual model; (2) ill-defined boundaries and roles of the professional which make for diminution of professional identity; (3) group responsibility deteriorating into a state of "no responsibility"; (4) the possibility of lack of personal attention; (5) the values of the therapeutic community possibly being inappropriate in society at large; (6) difficulties of program evaluation and research; and (7) the unavailability of staff especially trained for the therapeutic community.

Conjoint Family Therapy

A form of therapy closely related to group therapy, conjoint family therapy, consists of treating the patient in conjunction with "other members of his family together as a functioning natural group" (Jackson & Weakland, 1961, p. 30). The underlying theory is that the therapist is dealing with a "sick family," not merely a "sick patient" (Jackson, 1967). A novel variation of Jackson's system is that of Satir (1967) who places the accent on psychological health rather than psychopathology by calling for well-family checkups as a preventive measure.

In Great Britain, *family psychiatry* developed by Howells (1962, 1963, 1968b, 1968c), has as its goal the production of an "emotionally healthy family," since the family members sent for referral are merely an indicator of that family's psychopathology. Family psychotherapy may employ the following techniques: (1) individual therapy; (2) didactic therapy (joint therapy); family group therapy (conjoint family therapy); and nonfamily group therapy.

Numerous other forms of group therapies exist both in fact and in theory, such as: Daytop Lodge, group therapy for drug addicts (Shelly & Bassin, 1965); the new group therapy (Mowrer, 1964) consisting of laymen operations, numbering about 265 throughout the country, and affiliated with the American Conference of Therapeutic Self-Help Clubs; multiple impact therapy, and many others.

Physiodynamic Therapies

Since the discovery of psychoanalysis by Freud, the field of psychotherapy has developed fruitfully in a variety of directions. In addition to psychotheraphy, and allied to it, are the physical or physiodynamic therapies, including shock therapies, psychosurgery, and drug therapy.

Malarial Treatment of General Paresis

In 1887, Wagner-Jauregg (1968) accidentally discovered the therapeutic effects of malaria on general paresis, and in 1917 injected the blood of a malarial patient into that of one suffering from syphilitic infection, and consequently hit upon malarial therapy.

Electroshock Therapy

Cerletti (1950, 1954, 1968) reported that he and his associate L. Bini in 1937 successfully treated a schizophrenic patient by applying a 60-cycle alternating current to produce convulsion by electrodes placed on the patient's head. On the conclusion of EST, the schizophrenic whose only speech previously was gibberishness "sat up of his own accord, looked about him calmly with a vague smile, as though asking what was expected of him. I asked him, 'What has been happening to you?' He answered with no more gibberish: 'I don't know; perhaps I have been asleep' " (Cerletti, 1968, pp. 363–364).

Insulin Shock Therapy

In a series of articles in the *Wiener medizinische Wochenschrift* in 1934 to 1935, Sakel (1938) reported that his success with insulin shock therapy with schizophrenics began as early as 1927. "The main therapeutic principle lay in the inducement of a pathophysiological condition of insulin hypoglycemia with one of two clinical manifestations, comahybernation or convulsion. These conditions I term 'shock' " (1954, p. 264). Sakel's method underwent three phases: adaptation; shock; and polarization. He claimed as high as 86 percent success with cases of schizophrenia that had not been ill over a year.

Metrazol Convulsive Therapy and Carbon Dioxide Therapy

A convulsive treatment with the intravenous use of metrazol was developed by Meduna (1936, 1954a, b) and introduced in 1934. The convulsive reaction to metrazol is comparable to that of epilepsy (grand mal). A brief coma, following convulsion, is accompanied by an improvement in respiration and relaxation, with a gradual clearing in consciousness. Meduna deduced the existence of a "biologic antagonism between the schizophrenic and the epileptic process" (Meduna, 1968, p. 367), because of the rarity of epileptic convulsion in schizophrenia.

Later, Meduna (1954a, b) developed a carbon dioxide psychotherapy for use with neurotics. Essentially it is a desensitization process whereby through repeated inhalations of CO_2 "for a protracted period of time, the patient regains a normal homeostatic balance; and his excitability to old and new pathogenic influences becomes so lowered that the particular influences cease to be pathogenic" (1948). Loss of consciousness usually occurs before 20 to 25 respirations of CO_2, during which time psychomotor excitement is perceptible as well as sensory and other phenomena. Three types of abreaction may take place: "conscious realistic, conscious allegoric, and unconscious realistic ... explained by *inhibition of cortical inhibitory functions*" (1958, p. 86). Unless considerable improvement occurs by 20 to 30 treatments, this form of therapy is of no avail.

Psychosurgery: Prefrontal Leucotomy and Prefrontal Lobotomy

Following Fulton and Jacobsen's (1935) successful experimental surgery on the frontal brain region of monkeys, alleviating anxiety and frustration, Moniz (1954) developed bilateral prefrontal leucotomy, the severance of the association tracts joining the prefrontal brain areas and the thalamic centers by drilling holes on either side of the forehead through the skull and cutting the cores in brain tissue. Moniz believed that the operation, first performed on December 27, 1935, would cause new synaptic paths, and accordingly new behavior patterns. He felt that disordered behavior of established "synaptic relations must be altered, and the paths in which the impulses revolve in constant passage must be modified, so that the ideas which are connected with them will be modified and the thought will take another course" (1968, p. 376).

The psychosurgery of the Portuguese psychiatrist, Moniz, reached a second stage of sophistication in 1942 in the United States with the efforts of Freeman and Watts (1950) and their technique of prefrontal lobotomy. Though Freeman (1962) claims a renewed interest in psychosurgery developing in England, this surgical technique is rapidly reaching a point of historical value only. The white matter of the prefrontal lobes is reached by an instrument capable of severing the nerve paths connecting the prefrontal areas and the nuclei of the thalamus.

The white matter in the frontal lobes is cut approximately in the plane of the coronal suture. A burr hole is made through or near the suture line and with a long cannula the sphenoidal ridge is identified. With the coronal suture and the spenoidal ridge as landmarks, the nerve pathways can be sectioned in the desired plane. The lobotomy may be performed with a blunt knife-like instrument or with a special leucotome (Freeman & Watts, 1968, p. 378).

Sleep Therapy, Narcoanalysis, Hypnoanalysis, and Autogenic Training

Drug-induced narcosis accompanied with psychotherapy and abreaction in the drugged state produced by sodium pentothal and sodium amytal were techniques developed by Grinker and Spiegel (1945) in World War II, and by Horsley (1943) in Great Britain. The drugs, augmenting abreaction, served to release intense guilt feelings as well as hostility and fear. As early as 1931 Horsley discovered the effectiveness of nembutal as a psychotherapeutic agent. Grinker and Spiegel, who refer to their systems as narcosynthesis, claim that it is more than a

process of recapture by the ego of alienated ideas and emotions. It is also the synthesis of related feelings that have been separated by the process of dissociation. Thus, under pentothal, hostility and fear may be recombined as derivatives of the reaction to the same stress. The patient becomes aware that his anger is due to his being left unprotected in a fearful situation (1945, p. 393).

Jacobson's (1938) *progressive relaxation,* and the *autogenic training* of Schultz and Luthe (1959) are attempts at a synthesis of physiologic processes with psychotherapy. Combining hypnosis with their system, Schultz and Luthe developed six steps as the core of autogenic training: "heaviness and warmth in the extremities, regulation of cardiac activity and respiration, abdominal warmth and cooling of the forehead" (1959, p. 1). In addition, there are "autogenic standard exercises," such as, training postures, verbal formulae, meditative exercises, organ-specific exercises, intentional formulae. Organ-specific exercises and intentional formulae are adjuncts of the standard exercises, used as supplements to them.

Hypnoanalysis finds its strongest protagonist in Wolberg (1964, 1977) who contends that all persons are capable of being hypnotized, though his success is limited to 90 percent, with a correlation existing between a person's suggestibility and his hypnotic susceptibility. Neurotics respond to hypnotic therapy, but those with character disorders do not, and psychotics cannot be significantly aided by this mode of therapy. At best, hypnosis is a tool.

Sleep therapy, a form of treatment currently employed in the Soviet Union rather than in the United States, is used for both schizophrenics and neurotics. Andreev (1960) reports that the most effective results ensue from sleep that is closest to natural rather than narcotic induced. Hypnosis, conditioned reflex, and at times minute doses of hypnotic drug may be used toward this end. With neurotics, psychotherapy is an indispensable accompaniment, since sleep's value is only "restorative and protective in character."

In addition to the types of psychotherapy discussed, there are numerous others treating specialized areas or types of individuals, such as psychotherapy with children (Hammer & Kaplan, 1967); pastoral psychotheraphy, counseling by trained clergy (Clinebell, 1966); counseling juvenile delinquents (Slavson, 1965a); psychotherapy via psychopharmacology (Wortis, 1962); poetry therapy (Leedy, 1969); and Daytop Lodge approach to drug addiction (Shelly & Bassin, 1965).

Crisis Intervention

In crisis intervention, explain Hinsie and Campbell, "the focus is on transitional-developmental and accidental-situational demands for novel adaptational responses. Because minimal intervention at such times tends to achieve maximal and optimal effects, such a model is more readily applicable to population groups than the medical model" (1970, p. 606). Crisis intervention means precisely what the word connotes, an intervening on the part of anyone who can be helpful in a crisis or emergency situation as in an earthquake disaster, fire, storm, or other crisis situation. In such situations, ordinary people are often more effective than experts. "Some persons with little formal training," observed Albee, "are often as effective, or even more effective, in human intervention with disturbed people than are the experts" (1974, p. viii). There are situations in which the person who happens to be there is in a position to be the most effective. This is also true in general medicine. A case in point is the individual who is on the spot to administer CPR (cardio-pulmonary resuscitation) to a person who has just lost consciousness and is without a heartbeat.

In addition to natural disasters, other crises of a more personal nature can arise, such as the death of a person important to one, a divorce, and a host of other traumatic vicissitudes of life. Accordingly, Aguiler and Messick define crisis as a turning point in which "a person faces a problem that he cannot readily solve by using the coping mechanisms that have worked for him before. As a result, his tension and anxiety increase, and he becomes less able to find a solution. A person in this situation feels helpless—he is caught in a state of great emotional upset and feels unable to take action on his own to solve his problem" (1974, p. 1). The objective of crisis intervention, then, is to reestablish equilibrium in such an individual.

Characteristics of an effective counselor dealing with an individual in a crisis situation include emotional maturity, the ability to communicate both verbally and through nonverbal behavior, a self-awareness of one's own feelings, empathy, warmth, genuineness, and previous experience with crises. "Counselors who themselves experienced crisis with some degree of success are more apt to be able to help clients through a crisis period than those who have not" (Getz, Wiesen, Sue & Ayers, 1974, p. 28).

42.

Carl R. Rogers

CLIENT-CENTERED THERAPY

A. CONDITIONS OF THE THERAPEUTIC PROCESS

For therapy to occur it is necessary that these conditions exist.

1. That two persons are in *contact.*

2. That the first person, whom we shall term the client, is in a state of *incongruence,* being *vulnerable,* or *anxious.*

3. That the second person, whom we shall term the therapist, is *congruent* in the *relationship.*

4. That the therapist is *experiencing unconditional positive regard* toward the client.

5. That the therapist is *experiencing* an *empathic* understanding of the client's *internal frame of reference.*

6. That the client *perceives,* at least to a minimal degree, conditions 4 and 5, the *unconditional positive regard* of the therapist for him, and the *empathic* understanding of the therapist.

* * *

B. THE PROCESS OF THERAPY

When the preceding conditions exist and continue, a process is set in motion which has these characteristic directions:

1. The client is increasingly free in expressing his *feelings,* through verbal and/or motor channels.

From "A theory of therapy, personality, and interpersonal relationships as developed in the client-centered frame-work" by Carl R. Rogers. In *Psychology: A Study of a Science* by S. Koch. Copyright 1959 by McGraw-Hill Book Company. Reproduced with permission.

2. His expressed feelings increasingly have reference to the *self,* rather than nonself.

3. He increasingly differentiates and discriminates the objects of his *feelings* and *perceptions,* including his environment, other persons, his *self,* his *experiences,* and the interrelationships of these. He becomes less *intensional* and more *extensional* in his *perceptions,* or to put it in other terms, his experiences are more *accurately symbolized.*

4. His expressed *feelings* increasingly have reference to the *incongruity* between certain of his *experiences* and his *concept of self.*

5. He comes to experience in awareness the threat of such *incongruence.*

a. This *experience of threat* is possible only because of the continued *unconditional positive regard of* the therapist, which is extended to *incongruence* as much as to *congruence,* to *anxiety* as much as to absence of *anxiety.*

6. He *experiences* fully, in *awareness,* feelings which have in the past been *denied to awareness,* or *distorted in awareness.*

7. His *concept of self* becomes reorganized to assimilate and include these *experiences* which have previously been *distorted in* or *denied to awareness.*

8. As this reorganization of the *self-structure* continues, his *concept* of *self* becomes increasingly *congruent* with his *experience;* the *self* now including *experiences* which previously would have been too *threatening* to be in *awareness.*

a. A corollary tendency is toward fewer perceptual *distortions in awareness,* or *denials to awareness,* since there are fewer *experiences* which can be *threatening*. In other words, *defensiveness* is decreased.

9. He becomes increasingly able to *experience,* without a feeling of *threat,* the therapist's *unconditional positive regard.*

10. He increasingly feels an *unconditional positive self-regard.*

11. He increasingly *experiences* himself as the *locus of evaluation.*

12. He reacts to *experience* less in terms of his *conditions of worth* and more in terms of an *organismic valuing process.*

* * *

C. OUTCOMES IN PERSONALITY AND BEHAVIOR

There is no clear distinction between process and outcome. Items of process are simply differentiated aspects of outcome. Hence the statements which follow could have been included under process. For reasons of convenience in understanding, there have been grouped here those changes which are customarily associated with the terms outcomes, or results, or are observed outside of the therapeutic relationship. These are the changes which are hypothesized as being relatively permanent:

1. The client is more *congruent,* more *open to his experience,* less *defensive.*

2. He is consequently more realistic, objective, *extensional* in his *perceptions.*

3. He is consequently more effective in problem solving.

4. His *psychological adjustment* is improved, being closer to the optimum.

   a. This is owing to, and is a continuation of, the changes in *self-structure* described in *B*7 and *B*8.

5. As a result of the increased *congruence* of *self* and *experience* (*C*4 above) his *vulnerability* to *threat* is reduced.

6. As a consequence of *C*2 above, his perception of his *ideal self* is more realistic, more achievable.

7. As a consequence of the changes in *C*4 and *C*5 his *self* is more *congruent* with his *ideal self.*

8. As a consequence of the increased *congruence* of *self* and *ideal self* (*C*6) and the greater *congruence* of *self* and *experience,* tension of all types is reduced—physiological tension, psychological tension, and the specific type of psychological tension defined as *anxiety.*

9. He has an increased degree of *positive self-regard.*

10. He *perceives* the *locus of evaluation* and the locus of choice as residing within himself.

   a. As a consequence of *C*9 and *C*10 he feels more confident and more self-directing.

   b. As a consequence of *C*1 and *C*10 his values are determined by an *organismic valuing process.*

11. As a consequence of *C*1, and *C*2, he *perceives* others more realistically and accurately.

12. He *experiences* more *acceptance* of others, as a consequence of less need for distortion of his perceptions of them.

13. His behavior changes in various ways.

   a. Since the proportion of *experience* assimilated into the *self-structure* is increased, the proportion of behaviors which can be "owned" as belonging to the *self* is increased.

   b. Conversely, the proportion of behaviors which are disowned as *self-experiences,* felt to be "not myself," is decreased.

   c. Hence his behavior is *perceived* as being more within his control.

14. His behavior is perceived by others as more socialized, more *mature.*

15. As a consequence of *C*1, 2, 3, his behavior is more creative, more uniquely adaptive to each new situation and each new problem, more fully expressive of his own purposes and values.

43.

Joseph Wolpe

BEHAVIOR THERAPY

PSYCHOTHERAPY BY RECIPROCAL INHIBITION

The aim of behavior is always to change habits judged undesirable. The achievement of this aim depends on the application of one or more of three categories of conditioning operations.

1. Counterconditioning

A basic premise about neuroses is that they are persistent unadaptive learned habits of reaction. . . . Almost universally, anxiety is a prominent constituent of neurotic reaction; and since anxiety involves a primitive (subcortical) level of neural organization, its unlearning can be procured only through processes that involve this primitive level. Neurotic anxiety cannot be overcome purely by intellectual action—logical argument, rational insight—except in the special case where it stems entirely from misconceptions. . . .

The elimination of anxiety response habits is usually accomplished by the inhibition of anxiety by a competing response. The formal process is the development of conditioned inhibition through reciprocal inhibition (Wolpe, 1954). *If a response inhibitory of anxiety can be made to occur in the presence of anxiety-evoking stimuli it will weaken the bond between these stimuli and the anxiety.* In human neuroses, a considerable number of responses

Reprinted with permission from Joseph Wolpe, *The Practice of Behavior Therapy.* Copyright 1969 by Pergamon Press.

which empirically inhibit anxiety have been successfully used to overcome neurotic anxiety-response habits as well as other neurotic habits. For example, assertive responses . . . are used to overcome neurotic anxieties that inhibit effective action towards those persons with whom the patient has to interact. The essence of the therapist's role is to encourage the outward expression, under all reasonable circumstances, of the feelings and action tendencies previously inhibited by anxiety. Each act of assertion to some extent reciprocally inhibits the concurrent anxiety and slightly weakens the anxiety response habit. The reduction of anxiety drive is the main reinforcing agent of this habit change. Similarly, relaxation responses can be employed to bring about systematic decrements of anxiety response patterns to many classes of stimuli. . . .

The reciprocal inhibition principle also comes into play in overcoming responses other than anxiety. It is the basis of the conditioned inhibition of obsessional and compulsive habits by aversion therapy. . . . In this a painful faradic shock or similar stimulus inhibits the undesired behavior, with the result that conditioned inhibition of the latter is established, and accumulates with repetition. There are also many instances of positive conditioning which *ipso facto* include the conditioned inhibition of previous habits of response to the antecedent stimuli concerned. For example, when assertive behavior is instigated, while the expression of "positive" feelings produces conditioned inhibition of anxiety, the motor actions involved in such expression inhibit and consequently displace the previous motor habit. It should be noted that here the reinforcement comprises the various "rewarding" consequences of the new response.

2. Positive Reconditioning

The conditioning of new motor habits or ways of thinking may accompany the overcoming of unadaptive autonomic responses, as in the example just given. But frequently new habits of action or of thought are needed in contexts that do not involve anxiety. An instance of this is the conditioning treatment of enuresis nocturna. By arranging for the patient to be awakened by an alarm as soon as the first drop or urine is excreted during sleep, the waking reaction is conditioned to the imminence of urination, and this subsequently leads to the development of an inhibition of the tendency to urinate in response to bladder stimulation during sleep. (Gwynne Jones, 1960, Lovibond, 1963). A further example is the conditioning of effective study habits in individuals who have unproductive habits and fritter away their time when they should be working (Sulzer, 1965).

Successful conditioning of new habits always involves the use of "rewards" of one kind or another. It sometimes suffices to supply these on an *ad hoc* basis, but in recent years there has been increasing formal use of Skinner's (1953) operant conditioning principles to remove and replace undesirable habits. In order to establish a new behavior pattern in a particular situation, the desired response has to be elicited and each time rewarded, while the undesired behavior is consistently not rewarded and even punished. For example, anorexia nervosa has been successfully treated by making social rewards such as the use of a radio or the granting of companionship contingent on eating, with-

drawing these rewards when the patient fails to eat (Bachrach, Erwin and Mohr, 1965). Various types of behavior in schizophrenics have been treated on the same principle (Lindsley, 1956, Williams, 1959, Ayllon, 1963, Davison, 1964) and major and lasting changes of behavior have been produced, even in patients who had been hospitalized for years. . . .

3. Experimental Extinction

This is the progressive weakening of a habit through the repeated nonreinforcement of the responses that manifest it. Thus, behavior that depends on food reinforcement becomes progressively weaker if its occurrences are not followed by food. The same is usually true of avoidance behavior if it is not reinforced by an occasional shock. The very evocation of the response has effects that are self-weakening (whether or not it should ultimately be proved that this depends on the fatigue-associated reactive inhibition mechanism proposed by Hull (1943).

Therapeutic techniques based on the extinction mechanism, introduced a quarter of a century ago by Dunlap (1932) under the name "negative practice," have in recent years again been employed in the treatment of such motor habits as tics (e.g. Yates, 1958). In correlation with a very large number of unreinforced trials spontaneous evocations of the undesired movement are progressively lessened.

* * *

THE TECHNIQUE OF SYSTEMATIC DESENSITIZATION

The problems posed by the patient are carefully considered by the therapist, and if changed behavior is required in social, sexual or other life situations, this will usually be given attention first. If systematic desensitization is also indicated, it is started as soon as possible in parallel with whatever measures have been instituted in life situations. The technique involves three separate sets of operations:

1. Training in deep muscle relaxation;
2. The construction of anxiety hierarchies;
3. Counterposing relaxation and anxiety-evoking stimuli from the hierarchies.

I. Training in Relaxation

The method of relaxation taught is essentially that of Jacobson (1938), but instruction is completed in the course of about six interviews, in marked contrast to Jacobson's very prolonged training schedules. The patient is asked to practice at home for two fifteen-minute periods a day.

In introducing the subject of relaxation, I tell the patient (who has usually already gained a general idea of the nature of conditioning therapy) that relaxation is just one of the methods in our armamentarium for combating anxiety. I continue as follows:

Even the ordinary relaxing that occurs when one lies down often produces quite a noticeable calming effect. It has been found that there is a definite relationship between the extent of muscle relaxation and the production of emotional changes opposite to anxiety. I am going to teach you how to relax far beyond the usual point, and with practice you will be able to 'switch on' at will very considerable emotional effects of an 'anti-anxiety' kind.

There is no established sequence for training the various muscle groups in relaxation, but whatever sequence is adopted should be systematic. My own practice is to start with the arms because they are convenient for purposes of demonstration and easy to check on. The head region is next because the most marked anxiety-inhibiting effects are usually obtained by relaxations there.

2. The Construction of Hierarchies

An anxiety hierarchy is a list of stimuli on a common theme ranked in descending order according to the amount of anxiety they evoke. In some anxiety neuroses the rank order of the stimuli is an exceedingly difficult matter. . . .

The theme, or common core, of a neurosis is usually derived from extrinsic stimulus situations disturbing to the patient—like spiders or criticisms; but sometimes the core subsists in response-produced stimuli. A variety of physically disparate stimulus situations may all induce a common response. For example, a case of claustrophobia (Wolpe, 1961) had the same kind of trapped feeling when she had irremovable nail polish on her fingers or was wearing a tight ring as when she was physically confined. Such commonality of response is the basis of secondary generalization (Hull, 1943, p. 191).

Hierarchy construction usually begins at about the same time as relaxation training, and is subject to alterations or additions at any time. It is important to note that both the gathering of data and its subsequent organizing are done in an ordinary conversational way and *not under relaxation,* since the patient's *ordinary* responses to stimuli are what the therapist needs to know.

The raw data from which the hierarchies are constructed come from four main sources: (a) the patient's history . . . ; (b) responses to the Willoughby Questionnaire, which reveals anxieties mainly in certain interpersonal contexts: (c) a Fear Survey Schedule (Wolpe & Lang, 1964) . . . and (d) special probings into all possible situations in which the patient feels unadaptive anxiety. It frequently helps to assign the patient the homework task of listing all situations, thoughts, or feelings that he finds disturbing, fearful, embarrassing, or in any other way distressing.

When all the identified sources of neurotic disturbance have been listed, the therapist classifies them into themes. Usually there is more than one theme. In most cases these are fairly obvious, but there are many exceptions. For example, a fear of going to movies, parties and other public situations may suggest a claustrophobia and yet really be a basic fear of scrutiny. Frequently, fear and avoidance of social occasions turns out to be based on fear of criticism or of rejection; or the fear may be a function of the mere physical presence of people, varying with the number to whom the patient is exposed. One patient's ostensible fear of social situations was really a conditioned anxiety response to the smell of food in public places. A good example of the importance of correct identification of relevant sources of anxiety is to be found in a previously reported case (Wolpe, 1958, p. 152) where a man's impotence turned out to be due to anxiety not related to any aspect of the sexual situation as such, but to the idea of trauma. In the context of an attempt at defloration, anxiety had been conditioned to the sexual act. In this instance the strategy of treatment was shifted by this revelation from *in vivo* use of the sexual response to systematic desensitization to tissue damage.

It is not necessary for the patient actually to have experienced each situation that is to be included in a hierarchy. The question posed is, "If you were today confronted by such and such a situation, *would you expect* to be anxious?" To answer this question he has to *imagine* the situation concerned, and it is generally almost as easy to imagine a supposed event as one that has at some time occurred. The temporal setting of an imagined stimulus configuration scarcely affects the responses to it. A man with a phobia for dogs will usually have about as much anxiety at the idea of meeting a bulldog on the way home tomorrow as at recalling an actual encounter with this breed of dog.

The following list of fears from a recent patient will be used to illustrate some of the intricacies of hierarchy construction. This list is reproduced exactly as the patient presented it.

Raw List of Fears

1. High Altitudes	11. Fire
2. Elevators	12. Fainting
3. Crowded Places	13. Falling Back
4. Church	14. Injections
5. Darkness—	15. Medications
Movies, etc.	16. Fear of the
6. Being Alone	Unknown
7. Marital Relations	17. Losing My Mind
(pregnancy)	18. Locked Doors
8. Walking any	19. Amusement Park
Distance	Rides
9. Death	20. Steep Stairways
10. Accidents	

With the help of a little clarification from the patient the items were sorted into categories, thus:

A. Acrophobia

1. High Altitudes	20. Steep Stairways
19. Amusement Park	
Rides	

B. Claustrophobia

2. Elevators	5. Movies (darkness
3. Crowded Places	factor)
4. Church	18. Locked Doors

C. Agoraphobia

6. Being Alone	8. Walking any Distance (alone)

D. Illness and its Associations

12. Fainting	14. Injections
13. Falling Back	15. Medication

E. Basically Objective Fears

7. Marital Relations	11. Fire
(pregnancy)	16. Fear of the
9. Death	Unknown
10. Accidents	17. Losing My Mind

3. Desensitization Procedure: Counteracting Anxiety by Relaxation

The stage is now set for the conventional desensitization procedure—the patient having attained a capacity to calm himself by relaxation, and the therapist having established appropriate hierarchies. It is natural to hope for a smooth therapeutic passage, and such is often the case but there are many difficulties that may encumber the path. I shall first describe the technique and the characteristic course of the uncomplicated process of desensitization.

The assessment of a patient's ability to relax depends partly upon his reports of the degree of calmness that relaxing brings about in him, and partly upon impressions gained from observing him. By the second or third lesson, most patients report calmness, ease, tranquility or sleepiness. A few experience little or no change of feeling. It would, of course, be a boon to have objective indicators to determine degree of relaxation. Jacobson (1939, 1964) has used the electromyogram, but mainly as a corroborative measure. It is too laborious for routine use. Meanwhile, fortunately, the reports of patients usually serve as a sufficiently reliable guide to their emotional state, especially with the help of the subjective anxiety scale (see above). Quite a number of patients, especially those who have little or no current anxiety, report a positive feeling of calm after only one or two sessions of relaxation training. In some fortunate individuals there appears to be a kind of relaxation-radiation zone (usually in the arms or face); and these report a diffuse spread of relaxation to many regions with correlated growth of calmness when the radiation zone is relaxed. If the hierarchies are ready early it is my practice to start desensitization with those who can

attain distinct emotional calm before concluding the relaxation training (though this is continued during subsequent interviews).

In embarking upon a desensitization program it is of course highly desirable for the patient to achieve a positive feeling of calm, i.e., a negative of anxiety; but it is *not* mandatory and one is always well satisfied with zero subjective units of disturbance (*suds*). In a fair number who have considerable levels of current anxiety [whether or not this is pervasive ('free-floating') anxiety], it has been found that a substantial lowering of the level—say, from 50 to 15 *suds*—may afford a sufficiently low anxiety baseline for successful desensitization. Apparently, an anxiety-inhibiting 'dynamism' can inhibit small quanta of intercurrent anxiety even when it does not fully overcome current anxiety. Desensitizing effects are only rarely obtainable with levels in excess of 25 *suds;* and in some individuals a zero level is a *sine qua non.*

REFERENCES

Ayllon, T. Intensive treatment of psychotic behavior by stimulus satiation and food reinforcement. *Behaviour Research and Therapy,* 1963, **1**, 53.

Bachrach, A. J., Erwin, W. J., & Mohr, J. P. The control of eating behavior in an anorexic by operant conditioning techniques. In L. Ullman and L. Krasner (Eds.), *Case studies in behavior modification.* New York: Holt, Rinehart, and Winston, 1965.

Davison, G. C. A social learning therapy programme with an autistic child. *Behaviour Research and Therapy,* 1964, **2**, 149.

Dunlap, K. *Habits: their making and unmaking.* New York: Liveright, 1932.

Hull, C. L. *Principles of behavior.* New York: Appleton-Century, 1943.

Jacobson, E. *Progressive relaxation.* Chicago: University of Chicago Press, 1938.

Jacobson, E. Variation of blood pressure with skeletal muscle tension and relaxation. *Annals of Internal Medicine,* 1939, **12,** 1194.

Jacobson, E. Variation of pulse rate with skeletal muscle tension and relaxation. *Annals of Internal Medicine,* 1940, **13,** 1619.

Lindsley, O. R. Operant conditioning methods applied to research in chronic schizophrenia. *Psychiatric Research Reports,* 1956, **5,** 118.

Lovibond, S. H. The mechanism of conditioning treatment of enuresis. *Behaviour Research and Therapy,* 1963, **1,** 17.

Skinner, B. F. *Science and human behavior.* New York, Macmillan & Co., 1953.

Sulzer, E. S. Behavior modification in psychiatric adult patients. In L. Ullman and L. Krasner (Eds.), *Case studies in behavior modification,* New York, Holt, Rinehart, and Winston, 1965.

Williams, C. D. The elimination of tantrum behavior by extinction procedures, case report. *Journal of Abnormal and Social Psychology,* 1959, **59,** 269.

Wolpe, J. Reciprocal inhibition as the main basis of psychotherapeutic effects. *Archives of Neurology and Psychiatry,* 1954, **72,** 205.

Wolpe, J. *Psychotherapy by reciprocal inhibition.* Stanford: Stanford University Press, 1958.

Wolpe, J. The systematic desensitization treatment of neuroses. *Journal of Nervous and Mental Disease,* 1961, **112,** 189.

Wolpe, J., & Lang, P. J. A fear survey schedule for use in behavior therapy. *Behaviour Research and Therapy,* 1964, **2,** 27.

Yates, A. J. The application of learning theory to the treatment of tics. *Journal of Abnormal and Social Psychology,* 1958, **56,** 175.

44.

Albert Bandura

MODELLING THERAPY

One of the fundamental means by which human behaviour is acquired and modified is through modelling or vicarious processes. Research conducted within the broad framework of social learning theory (Bandura, 1965; Bandura and Walters, 1963) provides considerable evidence that virtually all learning phenomena that result from direct experiences can occur vicariously, as a function of observing other people's behaviour and its consequences

for them. Thus, for example, persons can acquire complex response patterns through exposure to the performances of exemplary models; emotional responses can be conditioned, through observation, by witnessing the affective reactions of others undergoing painful or pleasurable experiences; fearful and avoidant responsivity can be extinguished vicariously through observing modelled approach behaviour toward feared objects without any adverse consequences happening to the performer; inhibitions can be induced by witnessing the behaviour of others being punished; and, finally, the expression of well-learned responses can be enhanced and socially reg-

From Albert Bandura, "Modelling approaches to the modification of phobic disorders." In Ruth Porter (Ed.), *The role of learning in psychotherapy.* London: J. & A. Churchill, 1968. Pp. 201-217. Reprinted by permission.

ulated through the actions of influential models. Modelling procedures are, therefore, ideally suited for effecting diverse changes in psychological functioning.

A comprehensive review of the numerous psychotherapeutic applications of modelling approaches is beyond the scope of this paper. Instead attention will be focused mainly on a series of experiments designed both to establish the efficacy of modelling procedures for treating phobic conditions, and to delineate some of the variables governing the process of vicarious extinction. The findings derived from this programme of research will be discussed at length, followed by some speculations on the probable mechanisms through which vicarious extinction effects are produced.

New therapeutic approaches are traditionally promoted enthusiastically and it is not until after the methods have been applied clinically for some time by a coterie of advocates that objective tests of efficacy are conducted. Usually the methods are unceremoniously retired by subsequent controlled studies. Workers in psychotherapy have, therefore, come to view any new therapeutic approach as a passing fad. When laboratory tests of efficacy precede clinical application, new methods are subjected to close scrutiny at each stage of development, and those that evolve are likely to produce outcomes sufficiently favourable to weather the test of time.

All the studies reported in this paper employ essentially the same basic experimental design. Subjects are first given an objective test of avoidance behaviour in which they are asked to perform progressively more threatening interactions with a phobic object. Those who are sufficiently fearful to qualify for the project are then assigned, on the basis of the severity of their avoidance behaviour, to various treatment conditions.

Evidence that deviant behaviour can be modified by a particular method is of limited therapeutic significance unless it can be demonstrated that established response patterns generalize to stimuli beyond those encountered in treatment, and that induced changes endure after the formal therapeutic conditions have been discontinued. Therefore the administration of tests for avoidance behaviour toward different phobic objects is repeated after the subjects have completed the treatment programme, to measure transfer effects. The assessment procedures are repeated after one month to determine how well the behavioural changes have been maintained.

Since the absence of anticipated aversive consequences is a requisite for fear extinction, the modelling displays most likely to have strong effects on phobic observers are those in which performances that the observers regard as hazardous are repeatedly shown to be safe in a variety of threatening circumstances. But the presentation of modelled approach responses toward the most aversive situations at the outset is apt to generate in observers high levels of emotional arousal that can impede vicarious extinction. The efficacy of modelling procedures may, therefore, partly depend on the manner in which the modelled performances are presented.

Avoidance responses can be extinguished with minimal distress if subjects are exposed to a graduated sequence of modelling activities beginning with displays that have low arousal value. After emotional reactions to attenuated threats have been extinguished, progressively more aversive modelling cues, which are weakened by generalization of anxiety extinction from preceding displays, are gradually introduced and neutralized. Stimulus graduation is not a necessary condition for vicarious extinction, but it permits greater control over the change process and elicits less anxiety than approaches with repeated exposure to modelling events having high threat value.

VICARIOUS EXTINCTION OF PHOBIC BEHAVIOUR

Our initial study (Bandura, Grusec and Menlove, 1967) was a stringent test of the degree to which strong avoidance behaviour can be extinguished through modelling procedures. We also investigated whether the induction of positive affective responses in observers during exposure to modelling cues that potentially are threatening expedites vicarious extinction.

Young children, who exhibited a strong fear of dogs, were assigned to one of four treatment conditions. One group participated in eight brief sessions during which they observed a fearless peer-model exhibit progressively more fear-arousing interactions with a dog. For these children, the modelled approach behaviour was presented within a highly positive party context designed to counteract anxiety reactions. When the jovial party was well under way, a dauntless four-year-old boy entered the room with a dog in tow, and performed pre-arranged sequences of interactions with the dog for approximately three minutes during each session. The fear-provoking properties of the modelled displays were gradually increased from session to session by varying simultaneously the physical restraints on the dog, the directness and intimacy of the modelled approach responses, and the duration of interaction between the model and the dog.

A second group of children observed the same graduated performances, but in a neutral context. In the two treatment conditions described, the stimulus complex contained both modelling cues and repeated observation of the phobic stimulus. Therefore, in order to evaluate the effects

of exposure to a feared animal alone, a third group of children observed the dog in the positive context but without the model. A fourth group participated in the positive activities but was never exposed to either the dog or the modelled displays.

Children's phobic behaviour toward two different dogs was measured separately, after the treatment programme and again a month later. The avoidance test consisted of a graded sequence of interactions with the dog. The children were asked, for example, to approach and pet the dog, to release it from a playpen, remove its leash, feed it with dog biscuits, and spend a fixed period of time alone in the room with the animal. The final and most difficult set of tasks required the children to climb into the playpen with the dog and, after having locked the gate, to pet it and remain alone

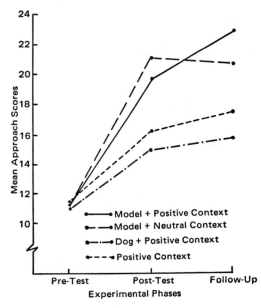

FIGURE 44-1. Mean Approach Scores Achieved by Children with Dog Phobias in Each of the Treatment Conditions on Three Different Periods of Assessment. From Albert Bandura, J.E. Grusec, and F.L. Menlove, *Journal of Personality and Social Psychology*, vol. 5, p. 16. Copyright 1967 by the American Psychological Association. Reprinted by permission of the publisher and author.

with it under these confining fear-arousing conditions.

As shown in Figure 44-1, the modelling treatment produced stable and generalized reduction in avoidance behaviour. The two groups of children who had observed the peer-model interact without anxiety with the dog displayed significantly greater approach behaviour toward both the experimental and an unfamiliar animal than children in the third and fourth groups (exposure to the dog alone and control conditions with neither dog nor model), who did not differ from each other. The positive context, however, did not contribute much to the favourable outcomes obtained. A more stringent criterion of therapeutic efficacy is the percentage of participants who could manage the final set of tasks. That is, the majority (67 per cent) of children receiving the modelling treatment were eventually able to remain alone in the room and confined with the dog in the playpen; in contrast, this terminal task was attained by relatively few children in the two control conditions.

VICARIOUS EXTINCTION AS A FUNCTION OF MULTIPLE MODELLING

One would expect, from knowledge of generalization processes, that vicarious extinction would be partly governed by the variety of modelling stimulus elements that are neutralized. That is, exposure to multiple models who exhibit fearless behaviour toward variant forms of phobic object should produce relatively thorough extinction of arousal reactions, and hence, extensive reduction in avoidance behaviour. On the other hand observers whose emotional responsiveness to a restricted set of aversive modelling elements is extinguished tend to achieve weaker extinction effects. This proposition was tested in a

second experiment (Bandura and Menlove, 1968) employing the same assessment methodology with children who displayed severe avoidance behaviour to dogs. In this project the modelled performances were presented in a series of brief cine-films in order to test the efficacy of symbolic modelling techniques, which lend themselves readily to psychotherapeutic applications.

One group of children, who participated in a single modelling treatment, observed a fearless male model display the same progressively more fear-arousing interactions with a dog as in the preceding experiment. The second group of children, receiving multiple modelling treatments, observed several different girls and boys of varying ages interacting positively with various breeds of dogs of different sizes. The size and fearsomeness of the dogs

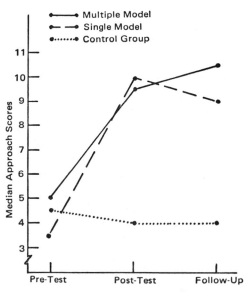

FIGURE 44-2. Median Approach Scores Obtained by Children with Dog Phobias in Each of Three Conditions at Different Phases of the Experiment. (From Albert Bandura and F.L. Menlove, *Journal of Personality and Social Psychology*, vol. 8, p. 99, Copyright 1968 by the American Psychological Association. Reprinted by permission of the publisher and author.)

were progressively increased from small dogs that were not threatening in appearance to massive animals that were. Children assigned to a control group were shown cine-films without dogs.

As in the previous experiment, children who observed approach behaviour modelled without any adverse consequences to the performer displayed enduring and generalized reduction in avoidance behaviour, whereas the controls did not show such changes (Figure 44-2). Comparison of the performance of the most difficult terminal tasks by children presented with the single modelling display and those who witnessed the multiple modelling, showed that the latter treatment is more effective in completely eliminating phobic behaviour. As a further test of the therapeutic value of symbolic modelling, the control group of children were given the multiple modelling treatment after the main experiment had been completed. These children, whose avoidance behaviour remained unchanged in several tests conducted during the control period, displayed, after the treatment, a sharp increase in their ability to approach dogs.

Comparison of the results of the two experiments suggests that symbolic modelling is less powerful than live demonstrations of essentially the same behaviour. Although the single modelling treatment effected significant reductions in children's avoidance responses, it did not sufficiently weaken their fears to enable them to carry out the most frightening terminal approach behaviour (being confined with the dog in the playpen). But the diminished efficacy of symbolic modelling can be offset by a broader sampling of models and aversive stimulus objects. Children who received this diverse modelling treatment not only showed continued improvement in approach behaviour between post-test and follow-up periods, but

also achieved terminal performances at rates comparable to equally severely phobic children who, in the previous experiment, had observed fearless behaviour by a single real-life model.

The potency of modelling influences in the transmission of anxiety responses is widely acknowledged, but the therapeutic value of these influences has sometimes been questioned (Jersild and Holmes, 1935) on the grounds that fears persist even though modelling frequently occurs under ordinary conditions of life. The effectiveness of any principle of learning depends not only on its validity but also on the manner in which it is implemented. Inconsistent, haphazard and inadequately sequenced learning experiences will produce disappointing results regardless of the cogency of the principle supposedly guiding the treatment programme.

In many instances weak fears are undoubtedly extinguished, or substantially reduced, through fortuitous naturalistic modelling. But carefully planned modelling experiences are essential for the modification of more tenacious phobias. There is some evidence (Bandura and Menlove, 1968) that parents of children who exhibit severe fearfulness make no attempt to overcome their children's fears because they (the parents) suffer from similar fears. Consequently they seldom model fearlessness and, on the rare occasion when they do so, the modelling endeavours do not consist of the carefully graded presentation of threatening stimuli without which this method is not only likely to be ineffective, but may actually exacerbate anxiety reactions. A not uncommon domestic modelling scene, for example, is one in which a parent is busily petting a dog that is jumping about, while simultaneously bidding the child, who is clinging fearfully, to touch the bounding animal. By contrast, the modelling treatments, in addition to utilizing the principle of graduation to reduce anxiety arousal, involved concentrated exposures to modelling displays under protected observation conditions, and extensive variations of the characteristics of the model, the intimacy of approach behaviour, and the aversive properties of the feared object. Had the modelling sequences been presented in a widely dispersed and haphazard fashion, and restricted to the more reserved petting responses by adults (whom children are likely to discriminate as better able to protect themselves), the vicarious extinction outcomes might have been relatively weak and unpredictable.

In addition to exposure variables, qualitative aspects of the modelled behaviour are likely to exercise some degree of control over vicarious extinction outcomes. It has been shown in studies of vicarious emotional conditioning (Bandura and Rosenthal, 1966; Berger, 1962) that negative affection expressions by models can serve as powerful arousal cues for observers. One would expect modelled approach responses accompanied by positive affective expressions to engender less anxiety arousal and, hence, faster extinction than if the model showed fearful reactions while performing the same behaviour. Parental modelling efforts intended to overcome children's fears are frequently nullified when parents suffer similar apprehensions and force themselves into tense contact with the feared objects. In the present experiments the models frequently expressed pleasant emotional reactions as they performed approach responses in a relaxed manner.

COMPARATIVE EFFICACY OF MODELLING AND DESENSITIZATION TREATMENT APPROACHES

Our third project (Bandura, Blanchard and Ritter, 1968) used an elaborate experimental design that assessed the comparative efficacy of modelling and desensitization treatment approaches for producing affective, behavioural and attitudinal changes. The participants were adolescents and adults with snake phobias that unnecessarily restricted their psychological functioning in various ways. This type of behaviour disorder was selected for study partly because snake phobias have been frequently employed in evaluating the potency of different forms of behavioural therapy and substantial data have been accumulated on the results (Davison, 1968; Lang, Lazovik and Reynolds, 1965; Schubot, 1966). Apart from the comparative data, this paradigm is well suited for laboratory investigations of extinction processes because avoidance behaviour can be effectively measured and extra-experimental encounters with snakes that might confound the effects of treatment rarely occur or can be easily controlled.

In the initial phase of the experiment the participants were given a behavioural test that measured the strength of their avoidance of snakes. They also completed a comprehensive fear inventory to determine whether the elimination of anxieties about snakes is associated with concomitant changes in other areas of anxiety. Attitudinal ratings on several scales describing various encounters with snakes, and on evaluative dimensions of the semantic differential technique, were also obtained. The latter measures were included to furnish the data on the inadequately explored attitudinal effects of behavioural changes induced through social-learning methods. The attitude scales were always given before and after the snake-avoidance test to permit evaluation of the reciprocal interaction between attitudinal and behavioural changes.

The cases were individually matched according to their avoidance behaviour, and assigned to one of four conditions.

One group participated in a self-regulated symbolic modelling treatment in which the clients observed a graduated film depicting young children, adolescents and adults engaging in progressively more fear-provoking interactions with a large king snake. To increase the therapeutic power of this method two other features were added. First, clients were taught to induce and to maintain anxiety-inhibiting relaxation throughout the period of exposure. A self-managed modelling treatment should permit greater control over extinction outcomes than one in which a person is exposed to a sequence of aversive modelling cues without regard to his anxiety reactions. Therefore the rate of presentation of the modelling stimuli was regulated by the client through a projector equipped with remote-control starting and reversing devices. Clients were instructed to stop the film whenever a particular modelled performance proved anxiety-provoking, to reverse the film to the beginning of the aversive sequence, and to reinduce deep relaxation. They then re-viewed the threatening scene repeatedly in this manner until it was completely neutralized before proceeding to the next item in the graduated sequence. After the clients became skilled in the stimulus presentation and self-induction of relaxation, the therapist absented himself from the situation so that the clients themselves conducted their own treatment until their anxieties to the depicted scene were thoroughly extinquished.

The second group of clients received a live-modelling-guided participation form of treatment in which, after observing intimate snake-interaction behaviour repeatedly modelled by the therapist, they were aided, through demonstration, to perform progressively more approach responses toward a snake. At each step the therapist himself performed fearless be-haviour, and gradually led the clients into touching, stroking, and then holding the middle of the snake's body with gloved and then bare hands, while he held the snake by the head and tail. When clients no longer felt any apprehension about touching the snake under these secure conditions, anxieties about contact with the snake's head area and entwining tail were extinguished. The therapist again performed the tasks fearlessly, and then he and the client performed the responses jointly; as clients became less fearful the therapist gradually reduced his participation and control over the snake until eventually the clients were able to hold the snake in their laps without assistance, to let the snake loose in the room and retrieve it, and to let it crawl freely over their bodies. Progress through the graded approach tasks was paced according to the clients' apprehensiveness. When they reported being able to perform one activity with little or no fear, they were eased into a more difficult interaction.

Clients assigned to the third group received the standard form of counter-conditioning therapy devised by Wolpe (1958). In this procedure deep relaxation was successively paired with imaginal representations of snake scenes arranged in order of increasing aversiveness. As in the other conditions, treatment was continued until the clients' anxiety reactions were totally extinguished or the maximum time (6 hours) allotted for treatment (not counting relaxation training) was completed. The maximum contact with snakes, either live or in symbolic form, was thus equated across treatments.

Clients assigned to the control group participated in the behavioural and attitudinal assessments without receiving any intervening treatment. This group was included primarily to furnish a control for changes resulting from repeated measurements. A relationship pseudotherapy was not used because several previous investigations have shown that snake avoidance behaviour is unaffected by such experiences. In addition, the controls were subsequently used to test a variation of the symbolic modelling treatment. To evaluate the reliability of treatment outcomes the procedures were administered by two therapists, one female and the other male, with different personality characteristics.

After the treatment series was completed the assessment procedures were readministered to all subjects. The behavioural test, using two snakes of strikingly different colours, consisted of series of tasks requiring subjects to approach, look at, touch and hold a snake with gloved and bare hands; to remove the snake from its cage, let it loose in the room, and then replace it in the cage; to hold it within five inches of their faces; and, finally, to tolerate the snake in their laps while they held their hands passively at their sides. Immediately before and during the performance of each task clients rated the intensity of their fear on a ten-interval scale to provide a measure of affective changes associated with the different methods of treatment.

Behavioural Changes

The results of the behavioural test, summarized graphically in Figure 44-3, show that the control subjects are essentially unchanged in avoidance behaviour; symbolic modelling and desensitization treatments substantially reduced phobic behaviour; while live modelling combined with guided participation proved to be an unusually powerful treatment and eliminated snake phobias in virtually all subjects (92 per cent).

Affective Changes

The modelling procedures not only extinguished strong, long-standing avoidance behaviour, but also effectively neutralized the anxiety-arousing properties of the phobic stimuli. Both of the modelling treatments achieved marked decrements in anticipatory and performance anxiety. Although subjects who had received desensitization treatment also experienced less emotional arousal while approaching the snakes in the various ways described, their fear was significantly less reduced than the fear shown by subjects in the modelling conditions.

Attitudinal Changes

Because cognitive and attitudinal changes have been systematically assessed

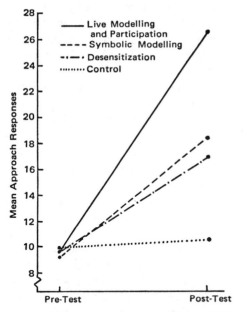

FIGURE 44-3. Mean Number of Approach Responses Performed by Clients with Snake Phobias, Who Received Either Systematic Desensitization, Symbolic Modelling, Live Modelling Combined with Guided Performance, or No Treatment. Each of the Groups Contains 12 Subjects. (From Bandura, A., Blanchard, E., & Ritter, B. *Journal of Abnormal Psychology*, volume 87, pp. 50–70. Virginia: American Psychological Association. Copyright 1978 by the American Psychological Association. Reprinted by permission of the publisher and author.

in applications of behavioural therapies, it has been generally assumed that these types of approaches alter behaviours only. One can distinguish between three basic strategies of attitude change. The *information-oriented* approach attempts to modify the subjects' attitudes by altering their beliefs about the attitude object through various forms of persuasive interpretation. This method produces changes in attitudes but generally has little effect on overt actions (Festinger, 1964; Fleischmann, Harris and Burtt, 1955; Levitt, 1965; Maccoby *et al.*, 1962). A second general strategy involves an *affect-oriented* approach wherein both evaluations of, and behaviour toward, particular attitude objects are modified by altering their affective properties, usually through vicarious or direct conditioning procedures. The third approach, which is often used in social learning (Bandura, 1969) and in experimental social psychology (Brehm and Cohen, 1962; Festinger, 1957), relies upon a *behaviour-oriented* strategy. The results of this procedure have provided considerable evidence that enduring attitudinal changes can be induced most effectively by getting a person to engage in new behaviour in relation to the attitude object without untoward consequences. The relative superiority of the behavioural approach probably stems from the fact that a basic change in behaviour and the resultant experiential feedback provide an objective and genuine basis for new evaluations.

The results of the present experiment show that applications of social learning therapies have important attitudinal consequences. Both symbolic modelling and desensitization, which primarily involve extinction of the negative affect aroused by aversive stimuli, produced favourable changes in attitudes toward snakes. Consistent with theoretical expectation, the treatment condition that reduced the anxiety-arousing properties of snakes and enabled subjects to engage in intimate interactions with snakes effected the greatest attitudinal changes.

Positive Transfers of Anxiety Decrements

The difference between psychodynamic and social-learning approaches to psychotherapy is often misconstrued as the difference between treatment of causes and of symptoms. But one cannot eliminate behaviour as such, except perhaps through direct removal of the requisite neurophysiological systems. Response patterns can be modified only by altering the conditions that regulate their occurrence. Psychodynamic and social-learning therapies are, therefore, equally concerned with modifying the "causes" of deviant behaviour; however, these theories differ (often radically) in what they regard these determinants to be—a crucial difference which, in turn, influences the types of psychological events favoured in the respective treatments. It would be more accurate and advantageous to redefine the cause-symptom treatment controversy as being primarily concerned with the question of whether a particular form of therapy chooses to modify conditions that, in reality, exercise strong, weak, or no significant control over the behaviour in question. One would predict from this point of view that favourable changes induced in one area of behaviour will tend to set in motion beneficial changes in related areas of psychological functioning.

Analysis of the fear inventory scores in our studies does indeed reveal some degree of reduction of fear towards situations beyond the specifically treated phobia, the decrements being roughly proportional to the potency of the treatments employed.

Untreated controls showed no changes in either the number or intensity of their fears; desensitization produced a decrease only in the severity of fears towards other animals; and symbolic modelling was accompanied by a reduction in the number of animal fears and a general diminution in the intensity of anxiety in several other areas of functioning. Live modelling combined with participation, on the other hand, effected widespread reductions of fear in relation to a variety of threats involving both interpersonal and nonsocial events.

The positive transfer obtained in this study probably reflects the operation of at least two somewhat different processes. The first involves generalization of extinction effects from treated stimuli to related sources of anxiety. The second entails positive reinforcement of a sense of capability through success, which mitigates emotional responses to potentially threatening situations. In a follow-up questionnaire most of the clients reported that, having successfully overcome a phobia that plagued them for most of their lives, they felt increased confidence that they could cope effectively with other fear-provoking events.

Under conditions where a given treatment procedure exercises weak behavioural control, many other variables (such as the personality characteristics of the therapists, attributes of the clients and minor technical variations) will emerge as influential determinants of change. But if a method is sufficiently powerful it should be able to override such influences. To demonstrate that in the cases that showed only partial improvement the major deficits resided in the method rather than in the client, all subjects who failed to achieve terminal performances, including the controls, were subsequently treated with the live modelling and guided partici-

pation techniques. Snake phobia was thoroughly extinguished in all these subjects, within a few brief sessions, regardless of their age, sex, anxiety proneness and the severity of the avoidance behaviour. Moreover, this supplementary treatment produced further reductions in fearfulness toward both the phobic stimuli and other types of threats, and additional attitudinal changes.

A one-month follow-up assessment revealed that the beneficial changes produced in behaviour, attitudes and emotional responsiveness were effectively maintained. The clients also gave evidence that the behavioural improvements had generalized to real-life situations. They were able to participate in recreational activities such as camping, hiking and gardening which they formerly avoided because of their dread of snakes; they no longer experienced marked distress when unexpectedly confronted with snakes in the course of their social or occupational activities; and they were able to handle harmless snakes, and a few even served as model therapists for their own children and faint-hearted friends. These favourable outcomes illustrate the need for new psychological facilities that offer brief and highly efficacious treatments for specific types of behaviour dysfunction. Vast numbers of people, who otherwise endure unnecessary restrictions in certain areas of their lives, could benefit from such services.

Ritter (1968) has achieved a uniform degree of success with group modelling procedures in children with snake phobias. Groups of children participated in two 35-minute sessions in which they either merely observed several fearless children exhibit intimate interactions with a snake, or received a modelling-guided participation form of treatment during which the therapist displayed positive responses toward the snake and then gradually eased the children into performing the feared behaviour. Snake phobias were completely extinguished in 53 per cent of the children by modelling alone and in 80 per cent of the children after modelling combined with guided participation. The results of these projects indicate that a powerful form of therapy is one in which therapeutic agents themselves model the desired behaviour and arrange optimum conditions for clients to engage in similar activities until they can perform the behaviour skillfully and fearlessly. The therapeutic outcomes associated with this approach are sufficiently promising to warrant its further extension to other types of anxieties and phobias.

In a recently completed experiment, O'Connor (1968) employed symbolic modelling in treating pre-school children who showed extreme social withdrawal, a behaviour disorder that reflects both deficits in social skills and fear of close interpersonal contacts. One-half of this group of children were shown a control film, while a matched group of isolates observed a talkie depicting timid children initially watching ongoing social activities at a distance but eventually joining and interacting with the children, with evident positive consequences. In a behavioural assessment conducted immediately after the treatment session the controls remained markedly withdrawn, whereas children who had received the symbolic modelling showed a fivefold increase in social interaction.

Within the modelling-guided participation treatment there are three processes operative that might contribute in varying degrees to such striking psychological changes. These are observation of fearless behaviour being modelled without any unfavorable consequences, incidental information received regarding the feared objects, and direct personal interactions with threatening objects, without adverse effects. In an experiment aimed at isolating the relative influence of these component variables, Blanchard (1968) matched subjects in terms of their snake-avoidance behaviour and assigned them to one of four conditions. One subject in each quartet received the standard procedure, which includes the benefits of modelling, incidental information and guided interaction with a snake. A second subject simultaneously observed the modelling sessions and listened to the verbal interchanges thus being exposed to both modelling and information influences. The third subject received only the modelling component, while the fourth, who merely participated in the testing procedures, experienced none of the constituent influences. Modelling accounted for a major part of the psychological changes, and guided participation also contributed a significant increment, particularly to approach behaviour and fear reduction. On the other hand, informational influences had no effects on either attitudes, emotional arousal or approach behaviour.

MECHANISMS UNDERLYING VICARIOUS EXTINCTION

Research is also needed to clarify the mechanisms through which modelling combined with guided participation achieves such uniformly powerful extinction effects. The findings of the studies described, particularly those based on a paradigm of non-response extinction, can perhaps be best explained in terms of a dual-process theory of avoidance behaviour (Rescorla and Solomon, 1967). According to this view, conditioned aversive stimuli evoke emotional arousal which has both autonomic and central components. It is further assumed that these arousal processes, especially those involving central systems, exert some degree of mediating control over instrumental avoidance responses. The influential role of arousal mediators is most clearly demonstrated by experiments in which avoidance responses to a given stimulus are established through prior classical pairings of that stimulus with aversive experiences. The skeletal muscles of the experimental animals are immobilized by curare to prevent avoidance responses from being conditioned directly to the external stimuli (Rescorla and Solomon, 1967; Solomon and Turner, 1962).

It follows from the dual-process theory that if the arousal capacity of a phobic stimulus is extinguished, then both the motivation and one set of controlling stimuli for avoidance behaviour are removed. Neutralization of an aversive stimulus through classical extinction procedures alone markedly facilitates subsequent elimination of avoidance behaviour (Black, 1958). It has been further shown (Bandura, Blanchard and Ritter, 1968) that emotional arousal can be effectively extinguished on a vicarious basis when observers merely witness models exhibiting approach responses toward feared objects without experiencing any adverse consequences. The more thoroughly emotional arousal to threatening stimuli is vicariously extinguished the greater is the reduction in avoidance behaviour (Blanchard, 1968). In accordance with these findings, the process of change associated with the powerful procedure involving modelling combined with guided participation may be conceptualized as follows. Repeated modelling of approach responses decreases the arousal potential of aversive stimuli below the threshold for activating avoidance responses, thus enabling subjects to engage, albeit somewhat anxiously, in approach behaviour. The favourable outcomes resulting from direct contact with threatening events further extinguish any residual anxiety and avoidance tendencies. Without the benefit of previous vicarious extinction the reinstatement of severely inhibited behaviour generally requires a tedious and protracted treatment programme. After approach behaviour towards formerly avoided objects has been fully restored the resultant new experiences give rise to substantial reorganization of attitudes.

SUMMARY

This paper is principally concerned with modelling processes whereby phobic behaviour is successfully extinguished through observation of modelling approach behaviour without adverse consequences accruing to the fearless performers. Results of several laboratory investigations reveal that live modelling combined with guided participation is an unusually powerful treatment that effects stable and generalized extinction of phobic behaviour in virtually all cases. Moreover, modelling procedures, both singly and in combination with guided performance, produce a marked reduction in emotional responsivity, substantial attitudinal changes, and anxiety decrements in areas of functioning beyond the specifically treated phobia.

A major factor in modelling procedures that expedites behavioural changes is assumed to be vicarious extinction of arousal reactions to aversive stimuli below the level for activating avoidance responses; this extinction thus enables the clients to approach the phobic objects. Direct contact with threats that are no longer objectively justified provides a variety of new experiences which, if favourable, further extinguish residual anxiety and augment attitudinal changes.

Laboratory findings suggest that a

powerful form of therapy is one in which therapeutic agents themselves model the desired behaviour and arrange optimal conditions for clients to engage in similar activities until they can perform the behaviour skillfully and fearlessly.

REFERENCES

Bandura, A. In L. Berkowitz (Ed.), *Advances in experimental social psychology*. New York: Academic Press, 1965. Pp. 1-55.

Bandura, A. *Principles of behavioral modification*. New York: Holt, Rinehart & Winston, 1969.

Bandura, A., Blanchard, E. B., & Ritter, B. J. The relative efficacy of desensitization and modelling therapeutic approaches for inducing behavioral, affective and attitudinal changes. Unpublished manuscript, Stanford University, 1968.

Bandura, A., Grusec, J. E., & Menlove, F. L. *Journal of Personality and Social Psychology*, 1967, **5**, 16-23.

Bandura, A., & Menlove, F. L. *Journal of Personality and Social Psychology*, 1968, **8**, 99-108.

Bandura, A., & Rosenthal, T. L. *Journal of Personality and Social Psychology*, 1966, **3**, 54-62.

Bandura, A., & Walters, R. H. *Social learning and personality development*. New York: Holt, Rinehart & Winston, 1963.

Berger, S. M. *Psychological Review*, 1962, **69**, 450-466.

Black, A. H. *Journal of Comparative and Physiological Psychology*, 1958, **51**, 519-524.

Blanchard, E. B. Doctoral thesis, Stanford University, Faculty of Arts and Science, 1968.

Brehm, J. W., & Cohen, A. R. *Explorations in cognitive dissonance*. New York: Wiley, 1962.

Davison, G. C. *Journal of Abnormal Psychology*, 1968, **73**, 91-99.

Festinger, L. *A theory of cognitive dissonance*. Evanston, Ill.: Row and Peterson, 1957.

Festinger, L. *Public Opinion Quarterly*, 1964, **28**, 404-417.

Fleishmann, E., Harris, E., & Burtt, H. *Leadership and supervision in industry*. Columbus, Ohio: Ohio State University Bureau of Educational Research, 1955.

Jersild, A. T., & Holmes, F. B. *Journal of Psychology*, 1935, **1**, 75-104.

Lang, P. J., Lazovik, A. D., & Reynolds, D. J. *Journal of Abnormal Psychology*, 1965, **70**, 395-402.

Levitt, T. *Industrial purchasing behavior*. Cambridge, Mass.: Harvard University Press, 1965.

Maccoby, N., Romney, A. K., Adams, J. S., & Maccoby, E. E. *"Critical periods" in seeking and accepting information*. Stanford: Stanford University Institute for Communication Research, 1962.

O'Connor, R. D. Modification of social withdrawal through symbolic modelling. Unpublished manuscript, Stanford University, 1968.

Rescorla, R. A., & Solomon, R. L. *Psychological Review*, 1967, **74**, 151-182.

Ritter, B. J. *Behavior Research Therapy*, 1968, **6**, 1-6.

Schubot, E. D. Doctoral thesis, Stanford University, Faculty of Arts and Science, 1966.

Solomon, R. L., & Turner, L. H. *Psychological Review*, 1962, **69**, 202-219.

Wolpe, J. *Psychotherapy by reciprocal inhibition*. Stanford: Stanford University Press, 1958.

45.

Albert Ellis

RATIONAL-EMOTIVE PSYCHOTHERAPY

RATIONAL-EMOTIVE PSYCHOTHERAPY DEFINED

Rational-emotive psychotherapy is a comprehensive approach to psychological treatment and to education that not only employs emotive and behavioristic methods but also significantly stresses and undermines the cognitive element in self-defeating behavior. Humans are exceptionally complex, so that there is no simple way in which they become "emotionally disturbed," nor no single manner in which they can be helped to overcome their disturbances. Their psychological problems arise from their misperceptions and mistaken cognitions about what they perceive; from their emotional underreactions or overreactions to normal and to unusual stimuli; and from their habitually dysfunctional behavior patterns, which encourage them to keep repeating nonadjustive responses even when they know they are behaving poorly. Consequently, a three-way, rational-emotive-behavioristic approach to their problems is desirable; and rational-emotive therapy (RET, for short) provides this multifaceted attack.[1]

Primarily, RET employs a highly active, cognitive approach. It is based on the assumption that what we label our "emotional" reactions are mainly caused by our conscious and unconscious evaluations, interpretations, and philosophies. Thus, we feel anxious or depressed because we strongly convince ourselves that it is not only unfortunate and inconvenient but that *it is terrible and catastrophic* when we fail at a major task or are rejected by a significant person. And we feel hostile because we vigorously believe that people who behave unfairly not only *had better not* but *absolutely should not* act the way they indubitably do and that it is *utterly insufferable* when they frustrate us.

THE RATIONAL-EMOTIVE ORIENTATION

Like stoicism, a school of philosophy that originated some twenty-five hundred years ago, RET holds that there are virtually no legitimate reasons for people to make themselves terribly upset, hysterical, or emotionally disturbed, no matter what kind of psychological or verbal stimuli are impinging on them. It encourages them to feel strong *appropriate* emotions—such as sorrow, regret, displeasure, annoyance, rebellion, and determination to change unpleasant social conditions. But it holds that when they experience certain self-defeating and *inappropriate* emotions—such as guilt, depression, rage, or feelings of worthlessness—they are adding an unverifiable, magical hypothesis (that things *ought* or *must* be different) to their empirically based view (that certain things and acts are reprehensible or inefficient and that something *had better* be done about changing them).

Because rational-emotive therapy is a highly structured and workable theory, the therapist can almost always see the few central irrational philosophies that clients

By permission of the author.

are vehemently propounding to themselves and through which they are foolishly upsetting themselves. The therapist can show clients how these ideas cause their problems and their symptoms; can demonstrate exactly how clients may forthrightly question and challenge these ideas; and can often induce them to work to uproot these ideas and to replace them with scientifically testable hypotheses about themselves and the world that are not likely to get them into future emotional difficulties.

THE COGNITIVE ASPECT OF THE THEORY

The cognitive part of the theory and practice of RET may be briefly stated in ABC form as follows:

At Point A there is an **activity, action,** or **agent** that you become disturbed about. Example: You go for an important job interview; or have a fight with your mate, who unfairly screams at you.

At point (R)B, you have a **rational belief** (or a **reasonable belief** or a **realistic belief**) about the **activity, action** or **agent** that occurs at point A. Example: "It would be unfortunate if I were rejected at the job interview." Or: "How annoying it is to have my mate unfairly scream at me!"

At point (I)B, you have an **irrational belief** (or an **inappropriate belief**) about the **activity, action,** or **agent** that occurs at point A. Example: "It would be catastrophic if I were rejected at the job interview." Or: "My mate is a horrible person for screaming at me!"

Point (R)B, the **rational belief,** can be supported by empirical data and is appropriate to the reality that is occurring, or that may occur, at point A. For it normally *is* unfortunate if you are rejected at an interview for an important job; and it *is* annoying to be unfairly screamed at by your mate. It would hardly be rational or

realistic to think: "How great if I am rejected at the job interview!" Or: "It is wonderful to have my mate scream at me!"

Point (I)B, the **irrational belief,** cannot be supported by any empirical evidence and is inappropriate to the reality that is occurring, or that may occur, at point A. For it hardly would be truly catastrophic, but only (at worst) highly inconvenient, if you were rejected for an important job interview. It is unlikely that you would never get another job; that you would literally starve to death; or that you would have to be utterly miserable at any other job you could get. And your mate is not a horrible person for screaming at you, but merely a person who behaves (at some times) horribly and who (at other times) has various lovable traits.

(I)B's or **irrational beliefs,** moreover, state or imply a *should, ought,* or *must*— an absolutistic *demand* or *dictate* that you obtain what you want. For, by believing it *catastrophic* or *awful* to be rejected for an important job interview, you explicitly or implicitly believe that you *should* or *must* be accepted at that interview. And by believing that your mate is a horrible person for screaming at you, you overtly or tacitly believe that he or she *ought* or *must* be nonscreaming. There is, of course, no law of the universe (except in his or her muddled head!) that says that you *should* do well at an important job interview, nor that your mate *must* not scream at you.

At point (R)C, you feel **rational consequences** or **reasonable consequences** of (R)B's (**rational beliefs**). Thus, if you rigorously and discriminately believe, "It would be unfortunate if I were rejected at the job interview," you feel concerned and thoughtful about the interview; you plan in a determined manner how to succeed at it; and if by chance you fail to get the job you want, you feel disappointed, displeased, sorrowful, and frustrated. Your actions and feelings are *appropriate* to the situation that is occurring or may occur at point A; and they tend to help you succeed at your goals or feel suitably regretful if you do not achieve these goals.

At point (I)C, you experience **irrational consequences** or **inappropriate consequences** of your (I)B's (**irrational beliefs**). Thus, if you childishly and dictatorially believe "It would be catastrophic if I were rejected at the job interview. I couldn't stand it! What a worm I would then prove to be! I *should* do well at this important interview!" you tend to feel anxious, self-hating, self-pitying, depressed, and enraged. You get dysfunctional, psychosomatic reactions, such as high blood pressure and ulcers. You become defensive, fail to see your own mistakes in this interview, and rationalizingly blame your failure on external factors. You become preoccupied with how hopeless your situation is, and refuse to do much about changing it by going for other interviews. You generally experience what we call *disturbed, neurotic,* or *overreactive* symptoms. Your actions and feelings at point (I)C are *inappropriate* to the situation that is occurring or may occur at point B, because they are based on magical demands regarding the way you and the universe presumably *ought to* be. And they tend to help you fail at your goals or feel horribly upset if you do not achieve them.

These are the ABC's of emotional disturbance or self-defeating attitudes and behavior, according to the RET theory. Therapeutically, these ABC's can be extended to (D)E's, which constitute the cognitive core of the RET methodology.

At point D, you can be taught (or can teach yourself) to **dispute** your (I)B's (**irrational beliefs**). Thus, you can ask yourself, "*Why* is it catastrophic if I am rejected in this forthcoming job interview? How would such a rejection *destroy* me? Why couldn't I *stand* losing this particular job? Where is the evidence that I would be a *worm* if I were rejected? Why *should* I have to do well at this important interview?" If you persistently, vigorously **dispute** (or *question* and *challenge*) your own (I)B's (**irrational beliefs**) which are creating your (I)C's (**inappropriate consequences**), you will sooner or later come to see, in most instances, that they are unverifiable, unempirically based, and superstitious; and you will be able to change and reject them.

At point (C)E, you are likely to obtain the **cognitive effect** of **disputing** your (I)B's (**irrational beliefs**). Thus, if you ask yourself, "Why is it catastrophic if I am rejected in this forthcoming job interview?" you will tend to answer: "It is not; it will merely be inconvenient." If you ask, "How would such a rejection destroy me?" you will reply: "It won't; it will only frustrate me." If you ask, "Why couldn't I stand losing this particular job?" you can tell yourself: "I can! I won't like it; but I can gracefully lump it!" If you ask, "Where is the evidence that I would be a worm if I were rejected?" you can respond: "There isn't any! I will only feel like a worm if I *define myself as, think of myself as* a worm!" If you ask, "Why *should* I *have* to do well at this important interview?" you will tell yourself: "There's no reason why I should *have* to do well. There are several reasons why *it would be nice; it would be very fortunate* if I succeeded at this job interview. But they never add up to: "Therefore I *must!*"

At point (B)E, you will most likely obtain the **behavioral effect** of **disputing** your (I)B's (**irrational beliefs**). Thus, you will tend to be much less anxious about your forthcoming job interview. You will become less self-hating, self-pitying, and enraged. You will reduce your psychosomatic reactions. You will be able to act less defensively. You will become less unconstructively preoccupied with the possibility or the actuality of failing at the job interview and will more constructively devote yourself to succeeding at it or taking other measures to improve your vocational condition if you fail at it. You will become significantly less "upset," "disturbed," "overreactive," or "neurotic."

On the cognitive level, then, rational-emotive therapy largely employs direct philosophic confrontation. The therapist actively demonstrates to clients how, every time they experience a dysfunctional emotion or behavior or **consequence,** at point C, it only indirectly stems from some **activity** or **agent** that may be occurring (or about to occur) in their life at point A, and it much more directly results from their interpretations, philosophies, attitudes, or **beliefs,** at point B. The therapist then teaches the clients how to scientifically (empirically and logically) **dispute** these beliefs, at point D, and to persist at this **disputing** until they consistently come up, at point E, with a set of sensible **cognitive effects,** (C)E's, and appropriate **behavioral effects,** (B)E's. When they have remained, for some period of time, at point E, the clients have a radically changed philosophic attitude toward themselves, toward others, and toward the world. They are thereafter much less likely to keep convincing themselves of (I)B's (**irrational beliefs)** and thereby creating (I)C's (**inappropriate consequences)** or emotional disturbances.

BEHAVIORISTIC TECHNIQUES OF RATIONAL-EMOTIVE THERAPY

In addition to its cognitive methods, RET has exceptionally important behavioristic techniques that it consistently uses. It especially uses activity homework assignments, which the therapist or the client's therapy group assign to the client during various sessions, and later check up to see whether they are completed. Such assignments may consist of the client's being asked to initiate contacts with three new people during a week's period; to visit her nagging father-in-law instead of trying to avoid him; or to make a list of her job-hunting assets and of several means of looking for a better job. These assignments are given in order to help the clients take risks, gain new experiences, interrupt their dysfunctional habituations, and change their philosophies regarding certain activities. Eysenck, Pottash and Taylor, and A. Lazarus have indicated that the RET homework assignments overlap significantly with some of the methods of behavior therapy.[2] In any event, they are an integral and important part of RET.[3]

Emotive Release

A third major emphasis in RET is on emotive release. Thus, the rational-emotive therapist usually takes a no-nonsense-about-it, direct-confrontation approach to clients and their problems. She forces or persuades the clients to express themselves openly and to bring out their real feelings, no matter how painful it may first be for them to do so. Frequently, the therapist ruthlessly reveals and attacks the clients' defenses—while simultaneously showing them how they can live without these defenses and how they can unconditionally accept themselves whether or not others highly approve of them. The therapist does not hesitate to reveal his or her own feelings, to answer personal questions, and to participate as an individual in rational marathon encounters. She gives the clients unconditional rather than conditional positive regard and teaches them the essence of rational-emotive philosophy: namely, that no humans are to be condemned for anything, no matter how execrable their acts may be. Their *deeds* may be measurable and heinous, but they are never to be rated or given report cards *as people*. Because of the therapist's full acceptance of them as human beings, the clients are able to express their feelings much more openly than in their everyday life and to accept *themselves* even when they are acknowledging the inefficiency or immorality of some of their *acts*.

In many important ways, then, RET uses expressive-experiential methods and behavioral techniques. It is not, however, primarily interested in helping clients *feel* better but in showing them how they can *get* better. In its approach to marathon group therapy, for example, RET allows the participants plenty of opportunity to encounter each other on a gut level, to force themselves to stay in the here and now, to face their own emotional and sensory reactions to themselves and to other members of the group, and to be ruthlessly honest with themselves and others. RET, however, does not merely begin and end on a purely basic encounter or sensitivity training level—and thereby risk opening up many people without showing them how to put themselves together again. Instead, the rational-oriented marathon also shows the participants exactly what they are telling themselves to create their negative feelings toward themselves and others, and how they can change their internalized and uncritically accepted (I)B's (**irrational beliefs**). Ultimately they can spontaneously feel and behave in a less self-defeating manner and actualize their potential for happy, nondefeating lives.

RET AS THE APPLICATION OF LOGIC AND SCIENTIFIC METHOD

Basically, RET is an extension of the scientific method to human affairs. People, for biological as well as environmental reasons, tend to think magically, superstitiously, unrealistically, and unscientifically about themselves and the world around them. In science, we teach people to set up hypotheses about external reality and then to vigorously question and challenge these hypotheses—to look for empirical evidence for and against them, before they are cavalierly accepted as truths. In rational-emotive therapy, the therapist teaches his clients to scientifically question (to dispute) their self-defeating hypotheses about themselves and others. Thus, if you believe—as, alas, millions of people tend to believe—that you are a worthless person because you perform certain acts badly, you are not merely taught to ask, "What is truly bad about my acts? Where is the evidence that they are wrong or unethical?" More importantly, you are shown how to ask yourself, "Granted that some of my acts may be mistaken, why am *I* a totally bad *person* for performing them? Where is the evidence that I must always (or mainly) be right in order to consider myself worthy? Assuming that it is *preferable* for me to act well or efficiently rather than badly or inefficiently, why do I *have* to do what is preferable?"

Similarly, when you perceive—and let us suppose that you correctly perceive—the erroneous and unjust acts of others, and when you make yourself (as you may all too frequently make yourself!) enraged at these others and try to hurt or annihilate them, you are taught by the rational-emotive therapist to stop and ask yourself: "Why is my hypothesis that these error-prone people are no damned good a true hypothesis? Granted that *it would be better* if they acted more competently or fairly, why *should* they have to do what would be better? Where is the evidence that people who commit a number of mistaken or unethical acts are doomed to be forever wrong? Why, even if they persistently behave poorly, should they be totally damned, excommunicated, and consigned to some kind of hell?"

Rational-emotive therapy teaches the individual to generalize adequately but to watch his *over*generalizing; to discriminate his desires, wants, and preferences from his assumed needs, necessities, or dictates; to be less suggestible and more thinking; to be a long-range hedonist, who enjoys himself in the here and now and the future, rather than merely a short-range hedonist, who thinks mainly of immediate gratification; to feel the appropriate emotions of sorrow, regret, annoyance, and determination to change unpleasant aspects of his life while minimizing the inappropriate emotions of worthlessness, self-pity, severe anxiety, and rage. RET, like the science of psychology itself and like the discipline of general semantics, particularly teaches the client how to *discriminate* more clearly between sense and nonsense, fiction and reality, superstition and science.[4] While using many behavioristic and teaching methods, it is far from being dogmatic and authoritarian. Rather, it is one of the most humanistically oriented kinds of therapy in that it emphasizes that humans can fully accept themselves just because they are alive, just because they exist; that they do not have to prove their worth in any way; that they can have real happiness whether or not they perform well and whether or not they impress others; that they are able to create their own meaningful purposes; and that they need no magic nor gods on whom to rely. The humanistic-existentialist approach to life is therefore as much a part of rational-emotive psychotherapy as is its rational, logical, and scientific methodology.[5]

VALIDATION OF RATIONAL-EMOTIVE PSYCHOTHERAPY

RET, like many other modern forms of psychotherapy, is backed by a good many years of clinical experience by the author and various other rational-emotive therapists.[6] RET is also supported by several studies demonstrating its clinical effectiveness under controlled experimental conditions.[7] Finally, RET has been empirically confirmed, in terms of some of its major theoretical hypotheses, by a great many experimental studies.[8]

A concrete example of the rational-emotive approach to psychotherapy is given in a paper entitled "Rational-Emotive Therapy."[9]

Let me quote from this paper:

One of my recent clients, a young male, came to therapy because he was becoming increasingly impotent with his bride of four months, and he was also losing confidence in his work as a dentist. He had the usual kind of family history, with an overly protective mother, a highly critical father, and a competitive younger brother; but we hardly mentioned this in the course of our sessions, except for a ten-minute exposition during the first session. Most of our time together, at the beginning, was spent in directly showing him that he believed very strongly that he had to succeed in life in order to be a worthwhile human being, and that he especially had to succeed in penile-vaginal intercourse in order to prove himself as a man. When I demonstrated to him that with this kind of demanding, self-denigrating view of himself he couldn't help being terribly anxious sexually and when he vigorously began to ask himself, "Why *must* I be great in bed in order to accept myself as a person?" he immediately began to function better sexually. Then, when I gave him the homework assignment of letting himself come to full orgasm through oral-genital relations—which he had previously never even considered doing, because he thought it unmanly to use this method for anything but love play preceding intercourse—he radically changed his sexual philosophy, began to have sex with his wife for enjoyment rather than for the purpose of proving himself, and became more potent than he had ever previously been in his life. Also, although we had rarely talked about his work, he clearly saw that he was demanding perfection of himself as a dentist, just as he was insisting that he be a perfect lover. He took a much more enjoying and less obligatory attitude toward his profession; and he gained considerably more confidence and skill in his activity. Although I saw this client for a total of only ten sessions, his symptomatic improvement as well as his basic personality structure were helped more than those of many other clients I have seen for scores of sessions when I employed psychoanalytic or other more passive therapeutic methods.

APPLICATIONS OF RATIONAL-EMOTIVE PSYCHOTHERAPY

Rational-emotive psychotherapy has a great many therapeutic applications, some of which are unavailable to various other modes of psychotherapy. For one thing, it is relevant and useful to a far wider range of client disabilities than are many other therapies. Harper, Patterson, and others have shown that many techniques, such as classical psychoanalysis, can only be effectively employed with a relatively small number of clients and are actually contraindicated with other individuals (such as schizophrenics).[10] Rational-emotive therapy, however, can be employed with almost any kind of person the therapist is likely to see, including those who are conventionally labeled as psychotic, borderline psychotic, psychopathic, and mentally retarded. This is not to say that equally good results are obtained when it is employed with these most difficult individuals as are obtained with run-of-the-mill neurotics. But the main principles of RET can be so simply and efficiently stated that even individuals with very serious problems, some of whom have not been reached by years of previous intensive therapy, can often find significant improvement through RET.

Rational-emotive principles can be used with many kinds of individuals to help prevent them from eventually becoming emotionally disturbed. Outstanding in this respect is RET's application to education. The Institute for Advanced Study in Ra-

tional Psychotherapy in New York City not only operates a postdoctoral training institute and a moderate-cost clinic but also runs a private school for normal children. At this school, the pupils are taught a rational-emotive philosophy by their regular teachers, in the course of classroom activities, recreational affairs, therapy groups, and other games and exercises. They are taught, for example, not to catastrophize when they do not achieve perfectly, not to enrage themselves against others when these others act badly, and not to demand that the world be nicer and easier than it usually is. As a result of this teaching, these pupils seem to be becoming remarkably less anxious, depressed, self-hating, and hostile than other children of equivalent age."[11]

Rational-emotive ideas also have application to politics, to problems of the generation gap, to the treatment and prevention of violence and murder, and to various other areas of life.[12] Because it is deeply philosophic, because it realistically accepts individuals where they are and shows them how they can obtain their fuller potentials, and because it is not only oriented toward individuals with emotional disturbances but toward all types of people everywhere, RET is likely to be increasingly applied to the solution of many kinds of human problems.

Is RET really more effective than other forms of psychotherapy? The evidence is not in that will answer this question. Clinical findings would seem to indicate that it benefits more people than do most other methods; that it can obtain beneficial results in surprisingly short order in many instances; and that the level of improvement or cure that is effected through its use is more elegant and deep-seated than that obtained through other methods. This clinical evidence is partly substantiated through controlled studies of therapeutic outcome. My hypothesis, backed by almost a hundred such studies, is that RET is a more effective procedure than methods that emphasize purely cognitive or emotive or behavioral approaches because it is active-directive, comprehensive, unusually clear and precise, and hard-headed and down-to-earth.

CHARACTERISTICS OF RET

Rational-emotive therapy is also philosophically unambiguous, logical, and empirically oriented. This can be especially seen in its viewpoint on the most important of therapeutic problems: that of human worth. Nearly all systems of psychotherapy hold that people are worthwhile and can esteem themselves when they discover how to relate well to others and win the love they need or when they perform adequately and fully actualize themselves. Freud held that people solve their basic problems through work and love.[13] Adler emphasized the necessity of their finding social interests.[14] Sullivan stressed achieving adequate interpersonal relations.[15] Glasser insists that they need both love and achievement.[16] Branden demands competence and extreme rationality.[17] Even Rogers, who presumably emphasizes unconditional positive regard, actually holds that the individual can truly accept himself only when someone else, such as a therapist, accepts him or loves him unconditionally; so that this self-concept is still dependent on some important element outside himself.[18]

RET, on the contrary, seems to be almost the only major kind of psychotherapy that holds that humans do not need *any* trait, characteristic, achievement, purpose, or social approval in order to accept themselves. In fact, I contend, they do not have to rate themselves, esteem themselves, or have any self-measurement of self-concept whatever.

I have elsewhere shown in detail how it is really impossible for people to have valid self-images and why it is enormously harmful if they attempt to construct one.[19] Suffice it to say here, in brief summation, that ego ratings depend on the summation of the ratings of the individual's separate traits (such as competence, honesty, talents, etc.). It is not legitimate to add and average these traits any more than it is legitimate to add apples and pears. Moreover, if you finally arrive, by some devious means, at a global rating of your being (or of your "self"), you thereby invent a magical heaven (your "worth," your "value," your "goodness") and a mystical hell (your "worthlessness," your "valuelessness," your "badness"). This deification or devilification of the individual is arrived at tautologically, by definition. It has no real relation to objective reality. It is based on the false assumption that you *should* or *must* be a certain way and that the universe truly *cares* if you are not what you *ought to* be. It refuses to acknowledge the fact that all humans are, and probably always will be, incredibly *fallible*. And it almost always results in your harshly condemning and punishing yourself or defensively pretending that you are "worthy" and "good" in order to minimize your anxiety and self-deprecation. Finally, since self-ratings invariably involve ego-games wherein you compare your self-esteem to that of others, they inevitably result in your deifying and damning other humans in addition to yourself; and the feelings of intense anxiety and hostility that thereby occur constitute the very core of what we usually call *emotional disturbance*.

Rational-emotive therapy, by solidly teaching people to avoid *any* kind of self-rating (and only, instead, to measure their characteristics and performances, so that they may help correct them and increase their enjoyment), gets to the most elegant and deepest levels of personality change. It offers no panacea to human unhappiness, sorrow, frustration, and annoyance. But it importantly reveals, attacks, and radically uproots the major sources of needless self-defeating and socially destructive behavior.

FOOTNOTES

[1] A. Ellis, "What *Really* Causes Therapeutic Change," *Voices* 4, no. 2 (1968): 90-97.

[2] H. J. Eysenck, ed., *Experiments in Behaviour Therapy* (New York: Macmillan, 1964); A. Lazarus, *Beyond Behavior Therapy* (New York: McGraw-Hill, 1971); R. R. Pottash and J. E. Taylor, "Discussion of Albert Ellis: Phobia Treated with Rational-Emotive Psychotherapy," *Voices* 3, no. 3 (1967): 38-41.

[3] A. Ellis, *How to Live with a "Neurotic,"* rev. ed. (New York: Crown, 1975); A. Ellis, *Reason and Emotion in Psychotherapy* (New York: Lyle Stuart, 1962); A. Ellis, *Homosexuality* (New York: Lyle Stuart, 1965); A. Ellis, *Sex and the Liberated Man,* rev. ed. (New York: Lyle Stuart, 1976); A. Ellis, J. L. Wolfe, and S. Moseley, *How to Prevent Your Child from Becoming a Neurotic Adult* (New York: Crown, 1966); A. Ellis and R. A. Harper, *A New Guide to Rational Living* (Englewood Cliffs, N.J.: Prentice-Hall, and Hollywood, Calif.: Wilshire, 1975); A. Ellis and R. A. Harper, *A Guide to Successful Marriage* (New York: Lyle Stuart, and Hollywood Calif.: Wilshire, 1968); M. Maultsby, Jr., *Help Yourself to Happiness* (New York: Institute for Rational Living, 1975); K. T. Morns and H. M. Konitz, *Rational-Emotive Therapy* (Boston: Houghton Mifflin, 1975).

[4] A. Korzbyski, *Science and Sanity* (Lancaster, Pa.: Lancaster Press, 1933); Ellis, *How to Live with a "Neurotic."*

[5] A. Ellis, "A Weekend of Rational Encounter," in *Encounter,* ed. A. Burton (San Francisco: Jossey-Bass, 1969), pp. 112-27; idem, *Humanistic Psychotherapy* (New York: Julian Press/McGraw-Hill Paperbacks, 1974).

[6] B. Ard, "Bruising the Libido," *Rational Living* 1, no. 2 (1966): 19-25; B. Ard, "The A-B-C of Marriage Counseling," *Rational Living* 2, no. 2 (1967): 10-12; B. Ard, "Rational Therapy in Rehabilitation Counseling," *Rehabilitation Counseling Bulletin* 12 (1968): 84-88; R. Callahan, "Overcoming Religious Faith," *Rational Living* 2, no. 1 (1967): 16, 21; L. Diamond, "Defeating Self-Defeat; Two Case Histories," *Rational Living* 2, no. 1 (1967): 13-14; L. Diamond, "Restoring Amputated Ego," *Rational Living* 2, no 2 (1967): 15; Ellis, *Reason and Emotion in Psychotherapy;* Ellis, *Homosexuality;* A. Ellis, *The Art and Science of Love* (New York: Lyle Stuart and Bantam, 1965); A. Ellis, Wolfe, and S. Moseley, *How to Prevent Your Child from Becoming a Neurotic Adult; A.* Ellis and J. M. Gullo, *Murder and Assassination* (New York: Lyle Stuart, 1971); A. Ellis and R. A. Harper, *A New Guide to Rational Living; A.* Ellis and R. A. Harper, *A Guide to Successful Marriage;* M. D. Glicken, "Counseling Children," *Rational Living* 1, no. 2 (1966): 27, 30; M. D. Glicken, "Rational Counseling: A New Approach to Children," *Journal of Elementary Guidance and Counseling* 2, no. 4 (1968): 261-67; I. Greenberg, "Psychotherapy: Learning and Relearning," *Canada's Mental Health,* supplement no. 53 (1966); M. Grossack, "Why Rational-Emotive Therapy Works," *Psychological Reports* 16 (1965): 464; M. Grossack, *You Are Not Alone* (Boston: Marlborough Books, 1975); J. M. Gullo, "Useful Variations on Rational-Emotive Therapy," *Rational Living* 1, no. 1 (1966): 44-45; J. M. Gullo, "Counseling Hospital Patients," *Rational Living* 1, no. 2 (1966): 11-15; P. A. Hauck, *The Rational Management of Children* (New York: Libra, 1967); Lazarus, *Behavior Therapy and Beyond* (New York: McGraw-Hill, 1971); W. Knaus, *Rational-Emotive Education* (New York: Institute for Rational Living, 1974); E. E. Wagner, "Techniques of Rational Counseling," *High Spots* 3, no. 6 (1963): 2; E. E. Wagner, "Counseling Children," *Rational Living* 1, no. 2 (1966): 26, 28-30; M. C. Maultsby, Jr., *Help Yourself to Happiness* (New York: Institute for Rational Living, 1975); P. Hauck, *Overcoming Depression* (Philadelphia: Westminster Press, 1973); P. Hauck, *Overcoming Frustration and Anger* (Philadelphia: Westminster Press, 1974).

[7] A. Deloreto, "A Comparison of the Relative Effectiveness of Systematic Desensitization, Rational-Emotive and Client-Centered Group Psychotherapy in the Reduction of Interpersonal Anxiety in Introverts and Extroverts," Ph.D. thesis, Michigan State University, 1969; P. L. Russell and J. M. Brandsma, "A Theoretical and Empirical Integration of the Rational-Emotive and Classical Conditioning Theories," *Journal of Consulting and Clinical Psychology* 42 (1974): 389-397; D. E. Burnhead, "The Reduction of Negative Affect in Human Subjects," Ph.D. thesis, Western Michigan University, 1970; A. P. MacDonald and R. G. Ganes, "Ellis' Irrational Values," *Rational Living* 7(2) (1972): 25-28; D. H. Michenbaum, *Cognitive Behavior Modification* (Morristown, N.J.: General Learning Press, 1974); L. D. Trexler, "Rational-Emotive Therapy, Placebo, and No-Treatment Effects on Public-Speaking Anxiety," Ph.D. thesis, Temple University, 1971; M. Grossack, T. Armstrong, and G. Lussiev, "Correlates of Self-Actualization," Journal of Humanistic Psychology 6 (1966): 87; T. O. Karst and L. D. Trexler, "Initial Study Using Fixed-Role and Rational-Emotive Therapy in Treating Public-Speaking Anxiety," *Journal of Consulting and Clinical Psychology* 34 (1970): 360-66; S. Krippner, "Relationship Between Reading Improvement and Ten Selected Variables," *Perceptual and Motor Skills* 19 (1964): 15-20; J. C. Lafferty, D. Dennerll, and P. Rettich, "A Creative School Mental Health Program," *National Elementary Principal* 43, no. 5 (1964): 28-35; M. Maultsby, "Psychological

and Biochemical Test Change in Patients Who Were Paid to Engage in Psychotherapy," mimeographed (Department of Medicine, University of Wisconsin, 1970); M. Maultsby, "Systematic, Written Homework in Psychotherapy," *Rational Living* 5, no. 1 (1970) (A clinical study of 87 unselected OPD patients); K. L. Sharma, "A Rational Group Therapy Approach to Counseling Anxious Underachievers," Ph.D. thesis, University of Alberta, 1970; H. W. Zingle, "A Rational Therapy Approach to Counseling Underachievers," Ph.D. thesis, University of Alberta, 1965; W. R. Maes and R. A. Heimann, "The Comparison of Three Approaches to the Reduction of Test Anxiety in High School Students," (Washington, D.C.: U.S. Office of Education, 1970).

[8] A. H. Argabrite and L. J. Nidorf, "Fifteen Questions for Rating Reason," *Rational Living* 3, no. 1 (1968): 9-11; T. X. Barber, *Hypnosis: A Scientific Approach* (Cincinnati: Van Nostrand Reinhold, 1969); L. Berkowitz, J. P. Lepinsky, and E. J. Angulo, "Awareness of own Anger Level and Subsequent Aggression," *Journal of Personality and Social Psychology* 11 (1969): 292-300; W. A. Carlson, R. M. W. Travers, and E. A. Schwab, "A Laboratory Approach to the Cognitive Control of Anxiety" (Paper presented at the American Personnel and Guidance Association Meeting, Las Vegas, March 31, 1969); R. C. Conklin, "A Psychometric Instrument for the Early Identification of the Underachievers," Master's thesis, University of Alberta, 1965; S. W. Cook and R. E. Harris, "The Verbal Conditioning of the Galvanic Skin Reflex," *Journal of Experimental Psychology* 21 (1937): 201-10; R. L. Davies, "Relationship of Irrational Ideas to Emotional Disturbance," M.Ed. thesis, University of Alberta, 1970; A. Ellis, "Outcome of Employing Three Techniques of Psychotherapy," *Journal of Clinical Psychology* 13 (1957): 344-50; H. J. Geis, "A Study of Shame and Guilt," Ph.D. thesis, New York University, 1968; B. J. Hartman, "Sixty Revealing Questions for Twenty Minutes," *Rational Living* 3, no. 1 (1968): 7-8; R. G. Jones, "A Factored Measure of Ellis's Irrational Belief System, with Personality and Maladjustment Correlates," Ph.D. thesis, Texas Technological College, 1968; R. Lazarus, *Psychological Stress and the Coping Process* (New York: McGraw-Hill, 1966); Maultsby, "Systematic, Written Homework in Psychotherapy"; N. Miller, "Learning of Visceral and Glandular Responses," *Science* 163 (January 31, 1969): 34-45; O. H. Mowrer, "Preparatory Set (Expectancy)—A Determinant in Motivation and Learning," *Psychological Review* 45 (1938): 62-91; S. Schacter, "The Interaction of Cognitive and Physiological Determinants of Emotional States," *Advances in Experimental Social Psychology*, vol. 1, ed. L. Berkowitz (New York: Academic Press, 1964); S. Schacter and J. E. Singer, "Cognitive, Social and Physiological Determinants of Emotional State," *Psychological Review* 69 (1962): 379-99; G. L. Taft, "A Study of the Relationship of Anxiety and Irrational Beliefs," Ph.D. thesis, University of Alberta, 1965; S. Valins, "Cognitive Effects of False Heart-Rate Feedback," *Journal of Personality and Social Psychology* 4 (1966): 400-408; E. Velten, "A Laboratory Task for Induction of Mood States," *Behavior Research and Therapy* 6 (1968): 473-82.

[9] A. Ellis, "Rational-Emotive Therapy," *Journal of Contemporary Psychotherapy* 1 (1969): 82-90.

[10] R. A. Harper, *Psychoanalysis and Psychotherapy: Thirty-Six Systems* (Englewood Cliffs, N.J.: Prentice-Hall, 1959); R. A. Harper, *The New Psychotherapies* (Englewood Cliffs, N.J.: Prentice-Hall, 1975); C. H. Patterson, *Theories of Counseling and Psychotherapy* (New York: Harper & Row, 1966).

[11] A. Ellis, "Teaching Emotional Education in the Classroom," *School Health Review* (November 1969): 10-14; W. Knaus, Rational-Emotive Education (New York: Institute for Rational Living, 1974).

[12] A. Ellis, "Toward the Understanding of Youthful Rebellion," in *A Search for the Meaning of the Generation Gap*, ed. P. R. Frank (San Diego: San Diego County Department of Education, 1969): 85-105; Ellis and Gullo, *Murder and Assassination* (New York: Lyle Stuart, 1972).

[13] S. Freud, *Collected Papers* (New York: Collier, Macmillan, 1963).

[14] A. Adler, *What Life Should Mean to You* (New York: Capricorn Books, 1958); idem, *Social Interest* (New York: Capricorn Books, 1964).

[15] H. S. Sullivan, *The Interpersonal Theory of Psychiatry* (New York: Norton, 1968).

[16] W. Glasser, *Reality Therapy* (New York: Harper & Row, 1964); idem, *Schools without Failure* (New York: Harper & Row, 1969).

[17] N. Branden, *The Psychology of Self-Esteem* (Los Angeles: Nash, 1970).

[18] C. R. Rogers, *On Becoming a Person* (Boston: Houghton Mifflin, 1961).

[19] A. Ellis, "Psychotherapy and the Value of a Human Being," in *Value and Evaluation: Essays in Honor of Robert S. Hartman*, ed. J. W. Davis (Knoxville: University of Tennessee Press, 1972).

46.

Viktor E. Frankl

LOGOTHERAPY

It is the contention of some authors that in existential psychiatry, logotherapy is the only school which has evolved psychotherapeutic techniques. Man's primary concern is to find and fulfill meaning and purpose in life. Today, however, ever more patients relate the feeling of a profound meaninglessness. In logotherapy, this inner void is referred to as the "existential vacuum." According to existential analysis (*Existenzanalyse*) which underlies logotherapy, there are two specifically human phenomena, the "capacity of self-transcendence" and the "capacity of self-detachment." They are mobilized by two logotherapeutic techniques, "de-reflection" and "paradoxical intention," respectively. Both lend themselves particularly to the short-term treatment of sexual as well as obsessive-compulsive and phobic neuroses, especially in cases in which the anticipatory anxiety mechanism is involved.

Most of the authors agree in that logotherapy falls under the category of existential psychiatry. Pertinent statements have been made by Allport [1], Ungersma [2], Tweedie [3, 4], Leslie [5], Kaczanowski [6], Crumbaugh [7] and Pervin [8]. In fact, as early as in the thirties I coined the word *Existenzanalyse* as an alternative name for logotherapy. Later on, when American authors started publishing in the field of logotherapy they introduced the term "existential analysis" [9] as a translation of *Existenzanalyse*. Unfortunately, other authors did the same with the word *Daseinsanalyse*—a term which, in the forties, had been selected by Ludwig Binswanger, to denote his own teachings, and henceforth existential analysis became quite an am-

biguous word. In order not to add to the confusion which had been aroused by this state of affairs, I decided to refrain more and more from using the term existential analysis in so far as my publications in English were concerned—at the risk, to be sure, to speak of logotherapy even in a context where no therapy in the strict and proper sense of the word was involved. What I call medical ministry [10], e.g., forms an important aspect of the practice of logotherapy but is indicated precisely in those cases where actual therapy is impossible—simply because the patient is confronted and facing an incurable disease. To be sure, in the widest possible sense logotherapy is treatment even then; it is treatment of the patient's attitude toward his unchangeable fate.

Logotherapy goes beyond *Daseinsanalyse* or, to adopt the translation by Scher, ontoanalysis in that it is not only concerned with ontos or being, but also with logos or meaning. This may well account for the fact that logotherapy is more than mere analysis, namely, as the very name indicates, therapy. In a personal conversation Ludwig Binswanger felt that, as compared with ontoanalysis, logotherapy was more activistic, and even more, that logotherapy could lend itself as the therapeutic supplement to ontoanalysis.

Logotherapy has not only been subsumed under the heading existential psychiatry but also has been acclaimed, within this province, as the only school which has succeeded in developing what one might be justified in calling a technique. This at least is the contention of such authors as

From Viktor E. Frankl, "Logotherapy." *Israel Annals of Psychiatry and Related Disciplines,* 1967, **5**, 142-155. Reprinted by permission.

Ungersma [2], Tweedie [3, 4], Leslie [5], Kaczanowski [40, 6] and Crumbaugh [7]. This does not imply that we logotherapists are too proud of this fact. For long we have come to realize that what counts and matters in therapy is not techniques but rather the human relation between doctor and patient, or the personal and existential encounter.

By way of a deliberate oversimplification for didactic purposes one could define logotherapy by the literal translation as healing through meaning [11]. What in logotherapy is called the will to meaning [1] indeed occupies a central place in the system. It refers to the fact which reveals itself to a phenomenological analysis, namely, that man is basically striving to find and fulfill meaning and purpose in life.

Today, the will to meaning is often frustrated. In logotherapy, one speaks of existential frustration. Patients who fall into this diagnostic category usually complain of a sense of futility and meaninglessness or emptiness and void. In logotherapy, this condition is termed "existential vacuum." As to its etiology it seems to me to be due to the following facts. First, in contrast to an animal, no drives and instincts tell man what he must do. Second, in contrast to former times, no conventions, traditions and values tell him what he should do. Soon, one may predict, he will not even know what he basically wishes to do. All the more he simply will wish to do what other people do, or he just will do what other people want him to do. That is to say, he will fall prey to conformism or totalitarianism, respectively, the first being representative for the West, the second being representative for the East.

The existential vacuum constitutes the mass neurosis of our age. In a recent publication, a Czechoslovakian psychiatrist, Stanislav Kratochvil [12], has pointed out that existential frustration makes itself felt even in Communist countries.

In cases in which existential frustration produces neurotic symptoms, one is dealing with a new type of neurosis which I call "noogenic neurosis." It goes to the credit of Crumbaugh to have developed a special test diagnostically to differentiate the noogenic neurosis from the conventional neuroses. After publishing the results obtained by his Purpose-in-life Test (PIL) together with Maholick [13] he delivered an amplified version before the annual meeting of The American Psychological Association, the data having been based on a total of 1,151 subjects. Crumbaugh arrived at the conclusion that "noogenic neurosis exists apart from the conventional diagnostic categories" and is not "identical with any of the conventional diagnostic syndromes." It represents "a new clinical syndrome which cannot be adequately comprehended under any of the classical descriptions. Present results lend support" and are "favorable to Frankl's concepts of noogenic neurosis and existential vacuum. The low correlation between the PIL and educational level implies on the one hand that purposeful, meaningful lives are not limited to those with educational opportunity, and on the other that education alone by no means assures the attainment of meaning in life."[14]

Along with the empirical corroboration and confirmation of logotherapeutic concepts as furnished by Crumbaugh statistical research has been conducted referring to the frequency of noogenic neurosis. Werner [15] in London, Langen and Volhard [16] in Tübingen, Prill [17] in Würzburg, and Niebauer [18, p. 753] in Vienna agree in so far as they estimate that about 20 per cent of the neuroses one encounters are noogenic in nature.

It goes without saying that meaning and purpose in life cannot be prescribed like a drug. It is not the job of a doctor to *give* meaning to the patient's life. But it may well be his task, through an existential analysis, to enable the patient to *find* meaning in life. Again it was Crumbaugh and Maholick [19] who, to my knowledge for the first time, have pointed to the fact that finding meaning in a situation has something to do with a Gestalt perception. This assumption is confirmed by Wertheimer [20], who explicitly states that a quality of "requiredness" is inherent in the situation and, what is even more, "the demands and 'requirements' " of the situation are "objective qualities."

According to logotherapeutic teachings, meaning is not really lacking in any life situation. This is due to the fact that even the negative aspects of human existence such as suffering, guilt, and death can still be turned into something positive, provided that they are faced with the right attitude. Needless to say, meaning can be found only in unavoidable suffering whereas accepting avoidable pain would form some sort of masochism rather than heroism. As a matter of fact, unavoidable suffering is inherent in the human condition and the therapist should take heed not to reinforce the patient's evasive denial of this existential fact.

Alongside the will to meaning stands the will to power and what one could call the will to pleasure. In the final analysis, the direct intention of pleasure or the pursuit of happiness as it usually is referred to, defeats and thwarts itself. The more an individual aims at pleasure the more he misses the aim. In logotherapy we speak in this context of hyperintention.

Along with this pathogenic phenomenon and associated with it we may observe and meet another one, i.e., what in logotherapy is called hyperreflection. Hyperreflection means excessive attention. Spontaneity and activity are impeded and inhibited if too much made a target of attention. Consider the centipede who, as a story has it, was asked by his enemy in which sequence he moved his legs. The effect was that the centipede paid attention to the problem, and by so doing was incapacitated to move his legs at all. He is said to have died from starvation. Should we say that he died from fatal hyperreflection?

In logotherapy hyperreflection is counteracted by dereflection. One of those domains in which this technique is applied is that of sexual neuroses, be it frigidity or impotence. Sexual performance or experience are strangled to the same extent to which they are made either an object of attention or an objective of intention. As far as frigidity is concerned, the reader is referred to an instructive and illustrative case I have included in my book, *Man's Search for Meaning* [1, pp. 194 f.]. In cases of impotence, hyperintention is frequently due to the fact that the patient approaches sexual intercourse as something which is demanded of him. I have elaborated on this aspect of the etiology of impotence elsewhere (21, pp. 159 ff.). A logotherapeutic technique has been developed in order to remove the demand quality the patient attaches and attributes to sexual intercourse. I have discussed this technique in a paper at a symposium on logotherapy in London [22]. Yet the logotherapeutic treatment of sexual neurosis is applicable regardless of whether or not one adopts the logotherapeutic theory. In the Neurological Department of the Poliklinik Hospital in Vienna, I have entrusted an outpatient ward for patients with sexual neuroses to a psychoanalytically trained physician who uses in the given setting the logotherapeutic rather than the psychoanalytic technique.

Whereas dereflection is part and parcel of the logotherapeutic treatment of sexual neurosis there is another logotherapeutic technique which lends itself to the short-term treatment of obsessive-compulsive and phobic patients. This technique is called paradoxical intention. I have described it as early as 1946 in my book, *The Doctor and the Soul* [10], and in a paper [23] reprinted in another of my books [24].

To put it in a nutshell, paradoxical intention means that the patient is encouraged to do, or wish to happen, the very things he fears. In order to understand the therapeutic efficiency of this technique we must consider the phenomenon called "anticipatory anxiety." By this I mean the response and reaction to an event in terms of the fearful expectation of the recurrence of the event. However, fear tends to make come true precisely that which one is afraid of and in the same vein anticipatory anxiety triggers off what the patient so fearfully expects to happen. Thus a vicious circle is established. A symptom evokes a phobia and the phobia provokes the symptom. The recurrence of the symptom then reinforces the phobia.

The patient is caught in a cocoon. A circle formation is built up or, as we might say as well, a feedback mechanism is established. How can we break up the vicious circle? It can be managed in two ways, first by pharmacotherapy and second by psychotherapy, unless we decide to combine both. This is necessary in severe cases.

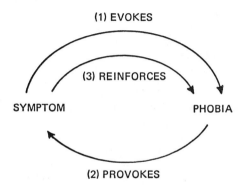

(1) EVOKES

(3) REINFORCES

SYMPTOM   PHOBIA

(2) PROVOKES

It is possible even to start with pharmacotherapy. This holds for those cases with agoraphobic symptoms in which hyperthyroidism is an underlying factor [25], or cases of claustrophobia which I could trace to latent tetany [26]. One should bear in mind, however, that the organic factor involved in such cases provides no more than a mere inclination to anxiety while the full-fledged anxiety neurosis does not develop unless the anticipatory anxiety mechanism comes into play. Therefore, to unhinge the circle one must attack it on the psychic pole as well as on the organic pole. And the first is precisely the job done by paradoxical intention.

What then is going on when paradoxical intention is applied? Encouraging the patient to do, or wish to happen, the very things he fears entails and engenders an inversion of intention. The pathogenic fear is replaced by a paradoxical wish. By the same token, however, the wind is taken out of the sails of anticipatory anxiety.

The intention of a phobic individual is to escape and avoid those situations which arouse fear and anxiety. In logotherapy, we speak of flight from fear. We may observe it in those cases, e.g., in which anxiety itself is the target of fear. In these cases the patient himself speaks of "fear of fear." He really fears the potential effects of fear, be it a faint, a coronary or a stroke.

According to logotherapeutic findings and teachings, flight from fear is a pathogenic pattern [28]. More specifically it is the phobic pattern. But the development of a phobia can be obviated by confronting one with the situation he begins to fear.

Alongside flight from fear there are two more pathogenic patterns, namely, fight for pleasure and fight against obsessions and compulsions. Fight for pleasure is identical with hyperintention of pleasure, that is to say, one of the major factors underlying sexual neuroses. Fight against obsessions and compulsions in turn is the pathogenic pattern underlying obsessive-compulsive neuroses. Obsessive-compulsive neurotics are plagued by the idea that they might commit suicide or even homicide or that the strange thoughts which haunt them might be signs of imminent, if not present, psychosis. In other words, they fear the potential effects or the potential cause of the strange thoughts. The phobic individual fears the potential effects of fear, I have said, and this "fear of fear" prompts him to set out on his flight from fear. This phobic pattern is paralleled by the obsessive-compulsive pattern. The obsessive-compulsive neurotics also display fear. But they do not exhibit "fear of fear" but rather fear of themselves, and their response and reaction to this fear is fight against obsessions and compulsions rather than flight from fear. But the more the patients fight their obsessions and compulsions the stronger these symptoms become. In other words, alongside the circle formation built up by anticipatory anxiety in phobic cases, there is another feedback mechanism which we may encounter in the obsessive-compulsive neurotics. Pressure induces counterpressure, and counterpressure, in turn, increases pressure. Conversely, if one succeeds in making the patient stop fighting his obsessions and compulsions—and this may well be accomplished by paradoxical intention—these symptoms soon diminish and finally atrophy.

Having discussed the theory let us turn to the practice of paradoxical intention. Let us take up a case report:

The patient refused to leave his house because every time he did he had attacks of fear that he would collapse on the street. Every time he did leave his house he returned after a few steps. He ran away from his fear. Admitted to my department, a thorough checkup made certain that there was nothing wrong with his heart. One of the doctors told him that. Then he suggested the patient should go out on the street and try to get a heart attack. He told him, "Tell yourself that yesterday you had two heart attacks, and today you have time to get three—it's still early in the morning. Tell yourself that you will have a nice, fat coronary, and a stroke to boot." For the first time the patient was able to break through his cocoon in which he had enclosed himself.

Another instance of paradoxical intention is the following case history that Gerz [29] presented:

It concerns a fifty-six-year-old lawyer, who was married and the father of an eighteen-year-old son. His neurosis began seventeen years ago, when he was still in private practice. "All of a sudden, out of a clear blue sky, an awful obsession came into my mind that I had defrauded the government by underestimating my income tax by some three hundred dollars, even though I made it out as honestly as I knew how. I began to worry that it might be several hundred dollars more. Try as I might, I could not get these ideas out of my head." The patient imagined himself being prosecuted for fraud, going to jail, receiving newspaper publicity, and finally losing his job. He was hospitalized at a private sanitarium, receiving psychotherapy and twenty-five treatments with electro-convulsive therapy, without improvement. Meanwhile he had to give up his law practice and to take a job as a court clerk. Further obsessions developed. They shifted from day to day, and week to week. He developed the habit of checking and rechecking things, such as the wheels of his car and things he did at his office. He became obsessed about his insurance policies, fearing that perhaps one had expired or that one did not include the protection he wanted. It was at this time that he bought special insurance from Lloyds, because he feared he might make a mistake in court and be sued. He felt compelled to check and recheck everything, including his various insurance policies locked in a special steel box in a safe at home. The policies themselves were in envelopes secured by a number of strings. His fear of being sued was so great that off and on he had to go through the involved procedure of taking out his policies and making sure he was insured properly; and when he finally had put them back into the steel box in the safe, he wondered whether he had really checked everything. He had to repeat this process over and over until he finally "felt certain" that he was "safe." In court he became so completely incapacitated that he needed to be hospitalized. It was at this time that Dr. Gerz began treating him with paradoxical intention. He was in logotherapy for four months three times weekly, and was instructed to use the following "paradoxical intentions": "I don't give a damn any more. Hell, who wants to be a perfectionist? I hope I get sued very soon, the sooner the better." Dr. Gerz instructed him to try "to get sued three times a day and get his money's worth from Lloyds of London!" He was told to wish that he would make many, many mistakes, really mess up his work, and show his secretaries that he was the greatest "mistake maker" in the world. No doubt, Dr. Gerz's complete lack of anxiety could be adopted by the patient, as a humourous situation was created and as Dr. Gerz kept telling the patient on each visit: "For heaven's sake, are you still around! I've been looking through the newspapers hoping to read about the big scandalous lawsuit." At these comments the patient would burst into laughter, and he finally adopted the attitude of: "To hell with everything. I don't care if I make mistakes; I don't give a damn what happens. Let 'em sue me." He would laugh and say: "My insurance companies will go bankrupt." About a year after therapy began, he said: "This formula has worked a miracle for me. Dr. Gerz has made a new person out of me in four months. I occasionally get a worry, but now I am able to cope with it. I know how to handle it."

Weisskopf-Joelson [30] makes the following statement:

"I have made use of 'paradoxical intention' with many of my patients, including myself, and I have found it very effective. For example, a university student complained about being anxious with regard to an oral report to be given—let us say—on Friday. I advised him to take his appointment calendar and to write on every page of the week, with large letters, the word 'ANXIETY.' As it were—I asked him to plan for an anxious week. He was much relieved after doing this because now he was suffering from anxiety only, but not from anxiety about anxiety."

In recent years many reports were published on the use of paradoxical intention.

In addition to David (Buenos Aires), mention may be made of the associates of Ernst Kretschmer (Tübingen), Langen and Volhard, Prill (Gynecological University Clinic of Würzburg), and Rehder (Hamburg). At the Fourth International Congress for Psychotherapy (1958), Ledermann declared: "The results (of logotherapy) are not to be denied. I have found the method helpful in cases of obsessional neurosis." Frick (Bolzano, Italy) goes still further by stating that there are cases of severe obsessive-compulsive neurosis in which a logotherapeutic procedure is the "only therapeutic way," and refers to some cases in which electro-shock therapy had failed and logotherapy alone proved successful. Lopez-Ibor (Madrid) makes a similar statement. In addition to my associates, Kocourek and Niebauer, N. Toll reports that she has been using it successfully for over six years. Bazzi (Rome) has even worked out special indications in which paradoxical intention should be applied and those in which the autogenic training method of Schultz is indicated [31].

There is evidence that paradoxical intention even works in chronic cases [32]. For example, in the German *Encyclopaedia of Psychotherapy* [18, p. 757] the case of a sixty-five-year-old woman is described who for 60 years had suffered from a handwashing compulsion. A member of my staff successfully applied the paradoxical intention technique in this case.

J. Lehembre has tried paradoxical intention on children, at the Departments of Psychiatry and Pediatrics of the Universities of Utrecht and Nijmegen. He has been successful in most of the cases. In his report [33] he makes the point that only in a single case symptom substitution has been observed.

Jasper's dictum, "in philosophy, being new speaks against being true," may also hold for psychotherapy. Unwillingly and unwittingly, paradoxical intention has certainly been used all along. With regard to unwilling use, an example was reported to me by the Head of the Department of Psychiatry at the University of Mainz in West-Germany. When he was in Junior High School his class was to present a play. One of the characters was a stutterer and so they gave this role to a student who actually stuttered. Soon, however, he had to give up the role because it turned out that when standing on the stage he was completely unable to stutter. He had to be replaced by another boy.

With regard to unwitting use, an instance of paradoxical intention is the following:

One of my American students who had to take his exams from me and in this setting was to explain paradoxical intention resorted to the following autobiographical account: "My stomach used to growl in company of others. The more I tried to keep it from happening, the more it growled. Soon started to take it for granted that it would be with me rest of my life. Began to live with it—laughed with others about it. Soon it disappeared."

In this context, I should like to place emphasis on the fact that my student adopted a humorous attitude toward a symptom. In fact, paradoxical intention should always be formulated in as humorous a manner as possible. Humor is indeed a definitely human phenomenon; after all, no beast is capable of laughing. What is even more important, humor allows man to create a perspective, to put a distance between himself and whatever may confront him. By the same token, humor allows man to detach himself and thereby to attain the fullest possible control over himself. To make use of the human capacity of self-detachment is what paradoxical intention basically achieves. Keeping this in mind, it seems no longer true that we do not yet take humor earnestly and seriously

enough (*dass wir den Humor noch nicht ernst genug nehmen*) as Konrad Lorenz [34, p. 411] contends in his most recent book.

What comes to mind, however, is a question which once was raised by Gordon W. Allport after I had read a paper at Harvard University. It is the question whether or not that sound sense of humor which is inherent in the technique of paradoxical intention is equally available in each and every patient. I insisted that in principle each and every human being by virtue of his humanness is capable of detaching himself from himself and laughing about himself. But there are certainly quantitative differences in the degree to which the human capacity for self-detachment and the sound sense of humor[1] can be mobilized. An example of a low degree is the following:

I had a man in my Department, a guard in a museum who could not stay on his job because he suffered from deadly fears that someone would steal a painting. During a round I made with my staff, I tried paradoxical intention with him: "Tell yourself they stole a Rembrandt yesterday and today they would steal a Rembrandt and a Van Gogh." He just stared at me and said, "But, Herr Professor, that's against the law!" This man simply was too feeble-minded to understand the meaning of paradoxical intention.

In this respect paradoxical intention or for that matter logotherapy is not an exception. It is the rule that psychotherapy—each and every method of psychotherapy—

---

[1] Speaking of humor I am justified in defining paradoxical intention in terms of a joke: A boy who came to school late offered as an excuse to the teacher the fact that the icy streets were so slippery that whenever he moved one step forward he slipped two steps back again. Thereupon the teacher retorted: But now I have caught you in a lie—if this had been true, you never could have succeeded in arriving at school," whereupon the boy replied: "Why not? I just turned around and went home." Wasn't this paradoxical intention? Wasn't the boy successful through an inversion of the original intention?

is not applicable to each patient with the same degree of success. Even more, not every doctor is capable of handling each and every method of psychotherapy with the same degree of skill. That is why I am used to comparing the method of choice in a given case with an equation with 2 unknowns:

$$\Psi = x + y$$

The first unknown represents the unique personality of the patient. The second unknown represents the unique personality of the doctor. Both have to be taken into account if in a given case the method of psychotherapy is to be chosen. What holds for psychotherapy is also true of logotherapy.

Logotherapy is no panacea. For this if for no other reason it is justified to combine logotherapy with other methods as it has been propounded, among others, by Ledermann (hypnosis [35], Bazzi (relaxation training after Schultz [31], Kvilhaugh (behavior therapy [36], Vorbusch [37], Kratochvil (activation training after Bojanovsky and Chloupkova) and also Gerz (pharmacotherapy [38]).

On the other hand, the remarkable results obtained by paradoxical intention cannot be explained merely in terms of suggestion. Actually, our patients often set out to use paradoxical intention with a strong conviction that it simply cannot work and yet they finally succeed. In other words, they do succeed not because, but rather in spite of, suggestion. Benedikt [39] subjected his patients to test batteries in order to evaluate their susceptibility with respect to suggestion. It turned out that these patients were even less susceptible to suggestion than the average. But paradoxical intention was successful in these cases.

Gerz [29, 32] and Tweedie [4, 5] have proved that paradoxical intention must not be confounded with persuasion. However, it is my contention that in some cases paradoxical intention cannot be launched without being preceded by persuasion. That is particularly true of obsessions with blasphemy, for the treatment of which a special logotherapeutic technique has been devised [21, p. 239].

Most of the authors who have practiced paradoxical intention and published their work agree that it is a short term procedure. The assumption, however, "that the durability of results corresponds to the length of therapy" is one of "the illusions of Freudian orthodoxy," to quote Gutheil [41]. It is also "a completely baseless assertion," to cite the grand old man of German psychotherapy, J. H. Schultz [42], "that symptom removal must be followed by substitute symptoms." Weisskopf-Joelson [43, 44], has expressed the same view. "Psychoanalytically oriented therapists," she says, "might argue no real improvement can be achieved with methods such as logotherapy, since the pathology in 'deeper' layers remains untouched, while the therapist limits himself to the strengthening or erecting of defenses. Such conclusions are not free of danger. They may keep us from the awareness of major sources of mental health because these sources do not fit into a specific theoretical framework. We must not forget that such concepts as 'defenses,' 'deeper layers,' and 'adequate functioning of a superficial level with underlying pathology' are theoretical concepts rather than empirical observations." By contrast the results obtained by paradoxical intention do deserve to be qualified as empirical observations. G. Golloway contends that paradoxical intention does not resolve the "underlying conflict." But this "does not detract from paradoxical intention as a successful technique. It is no insult to surgery that it does not cure the diseased gall bladder it removes. The patient is better off."

For this reason many psychoanalysts have been using the paradoxical intention technique successfully. Some workers in the field try to explain this success and specifically to explain it in psychodynamic terms [24, 32]. To cite another instance, Müller-Hegemann [45] (Leipzig) interprets paradoxical intention in terms of a "neurophysiologically oriented approach." Anyway, he "has observed favorable results in the last years in patients suffering from phobias" and therefore considers paradoxical intention "to have much merit." Again, it should be noted that even doctors who adhere to theories different from the one which underlies logotherapy include paradoxical intention in their armamentarium [49, 50].

Attempts have been made to clarify the indications for logotherapy. For example, Gerz feels that paradoxical intention is a specific and effective treatment of phobic and obsessive-compulsive conditions. It "lends itself in the acute cases to short-term therapy." [29]

With respect to statistics Gerz reported: "88.2% of all patients recovered or made considerable improvement. Most of these cases suffered from their illness up to 24 years." [29] "Those who have been sick for several years need up to 12 months of bi-weekly sessions to bring about recovery. Most acute cases who are sick for a few weeks or months respond to paradoxical intention within about 4 to 12 sessions." [32]

To be sure, "it is understandable that the psychiatrist with many years of psychoanalytic training might tend to be prejudiced and to reject paradoxical intention without having tried it." [32] However, even if much of the resistance to paradoxical intention or for that matter logotherapy were not due to financial but rather emotional grounds such as the adherence

and obedience to a sect, the sectarian is admonished by Freud that "reverence before the greatness of a genius is certainly a great thing. But our reverence before facts should exceed it." [46]

As compared with the indications for logotherapy, it is even more important to delineate where paradoxical intention is counterindicated. It is strictly counterindicated in psychotic depressions. For such patients a special logotherapeutic technique is reserved whose guiding principle is the decrease of that burden of guilt feelings on the part of the patient which is due to his tendency to self-accusations [21, pp. 261 ff.]. It would be a misconception of existential psychiatry to interpret these self-accusations as indicating that a patient suffering from endogenous depression not only feels guilty, but really is guilty, "existentially guilty," and hence depressed. This would amount to mistaking an effect for the cause. Even more, such an interpretation would reinforce the patient's guilt feelings to the extent that his suicide might well be the result. Incidentally, logotherapy offers a special test to evaluate the suicide risk in a given case [21, p. 262].

As far as schizophrenic patients are concerned, logotherapy is far from providing a causal treatment. As a psychotherapeutic adjunct, however, the aforementioned logotherapeutic technique called dereflection is also recommended for such patients [21, p. 260, pp. 264 f.]. The volume, *Modern Psychotherapeutic Practice* [47], includes some tape-recorded sessions with schizophrenic patients to demonstrate the way in which dereflection can be utilized [51].

Burton [48] recently stated that "the last 50 years of therapeutic psychiatry have made a fetish of the deep personal history of the patient. Freud's startling cures of supposed unremitting hysterias led us to seek a similar traumatic experience in every patient and to reify insight as curative, something we are only now recovering from." But even if one assumes that neuroses or even psychoses are caused by what is supposed to cause them in terms of psychodynamic hypotheses, logotherapy would still be indicated in terms of a noncausal treatment [43, 44]. For one must consider the fact that as long as there is an existential vacuum in the patient, the symptoms will rush into it. That is why the "logotherapeutic encounter," as Crumbaugh [7] contends, "continues beyond where most therapies, especially analytically oriented methods, stop: it holds that unless purposeful goals and commitment to them are attained, therapy will have been for naught as the pathological etiology will remain and the symptom will later return."

It is the contention of some authors that in existential psychiatry, logotherapy is the only school which has evolved psychotherapeutic techniques. Even more, it has been said that logotherapy adds a new dimension to psychotherapy; more specifically, that it adds to it the dimension of the distinctively human phenomena. In fact, two specifically human phenomena, the capacity of self-transcendence and the capacity of self-detachment, are mobilized by two logotherapeutic techniques, dereflection and paradoxical intention, respectively. Petrilowitsch (Mainz) ascribes the surprising and astonishing results obtained by the two logotherapeutic techniques to the fact that logotherapy does not remain and stay in the dimension of neurosis, i.e., in the dimension of dynamics or conditioning processes. In contrast to behavior therapy, e.g., logotherapy is not satisfied with reconditioning but opens the dimension of the very humanness of man and draws upon the resources which are available in the humanitas of the homo patiens.

The findings of the pioneering schools are not annulled by logotherapy but rather overarched by it. This equally holds for scientific approaches such as Watsonian behaviorism, Pavlovian reflexology, Freudian psychoanalysis and Adlerian psychology. Now the findings of these schools are seen in the light of a higher, the human, dimension. They are not nullified by logotherapy but rather reinterpreted and reevaluated by it—or, as the Norwegian psychotherapist Bjarne Kvilhaugh [36] put it—they are rehumanized by logotherapy.

REFERENCES

1. Frankl, V. E. Preface by Gordon W. Allport. *Man's search for meaning: An introduction to logotherapy.* New York: Washington Square Press, 1963.
2. Ungersma, A. J. *The search for meaning: A new approach to psychotherapy and pastoral psychology.* Philadelphia: The Westminster Press, 1961.
3. Tweedie, D. F. *Logotherapy and the Christian faith: An evaluation of Frankl's existential approach to psychotherapy.* Grand Rapids: Baker Book House, 1965.
4. Tweedie, D. F. *The Christian and the couch: An introduction to Christian logotherapy.* Grand Rapids: Baker Book House, 1963.
5. Leslie, R. C. *Jesus and logotherapy: The ministry of Jesus as interpreted through the psychotherapy of Viktor Frankl.* New York: Abingdon Press, 1965.
6. Kaczanowski, G. In Arthur Burton, *Modern psychotherapeutic practice: Innovations in technique.* Palo Alto: Science and Behavior Books, 1965.
7. Crumbaugh, J. C. The application of logotherapy. *Journal of Existentialism,* 1965, **5,** 403-12.
8. Pervin, L. A. Existentialism, psychology, and psychotherapy. *American Psychologist,* 1960, **15,** 305-9.
9. Polak, P. Frankl's existential analysis. *American Journal of Psychotherapy,* 1949, **3,** 517.

10. Frankl, V. E. *Arztliche Seelsorge: Grundlagen der Logotherapie und Existenzanalyse.* (7th exp. ed.) Vienna: Deuticke, 1966.

11. Fabry, J. B. *The pursuit of meaning: Logotherapy applied to life.* Boston: Beacon Press, 1968.

12. Kratochvil, S. Ka psychoterapii existencialni frustrace. *Ceskoslovenska Psychiatrie,* 1961, **57,** 186.

13. Crumbaugh, J. C., & Maholick, L. T. An experimental study in existentialism: The psychometric approach to Frankl's concept of noogenic neurosis. *Journal of Clinical Psychology,* 1964, **20,** 200.

14. Crumbaugh, J. C. Cross-validation of purpose-in-life test based on Frankl's concepts. *Journal of Individual Psychology,* 1968, **24,** 74.

15. Werner, T. A. Opening paper read before the Symposium on Logotherapy, International Congress of Psychotherapy, Vienna, 1961.

16. Volhard, R., & Langen, D. Mehrdimensionale Psychotherapie. *Zeitschrift für Psychotherapie und Medizinische Psychologie,* 1953, **3,** 1.

17. Prill, H. J. Organneurose und Konstitution bei chronisch-funktionellen Unterleibsbeschwerden der Frau. *Zeitschrift für Psychotherapie und Medizinische Psychologie,* 1955, **5,** 215.

18. Kocourek, K., Niebauer, E., & Polak, P. Ergebnisse der klinischen Anwendung der Logotherapie. In V. E. Frankl, V. E. von Gebsattel, and J. H. Schultz (Eds.) *Handbuch der Neurosenlehre und Psychotherapie,* Vol. 3. Munich-Berlin: Urban & Schwarzenberg, 1959.

19. Crumbaugh, J. C., & Maholick, L. T. The case for Frankl's "Will to Meaning." *Journal of Existential Psychiatry,* 1963, **4,** 43.

20. Wertheimer, M. Some problems in the theory of ethics. In M. Henle (Ed.) *Documents of gestalt psychology.* Berkeley: University of California Press, 1961.

21. Frankl, V. E. *The doctor and the soul: From psychotherapy to logotherapy,* (2d. exp. ed.) New York: Knopf, 1965.

22. Frankl, V. E. Logotherapy and existential analysis: A review. *American Journal of Psychotherapy,* 1966, **20,** 252.

23. Frankl, V. E. Paradoxical intention: A logotherapeutic technique. *American Journal of Psychotherapy,* 1960, **14,** 520.

24. Frankl, V. E. *Psychotherapy and existentialism: Selected papers on logotherapy.* New York: Washington Square Press, 1967.

25. Frankl, V. E. Psychische Symptome und neurotische Reaktionen bei Hyperthyreose. *Medizinische Klinik,* 1956, **51,** 1139.

26. Frankl, V. E. Über somatogene pseudoneurosen. *Wiener Klinische Wochenschrift,* 1956, **68,** 280.

28. Frankl, V. E. Angst und Zwang. Zur Kenntnis pathogener Reaktionsmuster. *Acta Psychother.,* 1953, **1,** 111.

29. Gerz, H. O. Experience with the logotherapeutic technique of paradoxical intention in the treatment of phobic and obsessive-compulsive patients. *American Journal of Psychiatry,* 1966, **123,** 548.

30. Weisskopf-Joelson, E. The present crisis in psychotherapy. *The Journal of Psychology,* 1968, **69,** 107.

31. Bazzi, T. Considerations sur les limitations et les contraindications de la logotherapie. Paper read before the Fourth International Congress of Psychotherapy in Barcelona, Spain, 1958.

32. Gerz, H. O. The treatment of the phobic and the obsessive-compulsive patient using paradoxical intention sec. Viktor E. Frankl. *Journal of Neuropsychiatry,* 1962, **3,** 375.

33. Lehembre, J. L'intention paradoxale, procedé de psychotherapie. *Acta Neurologica et Psychiatrica Belgica,* 1964, **64,** 725.

34. Lorenz, K. *Das sogenannte Böse.* Vienna: Borotha-Schoeler, 1963.

35. Ledermann, F. K. Clinical applications of existential psychotherapy. *Journal of Existential Psychiatry,* 1962, **3,** 45.

36. Kvilhaugh, B. Klinische Erfahrungen mit der logotherapeutischen Technik der paradoxen Intention beziehungsweise deren Kombination mit anderen Behandlungsmethoden (Bericht über 40 Fälle). Paper read before the Austrian Medical Society of Psychotherapy, Vienna, July 18, 1963.

37. Vorbusch, H. J. Die Behandlung schwerer Schlafstörungen mit der paradoxen Inten-

tion. Paper read before the Austrian Medical Society of Psychotherapy, Vienna, June 1, 1965.

38. Gerz, H. O. Severe depressive and anxiety states. *Mind*, 1963, **1**, 235.

39. Benedikt, F. Zur Therapie angst- und zwangsneurotischer Symptome mit Hilfe der "paradoxen Intention" und "Dereflexion" nach V. E. Frankl. *Dissertation*. University of Munich Medical School, 1966.

40. Kaczanowski, G. Frankl's logotherapy. *American Journal of Psychiatry*, 1960, **117**, 563.

41. Gutheil, E. A. Proceedings of the Association for the Advancement of Psychotherapy. *American Journal of Psychotherapy*, 1956, **10**, 134.

42. Schultz, J. H. Analytische und organismische Psychotherapie. *Acta Psychotherapeutica Psychosomatica et Orthopaedagogica*, 1953, **1**, 33.

43. Weisskopf-Joelson, E. Some comments on a Viennese school of psychiatry. *Journal of Abnormal and Social Psychology*, 1955, **51**, 701.

44. Weisskopf-Joelson, E. Logotherapy and existential analysis. *Acta Psychotherapeutica Psychosomatica et Orthopaedagogica*, 1958, **6**, 193.

45. Müller-Hegemann, D. Methodological approaches in psychotherapy. *American Journal of Psychotherapy*, 1963, **17**, 554.

46. Freud, S. Über Forel: Der Hypnotismus, seine Bedeutung und seine Handhabung. *Wiener medizinische Wochenschrift*, 1889, **34**, 1098.

47. Frankl, V. E. Fragments from the logotherapeutic treatment of four cases. In Arthur Burton, *Modern psychotherapeutic practice: Innovations in technique*. Palo Alto: Science and Behavior Books, 1965.

48. Burton, A. Beyond the transference. *Psychotherapy: Theory, Research & Practice*, 1964, **1**, 49.

49. Victor, R. G., & Krug, C. M. Paradoxical intention. *American Journal of Psychotherapy*, 1967, **21**, 808.

50. Havens, L. Paradoxical intention. *Psychiatry & Social Science Review*, 1968, **2**, 16.

51. Frankl, V. E. *The will to meaning: Foundations and applications of logotherapy*. New York: The New American Library, 1970.

47.

William S. Sahakian

PHILOSOPHICAL PSYCHOTHERAPY

Philosophical psychotherapy is not an innovation that has emerged as a gimmick, but has had years of testing in classroom and clinical settings. With the au-

From William S. Sahakian, "Philosophical psychotherapy," *Psychologia*, 1974, vol. 17, No. 4, pp. 179–185. "Stoic philosophical psychotherapy," *Journal of Individual Psychology*, 1969, vol. 25, pp. 32–35. "Philosophical psychotherapy: An existential approach," *Journal of Individual Psychology*, 1976, vol. 32, pp. 62–68.

thor, it first appeared in classroom lectures and discussions when students reported with amazing regularity that his lectures were more than the usual informative talks; they were psychologically therapeutic experiences. Since the lectures were not planned to possess therapeutic value, it seemed worthwhile to analyze, review, and research the entire lecture series for an explanation as to why certain lectures and classroom discussions should affect students therapeutically. It was during this study that philosophy as a psychotherapeutic instrument was discovered and transferred to client-oriented situations.

It is not new that a person's psychological stance is often and to a considerable extent predicated on his philosophical convictions. But William James (1907) believed the opposite, namely, that a person's psychological constitution determined his philosophy so that the tough-minded personality was empiricistic, materialistic, pessimistic, fatalistic, and sceptical; whereas the tender-minded person was rationalistic, idealistic, optimistic, "free-willist," and dogmatic. Perhaps it was the enormous influence engendered by James that had scholars thinking in terms of the psychological affecting the theoretical beliefs of an individual that detoured us from the possibility that the reverse could be equally effective, if not entirely true. That is, it may be the case that the philosophical convictions of a person determine his psychological attitude, and it was mistakenly taken to be the opposite. The author's current position is that both are active, with one's philosophical *Weltanschauung* being in the ascendency.

The conception of one's philosophical beliefs affecting his psychological outlook and behavior is far from new, for it dates as far back as Epicurus and Epictetus. Epicurus, dealing with the anxieties of a youth, admonished him [the youth, Menoeceus] to have a salutary philosophy, for anxieties are couched in jaundiced philosophies.[1] The Stoics also dealt with psychological tensions from a philosophical orientation. Epictetus counselled that when life's vicissitudes that cannot be changed become an inscrutable problem, then a shift in attitude from one of anxious concern to one of stoical indifference will transform the situation into a reasonably tolerable one.[2] Moving from these ancient philosophers to the modern period, at least two notable philosophers can be found who have espoused a philosophical base for psychotherapy. The first of these, Schopenhauer, offered two recommendations: (1) the mental immersion into the depths of profound philosophy results in an alleviation of one's mental anguish, and (2) the psychological embracement of one's miseries, as it were, has the effect of attenuating their painful affects.[3] The first is effected by psychologically soaring to a realm above one's passions, anxieties, and driving forces to an elevated state of relative tranquility or escape from them, while the latter eliminates the intensity of *pressure* of painful experiences such as fears, crises, impending calamities, and the like. The second of these modern philosophical psychologists, Nietzsche, propounded the hypothesis that if a person has a "why" of living, he can overcome any "how."[4] That is, if a person has a reason for living, then he can endure any obstacle that he may confront in life.[5] Alfred Adler's theory of fictional finals,[6] a view that he derived from the philosopher Hans Vaihinger's *Philosophy of "as if,"*[7] possesses a comparable effect to Nietzsche's dictum.

PHILOSOPHICAL PSYCHOTHERAPY DEFINED

From what has been said it can be surmised that philosophical psychotherapy may be defined as any system that utilizes beliefs, attitudes, convictions, a person's *Weltanschauung* or philosophy of life, as a vehicle to alter, control or cope with his psychological or emotional problems, thereby changing his behavior pattern, psychological or emotional state, hence rectifying a maladjusted condition.

That beliefs affect our psychological state and behavior is an experience common to everyone. Evidence of this fact is so abounding that a simple instance or example attesting to it should suffice. If, while flying aboard a passenger airplane, the captain should announce that the landing gear is jammed and that the plane may have to crash-land, the passengers would be anxiously apprehensive even though the captain for some ulterior motive may have fabricated this deceit (or even if the landing gear is operative, but the captain's signaling device is in error). Note that a belief, notwithstanding its being an erroneous one, has potent psychological effects upon us and our behavior. Another example is that of a representative of the police or army delivering an erroneous message to a person informing him that his son has been killed. The news, despite its being false, can have severe psychological effects upon one as long as it is believed. It is said that Abraham Lincoln suffered more from worries about things that never occurred than from those that materialized.

Although many neurotics and others suffer in the same manner as do those victimized by false calamitous beliefs, the point is not whether beliefs are false (these illustrations were merely supplied to demonstrate the potency of even false notions), but that beliefs per se, whether true or false, motivate the individual. But philosophical psychotherapy is not simply a question of beliefs, it is a question of conviction, attitude, response, and choice. It is a question of undermining unsavory beliefs, disarming their power, establishing a posture toward them.

The author has had a number of individuals who, after having undergone Freudian psychotherapy, despairingly report that their maladjusted behavior (neurosis) is an indelible product of their childhood years and consequently is unavoidable. Their fatalistic beliefs derived from psychoanalyses rendered the wills of these individuals paralyzed with the resultant belief that they could not by choice extricate themselves from their predicament by a deliberate change of their behavior. These are cases where a belief in one's inability to choose to change left his autonomous will in a prostrate condition.

The reason why a person is the victim of his past experiences and of his complexes is that he *believes* that he has been duped, "brain-washed," or psychologized by his own tragic misinformation or an imprudent psychotherapist's unsalutary philosophy. As soon as a person *ceases* to believe that he can do no other but what his past experiences dictate that he must do, then he will experience a liberation that allows him the free choices that are truly within his possession and power of exercise. Beliefs possess the power to condition a person, and beliefs gained in therapy are a form of the conditioning process. The author has known individuals in therapy who (on advice to exercise their choices) do so with laborious effort because they have been in a sense hypnotically conditioned to believe in the paralysis of their genuinely autonomous state.[8] As the perceptive mind of Peirce observed, a belief is "that upon which a man is prepared to act"; and "beliefs are really rules for action, and the whole function of thinking is but one step in the production of habits of action."[9] Adler was convinced of the effect philosophy exerts on man. He saw "no reason to be afraid of metaphysics; it has had a great influence on human life and development."[10]

THE CHARACTER OF PHILOSOPHICAL PSYCHOTHERAPY

In philosophical psychotherapy, a person's attitude, which is inextricably interwoven with his beliefs, is of paramount importance. The Stoics believed that if a condition was unalterable, then it was imperative to change one's attitude in order to cope with the confronting situation. If concern for one's predicament is incapable of bringing about a suitable alteration of conditions, then alter your attitude. External conditions and internal attitudes play such a reciprocal role that a restructuring of one causes a concomitant reorganization of the other. The Stoic, Epictetus, advises that if you cannot change your situation, then assume an attitude of indifference toward it. The failure to be concerned about a situation causes a discharge in the forces that the distasteful condition may have exerted upon you. A young college student who was once faced with close prospects of death and its attending anxiety came abruptly to the rude realization that death is much too imminently near even for a young man. Subsequent to this experience his attitude was of extreme indifference to the values ordinarily countenanced by the general public, and he, with an air of indifference, was free from most of the petty anxieties that disturb the tranquility of the average person. One technique the author has advised in dealing with daily anxieties is to assume the mental stance that life is too brief to be concerned with them and a carefree attitude (of "Who cares," "I can't be bothered, life is too short," or "Who gives a damn,") will often aid in alleviating tension.

Another stoically philosophical stance is a device used to remain emotionally unperturbed, or to set oneself emotionally beyond the distance of persons who normally would prove distressing. The Stoics believed that you cannot be emotionally disturbed unless you will to become so, that is, unless you allow your will to be broken. For example, if you are emotionally upset by an insulting word or action of a person, it is not he that is distressing but the fact

that you permitted him control over yourself. You granted him the emotional powers by allowing him to break your will. Had you retained your will in your own discreet possession, then no person could inflict emotional disturbances upon you. The author recommends that in cases where many persons or situations are emotionally distressing, one can often maintain a composure free from repression by understanding the matter and readjusting his attitude. To illustrate, there was a man who asserted that he was fast reaching the point where he was no longer going to drive his car because the reckless and discourteous drivers on the road were more than he could cope with emotionally. It was recommended to this man that he readjust his attitude toward driving by making up his mind that in venturing upon the road one must expect a certain percentage of discourteous drivers out of the enormous numbers of cars on the congested city roads. He found that with the necessary change of attitude, not only was he able to cope with those drivers causing him perturbation but that it seemed as if there were fewer of this type of driver on the road than he realized.

Another individual who was easily provoked by others found that attitudinal changes provided a decided control over the matter. Instead of becoming disturbed when insulted, he assumed a philosophical attitude of indifference by thinking to himself that the would-be insulter was simply ignorant of the facts or that he was simply a stupid person who knew no better. Thoughts such as these do more than acquiesce the emotions; they remove the tension required for emotions to generate. Accordingly, it is not a question of repressing the emotions, since emotional pressure is not present to repress. This method is far superior to the Freudian technique of giving vent to one's emotions, for Freud's recommendation often proves detrimental to self and others, to others because they become the object of one's emotional venom and its destructive effects, to oneself because the regular unbridled expression of one's feelings develops into a trait, a personality characteristic dominating the individual and potent enough to motivate the personality by its own functional autonomy as Allport has argued.[11]

The Effectiveness of Philosophical Psychotherapy

Philosophical psychotherapy may require other therapeutic techniques to supplement it, but it is an unusually effective complement to nearly all systems. The value of philosophical psychotherapy can be readily seen and appreciated by those who are aware of the importance of changing a patient's attitude under the assumption that "the conscious as well as the unconscious is determined by subjective values and interests."[12] One of the most efficient methods of altering a person's psychological posture is by changing his philosophical outlook. One may even go so far as to assert that in certain instances a symptom is produced or controlled or eliminated by a change in a patient's philosophical attitude. One's beliefs play an important role in reinforcing or eliminating symptoms.

The present section deals with the application of Stoic philosophy to psychotherapy. According to the psychology of the Stoics, what cannot be changed should be accepted or else treated with philosophical indifference.[13] A fact which is not accepted by a person may cause him great distress; that is, if he is confronted with a problem or situation that he cannot change but nevertheless strives doggedly to dispel, he will merely succeed in intensifying the emotional tension and stress, causing him more misery than the problem that he is seeking to resolve. Emotional exhaustion compounded by a sense of defeat or despair in combatting one's psychological disturbances is often more distressing than the original ailment. It is in these cases that philosophical psychotherapy is definitely indicated: Instead of removing the object of complaint of a person, you alter his philosophical attitude or posture.

TECHNIQUE OF PHILOSOPHICAL PSYCHOTHERAPY

Philosophical psychotherapy lends itself to phenomenological theories of personality such as those of Rogers and Frankl.[14] For Rogers, the important consideration is that which the individual experiences as reality, his phenomenological field of experience and not reality per se. For example, a thirsty person races anxiously to a pool of water whether it is actually a mirage or genuine reality. For Rogers, anxiety is an alarm, but in philosophical therapy (after an attempt via the usual modes of therapy have failed to eliminate the cause or source of anxiety), one seeks to shut off the alarm, because it is then regarded as a false alarm. Anxiety is triggered off unnecessarily. In this situation and at this point, it is no longer advisable to continue to remove the threat, since continued failure often proves demoralizing. At this point, philosophical therapy is indicated, that is, ignore the threatening object, and attenuate the pressure. Ordinarily, in such cases, the object of threat is not the primary or direct source of discomfort, for the primary source is the attempt to combat or cope with the object of tension. Not only is this a common experience in the life of a neurotic, but it is found in everyday experiences of reasonably well-adjusted persons. There was the predicament of a clergyman who was about to perform religious services and reported that the prospects of performing such services were overwhelmingly terrifying, because the clergyman felt that it was impossible to measure up to the expectations of the congregation either morally or academically. The clergyman sought to remove the source of tension (performing services) by providing a socially acceptable excuse, such as obtaining a substitute cleric to conduct the services. The author's counsel in this matter, proceeding along the lines of philosophical psychotherapy, was to allow the assumed source of tension (conducting services) remain as it was but to remove the actual source of tension, namely, the beliefs and attitudes displayed. Our dialogue proceeded in the following manner (after the expression of the clergyman's feeling of tension owing to a sense of moral and intellectual incompetence):

"In a religious service does the clergyman perform for the congregation? Is the congregation gathered together to observe how marvelous the clergyman is?"

"No, he performs for no one."

"Is he there to display his intellectual talents in order to win the praise and admiration of his congregation?"

"No, the purpose of a religious service is to praise God, the clergy being merely the instrument toward this end. The people are in church for the sole purpose of worshipping God, and it would be improper for the clergyman to display ostentatiously his charming personality or anything else to distract the people from the principal purpose of the church service."

"Then, you are not on exhibition?"

"You are right! I feel a great deal better."

Frankl often uses a form of philosophical psychotherapy in his logotherapy, especially in relation to what he terms the *tragic triad* (pain, death, and guilt).[15] In cases where a person cannot remove suffering, he can alter his attitude toward it. The author was confronted with a case in which the individual concerned suffered a calamitous experience, his best friend being killed tragically by a tractor overturning upon him. Our conference proceeded somewhat as follows:

"I'm distraught, angry, and want to curse someone for what happened. If there is a God, why did he allow it to occur?"

Ironically, this man said that he did not believe in God; then he proceeded to curse God—his emotional upheaval causing his irrational outburst and contradiction. He went on to say:

"I can't understand it. Here is a fine young man, a good person with a good family that needed him. Now what are they supposed to do? I hate the world; there is no justice in it. Why is there evil? Why do good people have to suffer? What is the meaning of it all?"

Ordinarily, in such a case the psychotherapist would permit the emotionally troubled man to continue to expel all of his emotional ejaculations to the point of emotional depletion as a cathartic experience. Allport would argue that this man may continue to express his emotional evincings to a point where it becomes not only a personality trait but one that is cardinal and functioning autonomously, and that would be disastrous. In this instance, the man was allowed to vent his feelings until he reached a point where he sought a respite from emoting and awaited a response from the psychotherapist. At this juncture he was sympathetically told:

"Suffering has a peculiar effect on persons, usually developing in them one of two types of characteristics: The first is a vengeful personality, with a profound hatred of everything and everyone because of the injustice sensed in his experience of suffering. His embittered attitude permeates his world as a style of life. The second, however, is a mellowed personality who has emerged with insight and maturity, and exhibits a profound compassion and understanding for the suffering of others as a fellow-sufferer, as a comrade in misery. Misery often unites people together as Albert Schweitzer noted in his experiences in darkest Africa and as members of Alcoholics Anonymous are keenly aware. Which type will you choose to be, or which type will you allow yourself to fall prey to becoming?"

To my amazement, he retorted:

"You are absolutely right, the experience of suffering does place a person in an advantageous position to appreciate the suffering of others, and he can become mellowed and matured in a manner that no one else can. In a sense, one is privileged to suffer, for it can make him superior to others, sharing experiences and a level of living unknown to others."

Note the philosophical and not the psychological approach employed. It was not necessary to see this man for a number of times and permit him to expel his emotions, excusing it as catharsis. His emotions were self-contained once his philosophical attitude was altered and he accepted his circumstances. His emotional tensions were not principally aroused from the tragedy but from his attitude toward, and philosophical interpretation or beliefs concerning, the tragedy.

CASE STUDIES

Case One

A woman in her fifties, after having undergone brain surgery, complained of headaches localized behind the left ear. After careful examination, her physicians concluded that the operation was quite successful and that they could find nothing physically wrong with her, and recommended that she see the clinic's psychiatrist. Some months later, when she came to my attention, she had had no less than a dozen visits with the clinic's psychiatrist but to no avail.

Knowing that she had competent psychiatric care, I decided to proceed along another approach, namely philosophical psychotherapy. On the conclusion of a

brief introductory chat, enabling us to become better acquainted with each other, I explored her attitude regarding her ailment by engaging in the following dialogue with her:

"Is the pain severe?"
"Yes, at times."
"Is it endurable?"
"Not at times, and I think that it is getting worse."
"Is it very painful at this moment?"
"Excruciating!"
"Do you feel that the pain will become so intense that it will drive you out of your mind?"
"How did you know that? That is precisely what terrifies me; I am afraid that I am going insane, that is, the pain will get worse until I lose my mind."

At this point it was decided to employ Stoic psychotherapy. The patient would be offered the choice of accepting her condition laden with pain instead of fighting it, which she had been doing up to now. What she did not realize was that she was suffering from a dual pain, one which she had localized in the brain, and the other, the strain of emotional tension. Apparently, the latter was the less endurable of the two and had a concomitant aggravating effect upon the former.

The dialogue with the patient continued:

"Why do you want to get rid of the pain?"
"Nobody wants pain," she said looking at me as if I were rather peculiar for asking such an asinine question.
"If you could feel confident that no matter how severe the pain in your head becomes it will, nevertheless, not drive you to 'insanity' as you put it, do you think it would then be possible for you to endure the headache?"
"Why? Won't it?"
"But do you think that you could endure it?"
"Yes, I'm sure that I can."
"What if I were to tell you that your headache will never cause 'insanity'; and if you were ever to become 'insane' it would not be from your head pain?"
"Is that true?"
"Actually, a person becomes adapted to pain."

"Truly?"

"It is true."

Then smilingly she said: "I don't think that you will believe it but the pain in my head has subsided considerably, and I know that I can endure it."

When the tension that she had suffered was alleviated, she accepted her condition and was reasonably content, which indicates that it was not the head pain (regardless of whether it was psychological, psychosomatic, or otherwise) that distressed her, but the strenuous emotional confrontation with what she thought was a grave problem. Note that the symptom had "subsided considerably" through this dialectical method.

Case Two

This second case is that of a man in his late thirties complaining of neurotic symptoms though he had been to a number of psychiatrists. When he came to me it was uncertain whether he expected a miracle or was just shopping for another psychotherapist. It was quite obvious in this case that, owing to the failure of a number of psychiatrists, Stoic philosophical psychotherapy might possibly succeed where the other methods had failed. At least it was worth the attempt. He had a number of persistent neurotic symptoms with which he was wrestling, with the hope of conquering them. Instead of gaining any control over them, he had become worse by succumbing to despair and by depleting himself emotionally. It became quite clear that the tense, emotional strain exerted in combatting his neurosis was more painfully distressing than the neurosis itself. After some time, our session took the following dialectical course:

"You have told me of some of your neurotic symptoms and you say that you want me to help you to eradicate them. Why?"

"What do you mean, 'Why?' Any normal person would want to get rid of them. They are tormenting problems and disturb me terribly. They have made me miserable for a long time."

"Have you ever tried to live with them; accept them? Some crippled people have learned to live with their ailment. They do not spend every hour of their waking day or an entire lifetime striving to gain mastery over their problem. They accept their plight and learn to live with it, as do many other people who are handicapped victims. Some persons with the loss of an arm or with a heart condition learn to live within the limitations of their handicap; they do not waste their time and exhaust themselves vainly combatting their problem. Is it not possible for you also to do something comparable?"

After staring at me with a meaningless look for almost a minute, the patient's eyes and face lit up, and he smiled broadly (a smile that never left his face for the remainder of the session) and said:

"Why didn't the other psychotherapists tell me this long ago? Of course I can accept it and live with it. In fact, I feel better already. It is most ironic that I should come to a therapist, requesting that he cure me, and then have him tell me to keep my problem."

Two weeks later I saw this man, and with a similar smile and sense of relief he reported that he was "all better." Six months later, he was still content. The goal of Stoic psychotherapy is not happiness, but tranquility. In Stoic tranquility, there is neither anguish nor joy.[16]

CONCLUSION

Actually, what is most distressing to many neurotics and others is the emotional stress exerted to combat their problem, creating an emotional exhaustion, a state of doubt and insecurity, that readily stimulates or triggers anxiety at the slightest provocation. What needs to be accomplished in these cases is the removal of the superimposed emotional stress that comes with the fighting of the symptoms and not the symptoms per se.

Stoic psychotherapy may work here. The emotional block is removed by eliminating the driving force, namely, the unrelenting determination to control neurotic symptoms. Eliminate the tension created by the determination to gain mastery over the symptoms and the symptoms themselves may dissipate. If you cannot remove the problem, then change the attitude that is assumed toward it, and you will discover that you may have effectively dealt with two problems: the original neurosis and the distressing emotional tension expended in wresting it.

In closing we should like to point out that the motto of the "Introduction" of Adler's *The Neurotic Constitution* is a quotation from a leading Stoic, Seneca: "Everything depends on one's opinion. . . . We suffer according to our opinion. One is as miserable as one believes oneself to be.—*Epist.* 78, 13."[17]

PHILOSOPHICAL PSYCHOTHERAPY: AN EXISTENTIAL APPROACH

The Nature of Existential Psychotherapy

In this section, attention is centered on existential philosophy as a psychotherapeutic vehicle. Philosophical psychology in the nonscholastic and nonrationalistic sense is not new to empirical or clinical psychology, as is evidenced by the writings of Kierkegaard.[18]

Adherents of contemporary existential psychology and psychotherapy have learned of Kierkegaard's existential psychology through Heidegger,[19] but the philosopher who applied it directly to psychotherapy, terming it *existential psychoanalysis,* was Sartre.[20] Sartre also developed a phenomenological or existen-

tial theory of consciousness. Psychologists such as May[21] and psychiatrists such as Binswanger,[22] Condrau and Boss[23] look to Heidegger for their lead, while the psychiatrist Frankl[24] takes his lead from the phenomenological philosopher Scheler.[25] Rogers also identifies himself as a phenomenologist.[26] Recently, Maddi has joined the ranks of existentialist psychologists,[27] as has Thorne.[28] Adler is seen as related to the existentialist stream of development.[29] "The ceaseless task of unfolding issues of freedom, choice, and meaning is essential to the notion of humanism. This has been a cornerstone of Adlerian psychology."[30] Stern asserts that Sartre's position is decidedly nearer to Adler's than to Freud's. "There is no doubt that Sartre's 'original choice' is the counterpart of Adler's goal, and Sartre's 'fundamental project' is the replica of Adler's life plan."[31]

Objective of Existential Psychotherapy

The goal of existential therapy is *authenticity,* not tranquility as is the aim in Stoic therapy, nor happiness as is the goal in some other forms of therapy. For Kierkegaard, authenticity is the willingness to be oneself, standing "transparently" before God;[32] for Heidegger, it is to be genuine, to make one's own (autonomous) choices, to avoid losing one's identity by blending in with the crowd.

Pleasure or happiness is not desired, because the pursuit of pleasure inevitably terminates in despair.[33] The person who constantly seeks pleasure is fundamentally a desperate individual, as exemplified by the so-called jet set whose members are driven to such lengths for a taste of pleasure: by breakfasting in New York, lunching in Los Angeles, and supping in Acapulco to extract a "kick" out of life. Such behavior is an act of desperation, as is the "doing-the-town" itinerary of those who go from nightclub to nightclub to escape ennui.

A philosophy of pleasure is a philosophy of despair. It is an indication of extreme boredom from which one is prepared to do virtually anything to extricate oneself. A Freudian system of psychological hedonism tends toward despair, hence to "existential frustration" or "existential neurosis." Frankl, repudiating pleasure as the goal of human existence, cited the case of a woman in a concentration camp who sought to take her own life because the future offered no promise of pleasure. Frankl, challenging this hedonistic philosophy, countered that the woman was posing the wrong question. Her query should have been: "What can life expect from me?"[34]

In existential philosophy and psychotherapy, *choice, freedom,* and *responsibility* are the aims, not pleasure. Pleasure will not see a person through life, but a *raison d'être* will, and this will carry a person through life's severest vicissitudes. As Nietzsche said: "If we have our own reason for living, we shall endure almost any mode of life."[35] By freely choosing our mode of existence, we develop our personality according to our individual preference.

Characteristics of Existential Psychotherapy

The existential psychotherapist is convinced that his client can freely choose his personality at any stage of life, and in any condition of human existence. "Empirical psychoanalysis tries to determine the complex," asserted Sartre, "while existential analysis tries to determine the original choice."[36] A patient's past does not have the control over him that psychoanalysts fancy; an individual's future rests in his own hands. A person is a *being-for-the-future,* not the victim of the past. The reason a person is victimized by his past

experiences is that he *believes* he is, and so is committed in practice to that belief. Actually, he has been "brainwashed" by a fatalistic philosophy as found in psychoanalysis. As soon as a person ceases to believe that he can do no other but what his past dictates, then he will experience the freedom that he genuinely possesses and can now exercise it. Belief directs a person. Many people have become so committed to the deterministic views of psychoanalysis that when they think and act independently, they do so only with enormous effort and difficulty.[37] As Peirce observed, a belief is "that upon which a man is prepared to act. Beliefs are really rules for action, and the whole function of thinking is but one step in the production of habits of action."[38] Adler, too, was convinced of the effect philosophy exerts on an individual. He saw "no reason to be afraid of metaphysics; it has had a great influence on human life and development."[39]

Existentialists hold that the essential nature of a person is freedom. It is necessary for this freedom to be expressed for one to find one's wholesome self. According to Sartre, we are our choices, and psychoanalysis results in "a lie without a liar; it allows me to understand how it is possible for me to be lied to without lying to myself . . . : it replaces the duality of the deceiver and the deceived, the essential condition of the lie, by that of the 'id' and the 'ego.'"[40] Stern and Sartre emphasize the unity of the individual, his relative indeterminism, and his responsibility for his choices.[41]

Prior to Sartre, both Kierkegaard and Heidegger asserted that we are our choices, but with a different inflection. Kierkegaard modified Socrates' dictum from "know thyself" to "choose thyself." An authentic self (Heidegger) or a transparent self (Kierkegaard) is not alienated from the past, or even from the present, but integrates past and present with the *future*. A person's future is as much a part of him as is the past and present, directing him to his authentic self. An individual is more than a being-in-the-world (a phenomenological existence incorporating surrounding reality), he is a being-for-the-future. His futural existence has a bearing on his present existence—his motivation and behavior. Adlerian therapy aims at a durable adjustment by integrating the future with the present. "When I speak of active adaptation," remarked Adler, "it is a question rather of adaptation *sub specie aeternitatis* [under the aspect of the eternal], for only that physical and psychical development is 'right' which can be reckoned as right for the uttermost future."[42]

To appreciate existential psychotherapy, two case studies will serve to elucidate its tenets in practice.

CASE STUDIES

Case One
(Illustrating Being-of-the-Future)

A male in his thirties, despondent over an affair of unrequited love, sought to do away with himself. Insisting on immediate psychotherapy, he came to the therapist's office without an appointment and there played his small portable tape recorder, containing his final statement to those he loved. He announced that although he had wanted to take his life in the past, this was the first time that he knew for certain he would follow through with his suicidal plan.

In this session he spent a considerable period of time dwelling on his bleak past, and he talked incessantly of episodes in his life which terminated in failure, discouragement, and misfortune. After summarizing his life as one of disvalue, he pointed out

that the pattern of his existence was miserable and fixed by previous experiences. To validate what the future held in store for him, he used the past as his monitor, as if it held the reins of the future.

The client, who was a person of high potential, had moderate ambitions well within his grasp. During this and subsequent sessions, it was pointed out that he was much more than a being-of-the-past, that he was also a being-for-the-future and must allow that future to assist him. The therapist said he believed his patient had great potential that made for a promising future, and that he could "cash in" and live on the promise of that future.

The client constantly harped on past episodes of unhappiness, using them as a forecast of the future. Eventually, he learned to see past experiences as unreliable predictors and to draw on the future for direction in decision-making.

Once he became identified with the future instead of the past, his attitude changed to his benefit. With this philosophical conversion, there was a concomitant transformation in emotions, attitude, behavior, and other personality factors. Subsequent to the first session, this man required only reinforcement of the philosophical attitude acquired during the initial meeting. A year later, he was still doing well, free from suicidal inclinations.

Case Two (Illustrating Choice, Decision, and Authenticity)

A married woman of thirty, who had previously undergone psychoanalysis, said she hated herself and had wanted to take her life on several occasions. She suffered from what one might identify as an existential neurosis, since she had lost her purpose in life, was floundering mentally, and was confused as to her identity. Fearing that life was "passing her by" before she had an opportunity to live, she wanted to know before it was too late precisely what truth or meaning life had for her, and if indeed it had any meaning at all.

Behind her search for answers was a desire to be told exactly what to think and do. She revealed that since childhood she never was allowed to make a decision. Her mother invariably made them for her, even to this day, and now the situation was compounded by three in-laws joining mother in making choices for her. After six months of therapy, she (for the first time in her life that she could remember) made two decisions that she felt were autonomous. Having made them, she experienced a feeling of exhilaration because she sensed that she was now a person in her own right, free and independent.

Her new-found autonomy was complicated owing to an emergence of a sense of responsibility, a concomitant of her new autonomy. Now able to make choices, she realized she was responsible for her decisions and her behavior, whereas previously she could lean on others.

She now yearned to find her authentic self, hoping that her inner integrity would accord her the values that she prized in human existence. She wanted to make responsible choices. She sought to divorce her husband but did not want this action to be detrimental to her two young sons. She had a lover, but she did not want this to affect her children or herself adversely. In her search for authenticity, she realized that she would have to reexamine her scale of values and decide responsibly, whereas previously she allowed her mind to entertain only those desires to which her personality was predisposed, without engaging in any critical evaluation. That is to say, she would permit herself to drift toward amorous pursuits without questioning their consequences. In consequence of her existential analysis an entirely different perspective and value orientation on her life and behavior resulted.

SUMMARY

Unlike other systems of psychotherapy whose objectives are happiness or tranquility, existential analysis seeks to bring about an authentic person through the exercise of choices. One must bring his true self to realization through commitment, decisions, and choices. Inasmuch as personality change is effected through choice, an individual chooses himself, that is, his personality is the product of his choices. While the therapist does not make choices for his client, he facilitates his client's endeavors toward this end.

REFERENCES

1. Epicurus, "The Extant Writings of Epicurus," in *The Stoic and Epicurean Philosophers*, ed. W. J. Oates (New York: Random, 1940).
2. Epictetus, *The Works of Epictetus* (Boston: Little, 1865).
3. A. Schopenhauer, *The World as Will and Idea* (London: Trubner, 1883).
4. F. Nietzsche, "The Twilight of the Idols," in *The Complete Works of Friedrich Nietzsche*, ed. O. Levy (New York: Macmillan, 1909-11).
5. Maxim 12 of "The Twilight of the Idols."
6. A. Adler, *The Practice and Theory of Individual Psychology* (New York: Littlefield, 1929; reprint by Humanities, 1971).
7. H. Vaihinger, *The Philosophy of "as if"* (New York: Barnes & Noble, 1935).
8. W. S. Sahakian, "A Social Learning Theory of Obsessional Neurosis," *Israel Annals of Psychiatry and Related Disciplines* 7 (1969): 70-75.
9. C. S. Peirce, *Collected Papers* (Cambridge, Mass.: Harvard University Press, 1931-36), 8 vols.

10. A. Adler, *Social Interest: A Challenge to Mankind* (New York: Capricorn Books, 1964): 275.

11. G. W. Allport, *Personality: A Psychological Interpretation* (New York: Henry Holt, 1937): idem, *Pattern and Growth in Personality* (New York: Holt, Rinehart and Winston, 1961).

12. H. L. Ansbacher and R. R. Ansbacher, eds., *The Individual Psychology of Alfred Adler* (New York: Basic, 1956), p. 9.

13. Epictetus, *Discourses* (Oxford: Clarendon, 1916).

14. V. E. Frankl, *The Will to Meaning: Foundations and Applications of Logotherapy* (New York: World Publishing, 1969): C. R. Rogers, "A Theory of Therapy, Personality, and Interpersonal Relationships, as Developed in the Client-Centered Framework," in *Psychology: A Study of a Science,* ed. S. Koch (New York: McGraw-Hill, 1959), vol. 3; C. R. Rogers, "The Phenomenological Theory of Personality," in *Psychology of Personality,* ed. W. S. Sahakian (Chicago: Rand McNally, 1977).

15. V. E. Frankl, *Psychotherapy and Existentialism* (New York: Washington Square Press, 1967).

16. H. N. Simpson, *Stoic Apologetics* (440 Linden Ave., Oak Park, Ill. 60302: Author, 1966).

17. A. Adler, *The Neurotic Constitution* (New York: Dodd, 1926; reprint by Books for Libraries, 1972).

18. S. Kierkegaard, *Fear and Trembling,* 2d ed. (Princeton: Princeton University Press, 1954); idem, *The Concept of Dread,* 2d ed. (Princeton: Princeton University Press, 1957).

19. M. Heidegger, *Being and Time* (New York: Harper & Row, 1962).

20. J.-P. Sartre, *Being and Nothingness* (New York: Philosophical Library, 1956), pp. 557-75; idem, *The Transcendence of the Ego: An Existentialist Theory of Consciousness* (New York: Noonday, 1957).

21. R. May, ed., *Existential Psychology,* 2d ed. (New York: Random, 1969).

22. L. Binswanger, *Being-in-the World* (New York: Basic, 1963).

23. G. Condrau and M. Boss, "Existential Analysis," in *Modern Perspectives in World Psychiatry,* ed. J. G. Howells (Edinburgh and London: Oliver & Boyd, 1968), pp. 488-518; M. Boss, *Psychoanalysis and Daseinsanalysis* (New York: Basic, 1953).

24. V. E. Frankl, *The Will to Meaning: Foundations and Applications of Logotherapy* (New York: World Publishing, 1969).

25. M. Scheler, *Formalism in Ethics and Non-Formal Ethics of Values* (Evanston, Ill.: Northwestern University Press, 1973).

26. C. R. Rogers, *Client-Centered Therapy: Its Current Practice, Implications, and Theory* (Boston: Houghton Mifflin, 1951); p. 532.

27. S. R. Maddi, "The Existential Neurosis," *Journal of Abnormal Psychology* 72 (1967): 311-25.

28. F. C. Thorne, "An Existential Theory of Anxiety," *Journal of Clinical Psychology* 19 (1963): 35-43.

29. A. Adler, *The Science of Living* (Garden City, N.Y.: Doubleday, 1969); p. vii.

30. R. D. Waldman, "A Theory and Practice of Humanistic Psychotherapy," *Journal of Individual Psychology* 25 (1969): 19-31.

31. A. Stern, "Existential Psychoanalysis and Individual Psychology," *Journal of Individual Psychology* 14 (1958): 40.

32. S. Kierkegaard, *Either/Or,* 2 vols. (Princeton: Princeton University Press, 1944).

33. S. Kierkegaard, *Concluding Unscientific Postscript* (Princeton: Princeton University Press, 1941): idem, *Either/Or.*

34. V. E. Frankl, *The Doctor and the Soul: From Psychotherapy to Logotherapy,* rev. ed. (New York: Knopf, 1965).

35. F. Nietzsche, *Twilight of the Idols: Or, How to Philosophize with a Hammer,* in COMPLETE WORKS OF FRIEDRICH NIETZSCHE, 17 vols., ed. O. Levy (New York: Macmillan, 1901-11), vol. 16, maxim 12.

36. Sartre, *Being and Nothingness,* p. 657.

37. W. S. Sahakian, "A Social Learning Theory of Obsessional Neurosis," *Israel Annals of Psychiatry and Related Disciplines* 7 (1969): 70-75.

38. C. S. Peirce, *Collected Papers,* 8 vols. (Cambridge, Mass.: Harvard University Press, 1931-66).

39. A. Adler, *Social Interest: A Challenge to Mankind* (New York: Capricorn Books, 1964), p. 275.

40. Sartre, *Being and Nothingness,* p. 51.

41. P. Rom and H. L. Ansbacher, "An Adlerian Case of a Character by Sartre?" *Journal of Individual Psychology* 21 (1965): 37.

42. Adler, *Social Interest,* p. 271.

48.

Arnold A. Lazarus

MULTIMODAL THERAPY

SEVEN MODALITIES

An arbitrary division created *sui generis* would simply turn back the clock on the composite theories and facts that psychologists have amassed to date. It is no accident that ever since the publication of Brentano's *Psychologie vom empirischen Standpunkte* in 1874, acts like ideation, together with feeling states and sensory judgments, have comprised the main subject matter of general psychology. In other words, psychology as the scientific study of behavior has long been concerned with sensation, imagery, cognition, emotion, and interpersonal relationships. If we examine psychotherapeutic processes in the light of each of these basic modalities, seemingly disparate systems are brought into clearer focus, and the necessary and sufficient conditions for long-lasting therapeutic change might readily be discerned.

Every patient-therapist interaction involves *behavior* (be it lying down on a couch and free associating, or actively role playing a significant encounter), *affect* (be it the silent joy of nonjudgmental acceptance, or the sobbing release of pent-up anger), *sensation* (which covers a wide range of sensory stimuli from the spontaneous awareness of bodily discomfort to the deliberate cultivation of specific sensual delights), *imagery* (be it the fleeting glimpse of a childhood memory, or the contrived perception of a calm-producing scene), and *cognition* (the insights, philosophies, ideas, and judgments that constitute our fundamental values, attitudes and beliefs). All of these take place within the context of an *interpersonal* relationship, or various interpersonal relationships. An added dimension with many patients is their need for medication or *drugs* (*e.g.,* phenothiazine derivatives and various antidepressants and mood regulators). Taking the first letter of each of the foregoing italicized words, we have the acronym BASIC ID. *Obviously, the proposed seven modalities are interdependent and interactive.*

* * *

Perhaps it is worth stressing at this point that the major hypothesis, backed by the writer's clinical data (8, 11), is that *durable*

From Arnold A. Lazarus, "Multimodal behavior therapy," *Journal of Nervous and Mental Disease,* vol. 156, pp. 406, 407, 409. © 1973 by The Williams & Wilkins Co., Baltimore.

MODALITY PROFILE

Modality	Problem	Proposed Treatment
Behavior	Inappropriate withdrawal responses	Assertive training
	Frequent crying	Nonreinforcement
	Unkempt appearance	Grooming instructions
	Excessive eating	Low calorie regimen
	Negative self-statements	Positive self-talk assignments
	Poor eye contact	Rehearsal techniques
	Mumbling of words with poor voice projection	Verbal projection exercises
	Avoidance of heterosexual situations	Re-education and desensitization
Affect	Unable to express overt anger	Role-playing
	Frequent anxiety	Relaxation training and reassurance
	Absence of enthusiasm and spontaneous joy	Positive imagery procedures
	Panic attacks (usually precipitated by criticism from authority figures)	Desensitization and assertive training
	Suicidal feelings	Time projection techniques
	Emptiness and aloneness	General relationship building
Sensation	Stomach spasms	Abdominal breathing and relaxing
	Out of touch with most sensual pleasures	Sensate focus method
	Tension in jaw and neck	Differential relaxation
	Frequent lower back pains	Orthopedic exercises
	Inner tremors	Gendlin's focusing methods (8, p. 232)
Imagery	Distressing scenes of sister's funera	Desensitization
	Mother's angry face shouting "You fool!"	Empty chair technique
	Performing fellatio on God	Blow up technique (implosion)
	Recurring dreams about airplane bombings	Eidetic imagery involing feelings of being safe
Cognition	Irrational self talk: "I am evil." "I must suffer." "Sex is dirty." "I am inferior."	Deliberate rational disputation and corrective self-talk
	Syllogistic reasoning overgeneralization	Parsing of irrational sentences
	Sexual misinformation	Sexual education
Interpersonal relationships	Characterized by childlike dependence	Specific self-sufficiency assignments
	Easily exploited/submissive	Assertive training
	Overly suspicious	Exaggerated role taking
	Secondary gains from parental concern	Explain reinforcement principles to parents and try to enlist their help
	Manipulative tendencies	Training in direct and confrontative behaviors

results are in direct proportion to the number of specific modalities deliberately invoked by any therapeutic system. Psychoanalysis, for instance, is grossly limited because penetrating insights can hardly be expected to restore effective functioning in people with deficient response repertoires—they need explicit training, modeling, and shaping for the acquisition of adaptive social patterns. Conversely, nothing short of coercive manipulation is likely to develop new response patterns that are at variance with people's fundamental belief systems. Indeed, insight, self-understanding, and the correction of irrational beliefs must usually precede behavior change whenever faulty assumptions govern the channels of manifest behavior. In other instances, behavior change must occur before "insight" can develop (8). Thus, cognitive restructuring and overt behavior training are often reciprocal. This should not be misconstrued as implying that a judicious blend of psychoanalysis and behavior therapy is being advocated. Psychoanalytic theory is unscientific and needlessly complex; behavioristic theory is often mechanistic and needlessly simplistic. The points being emphasized transcend any given system or school of therapy. However, adherence to social learning theory (1) as the most elegant theoretical system to explain our therapeutic sorties places the writer's identification within the province of behavior therapy—hence "multimodal behavior therapy." Perhaps the plainest way of expressing our major thesis is to stress that comprehensive treatment at the very least calls for the correction of irrational beliefs, deviant behaviors, unpleasant feelings, intrusive images, stressful relationships, negative sensations, and possible biochemical imbalance. To the extent that problem identification (diagnosis) systematically explores each of these modalities, whereupon therapeutic intervention remedies whatever deficits and maladaptive patterns emerge, treatment outcomes will be positive and long-lasting. To ignore any of these modalities is to practice a brand of therapy that is incomplete. Of course, not every case requires attention to each modality, but this conclusion can only be reached after each area has been carefully investigated during problem identification (*i.e.*., diagnosis).

* * *

REFERENCES

1. Bandura, A. *Principles of Behavior Modification.* Holt, Rhinehart and Winston, New York, 1969.
8. Lazarus, A. A. *Behavior Therapy and Beyond.* McGraw-Hill, New York, 1971.
11. Lazarus, A. A. Notes on behavior therapy, the problem of relapse and some tentative solutions. *Psychotherapy, 8:* 192–196, 1971.

49.

Jerome D. Frank

EFFECTIVENESS OF PSYCHOTHERAPY

Outcome research, despite progress in standardization of change measures and specification of therapeutic procedures, continues to fail to demonstrate significant differences in the effectiveness of these procedures for most conditions, suggesting that a more hopeful direction of research would be to explore therapeutically relevant qualities of the patient, the therapist, and their interaction. Based on clinical impressions and scattered research findings, suggestions are offered as to potentially promising research approaches to these areas.

After decades of research, the amount of well-established, clinically relevant knowledge about psychotherapeutic outcome still remains disappointingly meagre. Although some relationships between determinants and outcome have attained statistical significance, few are powerful enough to be clinically relevant, and most of those that have achieved this status are intuitively obvious. An example is the finding that patients who begin therapy at a high level of functioning terminate at higher levels than those who begin at low levels. In other words, the healthier one is to start with, the healthier one is at the end (Garfield, 1978).

From Jerome D. Frank, "The present status of outcome studies," *Journal of Consulting and Clinical Psychology,* vol. 47, pp. 310–315. Copyright 1979 by the American Psychological Association. Reprinted by permission of the publisher and author.

The reasons for this state of affairs are so familiar as to require only brief mention. Criteria for selection of patient samples are inadequate; therapies are so loosely defined that they permit large but undefinable variations in application by different therapists using ostensibly the same techniques; and measures of outcome are not standardized sufficiently so that results of different studies can accumulate. Furthermore, the choice of variables to be studied has been guided too much by the need to produce a publishable result and not enough by the search for significance. Thus, massive amounts of work have been done on variables determining acceptance of therapy and attendance, which at best are prerequisites to improvement. At worst, the tacit assumption that dropping out indicates failure of therapy is often misleading, in that many brief attenders may drop out because they have improved sufficiently so as not to feel the need of further treatment. The independent variables are too often actuarial ones, like age, sex, and social class, which at best are indirectly related to responsivity.

This presentation reviews four generalizations that outcome studies seem to have reasonably well established and then considers the main areas about which more information is needed and could be obtained, with occasional hunches as to the most promising lines to pursue.

THE CURRENT STATE OF KNOWLEDGE

By now it seems reasonably well established that all forms of psychotherapy—that is, planned, systematic efforts of a socially sanctioned, trained healer to relieve psychologically caused distress and disability through words and other symbolic interactions—are somewhat more effective than informal, unplanned help. Unfortunately, as appears from the studies of Sloane, Staples, Cristol, Yorkston, and Whipple (1975) and Smith and Glass (1977), these efforts are not impressively more effective. The latter found that the average difference between treated and untreated patients was about two thirds of a standard deviation. Since it is unclear how many of the studies included in reaching this figure were poorly controlled, the actual difference may be less.

The second generalization is that—except for the short-term superiority of behavior therapy for phobias, compulsions, obesity, and sexual problems, and possibly of cognitive therapy for the relief of depression—no one therapy has been shown to be overall significantly superior to any other, especially over the long term.

Third, follow-up studies seem to show consistently that whatever the form of therapy, most patients who show initial improvement maintain it (Lieberman, Yalom, & Miles, 1973). Moreover, when two therapies yield differences in outcome at the close of treatment, with rare exceptions these disappear over time, and the closing of the gap seems to depend more on patients who received the less successful therapy catching up to the others than on both groups regressing equally toward the mean. This suggests that the main beneficial effect of psychotherapy may be to accelerate improvement that would have occurred eventually in any case.

Even if therapy did no more than speed up natural recovery processes, however, appreciable shortening of the duration of a patient's distress and disability would nevertheless be sufficient to justify therapeutic efforts. To take an example of another form of treatment, electroconvulsive treatment for depression does not prevent relapses, but few would therefore deny its value.

The differences between immediate and long-term outcomes of psychotherapy suggest the probable importance of attempting to distinguish more sharply factors that produce improvement from those that maintain it (Liberman, 1978a).

Finally, the results of outcome research strongly suggest that more of the determinants of therapeutic success lie in the personal qualities of the patient and the therapist and in their interactions than in the therapeutic method.

The conclusions that all therapies do somewhat better than no therapy and that for the vast majority of patients one method has not been proven to be more effective than another rest on measures of central tendency or nose-counting. In view of the relative lack of clarity of most studies with respect to important variables, failures to obtain significant differences between populations should not be interpreted as indicating that such differences do not exist. As Garfield (1978) has put it: "A host of idiosyncratic studies of poorly defined populations with vaguely described therapies and exceedingly variable outcome criteria will not produce findings of any substance" (p. 225).

A particular source of weakness in outcome measures is their failure to do justice to the striking benefits achieved by a few patients under many forms of psychotherapy. Most therapists have witnessed improvement justifying the overused phrase "basic personality change" in an occasional patient—in fact, on the principle of intermittent reinforcement, these patients are probably what keep most of us going. Most improvement scales express mental health in terms of diminished disability—that is, they do not do adequate justice to these gratifying patients. The challenge is how to devise scales for appraising outcome and statistical procedures that take adequate account of rare but huge successes. To illustrate with a close analogy, although many attenders find participation in revival meetings psychologically rewarding, it is estimated that only 2 to 5% make a "decision for Christ" at a meeting, and only about 15% of them (less than half of 1% of the total) remain permanently converted (Argyle, 1958). Applying conventional outcome measures, we would probably class those who enjoy the experience as slightly improved, the maximally 5% who are temporarily converted as moderately improved, and the minuscule number of permanent converts as markedly improved, or perhaps even recovered. Thus, by statistical criteria, as producers of both immediate and long-term changes, the record of revival meetings is abysmal. Yet the tiny fraction who are permanently converted would justifiably claim that for them revival meetings are extremely effective.

This line of thinking suggests that instead of continuing to pursue the relatively unrewarding enterprise of statistically comparing the effectiveness of different therapies, we should focus on particular forms of therapy that seem to work exceptionally well with a few patients and seek to define the characteristics of both the therapy and the patients that lead to this happy result. David Malan's (1976) persistent and profitable pursuit of the determinants of the differential responses of patients to short-term psychoanalytically oriented therapy is an example.

Considerable progress is made with two other aspects of outcome research. The first is the development of measures of outcome that permit comparison of therapies with each other. Considerable progress has been made with this, particularly by the publication of *Psychotherapy Change Measures* (Waskow & Parloff, 1975). As a result, we can confidently expect increasing comparability of the outcome measures used by different researchers. Secondly, more detailed specification of different forms of therapy is making it possible to feel relatively confident that therapists who claim to be using the same method actually are doing so. Manuals have been devised for some behavioral and cognitive therapies and for crisis management, and this effort should certainly be encouraged. Both standardized measures of outcome and manuals may be largely irrelevant, however, to long-term open-ended therapies, especially those with an existential orientation. To the extent that the spontaneity of the therapist's actions is considered crucial and the patient's improvement is defined solely by changes in his or her subjective state, it is hard to see how either the therapy or the measures of benefit could ever be standardized. However, there is still so much to be learned from brief, highly structured psychotherapies that this caveat need not worry us for a long time to come.

PROBLEMS OF PATIENT SELECTION

Since research results to date suggest that the major determinants of therapeutic success appear to lie in aspects of patients' personality and style of life, the development of better criteria for their assignment to different therapies is a crucial need. A first step would be to try to purify the sample, as it were, by screening out candidates who would be expected to respond favorably to any form of help. These include patients with fluctuating conditions who enter therapy in the trough of a cycle, those in the midst of a crisis who can be expected to regain their equilibrium when it passes, and patients possessing good ego strength who are motivated by subjective distress to seek help. Incidentally, it may be that inclusion of patients who respond to any form of help accounts for the persistence of all schools of therapy. Patients naturally attribute their improvement to whatever they happen to be doing at the time, so they give credit to the therapy they are in, even though any other might have been equally successful. Since practitioners of all therapeutic schools have many such successes, their belief in the superiority of their method is similarly reinforced.

Another way of approaching the question of patient selection derives from the hypothesis that what brings patients to psychotherapy is a combination of specific symptoms plus demoralization, and that much of the improvement in all forms of psychotherapy results from the improvement in patients' morale brought about by features shared by all forms of therapy. Based on an epidemiological study of a stratified sample of city dwellers, Dohrenwend (Note 1) developed a demoralization index consisting of nine subscales: poor self-esteem, sadness, dread, anxiety, perceived physical health, unspecific psychophysiological complaints, helplessness-hopelessness, and confused thinking. It would be a simple matter to apply this scale to all patients seeking psychotherapy and to eliminate from research studies all those suffering from demoralization of brief duration, because they would probably respond to any form of help. One would have to also consider eliminating those whose demoralization is so prolonged and severe that they would be poor candidates for any therapy. Having excluded both these groups, we might not have enough patients left to study, to be sure, but this approach deserves to be tested.

Having eliminated patients who would or would not do well regardless of therapy, we need ways of classifying the remainder in terms of categories more relevant to different forms of therapy than the present diagnostic scheme, which has been based primarily on clinical descriptions. Three leads toward more psychotherapeutically relevant diagnostic categories have some experimental support, to which may be added a couple of purely speculative suggestions. It seems probable, first, that verbal, psychologically minded patients who have motivation for insight (Malan, 1976) do well in insight therapies, whereas those who are oriented to solving their problems by actions may do better in behavioral ones. Second, patients' expectations seem to have something to do with responsiveness to different forms of therapy. This is suggested by the well-established observation that once therapy is under way, all therapists, subtly or openly, indoctrinate patients into their therapeutic rationales and procedures. Furthermore, therapeutic success has been found to be related to congruence between patients' and therapists' expectations as to the therapeutic process, although this congruence with respect to outcome seems to be irrelevant (Wilkins, 1973).

The third promising lead is classification of patients in terms of locus of control. In our own research we stumbled on an interaction between locus of control and whether patients were led to believe that their improvement in therapy was the result of their own efforts or of a placebo pill. The internally controlled patients did significantly better than the externally controlled ones in the first condition, whereas the results were reversed in the second (Liberman, 1978b).

Other studies with related findings are

emerging. One, for example, found that cognitive relaxation procedures resulted in a greater decrement in heart rate and subjective distress in internally controlled than in externally controlled subjects, who responded better to muscular relaxation (Ollendick & Murphy, 1977). A study of reactions of test-anxious students to counseling and behavior therapies found that the internally controlled students preferred an optional amount of control in counseling, whereas the externally controlled felt that they were in too much control of therapy (Friedman & Dies, 1975). Mere straws in the wind, to be sure, but they may be harbingers of a gale!

Two other questions come to mind about possible personality attributes of patients related to choice of therapy, on which, to my knowledge, no research has been done. One is, Do persons who have strong investments in their bodies, such as athletes, physical education instructors, and actors, do particularly well in therapies that stress altering mental states through bodily manipulations and exercises such as bioenergetics?

The second question is, What characterizes persons who respond exceptionally well to abreactive techniques? These procedures have been used in the West at least since Mesmer, and they have never died out, but neither have they proved sufficiently effective overall to prevail. Rather, they seem to enjoy spurts of popularity interspersed with long periods of relative neglect. Presumably, this is because for most patients the improvement is not lasting, or perhaps because those who do experience marked and lasting benefits are too small a proportion of the patients treated by these methods to establish a statistical claim for the methods' validity. Could the success of emotional flooding therapies perhaps be related to the degree to which persons undergoing them are emotionally arous-

able? If so, would they be most useful with the most emotionally labile, the most phlegmatic, or is the optimal level of arousability somewhere between these extremes?

PROBLEMS OF THERAPIST EFFECTIVENESS

Two hypotheses concerning the qualities of therapists related to their therapeutic power, which are battered but refuse to die, are the "active personal participation" concept of Whitehorn and Betz (Dent, 1978; Razin, 1977; Whitehorn & Betz, 1975), operationalized by the A–B scale, and the warmth, genuineness, and empathy framework of Rogers and his colleagues (Truax & Carkhuff, 1967). Incidentally, since the ability of the therapist to offer high levels of either active personal participation or the Rogerian conditions seems largely to depend on the patient's responses, these elements are probably more appropriately viewed as properties of the therapist–patient interaction. The most encouraging findings using Rogerian dimensions have been reported by educators, who have found them to be positively related to student achievement (Aspy, 1969). Education is close enough to therapy to justify continuing exploration of the Rogerian dimensions' relation to therapeutic outcome.

Another lead is supplied by the study of Lieberman et al. (1973), which found that the most successful leaders of encounter groups, as measured by beneficial changes in members, displayed a combination of moderate stimulation, high caring, high meaning attribution, and moderate executive function.

Aspects of therapists that are difficult to pin down but may possibly be very relevant to their success are persuasiveness and what may be called healing ability. Pursuit of the latter leads quickly into the quicksands of the paranormal, such as clairvoyance, telepathy, and ability to speed plant growth or activate enzymes or produce spectacular auras on Kirlian photographs. Attempts to study such phenomena involve grave threats to the researcher's reputation as a sober scientist, so their pursuit can be recommended only to the most intrepid; but the rewards could be great.

It should be added that any research into the personal qualities of therapists related to their therapeutic efficiency is, of course, extremely threatening. The discovery that one lacks therapeutic personality characteristics could be disastrous, not only to one's pocketbook but also to one's self-esteem.

Finally, there is the promising area of goodness of match between patient and therapist along relevant dimensions. The word *relevant* needs to be stressed. Most of the matching that has been attempted has been on personality attributes determined by psychological tests or on demographic variables, which at best are only indirectly related to therapeutic success. The most promising lead that I have come upon in this area is level of conceptualization, developed by educators. A scale has been devised to measure the complexity with which persons conceptualize their subjective worlds (Carr, 1970). Although no conclusive studies have emerged, there is some evidence, which deserves to be pursued, that persons with lower conceptual levels respond best with structured therapy and a structured environment. Studies of smokers (Best, 1975), psychiatric outpatients treated by medical students, and alcoholics, as well as college students and delinquents, found that patients whose conceptual level was similar to that of their therapists did better than those in which there was a mismatch (Posthuma & Carr, 1975).

LIMITS TO OUTCOME RESEARCH

Given enough ingenuity, time, and effort, researchers could make considerably more progress with respect to the therapeutically relevant attributes of patients, therapists, and their interaction, and I personally believe this would be potentially the most rewarding line to pursue. There seem to be several built-in limits to the success of research on the outcome of psychotherapy, however, which I should like to mention in closing. The first is that since therapy does not occur in a social vacuum, many of the determinants of outcome lie outside the patient–therapist dyad, and therefore, no matter how sophisticated the focus on it, important sources of variance will be missed. Of these, intercurrent events in long-term therapy are especially significant, particularly with respect to maintenance of change (Voth & Orth, 1973). Whether these can ever be systematized remains to be seen. Even more difficult to evaluate—so much so that I can do no more than mention it as a possibility—is the role of the world view of the society in which the therapy occurs. At the very least, differences in world views of different cultures would be expected severely to limit the cross-cultural generalizability of findings. For example, Peruvian psychiatrists who work with the Indians have pointed out that attainment of mastery, cited by almost all North American psychotherapists as a major goal of treatment, would make no sense to their clientele. For them, the goal would be rather to learn to accept their fate or to restore their harmony with the spirit world. In addition, and perhaps more importantly, as this example suggests, the world view shared by patient and therapist may have more to do with the choice of procedures, selection of patients, and criteria of outcome than any of the variables I have already mentioned.

With respect to patients, the type of distress and disability for which many seek help are expressions of habitual maladaptive efforts to resolve internally or externally generated stresses. These efforts and the types of distress and disability they generate are protean, often idiosyncratic, and shift from time to time in the same patient. To the extent that this is so, it sets limits to any scheme of classification as related to therapy.

With respect to psychotherapeutic methods, until recently methodological problems have slowed research into group and family approaches, which may well be more powerful, by and large, than dyadic ones. As group creatures, humans are highly susceptible to group forces, especially if these are brought to bear by a strong leader operating within a belief system shared by the group members. Insofar as psychotherapy seeks to produce beneficial attitudinal and behavioral changes, group methods would appear to be more powerful than dyadic ones, a supposition supported by the fact that in most of the world, analogues of psychotherapy are conducted in groups.

Group therapy research involves a forbidding number and complexity of variables that must be taken into account. With the rapid advances of computer science, this problem is becoming more tractable. Lieberman et al. (1973) have blazed the way in their studies of encounter groups, and this should encourage similarly sophisticated research into therapy groups.

Other therapies that post particular difficulties for the researcher are those termed *humanistic* or *existential*. As already mentioned, they are conceptualized in ways that resist application of the scientific method, which consists of the systematic collection and analysis of shared data. To the extent that their effectiveness lies in a unique encounter between each patient and the therapist—an encounter, moreover, characterized by therapeutic improvisations—their scientific evaluation may permanently elude our efforts.

My overall conclusion is that the years of research on outcome, while they have yielded little in the way of definite and significant findings, have led to considerable advances with respect to the most fruitful questions to ask and the most appropriate methods for going about trying to answer them. Although we have not yet found many answers, we are becoming able to ask more cogent questions and to answer them in a more systematic and sophisticated fashion. This development supplies ground for hope that therapy research will make considerably more progress in the future than it has in the past.

REFERENCE NOTE

1. Dohrenwend, B. Personal communication, January 1978.

REFERENCES

Argyle, M. *Religious behaviour.* London: Routledge & Kegan Paul, 1958.

Aspy, D. N. The effect of teacher-offered conditions of empathy, positive regard, and congruence upon student achievement. *Florida Journal of Educational Research,* 1969, *11,* 39–48.

Best, J. A. Tailoring smoking withdrawal procedures to personality and motivational differences. *Journal of Consulting and Clinical Psychology,* 1975, *43,* 1–8.

Carr, J. E. Differentiation similarity of patient and therapist and the outcome of psychotherapy. *Journal of Abnormal Psychology,* 1970, *76,* 361–369.

Dent, J. K. *Exploring the psychosocial therapies through the personalities of effective therapists* (Publ. No. ADM 77-527). Washington, D.C.: U.S. Government Printing Office, 1978.

Friedman, M. L., & Dies, R. R. Reactions of internal and external test-anxious students to counseling and behavior therapies. *Journal of Consulting and Clinical Psychology,* 1975, *42,* 921.

Garfield, S. L. Research on client variables in psychotherapy. In S. L. Garfield & A. E. Bergin (Eds.), *Handbook of psychotherapy and behavior change* (2nd. ed.). New York: Wiley, 1978.

Liberman, B. L. The maintenance and persistence of change: Long-term follow-up investigations of psychotherapy. In J. D. Frank, R. Hoehn-Saric, S. D. Imber, B. L. Liberman, & A. R. Stone, *Effective ingredients of successful psychotherapy.* New York: Brunner/Mazel, 1978. (a)

Liberman, B. L. The role of mastery in psychotherapy: Maintenance of improvement and prescriptive change. In J. D. Frank, R. Hoehn-Saric, S. D. Imber, B. L. Liberman, & A. R. Stone, *Effective ingredients of successful psychotherapy.* New York: Brunner/Mazel, 1978. (b)

Lieberman, M. A., Yalom, I. D., & Miles, M. B. *Encounter groups: First facts.* New York: Basic Books, 1973.

Malan, D. H. *Toward the validation of dynamic psychotherapy: A replication.* New York: Plenum, 1976.

Ollendick, T. H., & Murphy, M. J. Differential effectiveness of muscular and cognitive relaxation as a function of locus of control. *Journal of Behavioral Therapy and Experimental Psychiatry,* 1977, *8,* 223–228.

Posthuma, A. B., & Carr, J. E. Differentiation matching in psychotherapy. *Canadian Psychological Review,* 1975, *16,* 35–43.

Razin, A. A–B variable in psychotherapy: Still promising after 20 years? In A. S. Gurman & A. M. Razin (Eds.), *Therapists' handbook for effective psychotherapy.* New York: Pergamon Press, 1977.

Sloane, R. B., Staples, F. R., Cristol, A. H., Yorkston, N. J., & Whipple, K. *Psychotherapy versus behavior therapy.* Cambridge, Mass.: Harvard University Press, 1975.

Smith, M. L., & Glass, G. V. Meta-analysis of psychotherapy outcome studies. *American Psychologist,* 1977, *32,* 752–760.

Truax, C. B., & Carkhuff, R. R. *Toward effective counseling and psychotherapy: Training and practice.* Chicago: Aldine, 1967.

Voth, H. M., & Orth, V. H. *Psychotherapy and the role of the environment.* New York: Behavioral Publications, 1973.

Waskow, I. E., & Parloff, M. B. (Eds.). *Psychotherapy change measures* (DHEW Publication No. ADM 74-120). Washington, D.C.: U.S. Government Printing Office, 1975.

Whitehorn, J. C., & Betz, B. J. *Effective psychotherapy with the schizophrenic patient.* New York: Aronson, 1975.

Wilkins, W. Expectancy of therapeutic gain: An empirical and conceptual critique. *Journal of Consulting and Clinical Psychology,* 1973, *40,* 69–77.

CHAPTER XII

Social Psychopathology

Social psychopathology, a young study yet in its infancy, has been gaining attention among psychopathologists in recent years partly due to the strides made by the milieu psychotherapists, partly owing to advances achieved by social psychopathologists dealing with statistics on social class and mental illness, and partly attributable to other factors, including sociopsychological hypotheses or theories of schizophrenia and studies in sociopathy.

Some researchers regard the community or society as well as individuals as being mentally ill. Frank (1936) sees the society as the patient and claims a growing realization "that our culture is sick, mentally disordered and in need of treatment"; while Halliday (1945a, 1948) postulates mental disorder as an index of the psychological health of a community, attributing the rising incidence of psychosomatic illness to "a response to noxious psychological factors of environment" (1938, p. 13). Fromm, too, viewing psychopathology from a social orientation, seeks to establish a "sane society" in the form of his proposed humanistic communitarian socialism (1955). He explains the psychosis of totalitarian movements in terms of man's craving to escape from his earlier won freedom that failed to afford the autonomy to construct a "meaningful life based on reason and love" (1941). Supplanting the Freudian concept of libidinal development, Fromm prefers a development of the "evolution of character in interpersonal terms" (1947), one of "humanistic psychoanalysis," the fundamental premise being "that the basic passions of man are not rooted in his instinctive needs, but in the specific conditions of human existence, in the need to find a new relatedness to man and nature after having lost the primary relatedness of the pre-human stage" (1955, p. viii). Fromm underscores the danger of alienation owing to its dehumanizing effect (1965). He develops his thought further by showing that humans have the capacity to love (1956) as well as the capacity to destroy (1964), the former being a "syndrome of growth" or the love of life, independence, and conquest over narcissism, and the latter being a "syndrome of decay," or the love of death, malignant narcissism, and in-cestuous symbiosis (1973).

In his experimental research, Calhoun (1962) encountered what he termed *behavioral sink*, a social psychopathological phenomenon occurring among congested populations of his domesticated albino rats in which their normal social behavioral patterns were disrupted, with pansexuality, "pathological togetherness," and disorganization dominant.

Social Class and Psychopathology

Sociocultural factors in psychopathology received a potent impact with the publication of *Social Class and Mental Illness* by Hollingshead and Redlich (1958), a study revealing the commensurate relationship between the lower social class and a corresponding higher rate of psychosis among them. An inverse relationship was found to exist between neurotic and psychotic among the upper and lower classes, so that neurosis declined from the higher to the lower classes while psychosis increased. Their research concluded that mental illness is correlated to social class, that the social position and status of the mentally-ill patient affects his treatment for his disorder because the treatment varies according to his respective class status, that specific classes exhibit specific types of psychopathology, and that social reaction to the presence of mental illness differs according to each class. These conclusions of Hollingshead and Redlich were subsequently verified in cross-cultural studies undertaken in some European nations (Kohn, 1968) and in Lebanon (Katchadourian & Churchill, 1969).

In a study dealing with social class and alcoholism, Schmidt and his group (1968) found facts corroborating the Hollingshead and Redlich study. They concluded that "class differences make it more likely that mental illness will develop in lower class persons, that it will last longer, and that it will be less adequately treated. Furthermore, for those lower class patients who come to the treatment agency, mental illness is like only one of a number of disturbances" (1968, p. 9).

In another study of schizophrenics of lower socioeconomic status in Puerto Rico by Hollingshead and Rogler (1962), mental illness was for the families of the ill studied virtually a way of life or part of their lives, and "eighty-five per cent of the sick families report a mentally ill member in either the husbands' or wives' family of orientation, while only fifty-five per cent of the well families report a mentally ill member in either the parental or the sibling generation" (1962, p. 394).

Downward Drift Hypothesis

Are the poorer classes more susceptible to schizophrenia or do schizophrenics tend to drift to the lower classes? In other words, Is the ghetto a breeding ground for mental illness? This is a debate that psychologists are currently attempting to resolve. There are studies that have shown schizophrenics to be downwardly mobile socially and occupationally (Turner & Wagonfeld, 1967), but other studies contradict these findings (Dunham, 1965). One attempt to resolve the matter was by conducting studies involving parents of schizophrenics. If the parents were from a higher class, then schizophrenics must have drifted to a lower class. Turner and Wagonfeld (1967) found this to be the case, and therefore merely being reared in lower classes proved no risk to becoming schizophrenic. Hence, there is no concentrated schizophrenic gene pool among the lower classes.

According to the downward drift hypothesis, persons who are schizophrenic-prone (according to the diathesis-stress theory) tend, over a number of generations, to be downward mobile in society. Since they terminate in the lower class, it follows that a relative excess of schizophrenic genes should be prevalent among lower class individuals. The Copenhagen study (Wender et al, 1973) did not corroborate the downward drift hypothesis. Kohn (1968), however, stated that his studies show a definite relationship between mental illness and the larger cities; in smaller cities the relationship became less conspicuous.

Social Class and Post-Hospital Performance

Freeman and Simmons (1959, 1963), studying social class and posthospital levels of performance, found that a critical factor that affects the course of the patient's posthospital experience consists of the values of, the part played by, or the attitude of the family members regarding tolerance of deviant behavior. They claim their findings support their hypothesis of a direct relationship existing between the patient's posthospital performance levels and the social class status of his family. "Tolerance of deviance on the part of family members has been posited as a key factor in the prolonged community tenure of former patients who function at inadequate levels" (Simmons & Freeman, 1959, p. 233).

In a subsequent study, Freeman and Simmons (1961) found that on the whole recent innovations endorsed in hospital regime and release practices failed to be accompanied by appropriate programs effective in extending the therapeutic process (as a treatment base) to the community and family of the patient. They suspect the reason may be that community agencies, owing to their exhausted resources, do not encourage former psychotics' participation in these programs; or that the patients' low socioeconomic status is a deterrent from seeking professional help in their respective communities. It is possible that the rehospitalization rate is low among these former patients because of their lack of contact with professionals and their relative nonidentity in larger communities.

Socially Shared Psychopathology

In a study on the sharing of disordered functioning by psychotics who are close associates, Gruenberg (1957) concluded: (1) social groupings do occur among mentally ill persons; (2) people can be bound together in groups owing to disordered functioning; (3) unusual health, rather than mental disorder, may be implied by one's alienation from his close associates; (4) ideas, attitudes, feelings, activities, and defense mechanisms are shared rather than the diagnostic groupings common among psychiatrists; (5) shared disordered functioning is more common among women; (6) leaders tend to be more seriously disordered; and (7) group size varies from a couple to a nation; mutual contact is unnecessary when the group shares the same mass media of communication.

In examining shared neurosis in a cultural and familial context, Cleveland and Longaker (1957) found neurotic patterning to be partially "reaction to cultural process through which family members experience their basic introduction to culturally-defined paths of behavior" (1957, p. 194). The neurotic is seen as an exaggeration of disparagement, a common maladjustive mode of our culture. Through the socialization process, especially via the family, cultural value conflicts and ambiguities confront the individual early in life, setting a fertile field for neurotic growth.

Clausen (1957) traces shared mental illness of adolescents through common drug use, the practice of which enhances group cohesiveness, bolsters solidarity, possibly serving as a symbol of "consensual pattern," and thereby augmenting the individual's sense of group membership.

Sociocultural Criterion of Psychopathology

Concluding from an examination of rare, unclassifiable, collective, and exotic psychotic syndromes that occur only in specific cultures and among certain groups while being absent in other societies, Arieti and Meth (1959) believe there is strong evidence for sociocultural etiology of mental disorder.

Mead (1967) carries this mode of reasoning one step further, questioning whether psychotic syndromes are significant only in respect to cultural norms in vogue in a given society. She cites the case of a colleague, an anthropologist, who was about to be attacked by a native with a spear readied to strike. While the children climbed trees, and shouted: "Don't hurt him; he'll be all right tomorrow"; the man's sister was summoned to calm the person temporarily mad. Rather than the attacker's behavior being considered deviant, "the only unusual element in this situation was the anthropologist, who hadn't climbed a tree in time," comments Mead.

The underlying philosophical rationale of the therapeutic community of Jones (1962, 1966) is that a sick society made one of its members ill, and it requires a wholesome therapeutic society to restore him to mental health. Jackson and Weakland (1961) find the mentally ill patient as a victim of a smaller society, that of a sick family.

Laing (1965, 1967) also considers psychosis as socioculturally designated, for he cites certain persons as "radically unsound," dangerous to self and others, but who socially are not regarded as psychotic, insane, or as persons fit for committal to a "madhouse." He observes:

A man who prefers to be dead rather than Red is normal. A man who says he has lost his soul is mad. A man who says that men are machines may be a great scientist. A man who says he *is* a machine is "depersonalized" in psychiatric jargon. A man who says that Negroes are an inferior race may be widely respected. A man who says his whiteness is a form of cancer is certifiable.

A little girl of seventeen in a mental hospital told me she was terrified because the Atom Bomb was inside her. That is a delusion. The statesmen of the world who boast and threaten that they have Doomsday weapons are far more dangerous, and far more estranged from "reality" than many of the people on whom the label "psychotic" is affixed (1965, pp. 11-12).

The growing consensus of mental illness as social deviation is also shared by Szasz (1963) who tacitly endorses Lemert's (1951) position of mental illness as "sociopathic behavior." Primary and secondary forms of socially deviant behavior are distinguishable, the latter form being intolerable to society. Goffman (1961) notes that imprisonment and confinement to a mental institution are quite alike, accordingly mental hospitalization serves as a form of social control as if mental disorder is a form of crime rather than an illness. "Instead of recognizing the deviant as an individual different from those who judge him, but nevertheless worthy of their respect, he is first discredited as a self-responsible human being, and then subjected to humiliating punishment defined and disguised as treatment" (Szasz, 1963, p. 108).

Social learning theorists would also view maladaptive behavior in sociocultural terms. Bandura (1968b) repudiates psychodynamic formulations of mental disorder for an explanation of deviant behavior under the aegis of social learning principles.

Considering the arbitrary and relativistic nature of the social judgment and definition of deviance, the main value of the normal-abnormal dichotomy is in guiding the sociolegal actions of societal agents concerned with the maintenance of an efficiently functioning society. This dichotomy, however, has little theoretical significance since there is no evidence that the behaviors so dichotomized are either qualitatively different or under the control of fundamentally different variables (1968b, p. 335).

Phillips (1968) entertains the thought that in technologically backward societies it may be that what in our society would be designated psychosis is normal for them because their entire society is in a state of immaturity. Consequently, in the rural society of Brazil it is normal to talk to God. Owing to belief in magical devices and supernaturalism, a person with certain psychotic symptoms (for Western society) would not be deviant in unsophisticated cultures. With the more advanced societies, there is a higher level of sophistication of personality development. In the estimation of Maher, mental deficiency is a phenomenon reached by culturally derived criteria:

What constitutes mentally retarded behavior depends to a large extent upon the society which happens to be making the judgment. An individual who does not create a problem for others in his social environment and who manages to become self-supporting is usually not defined as mentally retarded no matter what his test IQ may be. Mental retardation is primarily a socially defined phenomenon, and it is in large part meaningless to speak of mental retardation without this criterion in mind (1963, p. 238).

Preventive Psychiatry

One of the newer topics on the horizon of psychopathology is the prevention of mental disorder. It is comparable to today's general medicine, where there is a continuing and growing interest in preventive medicine. Crisis medicine, waiting for a person to become ill before taking any measures, has dominated medical practice of the past, but in preventive medicine people are monitored by their physicians with a view to averting their developing diseases such as heart disorders, diabetes, and other illnesses before the ailment takes root or develops to an advanced degree. Preferably, action is taken to forestall or prevent illness from occurring at all.

In the field of psychopathology, there is a move afoot toward paralleling the efforts currently found in the general practice medicine. With a view toward realizing this end, Albee (1985) founded the Vermont Conference on the Primary Prevention of Pychopathology, an organization that has met annually since 1975. The group, at the conclusion of these conferences, published their deliberations.

Epidemiology of Psychopathology

Has mental disorder reached epidemic proportions? Currently, 15% of the American population is mentally ill, 12% of adolescents and children under 18 years of age require treatment, over 20% of executives use cocaine, and unnumbered multitudes imbibe alcohol heavily. Add to these, criminal behavior, other forms of drug abuse, juvenile delinquency, and psychosexual dysfunctions, then one virtually establishes a case for claiming epidemic proportions for psychopathology. Albee claims that "there are tens of millions of emotionally handicapped children and adults in our society who need help, aren't getting it and, as things stand, never will get it" (1985, p. 61). The problem is compounded by the plight of an insufficient number of psychotherapists available to handle the case load. In the United States alone, psychologists and psychiatrists number only 45,000, leaving but one out of five of the 43,000,000 adults seeking treatment to receive any, while another 35,000,000 are left to fend for themselves.

What is the answer? According to Albee, prevention is one viable alternative that can reduce the numbers of the vast hordes of people seeking psychological treatment. One recourse is to treat people early enough to reduce the time spent in therapy, and thereby deter their condition from deteriorating. Thwarting the development of mental disturbance by treating people early enough is termed *secondary prevention,* while *primary prevention* is forestalling the disorder from arising at all. Primary prevention is the eradicating of the causes of mental disorder or the ability to recognize them and to deal with them in such a way as not to be infected by them.

50.

GEORGE W. ALBEE

PREVENTIVE PSYCHIATRY

The Question: If More Than 40 Million of Us Need Help for Mental and Emotional Problems, What Can Be Done?

Last September the National Institute of Mental Health (NIMH) reported that 19 percent of American adults (43 million people) are mentally ill. NIMH projected this astounding figure on the basis of carefully designed interviews with thousands of adults in New Haven, Baltimore and St. Louis.

The results received wide coverage in the press for a few days and then sank without a trace. There was no public panic. There were no vows from Washington or elsewhere to mount an all-out assault on the problem. There was nothing approaching the intense reaction and efforts aroused by the threats of Legionnaires' disease, AIDS or genital herpes, conditions that together infect only a small fraction of the people affected by mental and emotional disorders.

Estimating how many Americans are or will be mentally ill is not a new game. During the 1950s and early 1960s, the National Mental Health Association, a citizens group, proclaimed that 1 American in 10 would become mentally ill at some time. During the 1970s, Gerald Klerman, director of the Alcohol, Drug Abuse and Mental Health Administration (ADAM-

HA), said that, at any given moment, about 15 percent of the population is mentally ill, not just would be at some time. The new NIMH report raises the ante again. Does this mean that more Americans are suffering mental breakdowns than ever before? Probably not. There are real problems of objectivity and definition in measuring mental illness. Consider these facts:

Few mental problems can be diagnosed with laboratory or other objective tests. We can tell with virtual certainty whether a person has a coronary occlusion or a strep throat, diabetes or spinal cord damage. But to say someone is depressed or schizophrenic is to pass judgment on a pattern of behavior or on reported subjective experience, a much more difficult matter. In court trails, for example, psychiatrists called by the defense and by the prosecution regularly disagree on the mental fitness of a defendant at the time of the crime.

Similar differences in diagnosis occur outside the designedly contentious arena of the courts. Show a video-tape of an interview with a "disturbed person" to therapists from different countries and cultures and you will receive different diagnoses. Even within our own society the diagnosis will vary depending on what the therapist is told about the subject's social class. The same people will be diagnosed differently if they are seen as poor than if they are believed to be affluent. Appendicitis, a brain tumor and chicken pox are the same everywhere, regardless of culture or class; mental conditions, it seems, are not.

Another problem has to do with what is defined as mental illnesses. The number of "official" illnesses has fluctuated many times during this century. Early classifiers limited their attention largely to organic conditions, such as general paresis (brain syphilis) and delirium tremens, and to functional conditions such as schizophrenia, paranoia and manic-depressive psychosis. Freud then revised diagnostic thinking dramatically by focusing attention on the milder but more widespread neuroses such as hysteria, hypochondriasis, neurasthenia and phobia. More recently, criminal behavior, juvenile delinquency, alcoholism and drug abuse have been added to the list of "official" mental illnesses.

Periodically, the American Psychiatric Association publishes a *Diagnostic and Statistical Manual of Mental Disorders* (DSM). DSM I, published in 1952, listed 60 types and subtypes of mental illness. Sixteen years latter, DSM II expanded the number to 145. The current guide, DSM III, has 230 separate conditions, including tobacco dependence, developmental disorders and sexual dysfunctions. Clearly the more human problems that we label mental illnesses, the more people that we can say suffer from them. And, a cynic might add, the more conditions therapists can treat and collect health-insurance payments for.

At the same time, other kinds of mental disorder have ceased to exist. Neurosis no longer exists as a disease; its numerous manifestations have been included in other classifications or dropped in DSM III. The decision by the American Psychiatric Association in 1973 to remove homosexuality from its list of mental disorders overnight lowered the total number of Americans considered mentally ill by many millions. The decision to make a 70 IQ rather than an 84 IQ the cutoff point for defining mental retardation reduced by millions the number of retarded Americans. Sometimes it seems as though we are measuring mental difficulties with rubber yardsticks in the hands of the visually handicapped.

The experts who designed the NIMH study worked hard to overcome these difficulties. They succeeded to some extent. The study is a major landmark in epidemiology. But many of the problems that face interviewers in trying to count past and present mental illnesses remain. For example: Interviewers were asked to judge illness on the basis of what people were willing to divulge about alcohol or drug use, fears and anxiety, depression and obsessions. Institutionalized people were not included in the report, nor were the homeless, many of whom suffer from mental disorders. Thirteen percent of the individuals originally selected to be interviewed refused, and people in another 5 to 10 percent of the households refused even to identify the person slated to be interviewed. Women were overrepresented in the sample, perhaps because they were more likely to be home when interviewers visited, and no children were included, a significant omission since other research has shown that about 12 percent of those younger than 18 are in need of treatment.

There were other difficulties. The memory of people for their past emotional problems is uncertain and unreliable. If someone couldn't complete an interview because of serious illness, the interviewer asked someone else about the person. Interviewers made no attempt to differentiate among various kinds of organic mental illnesses because no medical histories, physical exams or lab tests were available. The study planners expected that older people would report more mental problems, past and present, than younger people did, since they had lived through the high-risk age periods for most conditions and into high-risk old age. But this didn't happen, for reasons that are not clear.

Beyond this, the study didn't report on many mental conditions listed in DSM III. For example, psychosexual dysfunctions that affect nearly a quarter of the adult population were not reported, probably because people are reluctant to discuss their sex lives with strangers. Tobacco use disorder, another condition that affects more than one adult in three, was not tallied. To push this numbers game to its ultimate absurdity, we could add the well-established statistic that, on the average, three other people are affected strongly by each person with a mental illness. Pull all these numbers together and we could end up with more mental disorders, serious and otherwise, than there are people in the United States.

This numerical absurdity helps make a point. While exactly how many people have mental or emotional problems is uncertain, the NIMH survey demonstrated that widespread, genuine distress does exist. Thomas Szasz, the great deflator of psychiatric pretensions, makes one critical error. When he calls mental illness a myth, he overlooks the fact that there are many seriously damaged people who, as children, were crippled by sexual exploitation, physical abuse, neglect, hostility and rejection. They have often grown up to be seriously damaged parents, incapable of managing their emotions or their lives. Many pass along emotional problems to their children, not genetically but behaviorally. Whether the NIMH figure of 19 percent is high or low, there are tens of millions of emotionally handicapped adults and children in our society who need help, aren't getting it and, as things stand, never will get it.

Fewer than one in five of the 43 million disturbed adult Americans projected by the NIMH study had received any treatment for six months prior to their interview. On an ABC News *Nightline* last fall that discussed the NIMH report, Fred Good-

win, director of intramural research at NIMH, told Ted Koppel that genetic factors and disturbed brain chemistry are largely responsible for mental illness, and that this knowledge would be a great relief to parents and others who have up until now been blamed for causing problems through faulty child-rearing.

When Koppel asked Timothy Johnson, ABC News medical editor, where individuals or families could turn for help with depression or other serious emotional problems, Johnson suggested finding a psychiatrist through a call to the family doctor or cleric for referral, or to the department of psychiatry at the nearest medical school. Someone should tell Johnson that there aren't that many family doctors, particularly for the poor, in the United States, and that the number of psychiatrists is shrinking. In 1959, when I did a national survey to determine the number of people entering the mental-health professions, nearly 10 percent of medical school graduates were going into the field of psychiatry. Today this figure is less than 5 percent. Psychologist Charles Kiesler estimated in the December 1980 issue of *American Psychologist* that there were only 45,000 psychiatrists, clinical psychologists and counseling psychologists delivering mental-health services in the United States at any one time.

Just for fun I did a little arithmetic. If fewer than one in five of America's 43 million disturbed adults has received treatment recently, 35 million have not. If only half of these were to try to see a professional for just five hour-long visits (an unrealistically small number for a serious emotional problem), the demand would occupy all the time of about 60,000 professionals for a year. This is more than twice the number of psychiatrists alone, and more than all the qualified therapists now available in this country. And, in fact, the demand is really much larger than these estimates suggest. The NIMH study did not count the many children who need help, nor have we allowed for the well-established fact that most psychiatrists and other therapists don't like to treat alcoholics, the poor, the aged and the psychotic. Finally, we need to remember that some common mental disorders (such as sexual problems) were not covered in the NIMH report.

This lack of people qualified to help is made worse by basic disagreement on what is most important in understanding and preventing mental disorders. On one side are professionals who favor a genetic-biochemical explanation that each mental disease has a separate physical cause; on the other are those who back a social-learning model—mental disorders result from faulty early learning of social coping skills, from low levels of competence, from low self-esteem and from poor support systems interacting with high levels of stress. The arguments used in the debate clearly are related to the political ideology of the proponents. Conservatives strongly favor a constitutional-organic disease explanation, largely because no major social change is called for if the problems are all inside the skin. The prevention model that they favor focuses narrowly on genetic counseling and on biochemical and brain research to discover the specific separate causes of each mental illness. They argue that there is no real proof that social stresses cause mental illnesses, and that the high rate of emotional disturbance among the very poor does not prove that poverty causes mental illness. Rather it may well be, they argue, that disturbed people "drift downward" from the middle and upper classes into poverty.

Psychiatrists H. Richard Lamb and Jack Zusman, writing in the January 1979 issue of *American Journal of Psychiatry,* state this view boldly: "The cause and effect relationship between social conditions and mental illness is extremely questionable," and "Major mental illness is probably in large part genetically determined and is probably therefore not preventable."

Those on the other side of the issue see the causes and prevention of mental illness much differently. Liberals, radicals and social environmentalists favor a prevention model that requires better parenting and social change to restore or increase social justice, to reduce powerlessness and to lessen the stresses of the competitive industrial society.

This viewpoint was expressed clearly by a leader in public-health research, the late John Cassel, a South African physician who taught at the University of North Carolina. In an article in the August 1976 issue of *American Journal of Epidemiology,* he wrote:

"A remarkably similar set of social circumstances characterizes people who develop tuberculosis and schizophrenia, become alcoholic, are victims of multiple accidents, or commit suicide. Common to all of these people is a marginal status in society. They are individuals who for a variety of reasons (e.g., ethnic minorities rejected by the dominant majority in their neighborhood; high sustained rates of residential and occupational mobility; broken homes or isolated living circumstances) have been deprived of meaningful social contact."

Historically, we have tried to help emotionally disturbed people live with their handicap and adjust as well as possible (rehabilitation or tertiary prevention); more recently we have tried to treat people early, with psychotherapy or drugs, to keep their problems from getting worse or perhaps to restore them to more normal functioning (secondary prevention); rarely have we tried to prevent problems from appearing in the first place (primary prevention).

Yet it seems to me that this strategy is

the most logical approach in trying to reduce the vast number of people who need help with mental or emotional problems. Instead of spending most of our time, money and energy on one-to-one treatment, we should develop large-scale preventive efforts along the lines developed by public-health pioneers in dealing with organic diseases such as polio, smallpox and measles. It is accepted public-health wisdom that widespread pathological conditions affecting millions can't be brought under control or eliminated by treating affected individuals. No number of heart transplants will reduce the incidence of heart disease. Most of the great plagues that have afflicted humankind through the centuries had been eliminated by effective primary prevention—working with large groups of people not yet affected by a disease to eliminate sources of infection or contagion and to build up their resistance to the disease. Once this fact is clearly understood, the logical necessity of prevention becomes clear.

In the case of mental disorders, the key elements are not bacteria, viruses or other noxious organic agents but a high level of current or past stress that may be engendered by many things, including serious marital problems; involuntary unemployment; sexual confusion and guilt; or a childhood history of serious neglect, physical abuse, sexual exploitation and lack of affection.

To lessen the incidence of mental disorders through prevention, we must reduce problems in three areas—organic factors, stress and exploitation of various kinds—and increase resources in three others—coping skills, self-esteem and support groups. To give just a few of many possible examples in each area, we can: reduce organic problems by improving nutrition during pregnancy and by reducing lead in the environment; reduce stress through

guaranteed employment and better care and housing for the elderly; lessen the abuse of children and exploitation of women and minorities of all kinds; improve competence through assertiveness training and courses on preparation for marriage; increase self-esteem through fairer press portrayals of the aged, the handicapped, women and minorities; and finally, and perhaps most important, encourage the further development of self-help movements and support groups such as home health-care programs, Meals on Wheels, daycare centers and Big Brother/Big Sister programs.

The rapid growth of support groups like these, made up of people whose experiences make them high-risk candidates for emotional and physical problems, is one of the most encouraging developments of recent years in the mental-health field. But we need more and larger self-help organizations. Research has made it very clear that individuals who have the support of such organizations are much better off emotionally than those who face their problems alone.

These groups and others—for people experiencing marital problems, for children of divorced, alcoholic or psychotic parents, for parents of handicapped children, for unmarried pregnant teenagers, for school dropouts—help both people who are already disturbed (secondary prevention) and those who are at risk but not yet affected (primary prevention). The talents and knowledge of mental-health professionals can best be used in encouraging such groups, monitoring their progress and providing expert consultation when it is requested.

For those of us who believe in this prevention approach to mental and emotional problems, there have been a few encouraging developments. Three new prevention-oriented journals have appeared recently, a dozen books reporting prevention research have been published and several new textbooks (solid evidence of professional interest) have appeared. The President's Commission on Mental Health, appointed by Jimmy Carter, responded to the report of its Task Panel on Prevention by recommending the establishment of a Center for Prevention at NIMH. A Division of Prevention and Special Mental Programs has been established, but with a meager budget and located in a setting largely unsympathetic to its mission.

Changing any social institution is exceedingly difficult, especially when strong economic interests benefit from the status quo. In spite of 25 years of strong efforts devoted to finding alternativs to the institutionalization of the mentally ill poor, our society still spends 70 percent of its mental-health dollars for the hospitalization and nursing-home care of a comparatively small number of seriously disturbed adults and confused elderly. Nearly all the other money spent on psychotherapy is paid by insurance companies to professionals in private practice. Community mental-health centers, once hailed as providing a door through which anyone might enter and find help, have never been adequately funded and now receive only 4 percent of the national mental-health dollar, almost none of it for efforts at prevention. The money spent by state agencies on primary prevention is even less. In the long run, however, prevention through social change that gives people more security and more power over their lives is our best hope—a faint but persistent hope.

51.

Paul H. Wender, David Rosenthal, Seymour S. Kety, Fini Schulsinger, and Joseph Welner

DOWNWARD DRIFT HYPOTHESIS OF SCHIZOPHRENIA

Previous epidemiological studies have generally shown an increased prevalence of schizophrenic disorders among lower socioeconomic status (SES) individuals, but the mechanism mediating this relationship has been unclear. Hypotheses that have been proposed include: a tendency for schizophrenics to move downward in the social hierarchy, the "downward drift hypothesis"; an increased schizophrenic gene pool in lower SES strata; and a provocative or inductive effect on psychopathology produced by factors associated with lower SES membership.

Naturalistic studies do not allow a separation of possible genetic and environmental indicators. To circumvent this problem, we studied these relationships in adopted populations. The findings of this study support only the downward drift hypothesis. The special attributes of this study population and the possible biases it may have introduced are discussed.

The hypothesis that there is a relationship between socioeconomic status (SES) and psychopathology, particularly schizophrenia, is widely held and reasonably well documented. Beginning with the finding of Faris and Dunham[1] that the highest rates of first admission for schizophrenia were found in areas of the city with the lowest SES and that these rates become

From *Archives of General Psychiatry*, 1973, vol. 28, pp. 318–325. Copyright 1973 by the American Medical Association.

progressively lower in higher SES groups, many studies have found the highest rates of mental illness among individuals with the lowest SES.

The relationship between social class and mental disorder is not clear-cut in all instances. In a careful review of the subject, Kohn[2] notes some findings that are possible exceptions to the hypothesis. The linear relationship between SES and schizophrenia breaks down in cities of medium size (population 100,000 to 500,000): in these cities the relationship between SES and mental illness is almost entirely accounted for by a concentration of cases in the very lowest SES (i.e., among the higher classes there is no correlation between SES and schizophrenia). In still smaller cities and rural populations the relationship between SES and mental disorder is absent.

A close inspection of the studies reveals a variety of methodological variations which might confuse the findings. These include the techniques of case ascertainment (hospital admission vs population survey), the methods of rate determination (prevalence vs incidence), and the diagnostic criteria employed. These methodological difficulties lead Kohn to conclude that despite the fact that

... the results of the studies of class and schizophrenia are hardly definitive ... [and may constitute] ... one more example of inadequate methods leading to premature false conclusions ... [that taken together]. ... A large number of studies point to the same conclusion: that rates of mental disorder, particularly of schizophrenia are highest at the lowest socioeconomic levels, at least in moderately large cities. ... .[2] (p. 162)

If there is a relationship between social class and psychopathology, how may it be interpreted? Three major explanatory hypotheses have been advanced. The first, the "sociogenic hypothesis," asserts that there are intrapersonal, familial, and extrafamilial concomitants of lowerclass status which favor, or at least fail to inhibit, the development of psychopathology. Among these factors would be included (and this list is not meant to be complete) such features as continuing economic difficulty, familial disorganization, inadequate education, maladaptive or inflexible attitudes and values, low self-esteem, and the feeling of inability to control or direct one's own life. Such factors might either lower the threshold to stress or be directly pathogenic themselves.

The second major hypothesis, the "downward drift hypothesis," can be divided into two related hypotheses. The first, which we shall designate the "narrow downward drift hypothesis," asserts that the higher rate of low SES among the disturbed population is a *consequence* of these individuals' psychopathology: sick people tend to become increasingly ineffectual socially and occupationally, and sink lower and lower in the social hierarchy.

A second variant of the downward drift hypothesis, which we designate as the "broad or intergenerational downward drift hypothesis," is not formally recognized. This hypothesis asserts that there is a genetic diathesis to mental illness and that the diathesis tends to produce a relative degree of social incompetence. As a result of this genetic diathesis acting over several generations, a form of evolutionary selection occurs, with this subpopulation sinking lower and lower in the social hierarchy until it eventually reaches its low and stable ecological niche.

What evidence can test these hypotheses? Only the narrow downward drift hypothesis can be subjected to unequivocal tests. One can follow the career of psychiatrically disturbed individuals and see if they tend to move downward. Such studies have been performed and their results are equivocal.

Tests of the broad downward drift and sociogenic hypotheses are likely to involve confounded variables: it has been demonstrated that there is a genetic diathesis for serious mental disorder (Heston,[3] Kety et al.[4] and Rosenthal et al.[5]). However, an individual with lower-class status may not only be subject to the stresses of such a status but may well be carrying a genetic diathesis for psychiatric disorder as well.

If we are to test the relative effects of class position and the effects of genetic diathesis, we must separate these two variables and this may be best done by studying adopted persons. One can determine the psychiatric status of adoptees born of low SES parents (and thus, according to one viewpoint, at greater risk for genetically determined disability) and compare them with adoptees born of higher SES parents who would presumably have lesser genetic risk. Similarly, one can control for the confounded biological factors by holding SES of birth constant and then testing the effects of differing SES among the adopting (i.e., rearing) parents.

We wish to emphasize that evaluations of the above hypotheses receive their most stringent tests only under certain conditions, and that *these conditions are not completely fulfilled in our experiments.* The "perfect" experiment utilizing adoption to separate "nature" and "nurture" effects would be one in which an unselected series of children were separated at birth from their biological parents and randomly assigned to a group of adopting parents. Obviously, we could not do this.

The population of parents whose offspring are placed for adoption do *not* comprise a random sample of the population that produces children; the population is very probably skewed, perhaps towards parents who may be more impulsive, inadequate, or less responsible than other parents. Similarly, the population of adopting parents is not a representative sample of parents rearing children. When the population of biological and adopting par-

ents in study 2 is compared with the social-class distribution of Copenhagen for the same time period, we find that the sample of biological parents is representative while the sample of adopting parents is of higher social class.

Moreover, it is likely that the lower-class parents who do adopt children are nonrepresentative in that in many instances (about one half) they have been prescreened. Such screened and "passed" lower-class parents would be expected to be better organized, economically more stable, and, perhaps, less psychologically disturbed than the average lower-class population of parents. Accordingly, the sociogenic hypotheses will receive only a weak test. If our findings indicate that lower SES rearing parents *do* produce more disturbed offspring, that hypothesis will have received support, but if they *do not,* we will not be able to say that the hypothesis is disproved since the adopted offspring may not have been subjected to *typical* lower SES rearing conditions.

The experiments about to be described should be read and interpreted with the above cautionary statements in mind. Additional comments on the possible effects of sampling biases will be found in the comment section.

METHODS AND PROCEDURES

The subjects employed in this analysis were adopted and nonadopted adults residing in Copenhagen. This group of individuals has been studied by us in several ongoing investigations assessing the roles of genetic and environmental factors in the cause of the schizophrenias. All of these studies use the strategy of studying adopted persons and their relatives as a method of separating genetic and experiential factors. Since the parents who transmit genetic factors and the parents who provide rearing experience are different, one can then independently assess the relationship between pathology in the offspring and pathology in each of these two sets of parents.

The two principal studies provide two methods of evaluating the relationship between social class and mental illness.

STUDY 1

In the first study, the "Extended Family Study," we studied the adopted and biological relatives of a group of adopted schizophrenic children and a group of matched nonschizophrenic adopted controls. The sample was collected as follows (for a more detailed discussion of the methodology, the reader should consult Kety et al.[4] and Rosenthal et al.[5]).

We began by obtaining a list of all persons in Copenhagen who had been adopted in the years 1924 through 1947. At the time the studies began (1964), these individuals ranged in age from 17 to more than 40 years. From this group we excluded all those who were adopted by biologically related persons. This left 5,483 adoptees from whom the following information was obtained: name, sex, and birthdate of the adoptee; age at time of first transfer to and formal adoption by the adopting parent; name and age of the biological and adopting mother; name, age, occupation, income and capital assets of the putative biological father and the adopting father.

The names of the adoptees were next compared with the files of the central psychiatric register in the Institute of Human Genetics, Copenhagen. This organization obtains the names and diagnoses of all patients psychiatrically diagnosed at inpatient and outpatient mental health facilities. The names were also checked with the approximately 10% of Danish facilities which do not report to the Institute. For all individuals with psychiatric diagnoses we obtained the clinical records and had them abstracted. Four psychiatrists then assessed these records and made independent diagnostic judgments.

The 33 adoptees independently diagnosed as schizophrenic constituted the "Index Group." From the sample of adoptees without documented histories of mental illness, we selected two groups of controls. The first group, 33 in number, were matched with the index cases pairwise on the following variables: sex, age, age at time of transfer to the adopting parents, and SES of the subject's adopting family. The SES was based on the occupation of the adoptive father, using criteria previously employed

in Denmark. This scale was first employed by Mednick and Schulsinger (unpublished manuscript) who adapted it from Svalastoga's study[6] of Danish social class.

SES RATING

0 *Unskilled worker:* e.g., agricultural laborer, unskilled factory worker

1 *Group leader,* but unskilled worker: supervisor of small group of employees or semiskilled worker, e.g., small shopkeeper, fisherman with small boat

2 *Skilled worker,* without own business: e.g., carpenter

3 *Subordinate clerk:* lowest level of white collar worker, e.g., salesman, proofreader.

4 *Skilled handworker with own business:* skilled handworker with one to three employees, semiskilled worker with more than 15 employees (e.g., factory foreman) or skilled non-academic personnel, e.g., kindergarten teacher, locomotive engineer

5 *Leaders or owners of small industries and "half-academic" occupations:* e.g., accountant, master printer (print shop owner), elementary school teacher

6 *Academic occupations:* people with 15 or more years of education after the Danish "students' examination," e.g., editor, minister, graduate engineer, architect, captain in army

7 *Advanced positions in business, professions, government:* e.g., chief of police, colonel in army, professor, physician in charge of a hospital

The second control group was selected by randomly choosing from the adoptee pool two subjects (with no known psychiatric diagnosis) for each index case, matching only for sex and date of adoption. This second group consisted of 66 individuals whose average age approximated that of the adoptees but whose adoptive families' SES were *not* matched with those of the index group. Finally, from the information available, we tabulated the SES of the adoptive and biological fathers of both groups. The distribution of SES for the biological fathers, the adoptive fathers, and the adoptees was compared with the year by year distribution of wage earners in Copenhagen. The results are shown in Table 51-1 and Figure 51-1. For purposes of analysis the SES ratings were collapsed into three categories: low, 0 to 2; middle, 3 to 5; high, 6 and 7. Since some of the eight occupational ratings fluctuated widely from year to year, failure to combine them would have gen-

TABLE 51-1
Study 1: Frequency Distribution of SES in the General Population, the Biological and
Adoptive Fathers, and the Adoptee*

Social Class	Sample and Frequency, %			
	General Population	Biological Fathers	Adoptive Fathers	Adoptees
Low	58	64	55	40
Middle	35	32	39	52
High	7	5	6	8

* x^2 (df = 2): General population vs. adoptees = 148, $P < .005$, general population vs. biological fathers = 1.86, NS; general population vs. adoptive fathers = .75, NS; adoptees vs. biological fathers = 23.3, $P < .005$; adoptees vs. adoptive fathers = 11.4, $P < .005$: biological fathers vs. adoptive fathers = 1.69, NS.

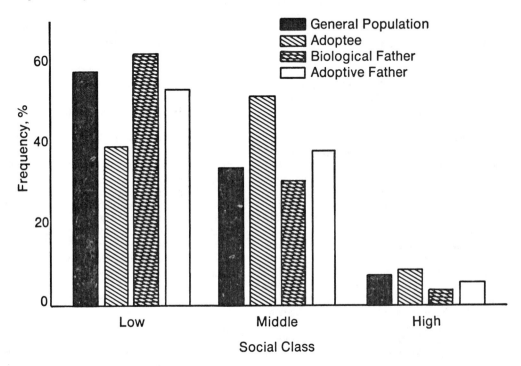

FIGURE 51-1. —Frequency Distribution of the Study Sample in Study 1 and the General Population.

erated irregular frequency plots and spuriously significant x^2. The SES distributions of the samples of biological fathers and adoptive fathers are representative of the general population, while those of the adoptees themselves are significantly higher.

The means and standard deviation of the three groups are shown in Table 51-2. There is no significant difference between the mean SES of the biological fathers of the index group and the biological fathers of the two control groups, nor between SES of the adoptive fathers of the index group and the second control group.

In the first control group, the SES of the

adoptive parents was expected to be the same as that of the index cases, since, as mentioned, the index and control groups were matched on this variable.

Comment. What is the relevance of these findings for the two major theories that attempt to explain the observed relationship between SES and schizophrenia? The first theory, the broad or intergenerational "downward drift" hypothesis, asserts that persons with the schizophrenia diathesis tend to have migrated downward over

TABLE 51-2
Study 1: Population and SES Characteristics of the Sample

Group	No.*	Men: Women	Age	SES of Father Biological†	Adoptive†
Index	33 (24)	18:15	36.1	2.1 ± 1.8	2.9 ± 1.8
Controls 1	33 (19)	18:15	35.9	2.3 ± 1.8	2.6 ± 1.7
Controls 2	66 (48)	36:30	35.3	2.2 ± 1.9	2.7 ± 1.7

* The numbers in parentheses represent the number of subjects for whom the SES of the biological father could be ascertained.

† Two-tailed *t*-tests: (1) any group of biological fathers vs. any other and any group of adoptive fathers vs. any other, NS; (2) any group of biological fathers vs. any group of adoptive fathers, NS; (3) total adoptive fathers vs. total biological fathers, $P < .05$.

several generations so that the lowest SES segment of the population should have a relative excess of "schizophrenia genes."

If schizophrenia is partially genetic in cause, the parents of schizophrenics, some of whom would have the diathesis for schizophrenia themselves, should in general have a SES lower than that of the general population, particularly the population of nonschizophrenics. In this sample the SES of the biological fathers of the schizophrenics was *not* lower than the SES of the fathers of the nonschizophrenics. Thus, this study does not provide corroborative evidence for the "broad downward drift" hypothesis. An alternative interpretation is, of course, that a genetic diathesis does not exist.

In order to test the "narrow downward hypothesis," we must examine the social class of the male index cases and controls. The reason for confining the analysis to men is that for our purposes social class, measured by occupational success, constitutes some measure of psychosocial adaptation. For women it is less adequate in this respect, since social class is either based on the single woman's occupation (in a society which did not encourage women to fulfill their greatest potential) or the married woman's husband's class. (One might reason that successful marriage is a measure of female social competence, but the measures are not directly comparable.)

For purposes of this analysis we may

compare the male index cases with either the matched controls from group 1 or with all the male controls (since the SES of the adoptive fathers in the two groups does not differ). We may compare either the average change in the subjects' SES (i.e., subject's SES minus adoptive father's SES) in the two groups, or we may compare the absolute level of SES in the index cases and control groups (Table 51-3). The index subjects' SES declines from that of the adoptive fathers, while that of the controls increases; the difference is significant ($P<.05$). Similarly, the mean SES of the index group is lower; this difference approaches significance ($P<.1$). Accordingly, these findings support the downward drift hypothesis.

The second theory, the "sociogenic" hypothesis, asserts that factors associated with low SES are pathogenic and favor the development of schizophrenia. This theory predicts a relationship between the SES of the adoptive families and the rate of schizophrenia in the adoptees: individuals developing schizophrenia would tend to come from rearing families of lower SES. Since control group 1 was matched with the index cases for SES of the adoptive family, we must compare the index group with the randomly selected controls in control group 2. The sociogenic hypothesis predicts that the SES of the adoptive fathers would be lower for the index group than for control group 2. Inspection of the findings in

TABLE 51-3
Male Index and Control Cases

Social Class	
Group	SES
Index (No. = 17)[1]	2.35 ± 1.54[3]
Total male controls (No. = 52)[2]	3.06 ± 1.61[3]

[1] One subject who was never employed and who was hospitalized from childhood was not included.
[2] Only subjects for whom SES data available for both subject and adoptive father.
[3] One-tailed *t*-test, index vs. total controls, $P < .1$.

Change of Social Class			
Group	SES Adoptive Father[1]	Subject	Change (Subject SES— Adoptive Father SES)
Index (No. = 17)	3.24 ± 1.89	2.35 ± 1.54	− .89 ± 2.50[2]
Control (No. = 52)	2.60 ± 1.61	3.06 ± 1.61	+ .46 ± 1.70

[1] The SES of the two groups of adoptive fathers does not differ significantly and so the change scores may be employed.
[2] One-tailed *t*-test, change in index vs. change in controls' SES, $P < .05$.

Table 51-2 reveals no such differences; these data do not substantiate the sociogenic hypothesis.

STUDY 2

In the second study we evaluated the consequences of schizophrenia in the biological parent with respect to psychopathology in the offspring, when the offspring had been separated from their biological parents in infancy.

Beginning with the list of 5,483 adoptees, we obtained the names and identifying data of their biological mothers and their putative biological fathers (of the latter, only 75% could be identified). The list of these biological parents was then cross-indexed with the central records of the Institute of Human Genetics. For those parents who had received psychiatric diag-

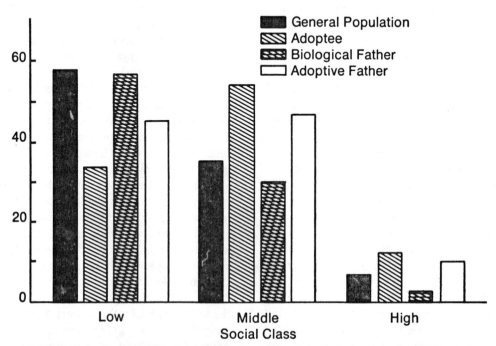

FIGURE 51-2 —Frequency Distribution of the Study Sample in Study 2 and the General Population.

TABLE 51-4
Study 2: Population and SES Characteristics of the Sample

Group	No.[1]	Biological	Adoptive	SES of Adoptee
Male index	35 (26)	2.1 ± 1.8	2.3 ± 2.0	3.1 ± 1.6
Female index	44 (36)	2.6 ± 1.8	3.6 ± 1.7	3.4 ± 1.5
Total	79 (62)	2.4 ± 1.8	3.0 ± 1.9	3.3 ± 1.5
Male controls	35 (25)	2.4 ± 1.6	2.7 ± 2.1	3.5 ± 1.7
Female controls	44 (35)	1.8 ± 1.3	3.3 ± 1.5[2]	3.7 ± 1.6
Total controls	79 (66)	2.1 ± 1.5	3.0 ± 1.8[3]	3.6 ± 1.7

[1] The numbers in parentheses represent the number of subjects for whom the SES of the biological father could be ascertained.
[2] Two-tailed *t*-test, $P < .01$.
[3] Two-tailed *t*-test, $P < .05$.

noses, we obtained and abstracted the clinical records. These records were independently rated by two raters and all cases diagnosed as schizophrenic, manic depressive, or probably schizophrenic were selected.

The offspring of these parents constituted the index group. For each index case we selected a control who did not have a parent with a file in the psychiatric register and who was matched (as closely as possible) for the following variables: sex, age, age of transfer to his adopting parents, and SES of his adoptive home. The distributions, means, and standard deviations for the SES of the respective groups are shown in Fig. 51-2 and Table 51.4.

As may be seen by comparing Table 51-4 with Table 51-1, there are no significant differences between the SES of the biological and adoptive fathers in studies 1 and 2 (Index cases, biological fathers: 2.3 in study 1 and 2.4 in study 2; control cases, biological fathers: 2.4 in study 1 and 2.1 in study 2; index cases, adoptive fathers: 3.1 in study 1 and 3.3 in study 2; control cases, adoptive fathers: 3.2 in study 1 [nonmatched controls] and 3.6 in study 2).

The index and control groups were then contacted and invited to receive a two-day psychiatric and psychological evaluation. In each group, 80% agreed. An experimental feature of considerable importance in eliminating the risk of assessment bias was the fact that the examining psychiatrist and psychologist were blind concerning the status of the biological parents of the subjects they saw: they did not know if the subject was a member of the index or control group. Following his interview with the subject, the psychiatrist prepared a lengthy summary which included the subject's personal history, history of psychopathology, and current level of psychological functioning. From the summaries of the 158 subjects examined (79 index cases and 79 controls) and 100 additional subjects, cards were prepared which summarized the subject's psychiatric diagnosis and current level of functioning.

The summary diagnoses, which did not indicate whether the cases were members of the index, control, or other groups, were then Q-sorted with a forced quasinormal distribution into 20 categories ranging from least to greatest psychiatric pathology. Five raters sorted the cards independently; the ten interrater correlations (product-moment) varied from 0.85 to 0.95, with a median of 0.91. Since raters agreed so well, we were able to determine a reliable psychopathology score for each subject. This score was his average placement in the Q-distribution by all five judges.

Comment. The psychopathology ratings, together with the available SES data, permitted investigation of the following questions:

1. What is the relationship between the SES of the biological parents and the degree of psychopathology in the offspring (for both the index and control groups)?

2. What is the relationship between the SES of the adoptive parents and the degree of psychopathology in the offspring (again, for both index and control groups)?

3. What is the relationship between the SES of the adoptee himself and his degree of psychopathology?

The questions again relate to the principal hypotheses accounting for the relationship between SES and psychopathology. An intergenerational downward drift hypothesis would assert that a low SES of the biological parents could be the consequence or a manifestation of a psychiatric disorder in them. Hence, lower SES in the biological parents would be expected to be correlated with higher psychopathology among their adopted-away offspring. Obviously, this relationship would have to be examined in the control rather than the index adoptees because in the latter group, both high and low SES parents were already psychotic since this was a condition for their selection.

The second question relates to the sociogenic hypothesis. If low SES is a provocative or causative factor of schizophrenia, lower SES in the adoptive parents should be associated with greater psychopathology in the subjects. This relationship can be examined in both the index and control groups. In the former, one can examine the effects (provocative) of low SES on individuals with a genetic predisposition to the disorder. In the latter group one can examine the effects of low SES as a causative factor in individuals without known genetic predisposition.

The third question relates to a narrow downward drift hypothesis which asserts that the relationship between low SES and mental illness is explained by the tendency of people with such illness to undergo downward social migration.

The correlation coefficients for the relationship between biological father's SES, adoptive father's SES, subject's SES, and the subject's psychopathology are shown for the index cases in Table 51-5 and for the control cases in Table 51-6. The combined population (i.e., of control and index cases taken together) is shown in Table 51-7.

Inspecting these data, it is seen that for both the index and control subject there is a significant positive correlation between the adoptive father's SES and the adoptee's SES: this is an expected finding. The SES of the offspring is correlated with the

TABLE 51-5

Study 2: Correlation Matrix of SES and Psychopathology of the Index Subjects

	Men (No. = 35)						Women (No. = 44)						Men and Women (No. = 79)					
	AF[1]	SES	BF[2]	SES	Adoptee SES[4]		AF[1]	SES	BF[2]	SES	Adoptee SES[4]		AF[1]	SES	BF[2]	SES	Adoptee SES[4]	
	N[3]	r[5]	N	r	N	r	N	r	N	r	N	r	N	r	N	r	N	r
Pathology score	35	-.01	26	-.05	30	-.02	44	-.21	36	.13	39	.01	79	-.07	62	.05	69	.02
Adoptive father's SES			26	.54[7]	30	.44[6]			36	.29	39	.32[6]			62	.42[7]	69	.40[7]
Biological father's SES					22	.04					32	.49[7]					54	.31[6]

[1] AF = adoptive father.
[2] BF = biological father.
[3] N = number of subjects; N is less than that of the total sample for BF SES because data were not available for all BFs.
[4] All subjects who were students (10) were excluded from adoptee SES correlations.
[5] Pearson product-moment correlation coefficients.
[6] Two-tailed t-test, $P < .05$.
[7] Two-tailed t-test, $P < .01$.

TABLE 51-6
Study 2: Correlation Matrix of SES and Psychopathology for the Control Subjects

	Men (No. = 35)						Women (No. = 44)						Men and Women (No. = 79)					
	AF[1] SES		BF[2] SES		Adoptee SES[4]		AF[1] SES		BF[2] SES		Adoptee SES[4]		AF[1] SES		BF[2] SES		Adoptee SES[4]	
	N[3]	r[5]	N	r	N	r	N	r	N	r	N	r	N	r	N	r	N	r
Pathology score	35	.40[6]	25	-.09	30	.10	44	.21	35	-.01	43	.17	79	.30[7]	60	-.06	73	.15
Adoptive father's SES			25	.36	30	.33			35	-.09	43	.44[7]			60	.10	73	.39[7]
Biological father's SES					22	.44[6]					34	.06					56	.16

[1] AF = adoptive father.
[2] BF = biological father.
[3] N = number of subjects; N is less than that of the total sample for BF SES because data were not available for all BFs.
[4] All subjects who were students (10) were excluded from adoptee SES correlations.
[5] Pearson product-moment correlation coefficients.
[6] Two-tailed t-test, $P < .05$.
[7] Two-tailed t-test, $P < .01$.

TABLE 51-7
Study 2: Correlation Matrix of SES and Psychopathology for the Total Sample. Combined Index and Control Cases.

	Men (No. = 50)						Women (No. = 55)						Men and Women (No. = 105)					
	AF[1] SES		BF[2] SES		Adoptee SES[4]		AF[1] SES		BF[2] SES		Adoptee SES[4]		AF[1] SES		BF[2] SES		Adoptee SES[4]	
	N[3]	r[5]	N	r	N	r	N	r	N	r	N	r	N	r	N	r	N	r
Pathology score	70	.15	51	-.09	60	.03	88	.02	71	.11	82	.08	158	.10	122	.02	142	.07
Adoptive father's SES			51	.45[6]	60	.39[6]			71	.16	82	.36[6]			122	.29[6]	142	.39[6]
Biological father's SES					44	.23					68	.19					112	.20

[1] AF = adoptive father.
[2] BF = biological father.
[3] N = number of subjects; N is less than that of the total sample for BF SES because data were not available for all BFs.
[4] All subjects who were students (10) were excluded.
[5] Pearson product-moment correlation coefficients.
[6] Two-tailed t-test, $P < .01$.
[7] Two-tailed t-test, $P < .01$.

SES of the rearing family. A second finding is that for the index cases there is a positive correlation between the biological father's SES and the adoptive father's SES; the correlation approaches significance for the female controls. This finding suggests that "selective placement" occurred. Children were probably not given to adoptive families at random, but an effort was made by those giving up the children to find adoptive homes similar to those of the biological parents.

With respect to the extended downward drift hypothesis, there is no correlation between the SES of the biological father and the psychiatric status of his offspring in the control group. Thus, in this study, the extended downward drift hypothesis is not substituted.

The narrow downward drift hypothesis would also predict that the index cases, who are much more likely to have the genetic diathesis, should have a lower average SES than the controls. As in study 1, this relationship is best examined for men for whom occupational level is a measure

of social functioning and for nonstudents (since students are arbitrarily assigned the SES of their rearing family).

The previous analyses have referred to the entire spectrum of psychopathology while most of the social class hypotheses deal specifically with schizophrenia. It is therefore useful to repeat these analyses confining them only to subjects in the schizophrenic spectrum. (The term "schizophrenic spectrum" has been used by us to refer to the group of individuals categorized as process schizophrenic, borderline schizophrenic, or schizoid, since these three disorders appear to represent points along a continuum of psychopathology. For the purpose of these analyses, a subject was designated as in the spectrum if his diagnosis was at least "clearly schizoid.") The results are shown in Table 51-8. The mean SES of the schizophrenic spectrum and nonschizophrenic spectrum subgroups do not differ significantly so that this hypothesis is not supported.

Finally, let us test the sociogenic hypothesis. It would predict that schizophrenic

TABLE 51-8
Study 2: Social Class Relationships for Male Nonstudents Who are
Within or Outside the Schizophrenic Spectrum

	SES				
	Schizophrenic Spectrum			Nonschizophrenic Spectrum	
Adoptee's SES	No.	SES		No.	SES
Index group	9	2.7 ± 1.6		21	2.9 ± 1.2
Control group	7	3.0 ± 1.4		23	3.3 ± 2.1
Total	16	2.8 ± 1.5		44	3.1 ± 1.5[1]
Adoptive Fathers' SES					
Index group	9	1.7 ± 1.2		21	2.5 ± 2.1
Control group	7	3.0 ± 2.0		23	2.6 ± 2.2
Total	16	2.2 ± 1.7		44	2.6 ± 2.2

Analysis of Variance			
Source	df	MS	F[2]
Schizophrenic spectrum vs. nonschizophrenic spectrum (A)	1	.629	.140
Index vs. control (B)	1	2.604	.582
A × B	1	4.517	1.009
Error	56	4.477	

Proportionate weights solution for unequal cell frequencies.

[1] *t*-test: total schizophrenic spectrum vs. total nonschizophrenic spectrum, $P = \text{NS}$.
[2] All Fs, NS.

spectrum offspring would be more likely to come from lower SES adopting families. Again, and for similar reasons, confining our analyses to nonstudent men, the analyses yield the data summarized in Table 51-8. The SES of the adoptive fathers of the schizophrenic and nonschizophrenic spectrum subgroups do not differ significantly; thus, this hypothesis also fails to obtain support with regard to the sociogenic hypothesis.

It is also of interest to inquire if there is a relationship between the SES of the rearing family and all types of psychopathology in the offspring. As may be seen in Tables 51-5, 51-6, and 51-7, there is a significant positive correlation between the adoptive parent's SES and adoptee psychopathology for the male group of controls. However, the direction of the correlation is *opposite* in sign to that predicted. The *positive* correlation between the adoptive father's SES and psychopathology in the offspring indicates that there was a greater degree of psychopathology among the offspring reared in *higher* SES families.

In summary, all three hypotheses relating schizophrenia and social class—the narrow downward drift hypothesis, the extended downward drift hypothesis, and the sociogenic hypothesis—failed to obtain support. Some possible interpretations of the results are discussed below.

COMMENT

In these two studies, we were able to demonstrate only one correlation between social class and psychopathology, whether we measured the latter in terms of global severity of illness or by the presence or absence of schizophrenic disorder. How can this be understood in the light of the previously well established relationship between SES and mental illness? Two possible explanations seem relevant. Both relate to the populations employed.

First, how general is the relationship between SES and mental illness? Kohn[2] states that upon examination of previous studies, he noticed a relationship between city size, SES, and mental illness: in large cities there was a clear-cut relationship between the two variables, but for small cities the relationship gradually became attenuated and finally disappeared. For cities of intermediate size (population 500,000) such as Oslo, the relationship between SES and mental illness is accounted for by a concentration of such illness in the lowest social strata but little or no such relationship occurs in the higher strata.

This raises the question whether Copenhagen "behaves" like a large or small city. At present, greater Copenhagen has a population of more than a million; in the interval during which the subjects were placed for adoption the city was smaller so it may have been expected to "behave" as a city of intermediate size. If this is so, psychopathology would be expected only in relationship with the lowest SES group. Since the range of SES among the biological parents was *not* skewed towards values lower than those of the population at large, the effects attributable to very low class placement may have been obscured. Similarly, the range of SES among the adopting parents was skewed towards higher values and a narrower range so the possible effects produced by lower SES rearing may likewise have been concealed.

The second possible explanation of our failure to find any relationship between SES and psychopathology concerns the special populations of parents that were employed. First, with respect to the biological parents, we must note that ordinarily in marriage we find some degree of assortative mating: like marries like. The SES of the mother and father tend to be similar and, hence, an estimate of the couple's SES based on the father's SES will be valid for the investigator's purpose.

In a population that places its children for adoption, and where the children are often illegitimate, assortative mating may not occur to the same extent. A fair number of the offspring may be the product of casual liaisons, perhaps between a lower SES mother and an upper SES father. In such instances an estimate of *parental* SES based on the *father's* SES would tend to be too high; calculations based on the mother's SES or the average of the two parents' SES might yield different results. Unfortunately, the mother's SES is too often difficult to ascertain reliably or meaningfully and therefore the effects of that variable are not testable. Second, there may be biases introduced by the self-selection involved in giving up children for adoption. In generating these samples of adopted subjects we obviously did not choose children at random and place them in adoptive homes; we accepted children who had been placed for adoption. It seems reasonable that there may be an association between giving up a child for adoption and parental psychopathology.

Most children placed for adoption are either illegitimate or come from homes unable to care for them. Since this is so, we could have obtained a nonrepresentative subsample of parents, those who are unable or unwilling to care for their children and who are perhaps themselves skewed towards greater psychopathology. This skewing would seem to be particularly likely for the upper SES parents in our sample. Such parents ordinarily would not be expected to place their children for adoption and one would expect this subgroup to have a disproportionate amount of parental psychopathology. Since all the best evidence indicates that there is a genetic component in schizophrenia, we may well have obtained a subgroup of upper-class parents with an increased likelihood of transmitting a predisposition of schizophrenia to the offspring they gave up for adoption.

From this viewpoint, the biological parents of the schizophrenic adoptees in study 2 would not necessarily be expected to be of lower SES than those of the control adoptees. Such patterns of self-selection tend to obscure the action of a biologically mediated downward drift effect. Another factor invalidating the test of the extended downward drift hypothesis in study 2 stems from the intentional selection of two contrasting populations of biological parents (those with a history of schizophrenic illness and those with no history of psychiatric illness). If there is a correlation between SES and schizophrenic illness, a *random* sample of lower-class parents would have a greater prevalence of schizophrenic illness than an upperclass sample. But in our study we were forced to examine the control parents who were a special subsample *without* known mental illness. Thus, the sampling technique itself militated against an adequate test of the intergenerational downward drift hypothesis.

Sampling bias may also have interfered with the testing of the sociogenic hypothesis. Factors generally associated with lower SES (increased family disruption, lower education, etc.) may be pathogenic. However, the sample of lower SES parents accepted by screening agencies as adopting parents would obviously be skewed towards healthier parents—perhaps those parents least affected by, or typical of, their SES position. It is possible that the average lower SES family is more pathogenic than the average upper SES parent, but that the best lower SES families are just as "good" as the average upper SES family. Thus our adopting parent sample, which may have contained the best of the lower SES parents (rather than average lower SES parents) may not have permitted a valid test of the possible relationship between class-associated parenting and psychopathology in the offspring.

In other words, it is possible that the range of rearing environments sampled was much smaller than the eight-point scale would indicate and that the environmental differences between 0 and 7 on our scale are less than those between 1 and 5 on the Hollingshead-Redlich scale. If this is so, the sociogenic hypothesis, like the downward drift hypothesis, would receive an inadequate test.

Lastly, the narrow downward drift hypothesis was supported only in study 1; in study 2 we did not find a correlation between the subjects' SES and their psychopathology score. There are two possible explanations. First, the narrow downward drift hypothesis may be true only for severe mental illness. In study 1 the index subjects were schizophrenics whose illness was severe enough to require hospitalization. On the other hand, the 158 adoptees in study 2 included only 44 subjects who had *some* form of schizophrenic disorder, and none had been ill enough to require hospitalization. Second, the mean age of the sample in study 2 is only 33 (±8); the age of risk for schizophrenia is generally assumed to be the age period between 15 and 45 years. Our subjects have lived through only slightly more than half this interval, so with the passage of time we may anticipate that the number of ill subjects and the severity of their illness will increase. With the passage of time, and the possible increase in severity of psychopathology, some of the subjects may indeed drift downward. Such a tendency may be revealed when the same subjects are followed up several years hence.

Interestingly, in study 2 we found a positive correlation between the control subjects' psychopathology score and their adoptive parents' SES. Since this relationship did not hold for index cases or female controls, one must suspect the finding of being a type 1 error (i.e., a false positive finding). The finding might, however, given a special hypothesis, make sense. If it is the case that there are some psychological characteristics, e.g., intelligence, which are partially determined genetically and which are also associated with SES, we might expect to find some discrepancies between adoptees' characteristics and those of their adopting parents.

Clinically, one sees high SES adopting parents, e.g., physicians, teachers, who are upset by the inability of their adopted children to meet their parent's academic expectations; in such instances one often sees frustrated children and disappointed parents. The implication of the hypothesis, and the observation, is that an adoptee's "fit" with his adopting family may produce difficulty and that his "fit" may be partially determined by genetic factors. In this population of adoptees it may be that the lack of fit between high SES expectations and low SES congenital characteristics may favor the development of psychopathology. Evidence against this interpretation is that there was apparently some selective placement for this group, i.e., the disparity was reduced because the subjects in higher SES adoptive homes tended to come from higher SES biological parents.

It is difficult to conceive of an adoptee population that would avoid the sampling biases discussed above and make possible more adequate tests of the downward drift and the sociogenic hypotheses. Such a population would need to be one in which the biological parents were not self-selected and the adopting parents were not pre-screened. The biological self-selection might be avoided by using parents who did not wish to give up their children for adoption, but whose children were placed because of parental death, e.g., war orphans.

The selection of adoptive parents might be avoided by utilizing the subsample who adopt "independently," not through agencies, and who had not been prescreened. Obviously, locating a population of adoptees whose biological and adoptive parents would meet the above requirements is virtually impossible, so that a more stringent test of these hypotheses by the adoptee method will not be soon forthcoming.

REFERENCES

1. Faris, R. E. L., and Dunham, H. W. *Mental disorders in urban areas.* Chicago: The University of Chicago Press, 1939.
2. Kohn, M. L., Social class and schizophrenia: A critical review, in D. Rosenthal and S. S. Kety (eds): *The transmission of schizophrenia.* London: Pergamon Press, 1968, pp 155-173.
3. Heston, L. L.: Psychiatric disorders in foster home reared children of schizophrenic mothers. *British Journal of Psychiatry,* 1966, 112:819-825, 1966.
4. Kety, S. S., et al. The types and prevalence of mental illness in the biological and adoptive families of adopted schizophrenics, in L. Rosenthal and S. S. Kety (eds): *The transmission of schizophrenia.* London: Pergamon Press, 1968, pp 345-363.
5. Rosenthal, D., et al. Schizophrenics' offspring reared in adoptive homes, in D. Rosenthal and S. S. Kety (eds): *The transmission of schizophrenia.* London: Pergamon Press, 1968, pp 377-391.
6. Svalastoga, K., *Prestige class and mobility.* Gyldendal, Copenhagen, 1959.

CHAPTER XIII

Classification and Statistics of Mental Disorders

Statistics on Mental Disorders

According to the National Institute of Mental Health (1967), admissions of patients for the first time to state and county mental hospitals in the United States in 1965 are as follows: Of the 135,476 patients (representing 273 of 290 hospitals), 4,900 were diagnosed as having acute brain syndromes (3,500 of them as alcoholics); 30,952 with chronic brain syndromes (more than half with cerebral arteriosclerosis); 32,971 with psychotic disorders (23,861 of whom were schizophrenics); 245 with psychophysiologic autonomic and visceral disorders; 14,869 with psychoneurotic reactions; 33,662 with personality disorders (approximately half of them with alcoholic addiction); 4,957 with transient situational personality disturbance; 3,629 with mental deficiency; 7,544 with mental disorder undiagnosed; and 1,747 without any mental disorder.

The largest single group is comprised of schizophrenia, with alcoholic disorders running rather closely behind. The only other large segments are composed of those with cerebral arteriosclerosis and neurosis.

The Commission on Professional and Hospital Activities (1974) produced a different set of statistical results. Those hospitalized for neurotic disorders virtually doubled the number of psychotics. Alcoholics came close to the number of hospitalized psychotics. The figures are:

Psychotics:

Paranoid Schizophrenia	12,063
Acute Schizophrenic Episode	3,962
Miscellaneous Schizophrenia	22,589
Childhood Psychosis	181
Involutional Melancholia	5,288
Miscellaneous Major Affective Disorders	13,193
Miscellaneous Psychoses	9,695
	66,971

Neuroses:

Anxiety Neurosis	38,995
Depressive Neurosis	67,183
Miscellaneous Neuroses (including Personality Disorders)	67,183
	128,806

Alcoholism:

Alcoholic Mental Disorder	10,090
Alcoholic Addiction	33,325
Miscellaneous Alcoholism	18,374
	61,789

Drug Related Mental Disorders:

Drug-Induced Mental Disorder	1,125
Opiate Dependence	3,449
Drug Dependence (except Opiate Dependence)	2,805
	7,379
Drug Addiction Including Alcoholism	69,168

Psychophysiologic disorders totaled 12,422; mental retardation 1,912; adjustment reaction of adolescence 5,371; adjustment reaction (other than adolescence) 7,296; miscellaneous mental disorders 13,087.

References to each "introduction" are found at the end of the final chapter.

52.

World Health Organization

INTERNATIONAL CLASSIFICATION OF MENTAL DISORDERS

PSYCHOSES (290-299)

Mental disorders in which impairment of mental function has developed to a degree that interferes grossly with insight, ability to meet some ordinary demands of life or to maintain adequate contact with reality. It is not an exact or well defined term. Mental retardation is excluded.

ORGANIC PSYCHOTIC CONDITIONS (290-294)

Syndromes in which there is impairment of orientation, memory, comprehension, calculation, learning capacity and judgement. These are the essential features but there may also be shallowness or lability of affect, or a more persistent disturbance of mood, lowering of ethical standards and exaggeration or emergence of personality traits, and diminished capacity for independent decision.

Psychoses of the types classifiable to 295-298 and without the above features are excluded even though they may be associated with organic conditions.

The term 'dementia' in this glossary includes organic psychoses as just specified, of a chronic or progressive nature, which if untreated are usually irreversible and terminal.

The term 'delirium' in this glossary includes organic psychoses with a short course in which the above features are overshadowed by clouded consciousness, confusion, disorientation, delusions, illusions and often vivid hallucinations.

Includes: psychotic organic brain syndrome

Excludes: nonpsychotic syndromes of organic aetiology (see 310.-)

From World Health Organization, *Manual of the International Statistical Classification of Diseases, Injuries, and Causes of Death: Based on the Recommendations of the Ninth Conference, 1975, and Adopted by the Twenty-Ninth World Health Assembly.* Vol. I. Geneva: World Health Organization, 1977. Pp. 177-213. Reprinted by permission.

psychoses classifiable to 295-298 and without the above features but associated with physical disease, injury or condition affecting the brain [e.g., following childbirth]; code to 295-298 and use additional code to identify the associated physical condition

290 Senile and Presenile Organic Psychotic Conditions

Excludes: psychoses classifiable to 295-298.8 occurring in the senium without dementia or delirium (295-298) transient organic psychotic conditions (293.-) dementia not classified as senile, presenile, or arteriosclerotic (294.1)

290.0 *Senile dementia, simple type*

Dementia occurring usually after the age of 65 in which any cerebral pathology other than that of senile atrophic change can be reasonably excluded.

Excludes: mild memory disturbances, not amounting to dementia, associated with senile brain disease (310.1) senile dementia: depressed or paranoid type (290.2) with confusion and/or delirium (290.3)

290.1 *Presenile dementia*

Dementia occurring usually before the age of 65 in patients with the relatively rare forms of diffuse or lobar cerebral atrophy. Use additional code to identify the associated neurological condition.

Brain syndrome with presenile brain disease
Circumscribed atrophy of the brain
Dementia in:
Alzheimer's disease
Pick's disease of the brain

Excludes: arteriosclerotic dementia (290.4)
dementia associated with other
cerebral conditions (294.1)

290.2 *Senile dementia, depressed or paranoid type*

A type of senile dementia characterized by development in advanced old age, progressive in nature, in which a variety of defusions and hallucinations of a persecutory, depressive and somatic content are also present. Disturbance of the sleep/waking cycle and preoccupation with dead people are often particularly prominent.

Senile psychosis NOS

Excludes: senile dementia:
NOS (290.0)
with confusion and/or delirium
(290.3)

290.3 *Senile dementia with acute confusional state*

Senile dementia with a superimposed reversible episode of acute confusional state

Excludes: senile:
dementia NOS (290.0)
psychosis NOS (290.2)

290.4 *Arteriosclerotic dementia*

Dementia attributable, because of physical signs [on examination of the central nervous system] to degenerative arterial disease of the brain. Symptoms suggesting a focal lesion in the brain are common. There may be a fluctuating or patchy intellectual defect with insight, and an intermittent course is common. Clinical differentiation from senile or presenile dementia, which may coexist with it, may be very difficult or impossible. Use additional code to identify cerebral atherosclerosis (437.0).

Excludes: suspected cases with no clear
evidence of arteriosclerosis (290.9)

290.8 *Other*

290.9 *Unspecified*

291 Alcoholic Psychoses

Organic psychotic states due mainly to excessive consumption of alcohol; defects of nutrition

are thought to play an important role. In some of these states, withdrawal of alcohol can be of aetiological significance.

Excludes: alcoholism without psychosis (303)

291.0 *Delirium tremens*

Acute or subacute organic psychotic states in alcoholics, characterized by clouded consciousness, disorientation, fear, illusions, delusions, hallucinations of any kind, notably visual and tactile, and restlessness, tremor and sometimes fever.

Alcoholic delirium

291.1 *Korsakov's psychosis, alcoholic*

A syndrome of prominent and lasting reduction of memory span, including striking loss of recent memory, disordered time appreciation and confabulation, occurring in alcoholics as the sequel to an acute alcoholic psychosis [especially delirium tremens] or, more rarely, in the course of chronic alcoholism. It is usually accompanied by peripheral neuritis and may be associated with Wernicke's encephalopathy.

Alcoholic polyneuritic psychosis

Excludes: Korsakov's psychosis:
NOS (294.0)
nonalcoholic (294.0)

291.2 *Other alcoholic dementia*

Nonhallucinatory dementias occurring in association with alcoholism but not characterized by the features of either delirium tremens or Korsakov's psychosis.

Alcoholic dementia NOS
Chronic alcoholic brain syndrome

291.3 *Other alcoholic hallucinosis*

A psychosis usually of less than six months' duration, with slight or no clouding of consciousness and much anxious restlessness in which auditory hallucinations, mostly of voices uttering insults and threats, predominate.

Excludes: schizophrenia (295.-) and paranoid
states (297.-) taking the form of
chronic hallucinosis with clear
consciousness in an alcoholic

291.4 Pathological drunkenness

Acute psychotic episodes induced by relatively small amounts of alcohol. These are regarded as individual idiosyncratic reactions to alcohol, not due to excessive consumption and without conspicuous neurological signs of intoxication.

Excludes: simple drunkenness (305.0)

291.5 Alcoholic jealousy

Chronic paranoid psychosis characterized by delusional jealousy and associated with alcoholism.

Alcoholic paranoia

Excludes: nonalcoholic paranoid states (297.-)
schizophrenia, paranoid type (295.3)

291.8 Other

Alcohol withdrawal syndrome

Excludes: delirium tremens (291.0)

291.9 Unspecified

Alcoholic:
mania NOS
psychosis NOS
Alcoholism (chronic) with psychosis

292 Drug Psychoses

Syndromes that do not fit the descriptions given in 295-298 (nonorganic psychoses) and which are due to consumption of drugs [notably amphetamines, barbiturates and the opiate and LSD groups] and solvents. Some of the syndromes in this group are not as severe as most conditions labelled "psychotic" but they are included here for practical reasons. Use additional E Code to identify the drug and also code drug dependence (304.-) if present.

292.0 Drug withdrawal syndrome

States associated with drug withdrawal ranging from severe, as specified for alcohol under 291.0 (delirium tremens) to less severe states characterized by one or more symptoms such as convulsions, tremor, anxiety, restlessness, gastrointestinal and muscular complaints, and mild disorientation and memory disturbance.

292.1 Paranoid and/or hallucinatory states induced by drugs

States of more than a few days but not usually of more than a few months duration, associated with large or prolonged intake of drugs, notably of the amphetamine and LSD groups. Auditory hallucinations usually predominate, and there may be anxiety and restlessness.

Excludes: the described conditions with confusion or delirium (293.-)
states following LSD or other hallucinogens, lasting only a few days or less ["bad trips"] (305.3)

292.2 Pathological drug intoxication

Individual idiosyncratic reactions to comparatively small quantities of a drug, which take the form of acute, brief psychotic states of any type.

Excludes: physiological side-effects of drugs [e.g., dystonias]
expected brief psychotic reactions to hallucinogens ["bad trips"] (305.3)

292.8 Other

292.9 Unspecified

293 Transient Organic Psychotic Conditions

States characterized by clouded consciousness, confusion, disorientation, illusions and often vivid hallucinations. They are usually due to some intra- or extracerebral toxic, infectious, metabolic or other systemic disturbance and are generally reversible. Depressive and paranoid symptoms may also be present but are not the main feature. Use additional code to identify the associated physical or neurological condition.

Excludes: confusional state or delirium superimposed on senile dementia (290.3)
dementia due to:
alcohol (291.-)
arteriosclerosis (290.4)
senility (290.0)

293.0 Acute confusional state

Short-lived states, lasting hours or days, of the above type.

Acute:
 delirium
 infective psychosis
 organic reaction
 post-traumatic organic psychosis
 psycho-organic syndrome
 psychosis associated with endocrine, metabolic
  or cerebrovascular disorder
Epileptic:
 confusional state
 twilight state

293.1 *Subacute confusional state*

States of the above type in which the symptoms, usually less florid, last for several weeks or longer, during which they may show marked fluctuations in intensity.

Subacute:
 delirium
 infective psychosis
 organic reaction
 post-traumatic organic psychosis
 psycho-organic syndrome
 psychosis associated with endocrine or
  metabolic disorder

293.8 *Other*

293.9 *Unspecified*

294 Other Organic Psychotic Conditions (Chronic)

294.0 *Korsakov's psychosis or syndrome (nonalcoholic)*

Syndromes as described under 291.1 but not due to alcohol.

294.1 *Dementia in conditions classified elsewhere*

Dementia not classifiable as senile, presenile or arteriosclerotic (290.-) but associated with other underlying conditions.

Dementia in:
 cerebral lipidoses
 epilepsy
 general paralysis of the insane
 hepatolenticular degeneration
 Huntington's chorea
 multiple sclerosis
 polyarteritis nodosa

Use additional code to identify the underlying physical condition

294.8 *Other*

States that fulfill the criteria of an organic psychosis but do not take the form of a confusional state (293.—, a nonalcoholic Karsakov's psychosis (294.0) or a dementia (294.1).

Mixed paranoid and affective organic psychotic states
Epileptic psychosis NOS (code also 345.-)

Excludes: mild memory disturbances, not
     amounting to dementia (310.1)

294.9 *Unspecified*

OTHER PSYCHOSES (295-299)

295 Schizophrenic Psychoses

A group of psychoses in which there is a fundamental disturbance of personality, a characteristic distortion of thinking, often a sense of being controlled by alien forces, delusions which may be bizarre, disturbed perception, abnormal affect out of keeping with the real situation, and autism. Nevertheless, clear consciousness and intellectual capacity are usually maintained. The disturbance of personality involves its most basic functions which give the normal person his feeling of individuality, uniqueness and self-direction. The most intimate thoughts, feelings and acts are often felt to be known to or shared by others and explanatory delusions may develop, to the effect that natural or supernatural forces are at work to influence the schizophrenic person's thoughts and actions in ways that are often bizarre. He may see himself as the pivot of all that happens. Hallucinations, especially of hearing, are common and may comment on the patient or address him. Perception is frequently disturbed in other ways; there may be perplexity, irrelevant features may become all-important and, accompanied by passivity feelings, may lead the patient to believe that everyday objects and situations possess a special, usually sinister, meaning intended for him. In the characteristic schizophrenic disturbance of thinking, peripheral and irrelevant features of a total concept, which are inhibited in normal directed mental activity, are brought to the forefront and utilized in place of the elements relevant and appropriate to the situation. Thus thinking becomes vague, elliptical and obscure, and its expression in speech sometimes incomprehensible. Breaks and interpolations in the flow of consecutive thought are frequent, and the patient may be convinced that his thoughts are being withdrawn by some outside agency. Mood may be shallow, capricious or incongruous. Ambivalence and disturbance of volition may appear as inertia, negativism or stupor. Catatonia may be present. The diagnosis "schizophrenia" should not be made unless there is, or has been evident during the same illness, characteristic disturbance of thought, perception, mood, conduct, or personality—preferably in at least two of these areas. The diagnosis should not be restricted to conditions running a protracted, deteriorating, or chronic course. In addition to making the diagnosis on the criteria just given, effort should be made to specify one of the following subdivisions of schizophrenia, according to the predominant symptoms.

Includes: schizophrenia of the types described in 295.0-295.9 occurring in children

Excludes: childhood type schizophrenia (299.9)
infantile autism (299.0)

295.0   *Simple type*

A psychosis in which there is insidious development of oddities of conduct, inability to meet the demands of society, and decline in total performance. Delusions and hallucinations are not in evidence and the condition is less obviously psychotic than are the hebephrenic, catatonic and paranoid types of schizophrenia. With increasing social impoverishment vagrancy may ensue and the patient becomes self-absorbed, idle and aimless. Because the schizophrenic symptoms are not clear-cut, diagnosis of this form should be made sparingly, if at all.

Schizophrenia simplex

Excludes: latent schizophrenia (295.5)

295.1   *Hebephrenic type*

A form of schizophrenia in which affective changes are prominent, delusions and hallucinations fleeting and fragmentary, behaviour irresponsible and unpredictable and mannerisms common. The mood is shallow and inappropriate, accompanied by giggling or self-satisfied, self-absorbed smiling, or by a lofty manner, grimaces, mannerisms, pranks, hypochondriacal complaints and reiterated phrases. Thought is disorganized. There is a tendency to remain solitary, and behaviour seems empty of purpose and feeling. This form of schizophrenia usually starts between the ages of 15 and 25 years.

Hebephrenia

295.2   *Catatonic type*

Includes as an essential feature prominent psychomotor disturbances often alternating between extremes such as hyperkinesis and stupor, or automatic obedience and negativism. Constrained attitudes may be maintained for long periods: if the patient's limbs are put in some unnatural position they may be held there for some time after the external force has been removed. Severe excitement may be a striking feature of the condition. Depressive or hypomanic concomitants may be present.

Catatonic:
agitation
excitation
stupor

Schizophrenic:
catalepsy
catatonia
flexibilitas cerea

295.3   *Paranoid type*

The form of schizophrenia in which relatively stable delusions, which may be accompanied by hallucinations, dominate the clinical picture. The delusions are frequently of persecution but may take other forms [for example of jealousy, exalted birth, Messianic mission, or bodily change]. Hallucinations and erratic behaviour may occur; in some cases conduct is seriously disturbed from the outset, thought disorder may be gross, and affective flattening with fragmentary delusions and hallucinations may develop.

Paraphrenic schizophrenia

Excludes: paraphrenia, involutional paranoid state (297.2)
paranoia (297.1)

295.4 *Acute schizophrenic episode*

Schizophrenic disorders, other than those listed above, in which there is a dream-like state with slight clouding of consciousness and perplexity. External things, people and events may become charged with personal significance for the patient. There may be ideas of reference and emotional turmoil. In many such cases remission occurs within a few weeks or months, even without treatment.

Oneirophrenia
Schizophreniform:
  attack
  psychosis, confusional type

Excludes: acute forms of schizophrenia of:
        catatonic type (295.2)
        hebephrenic type (295.1)
        paranoid type (295.3)
        simple type (295.0)

295.5 *Latent schizophrenia*

It has not been possible to produce a generally acceptable description for this condition. It is not recommended for general use, but a description is provided for those who believe it to be useful: a condition of eccentric or inconsequent behaviour and anomalies of affect which give the impression of schizophrenia though no definite and characteristic schizophrenic anomalies, present or past, have been manifest.

The inclusion terms indicate that this is the best place to classify some other poorly defined varieties of schizophrenia.

Latent schizophrenic reaction
Schizophrenia:
  borderline
  prepsychotic
  prodromal
  pseudoneurotic
  pseudopsychopathic

Excludes: schizoid personality (301.2)

295.6 *Residual schizophrenia*

A chronic form of schizophrenia in which the symptoms that persist from the acute phase have mostly lost their sharpness. Emotional response is blunted and thought disorder, even when gross, does not prevent the accomplishment of routine work.

Chronic undifferentiated schizophrenia

Restzustand (schizophrenic)
Schizophrenic residual state ·

295.7 *Schizoaffective type*

A psychosis in which pronounced manic or depressive features are intermingled with schizophrenic features and which tends towards remission without permanent defect, but which is prone to recur. The diagnosis should be made only when both the affective and schizophrenic symptoms are pronounced.

Cyclic schizophrenia
Mixed schizophrenic and affective psychosis
Schizoaffective psychosis
Schizophreniform psychosis, affective type

295.8 *Other*

Schizophrenia of specified type not classifiable under 295.0-295.7.

Acute (undifferentiated) schizophrenia
Atypical schizophrenia
Coenesthopathic schizophrenia

Excludes: infantile autism (299.0)

295.9 *Unspecified*

To be used only as a last resort.

Schizophrenia NOS
Schizophrenic reaction NOS
Schizophreniform psychosis NOS

296 **Affective Psychoses**

Mental disorders, usually recurrent, in which there is a severe disturbance of mood [mostly compounded of depression and anxiety but also manifested as elation and excitement] which is accompanied by one or more of the following: delusions, perplexity, disturbed attitude to self, disorder of perception and behaviour; these are all in keeping with the patient's prevailing mood [as are hallucinations when they occur]. There is a strong tendency to suicide. For practical reasons, mild disorders of mood may also be included here if the symptoms match closely the descriptions given; this applies particularly to mild hypomania.

Excludes: reactive depressive psychosis
        (298.0)
        reactive excitation (298.1)
        neurotic depression (300.4)

296.0 *Manic-depressive psychosis, manic type*

Mental disorders characterized by states of elation or excitement out of keeping with the patient's circumstances and varying from enhanced liveliness [hypomania] to violent, almost uncontrollable excitement. Aggression and anger, flight of ideas, distractibility, impaired judgement, and grandiose ideas are common.

Hypomania NOS
Hypomanic psychosis
Mania (monopolar) NOS
Manic disorder
Manic psychosis
Manic-depressive psychosis or reaction:
 hypomanic
 manic

Excludes: circular type if there was a previous attack of depression (296.2)

296.1 *Manic-depressive psychosis, depressed type*

An affective psychosis in which there is a widespread depressed mood of gloom and wretchedness with some degree of anxiety. There is often reduced activity but there may be restlessness and agitation. There is a marked tendency to recurrence; in a few cases this may be at regular intervals.

Depressive psychosis
Endogenous depression
Involutional melancholia
Manic-depressive reaction, depressed
Monopolar depression
Psychotic depression

Excludes: circular type if previous attack was of manic type (296.3)
 depression NOS (311)

296.2 *Manic-depressive psychosis, circular type but currently manic*

An affective psychosis which has appeared in both the depressive and the manic form, either alternating or separated by an interval of normality, but in which the manic form is currently present. [The manic phase is far less frequent than the depressive.]

Bipolar disorder, now manic

Excludes: brief compensatory or rebound mood swings (296.8)

296.3 *Manic-depressive psychosis, circular type but currently depressed*

Circular type (see 296.2) in which the depressive form is currently present.

Bipolar disorder, now depressed

Excludes: brief compensatory or rebound mood swings (296.8)

296.4 *Manic-depressive psychosis, circular type, mixed*

An affective psychosis in which both manic and depressive symptoms are present at the same time.

296.5 *Manic-depressive psychosis, circular type, current condition not specified*

Circular type (see 296.2) in which the current condition is not specified as either manic or depressive.

296.6 *Manic-depressive psychosis, other and unspecified*

Use this code for cases where no other information is available, except the unspecified term, manic-depressive psychosis, or for syndromes corresponding to the descriptions of depressed (296.1) or manic (296.0) types but which for other reasons cannot be classified under 296.0-296.5.

Manic-depressive psychosis:
 NOS
 mixed type
Manic-depressive:
 reaction NOS
 syndrome NOS

296.8 *Other*

Excludes: psychogenic affective psychoses (298.-)

296.9 *Unspecified*

Affective psychosis NOS
Melancholia NOS

297 Paranoid States

Excludes: acute paranoid reaction (298.3)
 alcoholic jealousy (291.5)
 paranoid schizophrenia (295.3)

297.0 *Paranoid state, simple*

A psychosis, acute or chronic, not classifiable as schizophrenia or affective psychosis, in which delusions, especially of being influenced, persecuted or treated in some special way, are the main symptoms. The delusions are of a fairly fixed, elaborate and systematized kind.

297.1 *Paranoia*

A rare chronic psychosis in which logically constructed systematized delusions have developed gradually without concomitant hallucinations or the schizophrenic type of disordered thinking. The delusions are mostly of grandeur [the paranoiac prophet or inventor], persecution or somatic abnormality.

Excludes: paranoid personality disorder
(301.0)

297.2 *Paraphrenia*

Paranoid psychosis in which there are conspicuous hallucinations, often in several modalities. Affective symptoms and disordered thinking, if present, do not dominate the clinical picture and the personality is well preserved.

Involutional paranoid state
Late paraphrenia

297.3 *Induced psychosis*

Mainly delusional psychosis, usually chronic and often without florid features, which appears to have developed as a result of a close, if not dependent, relationship with another person who already has an established similar psychosis. The delusions are at least partly shared. The rare cases in which several persons are affected should also be included here.

Folie à deux
Induced paranoid disorder

297.8 *Other*

Paranoid states which, though in many ways akin to schizophrenic or affective states, cannot readily be classified under any of the preceding rubrics, nor under 298.4.

Paranoia querulans
Sensitiver Beziehungswahn

Excludes: senile paranoid state (297.2)

297.9 *Unspecified*

Paranoid:
  psychosis NOS
  reaction NOS
  state NOS

298 Other Nonorganic Psychoses

Categories 298.0-298.8 should be restricted to the small group of psychotic conditions that are largely or entirely attributable to a recent life experience. They should not be used for the wider range of psychoses in which environmental factors play some [but not the *major*] part in aetiology

298.0 *Depressive type*

A depressive psychosis which can be similar in its symptoms to manic-depressive psychosis, depressed type (296.1) but is apparently provoked by saddening stress such as a bereavement, or a severe disappointment or frustration. There may be less diurnal variation of symptoms than in 296.1, and the delusions are more often understandable in the context of the life experiences. There is usually a serious disturbance of behaviour, e.g., major suicidal attempt.

Reactive depressive psychosis
Psychogenic depressive psychosis

Excludes: manic-depressive psychosis,
  depressed type (296.1)
  neurotic depression (300.4)

298.1 *Excitative type*

An affective psychosis similar in its symptoms to manic-depressive psychosis, manic type, but apparently provoked by emotional stress.

Excludes: manic-depressive psychosis,
  manic type (296.0)

298.2 *Reactive confusion*

Mental disorders with clouded consciousness, disorientation [though less marked than in organic confusion] and diminished accessibility often accompanied by excessive activity and apparently provoked by emotional stress.

Psychogenic confusion
Psychogenic twilight state

Excludes: acute confusional state (293.0)

298.3 *Acute paranoid reaction*

Paranoid states apparently provoked by some emotional stress. The stress is often misconstrued as an attack or threat. Such states are particularly prone to occur in prisoners or as acute reactions to a strange and threatening environment, e.g. in immigrants.

Bouffee délirante

Excludes: paranoid states (297.-)

298.4 *Psychogenic paranoid psychosis*

Psychogenic or reactive paranoid psychosis of any type which is more protracted than the acute reactions covered in 298.3. Where there is a diagnosis of psychogenic paranoid psychosis which does not specify "acute" this coding should be made.

Protracted reactive paranoid psychosis

298.8 *Other and unspecified reactive psychosis*

Hysterical psychosis
Psychogenic psychosis NOS
Psychogenic stupor

298.9 *Unspecified psychosis*

To be used only as a last resort, when no other term can be used.

Psychosis NOS

299 Psychoses with Origin Specific to Childhood

This category should be used only for psychoses which always begin before puberty. Adult-type psychoses such as schizophrenia or manic-depressive psychoses when occurring in childhood should be coded elsewhere under the appropriate heading—i.e., 295 and 296 for the examples given.

299.0 *Infantile autism*

A syndrome present from birth or beginning almost invariably in the first 30 months. Responses to auditory and sometimes to visual stimuli are abnormal and there are usually severe problems in the understanding of spoken language. Speech is delayed and, if it develops, is characterized by echolalia, the reversal of pronouns, immature grammatical structure and inability to use abstract terms. There is generally an impairment in the social use of both verbal and gestural language. Problems in social relationships are most severe before the age of five years and include an impairment in the development of eye-to-eye gaze, social attachments, and cooperative play. Ritualistic behaviour is usual and may include abnormal routines, resistance to change, attachment to odd objects and stereotyped patterns of play. The capacity for abstract or symbolic thought and for imaginative play is diminished. Intelligence ranges from severely subnormal to normal or above. Peformance is usually better on tasks involving rote memory or visuospatial skills than on those requiring symbolic or linguistic skills.

Childhood autism
Infantile psychosis
Kanner's syndrome

Excludes: disintegrative psychosis (299.1)
Heller's syndrome (299.1)
schizophrenic syndrome of childhood (299.9)

299.1 *Disintegrative psychosis*

A disorder in which normal or near-normal development for the first few years is followed by a loss of social skills and of speech, together with a severe disorder of emotions, behaviour and relationships. Usually this loss of speech and of social competence takes place over a period of a few months and is accompanied by the emergence of overactivity and of stereotypies. In most cases there is intellectual impairment, but this is not a necessary part of the disorder. The condition may follow overt brain disease—such as measles encephalitis—but it may also occur in the absence of any known organic brain disease or damage. Use additional code to identify any associated neurological disorder.

Heller's syndrome

Excludes: infantile autism (299.0)
schizophrenic syndrome of childhood (299.9)

299.8 *Other*

A variety of atypical infantile psychoses which may show some, but not all, of the features of infantile autism. Symptoms may include stereotyped repetitive movements, hyperkinesis, self-injury, retarded speech development, echolalia and impaired social relationships. Such disorders may occur in children of any level of intelligence but are particularly common in those with mental retardation.

Atypical childhood psychosis

Excludes: simple stereotypies without
psychotic disturbance (307.3)

299.9 *Unspecified*

Child psychosis NOS
Schizophrenia, childhood type NOS
Schizophrenic syndrome of childhood NOS

Excludes: schizophrenia of adult type
occurring in childhood
(295.0-295.8)

NEUROTIC DISORDERS, PERSONALITY DISORDERS AND OTHER NONPSYCHOTIC MENTAL DISORDERS (300-316)

300 Neurotic Disorders

The distinction between neurosis and psychosis is difficult and remains subject to debate. However, it has been retained in view of its wide use.

Neurotic disorders are mental disorders without any demonstrable organic basis in which the patient may have considerable insight and has unimpaired reality testing, in that he usually does not confuse his morbid subjective experiences and fantasies with external reality. Behaviour may be greatly affected although usually remaining within socially acceptable limits, but personality is not disorganized. The principal manifestations include excessive anxiety, hysterical symptoms, phobias, obsessional and compulsive symptoms, and depression.

300.0 *Anxiety states*

Various combinations of physical and mental manifestations of anxiety, not attributable to real danger and occurring either in attacks or as a persisting state. The anxiety is usually diffuse and may extend to panic. Other neurotic features such as obsessional or hysterical symptoms may be present but do not dominate the clinical picture.

Anxiety:
neurosis
reaction
state (neurotic)
Panic:
attack
disorder
state

Excludes: neurasthenia (300.5)
psychophysiological disorders
(306.-)

300.1 *Hysteria*

Mental disorders in which motives, of which the patient seems unaware, produce either a restriction of the field of consciousness or disturbances of motor or sensory function which may seem to have psychological advantage or symbolic value. It may be characterized by conversion phenomena or dissociative phenomena. In the conversion form the chief or only symptoms consist of psychogenic disturbance of function in some part of the body, e.g., paralysis, tremor, blindness, deafness, seizures. In the dissociative variety, the most prominent feature is a narrowing of the field of consciousness which seems to serve an unconscious purpose and is commonly accompanied or followed by a selective amnesia. There may be dramatic but essentially superficial changes of personality sometimes taking the form of a fugue [wandering state]. Behaviour may mimic psychosis or, rather, the patient's idea of psychosis.

Astasia-abasia, hysterical
Compensation neurosis
Conversion hysteria
Conversion reaction
Dissociative reaction or state
Ganser's syndrome, hysterical
Hysteria NOS
Multiple personality

Excludes: adjustment reaction (309.-)
anorexia nervosa (307.1)
gross stress reaction (308.-)
hysterical personality (301.5)
psychophysiological disorders
(306.-)

300.2 *Phobic state*

Neurotic states with abnormally intense dread of certain objects or specific situations which would not normally have that effect. If the anxiety tends to spread from a specified situation or object to a wider range of circumstances, it becomes akin to or identical with anxiety state, and should be classified as such (300.0).

Agoraphobia
Animal phobias
Anxiety-hysteria
Claustrophobia
Phobia NOS

Excludes: anxiety state (300.0)
obsessional phobias (300.3)

300.3 Obsessive-compulsive disorders

States in which the outstanding symptom is a feeling of subjective compulsion—which must be resisted—to carry out some action, to dwell on an idea, to recall an experience, or to ruminate on an abstract topic. Unwanted thoughts which intrude, the insistency of words or ideas, ruminations or trains of thought are perceived by the patient to be inappropriate or nonsensical. The obsessional urge or idea is recognized as alien to the personality but as coming from within the self. Obsessional actions may be quasiritual performances designed to relieve anxiety e.g., washing the hands to cope with contamination. Attempts to dispel the unwelcome thoughts or urges may lead to a severe inner struggle, with intense anxiety.

Anankastic neurosis
Compulsive neurosis

Excludes: obsessive-compulsive symptoms occurring in:
endogenous depression (296.1)
schizophrenia (295.-)
organic states, e.g., encephalitis

300.4 Neurotic depression

A neurotic disorder characterized by disproportionate depression which has usually recognizably ensued on a distressing experience; it does not include among its features delusions or hallucinations, and there is often preoccupation with the psychic trauma which preceded the illness, e.g., loss of a cherished person or possession. Anxiety is also frequently present and mixed states of anxiety and depression should be included here. The distinction between depressive neurosis and psychosis should be made not only upon the degree of depression but also on the presence or absence of other neurotic and psychotic characteristics and upon the degree of disturbance of the patient's behaviour.

Anxiety depression
Depressive reaction
Neurotic depressive state
Reactive depression

Excludes: adjustment reaction with depressive symptoms (309.0)
depression NOS (311)
manic-depressive psychosis, depressed type (296.1)
reactive depressive psychosis (298.0)

300.5 Neurasthenia

A neurotic disorder characterized by fatigue, irritability, headache, depression, insomnia, difficulty in concentration, and lack of capacity for enjoyment [anhedonia]. It may follow or accompany an infection or exhaustion, or arise from continued emotional stress. If neurasthenia is associated with a physical disorder, the latter should also be coded.

Nervous debility

Excludes: anxiety state (300.0)
neurotic depression (300.4)
psychophysiological disorders (306.-)
specific nonpsychotic mental disorders following organic brain damage (310.-)

300.6 Depersonalization syndrome

A neurotic disorder with an unpleasant state of disturbed perception in which external objects or parts of one's own body are experienced as changed in their quality, unreal, remote or automatized. The patient is aware of the subjective nature of the change he experiences. Depersonalization may occur as a feature of several mental disorders including depression, obsessional neurosis, anxiety and schizophrenia; in that case the condition should not be classified here but in the corresponding major category.

Derealization (neurotic)

300.7 Hypochondriasis

A neurotic disorder in which the conspicuous features are excessive concern with one's health in general or the integrity and functioning of some part of one's body, or, less frequently, one's mind. It is usually associated with anxiety and depression. It may occur as a feature of severe mental disorder and in that case should not be classified here but in the corresponding major category.

Excludes: hysteria (300.1)
  manic-depressive psychosis, depressed type (296.1)
  neurasthenia (300.5)
  obsessional disorder (300.3)
  schizophrenia (295.-)

300.8 *Other neurotic disorders*

Neurotic disorders not classified elsewhere, e.g., occupational neurosis. Patients with mixed neuroses should not be classified in this category but according to the most prominent symptoms they display.

Briquet's disorder
Occupational neurosis, including writer's cramp
Psychasthenia
Psychasthenic neurosis

300.9 *Unspecified*

To be used only as a last resort.

Neurosis NOS
Psychoneurosis NOS

301 Personality Disorders

Deeply ingrained maladaptive patterns of behaviour generally recognizable by the time of adolescence or earlier and continuing throughout most of adult life, although often becoming less obvious in middle or old age. The personality is abnormal either in the balance of its components, their quality and expression or in its total aspect. Because of this deviation or psychopathy the patient suffers or others have to suffer and there is an adverse effect upon the individual or on society. It includes what is sometimes called psychopathic personality, but if this is determined primarily by malfunctioning of the brain, it should not be classified here but as one of the nonpsychotic organic brain syndromes (310). When the patient exhibits an anomaly of personality directly related to his neurosis or psychosis, e.g., schizoid personality and schizophrenia or anankastic personality

and obsessive compulsive neurosis, the relevant neurosis or psychosis which is in evidence should be diagnosed in addition.

Character neurosis

301.0 *Paranoid personality disorder*

Personality disorder in which there is excessive sensitiveness to setbacks or to what are taken to be humiliations and rebuffs, a tendency to distort experience by misconstruing the neutral or friendly actions of others as hostile or contemptuous, and a combative and tenacious sense of personal rights. There may be a proneness to jealousy or excessive self-importance. Such persons may feel helplessly humiliated and put upon; others, likewise excessively sensitive, are aggressive and insistent. In all cases there is excessive self-reference.

Fanatic personality
Paranoid traits
Paranoid personality (disorder)

Excludes: acute paranoid reaction (298.3)
  alcoholic paranoia (291.5)
  paranoid schizophrenia (295.3)
  paranoid states (297.-)

301.1 *Affective personality disorder*

Personality disorder characterized by lifelong predominance of a pronounced mood which may be persistently depressive, persistently elated, or alternately one then the other. During periods of elation there is unshakeable optimism and an enhanced zest for life and activity, whereas periods of depression are marked by worry, pessimism, low output of energy and a sense of futility.

Cycloid personality
Cyclothymic personality
Depressive personality

Excludes: affective psychoses (296.-)
  cyclothymia (296.2-296.5)
  neurasthenia (300.5)
  neurotic depression (300.4)

301.2 *Schizoid personality disorder*

Personality disorder in which there is withdrawal from affectional, social and other contacts with autistic preference for fantasy and introspective reserve. Behaviour may be slightly eccentric or indicate avoidance of competitive situations. Apparent coolness and detachment may mask an incapacity to express feeling.

Excludes: schizophrenia (295.-)

301.3 *Explosive personality disorder*

Personality disorder characterized by instability of mood with liability to intemperate outbursts of anger, hate, violence or affection. Aggression may be expressed in words or in physical violence. The outbursts cannot readily be controlled by the affected persons, who are not otherwise prone to antisocial behaviour.

Aggressive:
 personality
 reaction
Aggressiveness
Emotional instability (excessive)
Pathological emotionality
Quarrelsomeness

Excludes: dyssocial personality (301.7)
 hysterical neurosis (300.1)

301.4 *Anankastic personality disorder*

Personality disorder characterized by feelings of personal insecurity, doubt and incompleteness leading to excessive conscientiousness, checking, stubbornness and caution. There may be insistent and unwelcome thoughts or impulses which do not attain the severity of an obsessional neurosis. There is perfectionism and meticulous accuracy and a need to check repeatedly in an attempt to ensure this. Rigidity and excessive doubt may be conspicuous.

Compulsive personality
Obsessional personality

Excludes: obsessive-compulsive disorder (300.3)
 phobic state (300.2)

301.5 *Hysterical personality disorder*

Personality disorder characterized by shallow, labile affectivity, dependence on others, craving for appreciation and attention, suggestibility and theatricality. There is often sexual immaturity, e.g., frigidity and over-responsiveness to stimuli. Under stress hysterical symptoms [neurosis] may develop.

Histrionic personality
Psychoinfantile personality

Excludes: hysterical neurosis (300.1)

301.6 *Asthenic personality disorder*

Personality disorder characterized by passive compliance with the wishes of elders and others and a weak inadequate response to the demands of daily life. Lack of vigour may show itself in the intellectual or emotional spheres; there is little capacity for enjoyment.

Dependent personality
Inadequate personality
Passive personality

Excludes: neurasthenia (300.5)

301.7 *Personality disorder with predominantly sociopathic or asocial manifestation*

Personality disorder characterized by disregard for social obligations, lack of feeling for others, and impetuous violence of callous unconcern. There is a gross disparity between behaviour and the prevailing social norms. Behaviour is not readily modifiable by experience, including punishment. People with this personality are often affectively cold and may be abnormally aggressive or irresponsible. Their tolerance to frustration is low; they blame others or offer plausible rationalizations for the behaviour which brings them into conflict with society.

Amoral personality
Antisocial personality
Asocial personality

Excludes: disturbance of conduct without specifiable personality disorder (312.-)
 explosive personality (301.3)

301.8 *Other personality disorders*

Personality:
 eccentric
 "haltlose" type
 immature
 passive-aggressive
 psychoneurotic

Excludes: psychoinfantile personality (301.5)

301.9 *Unspecified*

Pathological personality NOS
Personality disorder NOS
Psychopathic:
  constitutional state
  personality (disorder)

302 Sexual Deviations and Disorders

Abnormal sexual inclinations or behaviour which are part of a referral problem. The limits and features of normal sexual inclination and behaviour have not been stated absolutely in different societies and cultures but are broadly such as serve approved social and biological purposes. The sexual activity of affected persons is directed primarily either towards people not of the opposite sex, or towards sexual acts not associated with coitus normally, or towards coitus performed under abnormal circumstances. If the anomalous behaviour becomes manifest only during psychosis or other mental illness the condition should be classified under the major illness. It is common for more than one anomaly to occur together in the same individual; in that case the predominant deviation is classified. It is preferable not to include in this category individuals who perform deviant sexual acts when normal sexual outlets are not available to them.

302.0 *Homosexuality*

Exclusive or predominant sexual attraction for persons of the same sex with or without physical relationship. Code homosexuality here whether or not it is considered as a mental disorder.

Lesbianism

Excludes: homosexual paedophilia (302.2)

302.1 *Bestiality*

Sexual or anal intercourse with animals.

302.2 *Paedophilia*

Sexual deviations in which an adult engages in sexual activity with a child of the same or opposite sex.

302.3 *Transvestism*

Sexual deviation in which sexual pleasure is derived from dressing in clothes of the opposite sex. There is no consistent attempt to take on the identity or behaviour of the opposite sex.

Excludes: trans-sexualism (302.5)

302.4 *Exhibitionism*

Sexual deviation in which the main sexual pleasure and gratification is derived from exposure of the genitals to a person of the opposite sex.

302.5 *Trans-sexualism*

Sexual deviation centred around fixed beliefs that the overt bodily sex is wrong. The resulting behaviour is directed towards either changing the sexual organs by operation, or completely concealing the bodily sex by adopting both the dress and behaviour of the opposite sex.

Excludes: transvestism (302.3)

302.6 *Disorders of psychosexual identity*

Behaviour occurring in preadolescents of immature psychosexuality which is similar to that shown in the sexual deviations described under transvestism (302.3) and trans-sexualism (302.5). Cross-dressing is intermittent, although it may be frequent, and identification with the behaviour and appearance of the opposite sex is not yet fixed. The commonest form is feminism in boys.

Gender-role disorder

Excludes: homosexuality (302.0)
         trans-sexualism (302.5)
         transvestism (302.3)

302.7 *Frigidity and impotence*

Frigidity—dislike of or aversion to sexual intercourse, of psychological origin, of sufficient intensity to lead, if not to active avoidance, to marked anxiety, discomfort or pain when normal sexual intercourse takes place. Less severe degrees of this disorder that also give rise to consultation should also be coded here.

Impotence—sustained inability, due to psychological causes, to maintain an erection which will allow normal heterosexual penetration and ejaculation to take place.

Dyspareunia, psychogenic

Excludes: impotence of organic origin
         normal transient symptoms from
         ruptured hymen

transient or occasional failures of
erection due to fatigue, anxiety,
alcohol or drugs

302.8 *Other*

Fetishism
Masochism
Sadism

302.9 *Unspecified*

303 Alcohol Dependence Syndrome

A state, psychic and usually also physical,
resulting from taking alcohol, characterized by
behavioural and other responses that always include a compulsion to take alcohol on a continuous or periodic basis in order to experience
its psychic effects, and sometimes to avoid the
discomfort of its absence; tolerance may or may
not be present. A person may be dependent on
alcohol and other drugs; if so also make the
appropriate 304 coding. If dependence is associated with alcoholic psychosis or with physical complications, *both* should be coded.

Acute drunkenness in alcoholism
Chronic alcoholism
Dipsomania

Excludes: alcoholic psychoses (291.-)
    drunkenness NOS (305.0)
    physical complications of alcohol,
    such as:
     cirrhosis of liver (571.2)
     epilepsy (345.-)
     gastritis (535.3)

304 Drug Dependence

A state, psychic and sometimes also physical,
resulting from taking a drug, characterized by
behavioural and other responses that always
include a compulsion to take a drug on a
continuous or periodic basis in order to experience its psychic effects, and sometimes to avoid
the discomfort of its absence. Tolerance may or
may not be present. A person may be dependent
on more than one drug.

Excludes: nondependent abuse of drugs
    (305.-)

304.0 *Morphine type*

Heroin
Methadone

Opium
Opium alkaloids and their derivatives
Synthetics with morphine-like effects

304.1 *Barbiturate type*

Barbiturates
Nonbarbiturate sedatives and tranquillizers
 with a similar effect:
  chlordiazepoxide
  diazepam
  glutethimide
  meprobamate

304.2 *Cocaine*

Coca leaves and derivatives

304.3 *Cannabis*

Hemp
Hashish
Marijuana

304.4 *Amphetamine type and other*
    psychostimulants

Phenmetrazine
Methylphenidate

304.5 *Hallucinogens*

LSD and derivatives
Mescaline
Psilocybin

304.6 *Other*

Absinthe addiction
Glue sniffing

Excludes: tobacco dependence (305.1)

304.7 *Combinations of morphine type drug*
    with any other

304.8 *Combinations excluding morphine*
    type drug

304.9 *Unspecified*

Drug addiction NOS
Drug dependence NOS

305 Nondependent Abuse of Drugs

Includes cases where a person, for whom no
other diagnosis is possible, has come under

medical care because of the maladaptive effect of a drug on which he is not dependent (as defined in 304.-) and that he has taken on his own initiative to the detriment of his health or social functioning. When drug abuse is secondary to a psychiatric disorder, code the disorder.

Excludes: alcohol dependence syndrome (303)
 drug dependence (304.-)
 drug withdrawal syndrome (292.0)
 poisoning by drugs or medicaments (960-979)

305.0 *Alcohol*

Cases of acute intoxication or "hangover" effects.

Drunkenness NOS
Excessive drinking of alcohol NOS
"Hangover" (alcohol)
Inebriety NOS

Excludes: alcoholic psychoses (291.-)
 physical complications of alcohol, such as:
 cirrhosis of liver (571.2)
 epilepsy (345.-)
 gastritis (535.3)

305.1 *Tobacco*

Cases in which tobacco is used to the detriment of a person's health or social functioning or in which there is tobacco dependence. Dependence is included here rather than under 304.- because tobacco differs from other drugs of dependence in its psychotoxic effects.

Tobacco dependence

305.2 *Cannabis*

305.3 *Hallucinogens*

Cases of acute intoxication or "bad trips."

LSD reaction

305.4 *Barbiturates and tranquillizers*

Cases where a person has taken the drug to the detriment of his health or social functioning, in doses above or for periods beyond those normally regarded as therapeutic.

305.5 *Morphine type*

305.6 *Cocaine type*

305.7 *Amphetamine type*

305.8 *Antidepressants*

305.9 *Other, mixed or unspecified*

"Laxative habit"
Misuse of drugs NOS
Nonprescribed use of drugs or patent medicinals

306 Physiological Malfunction Arising From Mental Factors

A variety of physical symptoms or types of physiological malfunction of mental origin, not involving tissue damage and usually mediated through the autonomic nervous system. The disorders are grouped according to body system. Codes 306.0-306.9 should not be used if the physical symptom is secondary to a psychiatric disorder classifiable elsewhere. If tissue damage is involved, code under 316.

Excludes: hysteria (300.1)
 psychic factors associated with physical conditions involving tissue damage classified elsewhere (316)
 specific nonpsychotic mental disorders following organic brain damage (310.-)

306.0 *Musculoskeletal*

Psychogenic torticollis

Excludes: Gilles de la Tourette's syndrome (307.2)
 tics (307.2)

306.1 *Respiratory*

Air hunger
Hiccough (psychogenic)
Hyperventilation
Psychogenic cough
Yawning

Excludes: psychogenic asthma (316 and 493.9)

306.2 *Cardiovascular*

Cardiac neurosis
Cardiovascular neurosis
Neurocirculatory asthenia
Psychogenic cardiovascular disorder

Excludes: psychogenic paroxysmal tachycardia (316 and 427.9)

306.3 *Skin*

Psychogenic pruritus

Excludes: psychogenic:
  alopecia (316 and 704.0)
  dermatitis (316 and 692.-)
  eczema (316 and 691.9 or 692.-)
  urticaria (316 and 708.-)

306.4 *Gastrointestinal*

Aerophagy
Cyclical vomiting, psychogenic

Excludes: cyclical vomiting NOS (536.2)
  mucous colitis (316 and 564.1)
  psychogenic:
    cardiospasm (316 and 530.0)
    duodenal ulcer (316 and 532.-)
    gastric ulcer (316 and 531.-)
    peptic ulcer (316 and 533.-)

306.5 *Genitourinary*

Psychogenic dysmenorrhoea

Excludes: dyspareunia (302.7)
  enuresis (307.6)
  frigidity (302.7)
  impotence (302.7)

306.6 *Endocrine*

306.7 *Organs of special sense*

Excludes: hysterical blindness or deafness (300.1)

306.8 *Other*

Teeth-grinding

306.9 *Unspecified*

Psychophysiologic disorder NOS
Psychosomatic disorder NOS

307 Special Symptoms or Syndromes Not Elsewhere Classified

Conditions in which an outstanding symptom or group of symptoms is not manifestly part of a more fundamental classifiable condition.

Excludes: when due to mental disorders classified elsewhere
  when of organic origin

307.0 *Stammering and stuttering*

Disorders in the rhythm of speech, in which the individual knows precisely what he wishes to say, but at the time is unable to say it because of an involuntary, repetitive prolongation or cessation of a sound.

Excludes: dysphasia (784.5)
  lisping or lalling (307.9)
  retarded development of speech (315.3)

307.1 *Anorexia nervosa*

A disorder in which the main features are persistent active refusal to eat and marked loss of weight. The level of activity and alertness is characteristically high in relation to the degree of emaciation. Typically the disorder begins in teenage girls but it may sometimes begin before puberty and rarely it occurs in males. Amenorrhoea is usual and there may be a variety of other physiological changes including slow pulse and respiration, low body temperature and dependent oedema. Unusual eating habits and attitudes toward food are typical and sometimes starvation follows or alternates with periods of overeating. The accompanying psychiatric symptoms are diverse.

Excludes: eating disturbance NOS (307.5)
  loss of appetite (783.0)
  of nonorganic origin (307.5)

307.2 *Tics*

Disorders of no known organic origin in which the outstanding feature consists of quick, involuntary, apparently purposeless, and frequently repeated movements which are not due to any neurological condition. Any part of the body may be involved but the face is most frequently affected. Only one form of tic may be present, or there may be a combination of tics which are carried out simultaneously, alternatively or consecutively. Gilles de la Tourette's syndrome refers to a rare disorder occurring in individuals of any level of intelligence in which facial tics and tic-like throat noises become more marked and more generalized and in which later, whole words or short sentences [often with an obscene content] are ejaculated spasmodically and involuntarily. There is some overlap with other varieties of tic.

Excludes: nail-biting or thumb-sucking
(307.9)
stereotypies occurring in isolation
(307.3)
tics of organic origin (333.3)

307.3 *Stereotyped repetitive movements*

Disorders in which voluntary repetitive stereotyped movements, which are not due to any psychiatric or neurological condition, constitute the main feature. Includes head-banging, spasmus nutans, rocking, twirling, finger-flicking mannerisms and eye poking. Such movements are particularly common in cases of mental retardation with sensory impairment or with environmental monotony.

Stereotypies NOS

Excludes: tics:
NOS (307.2)
of organic origin (333.3)

307.4 *Specific disorders of sleep*

This category should only be used when a more precise medical or psychiatric diagnosis cannot be made.

(of nonorganic origin)
Hypersomnia
Insomnia
Inversion of sleep rhythm
Nightmares
Night terrors
Sleepwalking

Excludes: narcolepsy (347.0)
when of unspecified cause (780.5)

307.5 *Other and unspecified disorders of eating*

This category should only be used when a more precise medical or psychiatric diagnosis cannot be made.

(of nonorganic origin)
Infantile feeding disturbances
Loss of appetite
Overeating
Pica
Psychogenic vomiting

Excludes: anorexia:
nervosa (307.1)
of unspecified cause (783.0)

overeating of unspecified cause
(783.6)
vomiting:
NOS (787.0)
cyclical (536.2)
psychogenic (306.4)

307.6 *Enuresis*

A disorder in which the main manifestation is a persistent involuntary voiding of urine by day or night which is considered abnormal for the age of the individual. Sometimes the child will have failed to gain bladder control and in other cases he will have gained control and then lost it. Episodic or fluctuating enuresis should be included. The disorder would not usually be diagnosed under the age of four years.

Enuresis (primary) (secondary) of nonorganic origin

Excludes: enuresis of unspecified cause
(788.3)

307.7 *Encopresis*

A disorder in which the main manifestation is the persistent voluntary or involuntary passage of formed motions of normal or near-normal consistency into places not intended for that purpose in the individual's own sociocultural setting. Sometimes the child has failed to gain bowel control, and sometimes he has gained control but then later again became encopretic. There may be a variety of associated psychiatric symptoms and there may be smearing of faeces. The condition would not usually be diagnosed under the age of four years.

Encopresis (continuous) (discontinuous) of nonorganic origin

Excludes: encopresis of unspecified cause
(787.6)

307.8 *Psychalgia*

Cases in which there are pains of mental origin, e.g., headache or backache, when a more precise medical or psychiatric diagnosis cannot be made.

Tension headache
Psychogenic backache

Excludes: migraine (346.-)

pains not specifically attributable
to a psychological cause
(in):
back (784.5)
headache (784.0)
joint (719.4)
limb (729.5)
lumbago (724.2)
rheumatic (729.0)

307.9 *Other and unspecified*

The use of this category should be discouraged. Most of the items listed in the inclusion terms are not indicative of psychiatric disorder and are included only because such terms may sometimes still appear as diagnoses.

Hair plucking
Lalling
Lisping
Masturbation
Nail-biting
Thumb-sucking

308 Acute Reaction to Stress

Very transient disorders of any severity and nature which occur in individuals without any apparent mental disorder in response to exceptional physical or mental stress, such as natural catastrophe or battle, and which usually subside within hours or days.

Catastrophic stress
Combat fatigue
Exhaustion delirium

Excludes: adjustment reaction (309.-)

308.0 *Predominant disturbance of emotions*

Panic states, excitability, fear, depressions and anxiety fulfilling the above criteria.

308.1 *Predominant disturbance of consciousness*

Fugues fulfilling the above criteria.

308.2 *Predominant psychomotor disturbance*

Agitation states, stupor fulfilling the above criteria.

308.3 *Other*

Acute situational disturbance

308.4 *Mixed*

Many gross stress reactions include several elements but whenever possible a specific coding under .0, .1, .2 or .3 should be made according to the *preponderant* type of disturbance. The category of mixed disorders should only be used when there is such an admixture that this cannot be done.

308.9 *Unspecified*

309 Adjustment Reaction

Mild or transient disorders lasting longer than acute stress reactions (308.-) which occur in individuals of any age without any apparent pre-existing mental disorder. Such disorders are often relatively circumscribed or situation-specific, are generally reversible, and usually last only a few months. They are usually closely related in time and content to stresses such as bereavement, migration or separation experiences. Reactions to major stress that last longer than a few days are also included here. In children such disorders are associated with no significant distortion of development.

Excludes: acute reaction to major stress (308.-)
neurotic disorders (300.-)

309.0 *Brief depressive reaction*

States of depression, not specifiable as manic-depressive, psychotic or neurotic, generally transient, in which the depressive symptoms are usually closely related in time and content to some stressful event.

Grief reaction

Excludes: affective psychoses (296.-)
neurotic depression (300.4)
prolonged depressive reaction (309.1)
psychogenic depressive psychosis (298.0)

309.1 *Prolonged depressive reaction*

States of depression, not specifiable as manic-depressive, psychotic or neurotic, generally long-lasting; usually developing in association with prolonged exposure to a stressful situation.

Excludes: affective psychoses (296.-)
brief depressive reaction (309.0)
neurotic depression (300.4)

psychogenic depressive psychosis (298.0)

309.2 *With predominant disturbance of other emotions*

States, fulfilling the general criteria for adjustment reaction, in which the main symptoms are emotional in type [anxiety, fear, worry, etc.] but not specifically depressive.

Abnormal separation anxiety
Culture shock

309.3 *With predominant disturbance of conduct*

Mild or transient disorders, fulfilling the general criteria for adjustment reaction, in which the main disturbance predominantly involves a disturbance of conduct. For example, an adolescent grief reaction resulting in aggressive or antisocial disorder would be included here.

Excludes: disturbance of conduct NOS (312.-)
dyssocial behaviour without manifest psychiatric disorder (V71.0)
personality disorder with predominantly sociopathic or asocial manifestations (301.7)

309.4 *With mixed disturbance of emotions and conduct*

Disorders fulfilling the general definition in which both emotional disturbance and disturbance of conduct are prominent features.

309.8 *Other*

Adjustment reaction with elective mutism
Hospitalism in children NOS

309.9 *Unspecified*

Adjustment reaction NOS
Adaptation reaction NOS

310 Specific Nonpsychotic Mental Disorders Following Organic Brain Damage

Note: This category should be used only for conditions where the *form* of the disorder is determined by the brain pathology.

Excludes: neuroses, personality disorders or other nonpsychotic conditions

occurring in a form similar to that seen with functional disorders but in association with a physical condition; code to 300.-, 301.-, etc., and use additional code to identify the physical condition

310.0 *Frontal lobe syndrome*

Changes in behaviour following damage to the frontal areas of the brain or following interference with the connections of those areas. There is a general diminution of self-control, foresight, creativity and spontaneity, which may be manifest as increased irritability, selfishness, restlessness and lack of concern for others. Conscientiousness and powers of concentration are often diminished, but measurable deterioration of intellect or memory is not necessarily present. The overall picture is often one of emotional dullness, lack of drive and slowness; but, particularly in persons previously with energetic, restless or aggressive characteristics, there may be a change towards impulsiveness, boastfulness, temper outbursts, silly fatuous humour, and the development of unrealistic ambitions; the direction of change usually depends upon the previous personality. A considerable degree of recovery is possible and may continue over the course of several years.

Lobotomy syndrome
Postleucotomy syndrome (state)

Excludes: postcontusional syndrome (310.2)

310.1 *Cognitive or personality change of other type*

Chronic, mild states of memory disturbance and intellectual deterioration, often accompanied by increased irritability, querulousness, lassitude and complaints of physical weakness. These states are often associated with old age, and may precede more severe states due to brain damage classifiable under dementia of any type (290.-, and 294.-) or any condition in 293.- (Transient organic psychotic conditions).

Mild memory disturbance
Organic psychosyndrome of nonpsychotic severity

310.2 *Postconcussional syndrome*

States occurring after generalized contusion of the brain, in which the symptom picture may resemble that of the frontal lobe syndrome (310.0) or that of any of the neurotic disorders (300.0-300.9), but in which in addition, headache, giddiness, fatigue, insomnia and a subjective feeling of impaired intellectual ability are usually prominent. Mood may fluctuate, and quite ordinary stress may produce exaggerated fear and apprehension. There may be marked intolerance of mental and physical exertion, undue sensitivity to noise, and hypochondriacal preoccupation. The symptoms are more common in persons who have previously suffered from neurotic or personality disorders, or when there is a possibility of compensation. This syndrome is particularly associated with the closed type of head injury when signs of localized brain damage are slight or absent, but it may also occur in other conditions.

Postcontusional syndrome (encephalopathy)
Status post commotio cerebri
Post-traumatic brain syndrome, nonpsychotic

Excludes: frontal lobe syndrome (310.0)
           postencephalitic syndrome (310.8)
           any organic psychotic conditions
           following head injury
           (290.- to 294.0)

310.8 *Other*

Include here disorders resembling the postcontusional syndrome (310.2), associated with infective or other diseases of the brain or surrounding tissues.

Other focal (partial) organic psychosyndromes

310.9 *Unspecified*

311 Depressive Disorder, Not Elsewhere Classified

States of depression, usually of moderate but occasionally of marked intensity, which have no specifically manic-depressive or other psychotic depressive features and which do not appear to be associated with stressful events or other features specified under neurotic depression.

Depressive disorder NOS
Depressive state NOS
Depression NOS

Excludes: acute reaction to major stress with
           depressive symptoms (308.0)
           affective personality disorder
           (301.1)

affective psychoses (296.-)
brief depressive reaction (309.0)
disturbance of emotions specific to
   childhood and adolescence, with
   misery and unhappiness (313.1)
mixed adjustment reaction with
   depressive symptoms (309.4)
neurotic depression (300.4)
prolonged depressive adjustment
   reaction (309.1)
psychogenic depressive psychosis
   (298.0)

312 Disturbance of Conduct Not Elsewhere Classified

Disorders mainly involving aggressive and destructive behaviour and disorders involving delinquency. It should be used for abnormal behaviour, in individuals of any age, which gives rise to social disapproval but which is not part of any other psychiatric condition. Minor emotional disturbances may also be present. To be included, the behaviour—as judged by its frequency, severity and type of associations with other symptoms—must be abnormal in its context. Disturbances of conduct are distinguished from an adjustment reaction by a longer duration and by a lack of close relationship in time and content to some stress. They differ from a personality disorder by the absence of deeply ingrained maladaptive patterns of behaviour present from adolescence or earlier.

Excludes: adjustment reaction with
           disturbance of conduct (309.3)
           drug dependence (304.-)
           dyssocial behaviour without
           manifest psychiatric disorder
           (V71.0)
           personality disorder with
           predominantly sociopathic or
           asocial manifestations (301.7)
           sexual deviations (302.-)

312.0 *Unsocialized disturbance of conduct*

Disorders characterized by behaviours such as defiance, disobedience, quarrelsomeness, aggression, destructive behaviour, tantrums, solitary stealing, lying, teasing, bullying and disturbed relationships with others. The defiance may sometimes take the form of sexual misconduct.

Unsocialized aggressive disorder

312.1 *Socialized disturbance of conduct*

Disorders in individuals who have acquired the values or behaviour of a delinquent peer group to whom they are loyal and with whom they characteristically steal, play truant, and stay out late at night. There may also be promiscuity.

Group delinquency

Excludes: gang activity without manifest psychiatric disorder (V71.0)

312.2 *Compulsive conduct disorder*

Disorder of conduct or delinquent act which is specifically compulsive in origin.

Kleptomania

312.3 *Mixed disturbance of conduct and emotions*

Disorders involving behaviours listed for 312.0 and 312.1 but in which there is also *considerable* emotional disturbance as shown for example by anxiety, misery or obsessive manifestations.

Neurotic delinquency

Excludes: compulsive conduct disorder (312.2)

312.8 *Other*

312.9 *Unspecified*

313 Disturbance of Emotions Specific to Childhood and Adolescence

Less well differentiated emotional disorders characteristic of the childhood period. Where the emotional disorder takes the form of a neurotic disorder described under 300.-, the appropriate 300.- coding should be made. This category differs from category 308.- in terms of longer duration and by the lack of close relationship in time and content to some stress.

Excludes: adjustment reaction (309.-)
masturbation, nail-biting, thumb-sucking and other isolated symptoms (307.-)

313.0 *With anxiety and fearfulness*

Ill-defined emotional disorders characteristic of childhood in which the main symptoms involve anxiety and fearfulness. Many cases of school refusal or elective mutism might be included here.

Overanxious reaction of childhood or adolescence

Excludes: abnormal separation anxiety (309.2)
anxiety states (300.0)
hospitalism in children (309.8)
phobic state (300.2)

313.1 *With misery and unhappiness*

Emotional disorders characteristic of childhood in which the main symptoms involve misery and unhappiness. There may also be eating and sleep disturbances.

Excludes: depressive neurosis (300.4)

313.2 *With sensitivity, shyness and social withdrawal*

Emotional disorders characteristic of childhood in which the main symptoms involve sensitivity, shyness, or social withdrawal. Some cases of elective mutism might be included here.

Withdrawing reaction of childhood or adolescence

Excludes: infantile autism (299.0)
schizoid personality (301.2)
schizophrenia (295.-)

313.3 *Relationship problems*

Emotional disorders characteristic of childhood in which the main symptoms involve relationship problems.

Sibling jealousy

Excludes: relationship problems associated with aggression, destruction or other forms of conduct disturbance (312.-)

313.8 *Other or mixed*

Many emotional disorders of childhood include several elements but whenever possible a specific coding under .0, .1, .2 or .3 should be made according to the *preponderant* type of disturbance. The category of mixed disorders should only be used when there is such an admixture that this cannot be done.

313.9 *Unspecified*

314 Hyperkinetic Syndrome of Childhood

Disorders in which the essential features are short attention-span and distractibility. In early childhood the most striking symptom is disinhibited, poorly organized and poorly regulated extreme overactivity but in adolescence this may be replaced by underactivity. Impulsiveness, marked mood fluctuations and aggression are also common symptoms. Delays in the development of specific skills are often present and disturbed, poor relationships are common. If the hyperkinesis is symptomatic of an underlying disorder, code the underlying disorder instead.

314.0 *Simple disturbance of activity and attention*

Cases in which short attention span, distractibility, and overactivity are the main manifestations without significant disturbance of conduct or delay in specific skills.

Overactivity NOS

314.1 *Hyperkinesis with developmental delay*

Cases in which the hyperkinetic syndrome is associated with speech delay, clumsiness, reading difficulties or other delays in specific skills.

Developmental disorder of hyperkinesis

Use additional code to identify any associated neurological disorder

314.2 *Hyperkinetic conduct disorder*

Cases in which the hyperkinetic syndrome is associated with marked conduct disturbance but not developmental delay.

Hyperkinetic conduct disorder

Excludes: hyperkinesis with significant delays in specific skills (314.1)

314.8 *Other*

314.9 *Unspecified*

Hyperkinetic reaction of childhood or adolescence NOS
Hyperkinetic syndrome NOS

315 Specific Delays in Development

A group of disorders in which a specific delay in development is the main feature. In each case development is related to biological maturation but it is also influenced by nonbiological factors and the coding carries no aetiological implications.

Excludes: when due to a neurological disorder (320-389)

315.0 *Specific reading retardation*

Disorders in which the main feature is a serious impairment in the development of reading or spelling skills which is not explicable in terms of general intellectual retardation or of inadequate schooling. Speech or language difficulties, impaired right-left differentiation, perceptuo-motor problems, and coding difficulties are frequently associated. Similar problems are often present in other members of the family. Adverse psychosocial factors may be present.

Developmental dyslexia
Specific spelling difficulty

315.1 *Specific arithmetical retardation*

Disorders in which the main feature is a serious impairment in the development of arithmetical skills which is not explicable in terms of general intellectual retardation or of inadequate schooling.

Dyscalculia

315.2 *Other specific learning difficulties*

Disorders in which the main feature is a serious impairment in the development of other learning skills which are not explicable in terms of general intellectual retardation or of inadequate schooling.

Excludes: specific arithmetical retardation (315.1)
specific reading retardation (315.0)

315.3 *Developmental speech or language disorder*

Disorders in which the main feature is a serious impairment in the development of speech or language [syntax or semantics] which is not explicable in terms of general intellectual retardation. Most commonly there is a delay in the development of normal word-sound production resulting in defects of articulation. Omissions or substitutions of consonants are most frequent. There may also be a delay in the production of spoken language. Rarely, there is also a developmental delay in the comprehension of sounds. Includes cases in which delay is largely due to environmental privation.

Developmental aphasia
Dyslalia

Excludes: acquired aphasia (784.3)
elective mutism (309.8, 313.0 or 313.2)
lisping and lalling (307.9)
stammering and stuttering (307.0)

315.4 *Specific motor retardation*

Disorders in which the main feature is a serious impairment in the development of motor coordination which is not explicable in terms of general intellectual retardation. The clumsiness is commonly associated with perceptual difficulties.

Clumsiness syndrome
Dyspraxia syndrome

315.5 *Mixed development disorder*

A delay in the development of one specific skill [e.g., reading, arithmetic, speech or coordination] is frequently associated with lesser delays in other skills. When this occurs the coding should be made according to the skill most seriously impaired. The mixed category should be used only where the mixture of delayed skills is such that no one skill is preponderantly affected.

315.8 *Other*

315.9 *Unspecified*

Developmental disorder NOS

316 Psychic Factors Associated with Diseases Classified Elsewhere

Mental disturbances or psychic factors of any type thought to have played a major part in the aetiology of physical conditions, usually involving tissue damage, classified elsewhere. The mental disturbance is usually mild and non-specific and psychic factors [worry, fear, conflict, etc.] may be present without any overt psychiatric disorder. Use an additional code to identify the physical condition. In the rare instance that an overt psychiatric disorder is thought to have caused a physical condition, use a second additional code to record the psychiatric diagnosis.

Examples of the use of this category are:
psychogenic:
asthma 316 and 493.9
dermatitis 316 and 692.-
eczema 316 and 691.- or 692.-
gastric ulcer 316 and 531.-
mucous colitis 316 and 564.1
ulcerative colitis 316 and 556
urticaria 316 and 708.-
psychosocial dwarfism 316 and 259.4

Excludes: physical symptoms and physiological malfunctions, not involving tissue damage, of mental origin (306.-)

MENTAL RETARDATION (317-319)

A condition of arrested or incomplete development of mind which is especially characterized by subnormality of intelligence. The coding should be made on the individual's *current* level of functioning *without regard to its nature* or causation—such as psychosis, cultural deprivation, Down's syndrome etc. Where there is a specific cognitive handicap—such as in speech—the four-digit coding should be based on assessments of cognition *outside the area of specific handicap.* The assessment of intellectual level should be based on whatever information is available, including clinical evidence, adaptive behaviour and psychometric findings. The IQ levels given are based on a test with a mean of 100 and a standard deviation of 15—such as the Wechsler scales. They are provided only as a guide and should not be applied rigidly. Mental retardation often involves psychiatric disturbances and may often develop as a result of some physical disease or injury. In these cases, an additional code or codes should be used to identify any associated condition, psychiatric or physical. The Impairment and Handicap codes should also be consulted.

317 Mild Mental Retardation

Feeble-minded
High-grade defect
IQ 50-70
Mild mental subnormality
Moron

318 Other Specified Mental Retardation

318.0 *Moderate mental retardation*

Imbecile
IQ 35-49
Moderate mental subnormality

318.1 *Severe mental retardation*

IQ 20-34
Severe mental subnormality

318.2 *Profound mental retardation*

Idiocy
IQ under 20
Profound mental subnormality

319 Unspecified Mental Retardation

Mental deficiency NOS
Mental subnormality NOS

53.

National Institute of Mental Health

STATISTICS ON MENTAL DISORDERS

TABLE 53-1
Number, Percent Distribution, and Rate per 100,000 Civilian Population* of Additions to State and
County Mental Hospitals, by Diagnosis and Age: United States, 1969, 1974, and 1979

Diagnosis* and Age ‡	1969	1974	1979	1969	1974	1979	1969	1974	1979
	Number			Percent Distribution			Rate		
All diagnoses, total	458,918	434,345	380,371	100.0	100.0	100.0	231.6	206.2	171.6
Less than 18	27,973	26,141	22,863	6.1	6.0	6.0	40.1	38.3	35.5
18–44	250,179	258,578	247,605	54.5	59.5	65.1	369.2	335.1	280.8
45–64	136,640	117,537	87,408	29.8	27.1	23.0	332.9	271.2	197.3
65+	44,126	32,089	22,495	9.6	7.4	5.9	226.0	147.2	90.6
Mental retardation, total	13,163	13,508	9,446	2.9	3.1	2.5	6.6	6.4	4.3
Less than 18	2,589	2,500	1,691	0.6	0.6	0.4	3.7	3.7	2.6
18–44	8,023	8,546	6,159	1.7	2.0	1.6	11.8	11.1	7.0
45–64	2,233	2,128	1,341	0.5	0.5	0.4	5.4	4.9	3.0
65+	318	334	255	0.1	0.1	0.1	1.6	1.5	1.0
Alcohol and drug, total	109,275	122,292	103,751	23.8	28.2	27.3	55.2	58.1	46.8
Less than 18	958	1,616	1,937	0.2	0.4	0.5	1.4	2.4	3.0
18–44	56,218	69,814	63,053	12.3	16.1	16.6	83.0	90.5	71.5
45–64	48,029	46,242	34,795	10.5	10.6	9.1	117.0	106.7	78.5
65+	4,070	4,620	3,966	0.9	1.1	1.0	20.8	21.2	16.0
Organic brain syndrome, total	50,562	30,011	20,020	11.0	6.9	5.3	25.5	14.2	9.0
Less than 18	1,571	846	609	0.3	0.2	0.2	2.3	1.2	0.9
18–44	8,720	6,115	4,879	1.9	1.4	1.3	12.9	7.9	5.5
45–64	11,406	7,256	4,838	2.5	1.7	1.3	27.8	16.7	10.9
65+	28,865	15,794	9,694	6.3	3.6	2.5	147.9	72.5	39.1
Affective (formerly depression), total	47,146	42,649	42,249	10.3	9.8	11.1	23.8	20.2	19.1
Less than 18	974	1,034	1,280	0.2	0.2	0.3	1.4	1.5	2.0
18–44	22,395	24,244	26,950	4.9	5.6	7.1	33.0	31.4	30.6
45–64	20,042	14,231	11,481	4.4	3.3	3.0	48.8	32.8	25.9
65+	3,735	3,140	2,538	0.8	0.7	0.7	19.1	14.4	10.2
Schizophrenia, total	137,007	139,832	136,870	29.9	32.2	36.0	69.2	66.4	61.7
Less than 18	4,948	3,558	3,086	1.1	0.8	0.8	7.1	5.2	4.8
18–44	94,735	98,744	104,310	20.6	22.7	27.4	139.8	128.0	118.3
45–64	34,384	33,351	26,126	7.5	7.7	6.9	83.8	77.0	59.0
65+	2,940	4,179	3,348	0.6	1.0	0.9	15.1	19.2	13.5
Other psychoses, total	8.854	3,913	4,217	1.9	0.9	1.1	4.5	1.9	1.9
Less than 18	449	64	95	0.1	0.0	0.0	0.6	0.1	0.1
18–44	4,685	1,211	2,139	1.0	0.3	0.6	6.9	1.6	2.4
45–64	3,058	2,015	1,419	0.7	0.5	0.4	7.4	4.6	3.2
65+	662	623	564	0.1	0.1	0.1	3.4	2.9	2.3

continued

TABLE 53-1 continued

Diagnosis* and Age‡	1969	1974	1979	1969	1974	1979	1969	1974	1979
		Number		Percent	Distribution			Rate	
Other neuroses, total	12,452	6,639	3,292	2.7	1.5	0.9	6.3	3.2	1.5
Less than 18	719	356	181	0.2	0.1	0.0	1.0	0.5	0.3
18–44	8,136	4,364	2,310	1.8	1.0	0.6	12.0	5.7	2.6
45–64	3,142	1,638	654	0.7	0.4	0.2	7.7	3.8	1.5
65+	455	281	147	0.1	0.1	0.0	2.3	1.3	0.6
Personality disorders, total	31,678	24,728	17,302	6.9	5.7	4.5	16.0	11.7	7.8
Less than 18	3,507	2,042	1,717	0.8	0.5	0.5	5.0	3.0	2.7
18–44	22,613	19,214	14,128	4.9	4.4	3.7	33.4	24.9	16.0
45–64	5,269	3,169	1,300	1.1	0.7	0.3	12.8	7.3	2.9
65+	289	303	157	0.1	0.1	0.0	1.5	1.4	0.6
Other, total	48,781	50,773	43,224	10.6	11.7	11.4	24.6	24.1	19.5
Less than 18	12,258	14,125	12,267	2.7	3.3	3.2	17.6	20.7	19.0
18–44	24,654	26,326	23,677	5.4	6.1	6.2	36.4	34.1	26.8
45–64	9,077	7,507	5,454	2.0	1.7	1.4	22.1	17.3	12.3
65+	2,792	2,815	1,826	0.6	0.6	0.5	14.3	12.9	7.4

Notes: The data in this table, which are provided by the State agencies of mental health through the *Annual Census of Patient Characteristics, State and County Mental Hospital Inpatient Services, Additions and Resident Patients,* are reported for the fiscal year used by the particular State. For most States, it is the year ending June 30. These data will differ slightly from numbers of inpatient additions shown in table 2.3 (not reprinted here) that are based on responses to the *Inventory of Mental Health Facilities* by individual State and county mental hospitals, which are given the option to report on either a calendar- or fiscal-year basis. Information on the "State" hospital in Puerto Rico is excluded. Definitions of facility types and measures used are given in the appendix.

*The populations used in the calculations of these rates were obtained by averaging populations (provided by the Bureau of the Census and published in Series P-25 publications) for successive years as of July 1. For example, the population for 1979 was obtained by averaging the civilian populations as of July 1, 1978 and July 1, 1979.

†*Diagnostic Classification* The diagnostic classification can be found in *Diagnostic and Statistical Manual of Mental Disorders* (Second Edition), American Psychiatric Association, 1968. The codes corresponding to the diagnostic categories shown in the tables are as follows:

Diagnostic Groupings	Diagnostic Codes
Mental retardation	310–315
Alcohol and drug disorders	291, 303, 309.13; 294.3, 304, 309.14
Organic brain and syndromes (excl. alcoholism and drug)	290, 292, 293, 294 (except 294.3), 309.0, 309.2-309.9
Affective (formerly depression)	296, 298.0, 300.4
Schizophrenia	295
Other psychoses	297, 298.1-298.9, 299
Other neuroses	300.0-300.3, 300.5-300.9
Personality disorders	301
Other:	
Pre-adult disorders	307.0-307.2, 308
Other mental disorders	302, 305, 306, 307.3-307.4
Social maladjustment	316-317
No mental disorder	318
Undiagnosed	Includes only patients who have been admitted for suspected mental disorders, but for whom a diagnosis has not yet been established.

‡*Age* Additions during year. Age is reported as of the last birthday prior to addition.

SOURCES: (1969, 1974, 1979): National Institute of Mental Health. Unpublished data from the Survey and Reports Branch, Division of Biometry and Epidemiology.

TABLE 53–2
Number, Percent, Distribution, and Rate per 100,000 Civilian Population* of Resident Patients
in State and County Mental Hospitals at End of Year, by Diagnosis and Age:
United States, 1969, 1974, and 1979

Diagnosis and Age †	1969	1974	1979	1969	1974	1979	1969	1974	1979
	Number			Percent Distribution			Rate		
All diagnoses, total	369,969	215,586	139,546	100.0	100.0	100.0	185.8	101.9	625.9
Less than 18	12,841	10,036	7,245	3.5	4.7	5.2	18.4	14.8	11.3
18–44	101,158	79,841	53,866	27.3	37.0	38.6	147.9	102.2	60.3
45–64	144,550	71,045	38,123	39.1	33.0	27.3	349.6	163.4	86.0
65+	111,420	54,664	40,312	30.1	25.4	28.9	566.2	247.8	160.4
Mental retardation, total	31,699	19,699	11,386	8.6	9.1	8.2	15.9	9.3	5.1
Less than 18	2,065	1,542	829	0.6	0.7	0.6	3.0	2.3	1.3
18–44	12,817	9,565	5,872	3.5	4.4	4.2	18.7	12.2	6.6
45–64	12,867	6,521	3,245	3.5	3.0	2.3	31.1	15.0	7.3
65+	3,950	2,071	1,440	1.1	1.0	1.0	20.1	9.4	5.7
Alcohol and drug, total	23,411	22,602	8,980	6.3	10.5	6.4	11.8	10.7	4.0
Less than 18	162	304	248	0.0	0.1	0.2	0.2	0.4	0.4
18–44	6,395	10,433	3,887	1.7	4.8	2.8	9.4	13.3	4.3
45–64	11,971	9,278	3,168	3.2	4.3	2.3	28.9	21.3	7.1
65+	4,883	2,587	1,677	1.3	1.2	1.2	24.8	11.7	6.7
Organic brain syndrome, total	77,752	34,706	23,127	21.0	16.1	16.6	39.0	16.4	10.4
Less than 18	1,149	570	284	0.3	0.3	0.2	1.6	0.8	0.4
18–44	9,009	4,506	2,934	2.4	2.1	2.1	13.2	5.8	3.3
45–64	20,096	8,663	5,142	5.4	4.0	3.7	48.6	19.9	11.6
65+	47,498	20,967	14,767	12.8	9.7	10.6	241.4	95.0	58.8
Affective (formerly depression), total	23,688	12,803	8,592	6.4	5.9	6.2	11.9	6.0	3.9
Less than 18	234	237	276	0.1	0.1	0.2	0.3	0.3	0.4
18–44	3,544	4,034	2,967	1.0	1.9	2.1	5.2	5.2	3.3
45–64	10,103	4,461	2,491	2.7	2.1	1.8	24.4	10.3	5.6
65+	9,807	4,071	2,858	2.7	1.9	2.0	49.8	18.5	11.4
Schizophrenia, total	179,644	98,595	69,631	48.6	45.8	49.8	90.2	46.6	312.3
Less than 18	3,380	1,966	1,325	0.9	0.9	0.9	4.8	2.9	2.1
18–44	56,594	38,564	29,909	15.3	17.9	21.4	82.8	49.3	33.5
45–64	80,570	36,804	21,251	21.8	17.1	15.2	194.8	84.6	47.9
65+	39,100	21,261	17,146	10.6	9.9	12.3	198.7	96.4	68.2
Other psychoses, total	8,186	2,591	1,694	2.2	1.2	1.2	4.1	1.2	0.8
Less than 18	285	17	23	0.1	0.0	0.0	0.4	0.0	0.0
18–44	1,629	373	376	0.4	0.2	0.3	2.4	0.5	0.4
45–64	2,895	848	402	0.8	0.4	0.3	7.0	2.0	0.9
65+	3,377	1,353	893	0.9	0.6	0.6	17.2	6.1	3.6
Other neuroses, total	2,537	1,652	647	0.7	0.8	0.5	1.3	0.8	0.3
Less than 18	228	105	47	0.1	0.0	0.0	0.3	0.2	0.1
18–44	923	864	325	0.2	0.4	0.2	1.3	1.1	0.4
45–64	946	468	153	0.3	0.2	0.1	2.3	1.1	0.3
65+	440	215	122	0.1	0.1	0.1	2.2	1.0	0.5

continued

TABLE 53-2 continued

Diagnosis and Age †	1969	1974	1979	1969	1974	1979	1969	1974	1979
	Number			Percent Distribution			Rate		
Personality disorders,									
total	7,737	5,813	3,356	2.1	2.7	2.4	3.9	2.7	1.5
Less than 18	1,057	571	508	0.3	0.3	0.4	1.5	0.8	0.8
18–44	4,607	4,149	2,326	1.2	1.9	1.7	6.7	5.3	2.6
45–64	1,609	845	365	0.4	0.4	0.3	3.9	1.9	0.8
65+	464	248	157	0.1	0.1	0.1	2.4	1.1	0.6
Other, total	15,315	17,125	12,133	4.1	7.9	8.7	7.7	8.1	5.4
Less than 18	4,281	4,724	3,705	1.2	2.2	2.7	6.1	7.0	5.8
18–44	5,640	7,353	5,270	1.5	3.4	3.8	8.2	9.4	5.9
45–64	3,493	3,157	1,906	0.9	1.5	1.4	8.4	7.3	4.3
65+	1,901	1,891	1,252	0.5	0.9	0.9	9.7	8.6	5.0

Notes: The data in this table, which are provided by the State agencies of mental health through the *Annual Census of Patient Characteristics, State and County Mental Hospital Inpatient Services, Additions and Resident Patients,* are reported for the fiscal year used by the particular State. For most States, it is the year ending June 30. These data will differ slightly from numbers of inpatient additions shown in table 2.7 (not reprinted here) that are based on responses to the *Inventory of Mental Health Facilities* by individual State and county mental hospitals, which are given the option to report on either a calendar- or fiscal-year basis. Information on the "State" hospital in Puerto Rico is excluded. Definitions of facility types and measures used are given in the appendix.

*The populations used in the calculations of these rates are estimates of the U.S. civilian populations (provided by the Bureau of the Census and published in Series P-25 publications) as of July 1 for each respective year.

† *Diagnostic Classification* The diagnostic classification can be found in *Diagnostic and Statistical Manual of Mental Disorders* (Second Edition), American Psychiatric Association, 1968. The codes corresponding to the diagnostic categories shown in the tables are as follows:

Diagnostic Groupings	Diagnostic Codes
Mental retardation	310-315
Alcohol and drug disorders	291, 303, 309.13; 294.3, 304, 309.14
Organic brain syndromes (excl. alcoholism and drug)	290, 292, 293, 294 (except 294.3), 309.0, 309.2-309.9
Affective (formerly depression)	296, 298.0, 300.4
Schizophrenia	295
Other psychoses	297, 298.1-298.9, 299
Other neuroses	300.0-300.3, 300.5-300.9
Personality disorders	301
Other:	
Pre-adult disorders	307.0-307.2, 308
Other mental disorders	302, 305, 306, 307.3-307.4
Social maladjustment	316-317
No mental disorder	318
Undiagnosed	Includes only patients who have been admitted for suspected mental disorders, but for whom a diagnosis has not yet been established.

‡ *Age* Additions during year. Age is reported as of the last birthday at end of reported year.

SOURCES: (1969, 1974, 1979): National Institute of Mental Health. Unpublished data from the Survey and Reports Branch, Division of Biometry and Epidemiology.

TABLE 53-3

Number and Percent of Discharges from Non-Federal Short-Stay Hospitals, by No Diagnosis, Any Diagnosis, and Primary and/or Secondary Diagnosis* of Mental Disorder: United States, 1975, 1977, and 1980

Type of Discharge by Diagnosis	1975		1977		1980	
	Number (in 000s)	Percent	Number (in 000s)	Percent	Number (in 000s)	Percent
All discharges	34,043	100.0	35,902	100.0	37,832	100.0
No diagnosis of mental disorder	31,509	92.6	33,139	92.3	34,701	91.7
Any diagnosis of mental disorder	2,534	7.4	2,763	7.7	3,131	8.3
Primary diagnosis of mental disorder	1,494	4.4	1,625	4.5	1,692	4.5
Primary only	1,030	3.0	1,128	3.1	1,183	3.1
Primary and secondary	464	1.4	497	1.4	509	1.3
Secondary only	1,040	3.1	1,139	3.2	1,438	3.8

*For the purpose of brevity, the terms "primary diagnosis" and "secondary diagnosis" are substituted in this table for "first-listed diagnosis" and "second-or-later-listed diagnosis."

SOURCE: National Institute of Mental Health. Compiled from unpublished data from the National Hospital Discharge Survey.

TABLE 53-4

Number and Percent Distribution of Mental Disorder Discharges from Non-Federal Short-Stay Hospitals, by Sex and Average Length of Stay: United States, 1980

First-Listed Diagnosis	Number of Discharges						Average Length of Stay in Days		
	Total		Male		Female				
	Number (in 000s)	Percent	Number (in 000s)	Percent	Number (in 000s)	Percent	Total	Male	Female
All first-listed diagnoses	1,692	100.0	855	100.0	807	100.0	11.6	10.9	12.2
Mental retardation	12	0.7	5	0.6	7	0.9	11.2	7.5	13.9
Alcohol and drug related disorders	602	35.6	455	51.5	147	18.2	9.6	9.5	9.8
Organic brain syndromes other than alcohol and drug related	124	7.3	55	6.2	69	8.5	13.4	12.9	13.7
Affective disorders	325	19.2	103	11.6	222	27.5	14.1	13.1	14.6
Schizophrenia and related disorders	183	10.8	96	10.9	86	10.7	16.1	15.7	16.7
Other psychoses	53	3.1	24	2.8	28	3.5	13.0	11.2	14.6
Neuroses other than depressive	133	7.8	46	5.1	87	10.8	6.2	6.4	6.0
Personality disorders	54	3.2	25	2.8	29	3.6	13.5	11.7	15.1
Pre-adult disorders	10	0.6	7	0.8	*	*	18.5	21.3	*
Other mental disorders	197	11.7	68	7.7	129	16.0	10.2	10.6	10.0

*Does not meet standards of reliability or precision.

SOURCE: National Institute of Mental Health. Compiled from unpublished data from the National Hospital Discharge Survey.

TABLE 53–5

Number and Percent Distribution of Mental Disorder Discharges from Non-Federal Short-Stay Hospitals, by First-Listed Diagnosis and Age: United States, 1980

First-listed diagnosis	Total		Under 15 Years		15 to 44 Years		45 to 64 Years		65 Years and Over	
	Number (in 000s)	Percent	Number (in 000s)	Percent	Number (in 000s)	Percent	Number (in 000s)	Percent	Number (in 000s)	Percent
All first-listed diagnosis	1,692	100.0	46	100.0	954	100.0	450	100.0	243	100.0
Alcohol and drug related disorders	602	35.6	7	14.7	334	35.0	216	48.0	45	18.6
Organic brain syndromes other than alcohol and drug related	124	7.3	*	*	17	1.8	17	3.9	86	35.6
Affective disorders	325	19.2	*	*	183	19.1	91	20.3	48	19.7
Schizophrenia and related disorders	183	10.8	*	*	142	14.9	31	6.9	8	3.2
Other psychoses	53	3.1	*	*	23	2.4	12	2.6	18	7.3
Neuroses other than depressive	133	7.8	7	14.2	79	8.3	35	7.9	12	4.8
Personality disorders	54	3.2	*	*	46	4.9	5	1.2	*	*
Pre-adult disorders	10	0.6	7	14.2	*	*	–	–	–	–
Other mental disorders	210	12.4	16	34.7	126	13.2	39	8.7	25	10.5

Note: Asterisk (*) = does not meet standards of reliability or precision.

Short dash (–) = quantity or percent zero.

SOURCE: National Institute of Mental Health. Compiled from unpublished data from the National Hospital Discharge Survey.

TABLE 53–6

Average Length of Stay of Mental Disorder Discharges from Non-Federal Short-Stay Hospitals, by First-Listed Diagnosis and Age: United States, 1980

First-Listed Diagnosis		Length of Stay in Days by Age			
	Total	Under 15 Years	15 to 44 Years	45 to 64 Years	65 Years and Over
All first-listed diagnoses	11.5	13.5	11.0	11.3	13.7
Mental retardation	11.2	*	11.6	*	*
Alcohol and drug related disorders	9.6	6.5	9.5	9.9	9.5
Organic brain syndromes other than alcohol and drug related	13.4	*	10.0	10.9	14.9
Affective disorders	14.1	*	12.0	15.5	18.0
Schizophrenia and related disorders	16.1	*	16.1	15.1	17.9
Other psychoses	13.0	*	11.9	15.1	13.4
Neuroses other than depressive	6.2	4.2	6.2	6.6	6.0
Personality disorders	13.5	*	12.8	12.7	*
Pre-adult disorders	18.5	17.0	*	*	–
Other mental disorders	10.2	13.1	10.1	9.1	11.5

Note: Asterisk (*) = does not meet standards of reliability or precision.

Short dash (–) = quantity or percent zero.

SOURCE: National Institute of Mental Health. Compiled from unpublished data from the National Hospital Discharge Survey.

TABLE 53-7

Number and Percent of Discharges from Non-Federal Short-Stay Hospitals, by Second-to Seventh-Listed
Diagnoses of Mental Disorder: United States, 1980

Second-to Seventh-Listed Diagnosis	*All Cases, without regard to First-Listed Diagnosis*		*First-Listed Diagnosis of Mental Disorder*		*First-Listed Diagnosis other than Mental Disorder*	
	Number (in 000s)	*Percent*	*Number (in 000s)*	*Percent*	*Number (in 000s)*	*Percent*
All diagnoses	1,948	100.0	509	100.0	1,438	100.0
Mental retardation	54	2.8	10	2.0	44	3.0
Alcohol and drug related disorders	562	28.8	245	48.1	317	22.0
Organic brain syndromes other than alcohol and drug related	328	16.9	17	3.3	311	21.7
Affective disorders	234	12.0	39	7.6	195	13.5
Schizophrenia and related disorders	42	2.2	12	2.4	30	2.1
Other psychoses	71	3.7	12	2.3	60	4.1
Neuroses other than depressive	271	13.9	41	8.0	230	16.0
Personality disorders	88	4.5	62	12.1	26	1.8
Pre-adult disorders	12	0.6	6	1.2	6	0.4
Other mental disorders	286	14.7	66	12.9	221	15.3

SOURCE: National Institute of Mental Health. Compiled from unpublished data from the National Hospital
Discharge Survey.

References to Introductions

Abraham, K. Notes on the psychoanalytic investigation and treatment of manic-depressive insanity and allied conditions (1911). In *Selected papers of Karl Abraham.* New York: Basic Books, 1953. (a)

Abraham, K. The first pregenital stage of the libido (1916). In *Selected papers of Karl Abraham.* New York: Basic Books, 1953. (b)

Abraham, K. A short study of the development of the libido viewed in the light of mental disorders (1924). In *Selected papers of Karl Abraham.* New York: Basic Books, 1953. (c)

Abraham, K. *Selected papers.* New York: Basic Books, 1968.

Abramson, L. Y., Garber, J., & Seligman, M. E. P. Learned helplessness in humans: An attributional analysis. In J. Garber & M. E. P. Seligman (Eds.), *Human helplessness: Theory and applications.* New York: Academic Press, 1980.

Adler, A. *The neurotic constitution.* New York: Dodd & Mead, 1926.

Adler, A. *The practice and theory of individual psychology.* New York: Harcourt, Brace, 1927; London: Routledge & Kegan Paul, 1929.

Adler, A. *Social interest: A challenge to mankind.* London: Faber & Faber, 1938; New York: Putnam's, 1939.

Adler, A. *The science of living.* New York: Anchor, 1969.

Adler, K. A. Depression in the light of individual psychology. *Journal of Individual Psychology,* 1961, **17,** 56–67.

Adler, K. A. Life style, gender role, and the symptom of homosexuality. *Journal of Individual Psychology,* 1967, **23,** 67–78.

Agras, W. S., & Kraemer, H. C. The treatment of anorexia nervosa: Do different treatments have different outcomes? *Psychiatric Annals,* 1983, **13,** 928–935.

Aguilera, D. C., & Messick, J. M. *Crisis intervention: Theory and methodology.* St. Louis: C. V. Mosby, 1974.

Akiskal, H. S., & McKinney, W. T., Jr. Psychiatry and pseudopsychiatry. *Archives of General Psychiatry,* 1973, **28,** 367–373.

Akiskal, H. S., & McKinney, W. T., Jr. Overview of recent research in depression: Integration of ten conceptual models into a comprehensive clinical frame. *Archives of General Psychiatry,* 1975, **32,** 285–305.

Akiskal, H. S., & Tashjian, R. Affective Disorders: II. Recent Advances in Laboratory and Pathogenic Approaches. Hospital and Community Psychiatry, 1983, 34, 822-830.

Ainsworth, M. D. S., & Bell, S. M. Some contemporary patterns of mother-infant interaction in the feeding situation. In J. A. Ambrose (Ed.), *Stimulation in early infancy.* London: Academic Press, 1969.

Albee, G. W. *Mental health manpower trends.* New York: Basic Books, 1959.

Albee, G. W. Foreword. In D. C. Aguilera & J. M. Messick, *Crisis intervention: Theory and methodology.* St. Louis: C. V. Mosby, 1974.

Albee, G. W. The answer is prevention. *Psychology Today,* 1985, **19,** 60-62, 64.

Albert, R. S., Brigante, T. R., & Chase, M. The psychopathic personality: A content analysis of the concept. *Journal of General Psychology,* 1959, **60,** 17–28.

Alexander, F. Panel: Experimental study of psychophysiological correlations. Paper delivered at the Annual Meeting of the American Psychosomatic Society. Atlantic City, N.J.: May, 1959.

Alexander, F. The development of psychosomatic medicine. *Psychosomatic Medicine,* 1962, **24,** 13–23.

Alexander, F. Alcohol and behavior disorder-alcoholism. In S. P. Lucia (Ed.), *Alcohol and civilization.* New York: McGraw-Hill, 1963.

Alexander, F., Flagg, G. W., Foster, S., Clemens, T., & Blahd, E. Experimental studies of emotional stress: I. Hyperthyroidism. *Psychosomatic Medicine,* 1961, **23,** 104–114.

Alexander, F., & French, T. M. *Psychoanalytic therapy.* New York: Ronald Press, 1946.

Allen, C. *Homosexuality.* London: Staples Press, 1958.

Allinsmith, W., & Goethals, G. W. Cultural factors in mental health: Anthropological perspective. *Review of Educational Research,* 1956, **26,** 429–450.

Allport, G. W. *Personality: A psychological interpretation.* New York: Holt, 1937.

Allport, G. W. *Pattern and growth in personality.* New York: Holt, Rinehart & Winston, 1961.

American Medical Association. Committee on Alcoholism. *Manual on alcoholism.* Chicago: AMA, 1967.

American Psychiatric Association. *Diag-nostic and statistical manual of mental disorders.* 3rd ed. Washington, D.C.: American Psychiatric Association, 1980.

Andreev, B. V. *Sleep therapy in the neuroses.* New York: Consultants Bureau, 1960.

Angyal, A. *Neurosis and treatment: A holistic theory.* New York: Wiley, 1965.

Ansbacher, H. L. The structure of individual psychology. In B. B. Wolman (Ed.), *Scientific psychology.* New York: Basic Books, 1965.

Arbuckle, D. S. (Ed.) *Counseling and psychotherapy: An overview.* New York: McGraw-Hill, 1967.

Arieti, S. Schizophrenia: The manifest symptomatology, the psychodynamic and formal mechanisms. In S. Arieti (Ed.), *American handbook of psychiatry,* Vol. 1. New York: Basic Books, 1959.

Arieti, S. *American handbook of psychiatry.* New York: Basic Books, 1959–1966. 3 vols.

Arieti, S. Etiological considerations of schizophrenia. In S. C. Scher and H. R. Davis (Eds.), *The out-patient treatment of schizophrenia.* New York: Grune & Stratton, 1960.

Arieti, S. *The intrapsychic self: Feeling, cognition, and creativity in health and mental illness.* New York: Basic Books, 1967.

Arieti, S. *Interpretation of schizophrenia 1955,* 2nd ed. New York: Robert Brunner, 1974.

Arieti, S., & Meth, J. M. Rare, unclassifiable, collective, and exotic psychotic syndromes. In S. Arieti (Ed.), *American handbook of psychiatry.* Vol. 1. New York: Basic Books, 1959.

Artiss, K. L. *Milieu therapy in schizophrenia.* New York: Grune & Stratton, 1962.

Astrup, C. *Schizophrenia: Conditional reflex studies.* Springfield, Ill.: Charles C Thomas, 1962.

Astrup, C., & Noreik, K. *Functional psychoses: Diagnostic and prognostic models.* Springfield, Ill.: Charles C Thomas, 1966.

Auerback, A. (Ed.), *Schizophrenia: An integrated approach.* New York: Ronald Press, 1959.

Ausubel, D. P. *Drug addiction: Physiological,*

psychological, and sociological aspects. New York: Random House, 1958.

Ausubel, D. P. Causes and types of narcotic addiction: A psychosocial view. *Psychiatric Quarterly,* 1961, **35,** 523–531.

Axelrod, J. Neurotransmitters. In R. F. Thompson (Ed.), *Progress in psychobiology.* San Francisco: W. H. Freeman, 1976.

Bandura, A. Behavioral psychotherapy. *Scientific American,* 1967, **216,** 78–86.

Bandura, A. Modelling approaches to the modification of phobic disorders. In R. Porter (Ed.), *The role of learning in psychotherapy.* London: J. & A. Churchill, 1968. (a)

Bandura, A. A social learning interpretation of psychological dysfunctions. In P. London and D. Rosenhan (Eds.), *Foundations of abnormal psychology.* New York: Holt, Rinehart & Winston, 1968. (b)

Bandura, W. *Principles of behavior modification.* New York: Holt, Rinehart & Winston, 1969.

Bandura, A. Psychotherapy based upon modeling principles. In A. E. Bergin & S. L. Garfield (Eds.), *Handbook of psychotherapy and behavior change: An empirical analysis.* New York: Wiley, 1971.

Bandura, A. Self-efficacy: Toward a unifying theory of behavior change. *Psychological Review,* 1977, **84,** 191–215.

Barker, J. C. The medical aspects of sexual perversion. In W. A. R. Thomson (Ed.), *Sex and its problems.* Edinburgh: Livingstone, 1968.

Barron, F. Toward a positive definition of psychological health. Paper read before the American Psychological Association, 1955.

Bart, P. B. The sociology of depression. In P. M. Roman & T. M. Harrison (Eds.), *Explorations in psychiatric sociology.* Philadelphia: F. A. Davis, 1974.

Baruk, H. *Patients are people like us.* New York: William Morrow, 1977.

Batchelor, I. R. C. (Ed.). Affective reaction types. In D. Henderson & R. D. Gillespie, *Textbook of psychiatry for students and practitioners.* 10th ed. London: Oxford University Press, 1969. Pp. 210–245.

Bateson, G., Jackson, D. D., Haley, J., &

Weakland, J. Toward a theory of schizophrenia. *Behavioral Science,* 1956, **1,** 251–264.

Beck, A. T. Thinking and depression. *Archives of General Psychiatry,* 1963, **9,** 324–333.

Beck, A. T. Thinking and depression: II. Theory and therapy. *Archives of General Psychiatry,* 1964, **10,** 561–571.

Beck, A. T. *Depression: Causes and treatment.* Philadelphia: University of Pennsylvania Press, 1967.

Beck, A. T. The development of depression: A cognitive model. In R. J. Friedman & M. M. Katz (Eds.), *The psychology of depression: Contemporary theory and research.* New York: Wiley, 1974.

Beck, A. T. *Cognitive therapy and the emotional disorders.* New York: International Universities, 1976.

Beck, A. T., Rush, A. J., Shaw, B. S., & Emery, G. *Cognitive therapy of depression.* New York: Guilford Press, 1979.

Beck, A. T., Sethi, B. B., & Tuthill, R. W. Childhood bereavement and adult depression. *Archives of General Psychiatry,* 1963, **9,** 295–302.

Beck, S. J. *Psychological processes in the schizophrenic adaptation.* New York: Grune & Stratton, 1965.

Becker, J. *Affective disorders.* Morristown, N.J.: General Learning, 1977.

Becker, W. C. The process-reactive distinction: A key to the problem of schizophrenia. *Journal of Nervous and Mental Disease,* 1959, **129,** 442–449.

Beier, E. G. *The silent language of psychotherapy: Social reinforcement of unconscious processes.* Hawthorne, N.Y.: Aldine Publishing, 1966.

Bell, A. P., & Weinberg, M. S. *Homosexualities.* New York: Simon and Schuster, 1978.

Bellak, L. A multiple-factor psychosomatic theory of schizophrenia. *Psychiatric Quarterly,* 1949, **23,** 738–755.

Bellak, L. Toward a unified theory of schizophrenia: An elaboration of the multiple-factor psychosomatic theory of schizophrenia. *Journal of Nervous and Mental Disease,* 1955, **12,** 60–66.

Bellak, L. *et al. Manic-depressive psychosis*

and allied conditions. New York: Grune & Stratton, 1952.

Bender, L. Childhood schizophrenia. *American Journal of Orthopsychiatry*, 1947, **17**, 40–56.

Bender, L. Childhood schizophrenia. *Psychiatric Quarterly*, 1953, **27**, 663–687. (a)

Bender, L. Evidences from studies of childhood schizophrenia. *Archives of Neurology and Psychiatry*, 1953, **70**, 535. (b)

Bender, L. Twenty years of clinical research on schizophrenic children, with special reference to those under six years of age. In G. Caplan (Ed.), *Emotional problems of early childhood*. New York: Basic Books, 1955.

Benedek, T. F. Sexual functions in women and their disturbance. In S. Arieti (Ed.), *American handbook of psychiatry*. New York: Basic Books, 1959.

Benedict, P. K., & Jacks, I. Mental illness in primitive societies. *Psychiatry*, 1954, **17**, 337–389.

Berenson, B. G., & Carkhuff, R. R. (Eds.), *Sources of gain in counseling and psychotherapy: Readings and commentary*. New York: Holt, Rinehart & Winston, 1967.

Bergin, A. E., & S. L. Garfield (Eds.), *Handbook of psychotherapy and behavior change: An empirical analysis*. New York: Wiley, 1971.

Bergler, E. *Homosexuality: Disease or way of life?* New York: Hill & Wang, 1956.

Berne, E. *Transactional analysis in psychotherapy: A systematic individual and social psychiatry*. New York: Grove Press, 1961.

Berne, E. *The structure and dynamics of organizations and groups*. New York: Lippincott, 1963.

Berne, E. *Games people play: The psychology of human relationships*. New York: Grove Press, 1964.

Bernstein, A. The psychoanalytic technique. In B. B. Wolman (Ed.), *Handbook of clinical psychology*. New York: McGraw-Hill, 1965.

Bettelheim, B. Joey: A "mechanical boy." *Scientific American*, 1959, **200**, 116–127.

Bettelheim, B. *The empty fortress: Infantile autism and the birth of the self.* New York: Free Press, 1967.

Bibring, E. The mechanism of depression. In P. Greenacre (Ed.), *Affective disorders*. New York: International Universities, 1953, 1965.

Binswanger, L. Existential analysis and psychotherapy. In Frieda Fromm-Reichmann and J. L. Moreno (Eds.), *Progress in psychotherapy*. New York: Grune & Stratton, 1956.

Binswanger, L. The existential analysis school of thought. In R. May, E. Angel, and H. F. Ellenberger (Eds.), *Existence: A new dimension in psychiatry and psychology*. New York: Basic Books, 1958. (a)

Binswanger, L. The case of Ellen West. In R. May, E. Angel, and H. F. Ellenberger (Eds.), *Existence: A new dimension in psychiatry and psychology*. New York: Basic Books, 1958. (b)

Binswanger, L. *Being-in-the-world*. New York: Basic Books, 1963.

Bion, W. R. Differentiation of the psychotic from the non-psychotic personalities. *International Journal of Psychoanalysis*, 1957, **38**, 266–275.

Bion, W. R. *Experiences in groups*. New York: Basic Books, 1961.

Bleuler, E. *The theory of schizophrenic negativism*. New York: Journal of Nervous and Mental Disease Publishing, 1912.

Bleuler, E. *Textbook of psychiatry*. New York: Macmillan, 1924.

Bleuler, E. *Dementia praecox or the group of schizophrenias*. New York: International Universities Press, 1950.

Bliss, E. L. (Ed.) *Roots of behavior*. New York: Hoeber, 1962.

Block, M. A. Opportunities and limitations in the treatment of alcoholics by the internist. In J. Hirsh (Ed.), *Opportunities in the treatment of alcoholics*. Springfield, Ill.: Charles C Thomas, 1967.

Bolles, M., & Goldstein, K. A study of the impairment of "abstract behavior" in schizophrenic patients. *Psychiatric Quarterly*, 1938, **12**, 42–65.

Böök, J. A. A genetic and neuropsychiatric investigation of a North Swedish population: I. Psychoses. *Acta Genetica et Statistica Medica*, 1953, **4**, 1–100. (a)

Böök, J. A. Schizophrenia as a gene mutation. *Acta Genetica et Statistica Medica*, 1953, **4**, 133–139. (b)

Böök, J. A. Genetical etiology in mental illness. *Millbank Memorial Fund Quarterly*, 1960, **38**, 193–212.

Böök, J. A., Fraccaro, M., & Lindsten, J. Cytogenetical observations in mongolism. *Acta Paedopsychiatrica*, 1959, **48**, 453–468.

Borgatta, E. F., & Lambert, W. W. (Eds.), *Handbook of personality theory and research*. Chicago: Rand McNally, 1968.

Boskind-Lodahl, M., & Sirlin, J. The gorging-purging syndrome. *Psychology Today*, 1977, **10**, 50–52, 82–85.

Boskind-Lodahl, M., & White, Jr., W. C. The definition and treatment of bulimaria in college women—A pilot study. *Journal of the American College Health Association*, 1978, **27**, 84–86, 97.

Boss, M. The conception of man in natural science and daseinsanalysis. *Comprehensive Psychiatry*, 1962, **3**, 193–214.

Boss, M. *Psychoanalysis and daseinsanalysis*. New York: Basic Books, 1963.

Bosselman, B. C. *Neurosis and psychosis*. Springfield, Ill.: Charles C Thomas, 1964.

Bowlby, J. Grief and mourning in infancy and early childhood. *Psychoanalytic Study of the Child*, 1960, **15**, 9–52.

Bowlby, J. *Attachment and loss*. Vol. 3. *Loss: Sadness and depression*. New York: Basic Books, 1980.

Bowman, K. M., & Jellinek, E. M. Alcohol addiction and its treatment. In E. M. Jellinek (Ed.), *Alcohol and chronic alcoholism*. New Haven: Yale University Press, 1942.

Bowman, K. M., & Rose, M. In A. Auerback (Ed.), *Schizophrenia: An integrated approach*. New York: Ronald Press, 1959.

Brady, J. V., Porter, R. W., Conrad, D. G., & Mason, J. W. Avoidance behavior and the development of gastroduodenal ulcers. *Journal of the Experimental Analysis of Behavior*, 1958, **1**, 69–72.

Bragg, R. L. Risk of admission to mental hospital following hysterectomy or cholecystectomy. *American Journal of Public Health*, 1965, **55**, 1403–1410.

Brattemo, C. *Studies in metaphoric verbal behavior in patients with a psychiatric diagnosis of schizophrenia*. Stockholm: Skandinaviska Testförlaget, 1968.

Bray, G. To treat or not to treat—what is the question? In G. Bray (Ed.), *Recent advances in obesity research;* II. London: Newman, 1978. Pp. 248–265.

Brentano, F. *Psychologie vom empirischen Standpunkte*. Leipzig: Duncker und Humblot, 1874. Found translated in W. S. Sahakian (Ed.), *History of psychology: A source book in systematic psychology*. Itasca, Ill.: F. E. Peacock Publishers, 1968.

Brentano, F. Act psychology. In W. S. Sahakian (Ed.), *History of psychology: A source book in systematic psychology*. Itasca, Ill.: F. E. Peacock Publishers, 1968.

Breuer, J., & Freud, S. *Studies on hysteria*. London: Hogarth (1895), 1955.

Broadbent, D. E. *Perception and communication*. London: Pergamon Press, 1958.

Brock, H., & Del Giudice, C. Stealing and temporal orientation. *Journal of Abnormal and Social Psychology*, 1963, **66**, 91–94.

Brodsky, A., & Hare-Mustin, R. (Eds.). *Women and psychotherapy*. New York: Guilford Press, 1980.

Brown, G. W., Bone, M., Dalison, B., Wing, J. K. *Schizophrenia and social care: A comparative follow-up study of 339 schizophrenic patients*. London: Oxford University Press, 1966.

Bruch, H. Psychological antecedents of anorexia nervosa. In R. A. Vigersky (Ed.), *Anorexia nervosa*. New York: Raven Press, 1977. Pp. 1–10.

Bruch, H. *Eating disorders*. New York: Basic Books, 1973.

Bunney, W., & Davis, J. Norepinephrine in depressive reactions: A review of supporting evidence. *Archives of General Psychiatry*, 1965, **13**, 483–497.

Burton, A., Lopez-Ibor, J. J., & Mendel, W. M. *Schizophrenia as a life style*. New York: Springer, 1974.

Buss, A. H. Two anxiety factors in psychiatric patients. *Journal of Abnormal Psychology*, 1962, **65**, 426–427.

Buss, A. H. *Psychopathology*. New York: Wiley, 1966.

Button, A. D. The genesis and development of alcoholism: An empirically based schema. *Quarterly Journal of Studies on Alcohol,* 1956, **17,** 671–675.

Byrne, D. The repression-sensitization scale: Rationale, reliability and validity. *Journal of Personality,* 1961, **29,** 334–349.

Byrne, D. Repression-sensitization as a dimension of personality. In B. A. Maher (Ed.), *Progress in experimental personality research,* Vol. 1. New York: Academic Press, 1964.

Byrne, D., Golightly, C., & Sheffield, J. The repression-sensitization scale as a measure of adjustment: Relationship with the *CPI. Journal of Consulting Psychology,* 1965, **29,** 586–589.

Cain, A. H. *The cured alcoholic: New conceptions in alcoholism treatment and research.* New York: John Day Co., 1964.

Calhoun, J. B. A "behavioral sink." In E. L. Bliss (Ed.), *Roots of behavior.* New York: Hoeber, 1962.

Cameron, N. Reasoning, regression and communication in schizophrenics. *Psychological Monographs,* 1938, **50** (Whole No. 221).

Cameron, N., & Rychlak, J.F. *Personality development and psychopathology* (2nd ed.). Boston: Houghton Mifflin, 1985. Used by permission.

Campbell, M. Use of drug treatment in infantile autism and childhood schizophrenia: A review. In M. A. DiMascio, & K. F. Killam (Eds.), *Psychopharmacology: A generation of progress.* New York: Raven Press, 1978.

Campbell, M., Cohen, I. L., & Anderson, L. T. Pharmacology for autistic children: A summary of research. *Canadian Journal of Psychiatry,* 1981, **26,** 165–273.

Campbell, M., Hollander, C. S., Ferns, S., & Greene, L. W. Response to thyrotropin-releasing hormone stimulation in young psychotic children: A pilot study. *Psychoneuroendocrinology,* 1978, **3,** 195–201.

Cantor, S., Evans, J., Pearce, J., & Pezzot-Pearce, T. Childhood schizophrenia: Present but not accounted for. *American Journal of Psychiatry,* 1982, **139,** 758–762.

Carroll, B. J., Feinberg, M., Greden, J. F., Tarika, J., Albala, A. A., Haskett, James, N. McI., R. F., Kronfol, Z., Lohr, N., Steiner, M., de Vigne, J. P., & Young, E. A specific laboratory test for the diagnosis of melancholia. *Archives of General Psychiatry,* 1981, **38,** 15–22.

Casey, A. The effect of stress on the consumption of alcohol and reserpine. *Quarterly Journal of Studies on Alcoholism,* 1960, **21,** 208–215.

Catanzaro, R. J. (Ed.), *Alcoholism: The total treatment approach.* Springfield, Ill.: Charles C Thomas, 1968.

Cattell, R. B. *Personality and motivation: Structure and measurement.* New York: World Book, 1957.

Cattell, R. B. Advances in the measurement of neuroticism and anxiety in a conceptual framework of unitary-trait theory. *Annals of the New York Academy of Science,* 1962, **93,** 815–839.

Cattell, R. B. The nature and measurement of anxiety. *Scientific American,* 1963, **208,** 96–104.

Cattell, R. B. *The scientific analysis of personality.* Baltimore: Penguin Books, 1965.

Cattell, R. B. (Ed.) *Handbook of multivariate experimental psychology.* Chicago: Rand McNally, 1966.

Cattell, R. B. *Handbook of interpretive theory, psychometrics, and practical procedures.* San Francisco: Jossey-Bass, 1973.

Cattell, R. B., & Scheier, I. H. *The meaning and measurement of neuroticism and anxiety.* New York: Ronald Press, 1961.

Cerletti, U. Old and new information about electroshock. *American Journal of Psychiatry,* 1950, **107,** 87–91.

Cerletti, U. Electroshock therapy. *Journal of Clinical and Experimental Psychopathology & Quarterly Review of Psychiatry and Neurology,* 1954, **15,** 191–217.

Cerletti, U. Electroshock therapy. In W. S. Sahakian (Ed.), *History of psychology: A source book in systematic psychology.* Itasca, Ill.: F. E. Peacock Publishers, 1981.

Chapman, L. J. A reinterpretation of some pathological disturbances in conceptual breadth. *Journal of Abnormal and Social Psychology,* 1961, **62,** 514–519.

Chapman, L. J., & Chapman, J. P. Interpretation of words in schizophrenia. *Journal of Personality and Social Psychology,* 1965, **1,** 135–146.

Chapman, L. J., & Chapman, J. P. *Disordered thought in schizophrenia.* Englewood Cliffs, N.J.: Prentice-Hall, 1973.

Chapman, L. J., & Taylor, J. A. Breadth of deviate concepts used by schizophrenics. *Journal of Abnormal and Social Psychology,* 1957, **54,** 118–123.

Clausen, J. A. Social patterns, personality, and adolescent drug use. In A. H. Leighton, J. A. Clausen, and R. N. Wilson (Eds.), *Explorations in social psychiatry.* New York: Basic Books, 1957.

Cleckley, H. M. Psychopathic states. In S. Arieti (Ed.), *American handbook of psychiatry.* New York: Basic Books, 1959.

Cleckley, H. M. *The mask of sanity* (5th ed.) St. Louis: C. V. Mosby, 1976.

Cleveland, E. J., & Longaker, D. W. Neurotic patterns in the family. In A. H. Leighton, J. A. Clausen, and R. N. Wilson (Eds.), *Explorations in social psychiatry.* New York: Basic Books, 1957.

Clinebell, H. J. *Basic types of pastoral counseling.* Nashville, Tenn.: Abingdon Press, 1966.

Cole, J. O., & Wittenborn, J. R. (Eds.) *Pharmacotherapy of depression.* Springfield, Ill.: Charles C Thomas, 1966.

Coleman, J. C. *Abnormal psychology and modern life.* (3rd ed.) Glenview, Ill.: Scott, Foresman, 1964, 5th ed., 1976.

Commission on Professional and Hospital Activities. *Length of stay in PAS Hospitals.* Ann Arbor, MI: Commission on Professional and Hospital Activities, 1974.

Committee on Nomenclature and Statistics of the American Psychiatric Association. *Diagnostic and statistical manual: Mental disorders with special supplement on plans for revision.* Washington, D.C.: APA, 1980.

Condrau, G., & Boss, M. *Existential analysis.* In J. G. Howells (Ed.), *Modern perspectives in world psychiatry.* Edinburgh: Oliver & Boyd, 1968.

Conger, J. J. The effects of alcohol on conflict behavior in the albino rat. *Quarterly Journal of Studies on Alcohol,* 1951, **12,** 1–29.

Cooper, A., & Walk, A. *Recent developments in schizophrenia.* London: RMPA, 1967.

Cooper, P. J., & Fairburn, C. G. Binge-eating and self-induced vomiting in the community: A preliminary study. *British Journal of Psychiatry,* 1983, **142,** 139–144.

Corsini, R. J. (Ed.), *Current personality theories.* Itasca, Ill.: F. E. Peacock Publishers, 1977.

Courville, C. B. *Effect of alcohol on the nervous system of man.* Los Angeles: San Lucas Press, 1966.

Craft, J. *Ten studies into psychopathic personalities.* Bristol: John Wright, 1965.

Craig, W. J. Objective measures of thinking integrated with psychiatric symptoms. *Psychological Reports,* 1965, **16,** 539–546.

Crisp, A. H. Primary anorexia nervosa or adolescent weight phobia. *The Practitioner,* 1974, **212,** 525–535.

Crisp, A. H. Anorexia nervosa. *Proceeding of the Royal Society of Medicine,* 1977, **70,** 464–470.

Crisp, A. H. Some aspects of the relationship between body weight and sexual behaviour with particular reference to massive obesity and anorexia nervosa. *International Journal of Obesity,* 1978, **2,** 17–32.

Crisp, A. H., Palmer, R. L., & Kalucy, R. S. How common is anorexia nervosa? A prevalence study. *British Journal of Psychiatry,* 1976, **128,** 549–554.

Dally, P. Anorexia nervosa: Do we need a scapegoat? *Proceedings of the Royal Society of Medicine,* 1977, **70,** 470–474.

Dana, R. H. *Foundations of clinical psychology: Problems of personality and adjustment.* Princeton, N.J.: Van Nostrand, 1966.

Davies, E. B. (Ed.), *Depression.* Cambridge: Cambridge University Press, 1964.

DesLauriers, A. M. *The experience of reality in childhood schizophrenia.* New York: International Universities, 1962.

Deutsch, F., & Murphy, W. F. *The clinical interview.* New York: International Universities, 1955.

Dollard, J., & Miller, N. E. *Personality and*

psychotherapy. New York: McGraw-Hill, 1950.

Doust, J. W. L. Psychiatric aspects of somatic immunity. British Journal of Social Medicine, 1952, 6, 49–67. (a)

Doust, J. W. L. Dysplastic growth differentials in patients with psychiatric disorders. British Journal of Social Medicine, 1952, 6, 169–177. (b)

Drakeford, J. W. Integrity therapy. Nashville, Tenn.: Broadman, 1967.

Dublin, L. I. Suicide: A sociological and statistical study. New York: Ronald Press, 1963.

Dunaif, S. L., & Hoch, P. Pseudopsychopathic schizophrenia. In P. H. Hoch and J. Zubin (Eds.), Psychiatry and the law. New York: Grune & Stratton, 1955.

Dunham, H. W. Community and schizophrenia: An epidemiological analysis. Detroit: Wayne State University Press, 1965.

Dunlap, K. Habits: Their making and unmaking. New York: Liveright, 1932.

Durell, J., & Schildkraut, J. J. Biochemical studies of the schizophrenic and affective disorders. In S. Arieti (Ed.), American handbook of psychiatry. New York: Basic Books, 1966.

Ellis, A. Reason and emotion in psychotherapy. New York: Lyle Stuart, 1962.

Ellis, A. Sex and the liberated man. Secaucus, N.J.: Stuart, 1976.

Ellis, A. Rational-emotive psychotherapy. In D. S. Arbuckle (Ed.), Counseling and psychotherapy: An overview. New York: McGraw-Hill, 1967.

Ellis, A. Humanistic psychotherapy. New York: McGraw-Hill, 1973.

Ellis, A. Rational-emotive psychotherapy. In W. S. Sahakian (Ed.), Psychotherapy and counseling: Techniques in intervention. Boston: Houghton Mifflin, 1976.

Ellis, A. Rational-emotive therapy and cognitive behavior therapy. New York: Springer, 1983.

Ellis, A. Rational-emotive therapy. In R. Corsini (Ed.), Current psychotherapies. Itasca, Ill.: F. E. Peacock Publishers, 1984. Pp. 196–238.

Ellis, H. Studies in the psychology of sex. Vol. 2. New York: Random House, 1936.

Ellis, N. R. Handbook of mental deficiency: Psychological theory and research. New York: McGraw-Hill, 1963.

Ellison, G. D. Animal models of psychopathology: The low-norepinephrine and low-serotonin rat. American Psychologist, 1977, 32, 1036–1045.

English, O. S. Clinical observations on direct analysis. In O. S. English et al. (Eds.), Direct analysis and schizophrenia: Clinical observations and evaluations. New York: Grune & Stratton, 1961.

Enoch, M. D., Trethowan, W. H., & Barker, J. C. Some uncommon psychiatric syndromes. Bristol: John Wright, 1967.

Eriksen, C. W. The case for perceptual defense. Psychological Review, 1954, 61, 175–182.

Evans, R. I. (Ed.) R. D. Laing: The man and his ideas. New York: E. P. Dutton, 1976.

Eysenck, H. J. Criterion analysis—An application of the hypothetico-deductive method to factor analysis. Psychological Review, 1950, 57, 38–53.

Eysenck, H. J. The scientific study of personality. London: Routledge & Kegan Paul, 1952. Selections found in W. S. Sahakian, Psychology of personality: Readings in theory. 3d ed. Boston: Houghton Mifflin, 1977.

Eysenck, H. J. Dynamics of anxiety and hysteria. London: Routledge & Kegan Paul, 1957.

Eysenck, H. J. Learning theory and behavior therapy. Journal of Mental Science, 1959, 105, 61–75.

Eysenck, H. J. (Ed.), Handbook of abnormal psychology. London: Sir Isaac Pitman, 1960.

Eysenck, H. J. Handbook of abnormal psychology: An experimental approach. New York: Basic Books, 1961.

Eysenck, H. J. Crime and personality. London: Routledge & Kegan Paul, 1964.

Eysenck, H. J. Criterion analysis—An application of the hypothetico-deductive method to factor analysis. Psychological Review, 1950, 57, 39–44. An abridged form found in W. S. Sahakian, Psychology of *personality: Readings in theory.* Boston: Houghton Mifflin, 1977.

Eysenck, H. J., & Rachman, S. *The causes and cures of neurosis: An introduction to modern behaviour therapy based on learning theory and the principles of conditioning.* San Diego: Robert A. Knapp, 1965.

Fabry, J. B. *The pursuit of meaning: Logotherapy applied to life.* Boston: Beacon, 1968.

Fairbairn, R. *Object-relations theory of the personality.* New York: Basic Books, 1952.

Fairburn, C. A cognitive behavioural approach to the treatment of bulimia. *Psychological Medicine,* 1981, **11,** 707–711.

Fairweather, G. The effect of selected incentive conditions on the performance of psychopathic, normal and neurotic criminals in a serial rote learning situation. Unpublished doctoral dissertation, University of Illinois, 1954.

Federn, P. Psychoanalysis of psychoses. In P. Federn (Ed.), *Ego psychology and the psychoses.* New York: Basic Books (1943), 1952.

Federn, P. Mental hygiene of the ego in schizophrenia. In P. Federn (Ed.), *Ego psychology and the psychoses.* New York: Basic Books (1948), 1952.

Federn, P. The ego in schizophrenia. In P. Federn (Ed.), *Ego psychology and the psychoses.* New York: Basic Books (1949), 1952.

Federn, P. (Ed.), *Ego psychology and the psychoses.* New York: Basic Books, 1952.

Fenichel, O. *The psychoanalytic theory of neurosis.* New York: Norton, 1945.

Ferenczi, S. *Sex in psychoanalysis.* New York: Basic Books, 1950.

Ferenczi, S. *Further contributions to the theory and technique of psychoanalysis.* New York: Basic Books, 1952.

Ferster, C. B. Behavioral approaches to depression. In R. J. Friedman & M. M. Katz (Eds.), *The psychology of depression: Contemporary theory and research.* New York: Wiley, 1974.

Fish, B. Pharmacotherapy for autistic and schizophrenic children. In E. Ritvo (Ed.), *Autism: Diagnosis, current research and management.* New York: Spectrum, 1976.

Fish, B., & Ritvo, E. R. Psychoses of childhood. In J. D. Noshpitz (Ed.), *Basic handbook of child psychiatry.* Vol. 2. New York: Basic Books, 1979.

Fish, F. J. *Schizophrenia.* Bristol: John Wright, 1962.

Forbes, J. C., & Duncan, G. M. Effect of vitamin intake on adrenal cholesterol after acute alcoholic intoxication in rats. In H. E. Himwich (Ed.), *Alcohol: Basic aspects and treatment.* Washington, D.C.: American Association for the Advancement of Science, 1957.

Ford, C. S., & Beach, F. A. *Patterns of sexual behavior.* New York: Harper & Row, 1951.

Foulkes, S. H. *An introduction to group-analytic psychotherapy.* London: Heinemann, 1948.

Foulkes, S. H., & Anthony, E. J. *Group psychotherapy.* London: Penguin Books, 1957.

Fox, R. Introduction. In R. P. Maickel, *Biochemical factors in alcoholism.* Oxford: Pergamon Press, 1967.

Frank, J. D. The bewildering world of psychotherapy. *Journal of Social Issues,* 1972, **28,** 27–43.

Frank, J. D. The present status of outcome studies. *Journal of Consulting and Clinical Psychology,* 1979, **47,** 310–316.

Frank, J. D. Reply to Telch. *Journal of Consulting and Clinical Psychology, 1981,* **49,** 476–477.

Frank, L. K. Society as the patient. *American Journal of Sociology,* 1936, **42,** 335–344.

Frankenstein, C. *Psychopathy: A comparative analysis of clinical pictures.* New York: Grune & Stratton, 1959.

Frankl, V. E. Collective neurosis of the present day. *Internationales Journal für prophylaktische Medizin und Sozialhygiene,* 1958, **2,** 1–5. (a)

Frankl, V. E. On logotherapy and existential analysis. *American Journal of Psychoanalysis,* 1958, **18,** 28–37. (b)

Frankl, V. E. The spiritual dimension in existential analysis and logotherapy. *Jour-*

nal of Individual Psychology, 1959, **15,** 157–165.

Frankl, V. E. Paradoxical intention: A logotherapeutic technique. *American Journal of Psychotherapy,* 1960, **14,** 520–535.

Frankl, V. E. Logotherapy and the challenge of suffering. *Review of Existential Psychology and Psychiatry,* 1961, **1,** 3–7.

Frankl, V. E. Psychiatry and man's quest for meaning. *Journal of Religion and Health,* 1962, **1,** 93–103. (a)

Frankl, V. E. *Man's search for meaning: An introduction to logotherapy* (Rev. ed.) Boston: Beacon, 1962. (b)

Frankl, V. E. *The doctor and the soul: From psychotherapy to logotherapy* (Rev. ed.). New York: Knopf, 1966. (a)

Frankl, V. E. Logotherapy and existential analysis—A review. *American Journal of Psychotherapy,* 1966, **20,** 252–260. (b)

Frankl, V. E. *Psychotherapy and existentialism.* New York: Washington Square, 1967. (a)

Frankl, V. E. Logotherapy. *Israel Annals of Psychiatry and Related Disciplines,* 1967, **5,** 142–155. (b)

Frankl, V. E. *The will to meaning.* New York: World Publishing, 1969.

Frankl, V. E. *The unconscious God: Psychotherapy and theology.* New York: Simon & Schuster, 1975.

Frankl, V. E. *The unheard cry for meaning: Psychotherapy and humanism.* New York: Simon & Schuster, 1978.

Frazier, S. H., & Carr, A. C. *Introduction to psychopathology.* New York: Macmillan, 1964.

Freeman, H. E., & Simmons, O. G. Social class and post-hospital performance levels. *American Sociological Review,* 1959, **24,** 345–351.

Freeman, H. E., & Simmons, O. G. Treatment experiences of mental patients and their families. *American Journal of Public Health,* 1961, **51,** 1266–1273.

Freeman, H. E., & Simmons, O. G. *The mental patient comes home.* New York: Wiley, 1963.

Freeman, T. *Studies on psychosis: Descriptive, psychoanalytical and psychological aspects.* London: Tavistock, 1965.

Freeman, W. Psychosurgery. *American Journal of Psychiatry,* 1962, **119,** 621–628.

Freeman, W., & Watts, J. W. *Psychosurgery: In the treatment of mental disorders and intractable pain.* Springfield, Ill.: Charles C Thomas, 1950.

Freeman, W., & Watts, J. W. Prefrontal lobotomy. In W. S. Sahakian (Ed.), *History of psychology: A source book in systematic psychology.* 2d ed. Itasca, Ill.: F. E. Peacock Publishers, 1981.

French, T. M. *The integration of behavior.* Chicago: University of Chicago Press, 1952–54, 2 vols.

Freud, S. Psychoanalytic notes upon an autobiographical account of a case of paranoia. *Collected papers.* London: Hogarth (1911), 1925.

Freud, S. *A general introduction to psychoanalysis.* New York: Liveright (1916–17), 1935.

Freud, S. *The ego and the id.* London: Hogarth (1923), 1960.

Freud, S. *Collected papers.* London: Hogarth, 1946.

Freud, S. *The unconscious.* In S. Freud, *Collected papers.* London: Hogarth (1915), 1947.

Freud, S. Metaphysical supplement to the theory of dreams. In S. Freud, *Collected papers.* London: Hogarth (1916), 1947.

Freud, S. Neurosis and psychosis. In S. Freud, *Collected papers.* London: Hogarth (1924), 1947.

Freud, S. Mourning and melancholia. In S. Freud, *Collected papers.* London: Hogarth (1917), 1950.

Freud, S. *The interpretation of dreams.* In standard edition of the complete psychological works of Sigmund Freud. London: Hogarth (1900), 1953. Vols. IV, V.

Freud, S. *The collected papers of Sigmund Freud.* New York: Basic Books, 1959.

Freud, S. *The ego and the id.* New York: Norton (1923), 1960.

Freud, S. *New introductory lectures on psychoanalysis.* London: Hogarth, 1961, 1965.

Freud, S. *An outline of psychoanalysis.* New York: Norton (1940), 1963. (a)

Freud, S. *A general introduction to psychoanalysis.* London: George Allen & Unwin, 1963. (b)

Friedman, M., & Rosenman, R. H. *Type A behavior and your heart.* New York: Knopf, 1974.

Friedman, R. J., & Katz, M. M. (Eds.), *The psychology of depression: Contemporary theory and research.* New York: Wiley, 1974.

Fromm, E. *Escape from freedom.* New York: Norton, 1941.

Fromm, E. *Man for himself: An inquiry into the psychology of ethics.* New York: Holt, Rinehart & Winston, 1947.

Fromm, E. *The same society.* New York: Holt, 1955.

Fromm, E. *The art of loving.* New York: Harper & Row, 1956.

Fromm, E. Psychoanalysis and Zen Buddhism. In D. T. Suzuki, E. Fromm, and R. DeMartino, *Zen Buddhism and psychoanalysis.* New York: Grove Press, 1963.

Fromm, E. *The heart of man.* New York: Harper & Row, 1964.

Fromm, E. (Ed.), *Socialist humanism: An international symposium.* New York: Doubleday, 1965.

Fromm, E. *The anatomy of destructiveness.* New York: Holt, Rinehart & Winston, 1973.

Fromm-Reichmann, F. Psychoanalytic psychotherapy with psychotics: The influence of the modifications in technique on present trends in psychoanalysis. *Psychiatry,* 1943, **6,** 277–279.

Fromm-Reichmann, F. Recent advances in psychoanalysis. *Journal of the American Medical Women's Association,* 1949, **4,** 320–326.

Fromm-Reichmann, F. *Principles of intensive psychotherapy.* Chicago: University of Chicago Press, 1950.

Fromm-Reichmann, F., & Moreno, J. L. (Eds.), *Progress in psychotherapy.* New York: Grune & Stratton, 1956.

Fuller, J. L., & Thompson, W. R. *Behavior genetics.* New York: Wiley, 1960.

Fulton, J. F., & Jacobsen, C. E. The function of frontal lobes, a comparative study in monkeys, chimpanzees and man. *Abstracts of the Second International Neurological Congress.* London, 1935.

Garber, J., & Seligman, M. E. P. *Human helplessness.* New York: Academic Press, 1980.

Garmezy, N. Process and reactive schizophrenia. In M. M. Katz, J. O. Cole and W. E. Barton (Eds.), *The role and methodology of classification in psychiatry and psychopathology.* Chevy Chase, Md.: National Institute of Mental Health, 1968.

Garmezy, N. Process and reactive schizophrenia: Some conceptions and issues. *Schizophrenia Bulletin,* 1970, **2,** 30–74.

Garmezy, N., & Rodnick, E. H. Premorbid adjustment performance in schizophrenia: Implications for interpreting heterogeneity in schizophrenia. *Journal of Nervous and Mental Disease,* 1959, **129,** 450–466.

Gebhard, P. H., Gagnon, J. H., Pomeroy, W. B., & Christenson, C. V. *Sex offenders: An analysis of types.* New York: Harper & Row, 1965.

Geer, J., Davison, G. C., & Gatchel, R. I. Reduction of stress in humans through nonveridical perceived control of aversive stimulation. *Journal of Personality and Social Psychology,* 1970, **16,** 731–738.

Gershon, S., Holmberg, G., Mattson, N., & Marshall, A. Imipramine hydrochloride, autonomic and psychological functions. *Archives of General Psychiatry,* 1962, **6,** 112–117.

Gesell, A., & Ilg, F. L. *Child development.* New York: Harper & Row, 1949.

Getz, W., Wiesen, A. E., Sue, S., & Ayers, A. *Fundamentals of crisis counseling.* Lexington, Mass.: D. C. Heath, 1974.

Glasser, W. *Reality therapy: A new approach to psychiatry.* New York: Harper & Row, 1965.

Glasser, W. Reality therapy. In R. Corsini (Ed.), *Current psychotherapies.* Itasca, Ill.: F. E. Peacock Publishers, 1984. Pp. 320–353.

Goffman, E. *Asylums: Essays on the social situation of mental patients and other inmates.* New York: Doubleday, 1961.

Goldfarb, W. Effects of psychological deprivation in infancy and subsequent stimulation. *American Journal of Psychiatry*, 1945, **102**, 18–33.

Goldfarb, W. *Childhood schizophrenia.* Cambridge, Mass.: Harvard University Press, 1961.

Goldfarb, W. An investigation of childhood schizophrenia. *Archives of General Psychiatry*, 1964, **11**, 621–634.

Goldstein, K. *The organism.* New York: American Book, 1939.

Goldstein, K. *Human nature in the light of psychopathology.* Cambridge, Mass.: Harvard University Press, 1940.

Goldstein, K. Methodological approach to the study of schizophrenic thought disorders. In J. S. Kasanin (Ed.), *Language and thought in schizophrenia.* New York: Norton, 1964. Original publication: Berkeley: University of California Press, 1944.

Goldstein, K. The effect of brain damage on the personality. *Psychiatry*, 1952, **15**, 245–260.

Goldstein, K. The organismic approach. In S. Arieti (Ed.), *American handbook of psychiatry.* New York: Basic Books, 1959.

Goodwin, F. K., & Ebert, M. H. Lithium in mania: Clinical trials and controlled studies. In S. Gershon & B. Shopsin (Eds.), *Lithium: Its role in psychiatric research and treatment.* New York: Plenum, 1973. Pp. 237–252.

Gorham, D. R. *Clinical manual for the proverbs test.* Missoula, Mont.: Psychological Test Specialists, 1956. (a)

Gorham, D. R. A proverbs test for clinical and experimental use. *Psychological Reports*, 1956, **2**, 1–12. (b)

Gorham, D. R. Use of the proverbs test for differentiating schizophrenics from normals. *Journal of Consulting Psychology*, 1956, **20**, 435–440. (c)

Gottesman, I. I. Schizophrenia and genetics: Where are we? Are you sure? In L. C. Wynne, R. Cromwell, S. Matthysse (Eds.), *Nature of schizophrenia: New findings and future strategies.* New York: Wiley, 1978.

Gottesman, I. I., & Shields, J. Schizophrenia in twins: 16 years' consecutive admissions to a psychiatric clinic. *British Journal of Psychiatry*, 1966, **112**, 809–818.

Gottesman, I. I., & Shields, J. *Schizophrenia and genetics: A twin study vantage point.* New York: Academic Press, 1972.

Gottesman, I. I., & Shields, J. A critical review of recent adoption, twin and family studies of schizophrenia: Behavioral genetics perspectives. *Schizophrenia Bulletin*, 1976, **2**, 360–401.

Greenacre, P. Conscience in the psychopath. *American Journal of Orthopsychiatry*, 1945, **15**, 495–509.

Greenblatt, M., Grosser, G. H., & Wechsler, H. Differential response of hospitalized depressed patients to somatic therapy. *American Journal of Psychiatry*, 1964, **120**, 935–943.

Gregory, I. Genetic factors in schizophrenia. *American Journal of Psychiatry*, 1960, **116**, 961–972.

Gregory, I. *Fundamentals of psychiatry.* Philadelphia: Saunders, 1968.

Greiner, A. C., & Nicolson, G. A. Schizophrenia: Melanosis. *Lancet*, 1965, **2**, 1165–1167.

Grinker, R. R. The phenomena of depressions. In *Third World Congress of Psychiatry, Proceedings.* Montreal, Can.: University of Toronto Press, 1961, **1**, 160–164.

Grinker, R. R. *Psychiatry in broad perspective.* New York: Behavioral Publications, 1975.

Grinker, R. R., Miller, J., Sabshin, M., Nunn, R., & Nunnally, J. C. *The phenomena of depressions.* New York: Hoeber, 1961.

Grinker, R. R., & Nunnally, J. C. The phenomena of depressions. In M. M. Katz, J. O. Cole, & W. E. Barton (Eds.), *The role and methodology of classification in psychiatry and psychopathology.* Chevy Chase, Md.: National Institute of Mental Health, 1968.

Grinker, R. R., & Spiegel, J. P. *War neuroses.* New York: Blakiston, 1945.

Grinker, R. R., Werble, B., & Drye, R. C. *The borderline syndrome: A behavioral study of ego-functions.* New York: Basic Books, 1968.

Gruenberg, E. M. Socially shared psychopathology. In A. H. Leighton, J. A.

Clausen, & R. N. Wilson (Eds.), *Explorations in social psychiatry.* New York: Basic Books, 1957.

Guertin, W. H. An inverted factor analytic study of schizophrenia. *Journal of Consulting Psychology,* 1952, **16,** 371–375.

Guertin, W. H. Medical and statistical-psychological models for research in schizophrenia. *Behavioral Science,* 1961, **6,** 200–204. (a)

Guertin, W. H. Empirical syndrome groupings of schizophrenia hospital admissions. *Journal of Clinical Psychology,* 1961, **17,** 268–275. (b)

Gull, W. Anorexia nervosa. *Lancet,* 1888, **1,** 516–517.

Gutheil, E. A. Sexual dysfunctions in men. In S. Arieti (Ed.), *American handbook of psychiatry.* New York: Basic Books, 1959.

Hadley, J. M. *Clinical and counseling psychology.* New York: Knopf, 1958.

Halmi, K. A., Falk, J. R., & Schwartz, E. Binge-eating and vomiting: A survey of college population. *Psychological Medicine,* 1981, **11,** 697–706.

Hamilton, M. The assessment of anxiety states by rating. *British Journal of Medicine and Psychology,* 1959, **32,** 50–59.

Hammer, M., & Kaplan, A. M. *The practice of psychotherapy with children.* Homewood, Ill.: Dorsey Press, 1967.

Harlow, H. F., McGaugh, J. L., & Thompson, R. F. *Psychology.* San Francisco: Albion, 1971.

Hay, G. G., & Leonard, J. C. Anorexia nervosa and males. *Lancet,* 1979, **ii,** 574–576.

Hayman, M. *Alcoholism: Mechanism and management.* Springfield, Ill.: Charles C Thomas, 1966.

Heath, R. G. A biochemical hypothesis on the etiology of schizophrenia. In D. D. Jackson (Ed.), *The etiology of schizophrenia.* New York: Basic Books, 1960.

Heath, R. G. Schizophrenia: Biochemical and physiologic aberrations. *International Journal of Neuropsychiatry,* 1966, **2,** 597–610.

Heath, R. G. Catatonia induced in monkeys by antibrain antibody. *American Journal of*

Psychiatry, 1967, **123,** 1499–1504.

Heath, R. H. (Ed.), *Serological fractions in schizophrenia.* New York: Hoeber Medical Division, Harper & Row, 1963.

Hebb, D. O. *A textbook of psychology* (2nd ed.) Philadelphia: W. B. Saunders, 1966.

Heeley, A., & Roberts, G. Tryptophan metabolism in psychotic children. *Developmental Medicine and Child Neurology.* 1965, **7,** 46–49.

Heidigger, M. *Being and time.* New York: Harper & Row, 1962.

Heineman, C. E. A forced choice form of the Taylor Anxiety Scale. *Journal of Consulting Psychology,* 1953, **17,** 447–454.

Hetherington, E., & Klinger, E. Psychopathy and punishment. *Journal of Abnormal and Social Psychology.* 1964, **69,** 113–115.

Himwich, H. E. *Alcoholism: Basic aspects and treatment.* Washington, D.C.: American Association for the Advancement of Science, 1957.

Hinsie, L. E., & Campbell, R. J. *Psychiatric dictionary.* 4th ed. New York: Oxford University Press, 1970.

Hinsie, L. E., & Shatsky. J. *Psychiatric dictionary: With encyclopedic treatment of modern terms* (2nd ed.) New York: Oxford University Press, 1953.

Hirsch, J. *Opportunities in the treatment of alcoholics.* Springfield, Ill.: Charles C Thomas, 1967.

Hoch, P. H., & Polatin, P. Pseudoneurotic forms of schizophrenia. *Psychiatric Quarterly,* 1949, **23,** 248–276.

Hodern, A., Burt, C. G., & Holt, N. F. *Depressive states: A pharmatherapeutic study.* Springfield, Ill.: Charles C Thomas, 1965.

Hoffer, A. *Niacin therapy in psychiatry.* Springfield, Ill.: Charles C Thomas, 1962.

Hoffer, A., & Osmond, H. *The chemical basis of clinical psychiatry.* Springfield, Ill.: Charles C Thomas, 1960.

Hoffer, A., & Osmond, H. *How to live with schizophrenia.* 2nd ed. New Hyde Park, N.Y.: University Books, 1974.

Hoffer, A., Osmond, H., Callbeck, M. J., & Kahan, I. Treatment of schizophrenia with nicotinic acid and nicotinamide. *Journal of Clinical and Experimental Psychopathol-*

ogy & *Quarterly Review of Psychiatry and Neurology,* 1957, **18,** 131–158.

Hoffer, A., Osmond, H., & Smythies, J. Schizophrenia: A new approach, II. Result of a year's research. *Journal of Mental Science,* 1954, **100,** 29–45.

Hollingshead, A. B., & Redlich, F. C. *Social class and mental illness: A community study.* New York: Wiley, 1958.

Hollingshead, A. B., & Rogler, L. H. Lower socioeconomic status and mental illness. *Sociology and Social Research,* 1962, **46,** 387–396.

Horney, K. *The neurotic personality of our time.* New York: Norton, 1937.

Horney, K. *Self-analysis.* New York: Norton, 1942.

Horney, K. *Our inner conflicts.* New York: Holt, 1945.

Horney, K. *Neurosis and human growth.* New York: Norton, 1950.

Horsley, J. S. *Narco-analysis.* New York: Oxford University Press, 1943.

Hoskins. R. G. *The biology of schizophrenia.* New York: Norton, 1946.

Hoskins, R. G. Hormone therapy. *Journal of Clinical Psychopathology & Quarterly Review of Psychiatry and Neurology,* 1954, **14,** 363–372.

Howells, J. G. The nuclear family as the functional unit in psychiatry. *Journal of Mental Science,* 1962, **108,** 675–684.

Howells, J. G. *Family psychiatry.* Edinburgh: Oliver & Boyd, 1963.

Howells, J. G. (Ed.), *Modern perspectives in world psychiatry.* Edinburgh: Oliver & Boyd, 1968. (a)

Howells, J. G. *Theory and practice of family psychiatry.* Edinburgh: Oliver & Boyd, 1968. (b)

Howells, J. G. Family psychiatry. In J. G. Howells (Ed.), *Modern perspectives in world psychiatry.* Edinburgh: Oliver & Boyd, 1968. (c)

Hudson, J. I., Pope, Jr., H. G., & Jonas, J. M. Treatment of bulimia with antidepressants: Theoretical considerations and clinical findings. *Psychiatric Annals,* 1983, **13,** 965–969.

Hull, C. L. *Principles of behavior.* New York: Appleton-Century-Crofts, 1943.

Husserl, E. *Ideas: General introduction to pure phenomenology.* New York: Macmillan, 1931.

Hutt, C., & Hutt, S. J. Stereotypies and their relation to arousal: A study of autistic children. In S. J. Hutt & C. J. Hutt (Eds.), *Behaviour studies in psychiatry.* Oxford: Pergamon, 1970.

Iversen, S. D., & Iversen, L. L. *Behavioral pharmacology.* New York: Oxford University Press, 1975.

Jackson, D. D. Aspects of conjoint family therapy. In G. H. Zuk and I. Boszormenyi-Nagy (Eds.), *Family therapy and disturbed families.* Palo Alto, Calif., Science and Behavior Books, 1967.

Jackson, D. D., & Weakland, J. H. Conjoint family therapy: Some considerations on the theory, technique, and results. *Psychiatry,* 1961, **24,** 30–45.

Jacobs, P. A., Baikie, A. G., Court Brown, W. M., & Strong, J. A. The somatic chromosomes in mongolism. *Lancet,* 1959, **1,** 710.

Jacobson, E. *Progressive relaxation.* Chicago: University of Chicago Press, 1938.

Jacobson, E. Contributions to the metapsychology of cyclothymic depression. In P. Greenacre (Ed.), *Affective disorders.* New York: International Universities, 1953.

Jacobson, E. Transference problems in the psychoanalytic treatment of severely depressive patients. *Journal of the American Psychoanalytic Association,* 1954, **2,** 595–606.

Jahoda, M. *Current concepts of positive mental health.* New York: Basic Books, 1958.

Jaspers, K. Kausale und verstandliche Zusammenhange swischen Schichksal und der Psychose bei der Dementia Praecox. *Zeitschrift fur̈ Neurologie und Psychiatrie,* 1913, **14,** 158.

Jaspers, K. *General psychopathology.* Chicago: University of Chicago Press, 1963.

Jellinek, E. M. Phases of alcohol addiction. *Quarterly Journal of Studies on Alcohol,* 1952, **13,** 673–674.

Jellinek, E. M. *The disease concept of alcoholism.* New Haven: Hillhouse Press, 1960.

Jennings, A. N. Depressive and deprivation reactions in early childhood. In D. Maddison and G. M. Duncan (Eds.), *Aspects of depressive illness.* Edinburgh: Livingstone, 1965.

Johnson, C., & Larson, R. Bulimia: Analysis of mood and behavior. *Psychosomatic Medicine,* 1982, **44**, 341-351.

Jones. M. *Social psychiatry: A study of therapeutic communities.* London: Tavistock, 1952.

Jones, M. *The therapeutic community: A new treatment method in psychiatry.* New York: Basic Books, 1953.

Jones, M. The concept of a therapeutic community. *American Journal of Psychiatry,* 1956, **112**, 647-650.

Jones, M. *Social psychiatry: In the community, in hospitals, and in prisons.* Springfield, Ill.: Charles C Thomas, 1962.

Jones, M. Group work in mental hospitals. *British Journal of Psychiatry,* 1966, **112**, 1007-1011.

Jung, C. G. *Psychological types.* New York: Harcourt Brace Jovanovich, 1924.

Jung, C. G. *Contributions to analytical psychology.* New York: Harcourt Brace Jovanovich, 1928.

Jung, C. G. *Two essays on analytical psychology.* New York: Bollingen, 1953.

Jung, C. G. The practice of psychotherapy. In C. G. Jung, *The collected works of C. G. Jung.* 16, New York: Bollingen, 1966.

Jung, C. G. Analytic psychotherapy. In W. S. Sahakian (Ed.), *Psychotherapy and counseling: Studies in technique.* Boston: Houghton Mifflin, 1976.

Kaczanowski, G. K. Logotherapy—A new psychotherapeutic tool. *Psychosomatics,* 1967, **8**, 158-161.

Kagan, J., & Moss, H. A. *Birth to maturity: A study in psychological development.* New York: Wiley, 1962.

Kalin, N. H., Risch, S. C., Janowsky, D. S., & Murphy, D. L. Use of the Dexamethasone Suppression Test in clinical psychiatry. *Journal of Clinical Psychopharmacology,* 1981, **1**, 64-69.

Kallmann, F. J. *The genetics of schizophrenia.* New York: J. J. Augustin, 1938.

Kallmann, F. J. The genetic theory of schizophrenia—An analysis of 691 twin index families. *American Journal of Psychiatry,* 1946, **103**, 309-322.

Kallmann, F. J. Comparative twin study on the genetic aspects of male homosexuality. *Journal of Nervous and Mental Disease,* 1952, **115**, 283-298. (a)

Kallmann, F. J. Twin and sibship study of overt male homosexuality. *American Journal of Human Genetics,* 1952, **4**, 136-146. (b)

Kallmann, F. J. *Heredity in mental health and disorder.* New York: Norton, 1953.

Kallmann, F. J. The genetics of mental illness. In S. Arieti (Ed.), *American handbook of psychiatry.* New York: Basic Books, 1959.

Kallmann, F. J. Genetic factors in the etiology of mental disorders. *American Journal of Orthopsychiatry,* 1961, **31**, 445-451.

Kanner, L. Autistic disturbances of affective contact. *Nervous Child.* 1943, **2**, 217-250.

Kanner, L. Early infantile autism. *Journal of Pediatrics,* 1944, **25**, 211-217.

Kanner, L. *Childhood psychosis: Initial studies and new insights.* Washington, D.C.: V. H. Winston, 1973.

Kantor, R. E., & Herron, W. G. *Reactive and process schizophrenia.* Palo Alto, Calif.: Science and Behavior Books, 1966.

Kantor, R. E., Wallner. J. M., & Winder, C. L. Process and reactive schizophrenia. *Journal of Consulting Psychology,* 1953, **17**, 157-162.

Karpman, B. *The hangover: A critical study in the psychodynamics of alcoholism.* Springfield, Ill.: Charles C Thomas, 1957.

Katchadourian, H. A., & Churchill, C. W. Social class and mental illness in urban Lebanon. *Social Psychiatry,* 1969, **4**, 49-55.

Kazdin, A. E., & Wilcoxon, L. A. Systematic desensitization and nonspecific treatment effects: A methodological evaluation. *Psychological Bulletin,* 1976, **83**, 729-758.

Keiser, L. *The traumatic neurosis.* Philadelphia: Lippincott, 1968.

Keller, M. Definition of alcoholism. *Quarterly Journal of Alcoholism,* 1960, **21,** 125–134.

Kelly, G. A. *The psychology of personal constructs.* New York: Norton, 1955. 2 vols.

Kelly, G. A. *Selected Papers of. . . .*New York: Wiley, 1969.

Kendell, R. E. *The classification of depressive illnesses.* London: Oxford University Press, 1968.

Kety, S. S. Biochemical theories of schizophrenia. *Science,* 1959, **129,** 1528–1532, 1590–1596.

Kety, S. S. Recent biochemical theories of schizophrenia. In D. D. Jackson (Ed.), *The etiology of schizophrenia.* New York: Basic Books, 1960.

Kety, S. S. Biochemical theories of schizophrenia. *International Journal of Psychiatry,* 1965, **1,** 409–466.

Kety, S. S. Biochemical hypotheses and studies. In L. Bellak and L. Loeb (Eds.), *The schizophrenic syndrome.* New York: Grune & Stratton, 1969.

Kety, S. S. Toward hypotheses for a biochemical component in the vulnerability to schizophrenia. *Seminars in Psychiatry,* 1972, **4,** 233–238.

Kety, S. S. Problems in biological research in psychiatry. In J. Mendels (Ed.), *Biological psychiatry.* New York: Wiley, 1973.

Kierkegaard, S. *Concluding unscientific postscript.* Princeton, N. J.: Princeton University Press, 1941. (a)

Kierkegaard, S. *Fear and trembling.* Princeton, N. J.: Princeton University Press, 1941. (b)

Kierkegaard, S. *Sickness unto death.* Princeton, N. J.: Princeton University Press, 1941. (c)

Kierkegaard, S. *The concept of dread.* Princeton, N. J.: Princeton University Press, 1957.

Kiloh, L. G., Ball, J. R. B., & Garside, R. F. Prognostic factors in treatment of depressive states with imipramine. *British Medical Journal,* 1962, **1,** 1225–1227.

Kiloh, L. G., & Garside, R. F. The independence of neurotic depression and endogenous depression. *British Journal of Psychiatry,* 1963, **109,** 451–463.

Kimble, G. A., & Garmezy, N. *Principles of general psychology.* New York: Ronald Press, 1968.

King, G. F. Differential autonomic responsiveness in the process-reactive classification of schizophrenia. *Journal of Abnormal and Social Psychology,* 1958, **56,** 160–164.

Kingham, R. J. Alcoholism and reinforcement theory of learning. *Quarterly Journal of Studies on Alcohol,* 1958, **19,** 320–330.

Kinsey, A. C., Pomeroy, W. B., & Martin, C. E. *Sexual behavior in the human male.* Philadelphia: Saunders, 1948.

Kinsey, A. C., Pomeroy, W. B., Martin, C. E., & Gebhard, P. *Sexual behavior in the human female.* Philadelphia: Saunders, 1953.

Kisker, G. *The disorganized personality.* 3rd ed. New York: McGraw-Hill, 1977.

Klein, M. A contribution to the psychogenesis of manic-depressive states. *Contributions to psycho-analysis, 1921–1945.* London: Hogarth (1934). 1948. (a)

Klein, M. *Contributions to psycho-analysis, 1921–1945.* London: Hogarth, 1948. (b)

Klein, M. *The psychoanalysis of children.* New York: Grove Press, 1960.

Kline, N. S. *From sad to glad: Kline on depression.* New York: G. P. Putnam, 1974.

Knutson, A. L. New perspectives regarding positive mental health. *American Psychologist,* 1963, **18,** 300–306.

Koegel, R., & Covert, A. The relationship of self-stimulation to learning in autistic children. *Journal of Applied Behavioral Analysis,* 1972, **5,** 381–387.

Koegel, R., Firestone, P., Kramme, K., & Dunlap. G. Increasing spontaneous play by suppressing self-stimulation. *Journal of Applied Behavioral Analysis,* 1974, **7,** 521–528.

Kohn, M. L. Social class and schizophrenia: A critical review. In D. Rosenthal & S. S. Kety (Eds.), *The transmission of schizophrenia.* Oxford: Pergamon, 1968.

Kolb, L. C. *Noyes' modern clinical psychiatry.* Philadelphia: Saunders, 1968.

Kraft, A. M. The therapeutic community. In S. Arieti (Ed.), *American handbook of psychiatry.* New York: Basic Books, 1966.

Kubie, L. S. The fundamental nature of the distinction between normality and neurosis. *Psychoanalytic Quarterly,* 1954, **23,** 167–204.

Ladee, G. A. *Hypochondriacal syndromes.* Amsterdam: Elsevier, 1966.

Laing, R. D. *The divided self: An existential study in sanity and madness.* Baltimore: Penguin Books, 1965.

Laing, R. D. *The politics of experience.* New York: Pantheon, 1967.

Laing, R. D. *The man and his ideas.* In R. I. Evans (Ed.), *R. D. Laing: The man and his ideas.* New York: E. P. Dutton, 1976.

Lasegue, C. On hysterical anorexia. *Medical Times and Gazette,* 1973, **2,** 265–266.

Lazarus, A. A. *Behavior therapy and beyond.* New York: McGraw-Hill, 1971.

Lazarus, A. A. Multimodal behavior therapy: Treating the "Basic Id." *Journal of Nervous and Mental Disease,* 1973, **156,** 404–411.

Lazarus, A. A. *The practice of multimodal therapy: Systematic, comprehensive, and effective psychotherapy.* New York: McGraw-Hill, 1981.

Lazarus, R. S. Is there a mechanism of perceptual defense? A reply to Postman, Bronson and Gropper. *Journal of Abnormal and Social Psychology,* 1954, **49,** 396–398.

Leedy, J. J. (Ed.), *Poetry therapy.* Philadelphia: Lippincott, 1969.

Lehmann, H. E. Depression: Categories, mechanisms and phenomena. In J. O. Cole and J. R. Wittenborn (Eds.), *Pharmacotherapy of depression.* Springfield, Ill.: Charles C Thomas, 1966.

Leighton, A. H., Clausen, J. A., & Wilson, R. N. *Explorations in social psychiatry.* New York: Basic Books, 1957.

Lejeune, J., Gautier, M., & Turpin, R. Les chromosomes humains en culture de tissus. *Comptes Rendus Hebomadaires des Scéances de l'Académie des Sciences,* 1959, **248,** 602–606. (a)

Lejeune, J., Turpin, R., & Gautier, M. Le mongolisme: Premier exemple d'aberation autosomique humaine. *Annales de Gene-* *tique,* 1959, **1,** 41–49. (b)

Lemert, E. *Social pathology: A systematic approach to the theory of sociopathic behavior.* New York: McGraw-Hill, 1951.

Levitt, R. A. (Ed.), *Psychopharmacology: A biological approach.* Washington, D.C.: Hemisphere/Wiley, 1975.

Levitt, R. A., & Lonowski, D. J. Adrenergic drugs. In R. A. Levitt (Ed.). *Psychopharmacology: A biological approach.* Washington, D.C.: Hemisphere/Wiley, 1975.

Levy, R. I. The psychodynamic functions of alcohol. *Quarterly Journal of Studies on Alcohol,* 1958, **19,** 649–659.

Lewinsohn, P. M. A behavioral approach to depression. In R. J. Friedman & M. M. Katz (Eds.), *The psychology of depression: Contemporary theory and research.* New York: Wiley, 1974.

Liddle, G. W. Tests of pituitary-adrenal suppressibility in the diagnosis of Cushing's syndrome. *Journal of Clinical Endocrinology and Metabolism,* 1960, **20,** 1539–1560.

Lidz, T. The thyroid. In E. D. Wittkower and R. A. Cleghorn (Eds.), *Recent developments in psychosomatic medicine.* Philadelphia: Lippincott, 1954.

Lidz, T. *The person.* New York: Basic, 1968. Rev. ed., 1976.

Lidz, R. W., & Lidz, T. The family environment of schizophrenic patients. *American Journal of Psychiatry,* 1949, **106,** 332–345.

Lidz, T., Cornelison, A. R., Terry, D., & Fleck, S. The intrafamilial environment of the schizophrenic patient: II. Marital schism and marital skew. *American Journal of Psychiatry,* 1957, **114,** 241–248.

Lidz, T., Cornelison, A. R., Terry, D., & Fleck, S. The intrafamilial environment of the schizophrenic patient: VI. The transmission of irrationality. *Archives of Neurology and Psychiatry,* 1958, **79,** 305–316.

Lidz, T., Fleck, S., Alanen, Y. O., & Cornelison, A. Schizophrenic patients and their siblings. *Psychiatry,* 1963, **26,** 1–18.

Lidz, T. *et al. Schizophrenia and the family.* New York: International Universities, 1965.

Liem, J. H. Effects of verbal communications of parents and children: A comparison of normal and schizophrenic families. *Journal of Consulting and Clinical Psychology*, 1974, **42**, 438–450.

Lindesmith, A. R. Problems in the social psychology of addiction. In D. M. Wilner and G. G. Kassebaum (Eds.), *Narcotics*. New York: Blakiston, 1965.

Lindesmith, A. R. *Addiction and opiates* (2nd ed.). Hawthorne, N.Y.: Aldine Publishing, 1968.

London, P. The major psychological disorders. In P. London and D. Rosenhan (Eds.), *Foundations of abnormal psychology*. New York: Holt, Rinehart & Winston, 1968.

London, P., & Rosenhan, D. *Foundations of abnormal psychology*. New York: Holt, Rinehart & Winston, 1968.

Lorr, M. Measurement of the major psychotic syndromes. *Annals of the New York Academy of Science*, 1962, **93**, 851–856.

Lorr, M. (Ed.), *Explorations in typing psychotics*. Oxford: Pergamon Press, 1966.

Lorr, M. Syndromes of deviation. In E. F. Borgatta and W. W. Lambert (Eds.), *Handbook of personality theory and research*. Chicago: Rand McNally, 1968. (a)

Lorr, M. A typology for functional psychotics. In M. M. Katz, J. O. Cole and W. E. Barton (Eds.), *The role and methodology of classification in psychiatry and psychopathology*. Chevy Chase, Md.: National Institute of Mental Health, 1968. (b)

Lorr, M., Klett, C. J., & McNair, D. M. *Syndromes of psychosis*. New York: Macmillan, 1963.

Lorr, M., McNair, D. M., Klett, C. J., & Lasky, J. J. Evidence of ten psychotic syndromes. *Journal of Consulting Psychology*, 1962, **26**, 185–189.

Lotter, V. Epidemiology of autistic conditions in young children. *Social Psychiatry*, 1966, **1**, 124–137.

Lourie, R. S. Suicide and attempted suicide in children and adolescents. In L. Yochelson (Ed.), *Symposium on suicide*. Washington, D.C.: George Washington University School of Medicine, 1965.

Lovaas, O. I., Litrownik, A., & Mann, R. Response latencies to auditory stimuli in children engaged in self-stimulatory behavior. *Behavior Research Therapy*, 1971, **9**, 39–49.

Lu, Yi-chuang. Mother-child role relations in schizophrenia: A comparison of schizophrenic patients with nonschizophrenic siblings. *Psychiatry*, 1961, **24**, 133–142.

Lu, Yi-chuang. Contradictory parental expectations in schizophrenia. *American Medical Association Archives of General Psychiatry*, 1962, **6**, 219–234.

Lucia, S. P. *Alcohol and civilization*. New York: McGraw–Hill, 1963.

Ludwig, A. O. Rheumatoid arthritis. In E. D. Wittkower and R. A. Cleghorn (Eds.), *Recent developments in psychosomatic medicine*. Philadelphia: Lippincott, 1954.

Lykken, D. T. A study of anxiety in the sociopathic personality. *Journal of Abnormal and Social Psychology*, 1957, **55**, 6–10.

McCord, W., & McCord, J. *The psychopath: An essay on the criminal mind* (rev. ed.). Princeton, N. J.: Van Nostrand, 1964.

McIsaac, W. M. A biochemical concept of mental disease. *Postgraduate Medicine*, 1961, **20**, 111–118.

McKinney, W. T., Suomi, S. J., & Harlow, H. F. New models of separation and depression in rhesus monkeys. In J. P. Scott & E. C. Senay (Eds.), *Separation and depression: Clinical and research aspects*. Washington, D.C.: American Association for the Advancement of Science, 1973. Publication No. 94.

McNair, D. M., Lorr, M., & Hemingway, P. Further evidence for syndrome-based psychotic types. *Archives of General Psychiatry*, 1964, **11**, 368–376.

Maddi, S. R. The existential neurosis. *Journal of Abnormal and Social Psychology*, 1967, **72**, 311–325.

Maddison, D., & Duncan, G. M. *Aspects of depressive illness*. Edinburgh: Livingstone, 1965.

Maher, B. A. Intelligence and brain damage. In N. R. Ellis (Ed.), *Handbook of mental deficiency*. New York: McGraw–Hill, 1963.

Maher, B. A. *Principles of psychopathology:*

An experimental approach. New York: McGraw-Hill, 1966.

Maickel, R. P. *Biochemical factors in alcoholism.* Oxford: Pergamon Press, 1967.

Mahl, G. F. Effect of chronic fear on the gastric secretion of HCl in dogs. *Psychosomatic Medicine,* 1949, **11**, 30–44.

Mahl, G. F. Anxiety, HCl secretion, and peptic ulcer. *Psychosomatic Medicine,* 1950, **12**, 158–169.

Mahl, G. F. Relationship between acute and chronic fear and the gastric acidity and blood sugar levels in *Macaca mulatta* monkeys. *Psychosomatic Medicine,* 1952, **14**, 182–210.

Malis, G. Y. *Research on the etiology of schizophrenia.* New York: Consultants Bureau, 1961.

Malone, T. P., Whitaker, C. A., Warkentin, J., & Felder, R. E. Rational and nonrational psychotherapy. *American Journal of Psychotherapy,* 1961, **15**, 212–220.

Malzberg, B. *The alcoholic psychoses.* New Haven: Yale Center of Alcohol Studies, 1960.

Mandler, G. The interruption of behavior. In D. Levine (Ed.), *Nebraska symposium on motivation.* Lincoln: University of Nebraska Press, 1964.

Mark, V. H., & Ervin, F. R. *Violence and the brain.* New York: Harper & Row, 1970.

Martin, B. *Abnormal psychology: Clinical and scientific perspectives.* New York: Holt, Rinehart & Winston, 1977.

Maser, J. D., & Seligman, M. E. P. (Eds.) *Psychopathology: Experimental models.* San Francisco: W. H. Freeman, 1977.

Maslow, A. H. *Motivation and personality,* New York: Harper, 1954.

Maslow, A. H. Neurosis as a failure of personal growth. *Humanitas,* 1967, **3**, 153–169.

Maslow, A. H. *Toward a psychology of being* (3rd ed.). Princeton, N. J.: Van Nostrand, 1968.

Maslow, A. H., & Mittlemann, B. *Principles of abnormal psychology: The dynamics of psychic illness* (Rev. ed.). New York: Harper, 1951.

Masserman, J. H., & Yum, K. S. An analysis of the influence of alcohol on experimental neurosis in cats. *Psychosomatic Medicine,* 1946, **8**, 36–52.

Masters, W. H., & Johnson, V. E. *Human sexual response.* Boston: Little, Brown, 1966.

Mathis, J. L., Pierce, C. M., & Pishkin, V. *Basic psychiatry: A primer of concepts and terminology.* New York: Appleton-Century-Crofts, 1968.

May, R. Contributions of existential psychotherapy. In R. May, E. Angel and H. E. Ellenberger (Eds.), *Existence: A new dimension in psychiatry and psychology.* New York: Basic Books, 1958.

May, R. The existential approach. In S. Arieti (Ed.), *American handbook of psychiatry.* New York: Basic Books, 1959.

May, R. *Psychology and the human dilemma.* Princeton, N. J.: Van Nostrand, 1967.

May, R. (Ed.), *Existential psychology* (2nd ed.). New York: Random House, 1961, 1969, 1981.

May, R. *Power and innocence: A search for sources of violence.* New York: Dell, 1976.

May, R., Angel, E., & Ellenberger, H. F. (Eds.) *Existence: A new dimension in psychiatry and psychology.* New York: Basic Books, 1958.

Mead, M. The changing world of living. *Diseases of the Nervous System,* 1967, **28** (suppl.) 5–11.

Mednick, S. A. A learning theory approach to research in schizophrenia. *Psychological Bulletin,* 1958, **55**, 316–327.

Mednick, S. A. Learning theory and schizophrenia: A reply to a comment. *Psychological Bulletin,* 1959, **56**, 315–316.

Mednick, S. A., & Schulsinger, F. Some premorbid characteristics related to breakdown in children with schizophrenic mothers. In D. Rosenthal & S. S. Kety (Eds.), *The transmission of schizophrenia.* Oxford: Pergamon, 1968.

Meduna, L. J. New methods of medical treatment of schizophrenia. *Archives of Neurology and Psychiatry,* 1936, **35**, 361–363.

Meduna, L. J. Alteration of neurotic pattern by use of CO_2 inhalations. *Journal of Nervous and Mental Disease,* 1948, **108**, 373–379.

Meduna, L. J. *Oneirophrenia: The confusional state.* Urbana, Ill.: University of Illinois Press, 1950.

Meduna, L. J. The convulsive treatment: A reappraisal. *Journal of Clinical and Experimental Psychopathology & Quarterly Review of Psychiatry and Neurology,* 1954, **15,** 219–233. (a)

Meduna, L. J. The carbon dioxide treatment: A review. *Journal of Clinical and Experimental Psychopathology & Quarterly Review of Psychiatry and Neurology,* 1954, **15,** 235–249. (b)

Meduna, L. J. *Carbon dioxide therapy: A neurophysiological treatment of nervous disorders.* Springfield, Ill.: Charles C Thomas, 1958.

Meduna, L. J. Metrazol convulsive shock therapy. In W. S. Sahakian (Ed.), *History of psychology: A source book in systematic psychology.* Itasca, Ill.: F. E. Peacock Publishers, 1968.

Meehl, P. E. Schizotaxia, schizotypy, schizophrenia. *American Psychologist,* 1962, **17,** 827–838.

Melges, F., & Bowlby, J. Types of hopelessness in psychopathological process. *Archives of General Psychiatry,* 1969, **20,** 690–699.

Mendel, W. M. A phenomenological theory of schizophrenia. In A. Burton, J. J. Loper-Ibor, & W. M. Mendel, *Schizophrenia as a life style.* New York: Springer, 1974.

Mendels, J. (Ed.) *Biological psychiatry.* New York: Wiley, 1973.

Menninger, K. Toward a unitary concept of mental illness. In B. H. Hall (Ed.), *A psychiatrist's world.* New York: Viking, 1959.

Menninger, K. Concerning the advocacy of a unitary concept of mental illness. In L. Appleby, J. Sher, and J. Cummings (Eds.), *Chronic schizophrenia.* New York: Free Press, 1960.

Menninger, K. *The vital balance.* New York: Viking, 1963.

Menninger, K., Ellenberger, H., Pruyser, P., & Mayman, M. The unitary concept of mental illness. *Bulletin of the Menninger Clinic,* 1958, **22,** 4–12.

Meyer, A. *The commonsense psychiatry of....* New York: McGraw–Hill, 1948.

Meyer, A. *Collected papers of....* (Eunice E. Winters, Ed.). Baltimore: Johns Hopkins, 1951.

Mezan, P., & R. D. Laing: Portrait of a twentieth-century skeptic. In R. I Evans (Ed.), *R. D. Laing: The man and his ideas.* New York: E. P. Dutton, 1976.

Miller, N. E. Liberalization of the basic S-R concepts: Extensions to conflict behavior, motivation and social learning. In S. Koch (Ed.), *Psychology: A study of a science* (Vol. 2). New York: McGraw–Hill, 1959.

Miller, N. E. Experiments relevant to learning theory and psychopathology. In *Proceedings of the XVIII International Congress of Psychology.* Moscow, 1966. In W. S. Sahakian (Ed.), *Psychopathology today.* Itasca, Ill.: F. E. Peacock Publishers, 1970.

Miller, W. R., Rosellini, R. A., & Seligman, M.E.P. Learned helplessness and depression. In J. D. Maser & M.E.P. Seligman (Eds.), *Psychopathology: Experimental models.* San Francisco: W. H. Freeman, 1977.

Mills, I. H. Amitriptyline therapy in anorexia nervosa. *Lancet,* 1976, **ii,** 687.

Minuchin, S., Rosman, B., & Baker, L. *Psychosomatic families: Anorexia nervosa in context.* Cambridge, Mass.: Harvard University Press, 1978.

Moniz, E. How I succeeded in performing the prefrontal leukotomy. *Journal of Clinical Experimental Psychopathology,* 1954, **15,** 373–379.

Moniz, E. Prefrontal leukotomy. In W. S. Sahakian (Ed.), *History of psychology: A source book in systematic psychology.* Itasca, Ill.: F. E. Peacock Publishers, 1981.

Moreno, J. L. *Who shall survive? Foundations of sociometry, group psychotherapy and sociodrama.* Beacon, N. Y.: Beacon House, 1953.

Moreno, J. L. *Psychodrama.* Beacon, N. Y.: Beacon House, Vol. I, 1946, II, 1959, III, 1969. 4th ed., 1972.

Moreno, J. L. (Ed.) *The international handbook of group psychotherapy.* New York:

Philosophical Library, 1966. (a)

Moreno, J. L. Therapeutic aspects of psychodrama. *Psychiatric Opinion,* 1966, **3,** 36–42. (b)

Moreno, J. L. *Das Stegreif theater.* Beacon, N. Y.: Beacon House, 1970.

Morton, R. *Phthisiologica: Or a treatise of consumptions.* London, 1694.

Mowrer, O. H. On the dual nature of learning—A reinterpretation of "conditioning" and "problem-solving." *Harvard Educational Review,* 1947, **17,** 102–148.

Mowrer, O. H. Learning theory and the neurotic paradox. *American Journal of Orthopsychiatry,* 1948, **18,** 571–610.

Mowrer, O. H. *Learning theory and personality dynamics.* New York: Ronald Press, 1950.

Mowrer, O. H. Symposium, 1952, the therapeutic process. III. Learning theory and the neurotic fallacy. *American Journal of Orthopsychiatry,* 1952, **22,** 679–689.

Mowrer, O. H. Neurosis, psychotherapy, and two-factor learning theory. In O. H. Mowrer (Ed.), *Psychotherapy: Theory and research.* New York: Ronald Press, 1953.

Mowrer, O. H. "Sin," the lesser of two evils. *American Psychology,* 1960, **15,** 301–304.

Mowrer, O. H. *The crisis in psychiatry and religion.* Princeton, N. J.: Van Nostrand, 1961.

Mowrer, O. H. *The new group therapy.* Princeton, N. J.: Van Nostrand, 1964.

Mowrer, O. H. The behavior therapies, with special reference to modeling and imitation. *American Journal of Psychotherapy,* 1966, **20,** 439–461.

Mowrer, O. H. (Ed.) *Morality and mental health.* Chicago: Rand McNally, 1967. (a)

Mowrer, O. H. Communication, conscience and the unconscious. *Journal of Communication Disorders,* 1967, **1,** 109–135. (b)

Mullan, H., & Rosenbaum, M. *Group psychotherapy: Theory and practice.* New York: Free Press, 1962.

Mullan, H., & Sanguiliano, I. *Alcoholism: Group psychotherapy and rehabilitation.* Springfield, Ill.: Charles C Thomas, 1966.

National Council on Alcoholism, Inc. *New York City Alcoholism Study.* New York, 1962.

National Institute of Mental Health. *Patients in mental institutions. 1965. Part II. State and county mental hospitals.* Washington, D.C.: U. S. Department of Health, Education and Welfare, 1967.

Needleman, H. L. & Waber, D. The use of amitriptyline in anorexia nervosa. In R. A. Vigersky (Ed.), *Anorexia nervosa.* New York: Raven Press, 1977.

Neustatter, W. L. *The medical aspects of homosexuality.* In W. A. R. Thomson (Ed.), *Sex and its problems.* Edinburgh: Livingstone, 1968.

New York Academy of Medicine, Committee on Public Health. *Homosexuality.* New York: New York Academy of Medicine, 1964.

Nineteenth World Health Organization. *Manual of the international statistical classification of disease, injuries, and causes of death.* Geneva: World Health Organization, 1967.

Noyes, A. P., & Kolb, L. C. *Modern clinical psychiatry* (6th ed.). Philadelphia: Saunders, 1963.

Olds, J., & Milner, P. Positive reinforcement produced by electrical stimulation of septal area and other regions of rat brain. *Journal of Comparative & Physiological Psychology,* 1954, **47,** 419–427.

Ollendorff, R. H. V. *The juvenile homosexual experience and its effect on adult sexuality.* New York: Julian Press, 1966.

Orlinsky, D. E., & Howard, K. I. Gender and psychotherapeutic outcome. In A. Brodsky & Hare-Mustin (Eds.), *Women and psychotherapy.* New York: Guilford Press, 1980.

Ornitz, E. Childhood autism: A review of the clinical and experimental literature. *California Medicine,* 1973, **118,** 21-47.

Osmond, H., & Hoffer, A. Schizophrenia: A new approach. *Journal of Mental Science, 1959,* **105,** 656–673.

Osmond, H., & Hoffer, A. A comprehensive theory of schizophrenia. *International Journal of Neuropsychiatry,* 1966, **2,** 302–309.

Osmond, H., & Smythies, J. Schizophrenia: A new approach. *Journal of Mental Science,* 1952, **98,** 309–315.

Otis, L. S. Dissociation and recovery of a response learned under the influence of chlorpromazine or saline. *Science,* 1964, **143,** 1347–1348.

Overton, D. A. State-dependent or "dissociated" learning produced with pentobarbital. *Journal of Comparative and Physiological Psychology,* 1964, **57,** 3–12.

Paffenbarger, R. S., & McCabe, L. J. The effect of obstetric prenatal events on risk of mental illness in women of childbearing age. *American Journal of Public Health,* 1966, **56,** 400–407.

Partanen, J., Bruun, K., Markkanen, T. *Inheritance of drinking behavior: A study on intelligence, personality, and use of alcohol of adult twins.* Vol. 14. Helsinki: Finnish Foundation of Alcohol Studies, 1966.

Pavlov, I. P. *Conditioned reflexes.* London: Oxford University Press, 1927.

Payne, R. W. Cognitive abnormalities. In H. J. Eysenck (Ed.), *Handbook of abnormal psychology.* New York: Basic Books, 1961.

Payne, R. W. An object classification test as a measure of overinclusive thinking in schizophrenic patients. *British Journal of Social Clinical Psychology,* 1962, **1,** 213–221.

Payne, R. W., Caird, W. K., & Laverty, S. G. Overinclusive thinking and delusions in schizophrenic patients. *Journal of Abnormal and Social Psychology,* 1964, **68,** 562–566.

Payne, R. W., Mattussek, P., & George, E. I. An experimental study of schizophrenic thought disorder. *Journal of Mental Sciences,* 1959, **105,** 627–652.

Payne, R. W., & Sloane, R. B. Can schizophrenia be defined? *Diseases of the Nervous System,* 1968, **29** (Suppl.), 113–117.

Perls, F. S., Hefferline, R. E., & Goodman, P. *Gestalt therapy: Excitement and growth in the human personality.* New York: Dell, 1965.

Perls, F. S. *Ego, hunger and aggression: A revision of Freud's theory and method.* San Francisco, Calif.: Orbit Graphic Arts, 1966. (a)

Perls, F. S. Gestalt therapy and human po-
tentialities. In H. A. Otto (Ed.), *Explorations in human potentialities.* Springfield, Ill.: Charles C Thomas, 1966. (b)

Pepinsky, H. B., & Pepinsky, P. N. *Counseling: Theory and practice.* New York: Ronald Press, 1954.

Philips, I. (Ed.) *Prevention and treatment of mental retardation.* New York: Basic Books, 1966.

Phillips, E. L. *Psychotherapy: A modern theory and practice.* Englewood Cliffs, N. J.: Prentice-Hall, 1956.

Phillips, E. L., & Wiener, D. N. *Short-term psychotherapy and structured behavior change.* New York: McGraw-Hill, 1966.

Phillips, L. Case history data and prognosis in schizophrenia. *Journal of Nervous and Mental Disease,* 1953, **117,** 515–525.

Phillips, L. A social view of psychopathology. In P. London and D. Rosenhan (Eds.), *Foundations of abnormal psychology.* New York: Holt, Rinehart & Winston, 1968.

Piaget, J. *Judgment and reasoning in the child.* London: Routledge & Kegan Paul, 1928.

Piaget, J. *The child's conception of the world.* London: Routledge & Kegan Paul, 1929.

Piaget, J. *The child's conception of the physical causality.* London: Routledge & Kegan Paul, 1930.

Piaget, J. *The child and reality: Problems of genetic psychology.* New York: Grossman, 1973.

Piaget, J., & Inhelder, B. *The psychology of the child.* New York: Basic, 1969.

Pollack, M., Klein, D. F., Willner, A., Blumberg, A., & Fink, M. Imipramine-induced behavioral disorganization in schizophrenic patients: Physiologic and psychologic correlates. In J. Wortis (Ed.), *Recent advances in biological psychiatry.* Vol 7. New York: Plenum, 1965.

Pollmer, E. *Alcoholic personalities.* New York: Expositional Press, 1965.

Pope, Jr., H. G., & Hudson, J. I. Treatment of bulimia with antidepressants. *Psychopharmacology,* 1982, **78,** 176–179.

Quitkin, F. W., Rifkin, A., & Klein, D. F. Lithium in other psychiatric disorders. In S. Gershon & B. Shopsin (Eds.), *Lithium: Its role in psychiatric research and treat-*

ment. New York: Plenum, 1973. Pp. 295–315.

Rado, S. The problem of melancholia. *International Journal of Psycho-Analysis,* 1928, **9,** 420–438.

Rado, S. Hedonic control, action-self and the depressive spell. In P. H. Hoch and J. Zubin (Eds.), *Depression.* New York: Grune & Stratton, 1954.

Rado, S. The automatic motivating system of depressive behavior. *Comprehensive Psychiatry,* 1961, **2,** 248–260.

Rank, O. *Will therapy and truth and reality.* New York: Knopf, 1945.

Rank, O. The possibilities of therapy. *Journal of the Otto Rank Association,* 1968, **3,** 26–39.

Rank, O. Will therapy. In W. S. Sahakian (Ed.), *Psychotherapy and counseling: Studies in technique.* Chicago: Rand McNally, 1969.

Rank, O. *The trauma of birth.* New York: Harper & Row, 1973.

Rapoport, R. N. *Community as doctor: New perspectives on a therapeutic community.* London: Tavistock, 1960.

Rapoport, R. N. The therapeutic community. In D. L. Sills (Ed.), *Encyclopedia of the social sciences.* New York: Macmillan & Free Press, 1968.

Redlich, F. C. The concept of health in psychiatry. In A. H. Leighton, J. A. Clausen and R. N. Wilson (Eds.), *Explorations in social psychiatry.* New York: Basic Books, 1957.

Redlich, F. C., & Freedman, D. X. *The theory and practice of psychiatry.* New York: Basic Books, 1966.

Reich, W. *Character analysis.* New York: Farrar, Strauss & Giroux, 1972.

Reich, W. *The function of the orgasm.* New York: Farrar, Strauss & Giroux, 1973. (a)

Reich, W. *Selected writings.* New York: Farrar, Strauss & Giroux, 1973. (b)

Rimland, B. *Infantile autism.* New York: Appleton-Century-Crofts, 1964.

Rimm, D. C., & Somervill, J. W. *Abnormal psychology.* New York: Academic Press, 1977.

Ritvo, E. R. (Ed.) *Autism: Diagnosis, current research and management.* New York: Spectrum, 1976. (a)

Ritvo, E. R. Autism: From adjective to noun. In E. R. Ritvo (Ed.), *Autism: Diagnosis, current research and management.* New York: Spectrum, 1976. (b)

Ritvo, E. R., Freeman, B. J., Geller, E., Yuwiler, A. Effects of fenfluramine on 14 outpatients with the syndrome of autism. *Journal of the American Academy of Child Psychiatry,* 1983, **22,** 549–558.

Rogers, C. R. *Counseling and psychotherapy: New concepts in practice.* Boston: Houghton Mifflin, 1942.

Rogers, C. R. *Client-centered therapy: Its current practice, implications, and theory.* Boston: Houghton Mifflin, 1951.

Rogers, C. R. Client-centered therapy. In S. Arieti (Ed.), *American handbook of psychiatry.* New York: Basic Books, 1959.

Rogers, C. R. The therapeutic relationship: Recent theory and research. *Australian Journal of Psychology,* 1965, **17,** 95–108.

Roman, P. M., & Harrison, T. M. (Eds.) *Explorations in psychiatric sociology.* Philadelphia: F. A. Davis, 1974.

Rosen, E., & Gregory, I. *Abnormal psychology.* Philadelphia: Saunders, 1965.

Rosen, J. *Direct analysis: Selected papers.* New York: Grune & Stratton, 1953.

Rosenfeld, H. A. *Psychotic states: A psychoanalytical approach.* New York: International Universities, 1965.

Rosenhan, D. L. On being sane in insane places. *Science,* 1973, **179,** 250–258.

Rosenthal, D. (Ed.) *The Genain quadruplets: A case study and theoretical analysis of heredity and environment in schizophrenia.* New York: Basic Books, 1963.

Rosenthal, D. *Genetic theory and abnormal behavior.* New York: McGraw–Hill, 1970.

Rosenthal, D., & Kety, S. S. (Eds.) *The transmission of schizophrenia.* Oxford: Pergamon, 1968.

Rotter, J. B. *Social learning and clinical psychology.* New York: Prentice-Hall, 1954.

Rotter, J. B. *Clinical psychology.* New York: Prentice-Hall, 1964.

Russell, B. *Principles of mathematics* (2nd ed.). London: George Allen & Unwin, 1937.

Russell, G. Bulimia nervosa: An ominous variant of anorexia nervosa. *Psychological Medicine*, 1979, **9**, 429–448.

Russell, G. F. M. Anorexia nervosa: Its identity as an illness and its treatment. In J. H. Price (Ed.), *Modern trends in psychological medicine*, 1970, **2**, 131–164.

Russell, J. A. O. Psychosocial aspects of weight loss and amenorrhoea in adolescent girls. In N. Morris (Ed.), *Psychosomatic medicine in obstetrics and gynaecology.* Basel, Switz.: Karger, 1972. Pp. 593–595.

Rutter, M. Psychotic disorders in early childhood. In A. Cooper & A. Walk (Eds.), *Recent developments in schizophrenia.* London: RMPA, 1967.

Rutter, M. Concepts of autism: A review of research. *Journal of Child Psychology and Psychiatry*, 1968, **9**, 1–25.

Rutter, M. Infantile autism and other child psychoses. In M. Rutter & Hersov (Eds.), *Child psychiatry: Modern approaches.* Oxford: Blackwell Scientific Publications, 1977.

Rutter, M. Cognitive deficits in the pathogenesis of autism. *Journal of Child Psychology*, 1983, **24**, 513–531.

Saghir, M. T., & Robins, E. Homosexuality. *Archives of General Psychiatry*, 1969, **20**, 192–201. (a)

Saghir, M. T., Robins, E., & Walbran, B. Homosexuality II: Sexual behavior of the male homosexual. *Archives of General Psychiatry*, 1969, **21**, 219–229. (b)

Saghir, M. T., & Robins, E. *Male and female homosexuality: A comprehensive investigation.* Baltimore: Williams & Wilkins, 1973.

Sahakian, B. J., Bingham, S., Murgatroyd, P., Lean, M., & James, W. P. T. Food preferences, eating patterns, and caloric intake in normal and compulsive eaters. *Society for Neuroscience Abstracts*, 1971, **7**, 388.

Sahakian, B. J., Svendsen, A., & Klove, H. Environmental modification of stereotyped behavior in the autistic child (in press).

Sahakian, W. S. Stoic philosophical psychotherapy. *Journal of Individual Psychology*, 1969, **25**, 32–35. (a)

Sahakian, W. S. A social learning theory of obsessional neurosis. *Israel Annals of Psychiatry and Related Disciplines*, 1969, **7**, 70–75. (b)

Sahakian, W. S. Philosophical psychotherapy. In W. S. Sahakian (Ed.), *Psychotherapy and counseling: Techniques in intervention.* Boston: Houghton Mifflin, 1976. (a)

Sahakian, W. S. (Ed.) *Psychotherapy and counseling: Studies in technique.* (2nd ed.) Boston: Houghton Mifflin, 1976. (b)

Sahakian, W. S. Personalism. In R. J. Corsini (Ed.), *Current personality theories.* Itasca, Ill.: F. E. Peacock, 1977. (a)

Sahakian, W. S. *Psychology of personality. Readings in theory.* (3rd ed.) Boston: Houghton Mifflin, 1977. (b)

Sahakian, W. S. Logotherapy—for whom? In J. B. Fabry, R. P. Bulka, & W. S. Sahakian (Eds.), *Logotherapy in action.* New York: Jason Aronson, 1979.

Sahakian, W. S. Philosophical psychotherapy. In R. Herink (Ed.), *The psychotherapy handbook.* New York: Meridian book, New American Library, 1980. (a)

Sahakian, W. S. Philosophical psychotherapy: A variation of logotherapy. *International Forum for Logotherapy*, 1980, **3**, 37–40. (b)

Sahakian, W. S. *History of psychology: A source book in systematic psychology.* (2nd ed.) Itasca, Ill.: F. E. Peacock Publishers, 1981.

Sahakian, W. S. Therapeutic effects of philosophy. *Analecta Frankliana.* San Francisco: Institute of Logotherapy Press, 1982. Pp. 15–19.

Sahakian, W. S. Philosophical psychotherapy. *Encyclopedia of psychology.* New York: Wiley, 1984.

Sakel, M. The pharmacological shock treatment of schizophrenia. New York: *Journal of Nervous and Mental Disease*, 1938.

Sakel, M. The classical Sakel shock treatment: A reappraisal. *Journal of Clinical and Experimental Psychopathology & Review of Psychiatry and Neurology*, 1954, **15**, 255–316.

Salter, A. *Conditioned reflex therapy.* New York: Farrar, Straus, 1949.

Sampson, H., Messinger, S. L., & Towne, R.

D. *Schizophrenic women: Studies in marital crises.* New York: Atherton, 1964.

Sanders, R., Smith, R. S., & Weinman, B. S. *Chronic psychoses and recovery: An experiment in socio-environmental treatment.* San Francisco, Calif.: Jossey–Bass, 1967.

Sarason, S. B., & Doris, J. *Psychological problems in mental deficiency.* 4th ed. New York: Harper & Row, 1969.

Sarason, I. G. *Abnormal psychology: The problem of maladaptive behavior.* 2nd ed. Englewood Cliffs, N. J.: Prentice-Hall, 1976.

Satir, V. *Conjoint family therapy: A guide to theory and technique.* Palo Alto, Calif.: Science and Behavior Books, 1967.

Satir, V. You as a change agent. In V. Satir, J. Stachowiak, & H. A. Taschman (Eds.), *Helping families to change.* New York: Jason Aronson. 1975.

Satir, V., Stachowiak, J., & Taschman, H. S. (Eds.) *Helping families to change.* New York: Jason Aronson, 1975.

Schachter, S. Obesity and eating. *Science,* 1968, **161,** 751–756.

Schachter, S. Eat, eat. *Psychology Today,* 1971, **4,** 44–47, 78–79.

Schaefer, H. H., & Martin, P. L. *Behavioral therapy.* New York: McGraw–Hill, 1969.

Scheler, M. *Der Formalismus in der Ethik und die materiale Wertethik.* Bern: Franke, 1966.

Schildkraut, J. J. The catecholamine hypothesis of affective disorders: A review of supporting evidence. *American Journal of Psychiatry,* 1965, **122,** 509–522.

Schildkraut, J. Pharmacology—The effects of lithium on biogenic amines. In S. Gershon & B. Shopsin (Eds.), *Lithium: Its role in psychiatric research and treatment.* New York: Plenum, 1973. Pp. 57–73.

Schmidt, W., Suiart, R. G., & Moss, M. K. *Social class and the treatment of alcoholism.* Toronto: University of Toronto Press, 1968.

Schneider, R. *Psychopathic personalities.* Springfield, Ill.: Charles C Thomas, 1958.

Schofield, M. *The sexual behaviour of young people.* London: Longmans, Green, 1965. (a)

Schofield, M. *Sociological aspects of homosexuality: A comparative study of three types of homosexuals.* London: Longmans, Green, 1965. (b)

Schopler, E. Evolution in understanding and treatment of autism. *Triangle,* 1982, **21,** 51–57.

Schou, M. Special review: Lithium in psychotic therapy and prophylaxis. *Journal of Psychiatric Research,* 1968, **6,** 67–95.

Schultz, J. H., & Luthe, W. *Autogenic training.* New York: Grune & Stratton, 1959.

Scott, W. A. Research definitions of mental health and mental illness. *Psychological Bulletin,* 1958, **55,** 29–45

Scott, W. A. Conceptions of normality. In E. F. Borgatta & W. W. Lambert (Eds.), *Handbook of personality theory and research.* Chicago: Rand McNally, 1968.

Searles, H. F. Integration and differentiation in schizophrenia. *British Journal of Medical Psychology,* 1959, **32,** 261–281.

Seay, B., Hansen, E., & Harlow, H. F. Mother-infant separation in monkeys. *Journal of Child Psychology,* 1962, **3,** 123–132.

Seligman, M. E. P. *Helplessness: On depression, development, and death.* San Francisco: W. H. Freeman, 1975.

Shakow, D. Segmental set: A theory of the formal psychological deficit in schizophrenia. *Archives of General Psychiatry,* 1962, **6,** 17–33.

Shakow, D. Psychological deficit in schizophrenia. *Behavioral Sciences,* 1963, **8,** 275–303.

Shakow, D. Some observations on the psychology (and some fewer, on the biology) of schizophrenia. *Journal of Nervous and Mental Disease,* 1971, **153,** 300–316.

Shakow, D. Segmental set: The adaptive process in schizophrenia. *American Psychologist,* 1977, **32,** 129–139.

Shapiro, T., & Sherman, M. Long-term follow-up of children with psychiatric disorders. *Hospital and Community Psychiatry,* 1983, **34,** 522–527.

Shelly, J. A., & Bassin, A. Daytop Lodge—A new treatment approach for drug addicts. *Correct Psychiatry,* 1965, **11,** 186–195.

Shoben, E. J. A learning-theory interpretation

of psychotherapy. *Harvard Educational Review,* 1948, **18,** 129–145.

Shoben, E. J. Psychotherapy as a problem in learning theory. *Psychological Bulletin,* 1949, **46,** 366–392.

Shoben, J. S. Toward a concept of the normal personality. *American Psychologist,* 1957, **12,** 183–189.

Siegman, A. W. The relationship between future time perspective, time estimation and impulse control in a group of young offenders and a control group. *Journal of Consulting Psychology,* 1961, **25,** 470–475.

Silverman, C. *The epidemiology of depression.* Baltimore: Johns Hopkins Press, 1968.

Silverman, H. L. *Psychiatry and psychology: Relationships, intra-relationships, and interrelationships.* Springfield, Ill.: Charles C Thomas, 1963.

Silverman, S. *Psychological aspects of physical symptoms.* New York: Appleton-Century-Crofts, 1968.

Simmons, O. G., & Freeman, H. E. Familial expectations and posthospital performance of mental patients. *Human Relations,* 1959, **12,** 233–242.

Slavson, S. R. *A textbook in analytic group psychotherapy.* New York: International Universities, 1964.

Slavson, S. R. *Reclaiming the delinquent by para-analytic group psychotherapy and the inversion technique.* New York: Free Press, 1965. (a)

Slavson, S. R. Para-analytic group psychotherapy: A treatment of choice for adolescents. *Psychotherapy and Psychosomatics,* 1965, **13,** 321–331. (b)

Smythies, J. R. *Schizophrenia: Chemistry, metabolism and treatment.* Springfield, Ill.: Charles C Thomas, 1963.

Smythies, J. R. *Biological psychiatry: A review of recent advances.* London: William Heinemann Medical Books, 1968.

Snyder, S. H. *Madness and the brain.* New York: McGraw-Hill, 1974.

Snyder, S. H., Banerjee, S. P., Yamamura, H. I., & Greenberg, D. Drugs, neurotransmitters, and schizophrenia. *Science,* 1974, **184,** 1243–1253.

Spence, J. T., Carson, R. C., & Thibaut, J. W. (Eds.) *Behavioral approaches to therapy.* Morristown, N. J.: General Learning. 1976.

Spence, K. W., & Farber, I. E. Conditioning and extinction as a function of anxiety. *Journal of Experimental Psychology,* 1953, **45,** 116–119.

Spence, K. W., & Taylor, J. A. Anxiety and the strength of the UCS as determiners of the amount of eyelid conditioning. *Journal of Experimental Psychology,* 1951, **42,** 183–188.

Spence, K. W., & Taylor, J. A. The relation of conditioned response strength to anxiety in normal, neurotic and psychotic subjects. *Journal of Experimental Psychology,* 1953, **45,** 265–272.

Spitz, R. Anaclitic depression. *Psychoanalytic Study of the Child,* 1946, **2,** 313–342.

Stampfl, T. G., & Levis, D. J. *Implosive therapy: Theory and technique,* In A. Bandura et al., *Behavioral approaches to therapy.* Morristown, N. J.: Silver Burdett, 1976. Pp. 89–110.

Stein, L., & Wise, C. D. Possible etiology of schizophrenia: Progressive damage to the noradrenergic reward system by 6-hydroxydopamine. *Science,* 1971, **171,** 1032–1036.

Stekel, W. *Technique of analytical psychotherapy.* New York: Liveright, 1950.

Stekel, W. *Homosexuality.* New York: Liveright, 1948.

Stern, P. J. *The abnormal person and his world.* Princeton, N.J.: Van Nostrand, 1964.

Stevens, J. R. An anatomy of schizophrenia? *Archives of General Psychiatry,* 1973, **29,** 177–189.

Stock, D., & Thelen, H. *Emotional dynamics and group culture.* New York: New York University Press, 1958.

Storm, T., & Smart, R. G. Dissociation: A possible explanation of some features of alcoholism, and implication for its treatment. *Quarterly Journal of Studies on Alcohol,* 1965, **26,** 111–115.

Strauss, E. W. Norm and pathology of

I-world relations. *Diseases of the Nervous System,* 1961, **22,** 57–68.

Strauss, E. W. *Phenomenological psychology.* New York: Basic Books, 1966.

Suggs, R. C. *Marquesan sexual behavior.* New York: Harcourt, Brace Jovanovich, 1966.

Sullivan, H. S. Psychiatry: Introduction to the study of interpersonal relations. *Psychiatry,* 1938, **1,** 121–134.

Sullivan, H. S. *Conceptions of modern psychiatry.* New York: Norton, 1947. (a)

Sullivan, H. S. Therapeutic investigations in schizophrenia. *Psychiatry,* 1947, **10,** 121–125. (b)

Sullivan, H. S. Towards a psychiatry of peoples. *Psychiatry,* 1948, **11,** 105–116.

Sullivan, H. S. *The interpersonal theory of psychiatry.* New York: Norton, 1953.

Sullivan, H. S. *The psychiatric interview.* New York: Norton, 1954.

Sullivan, H. S. *Clinical studies in psychiatry.* New York: Norton, 1956.

Sullivan, H. S. *Schizophrenia as a human process.* New York: Norton, 1962.

Sullivan, H. S. *The fusion of psychiatry and social science.* New York: Norton, 1964.

Sutherland, E. H., & Cressey, D. R. *Principles of criminology* (6th ed.). Philadelphia: Lippincott, 1960.

Suzuki, D. T. *Introduction to Zen Buddhism.* London: Rider, 1949.

Suzuki, D. T., Fromm, E., & DeMartino, R. *Zen Buddism and psychoanalysis.* New York: Harper, 1960.

Szasz, T. S. The problem of psychiatric nosology. *American Journal of Psychiatry,* 1957, **114,** 405–413.

Szasz, T. S. The myth of mental illness. *American Psychologist,* 1960, **15,** 113–118.

Szasz, T. S. *The myth of mental illness: Foundations of a theory of personal conduct.* New York: Hoebner-Harper, 1961. (a)

Szasz, T. S. The uses of naming and the origin of the myth of mental illness. *American Psychologist,* 1961, **61,** 59–65. (b)

Szasz, T. S. *Law, liberty, and psychiatry: An inquiry into the social uses of mental health practices.* New York: Macmillan, 1963.

Szasz, T. S. *The second sin.* Garden City,

N. Y.: Doubleday, 1973.

Szasz, T. S. *Heresies.* Garden City, N. Y.: Doubleday, 1976.

Tähkä, V. *The alcoholic personality: A clinical study.* Helsinki: Finnish Foundation for Alcohol Studies, 1966.

Taylor, J. A. The relationship of anxiety to the conditioned eyelid response. *Journal of Experimental Psychology,* 1951, **41,** 81–92.

Taylor, J. A. A personality scale of manifest anxiety. *Journal of Abnormal and Social Psychology,* 1953, **48,** 285–290.

Telch, M. J. The present status of outcome studies: A reply to Frank. *Journal of Consulting and Clinical Psychology,* 1981, **49,** 472–475.

Temerlin, M. K. Suggestion effects in psychiatric diagnosis. *Journal of Nervous and Mental Disease,* 1968, **147,** 349 –353.

Temerlin, M. K. Diagnostic bias in community mental health. *Community Mental Health,* 1970, **6,** 110–117.

Thompson, G. N. The psychiatry of alcoholism. In G. N. Thompson (Ed.), *Alcoholism.* Springfield, Ill.: Charles C Thomas, 1956.

Thompson, M. G., & Schwartz, D. M. Life adjustment of women with anorexia nervosa and anorexia-like behaviour. *The International Journal of Eating Disorders,* 1982, **1,** 47–60.

Thompson, R. F. (Ed.) *Progress in psychobiology.* San Francisco: W. H. Freeman, 1976.

Thomson, W. A. R. (Ed.), *Sex and its problems.* Edinburgh: Livingstone, 1968.

Thorndike, E. L. *Animal intelligence.* New York: Macmillan, 1911.

Thorne, F. C. An existential theory of anxiety. *Journal of Clinical Psychology,* 1963, **19,** 35–43.

Thorne, F. C. An analysis of Szasz' "myth of mental illness." *American Journal of Psychiatry,* 1966, **123,** 652–656.

Tillich, P. Existentialism and psychotherapy. *Review of Existential Psychology and Psychiatry,* 1961, **1.**

Torrey, E. F. *The mind game: Witchdoctors and psychiatrists.* New York: Emerson Hall, 1972.

Torrey, E. F. Is schizophrenia universal? An open question. *Schizophrenia Bulletin,* 1973, **7,** 53–59.

Torrey, E. F. *The death of psychiatry.* Radnor, Pa.: Chilton, 1974.

Torrey, E. F., & Peterson, M. R. The viral hypothesis of schizophrenia. *Schizophrenia Bulletin,* 1976, **2,** 136–146.

Truax, C. B., & Carkhuff, R. R. *Toward effective counseling and psychotherapy: Training and practice.* Hawthorne, N.Y.: Aldine Publishing, 1967.

Turner, R. J., & Wagonfeld, M. O. Occupational mobility and schizophrenia. *American Sociological Review,* 1967, **32,** 104–113.

Uhr, L., & Miller, J. G. *Drugs and behavior.* New York: Wiley, 1960.

Ullmann, L. P., & Krasner, L. A. *Psychological approach to abnormal behavior* (2nd ed.). Englewood Cliffs, N.J.: Prentice-Hall, 1975.

U.S. Department of Health, Education, and Welfare. *Alcoholism.* Washington, D.C.: U.S. Government Printing Office, 1966.

Von Domarus, E. The specific laws of logic in schizophrenia. In J. S. Kasanin (Ed.), *Language and thought in schizophrenia.* Berkeley: University of California Press, 1944.

Wagner-Jauregg, J. R. Malarial treatment of general paresis. In W. S. Sahakian (Ed.), *History of psychology. A source book in systematic psychology.* Itasca, Ill.: F. E. Peacock Publishers, 1981.

Wallerstein, R. S. *et al., Hospital treatment of alcoholism: A comparative, experimental study.* New York: Basic Books, 1957.

Watts, A. W. *Psychotherapy east and west.* New York: Pantheon, 1961.

Watts, C. A. H. *Depressive disorders in the community.* Bristol: John Wright, 1966.

Weakland, J. H. The "double-bind" hypothesis of schizophrenia and three-party interaction. In D. D. Jackson (Ed.), *The etiology of schizophrenia.* New York: Basic Books, 1960.

Weinberg, M. S., & Williams, C. J. *Male homosexuals: Their problems and adaptations.* New York: Oxford University Press, 1974.

Weiner, I. B. *Psychodiagnosis in schizophrenia.* New York: Wiley, 1966.

Weiss, J. M. Effects of coping response on stress. *Journal of Comparative and Physiological Psychology,* 1968, **65,** 251–260.

Weiss, J. M. Somatic effects of predictable and unpredictable shock. *Psychosomatic Medicine,* 1970, **32,** 397–409.

Weiss, J. M. Effects of coping behavior in different warning signal conditions on stress pathology in rats. *Journal of Comparative and Physiological Psychology,* 1971, **77,** 1–13. (a)

Weiss, J. M. Effects of punishing the coping response (conflict) on stress pathology in rats. *Journal of Comparative and Physiological Psychology,* 1971, **77,** 14–21. (b)

Weiss, J. M. Effects of coping behavior with and without a feedback signal on stress pathology in rats. *Journal of Comparative and Physiological Psychology,* 1971, **77,** 22–30. (c)

Weiss, J. M., Glazer, H., & Pohorecky, L. Coping behavior and neurochemical changes in rats. Paper presented at the Kittay Scientific Foundation Conference, New York, March, 1974.

Weiss, J. M., Stone, E. S., & Harrell, N. Coping behavior and brain norepinephrine in rats. *Journal of Comparative and Physiological Psychology,* 1970, **72,** 153–160.

Weisskopf-Joelson, E. Some comments on a Viennese school of psychiatry. *Journal of Abnormal and Social Psychology,* 1955, **51,** 701–703.

Welsh, G. S. An anxiety index and an internalization ratio for the MMPI. *Journal of Consulting Psychologists,* 1952, **16,** 65–72.

Wender, P. H., Rosenthal, D. Kety, S. S., Shulsinger, F., & Welner, J. Social class and psychopathology in adoptees. *Archives of General Psychiatry,* 1973, **28,** 318–325.

Wender, P. H., Rosenthal, D., Kety, S. S., Schulsinger, F., & Welner, J. Crossfostering: A research strategy for clarifying the role of genetic and experimental factors in the etiology of schizophrenia. *Archives of*

General Psychiatry, 1974, **30,** 121–128.

Westwood, G. *A minority: A report on the life of the male homosexual in Great Britain.* London: Longmans, 1960.

Whitaker, C. A., & Malone, T. P. *The roots of psychotherapy.* New York: Blakiston, 1953.

Whitaker, C. A., Malone, T. P., & Warkentin, J. Multiple therapy and psychotherapy. In F. Fromm-Reichmann and J. L. Moreno (Eds.), *Progress in psychotherapy.* New York: Grune & Stratton, 1956.

Whitaker, C. A., Stock, D., & Lieberman, M. A. *Psychotherapy through the group process.* Englewood Cliffs, N.J.: Prentice-Hall, 1964.

White, R. W. (Ed.) *The study of lives.* New York: Atherton, 1964.

White, R. W. & Watt, N. F. *The abnormal personality.* 4th ed. New York: Ronald Press, 1973.

Williams, R. J. *Alcoholism: The nutritional approach.* Austin, Tex.: University of Texas Press, 1959.

Wing, L. Diagnosis, clinical description, and prognosis. In L. Wing (Ed.), *Early childhood autism.* New York: Pergamon, 1976. (a)

Wing, L. (Ed.) *Early childhood autism.* New York: Pergamon, 1976. (b)

Wishner, J. Neurosis and tension: An exploratory study of the relationship between physiological and Rorschach measures. *Journal of Abnormal and Social Psychology,* 1953, **48,** 253–260.

Wishner, J. The concept of efficiency in psychology and psychopathology. *Psychological Review,* 1955, **62,** 69–80.

Wittenborn, J. R., Dempster, A., Maurer, H., & Plante, M. Pretreatment individual difference as potential predictors of response to pharmacotherapy. *Journal of Nervous Disorders,* 1964, **139,** 186–194.

Wittkower, E. D., & Cleghorn, R. A. (Eds.), *Recent developments in psychosomatic medicine.* Philadelphia: Lippincott, 1954.

Wolberg, L. R. *Hypnoanalysis* (2nd ed.). New York: Grune & Stratton, 1964.

Wolberg, L. R. *Medical hypnosis* (2nd ed.). New York: Grune & Stratton, 1948.

Wolman, B. B. (Ed.) *Handbook of clinical psychology.* New York: McGraw-Hill, 1965.

Wolman, B. B. *Vectoriasis praecox or the group of schizophrenias.* Springfield, Ill.: Charles C Thomas, 1966.

Wolberg, L. R. *The technique of psychotherapy.* 3rd ed. New York: Grune & Stratton, 1977.

Wolpe, J. *Psychotherapy by reciprocal inhibition.* Stanford, Calif.: Stanford University Press, 1958.

Wolpe, J. *The practice of behavior therapy.* New York: Pergamon, 1969. Rev. ed., 1973.

Wolpe, J. Conditioning: The basis of modern psychotherapy. In L. D. Eron and R. C. Callahan (Eds.), *The relation of theory to practice in psychotherapy.* Hawthorne, N.Y.: Aldine Publishing, 1969.

Wolpe, J. *Theme and variations: A behavior therapy casebook.* New York: Pergamon Press, 1976.

Wolpe, J., & Lazarus. A. A. *Behavior therapy techniques: A guide to the treatment of neuroses.* New York: Pergamon, 1966.

Wolpe, J., Salter, A., & Reyna, L. J. (Eds.) *The conditioning therapies: The challenge in psychotherapy.* New York: Holt, Rinehart & Winston, 1964.

Wolpert, E. A. Manic-depressive illness as an actual neurosis. In E. Anthony & T. Benedek (Eds.), *Depression and human existence.* Boston: Little, Brown, 1975.

Wolpert, E. A. (Ed.) *Manic-depressive illness: History of a syndrome.* New York: International Universities Press, 1977.

Woolley, D. W. Participation of serotonin in mental processes. In M. Rinkel (Ed.), *Chemical concepts of psychosis.* New York: McDowell, Obolensky, 1958. (a)

Woolley, D. W. Serotonin in mental illness. *Research Publications of the Association of Nervous and Mental Disease,* 1958, **36,** 381–400. (b)

Woolley, D. W., & Shaw, E. A biochemical and pharmacological suggestion about certain mental disorders. *Science,* 1954, **119,** 587–588.

Woolley, D. W., & Shaw, E. Some serotonin-like activities of lysergic acid diethylamide. *Science,* 1956, **124,** 121–122.

World Health Organization. *Manual of the international statistical classification of disease, injuries, and causes of death.* Geneva: World Health Organization, 1977.

Wortis, J. Psychopharmacology and physiological treatment. *American Journal of Psychiatry,* 1962, **119,** 621–628.

Wynne, Cromwell, Matthysse (Eds.), *Nature of schizophrenia: New findings and future strategies.* New York: Wiley, 1978.

Yalom, I. D. *The theory and practice of group psychotherapy.* New York: Basic Books, 1970.

Yates, A. J. *Behavior therapy.* New York: Wiley, 1970.

Young, J. G., Kavanagh, M. E., Anderson, G. M., Shaywitz, B. A., & Cohen, D. J. Clinical neurochemistry of autism and associated disorders. *Journal of Autism and Developmental Disorders,* 1982, **12,** 147–165.

Yuwiler, A., Geller, E., & Ritvo, E. Neurobiochemical research. In E. Ritvo (Ed.), *Autism: Diagnosis, current research and management.* New York: Spectrum, 1976.

Zetzel, E. R. The predisposition to depression. *Canadian Psychiatric Association Journal,* 1966, **11** (Suppl.), 236–249.

Zubin, J., & Spring, B. Vulnerability—A new view of schizophrenia. *Journal of Abnormal Psychology,* 1977, **86,** 103–126.

Zubin, J., Sutton, S., Salzinger, K., Burdock, E. I., & Perex, D. A biometric approach to prognosis in schizophrenia. In P. H. Hoch and J. Zubin (Eds.), *Comparative epidemiology in the mental disorders.* New York: Grune & Stratton, 1961.

Zuk, G. H., & Boszormenyi-Nagy, I. (Eds.), *Family therapy and disturbed families.* Palo Alto, Calif.: Science and Behavior Books, 1967.

Name Index

Subject Index

THE BOOK MANUFACTURE

Psychopathology Today, Third Edition, was typeset by Compositors, Cedar Rapids, Iowa. It was printed and bound at Kingsport Press, Kingsport, Tennessee. Cover design was by Jane Rae Brown. Chicago, Illinois. Internal design was by the F.E. Peacock Publishers' art department. The typeface is Times Roman.